I AM A DAUGHTER OF THE CHURCH

MW00659292

I AM A DAUGHTER OF THE CHURCH

P. Marie-Eugéne, O.C.D.

A Practical Synthesis of Carmelite Spirituality

Volume II

Translated by
Sister M. Verda Clare, C.S.C.

Christian Classics™
A Division of
RCL • Resources for Christian Living™
Allen, Texas

Reprinted 1982, 1997

NIHIL OBSTAT
Rev. Albert Schlitzer, C.S.C., S.T.D.,
University of Notre Dame

IMPRIMATUR
John F. Noll, D.D.,
Bishop of Fort Wayne, Indiana

The Nihil Obstat and Imprimatur are official declarations that the material reviewed is free of doctrinal or moral error. No implication is contained therein that those granting the Nihil Obstat and Imprimatur agree with the contents, opinions, or statements expressed.

Copyright © 1955 by
The FIDES Publishers Association
21 W. Superior Street, Chicago, IL

Reprinted with the permission of
FIDES/Claretian, Notre Dame, IN
by Christian Classics

All rights reserved. No part of this book shall be reproduced or transmitted in any form or by any means, electronic or mechanical, including photocopying, recording, or by any information or retrieval system, without written permission from the Publisher.

Send all inquiries to:
CHRISTIAN CLASSICS™
A division of RCL • Resources for Christian Living™
200 East Bethany Drive
Allen, Texas 75002-3804

Toll Free 800–888–3065
Fax 800–688–8356

Printed in the United States of America

ISBN 0–87061–224–7

To Mary Immaculate Queen, under two of her earliest and latest titles in the Church, Our Mother of Sorrows and Our Lady of Mount Carmel, this translation is offered, with a suppliant's prayer that she may use it as an instrument to draw many souls in our country into the intimacy of a deeper love of her Son, our Lord Jesus Christ.

FOREWORD

I Am a Daughter of the Church is the sequel to *I Want to See God*. This second volume, then, continues the description of the soul's spiritual journey as given by Saint Teresa.

One might be surprised at the change of title in the middle of the way. Could it be that Saint Teresa, having set out to see God, took a new view by reason of the difficulties of the journey and, renouncing the seemingly impossible goal of her heroic adventure, resigned herself at length to take her place near us, within our familiar horizons, to live simply as a good Christian and thus work out her temporal destiny as a daughter of the Church?

Not so. Let us not expect this proud Castilian of Avila, ennobled still more by the divine call, to abdicate the goal she had glimpsed at the beginning. Never will she consent to lower her ideal, to adjust it to our weak half-measures. She describes it in terms increasingly clear and lofty the nearer she approaches it. Her desires become more vast and more ardent in the measure that she makes it more her own. Actually she was to see God as perfectly as one can here below, in what she calls the intellectual vision of the Holy Trinity. But the fact we must emphasize is that she arrived at the summits only after having discovered the Church and sacrificed to it everything.

In this contemplative, who opens up her soul in writing, doctrine and life are so closely united that one can understand both the one and the other only by studying them together. Thus in the reformed Convent of Saint Joseph of Avila, the details of which Teresa organized with a view to seeing God and living in His intimacy, what strikes her most forcibly is the fact of her belonging to the Church. The Church it is which she discovers in the new ardors arising from her soul. She was seeking Jesus alone, and the Whole Christ is revealed to her.

No, her call has not changed—but how amazingly enlarged are her horizons! Previously Teresa had looked only to God and herself; now her sole desire is to know Christ Jesus and His members. The goods she had so jealously accumulated for the discovery of God, these she now gives up inasmuch as the good of the Church requires it of her. More eager than ever for divine light and intimacy, yet she sacrifices her personal tranquillity and her solitude, in order to found convents dedicated to painful prayer for the Church; and she extends her Reform to the Friars so as to realize through them what her role as a woman prevents her from doing, herself, for souls. This contemplative takes on cares without number; she becomes a foundress whom we find on all the perilous roads of Spain. There comes a day when she must leave this work to return as prioress in that same Convent of the Incarnation which she had left ten years before, because it no longer provided sustenance to her soul. Received with protestations from the nuns, who do not want her, she stays there for three years. And by one of those paradoxical turns in which loving Wisdom affirms His sovereign power and liberty, it is in this same convent, once abandoned by Teresa the better to find God, that Jesus comes to her to elevate her to the perfect union of spiritual marriage.

Spiritual marriage is a contract in good and due form. God gives Himself definitively and reveals Himself constantly in an intellectual vision. There is no ring, however, to seal the union, but rather a nail which attaches to the Cross. Nor is there a call to nuptial intimacy, but rather an invitation to work like a true bride for the honor of the Spouse. The tranquil possession of God in this union is not a goal nor a coming to rest; it is a means for working more efficaciously. Christ Jesus espouses souls here below only to associate them more closely to His own immolation and to His works for His Church. This is the doctrine that Saint Teresa develops in the last chapters of the *Interior Castle*. She was in fact to work and to suffer until death came for her at Alba de Tormes as she was returning from Burgos, where she had made the most difficult of her foundations.

The approach of death sets free at length her ardent desires to see God. It causes to shine forth also a ray from the beyond, revealing to her that new name, inscribed on mysterious white stone and given, says the Apocalypse, to those who have conquered in the fight. This new name, Teresa's, is "Daughter of the Church." With radiant joy she repeats it and falls into ecstasy. The name for all eternity of Teresa of Avila, this the Church has expressed for us by inscribing on the base of her statue in Saint Peter's Basilica in Rome: *Mater Spiritualium.*

It would have been a betrayal of the Teresian message not to give to this fact the place that belongs to it. *I Want to See God* pointed out the essential aspiration of the Teresian soul. *I Am a Daughter of the Church* will set forth the quality of the Saint's love, the end of her life and of her work, the characteristic note of the vocation she has left to her disciples. It was necessary to show the twofold aspect found in the simple and single movement of this Teresian vocation. The two words of Saint Teresa, the one spoken at the point of departure and the other at the summits, re-echo moreover the twofold battle cry of Elias, prophet and patriarch of Carmel, whose daughter Teresa claims to be: "As the Lord liveth in whose sight I stand . . ." and "With zeal have I been zealous for the Lord."

The title, *I Am a Daughter of the Church,* will give rise to the hope, on the part of some, of finding in these pages a doctrine for the apostolate. Let us not forget that Saint Teresa is a contemplative addressing herself to contemplatives. Clearly, nevertheless, the contemplatives that she forms do become apostles, and apostles of first rank, for she makes of them perfect instruments of the Holy Spirit. Thus in default of a method for the apostolate, Saint Teresa offers us a method for the formation of an apostle.

The temptation came to me to develop this latter aspect of the Teresian teaching. But it would have added more weight to an already compact volume and would have been a departure from the plan decided upon for this work. Hence I have limited myself to the essential lines such teaching would follow. These will suffice, I think, to show that the instruments of the Holy Spirit which Saint Teresa presents to us are perfect apostles, of the quality of those whom Jesus established as the foundation pillars of His Church, of those whom the Holy Spirit places at the turning points of history to do the great things of God, of those that we are needing for our own time.

P. Marie-Eugène de l'E.-J., O.C.D.

A MESSAGE from the Archbishop's House, Brighton, Massachusetts

It is a most heartening thing that there is, in these days, a public which will read a book such as this one. There have been times in the history of the Church when it would be taken for granted that devout souls would interest themselves in such a rich spiritual treasury as this provides. In our own day, however, there is such a multiplicity of activity, such a diversity of good works to be accomplished, that many a soul which instinctively yearns for closer union with Almighty God finds itself so preoccupied with things of immediate moment that it is unable to unite itself in fullness of love with the Eternal.

In these years since the War, which have witnessed such a marked return to the principles of the great mystics and ascetics of the Church, we have come, along with all our many strivings, to attach new importance to the spirit of contemplation. Although the fully contemplative life is one which few are privileged to lead, every Christian soul must know its moments of contemplation if it is ever, in this life, to have some knowledge of the eternal realities which surround it. These realities are given to us not by way of intuition or of vision but only by a passage through difficult pathways into a full-grown spiritual maturity. We must spend the days of our lives as we grow older, striving for this maturity in order that at the end of life we may attain to that childlikeness which Our Saviour has set down as the prerequisite for entrance into the Kingdom of Heaven.

It is an interesting thing and one not without significance, I think, that the spiritual giants of Carmel, Saint John of the Cross and Saint Teresa of Avila, have become better known and better understood through the impact of their teachings upon the simple, childlike Carmelite Sister of Lisieux, Saint Therese of the Child Jesus and the Holy Face.

In her the great tradition of these spiritual masters was exemplified in the *Little Way* in which by her utter simplicity she was enabled to walk confidently with God. Father Marie-Eugène, O.C.D., has done a magnificent work for the cause of Christ and His Church in collating all the teaching from the Carmelite tradition into these two volumes. Although based in largest measure on the *Interior Castle* of St. Teresa, this work itself is only a development of the age-long Carmelite tradition of that interior prayer and contemplation of divine perfections which leads to unitive life with God.

Certainly, the meaning of these pages must bring to everyone, as it has brought to me, the recognition that it is not easy to be a saint, but that it is even more difficult, if not impossible, to determine not to be a saint. The way is made clear for us, and we are the happier that it is made clear through the teachings of such approved theologians as the great Carmelite doctors of the Church. We have been shown here how the marvelous mystery of God's love can so operate in us as to transform us completely, not only by making us free from the taint of sin but making our lives richer by progress in virtue; and beyond this, elevating us to a life lived in love in the presence of God.

Our thanks to Sister Verda Clare for having made available to us in English the scholarship and the deep spiritual sense with which Father Marie-Eugène has informed this entire treatise. May Almighty God use it as an instrument to bring a better understanding of the ways of His love to His chosen souls.

Richard Cushing

Archbishop of Boston

Translator's Note

In translating from the French this second volume on Carmelite spirituality, *Je suis fille de l'Eglise,* I again owe much to those whom I mentioned in the "Translator's Note" of the first volume which appeared under the title, *I Want to See God.* For Father Marie-Eugène's renewed granting of translation rights and for the never failing interest of my superiors, especially Mother Kathryn Marie, C.S.C., midwestern provincial and Mother M. Rose Elizabeth, C.S.C., our superior general, I am most grateful.

The second volume is honored above the first in bearing a message from His Excellency, the Most Reverend Richard J. Cushing, D.D., Archbishop of Boston. Its appropriateness for a book entitled as this one needs no comment.

Because of other obligations, Father Michael, O.C.D., was not free to continue to the end the reading of the manuscript. At his request, Father Christopher, O.C.D., of the Discalced Carmelite Priory in Brookline, Massachusetts, kindly assumed the task for the last section. Both made many valuable suggestions for the improvement of the translation.

As for the first volume, so now for the second, I am indebted to several publishers for permission kindly given to quote from accepted translations of other works:

To Sheed and Ward, for the *Complete Works of Saint Teresa,* 3 Vols., translated and edited by the late Allison Peers; also for the *Collected Letters of Saint Therese of Lisieux,* translated by F. J. Sheed. To Burns Oates and Washbourne, Ltd., for the *Works of Saint John of the Cross,* 3 Vols., translated and edited by Allison Peers; and *Soeur Therese of Lisieux,* the *Little Flower of Jesus,* an *Autobiography,* edited by T. N. Taylor. To Newman Press, for the *Letters of Teresa of Avila,* 2 Vols., translated and edited by Allison Peers. To P. J. Kenedy and Sons, for *Novissima Verba,* a revised translation by the Carmelite Nuns of New York.

Note should be taken that I used the latest revised edition of the *Works of Saint John of the Cross* for quotations in *I Am a Daughter of the Church;* it appeared in 1953 after the publication of *I Want to See God.*

I must repeat my expression of gratitude to the Reverend Louis Putz, C.S.C., and the Reverend Albert Schlitzer, C.S.C., both of the University of Notre Dame; to Vincent J. Giese of the Fides Publishers Association; and to Miss Anne Pavlina and Miss Carol Braunsdorf of Saint Mary's College, Notre Dame, Indiana, for their steady help in typing the manuscript.

In a special way I am indebted to Sister M. John Frederick, C.S.C., of the English Department of the Archbishop Cushing College for her generously careful help in preparing the manuscript at a time when, because of my new duties, I should otherwise have been obliged to delay publication.

I leave this volume beside the first one in the hands of Our Lady, our Queen now and forever, praying that its pages may help us become more like her Son, transformed more and more into the loving likeness of Christ unto eternal life.

SISTER M. VERDA CLARE, C.S.C.

The Archbishop Cushing College
Brookline, Massachusetts
Feast of Saint Thomas Aquinas
March 7, 1955.

Contents

NOTE: This is the fourth part of the two volume study of Carmelite spirituality. The first three parts: PERSPECTIVES, THE FIRST STAGES, and MYSTICAL LIFE AND CONTEMPLATION, are in Volume I, I WANT TO SEE GOD.

HOLINESS IN SERVICE OF THE CHURCH

Up to Union of the Will

We must now consider in detail the action of loving Wisdom.

The outpourings of her love are not given to souls at the whim of circumstance. She orders them toward the goal that she has set, and that we can discover. The final goal is the perfect reign of God in the soul through transforming love and the building up of the Church.

There is an intermediary end which marks a decisive stage: this is the conquest of the will, the master faculty of the soul.

The fourth Mansions prepare for the triumph of God in the soul, which will be made secure in the fifth Mansions by the union of will.

The progressive development of God's action up to union of the will, the effects of that action, the soul's cooperation, the union of will itself and what it prepares for, such will be the subject-matter of this fourth part.

CHAPTER I

The Beginnings of Contemplative Prayer

This prayer is a little spark of true love for the Lord which He begins to enkindle in the soul.[1]

At the beginning of the fourth Mansions, Saint Teresa writes:

> Before I begin to speak of the fourth Mansions, it is most necessary that I should do what I have already done—namely, commend myself to the Holy Spirit, and beg Him from this point onward to speak for me, so that you may understand what I shall say about the Mansions still to be treated.[2]

Let us join in this prayer of the Saint, which becomes more urgent still on the threshold of the fifth Mansions.

There is no doubt that God's intervention in the spiritual life, especially in the life of prayer, is a most delicate and complex problem. Even if Saint Teresa had not so stated, the heated discussions concerning contemplation, as well as the negative results of the inquiry opened by Msgr. Saudreau "in order to fix the terminology of mysticism and come to an understanding," [3] would be enough to convince us that it was so.

To be able to solve the spiritual and psychological problems raised by the interventions of God through particular help, Saint Teresa would like to have much learning.

[1] *Life*, xv; Peers, I, 91.
[2] IV Mansions, i; Peers, II, 230.
[3] Cf. *Vie spirituelle* (supplement), 1929–1931.

> For many purposes it is necessary to be learned; and it would be very useful to have some learning here, in order to explain what is meant by general or particular help (for there are many who do not know this) and how it is now the Lord's will that the soul should see this particular help (as they say) with its own eyes.[4]

How are we to distinguish that special help, which raises prayer entirely to the supernatural level, from the general help which assists human activity in ordinary prayer? The answer has already been given.[5] Nevertheless, let us underline in passing the criterion that Saint Teresa insistently stresses; one that enables her to give a definition of supernatural prayer. Speaking of the first kind of prayer she experienced that seemed to her supernatural, she describes it as:

> . . . one which, despite all our efforts, cannot be acquired by industry or diligence, though we can certainly prepare for it, and it must be a great help if we do.[6]

And again:

> For even if we wear ourselves to pieces with penances and prayers and all kinds of other things, we can acquire but little if the Lord is not pleased to bestow it.[7]

This distinction established, we have to study the first forms that the divine interventions take by way of particular help in prayer.

We must ask at the outset, what are the first forms of God's supernatural action in a soul? This question calls forth a twofold response according as one considers the logical order, that is, the order imposed by the normal development of the life of grace in a soul, or the chronological order, that is, the order which, in fact, God follows.

In our exposition, we shall follow the logical order; the chronological order, however, merits our attention for the mo-

[4] *Life,* xiv; 85.
[5] Cf. Vol. I: *I Want to See God,* on "The signs of contemplation," p. 467 ff.
[6] *Spiritual Relations,* v; Peers, I, 327. Addressed to P. Rodrigo Alvarez.
[7] *Life* xxiv; Peers, I, 84.

ment. This is the proper domain of the divine mercy. In the distribution of His gifts, divine Mercy is sovereignly free and consults only His good pleasure. "The Spirit breatheth where he will," says Jesus to Nicodemus.[8] The same Spirit gives to everyone "according as he will." [9] "So then there is question not of him who wills nor of him who runs, but of God showing mercy." [10]

Saint Teresa notes in this regard:

> God is sometimes pleased to show great favour to persons who are in an evil state. . . . It must be understood, I think, that such persons will not be in mortal sin at the time. They may be in an evil state, and yet the Lord will allow them to see a vision, even a very good one, in order to draw them back to Himself.[11]

The graces enumerated by the Saint, visions or interior words, inflowings of sweetness, very swift raptures, are not properly speaking contemplative graces. They do not elevate the soul to a contemplative state for any length of time; but, even though fleeting, they are precious and important graces. Usually they work a veritable conversion even when there is no question of withdrawing the soul from sin. They reveal the supernatural world as a living reality and open up horizons not dreamed of before. At the same time they dilate the soul, create in it great desires and imperious needs that nothing thereafter can fully satisfy, short of the plenitude of the divine life that was for an instant glimpsed.

Besides this call to the summits, such graces ordinarily bear within them lights for the future. It would be imprudent for the soul to try to interpret them on its own; but an experienced eye will easily see in them rather clear indications as to the form of perfection and the particular way that God desires for the soul He has thus captivated. For this twofold reason they are often of incalculable benefit to one entering upon the way of

[8] John 3:8.
[9] I Cor. 12:11.
[10] Rom. 9:16.
[11] *Way of Perfection,* xiv; Peers, 65.

prayer. One should therefore keep and cultivate the memory of them, not to glory and delight in them as if they were one's own, but to thank God for His graces and frequently to ponder, in the depths they open, the exigencies of divine Love. These first favors are painful and sweet wounds. Happy the souls thus afflicted; more happy still are they if their love is generous enough to revivify unceasingly this burning wound!

Although rather frequent, according to Saint Teresa, nevertheless profound mystical grace is something exceptional.

Ordinarily, divine Mercy submits to the laws of a progressive conquest in the soul; follows the logical order. Saint Teresa notes in a "Relation" to Father Alvarez, that it was that way with her:

> The first kind of prayer I experience which seems to me supernatural . . . is an interior recollection felt in the soul.[12]

This passive recollection is at the first stage of the divine invading and precedes the prayer of quiet, as the Saint points out in her different treatises and in the "Relation" already quoted. In the *Interior Castle* she writes:

> The effects of this kind of prayer are numerous; some of them I shall explain. First of all, I will say something (though not much, as I have dealt with it elsewhere) about another kind of prayer, which almost invariably begins before this one.[13]

The first beginnings of contemplative prayer then, according to Saint Teresa, are passive recollection and the prayer of quiet or of divine consolations.[14] Along with these two degrees of prayer mentioned by Teresa, and belonging to the same period of spiritual life, we must place the prayer of contemplative aridity or of faith, of which John of the Cross speaks at length in the *Ascent of Mount Carmel*.

[12] *Relations*, v; Peers, I, 327.

[13] IV Mansions, iii; Peers, II, 240. Cf. also *Life*, xiv; *Way of Perfection*, xxviii; *Relations*, v, already quoted.

[14] In the classification of the degrees of prayer given in the *Life*, these two supernatural prayers belong to the second degree, that is, to the second way of watering the garden with the noria (*Life*, xiv, xv).

A. Supernatural recollection

Although Saint Teresa had previously treated of supernatural recollection, it is not until the *Interior Castle* and the "Relation" to Father Alvarez, written at about the same time, that she distinguishes it clearly from the prayer of quiet. Then only is her gaze sufficiently penetrating and her pen supple enough to give us a special description of this form of recollection. Of it, she writes:

> It does not involve remaining in the dark, or closing the eyes, nor is it dependent upon anything exterior. A person involuntarily closes his eyes and desires solitude. . . . The senses and all exterior things seem gradually to lose their hold on him, while the soul, on the other hand, regains its lost control.
>
> It is sometimes said that the soul enters within itself and sometimes that it rises above itself; but I cannot explain things in that kind of language, for I have no skill in it. However, I believe you will understand what I am able to tell you, though I may perhaps be intelligible only to myself. Let us suppose that these senses and faculties (the inhabitants as I have said, of this castle, which is the figure that I have taken to explain my meaning) have gone out of the castle, and, for days and years, have been consorting with strangers, to whom all the good things in the castle are abhorrent. Then, realizing how much they have lost, they come back to it, though they do not actually re-enter it, because the habits they have formed are hard to conquer. But they are no longer traitors and they now walk about in the vicinity of the castle. The great King, Who dwells in the Mansion within this castle, perceives their good will, and in His great mercy desires to bring them back to Him. So, like a good Shepherd, with a call so gentle that even they can hardly recognize it, He teaches them to know His voice and not to go away and get lost but to return to their Mansion; and so powerful is this Shepherd's call that they give up the things outside the castle which had led them astray, and once again enter it.
>
> I do not think I have ever explained this before as clearly as here.[15]

The Saint wants to stress that supernatural recollection is something quite distinct from the active recollection so much praised by her in the *Way of Perfection*.[16] Active recollection

[15] IV Mansions, iii; Peers, II, 240.

[16] *Way of Perfection,* xvi; Peers, II, 106-10; and more especially xxviii, 113-8.

is an excellent method which disciplines the faculties, singularly facilitates prayer, and prepares one for perfect contemplation. It is "in our power," and anyone who wants to arrive at it "must not be discouraged." [17] Passive recollection, on the other hand, is a pure favor from God, to which we could not attain through our own efforts.

Let us once more let the Saint speak for herself, for such sublime experience as hers alone can enlighten us in such delicate matters:

> It is a great help if God grants us this favour (recollection). Do not suppose that the understanding can attain to Him, merely by trying to think of Him as within the soul, or the imagination, by picturing Him as there. This is a good habit and an excellent kind of meditation, for it is founded upon a truth—namely, that God is within us. But it is not the kind of prayer that I have in mind, for anyone (with the help of the Lord, you understand) can practice it for himself. What I am describing is quite different. These people are sometimes in the castle before they have begun to think about God at all. I cannot say where they entered it or how they heard their Shepherd's call: it was certainly not with their ears, for outwardly such a call is not audible. They become markedly conscious that they are gradually retiring within themselves; anyone who experiences this will discover what I mean: I cannot explain it better.[18]

This supernatural recollection is certainly, then, an effect of God's, a sign of His presence. The Master does not yet manifest Himself; but at a distance His power reveals itself in action. From afar He sounds a mysterious call. The soul has not heard it, has grasped nothing directly; but it feels itself calmed, enveloped by some unknown power in a mantle of recollection. Nothing more is needed to reveal to it the presence of the Master. It seems to be in a holy land. Its powers have become suddenly docile. A gentle force holds them, and the inflowing of its sweetness penetrates them with a loving reverence. Each one has resumed the place assigned to it by the divine order in the soul and thus remains in peaceful expectation, filled with delight. All are on the watch for their Divine Shepherd whom

[17] *Ibid.*, xxix; 120.
[18] IV Mansions, iii; 241.

they know is near, without however seeing Him or perceiving anything directly.

As in every direct action of God, there are degrees in this supernatural recollection. At times it seems to be produced by a call so lightly delicate that it is almost imperceptible; at other times it declares itself through a strong rapture, taking such possession of the faculties as to leave them powerless. In neophytes, as we call those who have not yet known supernatural favors, its sensible effects are usually rather notable; while in the case of souls attuned by experience to the divine, the impression it makes on them can be so delicate and subtle that the soul scarcely has cognizance of it.

It may be that this passive recollection will not be followed by any other supernatural manifestation; that it was given simply to calm interior agitation, or to make an active prayer of simple regard more peaceful. More often, however, it is the prelude to greater favors. In His mercy the Master Himself creates the dispositions of silent attention and peaceful submission that He wants to find at the time of His manifestations. Supernatural recollection heralds, then, and prepares the way for divine visits. Saint Teresa says, speaking of those who receive it:

> His call to them is a special one and aims at making them intent upon interior things.[19]

And again:

> A person involuntarily closes his eyes and desires solitude; and, without the display of any human skill there seems gradually to be built for him a temple in which he can make the prayer already described.[20]

This supernatural peace and recollection that God has sent as a messenger before Him remains in the soul after each one of His passings as the most authentic and most characteristic sign of His action. Our God is a God of peace.

[19] *Ibid.*
[20] *Ibid.*; 240.

B. Prayer of quiet or of divine taste

Having announced Himself by the prayer of passive recollection, God "begins to give us His Kingdom" [21] in the prayer of quiet. Saint Teresa has left in her writings many descriptions of this prayer, also called the prayer of divine taste. A rereading of the principal ones will here be helpful—not to enter upon comparisons in order to emphasize their differences but rather to throw light on their essential elements.

One of the earliest of these descriptions in point of time the Saint gives in the *Way of Perfection:*

Now, daughters, I still want to describe this Prayer of Quiet to you. . . . It is in this kind of prayer, as I have said, that the Lord seems to me to begin to show us that He is hearing our petition: He begins to give us His Kingdom on earth so that we may truly praise Him. . . .

This is a supernatural state, and, however hard we try, we cannot reach it for ourselves; for it is a state in which the soul enters into peace, or rather in which the Lord gives it peace through His presence, as He did to that just man Simeon. In this state all the faculties are stilled. The soul, in a way which has nothing to do with the outward senses, realizes that it is now very close to its God, and that, if it were but a little closer, it would become one with Him through union. This is not because it sees Him either with its bodily or its spiritual eyes . . . yet it sees that it is in the Kingdom (or at least is near to the King Who will give it the Kingdom), and it feels such reverence that it dares to ask nothing. . . .

The body experiences the greatest delight and the soul is conscious of a deep satisfaction. So glad is it merely to find itself near the fountain that, even before it has begun to drink, it has had its fill. There seems nothing left for it to desire. The faculties are stilled and have no wish to move, for any movement they make appears to hinder the soul from loving God. They are not completely lost, however, since two of them being free, they can realize in Whose Presence they are. It is the will that is in captivity now.[22]

In the book of her *Life,* Teresa writes on the same subject:

The powers are not lost, nor do they sleep. The will alone is occupied, in such a way that, without knowing how, it becomes captive. It allows itself to be imprisoned by God.[23]

[21] *Way of Perfection,* xxxi; Peers, II, 126.
[22] *Ibid.;* 126-8.
[23] *Life,* xiv; Peers, I, 83.

In these two descriptions it is clearly shown that in the prayer of quiet, God's action is exercised on the will. But then a confusion is possible between passive recollection and the prayer of quiet; they do not seem to be distinct.[24] In the *Interior Castle,* however, Saint Teresa with her riper experience gives a more simple description, more clear and luminous, which marks out more specifically the nature of the prayer of quiet, its origin, and its various effects.

In developing the comparison of the two basins as we have seen, the Saint says that one receives the waters brought from a distance by an aqueduct; but, she continues:

> To the other fountain the water comes direct from its source, which is God, and . . . its coming is accompanied by the greatest peace and quietness and sweetness within ourselves—I cannot say where it arises or how. . . . I do not think that this happiness has its source in the heart at all. It arises in a much more interior part, like something of which the springs are very deep; I think this must be the centre of the soul, as I have since realized and as I will explain hereafter. . . .
>
> Apparently, as this heavenly water begins to flow from this source of which I am speaking—that is, from our very depths—it proceeds to spread ineffable blessings, so that the soul itself cannot understand all that it receives there. The fragrance it experiences, we might say, is as if in those interior depths there were a brazier on which were cast sweet perfumes; the light cannot be seen, nor the place where it dwells, but the fragrant smoke and the heat penetrate the entire soul, and very often, as I have said, the effects extend even to the body. Observe—and understand me here—that no heat is felt, nor is any fragrance perceived: it is a more delicate thing than that; I only put it in that way so that you may understand it.[25]

While the will is held sweetly captive by the divine delights it is savoring, what is the state of the other powers? Saint Teresa shows that this can vary widely according to circumstances. At times, they have knowledge and hence a share of the sweet banquet of the will. They try to come to the aid of the will in order to deepen its quietude by their own efforts; [26] but

[24] Thus the Saint writes in the book of her *Life:* "I have already said that, in this first state of recollection and quiet, the faculties of the soul do not fail." (*Life,* xv; Peers, I, 88). She seems to assimilate recollection to quiet.

[25] IV Mansions, ii; Peers, II, 237-8.

[26] The Saint describes this work of the understanding in search of many words and reflections with which to give thanks for this benefit and piling up

they only succeed in agitating and troubling it. They are throwing logs on a spark at the risk of putting it out:

> The other two faculties understanding and memory help the will so that it may become more and more capable of enjoying so great a blessing, though sometimes it comes about that, even when the will is in union, they hinder it exceedingly. . . . At such a time they are like doves which are not pleased with the food given them by the owner of the dovecot, without their having worked for it, and go in search of food elsewhere, but are so unsuccessful that they return. Just so these faculties come and go, to see if the will will give them some part of what it is enjoying.[27]

These powers, by their restlessness, have made themselves incapable of tasting the divine delights.

At other times the understanding has no part in the banquet of the soul; and so it is greatly disturbed:

> It may come about that the soul is enjoying the highest degree of quiet, and that the understanding has soared so far aloft that what is happening to it seems not to be going on in its own house at all; it *really* seems to be a guest in somebody else's house, looking for other lodgings, since its own lodging no longer satisfies it and it cannot remain there for long together.[28]

Thus the fourth Mansions, characterized by quietude, are paradoxically mansions too of much restlessness.

Again, it may happen that all the faculties are plunged in these waves of living water and are inebriated by them. The soul is so much filled with the water of grace, writes the Saint, that:

> It is unable to go forward, and has no idea how to do so, yet neither can it turn back: it would fain have the fruition of exceeding great glory. It is like a person holding the candle in his hand, who is soon to die a death that he longs for; and in that agony it is rejoicing with ineffable joy. . . .
>
> The faculties retain only the power of occupying themselves wholly with God; not one of them, it seems, ventures to stir, nor can we

---

its sins and imperfections so as to make itself realize that it does not deserve such a grace. When it begins to hold discourse with itself and think out reflections, it will soon begin to fancy it is doing something worthwhile (*Life*, xv; Peers, I, 90-1).

[27] *Life*, xiv; Peers, I, 84.

[28] *Way of Perfection*, xxxi; Peers, II, 130.

cause any one of them to move except by trying to fix our attention very carefully on something else, and even then I do not think we could entirely succeed in doing so. Many words are spoken, during this state, in praise of God, but, unless the Lord Himself puts order into them, they have no orderly form. The understanding, at any rate, counts for nothing here; the soul would like to shout praises aloud, for it is in such a state that it cannot contain itself—a state of delectable disquiet. Already the flowers are opening: see, they are beginning to send out their fragrance.[29]

The kind of prayer thus described is the third degree of prayer, or the watering by irrigation, which Saint Teresa, in the book of her *Life,* clearly distinguishes from the prayer of quiet because, she says, the water of grace flows more abundantly and the virtues are stronger.[30]

But we find that she has changed her opinion in the "Relation" to Father Alvarez[31] and in the *Interior Castle;* here she attaches this prayer of inebriation to the prayer of simple quiet because the powers, although inebriated with grace, are not united to God. The sensible effects are more intense, the efficacy of grace is perhaps greater than in the prayer of quiet; but the mode of God's action is the same: the will alone is truly captivated.

Saint Teresa observes, moreover, in the *Interior Castle,* that here her explanation differs from what she has said elsewhere. She writes:

In this state the faculties are not, I think, in union, but they become absorbed and are amazed as they consider what is happening to them.

It may be that in writing of these interior things I am contradicting what I have myself said elsewhere. This is not surprising, for almost fifteen years have passed since then, and perhaps the Lord has now given me a clearer realization of these matters than I had at first.[32]

[29] *Life,* xvi; Peers, I, 96-7.
[30] *Ibid.,* xvii; 101.
[31] She writes in this "Relation": "From this prayer is wont to proceed what is called a sleep of the faculties; these, however, are not so completely absorbed or suspended that it can be called rapture. Though this is not complete union, the soul is sometimes—often, indeed—aware that the will alone is in union. "Relations" v; Peers, I, 328.
[32] IV Mansions ii; Peers, II, 238.

Such is the prayer of quiet that sweetly holds captive the will, "a little spark of true love for the Lord which He begins to enkindle in the soul," [33] a "pledge that He is already choosing it for great things if it will prepare itself to receive them." [34]

C. Contemplative dryness or prayer of faith

This name suggests a prayer apparently quite different from the prayer of quiet; yet it is the name applicable to the first forms of contemplation described by Saint John of the Cross in the *Ascent of Mount Carmel* [35] and in the *Dark Night of the Soul.*[36] In these chapters, there is a description in almost the same terms as those used by Saint Teresa of the signs indicating that a soul should pass from discursive meditation to the state of contemplation. These psychological signs are well known, and we have already considered them.[37] And so it will now be sufficient to describe this contemplative prayer by stressing its characteristic traits according to Saint John of the Cross.

For Saint John of the Cross, contemplation is a loving knowledge. It consists essentially in receiving light from the Sun that is God, constantly warming souls with His love.

The divine light, by reason of its transcendence, normally produces the effect of darkness in powers not adapted to receive it. Dark night is characteristic of contemplation. It is experienced in the powerlessness, the aridity, the distaste of the faculties, which are unable to apply themselves to operations to which they were previously habituated and in which they found contentment and profit.

Yet there is a certain peace even in this desolation. The soul enjoys being alone, without any particular considerations, in quiet and repose, without any activity of the powers, fixed in a

[33] *Life,* xv; Peers, I, 90.
[34] *Ibid.*
[35] *Ascent,* Bk. II, xiii, xiv; Peers, I, 108-19.
[36] *Dark Night,* Bk. I, viii, ix; Peers, I, 349-56.
[37] Cf. Vol. I: *I Want to See God,* p. 467 ff.

loving knowledge. So subtle and delicate is this, that at first the soul has no cognizance of it, missing keenly as it does the sensible satisfactions of which it is now deprived. These first forms of contemplative prayer are thus marked by dryness, powerlessness, desolation.

A little later, however, the soul is like one to whom water has been brought, says the Saint; then

> It drinks peacefully without labour, and is no longer forced to draw the water through the aqueducts of past meditations and forms and figures. So that, as soon as the soul comes before God, it makes an act of knowledge, confused, loving, passive and tranquil, wherein it drinks of wisdom and love and delight.[38]

Farther on the Saint describes a state in which

> The soul remains as it were in a great forgetfulness, so that it knows not where it has been or what it has done, nor is it aware of the passage of time. . . .
>
> The cause of this forgetfulness is the purity and simplicity of this knowledge which occupies the soul and simplifies, purifies and cleanses it from all apprehensions and forms of the senses and of the memory, through which it acted when it was conscious of time, and thus leaves it in forgetfulness and without consciousness of time. This prayer, therefore, seems to the soul extremely brief, although, as we say, it may last for a long period; for the soul has been united in pure intelligence, which belongs not to time.[39]

However they may differ, these first degrees of contemplative prayer show us an authentically supernatural action of God, exercised over the powers of the soul. A delightful flood of love or of light springs from a deep source and flows into the will or the understanding; and, in some circumstances, into both.

God who is the source remains far away. The faculties drink from the springs of living water, but God does not give Himself in immediate contact to the soul directly. There may be an inebriation of the faculties even to the point of mystical sleep, but there is not complete union, Saint Teresa would say.

[38] *Ascent,* Bk. II, xiv; Peers, I, 112.
[39] *Ibid.;* 116-7.

Moreover, the faculties receive this living water only intermittently. Contemplation is imperfect. And yet these first beginnings of supernatural prayer are truly a preparation for the prayer of perfect contemplation. Do they not sustain the faculties, make them more pliable, spiritualize them, purify them? In a word, this incipient contemplation is directed toward and is the pledge of union; for what God has begun, He will bring to completion if the soul is faithful.

When the soul has emerged from the state of beginners but has not yet arrived at perfect union, these first forms of supernatural prayer, quietude and contemplative dryness, will be its habitual climate. This will be the base from which God will at times elevate it higher and to which it will promptly return; for until the state of union is reached, these seizures of the soul by God, however accented they be, can be but transient.

CHAPTER II

God as Light and God as Love

Whatever is received is received according to the mode of the receiver.[1]

The explanation of the first forms of supernatural prayer brought to our attention several differences between the prayer described by Saint Teresa and that of Saint John of the Cross.

Saint Teresa speaks of supernatural recollection and quiet; Saint John of the Cross, of contemplation. Saint John of the Cross requires the convergence of three signs as an indication of contemplation; Saint Teresa gives only one.

But the difference is especially one of climate. Saint Teresa introduces us into an atmosphere abounding in those conditions that dilate the soul. Saint John of the Cross for his part detains us in one where there is less warmth, where aridity, powerlessness, and often even disquiet seem to prevail.

Saint John of the Cross asserts that one can have contemplation without adverting to it. Saint Teresa on the contrary constantly appeals to her own experience to describe the supernatural states; and to that of her readers, that they may understand them. To such a degree is this so, one might wonder whether the two are talking about the same period of the spiritual life.

Yet there is no doubt that both are speaking of the first manifestations of the supernatural action of God in prayer.

Moreover, running through the differences there are charac-

[1] An Aristotelian-Thomistic principle.

teristic points of agreement: certain traits of Saint John of the Cross's presentation appear to be borrowed from the descriptions given by Saint Teresa; and vice versa. Saint John of the Cross speaks of the soul which, having given itself to prayer, "drinks peacefully without labour, and is no longer forced to draw the water through the aqueducts of past meditations,"[2] while Saint Teresa insists on the disquiet and the tumult of certain faculties during the prayer of quiet.

Even if there were not these resemblances, one could not believe that two teachers of the same school, who for several years at the Convent of the Incarnation at Avila (1572–74) had daily opportunity for comparing their experiences, and who collaborated so closely in the spiritual direction of the nuns, could leave behind them a body of doctrine with irreconcilable differences.

We propose to explain and reconcile these differences. In doing so, we shall have to make certain repetitions. But these will not be in vain, if they help us to see these truths in a new light and draw from them some practical conclusions.

A. Light and love in the mystical experience

Supernatural contemplation, that simple gaze of faith perfected in its exercise by the gifts of the Holy Spirit, proceeds from a twofold supernatural activity: that of the soul, whose loving faith penetrates into divine truth, its proper object; and that of God who, through the gifts, simplifies faith, rendering it tranquil and contemplative.

This twofold activity yields a twofold fruit. Loving faith entering more deeply as it does into God-love, who gives Himself to all those who seek Him, draws from the divine riches of His grace. And God, through the gifts of the Holy Spirit, gives a certain experience of Himself and of His grace.

Of these two fruits the first is in itself independent of the

[2] *Ascent,* Bk. II, xiv; Peers, I, 112.

second, for the divine riches of grace can come to a soul without its being aware of the gift received; the second is united to the first in supernatural contemplation and gives to it its characteristic note.

It is this experience of God through the gifts that will here claim our special attention.

The action of God through the gifts of the Holy Spirit has its sole motive in the mercy of God. Hence it is entirely gratuitous. As we know, this mercy has no other laws than the divine good pleasure. God therefore raises to contemplation whom He wills, when He wills, and as He wills.

Having said this in order to guard us against any too rigorous systematization, cognizance must be taken of the fact that the divine mercy usually acts in a certain manner and according to certain laws of progression, which can be verified in the experience of the majority of souls.

Experience indicates first of all that this inflow arises from the inmost depths of the soul. Let us recall the symbolic vision of the *Interior Castle;* God is present in the seventh Mansions and from there sends forth light and impelling grace that will draw the soul to the unitive embrace of spiritual marriage.

In the prayer of quiet, Saint Teresa notes that the soul clearly perceives that the living waters of divine consolation have their source in God; that this happiness does not have its origin in the heart but that "it comes from a more interior part as from a depth; I think that this must be from the center of the soul." [3]

In this upsurging of divine life from the innermost depths of the soul there is a call. Sweetly but strongly the soul and its powers feel themselves drawn toward the source of the divine gift: God hidden in the intimate center of the soul. Thus this inflowing of God orientates the soul toward its own inner depths, creating in it that movement of interiorization which is to end in perfect union with God.

The senses and the most exterior powers are the first to expe-

[3] IV Mansions, ii; Peers, II, 237.

rience this interior action of God in the soul, which Saint Teresa compares to the flute-call of the Good Shepherd. This call is so delicate and gentle that the wandering faculties can scarcely hear it; yet in it they recognize His voice and experience passive recollection, the first form of supernatural prayer.

In the kind of contemplative prayer which follows recollection, namely, that of quiet and contemplative dryness, God's action is experienced in the more interior faculties, the will and understanding. In the prayer of union, it is the center of the soul that is touched by God Himself. We do not have to go farther. It is enough for us to determine the progressive movement of God's action in the soul, which, arising from its innermost center, extends to the exterior parts of the soul, becoming progressively interior as it becomes more intense.

We promised to return and explain the differences between the prayer of quiet of Saint Teresa and the contemplative dryness of Saint John of the Cross. We shall now do so.

God is light and love. In the infinite riches of the divine simplicity, these two attributes correspond to the two human faculties of knowing and of willing. God is light to the intellect and to faith, which is engrafted in it. He is love to the will and to supernatural charity. On His side God gives Himself as light by the gift of understanding, and He causes Himself to be experienced as love by the gift of wisdom.

Since contemplation is essentially an act of the virtue of faith perfected by the gifts, it tends toward God inasmuch as He is light. But charity too plays its part in contemplation, since it is charity which through the gifts renders faith contemplative; thus contemplation can rest in God as light only in and through love.

It is then as light and as love that God will give Himself in contemplation. Can one, however, distinguish this twofold aspect in the divine manifestation? Saint John of the Cross assures us that one or other of them is dominant even in the sublimest communications of God, those received in the substance of the soul itself. This distinction is more marked and more important in the first stages of contemplative prayer with which we are now concerned, and in which the divine action is received in the understanding or the will.

A study of these two manifestations of God-light and of God-love will make it possible to throw some light on the differences existing between Saint John of the Cross and Saint Teresa.

1. LIGHT AND THE GIFT OF UNDERSTANDING

God as light can be experienced as such only by the intellect. This is the general law enunciated and explained by Saint John of the Cross. We must know, he writes,

> The understanding in its bodily prison has no preparation or capacity for receiving the clear knowledge of God; for such knowledge belongs not to this state, and we must either die or remain without receiving it. Wherefore Moses, when he entreated God for this clear knowledge, was told that he would be unable to see Him, in these words: 'No man shall see Me and remain alive.' [4] Wherefore Saint John says: [5] 'No man hath seen God at any time.'

And the Saint adds:

> Thus it is that contemplation, whereby the understanding has the loftiest knowledge of God, is called mystical theology, which signifies secret wisdom of God; for it is secret even to the understanding that receives it. For that reason Saint Dionysius calls it a ray of darkness. . . . Aristotle says that, even as are the eyes of the bat with regard to the sun, which is total darkness to it, even so is our understanding to that which is greater light in God, which is total darkness to us. And he says further that, the loftier and clearer are the things of God in themselves, the more completely unknown and obscure are they to us. This likewise the Apostle affirms, saying: The lofty things of God are the least known unto men.[6]

The human understanding is not fitted to perceive this divine light. Yet it receives it and experiences it in the diverse effects that it produces. These effects will be considered at greater

[4] Exod. 33:20.
[5] John 1:18.
[6] *Ascent,* Bk. II, vii; Peers, I, 90-2.

length in connection with the *Nights;* but we think it necessary to point them out even now.

When the divine light falls upon the understanding it renders it incapable of any consecutive thoughts. Writing of a person arrived at this stage, Saint John of the Cross says that:

> He can no longer meditate or reason with his imagination, neither can take pleasure therein as he was wont to do aforetime; . . .
>
> He has no desire to fix his meditation or his sense upon other particular objects, exterior or interior. I do not mean that the imagination neither comes nor goes (for even at times of deep recollection it is apt to move freely), but that the soul has no pleasure in fixing it of set purpose upon other objects.[7]

This inability to meditate and, more generally, to resume its former habit of cursive activity, may result in a complete paralysis of the faculties.

The powerlessness is accompanied by an uneasiness that Saint John of the Cross says is caused by the meeting of two contraries, the light of God and the impurities of the soul:

> It is clear that this dark contemplation is in these its beginnings painful likewise to the soul; for, as this Divine infused contemplation has many excellences that are extremely good, and the soul that receives them, not being purged, has many miseries that are likewise extremely bad, hence it follows that, as two contraries cannot coexist in one subject—the soul—it must of necessity have pain and suffering, since it is the subject wherein these two contraries war against each other.[8]

A more complete inflowing of this divine light usually creates an impression of darkness at the same time as a confused and loving general knowledge:

> At times (that is, when it is purest), it becomes darkness, because it withdraws the understanding from its accustomed lights, from forms and from fancies, and then the darkness is more clearly felt and realized.[9]

The general and loving knowledge which characterizes supernatural contemplation has been many times described. We shall

[7] *Ibid.*, xiii; 108-9.
[8] *Dark Night,* Bk. II, v; Peers, I, 382.
[9] *Ascent,* Bk. II, xxiv; Peers, I, 116.

return to it here only to point out with Saint John of the Cross that it may be imperceptible not only in the beginning of contemplative prayer but also when this attains to great purity and perfect simplicity. Saint John of the Cross says:

> When this Divine light strikes the soul with less force, it neither perceives darkness nor observes light, nor apprehends aught that it knows, from whatever source; hence at times the soul remains as it were in a great forgetfulness.[10]

And he adds that this absence of all experience of light is more complete in the most elevated states:

> But here it must be made clear that this general knowledge whereof we are speaking is at times so subtle and delicate, particularly when it is most pure and simple and perfect, most spiritual and most interior, that, although the soul be occupied therein, it can neither realize it nor perceive it. This is most frequently the case when we can say that it is in itself most clear, perfect and simple; and this comes to pass when it penetrates a soul that is unusually pure and far withdrawn from other particular kinds of knowledge and intelligence, which the understanding or the senses might fasten upon. Such a soul, since it no longer has those things wherein the understanding and the senses have the habit and custom of occupying themselves, is not conscious of them, inasmuch as it has not its accustomed powers of sense. . . .
>
> This will be clearly understood by the following comparison. If we consider a ray of sunlight which enters through a window, we see that, the more the said ray is charged with atoms and particles of matter, the more palpable, visible and bright it appears to the eye of sense. . . . And if the ray were completely pure and free from all these atoms and particles, even from the minutest specks of dust, it would appear completely dark and invisible to the eye, since everything that could be seen would be absent from it—namely, the objects of sight. For the eye would find no objects whereon to rest, since light is no proper object of vision, but the means whereby that which is visible is seen; so that if there be no visible objects wherein the sun's rays or any light can be reflected, nothing will be seen. Wherefore, if the ray of light entered by one window and went out by another, without meeting anything that has material form it would not be seen at all.[11]

These affirmations of Saint John of the Cross enable us to sum up thus our analysis of the experience of the divine light:

[10] *Ibid.*
[11] *Ibid.;* 115-6.

the divine light cannot be perceived because the soul has no faculty apt for the receiving of it. It can only experience the privative effects of powerlessness, of suffering, or of darkness; painful effects these, which are nevertheless ordinarily pervaded with a certain sweetness that comes from love.

2. LOVE AND THE GIFT OF WISDOM

If the communications of God as light are privative and deceptive for the human faculties, those of God as love are, on the contrary, positive and delightful.

The disproportion between the divine Infinite and the human, which does not allow the understanding to perceive the divine light, does not hinder the will from experiencing God as love. The understanding can know a thing only by receiving it in some way into itself, hence something less than itself; but for the will to love, to enter into the beloved and there experience love, a contact suffices. It matters not if the two beings united in love appear to one another on a certain plane of equality, like two rivers whose waters meet, or if there is between them the disproportion of a drop of water and the ocean into which it falls: love effects its own work of compenetration and union, making them equal. Thus the will and the senses can receive God-love in spite of their deficiencies, unite with Him and experience Him according to their way of feeling and of knowing.

The Church teaches us that the supernatural charity we possess on earth is the same as we shall have in heaven. Faith and hope will fail as imperfect instruments; charity will abide forever. Only its mode of operation will change. It will grasp and enjoy its divine object no longer merely by faith but by vision face to face. But its nature will not change, since already here below it unites us to God really and intimately without any other intermediary than the darkness in which faith leaves it.

So even here below charity has within itself a certain corrective for the darkness in which faith leaves it. It establishes between the soul and supernatural realities a loving contact, a connaturalness that gives it, not indeed vision, but a certain supernatural perception and experimental knowledge of these same divine realities. The power that natural love has of creating in those it unites a mutual sympathy, a dilation of mind and heart in their daily contacts, a deeper understanding of one another—all this has its counterpart in the supernatural life of grace in the gift of wisdom.

In the first forms of contemplative prayer, of which we are here speaking, the gift of wisdom causes one to experience, not indeed God Himself, but the gift of His charity that God makes to the soul. It is love's movement in the soul, its hold on the will, its overflowing into the other faculties, even to the senses, that the soul discovers in the dilation and joy of heart that love brings it. "Grace is poured out into your hearts by the Holy Spirit." Thus the first stages of contemplative prayer throw light on this affirmation of Saint Paul. Later, the divine touches deep within the soul will give it experience of the rest of the apostle's text, "by the Holy Spirit who is given to you," by revealing to it the Holy Spirit in its inmost center.

The prayer of quiet and the prayer of sleep-of-the-powers are typical manifestations of God as love in the faculties of the soul. One has only to reread Saint Teresa's descriptions quoted in the preceding chapter to be convinced of this.[12]

3. UNITY OF CONTEMPLATION AND THE TWO CONTEMPLATIVE GIFTS

It has been remarked that while one could no better illustrate the manifestations of God as love than by citing the descriptions given by Saint Teresa in the fourth Mansions, on the other hand, the manifestations of God as light place us in a Joannine atmosphere. It was a description of these latter that brought us to the signs of contemplation as indicated by the holy doctor.

Saint Teresa speaks in fact of delightful and sweet love in

[12] Cf. preceding chapter, pp. 10 ff.

the will; Saint John of the Cross speaks of knowledge received in the understanding, which is blinded by it.

Are there, then, two distinct forms of contemplation: one, enlightening to the understanding, which would be that of Saint John of the Cross; the other, full of love, that of Saint Teresa?

To distinguish two forms of contemplation, one exclusive of the other, would be to run contrary to the very nature of contemplation, which proceeds at the same time from faith and from charity and produces both knowledge and love. It would be also to contradict the expositions set forth by Saint John of the Cross and Saint Teresa, whose very authority we were invoking.

To the two privative signs produced by the blinding effect of God's light as it falls on the faculties, Saint John of the Cross adds a third sign, the most certain, he says, and a positive one, and related to the gift of wisdom. He writes:

> The third and surest sign is that the soul takes pleasure in being alone, and waits with loving attentiveness upon God, without making any particular meditation, in inward peace and quietness and rest.[13]

This third sign is closely allied to the quietude described by Saint Teresa. And on the other hand, in Saint Teresa's descriptions of quietude, she points out its privative effects in the understanding:

> It may come about that the soul is enjoying the highest degree of quiet, and that the understanding has soared so far aloft that what is happening to it seems not to be going on in its own house at all; it really seems to be a guest in somebody else's house, looking for other lodgings, since its own lodging no longer satisfies it and it cannot remain there for long together.[14]

We find no more precise description in Saint John of the Cross, nor so picturesque, of the disarray of the understanding when the divine light strikes it. Saint Teresa frequently returns to this agitation of the understanding during the prayer of quiet,

[13] *Ascent,* Bk. II, xiii; Peers, I, 109.
[14] *Way of Perfection,* xxxi; Peers, II, 130.

saying that the understanding must then be treated like a madman.[15]

The communications of God as light and as love are thus with rare exceptions concomitant in contemplation, even in its early stages. It is by the communication of love that the soul first becomes aware of light in the understanding, affirms Saint John of the Cross. The third sign, the positive one, is necessary in order to determine the value of the two others. He writes:

> When it [general and loving knowledge] is communicated to the will also, which happens almost invariably, the soul does not cease to understand in the very least degree, if it will reflect hereon, that it is employed and occupied in this knowledge, inasmuch as it is conscious of a sweetness of love therein, without particular knowledge or understanding of that which it loves. It is for this reason that this knowledge is described as general and loving; for, just as it is so in the understanding, being communicated to it obscurely, even so is it in the will, sweetness and love being communicated to it confusedly, so that it cannot have a distinct knowledge of the object of its love.[16]

Referring to what we have said of the substantial identity of the divine manifestation made through the various gifts of the Holy Spirit, of their different tonality, and of their orientation toward particular ends, we can conclude that there is no essential difference between the manifestations of God as light and those of God inasmuch as He is love. They are but reflections of divine attributes cast upon the soul, which produce different effects but are the one identical essence of God.

These varying manifestations of God as light and as love are not in mutual opposition. Saint John of the Cross and Saint

[15] In order to reduce still more the differences between the contemplation of Saint Teresa and that of Saint John of the Cross, one can affirm, it seems to me, that during long years in which she remained in aridity, unable to make use either of her imagination or her understanding (*Life,* ix; *Way of Perfection,* xxxvi) Saint Teresa was in a contemplative state of which she perceived only the suffering. The Saint had already been favored with the prayer of union; and the memory of those graces, while rendering her faculties powerless, made her long for positive divine manifestations.

Not knowing the nature and value of these privative effects, she was only harrassed by them and awaited the outpourings of the gift of wisdom to speak of contemplation.

[16] *Ascent,* Bk. II, xiv; Peers, I, 118-9.

Teresa exchanged their experiences in their many conversations with each other. These mutual confidences caused no trouble or division of mind between them; rather did they transport them both in common ecstasy.

There are not two sorts of Christian contemplation. There is only one which leads the soul to God, One in three Persons, but which produces in different souls different effects.

These differences do in fact occur. The contemplation which Saint John of the Cross describes in the *Ascent of Mount Carmel* is not altogether identical with that of Saint Teresa in the book of her *Life* and the *Interior Castle.* Under pretext of unifying them, let us not yield to the temptation of making them uniform. The manifestations of God-light and God-love, although not excluding one another and being concomitant in every stage of contemplation, are revealed through forms of contemplation differing in tonality and spiritual climate.

Their different method of exposition, descriptive in the case of Saint Teresa, scientific in that of Saint John of the Cross, does not suffice to explain all their differences. These can be accounted for only by the difference in the experience.

But a new problem thus presents itself: Why was their experience different? The answer to this question is freighted with practical consequences. Let us try to find it.

B. Saint Teresa's experience and that of Saint John of the Cross

An easy explanation would be to attribute the differences simply to the action of God. We are indeed in the domain of the divine mercy, which disposes everything with strength and wisdom and loves to show forth His sovereign liberty by the diversity of His gifts. It was His good pleasure to give light to Saint John of the Cross and to Saint Teresa love. *Sit pro ratione voluntas.* The divine good pleasure would explain everything and would dispense us from further inquiry.

But to attribute thus exclusively to God and to His direct, immediate action in souls the different effects of contemplation, would seem to leave out of account the ordinary ways of divine Providence.

God's action does in fact make use of natural means; His omnipotence and wisdom are exalted in using for their purpose secondary causes. Only occasionally do they dispense with the act of these causes and enter themselves in the ordinary working out of God's Providence.[17] This law is so general that we are right in appealing to the direct and immediate causality of God only when we have made sure that the influence of natural secondary causes is not in play.

In the present case, the difference in the temperaments of Teresa and John of the Cross seems to afford a sufficient explanation for the particular forms of their experience.

"*Quidquid recipitur, ad modum recipientis recipitur.* Whatever is received is received according to the mode of the recipient," say the Scholastics. The sun lighting up a landscape reflects the varying colors of the objects on which its rays fall. The bright light entering through the panes of a stained-glass window casts on the floor its many rich warm hues. Water takes the form of its container. The troubled cry of a child arouses different emotions in its mother and in a stranger. God is a sun which shines, resplendent, over souls. He is an ocean from which each one draws according to the measure and the form of the vessel that he brings to it.

Think then of John of the Cross, an artist but especially a thinker, theologian, philosopher habituated to intellectual pursuits, and of Teresa, marvelously balanced with an ardent heart, refined sensibility, and a strong will. The divine Sun shines

[17] It is interesting to note with what critical finesse Saint John of the Cross has applied this principle to the study of interior words. He distinguishes the successive words, pronounced by the soul under the influence of a supernatural light and the formal words that the soul receives passively. In the successive words the faculties give a distinct verbal form to the general light of God; in the formal words it is God Himself who, by His direct action gives to the light a verbal form.

upon their souls and enlightens them with its burning rays. Their powers open up sincere and deep to this beneficent divine inflowing; but is it not normal that the same action should produce different effects? Whatever is received is received according to the mode of the recipient. Especially is this so when God's action, while fettering and subduing the faculties, does not however altogether suspend them. When the prayer of union is reached, they are deprived of their activity; but here, they can react and they do so according to their own personal mode. From this divine communication Saint John of the Cross draws especially light, emphasizing its privative effects in the understanding and that loving knowledge produced in the depths of the soul; while on her part Saint Teresa experiences the savor of love, and lays emphasis on the sweetness that captivates the will and arises from the inmost source which is God.

Does this solve the problem of the differences between Saint John of the Cross and Saint Teresa in their exposition of the early stages of contemplative prayer? Can one conclude that these manifestations of God as light and as love—manifestations which in these early stages reach no further than the faculties—are produced by the same bright rays of the divine Sun reflecting the different tones of the souls that receive them, and by the same living waters received according to the capacity and shape of the vessel? Can it be asserted that their differences are wholly explained by the differences in temperament of the souls who experience them? How could we dare to make such decided affirmations in this domain of mystery of God's direct, personal dealings with souls, of which He alone jealously guards the secret? In indicating a reasonable law of the divine action we have suggested an explanation which seems to hold in many cases. May divine Mercy preserve us from dogmatizing in His domain and from seeming to restrict His action within the rigid limits of our reasonable laws.[18]

[18] I ooking for God's action in the world and in events, one must avoid two contrary errors: practical naturalism, which sees only natural causes and attributes everything to them, and on the other hand a certain practical fide-

And yet, despite all the imprecision and uncertainty that there is in these suggestions, we think it possible to base on them a judgment and practical directives for the life of prayer in our time.

Today more than ever before there is widespread admiration of the marvelous richness of Saint Teresa's personality, the simplicity and sublimity of her soul, the astounding daring yet perfect balance of her ardent temperament. Countless souls are attracted by her prayer that is so alive and direct. But when they have made a certain progress in mental prayer, they generally find themselves more at home in the dry atmosphere of Saint John of the Cross's contemplation than in the delectations of Teresian quietude. The choice is not theirs; for they would probably have sought the fruitful riches of the spiritual Mother rather than the detachment of the Mystical Doctor. But that is how matters stand. Modern souls, after the example of Saint Therese of the Child Jesus, have experience rather of the privative effects of contemplation. Feeling themselves poor in God's sight, they have recourse to Saint Therese and through her to Saint John of the Cross.

How reconcile this sense of poverty in the presence of God and under the influence of His action with that of the actual, the concrete, the absolute, that is evinced in the current vogue of existential philosophies and of doctrines that touch upon every aspect of life? Could it not be because civilization has made us intellectualists if not truly intellectuals? The intellect in its pride and self-idolatry has complacently extended its empire over all things, arraigning them, itself included, before its tribunal, thus falling into agnosticism.

The mind dried up by its pride is thirsty for life. But even in

---

ism, which would see in all things the direct intervention of God. An enlightened spirit of faith, which, in particular cases, knows how to recognize God's direct intervention, knows also in a general way how to discover in events the role of secondary causes, and—dominating them—the primary activity of God who uses everything, even free causes, for the realization of His designs.

its relations with God it is proud and intellectualist, and can evidently accept only a light that dazzles and impoverishes it; but this time, in order to purify and enrich it.

It was undoubtedly to meet this attitude and this need of the modern soul that the Church has declared Saint John of the Cross, who was the Mystical Doctor of Carmel, a doctor of the Universal Church.

In this belief and in view of this need, we think it right to emphasize the teaching of the holy doctor concerning these first degrees of contemplative prayer.

CHAPTER III

The Dark Nights

Oh, night that guided me,
Oh, night more lovely than the dawn,
Oh, night that joined Beloved with lover,
Lover transformed in the Beloved! [1]

The two didactic treatises of Saint John of the Cross, the *Ascent of Mount Carmel* and the *Dark Night of the Soul,* are a commentary on the canticle of the night from which we have just read a stanza. In this commentary the Saint sets forth the principles which guide the soul in its ascent to the summit of union with God in love. In it we become at once aware of the symbolism of night in the doctrine of Saint John of the Cross. In the darkness of night the soul journeys toward God; it is the darkness that makes this journey safe and fruitful. This dark night is the whole spiritual itinerary of the soul toward God. The night and the journey are one same thing, writes the Saint, speaking of the soul: "this going forth from itself and from all things was a 'dark night.' " [2]

We are here at the heart of the doctrine of Saint John of the Cross but, at the same time, faced with a symbolism and a terminology which require some explanation. Let us consider the nature of this night, its necessity, its phases, and its diverse modes.

A. Nature of the dark night

Night for Saint John of the Cross means privation and detachment. The nights are the privations and purifications

[1] *Dark Night,* Bk. I, st.v; Peers, I, 326.
[2] *Ibid.;* 329.

through which the soul must pass to attain to union with God. They are called nights because "the soul journeys, as it were, by night, in darkness." [3] Saint John of the Cross begins his explanation of this by giving a reason taken from the philosophers:

> The soul, as soon as God infuses it into the body, is like a smooth, blank board upon which nothing is painted; and, save for that which it experiences through the senses, nothing is communicated to it, in the course of nature, from any other source. And thus, for as long as it is in the body, it is like one who is in a dark prison and who knows nothing, save what he is able to see through the windows of the said prison; and, if he saw nothing through them, he would see nothing in any other way. And thus the soul, save for that which is communicated to it through the senses, which are the windows of its prison, could acquire nothing, in the course of nature, in any other way.
>
> Wherefore, if the soul rejects and denies that which it can receive through the senses, we can quite well say that it remains, as it were, dark and empty.[4]

And he remarks:

> We are not treating here of the lack of things, since this implies no detachment on the part of the soul if it has a desire for them; but we are treating of the detachment from them of the taste and desire, for it is this that leaves the soul free and void of them, although it may have them; for it is not the things of this world that either occupy the soul or cause it harm, since they enter it not, but rather the will and desire for them, for it is these that dwell within it.[5]

Night therefore affects much more the appetite than the faculty in which it is directly experienced. And so the Saint writes:

> We here describe as night the privation of every kind of pleasure which belongs to the desire; for even as night is naught but the privation of light, and, consequently, of all objects that can be seen by means of light, whereby the visual faculty remains unoccupied and in darkness, even so likewise the mortification of desire may be called night to the soul. For, when the soul is deprived of the pleasure of its desire in all things, it remains, as it were, unoccupied and in dark-

[3] *Ascent*, Bk. I, i; Peers, I, 17.
[4] *Ibid.*, iii; 22.
[5] *Ibid.*; 23.

ness. For even as the visual faculty, by means of light, is nourished and fed by objects which can be seen, and which, when the light is quenched, are not seen, even so, by means of the desire, the soul is nourished and fed by all things wherein it can take pleasure according to its faculties; and, when this also is quenched, or rather, mortified, the soul ceases to be fed upon the pleasure of all things, and thus, with respect to its desire, it remains unoccupied and in darkness.[6]

Night then is not an annihilation of the intellect, but rather a mortification of the appetite. This important distinction must be kept in mind.

This night like the night of nature has three parts: evening, midnight, and dawn:

We may say that there are three reasons for which this journey made by the soul to union with God is called night. The first has to do with the point from which the soul goes forth, for it has gradually to deprive itself of desire for all the worldly things which it possessed, by denying them to itself; which denial and deprivation are, as it were, night to all the senses of man. The second reason has to do with the mean, or the road along which the soul must travel to this union—that is, faith, which is likewise as dark as night to the understanding. The third has to do with the point to which it travels,—namely God, Who, equally, is dark night to the soul in this life. These three nights must pass through the soul,—or rather, the soul must pass through them—in order that it may come to Divine union with God. . . .

These three parts of the night are all one night; but like night itself, it has three parts. For the first part, which is that of sense, is comparable to the beginning of night, the point at which things begin to fade from sight. And the second part, which is faith, is comparable to midnight, which is total darkness. And the third part is like the close of night, which is God, which part is now near to the light of day.[7]

For these various reasons, and especially because of the nature of God and of faith which attains to Him, the reign of darkness extends over the whole spiritual itinerary. It will have a particular aspect at each stage. For the moment we shall consider it in its general traits, common to all periods of the journey.

[6] *Ibid.;* 21.
[7] *Ibid.,* ii; 19-21.

B. Necessity of the dark night

To prove the necessity of the dark night, Saint John of the Cross devotes to it no less than nine chapters of the *Ascent of Mount Carmel* [8] and six of the *Dark Night*.[9] In these his logic is rigorous, concise, and absolute. Its conclusions are inescapable.

1. HARM CAUSED BY DESIRES AND AFFECTIONS IN GENERAL

a. *Private effects*

Our guide first points out to us the end to be attained: "the divine light of the perfect union of the love of God." [10] The means taken must be proportionate to such an end.

Here is the general argument:

> The reason is that two contraries (even as philosophy teaches us) cannot coexist in one person; and that darkness, which is affection for the creatures, and light, which is God, are contrary to each other, and have no likeness or accord between one another, even as Saint Paul explained to the Corinthians, saying: *Quae conventio luci ad tenebras?*[11] That is to say: What communion can there be between light and darkness? Hence it is that the light of Divine union cannot dwell in the soul if these affections first flee not away from it.[12]

Let us follow the reasoning of the holy doctor. Love establishes a certain equality and similarity between the one who loves and the object loved:

> Thus, he that loves a creature becomes as low as is that creature, and, in some ways, lower; for love not only makes the lover equal to the object of his love, but even subjects him to it. Wherefore in the same way it comes to pass that that soul that loves anything else becomes incapable of pure union with God and transformation in Him. For the low estate of the creature is much less capable of union with the high estate of the Creator than is darkness with light. . . . And even as he that is in darkness comprehends not the light, so the soul

[8] *Ibid.*, iv-xii; 23-56.
[9] *Dark Night*, Bk. I, ii-vii; Peers, I, 332-349.
[10] *Ascent*, Prologue; Peers, I, 11.
[11] II Cor. 6:14.
[12] *Ascent*, Bk I, iv; 24.

that sets its affections upon creatures will be unable to comprehend God; and, until it be purged, it will be able neither to possess Him here below, through pure transformation of love, nor yonder in clear vision.[13]

All the being of creation, then, compared with the infinite Being of God, is nothing. And therefore the soul that sets its affections upon the being of creation is likewise nothing in the eyes of God, and less than nothing; for, as we have said, love makes equality and similitude, and even sets the lover below the object of his love. And therefore such a soul will in no wise be able to attain to union with the infinite Being of God; for that which is not can have no agreement with that which is.[14]

The Saint enumerates the various goods of this world in order to apply the principle he has enunciated:

All the beauty of the creatures, compared with the infinite beauty of God, is the height of deformity, even as Solomon says in the Proverbs: *Fallax gratia, et vana est pulchritudo.* Favour is deceitful and beauty is vain. And thus the soul that is affectioned to the beauty of any creature is as the height of deformity in the eyes of God. And therefore this soul that is deformed will be unable to become transformed in beauty, which is God, since deformity cannot attain to beauty.[15]

So it is with the wisdom of this world and all human ingenuity, with all pleasures and delights of the will, with riches and the glory of all things created; attachment to any of them renders the soul unfit for transformation in God:

Wherefore, it is supreme ignorance for the soul to think that it will be able to pass to this high estate of union with God if first it void not the desire of all things, natural and supernatural, which may hinder it, according as we shall declare hereafter; for there is the greatest possible distance between these things and that which comes to pass in this estate, which is naught else than transformation in God. For this reason Our Lord, when instructing us in this way said through Saint Luke:[16] . . . He that renounces not all things that he possesses with his will cannot be My disciple. And this is evident; for the doctrine that the Son of God came to teach was contempt for all things, so that a man might receive as a reward the spirit of God in himself.

13 *Ibid.;* 24.
14 *Ibid.;* 25.
15 *Ibid.;* 25.
16 Luke 14:33.

For, as long as the soul rejects not all things, it has no capacity to receive the spirit of God in pure transformation.[17]

As usual Saint John of the Cross bases his teaching on Sacred Scripture, illustrating it with figures borrowed in abundance from the Bible:

Of this we have a figure in Exodus,[18] wherein we read that God gave not the children of Israel the food from Heaven, which was manna, until the flour which they had brought from Egypt failed them. . . .

And not only does the soul become incapable of receiving the Divine Spirit when it stays and pastures on other strange pleasures, but those souls greatly offend the Divine Majesty who desire spiritual food and are not content with God alone, but desire rather to intermingle desire and affection for other things.

This can likewise be seen in the same Scripture,[19] wherein it is said that, not content with that simplest of food, they desired and craved fleshly food. And that Our Lord was grievously offended that they should desire to intermingle a food that was so base and so coarse with one that was so noble and so simple; which though it was so, had within itself the sweetness and substance of all foods. Wherefore, while they yet had the morsels in their mouths, as David says likewise:[20] The wrath of God came down upon them, sending fire from Heaven and consuming many thousands of them; for God held it an unworthy thing that they should have a desire for other food when He had given them food from Heaven.[21]

Saint John of the Cross multiplies proofs and examples in his eagerness to communicate to us the burning conviction born of his own experience. He seems to fear not being able to do so. There is a note of desolation in his appeal:

Oh, did spiritual persons but know how much good and what great abundance of spirit they lose through not seeking to raise up their desires above childish things, and how they would find in this simple spiritual food the sweetness of all things, if they desired not to taste those things! But such food gives them no pleasure.[22]

[17] *Ascent,* Bk. I, v; 29.
[18] Exod. 16:3.
[19] Numb. 11:4.
[20] Ps. 77:31.
[21] *Ascent,* Bk. I, v; 29 ff.
[22] *Ibid.;* 30.

b. *Positive evils*

To this general argument set forth so strongly, Saint John of the Cross adds a more precise and detailed exposition to show us how the desires cause two principal evils to the soul. The first is privative and consists in the deprivation of the spirit of God. The second is positive and multiple: the desires weary the soul, torment it, darken it, stain and weaken it.

Of the privative harm the Saint has already spoken. But he returns to it to sum up in energetic terms:

> Wherefore, as in natural generation no form can be introduced unless the preceding, contrary form is first expelled from the subject, which form, while present, is an impediment to the other by reason of the contrariety which the two have between each other; even so, for as long as the soul is subjected to the sensual spirit, the spirit which is pure and spiritual cannot enter it. Wherefore our Saviour said through Saint Matthew:[23] . . . It is not meet to take the children's bread and to cast it to the dogs.[24]

The positive evils are treated at length. Saint John of the Cross conveys in these pages—one would like to quote them extensively—all his horror of sin, all his suffering at seeing so many souls remain in spiritual mediocrity because they only imperfectly mortify their desires. A few quotations will awaken in us the urge to read and analyze the text itself.

1. First of all there is the weariness produced by these desires:

> It is clear that the desires weary and fatigue the soul; for they are like restless and discontented children, who are ever demanding this or that from their mother, and are never satisfied. . . . And the soul that has desires is wearied and fatigued; for it is like a man that is sick of a fever, who finds himself no better until the fever leaves him, and whose thirst increases with every moment. . . . The soul is wearied and fatigued by its desires, because it is wounded and moved and disturbed by them as is water by the winds; in just the same way they disturb it, allowing it not to rest in any place or in any thing soever. And of such a soul says Isaias:[25] The heart of the wicked man is like the sea when it rages. . . .

[23] Matt. 15:20.
[24] *Ascent,* Bk. I, vi; 34.
[25] Is. 57:20.

The soul that would fain satisfy its desires grows wearied and fatigued; for it is like one that, being hungered, opens his mouth that he may sate himself with wind, when, instead of being satisfied, his craving becomes greater, for the wind is no food for him.[26]

2. This weariness, though overpowering, does not induce rest; it is the weariness of fever and fret.

The second kind of positive evil which the desires cause the soul is in their tormenting and afflicting of it. . . . Of these David says:[27] . . . They compassed me about like bees, wounding me with their stings, and they were enkindled against me, like fire among thorns; for in the desires, which are the thorns, increases the fire of anguish and torment. And even as the husbandman, coveting the harvest for which he hopes, afflicts and torments the ox in the plough, even so does concupiscence afflict the soul in its desire to attain that for which it longs. . . .

Of this there is a figure in the Book of the Judges, wherein it may be read that that strong man, Samson, who at one time was strong and free and a judge of Israel, fell into the power of his enemies, and they took his strength from him, and put out his eyes, and bound him in a mill, to grind corn, wherein they tormented and afflicted him greatly; and thus it happens to the soul in which these its enemies, the desires, live and rule; for the first thing that they do is to weaken the soul and blind it, as we shall say below; and then they afflict and torment it, binding it to the mill of concupiscence; and the bonds with which it is bound are its own desires.

Wherefore God, having compassion . . . calls us through Saint Matthew, saying:[28] All ye that go about tormented, afflicted and burdened with the burden of your cares and desires, go forth from them, come to Me, and I will refresh you and ye shall find for your souls the rest which your desires take from you.[29]

3. The third evil caused by the desires is still graver and more harmful, especially for the contemplative. Like the passions, they blind the soul. Just as the clouds and mists veil the rays of the sun, so do the desires shut out from the soul the light of God and of reason, blinding and darkening it.

The third evil that the desires cause in the soul is that they blind and darken it. Even as vapours darken the air and allow not the bright sun to shine; or as a mirror that is clouded over cannot receive within

[26] *Ascent,* Bk. I, vi; 35-6.
[27] Ps. 118:12.
[28] Matt. 11:28.
[29] *Ascent,* Bk. I, vii; 37-8.

itself a clear image; or as water defiled by mud reflects not the visage of one that looks therein; even so the soul that is clouded by the desires is darkened in the understanding and allows neither the sun of natural reason nor that of the supernatural Wisdom of God to shine upon it and illumine it clearly. And thus David, speaking to this purpose, says:[30] Mine iniquities have taken hold upon me, and I could have no power to see.

And at this time, when the soul is darkened in the understanding, it is stultified also in the will, and the memory becomes dull and disordered in its due operation. For these faculties in their operations depend upon the understanding. . . .

Desire blinds and darkens the soul; for desire, as such, is blind, since of itself it has no understanding in itself, the reason being to it always, as it were, a child leading a blind man. And hence it comes to pass that, whensoever the soul is guided by its desire, it becomes blind; for this is as if one that sees were guided by one that sees not. . . . Of little use are its eyes to a moth, since desire for the beauty of the light dazzles it and leads it into the flame. And even so we may say that one who feeds upon desire is like a fish that is dazzled, upon which the light acts rather as darkness, preventing it from seeing the harm which the fishermen are preparing for it. This is very well explained by David himself, where he says of such persons:[31] There came upon them the fire, which burns with its heat and dazzles with its light. . . .

Oh that men could know how great is the blessing of Divine light whereof they are deprived by this blindness which proceeds from their affections and desires, and into what great hurts and evils these make them to fall day after day, for so long as they mortify them not! For a man must not rely upon a clear understanding, or upon gifts that he has received from God, and think that he may indulge his affection or desire, and will not be blinded and darkened, and fall gradually into a worse estate. For who would have said that a man so perfect in wisdom and the gifts of God as was Solomon would have been reduced to such blindness and foolishness of the will as to make altars to so many idols and to adore them himself, when he was old?[32] And no more was needed to bring him to this than the affection which he had for women and his neglect to deny his desires and the delights of his heart.[33]

4. Thus blinded and subjected to instinct by the desires, the soul becomes defiled. This defilement comes from the creatures

[30] Ps. 39:13.
[31] Ps. 57:9.
[32] III Kings 11:4.
[33] *Ascent,* Bk. I, viii; 39-42.

to which its desires attach it inordinately. This is the fourth evil that desires cause the soul.

They stain and defile it, as is taught in Ecclesiastes, in these words:[34] He that touches pitch shall be defiled therewith. And a man touches pitch when he allows the desire of his will to be satisfied by any creature. . . . And just as gold or diamond, if it were heated and placed upon pitch, would become foul and be stained by it, inasmuch as the heat would have cajoled and allured the pitch, even so the soul that is hot with desire for any creature draws forth foulness from it through the heat of its desire and is stained by it. . . . And in the same way that traces of soot would defile a face that is very lovely and perfect, even in this way do disordered desires befoul and defile the soul that has them, the which soul is in itself a most lovely and perfect image of God. . . .

If we set out to speak of the foul and vile appearance that the desires can give the soul, we should find nothing, however full of cobwebs and worms it might be, not even the corruption of a dead body, nor aught else that is impure and vile, nor aught that can exist and be imagined in this life, to which we could compare it. For, although it is true that the disordered soul, in its natural being, is as perfect as when God created it, yet, in its reasonable being, it is vile, abominable, foul, black and full of all the evils that are here being described, and many more.[35]

5. The will itself is tainted by the desires. These weaken and weary it, dissipating its energies on various objects. This is the fifth evil wrought by the desires. The soul has no longer the strength to walk perseveringly in the path of virtue.

For as the strength of the desire, when it is set upon various aims, is less than if it were set wholly on one thing alone. . . . As hot water, when uncovered, readily loses heat, and as aromatic spices, when they are unwrapped, gradually lose the fragrance and strength of their perfume, even so the soul that is not recollected in one single desire for God loses heat and vigour in its virtue.

And the desires weaken the virtue of the soul, because they are to it like the shoots that grow about a tree, and take away its virtue so that it cannot bring forth so much fruit. . . . And indeed, they are also like leeches, which are ever sucking the blood from the veins. . . .

From this it is clear that the desires bring no good to the soul but rather take from it that which it has; and if it mortify them not, they will not cease till they have wrought in it that which the children of the viper are said to work in their mother; who, as they are growing

[34] Eccles. 13:1.
[35] *Ascent,* Bk. I, ix; 43-4.

within her womb, consume her and kill her, and they themselves remain alive at her cost.[36]

Such is the multiple harm done to the soul by evil desires. Certainly, presented thus logically and rigorously, and with such vivid illustrations, Saint John's description of the evils caused the soul by desires leaves an impression that is almost terrifying.

2. ONLY THE VOLUNTARY DESIRES ARE HARMFUL

But do all our desires then really expose us to all these evils? Saint John of the Cross distinguishes: only the voluntary desires which have for their object a mortal sin incur the first and gravest evil, namely, the privation of grace; but he adds, all the desires mortal, venial, or simply imperfections, if they are voluntary, produce positive harm in different degrees.[37] The holy doctor places emphasis on their voluntariness. He says:

I am not writing here of the other natural desires which are not voluntary, and of thoughts that go not beyond the first movements, and other temptations to which the soul is not consenting; for these produce in the soul none of the evils aforementioned. For, although a person who suffers them may believe that the passion and disturbance which they then produce in him are defiling and blinding him, it is not the case; rather they are bringing him the opposite advantages.[38]

And elsewhere he writes:

I am speaking of those [desires] that are voluntary, for the natural desires hinder the soul little, if at all, from attaining to union, when they are not consented to nor pass beyond the first movements.[39]

Of such sins as these which are not voluntary and surreptitious it is written that the just man shall fall seven times in the day and shall rise up again.[40] But of the voluntary desires, which, though they be for very small things, are, as I have said, intentional venial sins, and any one that is not conquered suffices to impede union.[41]

[36] *Ibid.*, x; 47-8.
[37] *Ibid.*, xii; 54 ff.
[38] *Ibid.*; 56.
[39] *Ibid.*, xi; 49.
[40] Prov. 24:6.
[41] *Ascent*, Bk. I, xi; 50.

After having clearly distinguished the voluntary tendencies from "the natural desires or first movements" which are "all those wherein the rational will has had no part, whether at first or afterward," and which it is impossible to mortify wholly in this life,[42] the Saint gives examples of voluntary desires and insists on their baneful effects:

> These habitual imperfections are, for example, a common custom of much speaking, or some slight attachment which we never quite wish to conquer—such as that to a person, a garment, a book, a cell, a particular kind of food, tittle-tattle, fancies for tasting, knowing or hearing certain things and suchlike. . . . For it comes to the same thing whether a bird be held by a slender cord or by a stout one; since, even if it be slender, the bird will be as well held as though it were stout, for so long as it breaks it not and flies not away.[43]

And the Saint appeals to his own experience to support such grave affirmations:

> We have seen many persons to whom God has been granting the favour of leading them a long way, into a state of great detachment and liberty, yet who, merely through beginning to indulge some small attachment, under the pretext of doing good, or in the guise of conversation and friendship, often lose their spirituality and desire for God and holy solitude.[44]

The eleventh chapter of the *Ascent of Mount Carmel* is one of the most striking of those comprising the didactic teaching of Saint John of the Cross. Vigorous, austere, exact, it tells all the demands that love makes before it can wholly triumph in the soul. As long as there remains in the soul an unmortified, voluntary desire, not only can it not aspire to the perfect embrace of divine love, but it must fear losing what it has gained.

3. EVILS CAUSED BY EACH ONE OF THE CAPITAL SINS

But Saint John of the Cross is not only the vigorous theorist as regards the ascetic demands of perfect love. He is also the spiritual director who, with paternal kindness places at our

[42] *Ibid.;* 49.
[43] *Ibid.;* 50.
[44] *Ibid.;* 52.

disposal his clear-sighted psychological penetration in order to help us discover in us those tendencies which can be purified only in this dark night of faith.

In one of the first chapters of the *Dark Night* we find a sketch, drawn with a master hand, of the imperfections of those beginners who are "like to children . . . in all they do."

> In order that this may be seen more clearly, and likewise how much these beginners in the virtues lack with respect to the works in which they so readily engage with the pleasure aforementioned, we shall describe it by reference to the seven capital sins, each in its turn, indicating some of the many imperfections which they have under each heading.[45]

It is impossible to sum up the twenty pages that Saint John of the Cross gives to this analysis of faults and tendencies. They are among the most useful and the most penetrating that the mystical doctor has written. Any soul who aspires to perfection ought to read them and reread them, meditating at length upon them. A few passages will acquaint us with their great value.

a. *This concerns spiritual pride:*

> As these beginners feel themselves to be very fervent and diligent in spiritual things and devout exercises, from this prosperity (although it is true that holy things of their own nature cause humility) there often comes to them through their imperfections, a certain kind of secret pride whence they come to have some degree of satisfaction with their works and with themselves. And hence there comes to them likewise a certain desire, which is somewhat vain, and at times very vain, to speak of spiritual things before others, and sometimes even to teach such things rather than to learn them. They condemn others in their heart when they see that they have not the kind of devotion which they themselves desire. . . . And such a degree of evil are some of these persons wont to reach that they would have none appear good save themselves. . . .
>
> Sometimes, too, when their spiritual masters . . . do not approve of their spirit and behaviour . . . they consider that they do not understand them, or that, because they do not approve of this and comply with that, their confessors are themselves not spiritual. . . .

With good-humored but penetrating irony the Saint lays bare the adroit dissemblings as well as the laughable ruses of pride:

[45] *Dark Night,* Bk. I, i; Peers, I, 331.

Presuming thus, they are wont to resolve much and accomplish very little. Sometimes they are anxious that others shall realize how spiritual and devout they are, to which end they occasionally give outward evidence thereof in movements, sighs and other ceremonies. . . . They are too much embarrassed to confess their sins nakedly, lest their confessors should think less of them. . . .

Some of these beginners, too, make little of their faults, and at other times become over-sad when they see themselves fall into them, thinking themselves to have been saints already; and thus they become angry and impatient with themselves, which is another imperfection.[46]

To throw more light on the picture, Saint John of the Cross paints the contrasting one of the truly humble:

These souls will give their heart's blood to anyone that serves God, and will help others to serve Him as much as in them lies. . . . But souls who in the beginning journey with this degree of perfection are, as I understand, and as has been said, a minority, and very few are those who we can be glad do not fall into the opposite errors.[47]

b. *His description of spiritual covetousness is briefer but made with great precision:*

Many of these beginners have also at times great spiritual avarice. . . . They are very disconsolate and querulous because they find not in spiritual things the consolation that they would desire. Many can never have enough of listening to counsels and learning spiritual precepts, and of possessing and reading many books which treat of this matter. . . . Furthermore, they burden themselves with images and rosaries which are very curious; now they put down one, now take up another; now they change about, now change back again; now they want this kind of thing, now that, preferring one kind of cross to another, because it is more curious. And others you will see adorned with agnusdeis and relics and tokens, like children with trinkets. Here I condemn the attachment of the heart, and the affection which they have for the nature, multitude and curiosity of these things, inasmuch as it is quite contrary to poverty of spirit.[48]

c. *The advice of Saint John of the Cross on the subject of spiritual luxury is particularly valuable.* He says:

Leaving apart the falling of spiritual persons into this sin, since my intent is to treat of the imperfections which have to be purged by the

[46] *Ibid.*, ii; 332 ff.
[47] *Ibid.;* 335.
[48] *Ibid.*, iii; 336.

dark night, they [these beginners] have many imperfections which might be described as spiritual luxury, not because they are so, but because the imperfections proceed from spiritual things. For it often comes to pass that, in their very spiritual exercises, when they are powerless to prevent it, there arise and assert themselves in the sensual part of the soul impure acts and motions, and sometimes this happens even when the spirit is deep in prayer, or engaged in the Sacrament of Penance or in the Eucharist. . . .

The first cause from which they often proceed is the pleasure which human nature takes in spiritual things. For when the spirit and the sense are pleased, every part of a man is moved by that pleasure. . . . Now as, after all, these two parts are combined in one individual, they ordinarily both participate in that which one of them receives, each after its manner; for, as the philosopher says, everything that is received is in the recipient after the manner of the same recipient. And thus, in these beginnings, and even when the soul has made some progress, its sensual part, being imperfect, oftentimes receives the Spirit of God with the same imperfection.[49]

Both the principles and the conclusion are clearly stated, and are of universal application and calculated to calm the fears of many delicate and pure souls that have attained to rather elevated degrees of the spiritual life.

The second cause whence these rebellions sometimes proceed is the devil, who, in order to disquiet and disturb the soul, at times when it is at prayer or is striving to pray, contrives to stir up these motions of impurity in its nature; and if the soul gives heed to any of these, they cause it great harm.[50]

The third cause whence these impure motions are apt to proceed . . . is often the fear which such persons have conceived for these impure representations and motions. Something that they see or say or think brings them to their mind, and this makes them afraid, so that they suffer from them through no fault of their own.[51]

These movements are more troublesome in the case of certain souls of "tender and frail a nature." Under the heading of spiritual luxury Saint John of the Cross adds that boastfulness, display, self-complacency with which certain persons speak of spiritual things and perform acts of piety. There also he deals with certain friendships made under the guise of spirituality:

[49] *Ibid.*, iv; 338-9.
[50] *Ibid.*; 339.
[51] *Ibid.*; 340.

. . . which oftentimes arise from luxury and not from spirituality; this may be known to be the case when the remembrance of that friendship causes not the remembrance and love of God to grow, but occasions remorse of conscience. For, when the friendship is purely spiritual, the love of God grows with it; and the more the soul remembers it, the more it remembers the love of God, and the greater the desire it has for God; so that, as the one grows, the other grows also.[52]

This is a golden rule, an infallible criterion. Saint Therese of the Child Jesus appreciated its importance, writing it on the back of a picture of Saint John of the Cross which she kept in her breviary.

d. *Anger too shows itself in the conduct of certain beginners:*

They very easily become irritated over the smallest matter—sometimes, indeed, none can tolerate them. This happens frequently after they have been very pleasantly recollected in prayer according to sense.[53]

They cannot bear with the deprivation of sweetness and delight and are like "the child when they take it from the breast of which it was enjoying the sweetness."

At times also these beginners "become irritated at the sins of others, and keep watch on those others with a sort of uneasy zeal. . . . [They] set themselves up as masters of virtue." Or again they "are vexed with themselves when they observe their own imperfectness, and display an impatience that is not humility; so impatient are they about this that they would fain be saints in a day." [54]

e. *Saint John of the Cross insists at length on the sin of spiritual gluttony:*

For there is scarce one of these beginners who, however good his progress, falls not into some of the many imperfections which come to these beginners with respect to this sin, on account of the sweetness which they find at first in spiritual exercises. . . . Some of these persons, attracted by the pleasure which they find therein, kill themselves with penances, and others weaken themselves with fasts, by performing

[52] *Ibid.*; 341.
[53] *Ibid.*, v; 342.
[54] *Ibid.*; 343.

more than their frailty can bear, without the order or advice of any. . . .

They set bodily penance before subjection and obedience, which is penance of the reason and discretion, and therefore a sacrifice more acceptable and pleasing to God than any beside. But this, when the other side of it is disregarded, is no more than the penance of beasts, to which they are attracted, exactly like beasts, by the desire and pleasure which they find therein. . . . And many of these the devil assails, stirring up this gluttony in them through the pleasures and desires which he increases within them, to such an extent that, since they can no longer help themselves. . . .

These persons, in communicating, strive with every nerve to obtain some kind of sensible sweetness and pleasure, instead of humbly doing reverence and giving praise within themselves to God. And in such wise do they devote themselves to this that, when they have received no pleasure or sweetness in the senses, they think that they have accomplished nothing at all. . . .

These persons have the same defect as regards the practice of prayer, for they think that all the business of prayer consists in experiencing sensible pleasure and devotion and they strive to obtain this by great effort, wearying and fatiguing their faculties and their heads. . . .

These persons who are thus inclined to such pleasures have another very great imperfection, which is that they are very weak and remiss in journeying upon the hard road of the Cross.[55]

f. *Envy and spiritual sloth with which Saint John deals in the last place are the fruits of pride and gluttony:*

[Envy causes beginners] to experience movements of displeasure at the spiritual good of others, which cause them a certain sensible grief at being outstripped upon this road, so that they would prefer not to hear others praised; for they become displeased at others' virtues and sometimes they cannot refrain from contradicting what is said in praise of them, depreciating it as far as they can; and their annoyance thereat grows because the same is not said of them, for they would fain be preferred in everything. . . .

With respect also to spiritual sloth, beginners are apt to be irked by the things that are most spiritual, from which they flee because these things are incompatible with sensible pleasure. . . . If once they failed to find in prayer the satisfaction which their taste required . . . they would prefer not to return to it: sometimes they leave it; at other times they continue it unwillingly. . . .

These persons likewise find it irksome when they are commanded to do that wherein they take no pleasure.[56]

[55] *Ibid.*, vi; 343 ff.
[56] *Ibid.*, vii; 347-9.

These imperfections into which among others beginners fall must be purified in the dark night. Saint John of the Cross makes this clear in the conclusions with which he ends the discussion of each particular imperfection of beginners.

C. Phases and modes of the dark night

1. PHASES

From the first chapter of the *Ascent of Mount Carmel,* Saint John of the Cross makes it plain that the dark night has two phases, the purification of the senses and the purification of the spirit:

> The first night or purgation is of the sensual part of the soul . . . and the second is of the spiritual part.[57]

In the book of the *Dark Night* we find the same division:

> The one night or purgation will be sensual, wherein the soul is purged according to sense, which is subdued to the spirit; and the other is a night or purgation which is spiritual; wherein the soul is purged and stripped according to the spirit, and subdued and made ready for the union of love with God. The night of sense is common and comes to many; these are the beginners. . . . The night of the spirit is the portion of very few, and these are they that are already practised and proficient.[58]

Thus the two phases of the dark night are quite distinct, both by reason of the parts of the soul in which they take place and because of the end to be attained. Let us be precise.

The dark night of sense takes place in the sensitive faculties, and subdues them to the spirit. These powers are the external and internal senses, including of course the imagination. But if it be asked if this night touches only the senses, we would say it seems to involve more.

The soul, we must remember, is substantially united to the body; and while logic clearly distinguishes the intellectual life with its faculties from sense life with its powers, this distinction is not so sharp in the moving reality of life.

[57] *Ascent,* Bk. I, i; Peers, I, 18.
[58] *Dark Night,* Bk I, viii; Peers, I, 349.

There are our intellectual faculties, or rather a part of them which is in constant relation with our sensitive powers. There is our sensitive memory with its images into which our intellect plunges to abstract from them universal ideas. Then our will is drawn by its sensible desires towards sensible goods, undergoing their influence before it succeeds in controlling it. Those parts of our intellectual faculties then which border on our sensitive powers, and in the measure that their activity is allied and dependent on them, belong themselves to the domain of our senses. Sense life is localized in a certain region of the soul rather than in a power. It is at the periphery, there where those operations are produced in which the sense powers have a predominant influence. The spirit is the center of the soul and includes all that region where purely intellectual operations are realized.

This localization can, alone, explain those distinctions familiar to the mystics who speak of the suburbs of the soul where the superficial powers are, namely, the sense powers properly so called, the senses and the imagination. Here too the mystics locate the understanding and a part of the will, respectfully reserving the secret depths of the soul for the intelligence and basic will. The first regions constitute the sense part, the second are the spirit. This terminology, however disconcerting it may be for the traditional science of psychology, corresponds to a localization of tumult and of peace experienced in the course of union with God. Rather frequently in fact does God's action in the soul diffuse peace in the depths of the soul, of the intellect and will, while the imagination and the understanding—the reasoning faculty—are restless and disturbed.

It is these superficial and wayward powers that the purification of the senses has for its purpose to accommodate to the spirit at the same time that it purifies the sensitive powers themselves, so that they will not be troublesome to the spirit when it is subject to the action of God.

2. MODES

Purification whether of the senses or of the spirit requires a twofold activity: that of God and that of the soul. Hence there is the active night which "consists in that which the soul can do, and does, of itself, in order to enter therein," and the passive night "wherein the soul does nothing, and God works in it." [59]

When he sets forth the imperfections of beginners, Saint John of the Cross constantly remarks upon the inability of human activity to destroy such faults. He writes:

> Neither from these imperfections nor from those others can the soul be perfectly purified until God brings it into the passive purgation of that dark night whereof we shall speak presently. It befits the soul, however, in so far as it can, to contrive to labour, on its own account, to purge and perfect itself, so that it may merit being taken by God into that Divine care wherein it becomes healed of all things that it was unable of itself to cure.[60]
>
> For, however assiduously the beginner practises the mortification in himself of all these actions and passions of his, he can never completely succeed—very far from it—until God shall work it in him passively by means of the purgation of the said night.[61]

Thus the active night must prepare for and merit the passive night which is alone efficacious. The latter, on the other hand, demands a cooperation from the soul that is more energetic and painful than all its ascetic efforts hitherto.

This spiritual journey of the soul called the dark night has then an active and a passive aspect, both so closely knit as to be inseparable. It has been aptly suggested that "if one wished to express this twofold aspect of the dark night, one could draw first a perpendicular line to symbolize the soul's own activity. Then at a certain point on it, one would draw an arc to meet the line again at the top, which would represent the action of God." [62] At the summit the action of God and the soul become one living flame of love.

[59] *Ascent,* Bk I, xiii; Peers, I, 56.
[60] *Dark Night,* Bk I, iii; Peers, I, 337.
[61] *Ibid.,* vii; 349.
[62] Cf. P. Lucien, *Introduction à la Montée du Carmel,* p. 7.

Thus the *Ascent of Mount Carmel* which describes the soul's active role in its purification and the *Dark Night of the Soul* which details God's action in it are inseparable one from another.

In truth the asceticism of the *Ascent* seems wholly contemplative. This is so not only in the sense that it prepares the soul for contemplation, but also because in order to understand it and apply it in its fulness, one must already have had, at least in a transitory form, some experience of supernatural contemplation. It is these divine communications which create in the soul a thirst for the infinite and make it feel the need of the night of purification.

This precisely is what Saint John of the Cross affirms in his Prologue to the *Ascent*. He says:

> Nor is my principal intent to address all, but rather certain persons of our sacred Order of Mount Carmel of the primitive observance, both friars and nuns—since they have desired me to do so—to whom God is granting the favour of setting them on the road to this Mount; who, as they are already detached from the temporal things of this world, will better understand the instruction concerning detachment of spirit.[63]

Consequently if it is true that this doctrine can in some cases prepare a soul to enter into the fourth Mansions, nevertheless it is only within these very Mansions themselves that the soul receives that light which reveals its inner depths, and which enables the soul to submit itself with full benefit to its guidance.

[63] *Ascent,* Prologue; Peers, I, 15.

CHAPTER IV

The Dark Night of Sense

On a dark night,
Kindled in love with yearnings—
Oh, happy chance!—
I went forth without being observed,
My house being now at rest.[1]

The dark night of the senses is studied by Saint John of the Cross under its twofold aspect, active and passive. These are two distinct nights although bearing on the same faculties: the active night being nothing else than the mortification of the appetites which is effected by the soul itself; the passive night being the work of God and of His direct action in the soul.

The active night itself includes two phases. The first phase, which is preparatory, corresponds to the first three Teresian Mansions. It is simply mentioned by Saint John of the Cross but not studied by him. The Saint sets out by taking up the case of "beginners at the time when God begins to bring them into the state of contemplation." [2] It is then that the active night enters upon its second phase, when it joins forces with the passive night in the purification of the soul.

In the first preparatory phase, in which God does not intervene directly in the spiritual life of the soul, the soul itself retains the initiative, directing the active dark night in its own way. In the second phase, on the contrary, where the active and

[1] *Canticle of the Dark Night,* st. i; Peers, I, 329.
[2] *Ascent,* Bk. I, i; Peers, I, 18.

passive nights progress simultaneously, God gradually takes over the direction of the spiritual life, taking the initiative away from the soul, and brings it into submission to His own action within it.

Consequently, in this second phase of the night of the senses, the more important and the only one that Saint John of the Cross studies, active night and passive night are closely united and must complete each other. The treatise on the *Dark Night of Sense* cannot be separated from the *Ascent of Mount Carmel* and ought to be studied at the same time. These two nights can have their full purifying effect only if their action is synchronized. But since God has now taken the initiative and assumed direction of the soul, and since the soul must submit, the passive night produced by Him must have precedence over the active night.

The latter, which is the soul's own part, must keep pace with it, responding to its demands.

This is why, after treating of the first steps in contemplative prayer, we think it necessary to speak of the passive night of the senses before dealing in detail with what ought to be the conduct of the soul during this period. It is God's purifying action that will regulate the cooperation of the soul, or the active night.

In the *Dark Night,* Saint John of the Cross writes apropos of the passive night in general:

> Since the night of sense is first in order and comes first, we shall first of all say something about it briefly, since more is written of it, as of a thing that is more common; and we shall pass on to treat more fully of the spiritual night, since very little has been said of this, either in speech or in writing, and very little is known of it, even by experience.[3]

This text lets us see the place, a minor one and of the second order, that the night of sense holds in the doctrine of Saint John of the Cross and in his treatise on the *Dark Night,* re-

[3] *Dark Night,* Bk. I, viii; Peers, I, 350.

served especially for the night of the spirit. These "few words," briefly stated in passing, give us in regard to the dark night of sense a doctrine that is found nowhere else in so concise and logical a form. A consideration of them will suffice us to learn the nature and cause of the dark night of sense, the stage at which it appears, its effects of suffering and of grace.

A. Nature and cause

Since, then, the conduct of these beginners upon the way of God is ignoble, and has much to do with their love of self and their own inclinations, as has been explained above, God desires to lead them farther. He seeks to bring them out of that ignoble kind of love to a higher degree of love for Him, to free them from the ignoble exercises of sense and meditation (wherewith, as we have said, they go seeking God so unworthily and in so many ways that are unbefitting), and to lead them to a kind of spiritual exercise wherein they can commune with Him more abundantly and are freed more completely from imperfections. For they have now had practice for some time in the way of virtue and have persevered in meditation and prayer, whereby, through the sweetness and pleasure that they have found therein, they have lost their love of the things of the world and have gained some degree of spiritual strength in God; this has enabled them to some extent to refrain from creature desires, so that for God's sake they are now able to suffer a light burden and a little aridity without turning back to a time which they found more pleasant.

When they are going about these spiritual exercises with the greatest delight and pleasure, and when they believe that the sun of Divine favour is shining most brightly upon them, God turns all this light of theirs into darkness, and shuts against them the door and the source of the sweet water which they were tasting in God whensoever and for as long as they desired. . . . And thus He leaves them so completely in the dark that they know not whither to go with their sensible imagination and meditation; for they cannot advance a step in meditation, as they were wont to do aforetime, their inward senses being submerged in this night, and left with such dryness that not only do they experience no pleasure and consolation in the spiritual things and good exercises wherein they were wont to find their delights and pleasures, but instead, on the contrary, they find insipidity and bitterness in the said things.[4]

Such is the beginning of the dark night. But, as the Saint stresses, this state of soul may have its origin in causes quite

[4] *Ibid.;* 350-1.

other than that of the divine action. Evil tendencies, lukewarmness, or melancholy also produce states of powerlessness and sadness. Hence the mystical doctor gives three principal signs for recognizing what is authentic:

> The first is whether, when a soul finds no pleasure or consolation in the things of God, it also fails to find it in any thing created; for, as God sets the soul in this dark night to the end that He may quench and purge its sensual desire, He allows it not to find attraction or sweetness in anything whatsoever.[5]

Saint John of the Cross takes care to make the true passive night discernible. Thus he gives a second sign which could not proceed from lukewarmness or melancholy; its presence indicates that these others are not active, at least to any notable degree:

> The second sign whereby a man may believe himself to be experiencing the said purgation is that ordinarily the memory is centered upon God, with painful care and solicitude, thinking that it is not serving God, but is backsliding, because it finds itself without sweetness in the things of God.[6]

The third sign recalls the first sign of contemplation given in the *Ascent of Mount Carmel* and consists in this:

> That the soul can no longer meditate or reflect in the imaginative sphere of sense as it was wont, however much it may of itself endeavour to do so.[7]

This inability to meditate, far from diminishing, only increases as the soul makes progress, as the Saint emphasizes.[8]

[5] *Ibid.*, ix; 352.
[6] *Ibid.*
[7] *Ibid.*; 355.
[8] A comparison between the signs given in the *Ascent of Mount Carmel*, Bk. II, xiii, xiv, to recognize the moment when the soul ought to pass to the state of contemplation and the signs given in the *Dark Night of Sense*, ix, to determine whether the soul is in the passive night of sense, shows that there is question of approximately the same period of the spiritual life.

However, the signs given in the *Ascent* are more general and more universal. In the *Dark Night*, the Saint places the ascent on privative suffering and shows it proceeding from prayer, and overflowing into the exterior life of the soul. The night is thus more sharply marked; perhaps it is more advanced than in the description given in the *Ascent of Mount Carmel*.

It is well to make use of all the signs in making a spiritual diagnosis of the soul.

It is God Himself, he repeats incessantly, who produces this purifying dryness. The contemplation infused by Him is its proximate cause:

For the cause of this aridity is that God transfers to the spirit the good things and the strength of the senses, which, since the soul's natural strength and senses are incapable of using them, remain barren, dry and empty. For the sensual part of a man has no capacity for that which is pure spirit, and thus, when it is the spirit that receives the pleasure, the flesh is left without savour and is too weak to perform any action. But the spirit, which all the time is being fed, goes forward in strength, and with more alertness and solicitude than before, in its anxiety not to fail God.[9]

Saint John of the Cross states the same truth over again under different forms, but the repetition is helpful, for each time he adds some new detail:

The reason is that, in this state of contemplation, which the soul enters when it forsakes meditation for the state of the proficient, it is God Who is now working in the soul; He binds its interior faculties, and allows it not to cling to the understanding, nor to have delight in the will, nor to reason with the memory.[10]

And again:

For God now begins to communicate Himself to it, no longer through sense, as He did aforetime, by means of reflections which joined and sundered its knowledge, but by pure spirit, into which consecutive reflections enter not; but He communicated Himself to it by an act of simple contemplation, to which neither the exterior nor the interior senses of the lower part of the soul can attain. From this time forward, therefore, imagination and fancy can find no support in any meditation, and can gain no foothold by means thereof.[11]

These different texts are mutually clarifying. They moreover provide the psychological explanation of those characteristic phenomena of the passive night of sense, namely, that powerlessness of the soul and its distaste for all exterior and sensible goods.

In infused contemplation God communicates Himself at this

[9] *Ibid;* 353.
[10] *Ibid.;* 354.
[11] *Ibid.;* 355.

period to the superior part of the soul, supplying it and the theological virtues residing there the sustenance and support that they formerly found in the operations of the senses. In the words of Saint John of the Cross, God "binds the interior powers," making them independent of those that are exterior, while submitting them to His own direction.

This liberation of the superior part leaves the senses themselves isolated as it were, deprives them of the direction they were accustomed to find in the intellectual faculties and of that satisfaction derived from this mutual interchange. Henceforward any activity on the part of the sensitive faculties ends only in fatiguing frustration and distressing impotence.

As for participating in the light and unction that God infuses into the superior part of the soul, the sensitive faculties are incapable of it for the moment, as they are not yet fitted to receive such communications. "The sense part remains without food, empty, dry," says Saint John of the Cross, "because the sense part has no capacity for what is pure spirit." This incapacity of the senses is the reason for the passive night of sense and the cause of the suffering that accompanies it. The sense powers, then, shall continue in this state of restless impotence, of dreary distaste, until they have been purified in this suffering and made worthy to participate in this divine banquet. When this work of adaptation is completed, the night of the senses comes to its close.

This exposition of Saint John of the Cross shows that the purification of sense extends to all desires and inclinations toward things external and sensible; and that this purification attains not only to the senses properly so-called, which are as it were windows on to the exterior and sensible world, but to all the faculties which share in any immediate way in the exercise of the senses. Hence it reaches the imagination, the understanding in its use of images, even the will itself insofar as it is drawn by its desires to sensible goods. And so both the sensitive and intellectual faculties are subjected to the dark night of sense; the intellectual faculties however only insofar as they operate in conjunction with the senses. It is this ensemble which constitutes, as we have said, the region of sense distinct from the spirit.

The dark night of sense, we can see, is only apparently a trial. Produced by God's action in the soul, it causes suffering to the senses only because it is yet too pure and too spiritual for their impurities and coarseness. In reality it is a priceless grace which is in itself a call to higher things and at the same time a real preparation for them.

B. Time and duration of the passive night

> Into this dark night souls begin to enter when God draws them forth from the state of beginners—which is the state of those that meditate upon the spiritual road—and begins to set them in the state of progressives—which is that of those who are already contemplatives.[12]

The passive night of sense begins then with the contemplation that produces it.

It covers the entire period of transition from meditation to contemplation. Being the effect of contemplation and having for its purpose the development of contemplation, it coincides with the first experiences of contemplation yet in the intermittent stage. The *Interior Castle* places the passive night of sense in the fourth Mansions.

Less preoccupied than we are perhaps with chronological precision, Saint John of the Cross affirms in a general way that when souls

> . . . have now had practice for some time in the way of virtue and have persevered in meditation and prayer, . . . and when they believe that the sun of Divine favour is shining most brightly upon them, God turns all this light of theirs into darkness, and shuts against them the door and the source of the sweet spiritual water which they were tasting in God whensoever and for as long as they desired.[13]

[12] *Ibid.*, i; 330.
[13] *Ibid.*, viii; 350.

According to the Saint, the passive night is normally preceded by a period of the active night of sense. Preparation is required to receive this gratuitous gift of God. It is because persons who leave the world accomplish energetically the purification of the active night, that they are introduced rather quickly into the passive night.

> To recollected persons this commonly happens sooner after their beginnings than to others, inasmuch as they are freer from occasions of backsliding, and their desires turn more quickly from the things of the world, which is what is needful if they are to begin to enter this blessed night of sense. Ordinarily no great time passes after their beginning before they begin to enter this night of sense; and the great majority of them do in fact enter it, for they will generally be seen to fall into these aridities.[14]

The duration and intensity of the trial are too variable for Saint John of the Cross to be able to give more than general indications concerning them:

> For all do not experience it after one manner, neither do all encounter the same temptations. For this is meted out by the will of God, in conformity with the greater or the smaller degree of imperfection which each soul has to purge away. In conformity, likewise, with the degree of love of union to which God is pleased to raise it, He will humble it with greater or less intensity or in greater or less time.[15]

In the light of his experience, the Saint establishes categories which are determined by the call of God and the fervor of the souls.

At first there are the weak:

> These He purges very gently and with slight temptations. Habitually, too, He gives them refreshments of sense so that they may not fall away, and only after a long time do they attain to purity of perfection in this life, some of them never attaining to it.[16]

These descriptions demonstrate Saint John of the Cross's knowledge of the science of God and man. A familiar friend of God, the Saint knows that divine mercy is not surprised by the

[14] *Ibid;* 351.
[15] *Ibid.,* xiv; 373.
[16] *Ibid.*

hesitations and fears of human weakness. It does not break the soul, nor impose upon it its best gifts, especially when these are painful, but stooping with love over this frailty, adapts itself to it, waiting patiently for its consent and surrender.

And in such a patient manner does God bear with souls that are weaker still:

> Other souls, which are weaker, God Himself accompanies, now appearing, now moving farther away, that He may exercise them in His love; for without such turnings away they would not learn to reach God.[17]

God mercifully contents Himself with this little; but how sad it is to know that these souls are so slow, that they do not understand the gift of God and correspond so weakly with it.

But there are other souls, valiant and strong, who rejoice God greatly because they brave the rigors of the dark night of the spirit to arrive at the state of perfect union with Him. God acts in them with energy and intensity, submitting them to very special trials:

> But the souls which are to pass on to that happy and high estate, the union of love, are wont as a rule to remain for a long time in these aridities and temptations, however quickly God may lead them, as has been seen by experience. It is time, then, to begin to treat of the second night.[18]

C. Effects of the passive night

The effects of the passive night are of two kinds inseparable one from the other but distinct: painful effects and beneficent effects.

1. PAINFUL EFFECTS

"The first purgation or night is bitter and terrible to the sense"—without comparison however with the second which is "horrible and awful to the spirit." [19] The night of sense is only a

[17] *Ibid.*
[18] *Ibid.*
[19] *Ibid.*, viii; 349-50.

preparation, the strait gate that gives access to the narrow way of the night of the spirit.[20] Its sufferings are not, however, negligible.

a. Certain sufferings have already been indicated in the description of the dark night. These are aridities and the powerlessness of the faculties which formerly found delight and joy in prayer, but which now, being deprived of them, find neither comfort nor taste in the things of God, any more than in things created.

This suffering attains even to the spiritual part of the soul which, although it actually receives the strengthening light of contemplation, is not conscious of this help in the beginning:

> But the spirit . . . if it is not immediately conscious of spiritual sweetness and delight, but only of aridity and lack of sweetness, the reason for this is the strangeness of the exchange; for its palate has been accustomed to those other sensual pleasures upon which its eyes are still fixed, and, since the spiritual palate is not made ready or purged for such subtle pleasure, until it finds itself becoming prepared for it by means of this arid and dark night, it cannot experience spiritual pleasure and good, but only aridity and lack of sweetness, since it misses the pleasure which aforetime it enjoyed so readily.[21]

Saint John of the Cross recalls in this connection the example of the Hebrew people being led by God into the desert and fed by Him with manna "containing within itself all sweetness,"

> . . . and, as is there said, it turned to the savour which each one of them desired. But withal the children of Israel felt the lack of the pleasures and delights of the flesh and the onions which they had eaten aforetime in Egypt, the more so because their palate was accustomed to these and took delight in them, rather than in the delicate sweetness of the angelic manna; and they wept and sighed for the fleshpots even in the midst of the food of Heaven.[22]

Powerlessness and distaste, following upon the facility and delight previously experienced, engender anguish of spirit as a rule:

[20] *Ibid.*, xi; 361.
[21] *Ibid.*, ix; 353.
[22] *Ibid.*

> The memory is ordinarily centred upon God, with painful care and solicitude, thinking that it is not serving God, but is backsliding, because it finds itself without sweetness in the things of God.[23]

The soul is at a loss and attributes to perhaps some hidden sins this change and apparent severity of God toward it. For a fervent soul, there is no suffering comparable to this.

> Spiritual persons suffer great trials, by reason not so much of the aridities which they suffer, as of the fear which they have of being lost on the road, thinking that all spiritual blessing is over for them and that God has abandoned them since they find no help or pleasure in good things.[24]

b. These sufferings, at least in the beginning, arouse them to activity which is now inopportune and can only increase their disquiet:

> Then they grow weary, and endeavour (as they have been accustomed to do) to concentrate their faculties with some degree of pleasure upon some object of meditation, thinking that, when they are not doing this and yet are conscious of making an effort, they are doing nothing. This effort they make not without great inward repugnance and unwillingness on the part of their soul, which was taking pleasure in being in that quietness and ease, instead of working with its faculties. So they have abandoned the one pursuit, yet draw no profit from the other.[25]

c. Saint John of the Cross points out that other sufferings can be brought on by pathological tendencies such as melancholy. These tendencies intervene in the passive night of sense, not as principal cause of the dryness—for "when mere humour is the cause, it spends itself in displeasure and ruin of the physical nature,"—but as secondary cause, and they increase its anguish.

In speaking of luxury, the Saint refers to several effects of melancholy. One could enumerate others, though of a very different kind, produced by this melancholy or other moods and

[23] *Ibid.*, 352.
[24] *Ibid.*, x; 356.
[25] *Ibid.*

tendencies. For example, there is that uneasiness in the sensitive part of the soul, that impression of void and emptiness which stir it up to feverish activity. These tendencies weigh heavily upon the soul, hampering all its efforts. The holy doctor holds out hope to the soul that the night of the spirit will overcome them all. This is indeed a precious hope and a light which gives much understanding of those matters that take place in the regions of the soul where sense meets spirit; it allows hope of the triumph of grace amid the disconcerting horrors of this night.

The valiant who are to pass the night of the spirit have been already subjected to a specially vigorous purgation in the night of sense. Saint John of the Cross says that these have

> . . . formidable trials and temptations of sense, which last for a long time, albeit longer in some than in others. For to some the angel of Satan presents himself—namely, the spirit of fornication—that he may buffet their senses with abominable and violent temptations, and may trouble their spirits with vile considerations and representations which are most visible to the imagination, which things at times are a greater affliction to them than death.
>
> At other times in this night there is added to these things the spirit of blasphemy, which roams abroad, setting in the path of all the conceptions and thoughts of the soul intolerable blasphemies. These it sometimes suggests to the imagination with such violence that the soul almost utters them, which is a grave torment to it.
>
> At other times another abominable spirit, which Isaiah calls *Spiritus vertiginis,* is allowed to molest them, not in order that they may fall, but that it may try them. This spirit darkens their senses in such a way that it fills them with numerous scruples and problems, so perplexing, as they judge, that they can never, by any means, be satisfied concerning them, neither can they find any help for their judgement in counsel or thought. This is one of the severest goads and horrors of this night, very closely akin to that which passes in the night of the spirit. . . .
>
> The interior trials which we are here describing . . . [are those] which most effectively purge sense of all favours and consolations to which it was affected with natural weakness, and by which the soul is truly humiliated in preparation for the exaltation which it is to experience.[26]

[26] *Ibid.,* xiv; 372-3.

2. BENEFICENT EFFECTS

a. *Adaptation of sense to spirit*

Holy Wisdom afflicts only to cure. The soul is aware of this truth, and Saint John of the Cross puts on her lips these words:

> Oh, happy chance!—
> I went forth without being observed,[27]

which indicate what has effected in the passive night of sense:

> This going forth is understood of the subjection to its sensual part which the soul suffered when it sought God through operations so weak, so limited and so defective as are those of this lower part; . . . It will be a matter of great pleasure and great consolation, to one that journeys on this road, to see how that which seems to the soul so severe and adverse, and so contrary to spiritual pleasure, works in it so many blessings. These, as we say, are gained when the soul goes forth, as regards its affection and operation, by means of this night, from all created things, and when it journeys to eternal things, which is great happiness and good fortune.[28]

This "secret, peaceful and loving infusion from God," [29] which is contemplation, liberates the spirit from its subjection to the senses, and calms the senses themselves little by little in this night, thus permitting the soul to have free and peaceful commerce with God, who communicates Himself to it through the gifts of the Holy Ghost. The Saint writes:

> When this house of sensuality was now at rest—that is, was mortified—its passions being quenched and its desires put to rest and lulled to sleep by means of this blessed night of the purgation of sense, the soul went forth, to set out upon the road and way of the spirit, which is that of progressives and proficients, and which, by another name, is called the way of illumination or of infused contemplation wherein God Himself feeds and refreshes the soul, without meditation, or the soul's active help.[30]

This adaptation of the senses to the action of God in the spirit, this silent peace, this overflowing of sweetness into the

[27] *Ibid.*, st. i; 325.
[28] *Ibid.*, xi; 361.
[29] *Ibid.*, x; 359.
[30] *Ibid.*, xiv; 371.

whole soul, all this is the essential effect of the passive night of sense.

b. *Particular effects*

To this principal effect there are added, notes Saint John of the Cross, some particular benefits which are very precious, an infusion of light and love.

1. The light of loving Wisdom, falling on the suffering soul, enlightens the soul in regard to itself:

> This is the first and principal benefit caused by this arid and dark night of contemplation: the knowledge of oneself and of one's misery. . . . These aridities and this emptiness of the faculties . . . make it [the soul] recognize its own lowliness and misery, which in the time of its prosperity it was unable to see. Of this there is a good illustration in the Book of Exodus, where God, wishing to humble the children of Israel and desiring that they should know themselves, commanded them to take away and strip off the festal garments and adornments wherewith they were accustomed to adorn themselves in the Wilderness, saying: Now from henceforth strip yourselves of festal ornaments and put on everyday working dress, that ye may know what treatment ye deserve. . . . At the time when it was clad as for a festival and found in God much pleasure, consolation and help, it was somewhat more satisfied and contented, since it thought itself to some extent to be serving God. . . . But, now that the soul has put on its other and working attire—that of aridity and abandonment—and now that its first lights have turned into darkness, it possesses these lights more truly in this virtue of self-knowledge, which is so excellent and so necessary, considering itself now as nothing and experiencing no satisfaction in itself; for it sees that it does nothing of itself; neither can it do anything. And the smallness of this self-satisfaction, together with the soul's affliction at not serving God, is considered and esteemed by God as greater than all the consolations which the soul formerly experienced and the works which it wrought, however great they were.[31]

2. This light, besides enlightening the soul with regard to its own misery, also enlightens it in reference to the greatness and transcendence of God. Saint John of the Cross delights in quoting Scripture to confirm this testimony of his own experience:

[31] *Ibid.*, xii; 362-3.

'Thy light shall shine in the darkness,' God will enlighten the soul, giving it knowledge, not only of its lowliness and wretchedness, as we have said, but likewise of the greatness and excellence of God. . . .

'Whom shall God teach His knowledge, and whom shall He make to understand the hearing?' To those, He says, that are weaned from the milk and drawn away from the breasts. . . .

In the desert land, waterless, dry and pathless, I appeared before Thee, that I might see Thy virtue and Thy glory.[32]

Illustrations are easy to find, and the Saint does not fail to avail himself of them to show that the night of sense is illuminating and that self-knowledge is acquired in this night:

. . . from this arid night comes first of all self-knowledge, whence, as from a foundation, rises this other knowledge of God. For which cause Saint Augustine said to God: 'Let me know myself, Lord, and I shall know Thee.' [33]

3. From this twofold light the soul learns that respect due to the divine majesty:

The soul learns to commune with God with more respect and more courtesy, such as one must ever observe in converse with the Most High. These it knew not in its prosperous times of pleasure and consolation, for that pleasant favour which it experienced made its desire toward God somewhat bolder than was fitting, and discourteous and ill-considered.[34]

In the darkness of the night of sense, the soul has perception of the divine transcendence. It takes its rightful place and assumes its proper attitude in His presence. It imitates Moses who before the burning bush, having put off his shoes, became so discreet and so attentive that the Scripture says [35] that not only did he not make bold to draw near to God but that he dared not even to look at Him. The soul too "having taken off the shoes of its desires and pleasures becomes very conscious of its wretchedness in the sight of God" as befits one about to hear the divine word.

4. This respectful attitude before God is a sign of the hu-

[32] *Ibid.;* 364-5.
[33] *Ibid.;* 365.
[34] *Ibid.;* 363.
[35] Exod. 3:6.

mility that the soul has acquired in this dark night. The spiritual vices previously described are purified; pride with all its train of imperfections, avarice, spiritual gluttony, envy, and the other vices:

> For it sees itself so dry and miserable, that the idea never even occurs to it that it is making better progress than others, or outstripping them, as it believed itself to be doing before. On the contrary, it recognizes that others are making better progress than itself.[36]
>
> Softened and humbled by these aridities and hardships and other temptations and trials wherein God exercises it during this night, it becomes meek with respect to God, and to itself, and likewise with respect to its neighbor. So that it is no longer angry with itself and disturbed because of its own faults, nor with its neighbor because of his faults, neither is it displeased with God, nor does it utter unseemly complaints because He does not quickly make it holy.[37]
>
> These times of aridity, then, cause the soul to journey in all purity in the love of God, since it is no longer influenced in its actions by the pleasure and sweetness of the actions themselves, as perchance it was when it experienced sweetness, but only by a desire to please God.[38]

5. Saint John of the Cross loves to enumerate still further benefits which the soul derives from these aridities, namely that "it practises several virtues together, as, for example, patience and longsuffering," [39] as well as charity and fortitude. It habitually "has remembrance of God, with fear and dread of backsliding on the spiritual road." [40]

> Besides these benefits which have been mentioned, the soul attains innumerable others by means of this arid contemplation. For often, in the midst of these times of aridity and hardship, God communicates to the soul, when it is least expecting it, the purest spiritual sweetness and love, together with a spiritual knowledge which is sometimes very delicate, each manifestation of which is of greater benefit and worth than those which the soul enjoyed aforetime.[41]

The latter benefits mentioned by Saint John of the Cross are no longer the purifying work of light, but the positive and creative work of love.

[36] *Dark Night,* Bk. I, xii; 366.
[37] *Ibid.,* xiii; 369.
[38] *Ibid.;* 370.
[39] *Ibid.;* 368.
[40] *Ibid.*
[41] *Ibid.;* 369.

This loving Wisdom, which produces the passive dark night, subjects the soul to a painful and liberating purgation only in order to caress and conquer it by love.

The passive inflowing of perfect love and its final triumph—these are the ultimate purpose of this night, whose shadows are now beginning to fall. And so the soul says:

Kindled in love with yearnings.[42]

This enkindling of love is not as a rule felt at the first, because it has not begun to take hold upon the soul, by reason of the impurity of human nature, or because the soul has not understood its own state, as we have said, and has therefore given it no peaceful abiding-place within itself. Yet sometimes, nevertheless, there soon begins to make itself felt a certain yearning toward God; and the more this increases, the more is the soul affectioned and enkindled in love toward God, without knowing or understanding how and whence this love and affection come to it, but from time to time seeing this flame and this enkindling grow so greatly within it that it desires God with yearning of love; even as David, when he was in this dark night, said of himself in these words, namely: 'Because my heart was enkindled (that is to say, in the love of contemplation), my reins also were changed': that is, my desires for sensual affections were changed, namely from the way of sense to the way of the spirit, which is the aridity and cessation from all these things whereof we are speaking. And I, he says, was dissolved in nothing and annihilated, and I knew not; for, as we have said, without knowing the way whereby it goes, the soul finds itself annihilated with respect to all things above and below which were accustomed to please it; and finds itself enamoured, without knowing how. And because at times the enkindling of love in the spirit grows greater, the yearnings for God become so great in the soul that the very bones seem to be dried up by this thirst, and the natural powers to be fading away, and their warmth and strength to be perishing through the intensity of the thirst of love, for the soul feels that this thirst of love is a living thirst. This thirst David had and felt, when he said: 'My soul thirsted for the living God.' Which is as much as to say: Living was the thirst of my soul. Of this thirst, since it is living, we may say that it kills.[43]

In the night and as a result of it, love has taken partial possession of the soul. The anguish that it feels is a testimony to the soul's embarrassment in the midst of its impurities; the

[42] *Ibid.*, xi; 359.
[43] *Ibid.*; 359-60.

thirst it experiences manifests its need for opening itself to God's action, its desire of victory.

"Oh, happy chance"

In yet a while the soul that is now a prey to this loving anguish will be able to drink in abiding peace of the fountain of living water. Thus sustained and strengthened, it will mark its first notable victory, the conquest of the will.

But that these conflicts, at once painful and peaceful, may be turned into victory, the soul itself must lend its cooperation in the active night of sense of which we must now speak.

CHAPTER V

Active Night of Sense During Prayer

There are many, yes, many souls who arrive at this degree, but there are very few who go beyond it, and I do not know to what to attribute the fault. For certain, it is not God's.[1]

Such is the assertion of Saint Teresa speaking of the early forms of contemplative prayer, recollection and quiet.

Apropos of the night of sense, which is at the same stage of the spiritual life, Saint John of the Cross says:

The night of sense is common and comes to many; these are the beginners.[2]

As to the night of the spirit, which leads to the union of love, he says:

The night of the spirit is the portion of very few.[3]

As to the causes of this partial failure of the greater number of those souls who have known the gift of God in the first stages of contemplative prayer, our two Saints maintain a wise and charitable reserve. "God knows why," says Saint John of the Cross. "For certain the fault is not God's," Saint Teresa emphatically says. Both were too familiar with the mystery that surrounds God's call and the soul's response to lay claim to dispelling all its obscurity. Both knew too well the weakness

[1] *Life,* xv; Peers, I.
[2] *Dark Night,* Bk. I, viii; Peers, I, 349.
[3] *Ibid.*

of human nature with its delays, its painful progress, its sudden little spurts ahead, not to fear breaking it finally by too downright assertions.

Yet without doubt they place some of the responsibility on lack of generosity and even insufficient knowledge. God's action in a soul, His direct action especially, awaits a fitting response. Not finding it God ceases His work in the soul.[4]

The problem is grave. Its issue is either failure or high sanctity. The glory of God and the good of the Church are at stake. In the kingdom of God, everything is measured by perfections. The failure of a soul that God has set on the way to the heights is a greater evil than the mediocrity of thousands of other souls who have never advanced beyond the lower slopes of the spiritual ascent. Such failures cause great pity in the kingdom of God: Saint John of the Cross is moved to deep sorrow by them.

Beginners in the spiritual life have at hand an abundance of books for their guidance. Beginners in contemplation, on the contrary, although their needs are particular and urgent are in want of them. It was this that determined Saint John of the Cross to write the *Ascent of Mount Carmel.* In the Prologue he says:

> To this end I have been moved, not by any possibility that I see in myself of accomplishing so arduous a task, but by the confidence which I have in the Lord that He will help me to say something to relieve the great necessity which is experienced by many souls, who, when they set out upon the road of virtue, and Our Lord desires to bring them into this dark night that they may pass through it to Divine union, make no progress. At times this is because they have no desire to enter it or to allow themselves to be led into it; at other times, because they understand not themselves and lack competent and alert directors who will guide them to the summit. And so it is sad to see many souls to whom God gives both aptitude and favour with which

[4] If God gives a soul such pledges, it is a sign that He has great things in store for it. It will be its own fault if it does not make great progress. But if He sees that, after He has brought the Kingdom of Heaven into its abode, it returns to earth, not only will He refrain from showing it the secrets of His Kingdom but He will grant it this other favour only for short periods and rarely (*Way of Perfection,* xxxi; Peers, II, 133).

to make progress (and who, if they would take courage, could attain to this estate), remaining in an elementary stage of communion with God, for want of will, or knowledge, or because there is none who will lead them in the right path or teach them how to get away from these beginnings.[5]

To meet these same needs of souls, Saint Teresa had already written the *Way of Perfection* and the *Interior Castle.* In these treatises there can be found a detailed explanation of the active night of sense and that of the spirit, that is, an explanation of what must be the conduct of the soul in order to prepare itself for and respond to God's action within it.

Elsewhere in their writings, our two Saints may seem more sublime; but nowhere as here do they approach so near to us in their role of teachers and doctors of the spiritual life. Because of the difference in their method of exposition, the concurrence of their teachings on this stage of the spiritual life throws marvelous light on its various aspects and constitutes a harmonious body of doctrine.

A. How to direct this active night

These beautiful promises must not mislead us, however, into expecting a doctrine with clear and exact formulas that one can easily apply to the various cases that occur.

1. DIFFICULTIES

a. *The diversity of souls*

In the strong light that shines upon these regions the diversity of souls seems to be like that of the angels, each one of whom constitutes a species. There are scarcely two souls, states Saint John of the Cross, that resemble each other by half. Their states are still more varied, so different are the graces by which they are led and the vibrations that the same spiritual experience can awaken in each one of them.

[5] *Ascent,* Prologue; Peers, I, 11-2.

How could one then, in the midst of such diversity, propose a uniform method answering to all needs?

Let us not forget, moreover, that we are here in the domain of divine Wisdom, who progressively assumes direction of the soul. It is written of this Wisdom that His thoughts are not our thoughts, and that His ways are not our ways. Sovereignly free, Wisdom obeys only Himself. And so reason is as powerless to enclose in a formula the strong and sweet rhythm of His action, as it is to invent a method for submitting to it. This submission, as one can guess, is entirely supple, characterized by faithfulness and liberty in love; it resists any formulation that would constrain and confine it.

We are here in trackless country, declares Saint John of the Cross. It would be vain to search out in order to follow the trace of those who have gone before. This is as invisible as that of the ship in the ocean it has crossed, or that of the bird in the air it has cleaved in its rapid flight. Hence the Saint rises up with vehemence against those who would undertake to regiment, with the aid of methods made to the measure of their own mind and experience, the progress of souls whom the Holy Spirit has begun to enlighten and direct Himself.

b. *The intermittence of contemplation*

There are other circumstances which render it still more difficult to make assertions in the matter that are too precise. In this period of transition, contemplation is as yet imperfect: imperfect first of all because intermittent. God intervenes only in fleeting moments. Thus the soul at times finds it possible, and consequently has the duty, to resume its former active prayer. Again, it is imperfect when the soul receives it, for it ordinarily affects only one or two powers, leaving the others powerless and confused. Thus two regions are created in the soul, with two different climates which require twofold consideration and a twofold treatment. How can precise counsels be given for needs and states so diverse?

c. *The soul's difficulty in understanding*

Even if it were possible to find fitting counsels and to formulate them precisely, the soul does not seem capable either of receiving them or of understanding them. It is indeed from the pitiable state in which the soul finds itself that most of its pains and difficulties come at this period.

In the regions where it has now entered, everything is disconcerting and painful. It finds itself in impenetrable darkness, unable to form any clear idea of things and of its own state. It has only a sad memory of its former joys, and is unable to savor any secret communication of which people speak to it, and of which it has at times a fleeting realization. Then there are the contrasts it perceives in itself; on the one hand, the profound experience of its own misery and poverty, and on the other, the discoveries it makes at times of deep supernatural realities.

How then, in this darkness that envelops it and in this languor in which it is ordinarily immersed, can the soul, who is like a sick person under treatment, assimilate any teaching or profit by it?

2. MEANS

Does this mean that we are to give up trying to bring it a little light even in its most desolate hours? Certainly not. But this light must be in the form that is suited to this state and these regions.

a. *Directives*

Methods are to be rejected. Precise counsels are on the whole inopportune. In order to guide us in these regions, Saint John of the Cross and Saint Teresa provide only general directions.

These directives can be found here and there in their writings, becoming more definite by repeated touches, delicate touches and at times precise, remaining nevertheless general. Their aim is to render the soul attentive to the inspiration of God and docile under His action. They indicate more a direction to be taken than a path to be followed, an attitude of soul to be kept rather than a virtue to be practised. Arrows ever pointing toward the Infinite, they constantly incite the soul forward to God. They incessantly repeat that in order to attain the divine goal and avoid every danger, it is necessary for the soul but also sufficient to remain simple, poor, free, to keep it's gaze fixed on God, as it travels through the desert to Him.

It will appear at first sight that there exists between the two Saints considerable difference, even at times opposition, of teaching. But upon returning to it with greater attention, one soon comes to see that the difference is rather one of approach and emphasis. Both were trying to meet the same needs, to render the soul more pliant and unfettered under the action of an identical grace from God. Thus their twofold teachings converge into a doctrinal synthesis that is astonishingly rich and profound, helpful and well adapted to the needs of a soul at this stage of the spiritual life.

b. *Profitable mistakes*

These directives, more calculated to direct the soul than to guide it in detail, will not save it from all error and ill-success, however great its good will. The science of love is a practical science in which humble experience is sovereign mistress. Mistakes and failures are often more instructive than victories; they alone prove the value and reveal the import of the directives of the masters. To stumble over the sidings or even to fall repeatedly through ignorance into the two ditches that border the particular way that the soul is to follow, indicates experimentally to it within what limits it must make its journey toward God. The science of love is a science of humility.

c. *Divine light*

Besides, one needs worry but little for such a soul. In the darkness it travels securely. Soon it will have assurance. Is the Master not awake within? It is not alone. It is the action of Wisdom itself that causes this darkness, this confusion. Divine Wisdom is present to the soul, living in it, operating in it, watching over all its ways. The soul is obscurely aware of this, and at times perceives it clearly. One must not, therefore, grieve too much over the sufferings and the dangers of this period. The soul is happy; happier than it has ever been. It is advancing in safety under the light of the living flame that is burning within, faintly as yet perhaps, but guiding it surely towards the mysterious goal fixed for it by God:

Without light or guide, save that
which burned in my heart.

This light guided me
More surely than the light of noonday,
To the place where he (well I knew who!) was awaiting me—
A place where none appeared.[6]

Saint John of the Cross, who has sung the brilliant radiance of that flame, has nevertheless taken up his pen to relieve the extreme necessity of those souls in whom such a flame is beginning to burn. A contradiction? No, indeed! There is a marvelous meeting of the divine and human in the supernatural life of the soul. Besides, the whole purport of our master's teaching is to show the soul how to discover, in the depths of this darkness and mist, the small flame that is burning there, to trim and strengthen it that its light may illumine and fill the whole soul.

Let us then gather up these precious directives which show the soul how it must, first in prayer and then at other times, practise at this period the gift of self, how it must grow in humility, and interior silence, if it would correspond to the de-

[6] *Ascent*, Prologue, st. iii-iv; Peers, I, 10.

mands of divine Wisdom. Let us not ask them to dispel the dark night that God has made, but to set up in it a few luminous signposts to direct us along the way.

B. Active night during prayer

At this stage of the spiritual life, the conduct of the soul during prayer will be governed by the necessity of adapting itself to the intermittent character of contemplation and its imperfect forms.

1. TWOFOLD DUTY

A twofold duty rests upon the soul; first, it must respect God's action within it when He is giving contemplation, and favor it by peaceful and silent surrender; second, it must resume its own activity when contemplation ceases or when its imperfect form, itself, calls for complementary activity.

a. *To respect God's action within by silence*

Saint John of the Cross excels in placing in relief the first of these duties. He writes:

> Wherefore, whatever be the time or season, when once the soul has begun to enter into this pure and restful state of contemplation, which comes to pass when it may no longer meditate and is unable to do so, it must not seek to gather to itself meditations, neither must it desire to find help in spiritual sweetness or delight, but it must stand in complete detachment above all this and its spirit must be completely freed from it, as Habacuc said [7] that he must needs do in order to hear what the Lord should say to him. "I will stand upon my watch," he says, "and I will fix my step upon my munition, and I will watch to see that which will be said to me." This is as though he had said: I will raise up my mind above all the operations and all the knowledge that can be comprehended by my senses, and above that which they can keep and retain within themselves: all this I will leave below. And I will fix the step of the munition of my faculties, not allowing them to advance a step as to their own operation, so that through contemplation I may receive that which is communicated to me from

[7] Hab. 2:1.

God. For we have already said that pure contemplation consists in receiving.[8]

The blessings that God communicates to the soul in this contemplation are ineffable. A whole transformation takes place, a transformation the marvels of which Saint John of the Cross tells us in the *Spiritual Canticle* and the *Living Flame of Love*. But God acts in us only if we are silent and peaceful.

> The blessings that this silent communication and contemplation leave impressed upon the soul without its perceiving them at the time are, as I say, inestimable; for they are the most secret and therefore the most delicate anointings of the Holy Spirit, which secretly fill the soul with spiritual riches and gifts and graces; for, since it is God Who does all this, He does it not otherwise than as God. . . .
>
> These blessings, with the greatest facility, by no more than the slightest act which the soul may desire to make on its own account, with its memory, understanding or will, or by the application of its sense or desire or knowledge or sweetness or pleasure, are disturbed or hindered in the soul, which is a grave evil and a great shame and pity.
>
> Oh, how grave a matter is this, and what cause it gives for wonder, that, while the harm done is inconspicuous, and the interference with those holy anointings almost negligible, the harm should be more serious, and a matter for deeper sorrow and regret, than the disquieting and ruining of many souls of a more ordinary nature which have not attained to a state of such supreme fineness and delicacy! It is as though a portrait of supreme and delicate beauty were touched by a clumsy hand, and were daubed with coarse, crude colours. This would be a greater and more crying and pitiful shame than if many more ordinary portraits were besmeared in this way. For when the work of so delicate a hand as this of the Holy Spirit has been thus roughly treated, who will be able to repair its beauty?[9]

In this passage, Saint John of the Cross is speaking of the higher degree of contemplation. But in the lower degrees, the divine action has the right to the same respect and requires the same attitude of silence. More compassionate with beginners, because of their lack of knowledge, the holy doctor is however no less urgent in recommending to them peace and silence:

[8] *Living Flame,* st. iii; Peers, III, 162.
[9] *Ibid.;* 164-5.

It is piteous, then, to see many a one who, though his soul would fain tarry in this peace and rest of interior quiet, where it is filled with the peace and refreshment of God, takes from it its tranquillity, and leads it away to the most exterior things, and would make it return and retrace the ground it has already traversed, to no purpose, and abandon the end and goal wherein it is already reposing for the means which led it to that repose, which are meditations. . . . And, as such souls know not the mystery of this new experience, the idea comes to them that they are being idle and doing nothing.[10]

These pitiful souls lose the blessings of incipient contemplation. Saint John of the Cross multiplies comparisons in order to set forth plainly the harm wrought by this agitation. The soul, he says, is like a child

. . . which, while receiving the milk that has been collected and brought together for it in the breast, is taken from the breast and then forced to try to gain and collect food by its own diligent squeezing and handling.[11]

Or again:

It is like a child, whom its mother tries to carry in her arms, while it strikes out with its feet and cries out to be allowed to walk, and thus neither makes any progress nor allows its mother to do so. Or it is as when a painter is trying to paint a portrait and his subject keeps moving: either he will be unable to do anything at all or the picture will be spoiled.[12]

This return to meditation produces a recrudescence of pain and disquiet such as we described in speaking of the sufferings of the purification of sense. The Saint says:

They labour greatly to this end (to proceed by discursive methods) and find little sweetness or none; rather the aridity and weariness and disquiet of their souls are increased and grow, in proportion as they labour for that earlier sweetness. They cannot find this in that earlier manner. . . .[13]

The more they persist after this manner, the worse is the state wherein they find themselves, because their soul is drawn farther away from spiritual peace.[14]

[10] *Ascent,* Bk. II, xii; Peers, I, 106-7.
[11] *Ibid.*, xiv; 112.
[12] *Living Flame,* st. iii; Peers, III, 178.
[13] *Ascent,* Bk. II, xii; Peers, I, 106.
[14] *Ibid.;* 107.

So they have abandoned the one pursuit, yet draw no profit from the other; for, by seeking what is prompted by their own spirit, they lost the spirit of tranquillity and peace which they had before.[15]

Both respect for God's interior action in the soul and the soul's own spiritual gain impose upon it the duty of remaining silent and peaceful in contemplation.

Testimony of Saint Teresa, precise and finely shaded, is not lacking at this point. But that we shall reserve until we are making practical application of the general principle to various forms of prayer at this period of the spiritual life.

b. *To complete it by activity*

In regard to the second duty of the soul at this stage, Saint Teresa vigorously asserts the need of the soul itself supplying by the exercises of its own faculties for the lack or the imperfection of contemplation.

The Saint in fact finds it necessary to insist upon this duty, especially in the case of the soul who has experienced this contact with God, but who cannot but desire to find it once more. She writes:

You will desire, then, my daughters, to strive to attain this way of prayer (of quiet), and you will be right to do so for, as I have said, the soul cannot fully understand the favours which the Lord grants it there or the love which draws it ever nearer to Himself.[16]

This is certainly a legitimate desire. But in order to realize it, must one not try to place oneself in the passive attitude that these supernatural states require and thus try to induce this special intervention of God? Is it not possible to find in the teaching of Saint John of the Cross advice to adopt habitually, during the period of transition, a passive attitude of this kind?

Foolishness! answers Saint Teresa.[17]

If His majesty has not begun to grant us absorption, I cannot understand how we can cease thinking in any way which will not bring us

[15] *Dark Night,* Bk. I, x; Peers, I, 356.
[16] IV Mansions, ii; Peers, II, 238.
[17] *Life,* xii.

more harm than profit, although this has been a matter of continual discussion among spiritual persons. For my own part, I confess my lack of humility, but their arguments have never seemed to me good enough to lead me to accept what they say. One person told me of a certain book by the saintly Fray Peter of Alcantara . . . we read it together, and found that he says exactly what I say.[18]

Let us note that in this passage the Saint is speaking of the soul that has already arrived at supernatural recollection. For all the more reason, it must not give itself up to passivity, when it is in no way aware of this special intervention of God. Elsewhere she writes:

It is very important that we should not try to lift up our spirits unless they are lifted up by the Lord: in the latter case we shall become aware of the fact instantly. It is specially harmful for women to make such attempts, because the devil can foster illusions in them.[19]

"But how," you will ask, "are we to gain them [supernatural favours] if we do not strive after them?" I reply that there is no better way than this one which I have described. There are several reasons why they should not be striven for.[20]

Having discussed this point, the Saint sets frequently forth elsewhere in her treatises the reasons for this imperative insistence. The first and principal reason is that such an attitude is tainted with pride. Contemplation is a gratuitous gift of divine Mercy. She says:

His Majesty is not obliged to grant them [these favours] to us, as He is obliged to grant us glory if we keep His commandments. . . .

There is some lack of humility in our thinking that in return for our miserable services we can obtain anything so great . . .

The first way in which you will see if you have humility is that if you have it you will not think you merit these favours and consolations of the Lord . . .[21]

Humility alone can call down upon itself these outpourings of God's mercy. Hence it is that humility is the supreme law, the most important disposition for the obtaining of the gift of contemplation:

[18] IV Mansions, iii; 242.
[19] *Life*, xii; Peers, I, 73.
[20] IV Mansions, ii; Peers, II, 239.
[21] *Ibid.*

It is certainly desirable that we should know how to obtain this favour. I will tell you what I have found out about it. . . . As well as acting, then, as do those who have dwelt in the Mansions already described, have humility and again humility! It is by humility that the Lord allows Himself to be conquered so that He will do all we ask of Him.[22]

Humility here is not merely a sentiment: it must express itself in an abiding attitude of soul. The humble soul will demean itself as a poor man who has nothing and has the right to nothing. Without however dissembling its legitimate desires for close union with God, it will submit to the humble labor of its faculties until God stoops to raise it to loving passive attention. We have these words of our Lord:

"When thou art invited to a wedding feast, do not recline in the first place. . . . But when thou art invited, go and recline in the last place; that when he who invited thee comes in, he may say to thee, 'Friend, go up higher!' Then thou wilt be honored in the presence of all who are at table with thee. For everyone who exalts himself shall be humbled, and he who humbles himself shall be exalted." [23]

The parable of the Gospel has a still more rigorous application on the spiritual plane than on a purely natural plane. It is towards the humble that God inclines in mercy while He humbles the proud: "For He has scattered the proud. . . . He has put down the mighty from their thrones and has exalted the lowly," [24] sang the Virgin Mary in her Magnificat.

In this period of spiritual life, the last place—the place which the humble person must always take—is this prayer of peaceful activity. It is this that will attract the grace of God, bidding the soul to go higher. Any other attitude will sooner or later be punished by the privation of those graces already granted.

Saint Teresa adds that an effort to put a stop to the activity of the faculties would produce uneasiness, suffering and stupidity. She writes in the book of her *Life:*

[22] *Ibid.;* 238-9.
[23] Luke 14:8-11.
[24] Luke 1:31-2.

What I say we must not do is to presume or think that we can suspend it ourselves; nor must we allow it to cease working: if we do, we shall remain stupid and cold and shall achieve nothing whatsoever. . . . To keep the faculties of the soul busy and to think that, at the same time, you can keep them quiet, is foolishness. . . . It is lost labour, and the soul feels slightly frustrated, like a man who is just about to take a leap and then is pulled back.[25]

In the *Interior Castle* she adds this remark:

The very effort which the soul makes in order to cease from thought will perhaps awaken thought and cause it to think a great deal.[26]

To condemn oneself then to passivity in order to attain to contemplation, is as presumptuous and unavailing as it is dangerous.

But what is the soul to do during this period? How is it to occupy itself without hindering the action of God which may be about to begin if it has not already done so? We shall try to answer this. But first let us hear Saint Teresa describe in broad outlines the attitude of the soul:

What we have to do is to beg like poor and needy persons coming before a great and rich Emperor and then cast down our eyes in humble expectation. When from the secret signs He gives us we seem to realize that He is hearing us, it is well for us to keep silence, since He has permitted us to be near Him and there will be no harm in our striving not to labour with the understanding—provided, I mean, that we are able to do so. But if we are not quite sure that the King has heard us, or sees us, we must not stay where we are like ninnies, for there still remains a great deal for the soul to do when it has stilled the understanding; if it did nothing more it would experience much greater aridity and the imagination would grow more restless because of the effort caused it by cessation from thought. The Lord wishes us rather to make requests of Him and to remember that we are in His presence, for He knows what is fitting for us. I cannot believe in the efficacy of human activity in matters where His Majesty appears to have set a limit to it and to have been pleased to reserve action to Himself. There are many other things in which He has not so reserved it, such as penances, works of charity and prayers; these, with His aid, we can practise for ourselves, as far as our miserable nature is capable of them.[27]

[25] *Life,* xii; Peers, I, 72.
[26] IV Mansions, iii; Peers, II, 243.
[27] *Ibid.;* 242.

These general counsels, which are at once so liberal and so finely shaded, might suffice were it not that this is a most important point in the spiritual life on which souls who have reached there cannot have too much enlightenment. Here then are a few practical corollaries drawn from the principles above. Subsequently we shall apply them to the different forms that prayer assumes at this period of transition.

2. PRACTICAL COROLLARIES

a. *To prepare for prayer*

Preparation must be made for prayer (that is, proximate preparation) by some reading or by the choice of a precise subject. This is the first duty of the soul during this period.

Saint Teresa has told us: we have not the right to await passively the coming of a special grace of contemplation. We must prepare ourselves for it by using the faculties that we have. Humility and good sense would dictate this.

But every director knows the repugnance, if not the resistance, of certain souls on this point. The soul is all filled with the remembrance and perhaps with the delight of the prayer of the morning or the evening before; it longs to recover that strengthening and obscure contact which it had. Is it not now being obliged to turn back? Last evening's preparation proved useless; it was a hindrance rather than a help. The director who insists on such preparation would seem to be one of those whom Saint John of the Cross castigates in the *Living Flame*, directors who understand nothing of the ways of the spirit and are overfond of formulas and methods. Of these the Saint says:

> They disturb and impede the peace of this quiet and hushed contemplation which God has been giving their penitents by His own power, and they cause them to follow the road of meditation and imaginative reading.[28]

[28] *Living Flame,* st. iii; Peers, III, 171.

We have already answered this objection by remarking that the best means for meriting the grace of contemplation is to keep oneself humbly in the last place, that is, keep the faculties peacefully occupied until God Himself elevates us higher. The objection obliges us nevertheless to be more precise as to the requisite preparation for prayer.

This preparation must take into account the progress that has already been made and the stage of the spiritual life at which the soul has arrived. During this period, when the soul is not enjoying supernatural contemplation, it is ordinarily incapable of giving itself to meditation properly so-called. This powerlessness, whether it be the fruit of mystical graces or of persevering efforts that have simplified the operations of the intelligence, now allows only the prayer of simplicity. Preparation for prayer will therefore be such as to introduce the soul at once into this prayer.

Hence preparation will avoid too much reading that would only weary the soul, and any multiplicity of thoughts that would only disturb it. It will turn to something quite simple, somewhat synoptic. It will be the selecting of some text of Scripture, a striking thought, some attitude of Our Lord, a word that will illumine and recollect the faculties, calm the soul, keep it occupied until it pleases the Master to elevate it to higher regions. These will permit it to find peace again when, in the course of the prayer, it has been carried away by distractions or troubled by the painful agitation of the exterior faculties.

Thus to find the thought, the image, or the word which will fix the attention of the soul or will recollect it at the beginning of prayer and then serve it as a shield or rallying point against disquiet during prayer, such is the purpose and the result of preparation for prayer during this period of transition.

Let us add two remarks before closing this section.

The first is that rather frequently it is enough for the soul to begin this preparation for it to feel itself immediately recollected in God and in supernatural prayer. Thus does the vigilant Master manifest the ardor of His desire to reward humility and to respond to the first advances of a soul particularly dear to Him.

The second remark, of great practical importance, can be put thus: When preparation does not succeed in providing sustenance for the faculties nor in recollecting them, it is still a guarantee against the temptation of idleness, and serves as a sign that the soul is in contemplative dryness. Although apparently of no use, never is it more precious; and it attains its end by placing the soul under the painful and real action of God.

b. *To persevere in active prayer until contemplation begins*

The soul must persevere in active prayer until it is elevated to contemplation. This second corollary does not seem to require any prolonged development after what we have just said concerning preparation. It will not be useless, however, to bring the testimony of Saint John of the Cross to bear on this point, especially since we have heard him recommend passivity. He writes in the *Ascent:*

> In order that there may be no confusion in this instruction it will be meet in this chapter to explain at what time and season it behooves the spiritual person to lay aside the task of discursive meditation as carried on through the imaginations and forms and figures above mentioned, in order that he may lay them aside neither sooner nor later than when the Spirit bids him; for, although it is meet for him to lay them aside at the proper time in order that he may journey to God and not be hindered by them, it is no less needful for him not to lay aside the said imaginative meditation before the proper time lest he should turn backward. For, although the apprehensions of these faculties serve not as proximate means of union to the proficient, they serve nevertheless as remote means to beginners in order to dispose and habituate the spirit to spirituality by means of sense, and in order to void the sense, in the meantime, of all the other low forms and images, temporal, worldly, and natural.[29]

[29] *Ascent,* Bk. II, xii; Peers, I, 108.

The Saint is concerned to determine carefully the moment when the soul is to leave aside active prayer. A little farther on he takes up the question directly:

With regard to that which has been said, there might be raised one question—if progressives (that is, those whom God is beginning to bring into this supernatural knowledge of contemplation whereof we have spoken) must never again, because of this that they are beginning to experience, return to the way of meditation and reasoning and natural forms. To this the answer is that it is not to be understood that such as are beginning to experience this loving knowledge must, as a general rule, never again try to return to meditation; for, when they are first making progress in proficiency, the habit of contemplation is not yet so perfect that they can give themselves to the act thereof whensoever they wish, nor, in the same way, have they reached a point so far beyond meditation that they cannot occasionally meditate and reason in a natural way, as they were wont, using the figures and the steps that they were wont to use, and finding something new in them. Rather, in these early stages, when, by means of the indications already given, they are able to see that the soul is not occupied in that repose and knowledge, they will need to make use of meditation until by means of it they come to acquire in some degree of perfection the habit which we have described. . . . For until they reach this stage, which is that of the proficient in this exercise, they use sometimes the one and sometimes the other, at different times.[30]

This is precious instruction, which enables the soul to escape the temptation of wanting to resume its prayer at the same point where it left it the morning or evening before, prompted by desire for supernatural delight or for a more powerful action on the part of God. Saint Teresa, in fact, warns us frequently:

For, as I have already said—and I should not like this to be forgotten—in this life of ours the soul does not grow in the way the body does, though we speak as if it did, and growth does in fact occur. But whereas a child, after attaining to the full stature of a man, does not diminish in size so that his body becomes small again, in spiritual matters the Lord is pleased that such diminution should take place.[31]

Hence the necessity, concludes the Saint, of returning to simple considerations when the soul is no longer perfectly united to God.

[30] *Ibid.*, xv; 120.
[31] *Life*, xv; Peers, I, 94.

c. *To return to activity when contemplation ceases*

A third corollary follows from this teaching, namely: ***in the course of mental prayer, the soul must return to meditation when it is no longer under the action of contemplative grace.*** Contemplation may cease during prayer either because God gives it only in a transitory way, or, more frequently, the soul is not faithful in corresponding with it. The soul lets itself at times be carried away by distractions, by the disquiet of the sense powers, or even by the inflowing of supernatural sweetness and in this way loses contact with God from whom the sweetness comes. The emptiness and idleness in which the soul then finds itself must be filled by an active seeking of God. Saint John of the Cross writes:

> The reason is that, if the soul at that time had not this knowledge of God or this realization of His presence, the result would be that it would do nothing and have nothing; for, having turned aside from meditation (by means whereof the soul has been reasoning with its faculties of sense), and being still without contemplation, which is the general knowledge whereof we are speaking, wherein the soul makes use of its spiritual faculties—namely, memory, understanding and will—these being united in this knowledge which is then wrought and received in them, the soul would of necessity be without any exercise in the things of God.[32]

The Saint concludes that then the soul must return to meditation. It is in such moments as this that the usefulness of the preparation is apparent, when the soul has lost contemplation through distractions and disquietude, and is left in painful and humiliating dryness. A simple and prompt return to the recollecting thought or image will often suffice for resuming contact with the divine reality; or at least it will provide the faculties with a luminous guide-mark and a support in the tempest, while awaiting their recovery of complete tranquillity.

After stating the necessity of return to meditation when contemplation ceases, Saint John of the Cross adds:

[32] *Ascent,* Bk. II, xiv; Peers, I, 113-14.

But here it must be made clear that this general knowledge whereof we are speaking is at times so subtle and delicate, particularly when it is most pure and simple and perfect, most spiritual and most interior, that, although the soul be occupied therein, it can neither realize it nor perceive it.[33]

We must repeat: Not every impression of idleness must be combated by a return to meditation, especially when the soul has already been favored with contemplation. The delicate problem of discerning contemplation frequently arises when the contemplation is present in a very simple and arid form. It is for the director to undertake this task and give the soul general directives in accord with its needs.

d. *To maintain silence or activity according to different faculties*

A final conclusion from the principles given will be still more difficult of application. Let us state it thus: *When contemplation is still in its imperfect stages, the soul will have to safeguard peace and silence in the faculties which are then under God's direct action, and at the same time continue to act with the powers that are free and in the measure that it can without disturbing the peace in the depth of the soul.* This is the point that was "a matter of continual discussion among spiritual persons" to whom Saint Teresa refers in the third chapter of the fourth Mansions. The question was to know precisely if passive recollection, unaccompanied by loving attention, imposed the obligation of suspending the understanding. We have already heard the Saint declare her mind on this point and find her justification in the book of "a holy religious called Peter of Alcantara," whose testimony had been cited in opposition to her. Faithful to the principle stated many times over, that passivity is a proud and sterile attitude in a soul awaiting the special action of God, Saint Teresa insists that in imperfect contemplation, the faculties that are not under God's action

[33] *Ibid.;* 115.

must continue to act insofar as their activity does not disturb the regions of the soul held captive by God.

It seems to us that the discussion of which Saint Teresa speaks came less from opposition of doctrine than from a lack of psychological penetration on the part of her opponents and from spiritual experience that was as yet incomplete in their case.

In the first experiences of contemplative prayer, the soul is entirely taken up with the unwonted sweetness it experiences in the things of God; or, on the contrary, with sadness arising from its powerless dryness, and with regret for the loss of its consolations of former times. The impression of plenitude, which accompanies every supernatural action, even in its least degree, overflows into the psychological consciousness and there creates an impression of complete envelopment or even of perfect union. Contemplative dryness creates the same impression of overflow, but this latter is of a painful emptiness in all the faculties. The soul is then too much surprised and disconcerted by the newness of its interior state to be able to understand itself under the grace it is receiving. It does not know how to make a precise distinction between its faculties; it can only testify to its powerlessness to reach beyond this plenitude and to leave certain faculties in repose while acting quietly with the others.

On the other hand, the sublime contemplative experience of Saint Teresa enabled her not only to pass successfully beyond these first stages but also to analyze them with marvelous psychological insight. As we have seen from her descriptions of the prayer of passive recollection and the prayer of quiet, she clearly distinguishes the divine action in the soul and its own activity, the regions of peace and those of disquiet.

Her teaching is eminently useful for the soul blind in these early stages. Now that its attention has been drawn to this point, it discerns more easily of itself during contemplation the truth of Saint Teresa's experience in the matter. What it previously had judged to be subtle and perhaps vain distinctions, become illuminating to it, and it is not slow to appreciate the marvelous efficacy of the counsels that flow from it. The Saint writes:

> I have already said that, in this first state of recollection and quiet, the faculties of the soul do not fail; but the soul has much satisfaction in God that, although the other two faculties may be distracted, yet, since the will is in union with God for as long as the recollection lasts, its quiet and repose are not lost.[34]

To keep occupied the powers that are free; to respect the repose of those that are under God's action by avoiding any undue activity that might disturb them; not to engage therefore at this period during prayer except in activity that is quiet and peaceful; these are the directives that sum up the teaching of our two masters in regard to this stage of the spiritual life.

But these general directives must take account of widely different situations in the practical domain, of states of soul so diverse that in order to grasp the whole import of the teaching we will find it useful to follow still our Saints in the application that they themselves make of it for prayers of this period.

We shall look to Saint Teresa's teaching, with its manifold and precise nuances, for the prayers of passive recollection and quiet; Saint John of the Cross will be our guide in contemplative dryness.

3. APPLICATION TO CONTEMPLATIVE PRAYER

a. *Passive recollection*

Reference has already been made to this passive recollection which, in the logical order and often chronologically, is the first kind of contemplative prayer to be experienced. Saint Teresa carefully distinguishes it from simple active recollection; yet it is only a "disposition to hear the divine words." Writing of souls experiencing this kind of prayer, she says:

> I think I have read that they are like a hedgehog or a tortoise withdrawing into itself; and whoever wrote that must have understood it

[34] *Life*, xv; Peers, I, 88.

well. These creatures, however, enter within themselves whenever they like; whereas with us it is not a question of our will—it happens only when God is pleased to grant us this favour.[35]

What is the soul to do whose faculties have become recollected at this quiet call of the good Shepherd?

Either this passive recollection is the prelude and preparation for a more intense action of God, and the soul has only to abandon itself to this action; or it is only a fleeting experience of God's direction, and He will not extend His action farther. In that case there is to be no hesitation. Saint Teresa writes:

> In the Prayer of Recollection it is unnecessary to abandon meditation and the activities of the understanding.[36]
>
> If His Majesty has not begun to grant us absorption, I cannot understand how we can cease thinking in any way which will not bring us more harm than profit.[37]

Since the faculties are not suspended in this recollection, they should avail themselves of their liberty to seek God actively, profiting by the great facility for this that passive recollection gives them.

> God gave us our faculties to work with, and everything will have its due reward; there is no reason, then, for trying to cast a spell over them—they must be allowed to perform their office until God gives them a better one.[38]

This activity, moreover, must be carried on "without violence and without noise," for

> . . . all these interior activities are gentle and peaceful, and to do anything painful brings us harm rather than help.[39]

Thus Saint Teresa gives us the impression that this activity of the faculties will be very much simplified and limited to holding one's attention fixed in a general way on God and His presence. She writes:

[35] IV Mansions, iii; Peers, II, 241.
[36] *Ibid.;* 243.
[37] *Ibid.;* 242.
[38] *Ibid.;* 243.
[39] *Ibid.;* 242.

As I understand it, the soul whom the Lord has been pleased to lead into this Mansion will do best to act as I have said. Let it try, without forcing itself or causing any turmoil, to put a stop to all discursive reasoning, yet not to suspend the understanding, nor to cease from all thought, though it is well for it to remember that it is in God's presence and Who this God is. If feeling this should lead it into a state of absorption, well and good; but it should not try to understand what this state is, because that is a gift bestowed upon the will. The will, then, should be left to enjoy it, and should not labour except for uttering a few loving words, for although in such a case one may not be striving to cease from thought, such cessation often comes, though for a very short time.[40]

These latter counsels already have connection with the prayer of quiet; they restate a point of her teaching which she thought well to develop more at length, since she considered it of practical import to a great number of souls:

May His Majesty give me grace to explain this clearly, for there are many, many souls that reach this state and few that pass beyond it, and I do not know who is to blame for this. Most certainly it is not God.[41]

b. *The prayer of quiet*

This prayer is described at length in the chapter already cited:

This prayer, then, is a little spark of true love for the Lord which He begins to enkindle in the soul.[42]

The soul feels satisfaction and peace,

. . . together with a very great joy and repose of the faculties and a most sweet delight. . . . It dares not move or stir, for it thinks that if it does so this blessing may slip from its grasp: sometimes it would like to be unable even to breathe.[43]

To describe this sweetness, numerous comparisons spring to Saint Teresa's mind:

Apparently, as this heavenly water begins to flow from this source of which I am speaking—that is, from our very depths—it proceeds to spread within us and cause an interior dilation, . . . so that the soul itself cannot understand all that it receives there. The fragrance it

[40] *Ibid.;* 243.
[41] *Life,* xv; Peers, I, 89.
[42] *Ibid.;* 90.
[43] *Ibid.;* 88.

experiences, we might say, is as if in those interior depths there were a brazier on which were cast sweet perfumes; the light cannot be seen, nor the place where it dwells, but the fragrant smoke and the heat penetrate the entire soul, and very often, as I have said, the effects extend even to the body.[44]

But in this prayer only the will is held captive, notes Saint Teresa:

> There seems nothing left for it [the soul] to desire. The faculties are stilled and have no wish to move, for any movement they may make appears to hinder the soul from loving God. They are not completely lost, however, since, two of them being free, they can realize in Whose Presence they are. It is the will that is in captivity now.[45]

The Saint makes the same remark in the *Interior Castle,*[46] and in the book of her *Life:*

> The faculties are not lost, nor do they sleep. The will alone is occupied, in such a way that, without knowing how, it becomes captive. It allows itself to be imprisoned by God, as one who well knows itself to be the captive of Him Whom it loves. Oh, my Jesus and Lord, how much Thy love now means to us! It binds our own love so straitly that at that moment it leaves us no freedom to love anything but Thee.[47]

The soul's duty is evidently to guard this peace of the will now a captive of Him who has taken hold of it. This peace is less threatened by exterior temptations than by the disquiet of the interior faculties, by the understanding and memory.

Saint Teresa, who seems to have suffered very much from the agitation of these faculties, returns in all her treatises to this interior struggle and the means of triumphing over it. The understanding, imagination, and the memory share at times in the joy of the will; frequently they seem not to know of it. In both cases their activity can be dangerous.

When they do share in the joy, they

[44] IV Mansions, ii; Peers, II, 238.
[45] *Way of Perfection,* xxxi; Peers, II, 127-8.
[46] IV Mansions, ii; Peers, II, 238.
[47] *Life,* xiv; Peers, I, 83-4.

. . . help the will so that it may become more and more capable of enjoying so great a blessing.[48]

But their help is in the main annoying for it brings agitation. Speaking of these two powers, the Saint says:

They are like doves which are not pleased with the food given them by the owner of the dovecot, without their having worked for it, and go in search of food elsewhere, but are so unsuccessful that they return. . . . They must reflect that they are benefiting the will; or sometimes the memory or the imagination may do it harm by trying to present it with a picture of what it is enjoying.[49]

As to the understanding, she writes:

By noise, I mean going about with the understanding in search of many words and reflections with which to give thanks for this benefit and piling up its sins and imperfections so as to make itself realize that it does not deserve it. It is now that all this movement takes place: the understanding brings forward its representations and the memory becomes active—and sometimes I myself find these faculties really wearisome.[50]

At other times, the understanding and other powers are reduced almost to folly:

The understanding checks its activity, or rather the activity is checked for it when it finds it cannot understand what it desires, and thus it roams about all over the place, like a demented creature, and can settle down to nothing.[51]

And elsewhere Saint Teresa says:

It may come about that the soul is enjoying the highest degree of quiet, and that the understanding has soared so far aloft that what is happening to it seems not to be going on in its own house at all; it really seems to be a guest in somebody else's house, looking for other lodgings, since its own lodging no longer satisfies it and it cannot remain there for long together.[52]

A strange impression, certainly! And yet is not this feverish

[48] *Ibid.;* 84.
[49] *Ibid.*
[50] *Ibid.,* xv; 90.
[51] IV Mansions, iii; Peers, II, 243-4.
[52] *Way of Perfection,* xxxi; Peers, II, 130.

disarray of the faculties normally to be expected in face of the immobility and silence of the will, their mistress, as is also the feeling of being no longer at home in one's own dwelling, when held captive by a mysterious power that reveals only its strength.

As we see, the prayer of quiet develops in very different climates. What is one to do to protect it against the blustering good will of the faculties or against their disquieting activity? Saint Teresa writes:

The will must be calm and discreet and realize that we cannot treat effectively with God by the might of our own efforts and that these are like great logs of wood being heaped up indiscriminately so that they will quench this spark. Let us recognize this and with all humility say: "Lord, what can I do here? What has the servant to do with her Lord? What has earth to do with Heaven?" Or let it utter any words of love which come to its mind, with the firm and sure knowledge that what it is saying is the truth; and let it take no notice of the understanding, which is merely making itself a nuisance. And if the will wishes to communicate its joy to the understanding, or strives to lead it into recollection (as will often happen in this union of the will and state of tranquillity), and the understanding is very much disturbed, it will do better to leave it alone than to run after it. Let it (the will, I mean) continue in the fruition of that favour, and be as recollected as the wise little bee, for if no bees entered the hive and they all went about trying to bring each other in, there would not be much chance of their making any honey.

The soul will lose a great deal if it is not careful about this, especially if it has a lively understanding, with the result that, when it begins to hold discourse with itself and think out reflections, it will soon begin to fancy it is doing something worthwhile if its discourses and reflections are at all clever.[53]

Here is a still more energetic statement on the subject of the understanding:

When the will finds itself in this state of quiet, it must take no more notice of the understanding than it would of a madman, for, if it tries to draw the understanding along with it, it is bound to grow preoccupied and restless, with the result that this state of prayer will be all effort and no gain and the soul will lose what God has been giving it without any effort of its own.[54]

[53] *Life,* xv; Peers, I, 91.
[54] *Way of Perfection,* xxxi; Peers, II, 130.

Liberated from the turmoil of the understanding and the other faculties, the will, surrendered "into the arms of love," [55] must not remain inactive:

> Mental prayer must not be completely given up, nor yet must vocal prayer, if we ever wish to turn to it and are able to do so; for, if the state of Quiet is intense, it becomes difficult to speak except with great distress.[56]

Thus there will be more or less activity according to the degree of quiet. Again, Saint Teresa states precisely what is fitting. She says that all the reason has to do with this state is:

> . . . to understand that there is no reason, save His goodness alone, why God should grant us so great a favour, and to realize that we are very near Him, and to beg favours of His Majesty, and to pray to Him for the Church and for those who have been commended to us and for the souls in purgatory—not, however, with any noise of words, though with a hearty desire that He may hear us. This is a prayer that comprises a great deal and achieves more than any amount of meditation on the part of the understanding. Let the will, in order to quicken its love, arouse within itself certain reasons which reason itself will picture to it when it sees itself in so much better a state. Let it make certain acts of love, too, concerning what it will do for Him to Whom it owes so much, without allowing the understanding to make any noise, as I have said, in its search for these clever reflections. A few little straws laid down with humility (and they will be less than straws if it is we who lay them down) are more to the point here, and of more use for kindling the fire, than any amount of wood—that is, of the most learned reasoning—which, in our opinion, will put it out in a moment.[57]

Here is another comparison by which the Saint tells us over again what sweetness and what peace must govern the necessary interventions of activity during this quiet:

> It is well to seek greater solitude so as to make room for the Lord and allow His Majesty to do His own work in us. The most we should do is occasionally, and quite gently, to utter a single word, like a person giving a little puff to a candle, when he sees it has almost gone out, so as to make it burn again; though, if it were fully alight, the only result of blowing it would be to put it out. I think the puff should

[55] IV Mansions, iii; Peers, II, 244.
[56] *Life,* xv; Peers, I, 92.
[57] *Ibid.;* 91.

be a gentle one because, if we begin to tax our brains by making up long speeches, the will may become active again.[58]

Moreover let the soul not be too much concerned about its own activity. Let it

. . . abandon itself into the arms of love, and His Majesty will teach it what to do next; almost its whole work is to realize its unworthiness to receive such great good and to occupy itself in thanksgiving.[59]

[58] *Way of Perfection,* xxxi; Peers, II, 130.
[59] IV Mansions, iii; Peers, II, 244.

CHAPTER VI

Contemplative Dryness Active Night of Sense (continued)

As the sun, when it rises in the morning, will enter your house if you open the shutter, even so will God, Who sleeps not in keeping Israel, . . . enter the soul.[1]

Contemplative dryness is the name we have given to the first forms of contemplation described by Saint John of the Cross.

Between this contemplative dryness and the delightful quiet of Saint Teresa we have noted points of resemblance that allow us to place them at the same stage of the spiritual life. Yet rather notable differences remain between them.

These two forms of contemplative experience introduce us into different spiritual climates. Teresian quiet produces its effects, positive and delightful ones, in the will. The Joannine dryness seems to affect particularly the understanding, and produces in it effects that are privative because dazzling with contemplative light.

The contemplative of our day is generally attracted to the Joannine climate, because he finds in it more affinity with his own experience. And so the doctrine of Saint John of the Cross is now enjoying a revival.

The great and strong contemplative, Saint Therese of the

[1] *Living Flame,* st. iii; Peers, III, 167.

Child Jesus, was drawn to Saint John of the Cross. She too, describing her prayer, speaks insistently of dryness, "the most absolute aridity." John of the Cross became her master and her mystical doctor. She knew from memory whole pages of his writings and used to recite them to her novices during recreation. She writes:

> I have obtained many spiritual lights through the works of Saint John of the Cross. When I was seventeen and eighteen they were my only food.[2]

These indications must not be neglected. They reveal actual needs, and invite us to study in more detail the conduct of the soul in this prayer of contemplative dryness during the night of sense.

To avoid all confusion, let us first say emphatically that the dryness in question is authentically contemplative; that is, that it bears the three signs required by Saint John of the Cross. Should these three signs not be found together in it, then according to the evidence, one should obey Saint John of the Cross himself and return to meditation and to the activity of the faculties, so as to provide sustenance for the exchange of friendship with God.

But when the dryness is recognized as the fruit of God's action within, then the soul has the twofold obligation already pointed out, namely, to respect the action of God and to complete it with one's own.

Saint John of the Cross likes to insist on the first duty, to the point of seeming to neglect the second.

This insistence, a little surprising at first view and seemingly in opposition to Saint Teresa's teaching, appears upon reflection to be perfectly justified by the privative character of this contemplation and by its consequences. Actually, delight is not ordinarily experienced in it, especially in the beginning, because the delight is too subtle for a soul taken up with the memory of former graces and the present struggle against the

[2] *Autobiography,* viii, 131.

wandering of the faculties. It is all the more necessary to affirm the existence of contemplation as it is the more hidden. And it is all the more useful to recall the demands of silence as this contemplative dryness, which especially affects intellectual temperaments, finds these souls more sensitive to the lack of light. Besides, it arouses in them more painful reactions of powerlessness, disquiet, and restlessness.

The stress put by Saint John of the Cross on respect for God's action by silence answers then to a particular need of these souls. It does not, moreover, imply any belittling of the soul's duty to cooperate actively.

The attitude to be maintained during dryness cannot be stated in all its details. It is marked by suppleness and tenacious fidelity. Two directives are helpful in maintaining it; these we can state as follows:

A. To tend by faith toward the peaceful region of the spirit and remain there.

B. To ignore the turmoil in the sense region of the soul and calm it at times by means of certain activities.

A. Tend by faith toward the peaceful region of the spirit

We are now in the passive night of sense, which is a passage from sense to spirit by adapting the first to the second. Contemplative light brings about this adaptation and effects this passage.

The first directive points out what must be the soul's active cooperation: The soul should second, by its docility, this passing from sense to spirit and cooperate actively with grace which affects it, by making acts of faith.

But will the soul understand this directive? And to second this passing from sense to spirit, must the soul be aware of it? And again, to direct oneself toward the region of the spirit, is it necessary to understand what "sense" and "spirit" mean in the concrete and where they are actually localized?

These localizations are familiar to the mystics who all speak of an "interior cell," of a "depth of the soul," of a more intimate and more peaceful region which is the seat of God's presence and action in the soul. For Saint John of the Cross, sense includes the sense powers as well as the intellectual faculties in their immediate relations with these senses: consequently, the periphery of the soul. Spirit designates its more interior parts.[3]

These notions will later become familiar to the soul; they will give light on its experience by defining it better. For the moment, they are merely speculative and do not refer to any precise experience. In the Teresian quiet there is an interior perception indicating that the sweetness arises from a deep source. In this way it is easy to identify the spirit with those profound regions which produce quiet. The soul understands that it is the movement from sense to spirit that frees it from the thrall of external things and leads it to the water springing up within it.

In contemplative dryness, at least in its beginnings, a thick and somber grayness envelops the soul and its faculties, seeming to make impossible any distinction between them and to reduce them one and all to the same powerlessness and immobility.

In this conjuncture, how is one to discover in what direction the spirit lies, or how second a movement from sense to spirit of which one seems to be wholly unaware?

Nevertheless there is a practical criterion within reach of the soul, the criterion of peace and silence. "The senses" for Saint John of the Cross are the suburbs of the soul where turmoil and agitation reign; the sensitive powers are there. "Spirit" properly speaking is the abode of God. It is there that He dwells and acts in peace, there that He lets Himself be grasped by faith, or at times, allows Himself to be experienced as the only and transcendent Reality. Spirit is the meeting place between God who gives Himself as Father and the soul who seeks

[3] Cf. *supra,* ch. iii, p. 50 ff.

Him with its filial grace. This divine dwelling is silent, because just as God begot His Eternal Son in the silence of eternity, so too does He engender souls to the life of grace in the silence of the spirit.

This sense of silence and peace that accompanies all spiritual generation is the first and most constant experience of the soul. One can attain to it even in contemplative aridity by means of an act of faith or other anagogical acts.

In fact faith, a theological virtue, "the only proportionate and proximate means for attaining God," elevates the intellect that submits to it; and with the intellect, the whole soul, bringing it into contact with God. Thus it leads one into the supernatural world and into that region of the spirit where God acts and gives Himself.

In this truly contemplative dryness, faith penetrates into its divine object, and is there perfected in its exercise by the action of God through the gifts of the Holy Spirit.

This action of God which makes faith a living faith, imparts to it at the same time something which, if not an experience of sweetness, nevertheless calms the soul and induces it to repose silently on its divine object.

Thus it is that the activity of living faith produces at very least, as a minimum of experience, a subtle impression of silence and of peace. This silence indicates to the soul the region of the spirit toward which it must tend and the acts it must perform in order to reach it. It will succeed in this, consequently, by making acts of faith or better, anagogical acts, that is, simple acts of a theological virtue which go beyond the premises or foundations, put aside inquiries and reasonings, and go directly to their divine object to rest in Him alone.

What forms are these to take? In order that it may be of general application, a directive here should be something of a simple pointer indicating the direction to the goal, leaving it to each one to find his own way through the pathless regions that lie between. And yet, on condition that one knows how to pass quickly beyond them and find his own way, several indications can be given, a few signposts can be set up. Means that have succeeded in other cases, especially when they have been proposed by the great masters, merit consideration.

1. LOVING ASPIRATION

John of Saint Samson, that saintly blind man who was a bright light of the Carmelite Reform of Touraine in the seventeenth century, recommends the exercise of "aspiration" to lead the soul into these peaceful regions of the spirit. He writes:

> Aspiration is a loving enflamed launching of the heart and spirit by which the soul, passing beyond itself and all created things, unites itself in close union with God in this ardent expression of its love. Those who are disposed to aspirations must put forth effort until their aspiration, having become more intense, is sweet to them and delightful.[4]

One will succeed in this by degrees. As the beginning, aspiration draws its support from visible things; little by little, it becomes more concise, more brief, it encompasses and contains in itself "truths stripped of the non-essential." Thus one arrives at "love itself." He continues:

> The love produced by aspiration is so strong in certain souls that the will enters all alone into the loving bosom of God whom it tastes beyond all understanding and expression, while the understanding remains at the door astonished as it were and suspended in its action. There ensues an outflow of love, inundating, ravishing, delighting the soul and covering it with its floods, in the midst of which the soul is God Himself, His spirit, His divinity, as much as a creature can be in this life.

This exercise of loving aspiration which carries the soul back to God on a refluent tide of loving acts, less and less impeded by formulas is, as John of Saint Samson assures us, sovereignly efficacious. It makes use of the act of love, which is the anagog-

[4] Cf. *Vie de Jean de Saint-Samson* by P. Sernin, pp. 141-43. Also by the same author, *Maximes spirituelles,* pp. 155-58. Cf. *Vie Spirituelle,* 1925, which gives a very instructive summary of the doctrine of Jean de Saint-Samson. See especially Chapter vi, p. 134 ff., on aspiration.

ical act par excellence, and thus fixes the soul through love in its divine object which is God-Love.

John of Saint Samson notes that the soul must not too soon attempt the exercise of aspiration, for love in beginners is not strong enough efficaciously to elevate them to such lofty acts.

The great blind mystic remarks also that this exercise is not suited to all souls, even contemplative.

It is suited

> . . . to those who draw notable profit from the mystical ways, especially if they are of an affective nature. Some souls are never suited for it, occupying themselves as they do in God and with God by that holy and loving speculation which, it too, is an excellent mystical way.[5]

2. ANAGOGICAL ACT OF FAITH

We find again under the pen of John of Saint Samson the distinction between affective temperaments, for whom contemplation is especially loving and who can rise to the divine source through love whose sweetness they experience, and intellectual temperaments, in whom contemplation is especially knowledge and consequently dryness. In these latter, to whom we have constantly to return, we find that the sentiment of love is less easily aroused and perhaps less frequently exercised. There contemplation is more arid than loving, more static than dynamic. The peace which forms its base may be accompanied by all kinds of impressions: immobility and absolute silence, a perception of God through an opaque cloud, the impression of a wall that impedes any progress, or even an impression of being repulsed. One can give only general characteristics of these states which are almost as numerous and as varied as souls themselves and the moments of contemplation experienced by each.

It is the exercise of the virtue of faith that best suits them. But how are they to make these acts in practice? Generally it will not be by using set formulas but rather by keeping the

[5] *Vie de Jean de Saint-Samson.*

gaze of the soul fixed on God, by maintaining an interior attitude which consists in an orientation of the soul toward Him, a peaceful and actual attention, and an opening up of itself to His action.

It is very true that it is by faith that contact with God is established and maintained. And ordinarily the gifts of the Holy Ghost perfect faith when it is acting. But we have no right to count on this divine intervention through the gifts being sufficiently marked as to suspend our faculties and act without our concurrence.

This dryness and helplessness oblige us to exercise our faith actively in a peaceful and subtle manner. We should keep it awake by a penetrating gaze on the divine Reality of which now we have only fleeting or dim glimpses, or again by some short, tense ejaculatory prayer continually repeated because each time it makes God present to us in a vivid way. Or perhaps it may be best to maintain a simple attitude of peace under God's action, or a patient waiting on God who has hidden Himself and reduced us to this powerlessness, in order that we may find Him at a deeper level.

By turns Saint Therese of the Child Jesus remains content in the dark underground where no light shines except "from the lowered eyes of the face of Jesus," or keeps her gaze fixed on the cloud that hides the divine Sun, willing to wait for its luminous rays until "that unending day when faith shall be no more." Saint Jane de Chantal counsels the soul in this state to remain motionless in the presence of the Master, like a canvas before the artist who is to animate it with a living design.

But beyond these particular modes, here is the teaching of Saint John of the Cross on the exercise of faith in these regions:

> At this time the soul must be led in a way entirely contrary to the way wherein it was led at first. If formerly it was given material for meditation, and practised meditation, this material must now be taken from it and it must not meditate; for, as I say, it will be unable to do so even though it would, and, instead of becoming recollected, it will become distracted. . . . For it turns from the quiet and peaceful

blessings which were secretly given to its spirit, to the work that it desires to do with sense. . . . Wherefore in this state the soul must never have meditation imposed upon it, nor must it make any acts, nor strive after sweetness or fervour; for this would be to set an obstacle in the way of the principal agent, who, as I say, is God. For God secretly and quietly infuses into the soul loving knowledge and wisdom without any intervention of specific acts, although sometimes He specifically produces them in the soul for some length of time. And the soul has then to walk with loving advertence to God, without making specific acts, but conducting itself, as we have said, passively, and making no efforts of its own, but preserving this simple, pure and loving advertence and determination, like one that opens his eyes with the advertence of love.

Since God, then, as giver, is communing with the soul by means of loving and simple knowledge, the soul must likewise commune with Him by receiving with a loving and simple knowledge and advertence, so that knowledge may be united with knowledge and love with love.[6]

If, as I say, and as in truth is the case, the soul receives this loving knowledge passively and after the supernatural manner of God, . . . this soul must be quite annihilated in its natural operations, disencumbered, at ease, quiet, peaceful, serene and adapted to the manner of God; exactly like the air, which receives the greater clarification and heat from the sun when it is pure and cleansed from vapours and at rest. Therefore the soul must be attached to nothing—to no exercise of meditation or reasoning; to no kind of sweetness, whether it be of sense or of spirit; and to no other kind of apprehension.[7]

It must stand in complete detachment above all this and its spirit must be completely freed from it, as Habacuc[8] said that he must needs do in order to hear what the Lord should say to him. "I will stand upon my watch," he says, "and I will fix my step upon my munition, and I will watch to see that which will be said to me." This is as though he had said: I will raise up my mind above all the operations and all the knowledge that can be comprehended by my senses, and above that which they can keep and retain within themselves: all this I will leave below. And I will fix the step of the munition of my faculties, not allowing them to advance a step as to their own operation, so that through contemplation I may receive that

[6] *Living Flame,* st. iii; Peers, III, 160-1.
[7] *Ibid.;* 161.
[8] Hab. 2:1.

which is communicated to me from God. For we have already said that pure contemplation consists in receiving.[9]

This text describes particularly well the peaceful isolation of the soul in the region of spirit.

The Saint does not tire of insisting on the detachment and peace necessary for faith to be pure. In this dryness, which at times resembles death, the soul must be strengthened against any intellectual activism that seeks its nourishment in distinct thought, as well as against discouragement that would sink into complete passivity. Faith must be kept alive, sound, free, like an antenna erected above all the noises of the world to receive the waves from the Infinite.

When in this way the soul voids itself of all things and achieves emptiness and surrender of them (which, as we have said, is the part that the soul can play), it is impossible, if the soul does as much as in it lies, that God should fail to perform His own part by communicating Himself to the soul, at least secretly and in silence. It is more impossible than that the sun should fail to shine in a serene and unclouded sky; for as the sun, when it rises in the morning, will enter your house if you open the shutter, even so will God, Who sleeps not in keeping Israel, still less slumbers,[10] enter the soul that is empty and fill it with Divine blessings.[11]

On the other hand, with what sadness the holy doctor speaks of the harm caused the soul by agitation voluntarily stirred up during contemplation:

These anointings, then, and these touches, are the delicate and sublime acts of the Holy Spirit. . . . These blessings, with the greatest facility, by no more than the slightest act which the soul may desire to make on its own account, with its memory, understanding or will, or by the application of its sense or desire or knowledge or sweetness or pleasure, are disturbed or hindered in the soul, which is a grave evil and a great shame and pity.

Oh, how grave a matter is this, and what cause it gives for wonder, that, while the harm done is inconspicuous, and the interference with those holy anointings almost negligible, the harm should be more serious, and a matter for deeper sorrow and regret, than the disquiet-

[9] *Living Flame,* st. iii; Peers, III, 162.
[10] Cf. Ps. 120:4.
[11] *Living Flame,* st. iii; 167.

ing and ruining of many souls of a more ordinary nature which have not attained to a state of such supreme fineness and delicacy! It is as though a portrait of supreme and delicate beauty were touched by a clumsy hand, and were daubed with coarse, crude colours. This would be a greater and more crying and pitiful shame than if many more ordinary portraits were besmeared in this way. For when the work of so delicate a hand as this of the Holy Spirit has been thus roughly treated, who will be able to repair its beauty.[12]

These quotations are taken from the *Living Flame of Love.* Consequently they might seem applicable only to the perfect contemplation of a soul that has arrived at the summit. Actually, just as there is but one supernatural contemplation, there is but one contemplative attitude. The one and the other are progressively perfected. Their development is in constant, very close mutual interdependence and is regulated from the beginning by the same laws.

Since the aridity of which we are treating is clearly contemplative, the soul must already know the perfect response to be given to God's action within it, and should try to realize the contemplative attitude to the full measure insofar as the intermittent character of the contemplation and its own as yet unadapted faculties permit.

It is the senses, clamorous and dull in their operation, which impede the perfect receiving of the breathings of the Holy Ghost. Is it possible to render them less noxious, to free oneself from their troublesome agitations? The second directive will answer this question.

B. How to ignore the noise of sense and bring it calm

The exercise of faith or even loving aspiration, although always opening up the soul to God's light, does not always succeed in establishing peace in the lower faculties. These latter are restless and demanding, thus thwarting the soul's escape

[12] *Ibid.;* 164-5.

into the region of the spirit. What can one do to quiet this noise? [13]

The duty of the soul is to pay no heed to this noise; rather to escape it by a more vigorous movement towards the region of the spirit. The stag pursued by the hounds, says Tauler, runs faster towards the source of living water. Saint John of the Cross notes that the soul that has already arrived at perfection excels in escaping the terrors produced by the devil in the region of sense by running to shelter in the dark hiding place of faith, in the realm of the spirit. The turmoil of the senses is an excellent means of purification and has its part in helping one to enjoy the silence of the spirit. But in this period of transition man's way in the spiritual life is less of his own choosing than at any other time. Whether it be his inexperience, as a beginner, that leads him to squander his strength in violent efforts; or the special disposition of his temperament, making him unable to support passivity; or even the obsessing preoccupation of the moment, that has invaded the field of the faculties, it is often difficult and at times even impossible for a soul to rise for an instant above the agitation, or at least to dominate it sufficiently to maintain the peace of the higher regions undisturbed. Fatigue comes upon one; the body itself grows weary

[13] Among the purely natural mystics, such as the Hindu mystics, we find a highly developed technique for calming the powers and simplifying their operations. Thus the *Baghavad Gita* presents to us several yogas or ways of asceticism to arrive at losing oneself in the One, namely devotion, spiritual works, and direct contemplation. (Cf. *Baghavad Gita* translated by Shri Aurobindo, and *Discipline monastique* by Swami Brahmananda.) We must remark that these techniques end only in a sublimation of the activity of the faculties and in a losing of self in the One or the Universal that they call God. Catholic mysticism seeks union with a personal God, living and distinct from us. It aspires to perfect union with Him and not to a pantheistic fusion. In its progress toward the One it relies on the effort of man, but especially on the action of God. Its rather developed technique, as it appears in the austere framework of the monastic contemplative Orders, is not a technique of force that wants to attain an end, but a technique of docility that wants to yield to the movement of grace and respect the liberty of God, who must work in us to will and to do.

Natural mysticism can produce a superman who has arrived at higher states. Catholic mysticism produces a child of God, moved by the spirit of God.

of immobility; enervation sets in. One must use discretion to avoid more grave disorders, or even to direct one's forces and sustain the effort of resistance.

1. DISCRETION

Will discretion demand that we leave prayer aside and engage in some activity in order to find diversion and rest? There are in fact times when diversion may be necessary. Saint Teresa tells us that in order to bear with certain repugnances or with a sort of frenzy that follows some graces of union, it is good to leave prayer for activity. She writes:

> The best medicine—I do not say for removing the trouble, for I know of none for that, but for enabling the soul to endure it—is to occupy oneself with external affairs and works of charity and to hope in God's mercy, which never fails those who hope in Him.[14]

The Saint gives the same advice to certain temperaments whose weakness cannot bear the sensible effects of contemplation. But it is a treatment for exceptional cases. In the case of the first named, reference is made to souls who are undergoing particularly painful trials of the sixth Mansions; in the second case, we are in the presence of temperaments whose weaknesses require careful vigilance. One could not, without danger, generalize the advice. In the case of contemplative dryness, to abandon prayer for activity on account of the aridity experienced, would ordinarily be to yield to a dangerous and often seductive temptation.

A dangerous temptation this, because of the harmful effects that we pointed out when giving the teaching of John of the Cross; all the more dangerous, since the diversion that the activity promises and the spiritual sweetness that it sometimes brings, make it very attractive. In fact, God at times makes Himself more sensibly present to the soul in the midst of its exterior occupations than during prayer. He seems in effect to withdraw Himself when the soul goes in search of Him and to

[14] VI Mansions, i; Peers, II, 274.

hide behind a thick veil, which lets through only a subtle impression of a faraway presence; while on the other hand He seems to return and to let His sweetness overflow even to the senses when the soul itself ceases from its painful interior search for Him, and opens itself to the exterior world by returning to its habitual occupations. This delightful experience seems to confirm the impression of sterility left by contemplative dryness, and to put a seal of certitude on the thought that contemplative prayer is only a waste of time. A subtle temptation assuredly, but certainly a temptation. Let us try to clarify this, for the danger is grave.

During contemplation and by means of it, light and love flow into the soul. The abundance of light and the simultaneous unfitness of the faculties to receive such light produce dryness and imperception. Their supernatural effects seem not to go beyond the region of the spirit; and hence the lower faculties are paralyzed or agitated.

But let the contemplation come to an end and the faculties resume their activity under habitual conditions. In this very activity, the soul becomes conscious of the work that has been wrought in it by contemplation, and the riches it has received. The faculties have become more penetrating, more apt for finding the divine in creatures; they themselves seem filled with light and with love. Only a moment previously the soul wearied itself in its search for a God who did not reveal Himself and who seemed nowhere to be found. And now this soul, whom aridity has filled with thirst for God, sees all things filled and overflowing with that hidden God and discovers the divine secrets hidden in their depths. The sacred texts shine with new lights; the maxims of the saints reveal their inner meaning; nature itself shows forth in all their beauty the vestiges of the God who created it. The soul is in festive mood. The faculties, now at peace, are bathed in light and overflow with supernatural delight.

Following as it does the dryness of contemplation, this feast of the soul might cause it to think it has arisen to a more elevated spiritual state. We know now that it is nothing of the kind. Actually it is the awareness of the benefits of contemplation that is creating this joy, and this awareness takes place only when contemplation has ceased. It is such a joy as the awareness of the good produced by restful sleep gives to the awakening, or, by the withdrawal of a painful surgical needle. The joy is for the awakening, but it is the sleep or the needle that has produced the benefit.[15]

What are we to think of one who would seek the joy of the awakening but refuse the immobility of the sleep? Such an attitude would be at least strange and would make one lose all, both benefit and joys. This would be the case of the soul so carried away by the spiritual delights found in activity following contemplative dryness, as to think it possible to enjoy these continually by leaving the dryness and giving itself up only to activity.

2. PATIENCE

Contemplative dryness is a benefit to the soul; it must be endured in spite of fatigue and temptations that would draw one away from it. Such is the law. But to endure without danger and without weakening, discretion and humble patience must be added to persevering energy. We have already said this apropos of the struggle against the distractions and dryness of the first period of the spiritual life.[16] But it must be repeated here, for discretion and patience were never more necessary; and they must now be ingenious.

It is a war of usury without profit, and a hard one, that must be waged against forces one cannot dominate in oneself. Such

[15] The study of the graces of complete union of the fifth Mansions or of the raptures of the sixth, will confront us with the same phenomenon. We shall see that it is the awakening of the faculties after these graces that suspended all conscious activity, which permits the soul to explore the substantial riches that it has received and fully to enjoy them.

[16] Cf. Vol. I: *I Want to See God,* p. 245 ff.

is the agitation of the faculties during contemplative dryness. In using violence against it, one would quickly exhaust one's forces and would disturb the peaceful action of contemplation. The faculties obey the will completely only when held under its immediate control. They are agitated during this dryness because the will is held captive by God. It can return to its domain only by leaving the divine contact. Violence and direct efforts to calm the agitation bring fatigue, therefore, and cause one to lose the contemplation rather than help it. Patience is the only efficacious remedy.

Nevertheless, when this agitation of the faculties is so great as to prevent the anagogical act from entering into the peace of the spirit, or when in the course of contemplation it threatens to invade the whole soul, then one can try to arrest its harmful effects by exercising some other calming influence over the faculties. It is a matter of finding some diversion that will quiet the senses for a time sufficient for the faculties to escape into the region of the spirit, or keep them in sufficient check so as not to disturb naked contemplation.

3. SEVERAL CALMING INFLUENCES

To find means of securing this happy evasion is an art. These means differ according to souls and often their efficacy is only passing. Each one must seek those that are suited to him and change them when they are no longer effective. Hence the indications that follow will offer suggestions rather than exact advice.

Saint Therese of the Child Jesus tells us that in her periods of dryness, which were certainly contemplative, she had recourse to vocal prayer in these moments of weariness:

> Sometimes when I am in such a state of spiritual dryness that not a single good thought occurs to me, I say very slowly the "Our Father" or the "Hail Mary," and these prayers suffice to take me out of myself, and wonderfully refresh me.[17]

[17] *Autobiography,* x, 163.

The slow recitation of a favorite prayer, a few ejaculations that usually give joy to the soul can stop the first movements of a rising tempest, at times even calm it when it has been let loose. Vocal prayer is the necessary companion of contemplation for certain temperaments whose long habits of activity render insupportable the passivity that contemplation imposes. It is thus that souls that seem not to be able to pray otherwise than vocally can be great contemplatives. This case is rather frequent among persons of very limited intellectual culture, yet whose exterior life and conversation bear witness to a very intimate union with God. For all contemplatives, moreover, vocal prayer can bring tranquillity; and they must have recourse to it from time to time. In vocal prayer made under these circumstances, the soul will devote itself less to penetrating the meaning of the words than to drawing from them that power of loving recollection that they contain.

The choice of a prayer to be said can be of great importance. A prayer that would place the faculties in the very atmosphere of actual contemplation is excellent. Such or such a psalm, for example, will express admirably the solitude of the soul, its feeling of powerlessness; another will express the trust that springs from the depths of silence and of misery in which it lies. Unity will thus be brought into the soul, at least for an instant, and with unity, calm. We must note here the particularly calming influence of prayer to the Blessed Virgin. Some souls always find in this an efficacious help. Others prefer a prayer of trust in divine mercy and a prayer of humility, which is always sweet to them, because God always stoops to the soul that humbly trusts in Him.

The attractions of grace are an excellent guide in making this choice. Experience will teach each one which prayers are most helpful to him and the ones to which, consequently, he has the duty to return more frequently.

This prayer for the most part will be a cry of the soul, an exclamation, an appeal for help. Or perhaps it may be some words that evoke a favorite subject of prayer or some supernatural light imprinted on the soul. Or again it may be the expression of some deep need of the soul, the aspiration of one's whole being. And for this reason they have the power to recollect the soul by their very utterance. The faculties return with docility, avid for the recollection in which they now find themselves. "My Lord and my God." "I am He who is, you are she who is not." "My God, have mercy on me." These are rich and powerful formulas that cradle in some way the sleep of the faculties, while the depths of the soul silently delight in the mysterious and substantial divine truth that the words express in human language.

The agitation will perhaps return; but to gain time is to gain much. It is even to gain everything, for it is less a matter of suppressing all agitation than of permitting the soul to maintain or to resume contact, in spite of obstacles, with Him who sheds upon it His ineffable light.

The attitude of the body during prayer is not a matter of indifference and can contribute to the calming of the soul. Need will sometimes be felt to take a physical attitude that expresses one's inner sentiment and which, bringing into harmony interior and exterior attitudes, will make for the unity of the whole being. But care must be taken lest the effort to procure this unity impose excessive physical fatigue or provoke enervation. Again, discretion is necessary. The physical attitude, while being restful, must not favor sleepiness; and while freeing the soul from annoying constraint, must be a support for it and sustain it in its painful and resolute waiting for God.

Nor must one forget the tranquillizing influence of the Eucharist. Experience shows too that merely to be near Jesus in the Host, or to enter a church where He resides, produces sensible effects of interior calm on certain souls of prayer. And to maintain these effects, they have only to make from time to time acts of faith in the divine Presence, to gaze at the tabernacle or to look toward it occasionally. This is not the moment to ask if these effects have a cause uniquely supernatural; it suffices for us to mention them so that the soul in quest of recollection may avail itself of this nearness of Jesus in the Blessed Sacrament in order to enthrall the interior senses.

For other souls, on the contrary, this nearness is rather a hindrance and a cause of agitation. Drawn at the same time by the attraction of Jesus in the Blessed Sacrament and by an intense need for recollection within themselves, they remain in suspense, uncertain, hesitating to choose, and still disturbed even after making their choice. For these souls, as indeed for many others, complete solitude seems preferable and more conducive to calm. It frees them from all interior and exterior constraint, from a certain unreasonable self-consciousness, from the fear of being singular and of letting the radiance of interior grace be seen; and it alone allows them to give themselves up completely to the divine rapture. Nowhere better than in solitude do they find God, living Spirit and overflowing Love, and perceive the gentle breathing of His divine presence and the delicate anointings of His action in its inmost depths. And, so, while not belittling the calming effects of the Eucharistic Presence, they do not hesitate to sacrifice this in favor of the nourishing silence of the desert. And who would blame them, when history shows us how numerous were the souls that the desert attracted, and how strengthened and filled with God it returned them to the world.

Such is the diversity of souls, of their grace and their needs. Each one, enlightened by his own experience and by wise direction, will have to find what is suited to him. Any premature choice of methods or of means might be harmful or might hinder progress. Thus will each one discover his own way to flee through the tumult to the peace and silence of the depths of his soul.

At times evasion will be impossible, either because the soul has delayed its flight and thought of it efficaciously only when it was already held fast, or because an image or strange thought imposed itself from the first with the force of an obsession, or because the tumult is exterior and one is unable to withdraw from it all.

There remains for the soul only to groan under its powerlessness, to call upon the help of God and the intercession of the saints, who bring calm with deliverance. Humble patience is not always a disposition that liberates one; but a humble person always derives from this turmoil a purification that is certainly more meritorious, and perhaps more efficacious, than that which the delight of silence procures. Let Saint Therese of the Child Jesus confide to us what she did in such circumstances:

> For a long time my place at meditation was near a Sister who fidgeted continually, either with her Rosary, or something else; possibly, as I am very quick of hearing, I alone heard her, but I cannot tell you how much it tried me. I should have liked to turn round, and by looking at the offender, make her stop the noise; but in my heart I knew that I ought to bear it tranquilly, both for the love of God and to avoid giving pain. So I kept quiet, but the effort cost me so much that sometimes I was bathed in perspiration, and my meditation consisted merely in suffering with patience. After a time I tried to endure it in peace and joy, at least deep down in my soul, and I strove to take actual pleasure in the disagreeable little noise. Instead of trying not to hear it, which was impossible, I set myself to listen, as though it had been some delightful music, and my meditation—which was not the "prayer of quiet"—was passed in offering this music to Our Lord.[18]

The same asceticism of humble patience is suitable for that dead calm which is still more disconcerting than the agitation of the faculties; for noise gives an impression of life and allows one to suspect at times the living Presence, while absolute calm creates certitude of the absence of the divine Reality for whom the soul is thirsting.

In the silence that comes from powerlessness, from emptiness, Saint Teresa thinks of her soul as a garden of which God Himself is the gardener:

> It used to give me great delight to think of my soul as a garden and of the Lord as walking in it. I would beg Him to increase the fragrance

[18] *Autobiography,* x, 169.

of the little buds of virtue which seemed to be beginning to appear, and to keep them alive so that they might bloom to His glory—for I wanted nothing for myself—and I would ask Him to prune away any of them He wished to, for I knew that the plants would be all the better if He did. I speak of pruning, for there come times when the soul feels like anything but a garden: everything seems dry to it and no water comes to refresh it, and one would think there had never been any kind of virtue in it at all. The soul suffers many trials, for the Lord wants the poor gardener to think that all the trouble he has taken in watering the garden and keeping it alive is lost. Then is the proper time for weeding and rooting out the smaller plants, and this must be done, however small they may be, if they are useless; for we know that no efforts of ours are availing if God withholds from us the water of grace, and we must despise ourselves as nothing and as less than nothing. By doing this we can gain great humility and then the flowers will begin to grow afresh.[19]

The humble patience of Saint Therese of the Child Jesus in the same circumstances borrows from her grace of spiritual poverty a special note of simplicity. What matter the manner of soul, provided that it remain peaceful and that God can act in it in full liberty?

Need I tell you, dear Mother, about the retreat before my profession? Far from receiving consolation, I went through it in a state of utter dryness and as if abandoned by God. Jesus, as was His wont, slept in my little barque. How rarely do souls suffer Him to sleep in peace! This Good Master is so wearied with continually making fresh advances that He eagerly avails Himself of the repose I offer Him, and, no doubt, He will sleep on until my great and everlasting retreat; but, instead of being grieved at this, I am glad.[20]

But it sometimes happens that she goes to sleep, the emptiness is so heavy. And she tells us the means she found not to be disturbed upon awakening:

Well, I am not distressed. I reflect that little children are equally dear to their parents whether they are asleep or awake; that, in order to perform operations, doctors put their patients to sleep; and finally that *"The Lord knoweth our frame, He remembereth that we are but dust."* [21]

[19] *Life,* xiv; Peers, I, 86-7.
[20] *Autobiography,* viii, 118.
[21] *Ibid.*

We must not make the mistake, however, of thinking there is question of laziness or of lack of concern. Saint Therese knows well how to keep her soul occupied during this period of aridity and emptiness that she sometimes experiences during her thanksgiving. She tells us the means she habitually uses:

> I picture my soul as a piece of waste ground and beg Our Blessed Lady to take away my imperfections—which are as heaps of rubbish—and to build upon it a splendid tabernacle worthy of Heaven, and adorn it with her own adornments. Then I invite all the Angels and Saints to come and sing canticles of love, and it seems to me that Jesus is well pleased to see Himself received so grandly, and I share in His joy. But all this does not prevent distractions and drowsiness from troubling me, and not unfrequently I resolve to continue my thanksgiving throughout the day, since I made it so badly in choir.[22]

We should like to be able to quote the whole of an admirable letter to Sister Marie of the Sacred Heart, September 14, 1896. With her gracious story of the little bird, Saint Therese describes her attitude of contemplation, carried on with her gaze steadily fixed on God throughout all the aridities and the mists, in spite of her weaknesses and even the sleep that intervene to hinder it or interrupt it.

> I see myself as a feeble little bird, with only a light down to cover me; I am not an eagle, yet I have an eagle's eyes and an eagle's heart, for in spite of my extreme littleness, I dare to gaze upon the divine Sun, the Sun of Love, and my heart feels within it all the eagle's aspirations. . . .
>
> With reckless abandon, it wants to stay gazing upon its divine Sun; nothing can affright it, not wind nor rain, and if dark clouds come and hide the Star of Love, the little bird does not move, it knows that beyond the clouds its Sun shines still, that its radiance is not for a single instant eclipsed. . . .
>
> When it wants to gaze upon the divine Sun and the clouds keep it from seeing a single ray, its little eyes close in spite of itself, its little head is hid under its little wing, and the poor little thing sleeps, still fancying that it is gazing upon its dearest Star! When it awakes, it is not all desolate, its little heart stays at peace; it resumes its task of love; it invokes the Angels and the Saints who mount up like eagles toward that consuming Fire, which it so much desires.[23]

[22] *Ibid.*, 126.
[23] *Collected Letters of Saint Therese of Lisieux*, 284-5.

What luminous truths and what deep wisdom there are in these words and in these means, apparently those of a child!

These experiences, told with so captivating a charm, present us not with methods to be adopted but with a lesson to be learned. They set before us the suppleness that the soul must have, an example of the variety of means suited to its tastes and circumstances. These means it must know how to discover if it would hold firm, peaceful and alive in its faith, and open itself wide to the power of the divine light that is striking it.

This is the thing that matters, only this: to watch peacefully in faith, looking up to that loving Wisdom whose presence is indicated by the darkness, in this mingling of silence and tumult. Out from the dark night divine Wisdom causes to spring up vivifying and transforming waters.[24]

[24] The teaching here given is the same as that given in the chapter on silence (Part III, ch. V) and especially that on faith (Part III, ch. X). It is of such practical importance that we could not insist on it too much nor present it under too many different aspects in order to make it more precise. Saint John of the Cross does not tire of repeating it under various forms in his treatises. *Translator's note:* Part III, MYSTICAL LIFE AND CONTEMPLATION, is to be found in *I Want to See God.*

CHAPTER VII
Active Night Outside of Prayer

> *If you have no wish either to hear about them [my counsels] or to practise them, continue your mental prayer all your life.*[1]

A. Absolute asceticism

In the *Way of Perfection,* following her exposition of the virtues necessary for the contemplative, Saint Teresa gives us this warning in energetic, almost blunt, form. Without detachment, without humility, without the gift of self, all realized in an absolute form, God does not grant the grace of contemplation. Or rather, the Saint is more precise: when a soul practises these virtues without bringing to them that absoluteness which ensures their perfection, God visits it from time to time as a master visits the workmen in his vineyard, but He does not treat it as one of His own by pouring out upon it all His gifts. In other words, contemplation is not developed apart from an absolute asceticism.

This is matter for surprise. Actually, the classical division of the spiritual life into two periods, the one active, the other passive, has created the impression that there is a time for acquiring the virtues by our own persevering efforts, and a time for loving and being loved by God in a dwelling where peace now reigns.

Saint Teresa seems to take a stand against such a notion. Here is a text already quoted, but one that will bear reading because of its importance:

[1] *Way of Perfection,* xvi; Peers, II, 64.

You will ask, my daughters, why I am talking to you about virtues when you have more than enough books to teach you about them and when you want me to tell you only about contemplation. My reply is that, if you had asked me about meditation, I could have talked to you about it, and advised you all to practise it, even if you do not possess the virtues. For this is the first step to be taken towards the acquisition of the virtues and the very life of all Christians depends upon their beginning it. . . .

But contemplation, daughters, is another matter . . . for this King does not allow Himself to be taken except by one who surrenders wholly to Him.[2]

The thought is very clear: at the beginning of the spiritual life, when the soul is still at the stage of discursive meditation, it is fidelity to prayer that is of most importance; when the soul has become contemplative, it is asceticism which must take the lead. To her daughters of the Convent of Saint Joseph of Avila who ask advice as to how to progress in contemplation that has become habitual, she answers by writing the *Way of Perfection,* of which the first twenty chapters expound the absolute asceticism that the contemplative must practise. She writes:

Leave others to wage their own conflicts, which are not light ones. The standard-bearer is not a combatant, yet none the less he is exposed to great danger, and, inwardly, must suffer more than anyone else, for he cannot defend himself, as he is carrying the standard, which he must not allow to leave his hands, even if he is cut to pieces. Just so contemplatives have to bear aloft the standard of humility and must suffer all the blows which are aimed at them without striking any themselves. Their duty is to suffer as Christ did, to raise the Cross on high, not to allow it to leave their hands, whatever the perils in which they find themselves, and not to let themselves be found backward in suffering. It is for this reason that they are given such an honourable duty.[3]

We must not interpret this comparison in the sense of an asceticism, as is proven by the explanation of the virtues given in the preceding pages.

There is scarcely need to mention, it seems so evident to anyone who has merely opened the treatises of Saint John of the

[2] *Ibid.;* 63-4.
[3] *Ibid.,* xviii; 74.

Cross, that the same teaching is to be found under the pen of the mystical doctor of Carmel. From the beginning of the *Ascent of Mount Carmel,* the Saint discloses to us the hard demands of divine love, showing us the only road that leads to the summit of Carmel, on which is written five times "nothing." And Saint John of the Cross adds this comment:

> In order to arrive at having pleasure in everything,
> Desire to have pleasure in nothing.
> In order to arrive at possessing everything,
> Desire to possess nothing.
> In order to arrive at being everything,
> Desire to be nothing.
> In order to arrive at knowing everything,
> Desire to know nothing.
> In order to arrive at that wherein thou hast no pleasure,
> Thou must go by a way wherein thou hast no pleasure.
> In order to arrive at that which thou knowest not,
> Thou must go by a way that thou knowest not.
> In order to arrive at that which thou possessest not,
> Thou must go by a way that thou possessest not.
> In order to arrive at that which thou art not,
> Thou must go through that which thou art not.
>
> Means for not impeding the All:
>
> When thy mind dwells upon anything,
> Thou art ceasing to cast thyself upon the All.
> For, in order to pass from the all to the All,
> Thou hast to deny thyself wholly in all.
> And, when thou comest to possess it wholly,
> Thou must possess it without desiring anything.
> For, if thou wilt have anything in having all,
> Thou hast not thy treasure purely in God.[4]

Such are the rules of the road that leads to the summit of Carmel. Such is the chart that governs the soul's participation in the work of transformation through love, the ideal presented by the masters of Carmel.

To many persons, these precepts will certainly seem exaggerated: they will see in them an impossible challenge to the moral energies of man. Others, on the contrary, will find them

[4] *Ascent,* Bk. I, xiii; Peers, I, 59-60.

luminous, and their very austerity will seem to them sweet. They will have the impression, on reading Saint Teresa and Saint John of the Cross, that these masters put into exact and clear words the demands that their own soul has heard murmured by its interior Master, and show them how to be faithful to these. The heroism of this asceticism, the spiritual climate into which it introduces them, becomes for them a source of peace and ensures their spiritual balance.

The latter have the advantage over the former of having a certain experimental knowledge of the absolute, of having perceived, at least in a confused light, something of the purity of God and of His demands from those who come to Him.

In other words, in order to understand the teaching of the *Ascent of Mount Carmel* and the *Way of Perfection,* one must be at least a beginner in contemplation. It is for such beginners and for those progressing in the way of contemplation that these treatises were written. Let us not doubt this. The absolute precepts that are found in them are the rigorously logical conclusions drawn from the radical opposition that exists between God and sin, between grace and evil tendencies, between spirit and flesh. Saint John of the Cross writes:

> Wherefore, as in natural generation no form can be introduced unless the preceding, contrary form is first expelled from the subject, which form, while present, is an impediment to the other by reason of the contrariety which the two have between each other; even so, for as long as the soul is subjected to the sensual spirit, the spirit which is pure and spiritual cannot enter it.[5]

The soul must work with all its strength to reduce this opposition. God requires of it this cooperation in order to produce, Himself, the inflowing of His grace. The treatises, the *Ascent of Mount Carmel* and the *Way of Perfection,* will be for the soul in this stage, not works that present a faraway ideal from which to draw inspiration, but manuals of life that furnish at

[5] *Ibid.,* vi; 33-4.

every instant the practical formula, adapted to the needs of the moment.

Hence it is toward the realization of the absolute that the soul must work with its whole power of resolute and at times violent asceticism. The growth of contemplation is at issue. It is necessary to insist on this. Contemplation and asceticism have been too often disassociated, as also the prayer of quiet and virtue. At times they have been placed even in opposition. This error is extremely harmful in practice, as it invites or at least permits the soul to repose when the practice of virtue is of urgent necessity.

Let us again read Saint Teresa who does not tire of saying this important truth over and over in various ways. Speaking of the palace of the soul, she writes:

> The important point is that we should be absolutely resolved to give it to Him for His own and should empty it so that He may take out and put in just what He likes. . . . And, as He refuses to force our will, He takes what we give Him but does not give Himself wholly until He sees that we are giving ourselves wholly to Him. This is certain, and, as it is of such importance, I often remind you of it. Nor does He work within the soul as He does when it is wholly His and keeps nothing back. I do not see how He can do so, since He likes everything to be done in order.[6]

But elsewhere, adds the Saint, with a touch of sadness:

> So niggardly and so slow are we in giving ourselves wholly to God that we do not prepare ourselves as we should to receive that precious thing which it is His Majesty's will that we should enjoy only at a great price.[7]

Saint John of the Cross makes the same demands in even clearer terms. For him, absolute poverty is equivalent to perfect divine union. And so, lack of resoluteness in practising detachment is the most apparent cause of the failure and halt of souls in the mystical ascent. In the *Living Flame of Love,* he writes:

[6] *Way of Perfection,* xxviii; Peers, II, 118.
[7] *Life,* xi; Peers, I, 63.

Here it behooves us to note the reason why there are so few that attain to this lofty state of the perfection of union with God. It must be known that it is not because God is pleased that there should be few raised to this high spiritual state, for it would rather please Him that all souls should be perfect, but it is rather that He finds few vessels which can bear so high and lofty a work. For, when He proves them in small things and finds them weak and sees that they at once flee from labour, and desire not to submit to the least discomfort or mortification, He finds that they are not strong and faithful in the little things wherein He has granted them the favour of beginning to purge and fashion them, and sees that they will be much less so in great things.[8]

We conclude that the active night of sense imposes duties no less rigorous outside of prayer than during prayer. Fidelity in patiently surrendering oneself to God's action in contemplation will be efficacious with the divine mercy only when a generous and absolute asceticism accompanies it.

There cannot be fidelity to the Spirit of God in the life of prayer without generosity in the practice of absolute asceticism outside of prayer.

But absolute asceticism cannot be realized all at once. A master is needed to regulate its progress. This master is Holy Wisdom, who has awakened in the soul, and whose inflowing light and action make new demands each day.

B. Realization of asceticism

It is by setting its pace with the action of God within it that the soul will realize the asceticism necessary for it in this night of sense.

The soul must not doubt but that the awakening of loving Wisdom, of which it has painful or savouring experience from time to time in prayer, signifies a desire on the part of God to possess it completely and that this taking of possession is already beginning to be realized. God watches over Israel; already He has a constant solicitude for that soul, and now He has begun to assert His rights over it in a particular way. There is

[8] *Living Flame,* st. ii; Peers, iii, 138.

no doubt but that He is preparing, with all the resources of His wisdom and all the tenderness of His love, for that complete outpouring of His graces of which these earlier favors are a pledge.

But how is the soul to discern this providential action and discover in a practical way this guiding light of God, which seems to be enveloped in darkness more mysterious than that of the most obscure contemplation. Here, even less than anywhere else, can we speak of precise method and signs. There can be given, however, a few indications that are both necessary and sufficient to enable the soul to bring its ascetical activity into line with God's action within it, and to submit itself to its guidance.

1. INTERIOR LIGHT

Whatever may be the contemplative dryness that the soul experiences during this period, God's light is never absent from it. This light is not always manifest in flashes that cleave the dark night, but rather in a diffuse way. Sometimes the soul is enlightened about God; always, about itself.

Like a car whose headlights throw their beams ahead, or better, like a bright star that illumines its course, God, in His invasion of the soul, sends luminous rays ahead, which put in sharp relief the obstacles in His way and even disclose the means to be taken to hasten His advance.

Then there come to light no longer just the usually observable external faults, but deeply rooted tendencies that are hidden. Perhaps there is a tendency to pride or selfishness, unknown for what it is, or that was cloaked with an honorable, if not supernatural, motive. Or perhaps it is a need for silence or for self-surrender, a desire to give oneself completely, that rise up from the obscure depths of the unconscious and urgently claim the attention of the soul.

At times the light particularizes, throwing into relief some apparently insignificant detail and demanding some small act or sacrifice which appears to be of little importance or even unreasonable.

More often, the light opens to view the store of evil in the inmost depths of the soul, that "sin" in the Pauline sense of the word, the ramifications of which reach into all the faculties and whose influence extends to all their acts.

Whatever form they take, these lights disconcert the soul as much by their precise demands or by the confused mass of sin they reveal, as by the fact that they affect the soul's own activity. There are times that it would gladly evade their demands; and even when it is intent on following through with them, it wonders in what measure it can and must.

Ordinarily these lights are a manifestation of the solicitude of the divine Master within, who causes them to shine out in the soul's path in the measure of its needs.

This detail that is shown up is an indication of deeper tendencies which, like certain dangerous reefs in the sea, emerge above the surface only by an almost imperceptible point. Or that unimportant thing that must be done is a proof of love to which the Master attaches special price; the future will disclose its importance. The indistinct mass of sin that appears, this is the depth of misery, the abyss of sin that taints our human nature, and that is so important to know in order to see ourselves in truth and take an attitude of humility before God.

The soul must treasure these indications which stand out clearly in the light of this inner beacon. If it did not respond to these demands, the light might be extinguished. The interior torment might cease, but the soul might come to a definite standstill in mediocrity. It would no longer see the fetters that bound it, preventing it from soaring toward God, nor be conscious of that weight of its misery which is necessary to deepen its humility and purify its confidence in God:

For as long as it [the soul] has this [any harmful attachment] there is no possibility that it will make progress in perfection, even though the imperfection be extremely slight. For it comes to the same thing whether a bird be held by a slender cord or by a stout one; since, even if it be slender, the bird will be as well held as though it were stout, for so long as it breaks it not and flies not away.[9]

The soul that has not availed itself of the light to break its fetters, or at least to renounce the evil tendency it has discovered, afterwards runs the risk of remaining definitely enchained, and, worse still, of no longer seeing what it is that rivets it in its immobility.

Nevertheless, since the supernatural and the natural closely intermingle in this period of transition, and since the soul cannot as yet sufficiently discern between the divine light and its counterfeits, one must not follow particular lights, especially if they are important or seemingly unreasonable, without first submitting them to an experienced director. In describing them the soul will take care to place them in their concrete circumstances which can alone explain them and reveal what is God's will in their regard. The spiritual guide will interpret them according to the laws of supernatural wisdom, which may even require the folly of the cross during this period, and he will encourage the soul to respond generously.

Those general and indistinct lights that enlighten the soul as to the depths of evil within it are of great practical value inasmuch as they purify it. They cannot however serve as a norm for ascetical practices, unless they become more particularized and are prudently interpreted.

These precisions are first of all found in ascetical treatises covering this period of spiritual life. Saint John of the Cross gives us a very penetrating analysis of the vices of beginners. Everywhere in her writings Saint Teresa has the most pertinent things to say about those subtle tendencies of our nature—venomous reptiles, adders, or even simple lizards (she calls them)—which complacently conceal themselves under the appearance of spiritual good. The soul, therefore, which is necessarily bemused in this period of transition, has need of more explicit en-

[9] *Ascent,* Bk. I, xi; Peers, I, 50-1.

lightenment from the masters who better understood the things of God and the soul.

This enlightenment will be supplied by one's spiritual director, by superiors, or even by those around us. May it not be said that there is nothing more hidden from us than these tendencies that appear in our whole conduct and are clearly evident to those around us. They are so much a part of us that we have long since become habituated to them, if indeed we have not come to the point of fully justifying them. If the light of God, in revealing them, breaks the charm or at least the peace of our good relations with them, we become disconcerted and cannot see them in detail. Let us consult a spiritual judge both perspicacious and charitable who will not shy away from showing us the multiple and visible forms of the tendency, thus indicating the points that call for our vigorous efforts.

2. PROVIDENTIAL EVENTS

In a more precise and more sure way than interior lights, providential events fix the duty of the soul in this period and determine its progress toward the realization of the absolute.

The action of divine Providence extends to all things. In what concerns men, it pursues only one end, which is the building up of the mystical body of Christ and consequently the sanctification of the elect who are its members. Necessary causes or free causes are instruments in the hands of divine Wisdom. With sovereign and delicate art He uses their power, their good will or hatred for the realization of His great work.

How doubt but that this Wisdom surrounds with solicitude these souls whom He has called, whom He has justified, and to whom He manifests by these experiences of His action in them His particular designs for their sanctification and perfect union with Himself. Jesus said to His apostles:

> And you will be hated by all for my name's sake; yet not a hair of your head shall perish.[10]

[10] Luke 21:17-8.

Can not this word of the Master be applied to all who are privileged by divine election? Would God really leave to chance the events that touch the lives of such souls and that would hinder His work of sanctification in them? The apostle very clearly answers this question:

> Now we know that for those who love God all things work together unto good, for those who, according to his purpose, are saints through his call.[11]

Later, when the soul has arrived at spiritual espousals, God will show Himself divinely jealous of that soul, to such a point that Saint Teresa writes:

> It seems that our Lord wants everyone to realize that such a person's soul is now His and that no one must touch it. People are welcome to attack her body, her honour, and her possessions, for any of these attacks will be to His Majesty's honour. But her soul they may not attack, for unless, with most blameworthy presumption, it tears itself away from its Spouse, He will protect it from the whole world, and indeed from all hell.[12]

While waiting till it has arrived at this high state, God watches over it with loving care, and by every means procures its sanctification, which is more important to Him than everything else in the world.

The soul must believe in this loving and efficacious solicitude of divine Wisdom. It must be aware of this in all that happens to it and draw from all events that touch it the grace and light that they are meant to bring it. Grace and light, all the more precious in that they are precise, practical, given at each instant; and because they come to the soul at a time when the darkness and dryness of its prayer, along with exterior difficulties, make its progress uncertain and hesitant.

A humble and loving submission will usually suffice for the soul to gather these treasures.

This submission becomes more difficult when some free agent intervenes in events touching the soul. It then appears

[11] Rom. 8:28.
[12] VI Mansions, iv; Peers, II, 292.

as if the free agent alone were acting. And the fact that it is a free agent and that it intervenes from definite known motives of its own, hides from us and thereby diminishes in our eyes its value as an instrument of the First Cause, who is God. The fixity of physical laws seems to us to leave more place for providential action. Thus our faith discovers more readily the prime causality of God in an accident resulting from natural causes than in one that is the result of malevolence. We forget that eternal Wisdom, which reaches from one end of the world to the other with strength and sweetness, makes play of obstacles, transforming them into means; that, simple and pure, it penetrates and uses with the same ease for the realization of its designs the freedom of the human will and the fixity of natural causes. It operates through the world as if in play, and finds its greatest triumphs in its relations with men. "*Ludens in orbe terrarum . . . deliciae meae cum filiis hominum.* Playing in the whole world . . . my delights are to be with the children of men." It is also in God's action, through and by secondary human causes, that our loving faith will find, it too, its most profitable and most frequent triumphs.

In the same practical order let it be emphasized that in the period of the spiritual life where we are, our faith must be more on the alert in regard to providential situations than to events. An event passes by and usually has limited influence. A situation, by hypothesis, abides and makes a more enduring impression. It is a more abundant source of light and of grace for our realization of the designs of God. The family circle in which we have been brought up, the education we have received, a natural quality, a physical or moral defect, an habitual incapacity, these can determine the vocation of a soul and bring efficacious graces for its sanctity.

Providence creates, adapts, modifies these situations according to the needs of those whom He loves, in order to give grace that is needed or to make known His demands in a clear and at times imperious way. On reading the lives of the saints, one might be led to think that they are the fruit of their surroundings or of situations in which they live. In reality, it is God who makes His saints and who, lovingly and progressively, presses them on to heroism, rousing in their souls those cries and aspirations that carry them to the heights. Tobias was put to trial because of his fidelity. Job, too, tried for his fidelity, accepted with peace and resignation his tribulations: "The Lord has given, the Lord has taken away, blessed be the name of the Lord." God tortures marvelously His saints, say the Carmelite theologians of Salamanca. It was these admirable torments, produced by the divine light on their soul and by situations that they had to endure, that assured their sanctity. May our admiration for them be less "reasonable" and let it, like them, look beyond secondary causes and see only the First Cause, God, who efficaciously willed their sanctification and gave them the means of attaining to it as a reward for their fidelity.

Some excellent spiritual books recount the advantages and the spiritual riches derived from abandonment to divine Providence, who directs all things for the good of those who love Him. There is a practical problem, however, for which they do not give the solution, and which presents itself in a more marked way in the fourth Mansions, a period of transition during which the supernatural and the natural are closely mingled —the intermittent and incomplete divine action leaving place for the activity of the faculties and even for personal initiative. The practical problem is this: in what measure must one surrender oneself and in what measure must one act? Should one peacefully accept events or has one the duty to react against them and even try to change them?

This is a problem that anyone who has experienced both the bearing of providential events on his soul and the efficacy of his own personal activity must propose to himself, and perhaps at times with a certain anxiety. Do we not find Saint Therese of the Child Jesus, although at a higher stage and already firmly fixed in her teaching of spiritual childhood and abandonment, also a prey to a certain uneasiness? In the beautifully consoling dream that she had at the end of her life, she asks her heavenly guest if the good God "does not want more from me than these poor little acts and desires that I offer Him." [13]

Thus we find again on the plane of action the obscurities that cause suffering in mental prayer. Must not the dark night envelop the will as it envelops the intellect? Both must leave the world of sense. The darkness that they find in it, which is a sign of purification, is providentially destined to orientate them toward a higher and more simple light.

It would seem useless at this period to try to find a speculative solution of the problem of passivity and activity. The soul should be resigned to the darkness and not seek to lay up treasures of light for its journey through the pathless places it is about to enter. On the contrary, light will be given at the opportune moment, in the way already indicated, on what direction it must follow or what attitude it must adopt. The Master reminds His apostles of this:

> He said to them, "When I sent you forth without purse or wallet or sandals, did you lack anything?" And they said, "Nothing." [14]

It is so with the soul at this stage, and such should be its reply from the spiritual point of view. Why then concern itself with provisions for the journey or with the principles which would reconcile its twofold obligation of self-abandonment and personal activity?

A more particular problem arises at times to torment and thwart the soul with regard to obedience. It happens that certain external events or the commands of a superior run directly counter to its inclinations or prevent it from following some interior light. For example, a soul feels a profound need of silence and recollection in order to develop its life of prayer, but circumstances or the will of the superior oblige it to undertake tasks which demand the maximum of effort and attention. What

[13] *Autobiography,* xi, 180.
[14] Luke 22:35.

must the soul do? Which manifestation of God's will is it to follow?

Without hesitation we reply: both are authentic manifestations of God's will; and both are to be obeyed. Ordinarily there will be no opposition between them. The Holy Spirit manifests His will in different ways and obliges the soul to reconcile them, to blend them into a perfect realization of His will. Something like the brakes on a car, this interior attraction towards recollection and silence controls by prudent moderation the outward pull of external events and the tasks imposed by obedience.

The interior attraction indicates where the goal lies and guarantees the necessary spiritual energy for attaining to it; the exterior indications show what path to take and what pace to keep. Activity and anxiety, which seemed to frustrate the soul's desire for silence, have in reality purified it. In limiting the moments for its enjoyment, they have eliminated spiritual gluttony and sloth, and at the same time have provided the faculties with that activity which their immobility during silence demands.

Those lights, which at first were repugnant to the soul, now bespeak the loving care of divine Wisdom who has taken the soul under His own direction, desiring to make it completely His own. Should it happen, nevertheless, in certain circumstances that either the will of the superior or external events stand in direct opposition to an interior attraction or a particular light, then the soul, after manifesting its state to the superior or director if possible, should unhesitatingly obey those external indications of God's will as being the most authentic, at least for the moment. To act otherwise would expose it to the danger of going astray. Following its own personal lights, it would lose God and no longer find only self.

3. PRUDENCE

The two directives just given aim at placing the soul under the guidance of divine Wisdom. Under such guidance it will discover the form and the degree of the asceticism necessary at this period.

Yet Saint Teresa reminds us of the necessity at this period for prudence guided by reason as enlightened by faith. There are many reasons for this. First of all there is the novelty of the states in which the soul now finds itself and of the manner in which it must comport itself. There are the tendencies which, mortified insofar as they appear outwardly, manifest themselves now on the spiritual level. Then there is presumptious self-confidence, accentuated by favors received and the feeling of strength resulting from them. The devil, too, finds these circumstances particularly favorable to his purpose. He knows that he must seize upon souls when they are going through this dark passage from sense to spirit, else they will escape from him altogether and save many other souls from his clutches. Here is a warning from Saint Teresa:

> I earnestly warn such people not to enter upon occasions of sin, because the devil sets much more store by one soul in this state than by a great number of souls to whom the Lord does not grant these favours. For those in this state attract others, and so they can do the devil great harm and may well bring great advantage to the Church of God. He may see nothing else in them except that His Majesty is showing them especial love, but this is quite sufficient to make him do his utmost to bring about their perdition. The conflict, then, is sterner for such souls than for others and if they are lost their fate is less remediable.[15]

And the Saint terminates her exposition of the fourth Mansions by giving this last word of advice:

> I have written at great length of this Mansion, as it is the one which the greatest number of souls enter. As the natural is united with the supernatural in it, it is here that the devil can do most harm; for in the Mansions of which I have not yet spoken the Lord gives him fewer opportunities.[16]

Saint Teresa mentions some of the special duties that prudence, so necessary in this period, imposes.

[15] IV Mansions, iii; Peers, II, 245.
[16] *Ibid.;* 246.

The soul first of all must avoid dangerous occasions. Its feeling of strength and its consciousness of the graces it has received might cause it to neglect the precautions it has been accustomed hitherto to take against its frailty. The Saint writes:

> There is one earnest warning which I must give those who find themselves in this state: namely, that they exert the very greatest care to keep themselves from occasions of offending God. For as yet the soul is not even weaned but is like a child beginning to suck the breast. If it be taken from its mother, what can it be expected to do but die? [17]

That is well said and puts in his place as a beginner the contemplative who is enjoying the prayer of quiet.

The occasions to be avoided are not only the occasions of sin but especially those that might withdraw the soul from prayer:

> That, I am very much afraid, will be the lot of anyone to whom God has granted this favour if he gives up prayer; unless he does so for some very exceptional reason, or unless he returns to it quickly, he will go from bad to worse. I am aware how much ground there is for fear about this and I have been very much grieved by certain people I know, in whom I have seen what I am describing; they have left Him Who in His great love was yearning to give Himself to them as a Friend, and to prove His friendship by His works.[18]

That perseverance, which Saint Teresa so often recommends particularly in the *Way of Perfection* [19] and her *Life*,[20] must be especially recommended at this period, not only because of the difficulties of prayer itself but still more because of the exterior importunities to which the soul is subject, solicitations which rather often answer an awakening need to enter the apostolate, and which constitute a real danger for the contemplative.

The first contemplative graces are usually apparent exteriorly and may be in consequence an occasion for some surprise. On the other hand the soul experiences the need of giving to others the riches that seem to it overflowing. Is this not the normal

[17] *Ibid.;* 245.
[18] *Ibid.*
[19] *Way of Perfection,* xxi-xxiii; Peers, II.
[20] *Life,* viii; Peers, I.

instinct of charity? Let us hear our wise spiritual mother on this point:

> There is another temptation which is very common—namely to desire that everyone should be extremely spiritual when one is beginning to find what tranquillity, and what profit spirituality brings. It is not wrong to desire this but it may not be right to try to bring it about unless we do so with such discretion and dissimulation that we give no impression of wanting to teach others. For if a person is to do any good in this respect, he must be very strong in the virtues so as not to put temptation in others' way. This I found out for myself—and that is why I realize it. When, as I have said, I tried to get others to practise prayer. . . .
>
> In addition, there is another great disadvantage in yielding to this temptation: namely, the harm caused to our own soul; for the utmost we have to do at first is to take care of our soul and to remember that in the entire world there is only God and the soul.[21]

That this advice is addressed not only to souls in the first Mansions but also to those who have tasted of contemplative prayer is proved by the allusion Saint Teresa makes to her personal experience at a time when she had arrived at the prayer of union. Besides, a little farther on we find very clear statements to this effect:

> In any one of these visits [third degree of prayer], brief as its duration may be, the Gardener, being, as He is, the Creator of the water, gives the soul water without limit; . . . the fruit grows and ripens in such a way that, if the Lord wills, the soul can obtain sufficient nourishment from its own garden. But He allows it to share the fruit with others only when it has eaten so much of it that it is strong enough not to consume it all by merely nibbling it, and not to fail to get profit from it, nor to omit to recompense Him Who has bestowed it, but to maintain others and give them food at its own cost while itself perhaps is dying of hunger.[22]

The third way of watering the garden, of which the Saint speaks in this passage, corresponds to that degree of prayer she calls the sleep of the powers and is superior to the simple prayer of quiet. At this stage one should not think of engaging in a personal apostolate. It is to be noted, nevertheless, that

[21] *Life,* xiii; 77.
[22] *Ibid.,* xvii; 101.

Saint Teresa is here addressing persons who have neither the ministry proper to the priesthood nor other duties of the apostolate, and who, in consequence, can contribute to their neighbor's spiritual welfare only out of the superabundance of the divine life in their own souls.

When the soul has arrived at the fourth degree of prayer, hence at the prayer of union, it can begin to give of its riches without harm to itself:

> Having now a clear realization that the fruits of this prayer are not its own, it can start to share them and yet have no lack of them itself. It begins to show signs of being a soul that is guarding the treasures of Heaven and to be desirous of sharing them with others and to beseech God that it may not be alone in its riches. Almost without knowing it, and doing nothing consciously to that end, it begins to benefit its neighbors.[23]

And when it has attained to the raptures that characterize the sixth Mansions, the soul no longer runs any danger. On the contrary, such dangers as the world presents are profitable to it because they provide an occasion of victory. It is like the captain of the fortress who "has mounted, or has been led up to the highest of its towers and has reared the standard aloft there in the name of God":

> From his position of security he looks down on those below. No longer does he fear perils; rather he desires them, for through them, as it were, he receives the assurance of victory.[24]

These counsels of Saint Teresa, which have absolute value only for contemplatives who are not dedicated to works of the apostolate, furnish nevertheless very precious directives for all those who, by duty of their state, are obliged to procure the spiritual good of their neighbor. This advice tells them how carefully, in these first periods of overflowing fervor, they must protect their union with God, even though it be already enriched with contemplative graces, against excessive activity in

[23] *Life,* xix; 112.
[24] *Ibid.,* xx; 127.

the apostolate and against the dangers that accompany such exercise.

In this urge toward the apostolate there is a certain presumption, which arises out of the feeling of graces received or, better, out of that share the senses had in the graces communicated to the spiritual faculties. Other dangers still more grave are attached to the sensible perceptions of the spiritual; these will be studied more completely with the help of Saint John of the Cross at the beginning of the dark night of the spirit.

We must now point out a particular case which, in appearance, would seem to belong to the sixth Mansions, but which in fact derives from the first contemplative prayers of the fourth Mansions. And it is in connection with the fourth Mansions that Teresa describes it at length:

> There is one peril of which I want to warn you, though I have spoken of it elsewhere; I have seen persons given to prayer fall into it, and especially women. . . . It is this: some women, because of prayers, vigils and severe penances, and also for other reasons, have poor health. When they experience any spiritual consolations, therefore, their physical nature is too much for them; and as soon as they feel any interior joy there comes over them a physical weakness and languor, and they fall into a sleep, which they call "spiritual," and which is a little more marked than the condition that has been described. Thinking the one state to be the same as the other, they abandon themselves to this absorption; and the more they relax, the more complete becomes this absorption, because their physical nature continues to grow weaker. So they get it into their heads that it is arrobamiento, or rapture. But I call it abobamiento, foolishness; for they are doing nothing but wasting their time at it and ruining their health.
>
> One person was in this state for eight hours; she was not unconscious, nor was she conscious of anything concerning God. She was cured by being told to take more food and sleep and to do less penance; for, though she had misled both her confessor and other people and, quite involuntarily, deceived herself, there was one person who understood her. I believe the devil would go to any pains to gain such people as that and he was beginning to make good progress with this one.[25]

Saint Teresa thought these phenomena important and numerous enough to devote to them a whole chapter of the *Book*

[25] IV Mansions, iii; Peers, II, 245-6.

of the Foundations, giving a detailed psychological description of them. The following passage presents the characteristic traits:

> What I understand to be the case here is that, when the Lord begins to comfort the soul, our nature, being so fond of pleasure, abandons itself so completely to this pleasurable condition that it would not move, or lose what it has gained, for anything in the world. For in truth this pleasure is greater than any worldly pleasure, and may be bestowed upon a person of weak constitution, or upon one whose mind (or, to put it better, whose imagination) has no natural versatility, but who, once he has begun to study a subject, continues his study and never seeks distraction; in such a case this is what happens here, according to the person's nature, constitution or weakness. Many people, when they begin to think of anything—not necessarily of a thing having to do with God—remain absorbed in it and look at objects without noticing them; such people are temperamentally slow and seem to be so absent-minded that they forget what they are going to say. And, oh, if such persons should become melancholy! They will begin to nurse a thousand pleasant delusions.[26]

Such sharply marked pathological cases are met with at times; fortunately they are rather rare. More frequently one finds cases less clearly characterized, in which the same defects show up under different appearances.

All these temperaments—and this is cause of the whole disorder—are affected by a psychical weakness. Hence any supernatural action of God upon them or even any spiritual impression affects their senses so intensely that one cannot but be mistaken at first in appraising the supernatural quality of an experience which has such a vibrant reaction in the senses. A simple passive recollection takes place and lo, the soul swoons as if it had been carried away in a rapture, with suspension of the faculties; a simple spiritual consolation produces a sleep of the powers that is prolonged indefinitely.

Because these persons are readily and deeply absorbed in prayer, and they find a certain delight in surrender to it, and because exterior activity, by contrast, awakens in them only distaste and a sense of powerlessness, they desire only contemplation and an intimate, profound union with God in the dark

[26] *Foundations,* vi; Peers, III, 27.

night. Because they register with great intensity, and even at times with finesse, every spiritual impression, and because the experience and language of the great spiritual masters no longer seem to hold for them a secret, they are thought to be remarkably endowed for the contemplative life. Their apparent abundance of spiritual favors can be the cause of grave error in the matter of spiritual direction. To believe in the attractions these souls have and to encourage the cultivation of them can have actually very harmful consequences in the physical order as well as on the moral and spiritual plane.

The soul, persuaded that it is receiving special favors, seeks their sensible effects—particularly this state of absorption—entertains them, and abandons itself to them.

One of the first and perhaps least of the disadvantages of this, according to Saint Teresa, is one that we can sum up in few words, namely, a loss of time and merit. The faculties are deprived of "the advantage which, if they proceed with care, they generally gain." [27]

Moreover, self-love is usually nourished by these phenomena, and it can grow to frightening proportions. For here the soul is not preserved from vain glory, as it is in every authentic mystical grace, by the sweet overpowering of the divine contact.

But most of all, these absorptions and strong vibrations of the sense powers use up physical energy; they "paralyze the faculties and senses," says Saint Teresa, "and hinder them from fulfilling the commands of the soul." [28] And the Saint sounds a grave warning to souls, who, thus mistaken, add to their fatigue further mortifications and fasts which, by increasing their weakness, favor these states still more:

> If they were to go on in that way, and to find no remedy, they would gradually lose their senses or die.[29]

[27] *Ibid.;* 28.
[28] *Ibid.*
[29] *Ibid.;* 27.

In order to supply a remedy, one must be prompt in discerning these states. This is not always easy, Saint Teresa testifies, inasmuch as an authentic action of God is rather frequently present in them; besides, such souls are of good faith and consequently one cannot consider and treat them as deluded visionaries. And on the other hand, since this psychical weakness and the nervosity that accompanies it often give to the natural gifts and the real moral qualities of the person so affected a brilliant appearance that is very attractive, one can understand that an ordinary prudence is insufficient to detect these cases in their first manifestations, and that a special gift, enlightened by experience, is necessary.

Saint Teresa gives several signs which help a diagnosis. One cannot resist a genuine rapture, while with a little effort one can arrest this absorption. True rapture lasts only a short time, although its effects may continue on for a while. On the other hand, absorption is usually prolonged for several hours, because the soul gives itself up to it. The most authentic sign is that a rapture that is from God produces notable effects of virtue, especially of humility; absorption, on the contrary, paralyzes and "leaves no more effect than if it had not happened, except for producing weariness in the body." [30]

We treat of these cases in connection with asceticism outside of prayer, since it is to asceticism that belong the efficacious remedies for preventing or stopping their development.

One should guide such temperaments away from any life that is purely contemplative. The role of Martha is best for them, whatever may be their attractions and even their seeming aptitudes for the role of Mary. If these persons are already committed to the contemplative life, it is essential to reduce the time that they devote to prayer, to withdraw them from it completely at certain times, and constantly to procure them the diversion of work. Moreover, one must dispense them from weakening mortifications, and strengthen them bodily by ap-

[30] *Ibid.*; 32.

propriate rests and more abundant nourishment. Saint Teresa writes:

> One person was in this state for eight hours; she was not unconscious, nor was she conscious of anything concerning God. She was cured by being told to take more food and sleep and to do less penance; for, . . . there was one person who understood her.[31]

This advice on moderation seems to lead us away from, if not actually to go against, the resolute realization of the absolute that we recognized as being indispensable for the growth of God's action in the soul at this stage. And yet, it is indeed absolute renouncement that one is imposing on that soul by depriving it of the sweet delights of prayer and making it go against its attractions that so readily it terms as divine and as a certain manifestation of the will of God.

The necessity of this form of renouncement gives us an idea how varied can be the demands God makes in His first captivation of souls, the prudence the director must have in identifying them, the supple docility the soul needs in order to fulfill them.

[31] IV Mansions, iii; Peers, II, 246.

CHAPTER VIII
Obedience

There is no path which leads more quickly to the highest perfection than that of obedience.[1]

The fourth Mansions make us think of verdant thickets with their vegetation spreading out, young, hardy, and full of promise, an entanglement of branches, of vines and of brambles, a shady copse that seems yet darker in contrast to the sunbeams that play through it, but from which life springs. We find in these Mansions a mingling of the natural and the supernatural, God's action intermittent and as yet imperfect in the soul, and surprising reactions in the faculties.

Shall we succeed in bringing clarity to this chaos? . . . One cannot multiply one's efforts here too much, for it is highly important for the glory of God that the soul should not let itself be brought to a standstill by the difficulties it now meets.

In short, as the preceding pages have shown, the soul must learn here to be submissive to the Wisdom of Love and pliant to His action. Hence a practical problem of obedience must be faced at every instant. And by the same token it can be said that obedience is the virtue that characterizes this period.

A study of the virtue of obedience must, then, bring light to the problem; it will allow us to sum up and to state distinctly the duties of the soul at this stage, showing them to us from a new angle.

[1] *Foundations,* v; Peers, III, 23.

A. Nature of obedience

Obedience is a virtue that unites man to God, making him submissive to the divine will as manifested by God Himself or His representatives. It has been said of this virtue that it is almost theological.[2] In fact, it is attached to the virtue of justice, which causes us to render to God what is His due. God has sovereign rights over us who are His creatures. Submission to His good pleasure and execution in all its details of the mission that He has confided to us are for us a duty that His absolute sovereignty imposes upon us.

Besides, the plan for the realization of which He asks us to work is infinitely wise. It is to procure at the same time the glory of God and our happiness. There is nothing but what is highly reasonable, wise and beneficial in all that God asks of us: this sovereign Master exercises His power only for our good, respecting our liberty. The wisdom of the designs of God, as well as His sovereign power, is the foundation therefore of our obedience.

The divine will is made known to us through various channels: First of all, that of the law inscribed by God in creatures, directing them to their providential end. In conformity with their nature, this law is physical and necessary for creatures deprived of reason; moral for man, since it respects his liberty and is addressed to his reason which explores its first principles to derive from them the ensemble of our natural duties toward God, toward ourselves, and toward our neighbor.

To the code of the natural law there are added the precepts of the evangelical law, formulated by Christ and leading man to his supernatural end.

God has also entrusted to His representatives—all those who, directly or indirectly, hold a share in authority—the right and the duty of manifesting His will. "There exists no authority except from God," proclaims the apostle, "and those who exist

[2] P. Jean de Jésus-Marie.

have been appointed by God. Therefore he who resists the authority resists the ordinance of God." [3]

Among these representatives of God, the Church occupies a special rank. Her spiritual mission, as well as the powers that she has received directly from Christ, assures to her authority a primacy that the entire world must recognize.

This divine delegation of authority confers on the secular power as on the Church the right to make general laws, to give special orders, to subdelegate a part of their authority. Thus each one constantly meets in every domain of his personal or social life a whole network of channels bringing him concrete and various manifestations of the divine will.

In certain cases God reserves it to Himself to manifest His will to souls by interior illuminations, and even to cause it to be carried out by the impulse of His spirit. It is this direct intervention of God in the life of the soul that constitutes both the grace and the difficulty of the fourth Mansions. It is this that puts the problem of obedience under a new light.

B. Excellence of obedience

"What I want to teach you most of all," writes Saint Jerome to the monk Rusticus, "is not to give yourself up to your own will."

Has it not often been said that obedience is the first of the moral virtues? Saint Gregory explains this primacy:

> Obedience is the only virtue which causes the other virtues to germinate in our souls and which maintains them after having implanted them.[4]

1. IT ENSURES ORDER

Obedience establishes exterior order in the city as well as in-

[3] Rom. 13:1-2.
[4] Saint Gregory, *Morals*, Bk. xxxv, Ch. xxxiv, n. 28.

terior order in the soul. Without it there is no coherence in the efforts of a group, nor proper subordination; and so it is considered as the principal strength of armies.

It is obedience that makes for the beauty and harmony of the celestial choirs. And so again Saint Gregory says:

> If alone the beauty of order explains why there is found so much obedience there where there is no sin, for how much more reason must there be subordination and dependence among us where sin would bring about so much confusion without this help.[5]

Cassian testifies that in the Thebaid the most detestable hermits were the sarabaïtes who took on themselves the care of procuring necessities, lived independently of the elders, did what pleased them, and spent night and day at work.

2. OBEDIENCE IS THE BEST SACRIFICE

The judgment of Cassian is an echo of the word of God that we find in Isaias: "Why have we fasted, and thou hast not regarded?" the people cry out. "Why have we humbled our souls, and thou hast not taken notice?" "Behold in the day of your fast," answers the Lord God, "your own wili is found." [6] No sacrifice could in fact be accepted by God unless accompanied by the offering of our human faculties par excellence, our intellect and free will. It is these that obedience immolates to God. And so it is written that "obedience is better than sacrifices." [7]

And because obedience is the most perfect of sacrifices,[8] it is proof and sign of the love that aspires to give: "He who has my commandments and keeps them, he it is who loves me," [9] the apostle of love emphasized. This seems so evident to him that he says:

[5] *Ibid., Epistles,* Bk. v, Epist. liv.
[6] Is. 58:3.
[7] I Kings 15:22.
[8] Saint John of the Cross, *Maxims,* 286.
[9] John 14:21.

He who says that he knows him, and does not keep his commandments, is a liar and the truth is not in him. But he who keeps his word, in him the love of God is truly perfected.[10]

3. OBEDIENCE IS UNITIVE WITH GOD

Obedience is more than proof of love; it is a unitive act of love. Its preeminence among the other virtues, the riches that it brings, its efficacy for the acquisition of perfection, these come from its unitive value.

Saint Thomas defines perfection: an adherence to the sovereign good. In the program for perfection as set forth by the vows of religion, obedience creates with the sovereign good that is God the union that poverty and chastity prepare for and stabilize by breaking attachments to exterior and sensible goods. Poverty and chastity have a mainly negative role; to obedience belongs the positive role of uniting the soul to God and to His will.

A text from *Ecclesiasticus* reveals to us the mystery of obedience and the source of its riches. It is written:

Fons sapientiae Verbum Dei in excelsis, et ingressus illius mandata aeterna. The word of God on high is the fountain of wisdom, and her ways are everlasting commandments.[11]

In a few words the inspired author, or rather Wisdom herself, tells us of her work, her origin and her descent among us. This Wisdom is God. She is the Word in the bosom of the Holy Trinity. She put order into the world while God created it; and she has ensured the order and regular movement of this world by establishing herself in the eternal laws that she has fixed for it. Let us reread the text: *ingressus illius.* Wisdom truly enters into the world through law. Law is more than a manifestation of the Word; it is His dwelling here below. O the incomparable dignity of law, a material temple that houses Wisdom, manifests her and gives her. It is this dignity and this

[10] I John 2:4-5.
[11] Ecclus. 1:5.

divine wealth of law that make the value and richness of obedience.

Obedience, in fact, is a submission of the will of man to the will of God made known by law or by a command. True obedience is not merely external submission, simple acceptance and execution of an order that has been received. It is a submission of the spirit which goes through the door of this material temple that is law, in order to find the divine presence that vivifies it and gives it its reason for being. Through the outside shell or rather the veil of the order that is received, or of the law, obedience seeks God and truly communes with Him.

Communion with God through obedience, is this not saying too much? Does this not seem to suggest a certain incarnation of God in the law and in superiors, who thus would give God to us in the manner of the Eucharistic species?

Let us preserve the distances that the transcendence of the mystery of the altar imposes, the presence in the sacred host of the immolated body and blood of Christ; and let us emphasize that the same words can have in different cases a more or less full meaning. These remarks made, we do not hesitate to say that supernatural obedience causes us to commune with Wisdom and hence with God, in the law and in superiors.

Thus in order to arrive at the stable adherence to God that is perfection, three means of communion with Him are offered us. The first of these is the Eucharistic Communion which gives us the presence and vivifying action of the body and blood, soul and divinity of Jesus in the state of immolation, and hence of the outpouring of His life. It is the sacrament par excellence, a sign signifying and producing grace *ex opere operato* and giving us the author of grace Himself. It is the sacrament that makes saints and builds up the Church.

Contemplation, through the contact with God that living faith establishes, surrenders one also to the vivifying inflowing of the light of the Word, which transforms the soul from brilliance to brilliance unto the likeness of God. This communion is made, by means of the dogmatic formula, through faith engrafted in the intellect. It is a communion in the delightful light of love.

The communion that is realized by supernatural obedience, through the veil that is the law and the superior, also truly attains to God and unites us with Him through love engrafted in the will.

The unitive efficacy of these three communions differs. That of the Eucharistic Communion, considered in itself, is incomparably the greatest. That of contemplation, which requires an intervention of God through the gifts of the Holy Spirit, takes second place—before communion through obedience, which keeps nevertheless its proper efficacy.

But if now we consider not their value in themselves but their frequency, we note that the Eucharistic Communion is possible only once a day; that supernatural contemplation is the privilege of certain souls and at certain times; while communion through obedience is a good for every moment. We can thus understand why the last named, by very reason of its frequency, takes its place in the spiritual life of souls among the most important and most efficacious means of sanctification. Speaking of perfection Saint Teresa says, "Obedience brings us the sooner to that happy state and is the best means of attaining it." [12] An analysis of the benefits that it procures through its communion with Wisdom, will help us to see this still better.

Communion with Wisdom obtains for us all the properties of divine wisdom itself. Wisdom is first of all light, for it has its source in the Word who is light in the bosom of God, and who enlightens every intellect coming into this world. Obedience causes us to participate in the light of divine wisdom.

The thoughts of God surpass our thoughts as the heavens, the earth. The designs of God are infinite as is the intellect that conceived them. Their transcendence renders them obscure to us and unfathomable. We know only the general formula of

[12] *Foundations,* v; Peers, III, 23.

this plan of God for the world; it holds in its mystery, even to the end of our life, the part in it that is entrusted to us. How then shall we be able to make sure the human cooperation, intelligent and free, that we owe to it? In the moving play of the passions and wills of men, in the complexity of exterior events, how are we to discover the present will of God for us?

Wisdom has put into the law and the commands of superiors the practical light that indicates to us the will of God. *"Omnia mandata tua veritas,"* [13] sings the Psalmist. *"Lucerna pedibus meis verbum tuum et lumen semitis meis."* [14] All thy statutes are truth. Thy word is a lamp to my feet, and a light to my paths. *"Declaratio sermonum tuorum illuminat et intellectum dat parvulis."* [15] The declaration of thy words giveth light: and giveth understanding to little ones.

It is by obedience that man captures that light and makes it enter into his life. Obedience walks always in the light. It imposes submission on the intellect only to make it pass beyond its own lights, at best limited, and enter into the resplendent light of God. Mysteriously but surely it makes known to the soul the paths that Wisdom has traced out for it, and leads it into those regions that Wisdom has prepared as its abode for eternity.

Concerning the Son who is the bright radiance of the glory of the Father, Saint Paul testifies that by Him God created all things, and that He upholds all things by the power of His Word.[16] Omnipotence and strength are, like light, properties of the Word that is Wisdom. And this strength, He communicates to His instruments. These receive it as one of the fruits of their communion with Wisdom through obedience.

"Viriliter agite et confortetur cor vestrum," it is written. Act strongly or, better, obey courageously and your heart will be strengthened. The strength gained through obedience is one of

[13] Ps. 118:86.
[14] Ps. 118:105.
[15] Ps. 118:130.
[16] Heb. 1:2-3.

the most mysterious fruits of communion with Wisdom. And yet it is a fact of experience. Whatever hesitations there may be in the beginning, obedience—no matter how weak—finds in adherence to the divine will the strength to continue on to the end to be attained.

The fruitfulness of obedience and its victories are the best proofs of the intervention of Wisdom to sustain its action. "An obedient man shall speak of victory," [17] say the Proverbs; of his successes, we might translate it.

Wisdom is eminently fruitful. "She reacheth from end to end mightily and ordereth all things sweetly." [18] The word of God shall not return to Him void; [19] it effects all that it expresses. That is, Wisdom works out all her designs according as she has ordained them.

By communing with Wisdom, the obedient soul makes this fruitfulness its own. Its activity participates in the fecundity of the divine activity with which it cooperates and is assured of the success reserved to the divine plan. It is because the saints through their obedience enter into the line of the decrees of Wisdom, that they are such admirable achievers. Their deeds resist time, so devastating to the most solid works, and withstand revolutions that overthrow civilizations.

Like the Church, which remains strong and serene in the midst of the most violent tempests, the great religious Orders founded by the saints survive, more fervent, the most bloody upheavals. The human instrument that God has laid hold of and that has given itself to Him may be weak. At times it will be little gifted naturally. And yet the light that it enjoys reaches farther than the intuitions of genius; the strength that sustains it lifts it above the hero; and so the fruitfulness of its activity is that which belongs to Wisdom herself.

The apostle who, in the Epistle to the Corinthians, had placed

[17] Prov. 21:28.
[18] Wis. 8:1.
[19] Is. 55:11.

in relief the disconcerting play of Wisdom, who delights in choosing what is foolish and weak in the eyes of the world to confound the wise and strong,[20] exalts at the same time this folly of the cross and the obedience that explains its fecundity, by emphasizing that obedience was the principle of the glorification of Christ:

> Have this mind in you which was also in Christ Jesus, who though he was by nature God, did not consider being equal to God a thing to be clung to, but emptied himself, taking the nature of a slave and being made like unto men. And appearing in the form of man, he humbled himself, becoming obedient to death, even to death on a cross. Therefore God also has exalted him and has bestowed upon him the name that is above every name, so that at the name of Jesus every knee should bend of those in heaven, on earth and under the earth, and every tongue should confess that the Lord Jesus Christ is in the glory of God the Father.[21]

The Epistle to the Hebrews adds a complementary thought to this praise of the fruitfulness of obedience:

> And he, Son though he was, learned obedience from the things that he suffered; and when perfected, he became to all who obey him the cause of eternal salvation.[22]

Wisdom descends here below through the law; obedience it is that receives her. Wisdom, "vapor of the power of God," [23] and obedience, humble human cooperation, ensure the reign of God here below. But their union has not merely this earthly triumph; they mount up to God to enjoy eternally their victory in a common glory in the bosom of God.

C. Qualities of obedience

Obedience becomes the perfect collaborator of Wisdom only by fulfilling certain conditions. To be well-ordered it must seek out the authorized representative of Wisdom; to become super-

[20] I Cor. 1:27.
[21] Phil. 2:7-11.
[22] Heb. 5:9.
[23] Wis. 7:25.

natural it must see in this representative the hidden God; and finally it must consent to the totality of the divine exigencies.

1. WELL-ORDERED OBEDIENCE

Well-ordered obedience is that obedience which gives to each one of God's representatives the submission due to the authority with which he is invested.

Wisdom, sovereign mistress and orderer of the world, makes known her will through the multiple channels of laws and superiors. The natural law, the Church, the State, by their positive laws and legitimate representatives, have established a complex network of obligations and prescriptions which hem man in on every side. The religious in his monastery finds, besides the obligations common to all Christians, other prescriptions multiplied as if at will, emanating from his rule, from the constitutions, the ceremonial, and the constant vigilance of his superiors, which regulate his entire life and govern all he does. In this apparent dedalus, how is he to put right order into his obedience and give to each authority the submission that is its due? Some observations are here necessary.

In keeping with the nature of Wisdom, who disposes all things strongly and sweetly from beginning to end, the various authorities delegated by her are in hierarchical order and have been established each in its proper domain. The natural law is at the basis of morality; the positive laws that make it explicit owe it a filial respect. The Church has the sovereign authority that its spiritual mission requires, which is the highest mission. The State rules over the temporal order and governs it by the acts of an administration that often is complicated. The authority of the Church takes precedence over that of a religious Order, which received from her the laws suited to its particular mission.

To order one's obedience will consist, then, in looking to the divine order established by Wisdom; in each case, seeking the legitimate authority—legitimate because delegated in this domain by Wisdom. Ordinarily the problem should be simple. Codes of law and well-advised specialists settle doubtful cases.

There would be no need to insist on this point, therefore, if it were not true that rather frequently, especially among those who have made profession of obedience, judgment is swayed by tastes and preferences. Among the laws to which we are subject, we tend to accord more importance to the ones that impose upon us more often and more closely their precise obligations. Thus it is that the laws of the Church will remain in the background of our consciousness or are even forgotten, while the regulations or even simple customs of monastic life will take on such importance that to fail in them—and especially to change them—will produce an emotion and mental disturbance that conscience ought to experience only for grave faults. Likewise, in a small closed group, one will be under the fascination of the nearest superior; his authority will be progressively extended to such a point that it soon will appear as the only one legitimate in all domains. Or again, among superiors, a lower superior will recognize real authority only in that higher one who seems to him holy or endowed with certain qualities that appeal to him, or with which he is in sympathy. In all circumstances he will go to that one; his decisions alone are without appeal. And yet it is not the natural qualities, nor the supernatural gifts, nor even sanctity that is the foundation of authority; it is uniquely its delegation by God. Scribes and Pharisees were anathematized by Christ Jesus; nevertheless the Master requires His disciples to obey them, for they are on the chair of Moses and have inherited his authority.

In those cases where one's judgment itself is falsified, the ordering of one's obedience will demand more than an intellectual effort; a moral setting right is needed to bring one to full light and perfect obedience.

It may also happen that two laws or two superiors conflict by laying down different or contradictory prescriptions in a domain that seems to belong to both. This is a delicate trial for the conscience of the one who must obey. Sometimes he himself has brought about the situation by making superfluous inquiries of superiors. The present perplexity will make him more discreet in the future. A more thorough consideration of the rights of each one of the superiors in question will usually allow one to discover the legitimate authority in contested cases. Obedience to the veritable representative of God, silence with regard to the other, will permit one to settle supernaturally the conflict.

A graver conflict may arise. There may be opposition between the desires of God clearly manifested to the soul in a supernatural way and those of the director or representative of the Church. We say "desires of God clearly manifested," so as to speak only of cases where the conflict is a real one and thus eliminate those manifestations that error or bad faith call divine. When there is real opposition between God's will as manifested to the soul and the will of superiors, and when there is question of external things to be done that are submitted to the authority of the Church, the soul will have order in its obedience by submitting it to the authority of the Church.

But does this not violate the rights of God, principle and source of all authority? Is not this to withdraw the soul from His sovereign action and hinder it from arriving at perfection, which is nothing else than God's complete possession of it? "For whoever are led by the Spirit of God, they are the sons of God," says the apostle.[24] Saint Augustine is more explicit: "The just man knows no law," thus affirming the preeminence, in the state of perfection, of love over the external constraint of law. And yet the word of Christ to His apostles is clear and imperative:

> Amen I say to you, whatever you bind on earth shall be bound also in heaven; and whatever you loose on earth shall be loosed also in heaven.[25]

[24] Rom. 8:14.
[25] Matt. 18:18.

When He departed from earth, Jesus left only one authority, that of the Church. He Himself submits to it and wants to accomplish no work nor exterior movement that she has not permitted. Ineffable mystery of the divine condescendence! It is on this disposition established by God that Saint Teresa relies when she affirms apropos of supernatural locutions:

> If what is said is of great importance and involves some action on the part of the hearer, or matters affecting a third person, one should not do anything about it, or consider doing anything, without taking the advice of a learned confessor, a man of clear insight and a servant of God, even though one may understand the locutions better and better and it may become evident that they are of God. For this is His Majesty's will, so by carrying it out we are not failing to do what He commands: He has told us that we are to put our confessor in His place, even when it cannot be doubted that the words are His.[26]

Will not the will of God be impeded in this way? The Saint does not think so. God Himself will act on any authority that seems to place an obstacle to it.

> Our Lord will speak to the confessor and if such is His pleasure will make him recognize the work of His spirit; if He does not, we have no further obligations. I consider it very dangerous for a person to do anything but what he has been told to do and to follow his own opinion in this matter.[27]

God reserves it to Himself to enlighten concerning the extraordinary ways of a soul the master entrusted with its direction, to whom it owes submission. What seemed to be a difficulty in ordering one's obedience casts new light on the marvelous ordering of Wisdom, who obliges herself to prove twice over that she is directly dictating her will to a soul.

Certainly, there are not always such difficulties involved in ordering one's obedience. Yet it was necessary to point them out, for experience proves that the most grave deviations from obedience, at times a matter of scandal, come from the fact that one did not know how to or did not want to recognize legiti-

[26] VI Mansions, iii; Peers, II, 283.
[27] *Ibid.*

mate authority, and that consequently one's action did not enter into the plan of divine Wisdom.

2. SUPERNATURAL OBEDIENCE

Supernatural obedience is that obedience which, by a glance, sees God in the law and the superior and thus offers to Him submission.

To make one's obedience supernatural is to add an important perfection to well-ordered obedience. It is through faith, in fact, that supernatural contact with God is established. Our Lord exacted faith of those who sought from Him some benefit. The faith of the Canaanite woman moves Him; that of the Centurion makes Him rejoice; while that of the woman of Capharnaum, with the flow of blood, wins from Him her cure by an act of daring faith. By causing one to adhere to God, faith establishes the contact that allows for the outpouring of divine mercy into the soul. This contact through faith is necessary for any supernatural communion with God. The pagan without faith who would receive the Eucharistic Bread would have only a physical contact with the sacred species and would not truly commune with Christ Jesus. Again, it is living faith that is the specific instrument of contemplation. As to obedience, if it is not supernatural, it obtains certain external effects already appreciable. But it can claim to be a communion with Wisdom and draw from this source its supernatural riches of light, of strength, and of fecundity only if it is armed with the antenna of faith, which lifts it up to God Himself. Each act of obedience, moreover, bears within it an unlimited capacity for the supernatural; it is with the measure of its faith that, ordinarily, the soul draws upon the supernatural and is enriched by it. Thus it is supremely important to actualize one's faith by obeying, in order to profit by this means of sanctification, which is constantly within our reach.

To actualize one's faith requires an effort—an effort that those especially for whom obedience offers few difficulties do not think of making. Docile or even passive by temperament, having no ideas of their own, and their will lacking energy to assert itself and to run any risk whatever, obedience seems to them usually if not always the easiest way. This facility in submitting oneself in everything can make excellent elements in a community or any mass group. But such souls run great danger of drifting along on a mediocre level and of surpassing it only rarely to go to God with a faith avid for a grace of which they do not feel the need. Their obedience is easy, but little or not at all supernatural.

A similar danger threatens those who are very much devoted to their superior. This legitimate devotedness is always praiseworthy when it remains discreet. It incurs the risk however of maintaining the soul in simply natural relations with the superior and of checking the flight of faith. It belongs to faith to pierce the veils, those "silvered surfaces" [28] that always conceal here below the gold of the divine presence, and to go beyond them to attain to God Himself. If it happens that these silvered surfaces are resplendent with beauty, their charms can become an obstacle that detains one, making one forget the incomparable treasure that they cover. Thus the eminent qualities of a superior and the affection one has for him, after being a means that so happily facilitates obedience, can be an obstacle that arrests the movement of faith toward God whom this superior represents. The illusion can be complete. One was obeying perfectly, so one thought. The superior is changed; obedience seems to have disappeared with the silvered surfaces that served as its support. The facility had caused one to give up the effort to rise above oneself, and the fine point of faith became dull through disuse.

On the other hand, for the one who does not find in his superior the qualities that please him, the effort at going beyond himself to God will appear necessary as the only means for remaining faithful to his duty. These difficulties are perhaps

[28] *Spiritual Canticle,* st. xi; Peers, II, 64.

providential in his regard. If it be that he himself is well gifted and destined later to guide others, it is extremely important that he first learn to commune with God through obedience. He could not be the faithful interpreter of the will of God for his subjects if he himself, through supernatural obedience, has not learned to open his soul to the light of God, and has not made it docile and supple under the divine impulse.

3. COMPLETE OBEDIENCE

This further quality aims at securing the perfection of the very act of obedience. A purely exterior submission would evidently not suffice. Obedience engages in the first place the will. It unites the human will to the divine will, submitting the human to the divine. Without any doubt obedience requires first of all the complete submission of the will.

But can one disassociate the will from the intellect, which enlightens it and decides its choices? God is our absolute master. Any homage that would be only partial would not be worthy of Him. Moreover, in order to be in communion with divine Wisdom, obedience must offer Him our entire being. To be perfect, obedience must be complete, human in the full sense of the word, submitting to God all our faculties and especially the highest, intellect and will.

The submission of the intellect poses a problem which we cannot hide. Made for the truth, as the will for the good, the intellect can submit only to the truth. No one can oblige it to constant and unconditional submission, if he cannot guarantee that he possesses always the truth. God Himself, and the infallible Church, have a right to that complete submission. The superior, although legitimately called by God to transmit His desires, is not thereby infallible. He has a right to the submission of the subject's will. Do the dangers of error that his special office still leave in him allow him to claim a complete submission of the intellect?

Here is a practical case to make the problem concrete. A religious employed at a task in which he is past master, receives from his superior the order to do it another way. Respectfully —as he must—he presents his experience and the disadvantages of the order given. The superior maintains his order. The religious executes it with all his good will. In spite of this, the result is what he had foreseen: it clearly appears that the superior was mistaken. Must the religious, then, in order to obey perfectly the order received, submit his judgment when the superior is mistaken? [29]

The solution to the problem lies in a distinction between speculative judgment and practical judgment. The speculative judgment is concerned with the thing itself that is commanded, without reference to the circumstances of the command, and can be reserved when one has the evidence on his side. Thus the subject could without failing in his duty formulate this judgment: "From my experience I can affirm that the best way of doing this work is the one that I regularly use."

The practical judgment on the other hand has for its object the concrete case, such as it is in this particular set of circumstances including the order of the superior. Here there must be submission of judgment, if obedience is to be complete. It can be formulated thus in the concrete case: "The best way to do this work in the present circumstances, given the order of the superior, is the way that he indicates."

Submission of the practical judgment is sufficient for the perfection of obedience. The order of the superior does not in itself involve the definition of a universal truth; at most it bears on the enunciation of a particular truth, the import of which does not extend beyond the order that is given.

But, it will be said, to submit to the practical judgment is to run the risk of adhering to error, since the grounds on which the commands were based may be contradicted by the results of

[29] We are taking an extreme and almost extraordinary case, although not impossible. Actually in such a case the superior will usually have, to give such an order, reasons that will be justified by experience.

executing the order received. This is to judge superficially of the value of obedience. It is indeed possible, as in the example cited above, that the material and external effects of the act of obedience may not correspond to the intention of the superior and of the one executing it; and that consequently there may be an error. But this error is only partial. It leaves to the act of obedience its highest value, which is submission to the will of God manifested authentically by the superior, even though he be mistaken.[30] This submission of intellect and will is what God considers first of all in the act of obedience. It is the perfume that is pleasing to Him, the homage that He expects from us and that He accepts. Hence it remains true that, even when the act of obedience ends in apparent failure, it is better to posit that act, because God wills it so. The practical judgment, which submitted by recognizing the excellence of that act under obedience, was not, then, erroneous.

We are touching here an important point on which we must insist. This submission not only of the will but of the judgment in matters that are obscure or even improbable to it is of such value in God's sight that it becomes the principal means by which man cooperates in the great works of God. Abraham had received the formal promise that he would be the father of a great people. The command is given him to sacrifice Isaac, his only son. He sets himself to work to obey. Thus it is that he merits the fulfillment of the promise, and he becomes the father of the faithful.

Saint Teresa, in 1571, was all taken up with her foundations, which had been extending for three years. In order to restore peace to the Convent of the Incarnation that the Saint had left to begin her Reform, Father Hernandez, Visitor, named her its prioress. She had to give up her work, go back to a convent where she was not wanted. Was the Father Visitor not cleverly

[30] The authority of the superior is independent of his judgment. And so his decisions, provided they are not tyrannical, draw their force from that authority and not from motives given to justify the decisions.

unburdening himself of a grievous embarrassment by passing it on to Teresa? Who did not see this? She accepted it nonetheless. Peace returned to the Incarnation; and it was there in the following year that the Saint received the grace of spiritual marriage.

The mystery of the Annunciation offers us a tableau more simple still and a lesson that is more moving. The archangel proposes the mystery: "How shall this happen, since I do not know man?" answers the Virgin. For her this is clouded with obscurity. "The Holy Spirit shall come upon thee and the power of the Most High shall overshadow thee." The angel has not scattered the cloud from the mystery. He has simply announced the direct intervention of God. "Behold the handmaid of the Lord; be it done to me according to thy word." The Virgin submits, and the mystery of the Incarnation enters immediately into effect.

Before the soul becomes, on the summits, the human cooperator in the loftiest works of God, its obedience must be the most constant and most faithful proof of its love.[31] Obedience must be the humble and daily exercise that supernaturally strengthens and renders docile the human faculties, surrenders them progessively to God's action, and merits for the soul, insofar as this is possible, the first of the definitive and deep raptures of God, the union of will.

[31] John 14:21.

CHAPTER IX

Union of the Will

This is the union which I have desired all my life; it is for this that I continually beseech Our Lord.[1]

Here now is finished the hard travail of the fourth Mansions. True, the toil of them was sustained by tastes of divine delights, but it was carried on in suffering, in the dark night of sense, according to the terminology of Saint John of the Cross.

A divine reward is offered to the soul, a veritable transformation: union of the will. Let us hear Saint Teresa speak of this. Her pretty comparison with the silkworm allows her to summarize the stages already reached, to place the new grace in its proper setting, and to point out its importance:

> You will have heard of the wonderful way in which silk is made—a way which no one could invent but God—and how it comes from a kind of seed which looks like tiny peppercorns. . . . When the warm weather comes, and the mulberry trees begin to show leaf, this seed starts to take life; until it has this sustenance, on which it feeds, it is as dead. The silkworms feed on the mulberry-leaves until they are full grown, when people put down twigs, upon which, with their tiny mouths, they start spinning silk, making themselves very tight little cocoons, in which they bury themselves. Then, finally, the worm, which was large and ugly, comes right of the cocoon a beautiful white butterfly. . . .
>
> The silkworm is like the soul which takes life when, through the heat which comes from the Holy Spirit, it begins to utilize the general help which God gives to all, and to make use of the remedies which He left in His Church—such as frequent confessions, good books and sermons. . . . The soul begins to live and nourishes itself on this food, and on good meditations, until it is full grown—and this is what concerns me now; the rest is of little importance.

[1] V Mansions, iii; Peers, II, 260.

When it is full-grown, then, as I wrote at the beginning, it starts to spin its silk and to build the house in which it is to die. . . .

Here, then, daughters, you see what we can do, with God's favour. May His Majesty Himself be our Mansion as He is in this Prayer of Union which, as it were, we ourselves spin.[2]

The Saint explains that for the construction of this divine dwelling, the part that is in our power is to give of ourselves and die to ourselves as do the little silkworms.

And, before we have finished doing all that we can in that respect, God will take this tiny achievement of ours, which is nothing at all, unite it with His greatness and give it such worth that its reward will be the Lord Himself. . . .

On, then, my daughters! Let us hasten to perform this task and spin this cocoon. . . . Let the silkworm die—let it die, as in fact it does when it has completed the work which it was created to do. Then we shall see God and shall ourselves be as completely hidden in His greatness as is this little worm in its cocoon. Note that, when I speak of seeing God, I am referring to the way in which, as I have said, He allows Himself to be apprehended in this kind of union.

And now let us see what becomes of this silkworm, for all that I have been saying about it is leading up to this. When it is in this state of prayer, and quite dead to the world, it comes out as a little white butterfly.[3]

The transformation wrought by the prayer of union is equivalent to a real metamorphosis. Such is the meaning of the comparison emphasized by Teresa herself:

I tell you truly, the very soul does not know itself. For think of the difference between an ugly worm and a white butterfly; it is just the same here.[4]

Before studying this profound action of God in the soul, we must mention a problem raised by the Teresian description and terminology.

When describing the same stage of the spiritual life, that is, the one that marks the end of the purification of sense, Saint John of the Cross does not speak of union of the will, but only

[2] *Ibid.*, ii; 253-4.
[3] *Ibid.*; 254-5.
[4] *Ibid.*; 255.

of contemplation. He says of the soul that God is about to lead onward:

> It is wont to pass a long time, even years, after leaving the state of beginners, in exercising itself in that of proficients. In this latter state it is like to one that has come forth from a rigorous imprisonment; it goes about the things of God with much greater freedom and satisfaction of the soul, and with more abundant and inward delight than it did at the beginning before it entered the said night. . . . It now very readily finds in its spirit the most serene and loving contemplation and spiritual sweetness without the labour of meditation.[5]

Have the differences that were previously noted between the two spiritual masters of Carmel[6] now grown to the point of complete disagreement in the description of the fifth Mansions?

What is the essential mark of that loving contemplation which has become habitual and easy, or of the union of will?

Let us first call attention to the brevity of Saint John of the Cross's description. Our Saint is a spiritual director. Now, just as the doctor goes to the sick and not to those who are well, the director ministers to souls in trouble and difficulty. In the spiritual journey Saint John of the Cross tarries, then, in the transition periods, which are the most painful and the most obscure. Being a prudent and compassionate director, he is the doctor of the dark nights. The periods of euphoria, such as the fifth Mansions, detain him very little, although ordinarily the soul passes a rather long time in them, even years, because there it finds tranquillity and enjoyment. His descriptions are limited to what we have quoted, short of a few lines.

Nor does it astonish us that in the few sentences given to this period, which for him is intermediary between the two nights, Saint John of the Cross should place in relief the con-

[5] *Dark Night,* Bk. II, i; Peers, I, 374. We would not dare to say that these descriptions correspond exclusively to the fifth Mansions of Saint Teresa, but they certainly include them, since they refer to the "very long time" that separates the dark night of sense (the beginning of the fourth Mansions) from the dark night of the spirit (sixth Mansions).

[6] Cf. *supra,* ch. ii, "God as Light and God as Love," p. 28 ff.

templative effects; both the logic of his explanation and the particular quality of his experience required that it be so. John attains especially to light, as has been said;[7] Teresa to love. The first therefore lays stress on sweet and delightful contemplation, the second speaks of the union of will, which is the fruit of love: two different aspects of the same state, the manifold riches of which are thus opened up to our view.

But, besides the fact that the very brevity of the texts of Saint John of the Cross precludes our seeing in them a complete exposition of this period and expecting to find precise data that the Saint did not intend to give, we think that Saint Teresa's descriptions of it, more developed as they are, are also nearer to life. And so, while we must use extensively the teaching of Saint John of the Cross for the fourth and the sixth Mansions, Saint Teresa's doctrine will be our only guide in the fifth Mansions.

The four chapters of the "fifth Mansions" are devoted to describing, first, a mystical grace of union (chapters one and two), then a state of union or union of the will properly speaking (chapters three and four). Usually, these two descriptions are disassociated. The first, having to do with an extraordinary grace, is left for the initiated and specialists; the second is studied because it is not a transitory grace but is an established state, and especially because Saint Teresa declares that one can attain to it by one's own efforts.

It seems to us that this disassociation arbitrarily breaks the unity of the Teresian fifth Mansions. It incurs the risk of misunderstanding the value of the union of will itself and of placing it in a false perspective.

Union of will constitutes, beyond doubt, the distinctive note of the fifth Teresian Mansions. The Saint wishes to study it and underline its importance. This is the union that is the object of her ardent desire.

[7] *Ibid.*

This is the union which I have desired all my life; it is for this that I continually beseech Our Lord.[8]

What is the role of the mystical grace in relation to the union of will? It is a "short cut" [9] to it. Hence two ways lead to this happy state: the short cut of mystical graces and the ordinary way of persevering effort.

But let us not study merely the ordinary way to the neglect of the short cut, under the plea that extraordinary graces are of only limited practical interest. Otherwise we should neglect a body of doctrine of the highest importance. For Saint Teresa, mystical graces are not only luminous signs that indicate the stages of the soul's progress, but also symbols that reveal the nature of the characteristic grace of each stage. In this case, the mystical grace indicates the profound regions of the soul where union of will takes place. The Saint's teaching is to be underlined as most opportune.

How many, actually, are the illusions apropos of this union of will! It is so easy to mistake for it a good persevering will, or a certain taste for the supernatural, or intense desires. Saint Teresa has hunted down these illusions; let us hear what she says.

I like the way in which some souls, when they are at prayer, think that, for God's sake, they would be glad if they could be humbled and put to open shame—and then try to conceal quite a slight failure. Oh, and if they should be accused of anything that they have not done—! God save us from having to listen to them! [10]

And again:

When I see people very diligently trying to discover what kind of prayer they are experiencing and so completely wrapt up in their prayers that they seem afraid to stir, or to indulge in a moment's thought, lest they should lose the slightest degree of the tenderness and devotion which they have been feeling, I realize how little they understand of the road to the attainment of union. They think that the

[8] V Mansions, iii; Peers, II, 260.
[9] *Ibid.*
[10] *Ibid.;* 262.

whole thing consists in this. But no, sisters, no; what the Lord desires is works.[11]

Saint Teresa is speaking to her daughters and so draws examples from their life. It would be easy to apply them to another milieu.

Another illusion, more subtle, would be for a soul to think that it has arrived at union of will if it does not grieve at the loss of one who is dear:

Do not think that if, for example, my father or my brother dies, I ought to be in such conformity with the will of God that I shall not grieve at his loss, or that, if I have trials or illnesses, I must enjoy bearing them. It is good if we can do this and sometimes it is a matter of common sense: being unable to help ourselves, we make a virtue of necessity.[12]

There are signs more profound than these that enable one to recognize genuine union of will. An analysis of the mystical grace of union will help us to discover them.

A. Mystical grace of union

Saint Teresa presents to us at first the mystical grace of union as a deepening of preceding favors. Thus she compares it to the most elevated form of quiet, which is the sleep of the powers, in order to point out the differences.

Do not think it is a state, like the last, in which we dream; I say "dream," because the soul seems to be, as it were, drowsy, so that it neither seems asleep nor feels awake. Here we are all asleep, and fast asleep, to the things of the world, and to ourselves (in fact, for the short time that the condition lasts, the soul is without consciousness and has no power to think, even though it may desire to do so). . . . In fact, it has completely died to the world so that it may live more fully in God. This is a delectable death, a snatching of the soul from all the activities which it can perform while it is in the body.[13]

There is, then, a veritable suspension of the activity of the

[11] *Ibid.;* 262-3.
[12] *Ibid.;* 261.
[13] *Ibid.,* i; 248. Cf. also: *Way of Perfection,* xxi; Peers, II.

powers, which takes the form of a swoon, with loss of consciousness. The Saint continues:

I do not know if it (the soul) has still life enough to be able to breathe. I have just been thinking about this and I believe it has not; or at least, if it still breathes, it does so without realizing it.[14]

Moreover, the loss of consciousness is very brief:

As long as such a soul is in this state, it can neither see nor hear nor understand: the period is always short and seems to the soul even shorter than it really is.[15]

The awakening is followed by anxiety:

The soul is doubtful as to what has really happened until it has had a good deal of experience of it. It wonders if the whole thing was imagination, if it has been asleep, if the favour was a gift of God, or if the devil was transfigured into an angel of light. It retains a thousand suspicions, and it is well that it should, for, as I said, we can sometimes be deceived in this respect, even by our own nature.[16]

This complete obscurity characterizes the mystical grace of union of the fifth Mansions. The mystical graces of the sixth Mansions will be received in light. The soul has certitude nevertheless, even in the obscurity, and this certitude is an essential aspect of the grace, so that Saint Teresa asserts that it is the surest sign of its authenticity.

I will give you a clear indication which will make it impossible for you to go wrong or to doubt if some favour has come from God. . . . God implants Himself in the interior of that soul in such a way that, when it returns to itself, it cannot possibly doubt that God has been in it and it has been in God; so firmly does this truth remain within it that, although for years God may never grant it that favour again, it can neither forget it nor doubt that it has received it.[17]

This certainty, independent of any vision, God alone can give, affirms the Saint.[18] It is such that of itself it makes known the presence of God in the soul.

[14] *Ibid.*
[15] *Ibid.;* 251.
[16] *Ibid.;* 249.
[17] *Ibid.;* 250-1.
[18] *Ibid.;* 251.

I know of a person who had not learned that God was in all things by presence and power and essence: God granted her a favour of this kind, which convinced her of this so firmly. . . .[19]

This certitude reveals to the soul what took place in the obscurity of God's direct action in it. The soul in its whole essence has been united with God. The testimony of the Saint is clear, although given only by way of allusion:

He will come into the centre of the soul without using a door, as He did when He came in to His disciples, and said *Pax vobis,* and when He left the sepulchre without removing the stone.[20]

She had already said:

His Majesty is in such close contact and union with the essence of the soul that he [the devil] will not dare to approach, nor can he even understand this secret thing.[21]

And, situating this grace in its relation to those that will come in the following Mansions, Saint Teresa says that it is the soul's first meeting with the divine Spouse.

He grants her [the soul] this mercy, desiring that she shall get to know Him better, and that, as we may say, they shall meet together, and He shall unite her with Himself. We can compare this kind of union to a short meeting of that nature because it is over in the very shortest time.[22]

B. Effects of mystical grace: union of will

In this meeting which comes to pass in a union of the whole soul with God,[23] and not simply of some one of its powers, the Master works a profound marvel!

Here is this soul which God has made, as it were, completely foolish in order the better to impress upon it true wisdom.[24]

[19] *Ibid.*
[20] *Ibid.*, 252.
[21] *Ibid.;* 249.
[22] *Ibid.*, iv; 265.
[23] *Ibid.*, i; 252.
[24] *Ibid.*, 251.

In the words of the *Canticle of Canticles,* the Saint says elsewhere:

God put her in the cellar of wine and ordained charity in her.[25]

What can this mean, if not that the divine contact has produced an abundant inflowing of charity.

This charity is in such abundance and of such quality that the soul retains the mark of it. The effects of these substantial touches of God are profound and immutable as is the essence of the soul that they affect. The mystical grace of union brings about an effective hold of God upon the soul; thereafter it bears the mark of a divine seal:

His will is that, without understanding how, the soul shall go thence sealed with His seal. In reality, the soul in that state does no more than the wax when a seal is impressed upon it—the wax does not impress itself; it is only prepared for the impress: that is, it is soft—and it does not even soften itself so as to be prepared; it merely remains quiet and consenting.[26]

But this possession of the soul by God after the grace of union, Saint Teresa warns us, is not yet definitive. It can be lost; and the devil does not fail to use his most subtle tricks to destroy it:

For this communication has been no more than (as we might say) one single short meeting and the devil will take great pains about combating it and will try to hinder the betrothal. . . .

I tell you, daughters, I have known people of a very high degree of spirituality who have reached this state, and whom, notwithstanding, the devil, with great subtlety and craft, has won back to himself. For this purpose he will marshall all the powers of hell, for as I have often said, if he wins a single soul in this way he will win a whole multitude. The devil has much experience in this matter.[27]

[25] *Ibid.,* ii; 257.

[26] *Ibid.*

[27] *Ibid.;* iv; 265. And in the following pages, Saint Teresa finely describes that subtle action of the devil as he succeeds in separating from God a soul already taken captive by Him: "The devil comes with his artful wiles, and, under colour of doing good, sets about undermining it in trivial ways, and involving it in practices which, so he gives it to understand, are not wrong; little by little he darkens its understanding, and weakens its will, and causes its self-love to increase, until in one way and another he begins to withdraw

The soul must wait for the spiritual betrothal before it is so firmly possessed by God that no enemy will be able to separate it from Him.[28]

Although it is true that the bonds created by the grace of union can be broken by the cleverness of the devil, yet the soul comes from this contact with God really transformed, so that

> . . . the very soul does not know itself. For think of the difference between an ugly worm and a white butterfly; it is just the same here.[29]

These words of the Saint, quoted before, recalling the change of the silkworm into a butterfly, tell us how extraordinarily profound and fruitful are the effects of the grace of union. An abundant inflowing of love comes from this touch of God in the soul. It is normal that it is the will that gives sign of the most powerful effects, since this is the faculty receptive of love. Captivated by God, it is entirely surrendered to His good pleasure:

> That soul has now delivered itself into His hands and His great love has so completely subdued it that it neither knows nor desires anything save that God shall do with it what He wills.[30]

This abandonment and suppleness of the will—which moreover admits of degrees and goes on being perfected—assures peace to the soul, says Saint Teresa,

> . . . in this life and in the next as well. Nothing that happens on earth will afflict it unless it finds itself in peril of losing God, or sees that He is offended—neither sickness nor poverty nor death, except when someone dies who was needed by the Church of God. For this soul sees clearly that He knows what He does better than it knows itself what it desires.[31]

The divine captivation has wrought a detachment which is an uprooting. This is one of the most sensible effects. The soul

---

it from the love of God and to persuade it to indulge its own wishes" (V Mansions, iv; 266).

[28] VI Mansions, iv; 292.

[29] V Mansions, ii; 255.

[30] *Ibid.;* 257.

[31] *Ibid.,* iii; 260.

is lost, as it were, in the midst of all that formerly concerned it. The Saint writes:

> To see, then, the restlessness of this little butterfly—though it has never been quieter or more at rest in its life! Here is something to praise God for—namely, that it knows not where to settle and make its abode. By comparison with the abode it has had, everything it sees on earth leaves it dissatisfied, especially when God has again and again given it this wine which almost every time has brought it some new blessing. It sets no store by the things it did when it was a worm—that is, by its gradual weaving of the cocoon. . . . It is no longer bound by ties of relationship, friendship or property. Previously all its acts of will and resolutions and desires were powerless to loosen these and seemed only to bind them the more firmly; now it is grieved at having even to fulfil its obligations in these respects lest these should cause it to sin against God. Everything wearies it, because it has proved that it can find no true rest in the creatures.[32]

This detachment, which makes the butterfly "feel a stranger to things of the earth," [33] and allows it no "rest in spiritual consolations or in earthly treasures," [34] is accompanied by burning ardors of love that produce vehement desires to glorify God.

> All that it can do for God seems slight by comparison with its desires.[35]

And these are efficacious desires, which ensure it strength to practise the austerities of apostolic immolation:

> For the weakness which it used to think it had when it came to doing penance is now turned into strength.[36]

This love creates in souls a strange solicitude for the things of God—strange because so new, strong, and painful:

> Oh, the greatness of God! Only a few years since—perhaps only a few days—this soul was thinking of nothing but itself. Who has plunged it into such grievous anxieties? [37]

[32] *Ibid.*, ii; 255-6.
[33] *Ibid.;* 256.
[34] *Ibid.*, iv; 264.
[35] *Ibid.*, ii; 255.
[36] *Ibid.*
[37] *Ibid.;* 257.

Saint Teresa insists on the suffering that comes to the soul through the love that has been infused:

> I know that the torment which a certain person of my acquaintance has suffered, and suffers still, at seeing the Lord offended, is so intolerable that she would far sooner die than suffer it.[38]

Its greatest grief is over the loss of Christian souls.[39]

> It finds itself so anxious to praise the Lord that it would gladly be consumed and die a thousand deaths for His sake. Then it finds itself longing to suffer great trials and unable to do otherwise. It has the most vehement desires for penance, for solitude, and for all to know God.[40]

In fact, the grace of union is always fruitful for others, even should the soul be unfaithful:

> For my own part I believe it is God's will that so great a favour should not be given in vain, and that if the soul that receives it does not profit by it others will do so. For, as the soul possesses these aforementioned desires and virtues, it will always profit other souls so long as it leads a good life, and from its own heat new heat will be transmitted to them. Even after losing this, it may still desire others to profit, and take pleasure in describing the favours given by God to those who love and serve Him.
>
> I knew a person to whom this happened . . . and she brought them very, very great profit.[41]

Such are the marvelous riches left in the soul by the grace of mystical union. The contact with God was of short duration; its fruits are permanent. Very happily, Saint Teresa distinguishes the mystical grace from its effects. The grace is extraordinary and reserved to certain souls; its effects, because they constitute the union of will that characterizes the fifth Mansions, are sovereignly desirable.

But can these desires be truly efficacious, however legitimate they may be? How can one make such fruits one's own without the mystical grace? Saint Teresa has solved the problem: the

[38] *Ibid.;* 258.
[39] *Ibid.;* 256.
[40] *Ibid.;* 255.
[41] *Ibid.,* iii; 259. Cf. also: *Life,* xix; Peers, I.

mystical grace is a short cut. There is an ordinary way open to all souls; for this, suspension of the powers is not necessary, as the Saint explains:

> The Lord can enrich souls in many ways and bring them to these Mansions by many other paths than the short cut which has been described.[42]

C. Ordinary way to union of will

Before entering upon this new way, Saint Teresa gives us grave warning that advance in it will be no less difficult for being ordinary:

> But note very carefully, daughters, that the silkworm has of necessity to die; and it is this which will cost you most; for death comes more easily when one can see oneself living a new life, whereas our duty now is to continue living this present life, and yet to die of our own free will. I confess to you that we shall find this much harder.[43]

The image of the short cut through a winding road seems to indicate that the latter is easier because the ascent is slower. But no; by the short cut, quick ascent and a certain facility; by the ordinary way, slow progress and hard asceticism.

We must not be surprised at this. The two ways: mystical grace and ordinary progress, lead indeed to the same end. Let us recall the effects of mystical union already described; two words sum them up: perfect love and absolute detachment. The difference in the way of acquiring them might, almost unconsciously, cause us to place less value on these words and the realities that they signify. This would be to put at stake union of the will, itself. It would not be genuine union without that high degree of love effected by a profound divine rapture, nor without the absolute detachment necessary for the reign of that love.

[42] *Ibid.*; 260.
[43] *Ibid.*

1. ASCETICISM OF DETACHMENT

We readily understand this: in order to arrive at the detachment from relatives, friends, and worldly goods that ensures perfect liberty of spirit and makes one feel "a stranger to things of the earth," [44] "we shall need to do a very great deal before we can attain to this higher state, and we must on no account be careless." [45]

This resolute labor will consist in the practice of the virtues, of obedience particularly, which sets free the will and judgment, and in the gift of self, which must be complete.

> But observe, daughters, that, if you are to gain this, He would have you keep back nothing; whether it be little or much, He will have it all for Himself, and according to what you know yourself to have given, the favours He will grant you will be small or great. There is no better test than this of whether or no our prayer attains to union.[46]

The sharp sword of active asceticism cannot of itself alone bring about such a liberation. The soul knows how to wield it only by following its own limited views, unconsciously egotistic. It spares itself without knowing it and provides itself with compensations. Besides, could it without apparent cruelty, without presumption or without wounding charity, deprive itself of necessary goods and break with legitimate affections like those of relatives and friends? Only the sword of God has the right to cut clean certain bonds; only it can pierce through into the depths that free. To do this, it makes use of various events and free secondary causes. The lives of the saints and the experience of souls whose valor has attracted God's purifying glance and merited this honor permit us to see with what merciful power Holy Wisdom excels in tormenting those whom He calls to perfect union.

[44] *Ibid.*
[45] *Ibid.*
[46] *Ibid.;* 248.

2. PRACTICE OF LOVE

The part the soul must play is not limited to the asceticism of detachment. More important still is the development of love. Union is the work of love. And so, with Saint John of the Cross, we must repeat that it is supremely important for the soul to exercise itself in holy love. There are some souls who attach such importance to this exercise of love that for them concern about detachment takes only second place. Such was Saint Therese of the Child Jesus. What has been said about the mystical grace of perfect union seems to justify their attitude. Detachment is in their case the fruit of infused love; hence love is both end and means. Why should it not be the same for those who ascend by the ordinary way? But even here, care must be taken that the detachment be real, for it alone is the authentic proof of the quality of love. Whatever may be said of the primacy of love, it is certain that love alone can give to the work of detachment its perfection and assure to the soul the self-surrender and suppleness that are the proper mark of genuine union of will.

What does this practice of love include? Speaking to her daughters, Saint Teresa puts them on guard against illusions created by intensity of feeling, especially against that anxious and gluttonous seeking for God that would want to find Him only in recollection and delights. We have already heard her affably laugh at those persons so "wrapt up" in their prayers that they seem afraid to stir lest they lose the slightest degree of tenderness and devotion, for

> . . . how little they understand of the road to the attainment of union. They think that the whole thing consists in this. But no, sisters, no; what the Lord desires is works. If you see a sick woman to whom you can give some help, never be affected by fear that your devotion will suffer, but take pity on her: if she is in pain, you should feel pain too; if necessary, fast so that she may have your food, not so much for her sake as because you know it to be your Lord's will. That is true union with His will.[47]

[47] *Ibid.*, iii; 263.

There, clearly stated, is the importance of acts in order to attain to this union, which resides in the will and not in the sense faculties. There must be, then, acts and acts over again truly to develop charity. Is not this the place to recall that only those acts develop virtue that put to use the whole strength of the virtue already acquired and hence are called intense: while weak acts, good in themselves but not exercising all the charity that has been acquired, run the risk of diminishing its strength rather than increasing it. This theological truth is of considerable practical importance. Moreover, intensity here means perfection of the act in itself and purity of intention, not necessarily effort or violence in performing the act.

Thus it appears that the development of charity and the union of will that is its fruit are bound up with imponderables. One person goes along accomplishing his duty, honestly, without apparent fervor as without slackness: his acts are good but weak. Another, his neighbor, differs little from him, but his awakened fervor keeps on faithfully attentive to purify his intention and to add to his acts that little nothing which gives them their perfection: his acts are good and intense. The latter, and he alone, is growing in the virtue of love. Years pass in a life that the two lead in common and that differentiates them but little exteriorly. And yet, the second attains at length to the prayer of union; while the first, better endowed perhaps, is lulled into an ease and routine that have arrested all progress.

3. THE INTERVENTION OF GOD

Just as the active effort of the soul cannot attain to the detachment and suppleness that we have seen comes through mystical grace, neither can it attain to the love that effects union of will. Certainly, it is always true to say that charity is a divine thing, and that only the Holy Spirit can put it in our hearts. It is also true that it can be an object of merit. But what we want to say precisely here is that the perfect love of union of will, even in the ordinary way, is not uniquely the fruit of the soul's merits. It is given by a merciful intervention of divine Wisdom. It is important to emphasize this truth, in order that union of will be not attributed solely to the efforts of the soul, and that even the ordinary way be not considered as exclusively ascetic.

For Saint Teresa, in fact, the work of the soul tends only to bringing about the dispositions "necessary to complete union with the will of God." [48]

She writes:

> And before we have finished doing all that we can do in that respect, God will take this tiny achievement of ours, which is nothing at all, unite it with His greatness and give it such worth that its reward will be the Lord Himself.[49]

He it is who "can enrich souls in many ways and bring them to these Mansions." [50]

Moreover, besides the fact that the union of two free beings requires the convergence of their mutual love, and hence the free sharing on the part of each one of them, union of will comes from God's captivation of the soul and leaves, consequently, the principal part to His action.

This direct intervention of God, who infuses His love, occurred before in the prayers of quiet and of contemplative dryness which, under different experiences, are wholly an infusion of love in the will.[51] Saint John of the Cross himself, in the few lines that he has given to it, notes as characteristic of this period facility in entering upon sweet and loving contemplation, as well as a certain spiritual delight.[52] It seems, then, that God progressively takes captive the soul by means of sweet or painful bonds, until union of will is effected.

And so, in order to distinguish from the ordinary way the

[48] *Ibid.;* 261.
[49] *Ibid.,* ii; 254.
[50] *Ibid.,* iii; 260.
[51] In the prayer of quiet especially, Saint Teresa likes to stress that only the will is constantly held captive. This prayer, then, is a direct preparation for union of will.
[52] *Dark Night,* Bk. II, i; Peers, I.

short cut that is mystical grace, we should stress much less the direct intervention of God, which is common and necessary to both, than the mode of that intervention. Saint Teresa, in a text already quoted, gives us the solution to the problem:

> The Lord can enrich souls in many ways and bring them to these Mansions by many other paths than the short cut which has been described.[53]

It is the suspension of the powers, hence the extraordinary and powerful way in which the grace is given, and not a special quality of that grace, which characterizes the short cut. Whatever be the way leading to it, union of will is constituted by God's loving possession of the will, which thus becomes self-surrendered and supple under His divine impulses.

A precious grace, "But alas," laments Saint Teresa, "that so few of us are destined to attain it!" [54] It is a sovereignly desirable grace, marking a stage of supreme importance in the way of perfection. Most of all, it is a point of departure for the last stages toward sanctity, for the realization of high destinies in the divine plan.

[53] V Mansions, iii; Peers, II, 260.
[54] *Ibid.*

CHAPTER X

The Mystery of the Church

That all may be one, even as thou, Father, in me and I in thee.[1]

Union of the will produces a veritable transformation of the soul. The effects of mystical grace have made this evident. An important stage has indeed been reached. And another is announced by this transformation, which places the soul at the threshold of a new world. True, this world does not yet appear except in a semi-brightness that leaves its forms but dimly perceptible, while revealing their grandeur. But the brightness is of a dawning vibrant with hope, which in the next mansions will turn to the full light of day and disclose great splendors.

Let us consider carefully these lights that form part of the riches of the union of will. They are as precious clues to the solution of important problems and give an orientation for new advance.

A. Zeal for souls

"The very soul does not know itself," [2] writes Saint Teresa. The change is attended with surprise and even anxiety, when it is produced suddenly by mystical grace.

The little white butterfly that has come out of the cocoon, whose wings have grown, no longer has a resting-place, for it

[1] John 17:21.
[2] V Mansions, ii; Peers, II, 255.

feels itself "a stranger to things of earth. But where will the poor little creature go?" [3]

This confusion is not merely the effect of a passing bewilderment. It comes upon a soul already established in detachment, a soul stirred by new and deep desires. True, it may long to return to those obscure regions whence it has come with the certitude "that God has been in it and it has been in God," [4] but there is now a burning and painful solicitude for God and for souls, which it had not known before to so intense a degree.

> Only a few years since—perhaps only a few days—this soul was thinking of nothing but itself. Who has plunged it into such grievous anxieties? [5]
>
> I know that the torment which a certain person of my acquaintance has suffered, and suffers still, at seeing the Lord offended, is so intolerable that she would far sooner die than suffer it.[6]

This is a new trait that the Saint wants to point out. At some length she reflects upon the Passion of our Lord, who "saw everything and was continually witnessing the great offenses which were being committed against His Father," [7] and upon her own ardent desire to suffer and die for the salvation of sinners. This suffering of the soul, due proportion kept, resembles that of Christ; and Saint Teresa says it is an essential mark of this spiritual stage:

> If anyone told me that after reaching this state he had enjoyed continual rest and joy, I should say that he had not reached it at all.[8]

In these pages where the Saint is treating, with her characteristic logic, of union of will—not with the formal logic of thought but the logic of description which embraces all that is

[3] *Ibid.;* 256. Considering the convergence of the two ways in the same union of will, after the example of Saint Teresa, we are describing the union of will by the effects of mystical grace. The sudden and deep action of this grace gives a clearer and more keen awareness of the change that has taken place.

[4] *Ibid.,* i; 251.

[5] *Ibid.,* ii; 257.

[6] *Ibid;* 258.

[7] *Ibid.*

[8] *Ibid.;* 256.

before it—she speaks of the immense work of conversion effected by great saints who had received such favors and corresponded with them.[9]

Without any doubt, the prayer of union gives the soul a deep concern for the salvation of souls. This is an important fact that we must remember.

Whence comes this zeal? Saint Teresa answers:

> I will tell you. Have you not heard concerning the Bride (I said this a little while back, though not with reference to the same matter) that God put her in a cellar of wine and ordained charity in her? Well that is the position here.[10]

Charity has been ordered by God Himself in the soul, toward its twofold object: God and neighbor. And, commenting on the double precept, the Saint writes:

> The surest sign that we are keeping these two commandments is, I think, that we should really be loving our neighbor. . . . And be certain that, the farther advanced you find you are in this, the greater the love you will have for God.[11]

The importance that the Saint now attaches to love of neighbor, even to the point of sacrificing one's devotions for acts of charity,[12] is an indication of a new state of soul. It is not long since Teresa was signalizing as a grave danger for the soul the urge to distribute the fruits of its garden. The recipient of that advice had drunk of the third water, the water of perfect quiet, which is the sleep of the powers.[13] After the grace of union, the soul, "having now a clear realization that the fruits of this prayer are not its own, can start to share them and yet have no lack of them itself." [14]

Even more is to be said: the soul thus strengthened not only can but must give of its riches, although still with prudence. It feels an urgent need to do so.

[9] *Ibid.*, iv; 266.
[10] *Ibid.*, ii; 257.
[11] *Ibid.*, iii; 261.
[12] *Ibid.*; 263.
[13] *Life*, xvii; Peers, I, 101.
[14] *Ibid.*, xix; 112. Cf. *supra*, ch. vii.

To explain this profound change by saying that God has ordered the soul's charity this way does not seem sufficient. Why does the ordering of charity actually require that the soul now turn toward its neighbor? Saint Teresa does not explicitly say why, for she disclaims being a theologian and having the ability to give reasons for many things that she has observed. Yet she gives us the key to the problem.

In developing the analogy of the silkworm, she makes this remark, singular at first sight:

> When it is full-grown, then, as I wrote at the beginning, it starts to spin its silk and to build the house in which it is to die. This house may be understood here to mean Christ. I think I read or heard somewhere that our life is hid in Christ, or in God (for that is the same thing), or that our life is Christ. (The exact form of this is little to my purpose.) [15]

This surprising statement, connected in no way with what the Saint has previously said, obliges her to explain what we can do, so that "His Majesty Himself [may] be our Mansion as He is in this Prayer of Union"; [16] it seems to introduce a new element, increasing the complexity of the description. But this thought is dispelled on a moment's reflection. Actually the statement reveals to us a spiritual experience, most important and of great interest. Saint Teresa was aware that in the prayer of union she entered into the living Christ, and that thereafter Christ was to be the dwelling place where her life would be hidden. What else is this than the discovery of her incorporation into the mystical body of Christ, the Church; the awareness of her belonging to the whole Christ. That incorporation into Christ should be experienced by her at this time as a living reality obscurely grasped is truly a great thing. We can understand the consequent change of attitude in her soul, which we have observed; and we shall not be surprised at a new orientation of her life. A mystery of union, a mystery of darkness, yet

[15] V Mansions, ii; Peers, II, 254.
[16] *Ibid.*

the source of resplendent light! Let us pause here a moment to give it thought.

B. The mystery of the Church

The prayer of union, or union of will, is a seizure of the will by loving Wisdom. The soul thereafter bears the impress of a divine seal,[17] which although not indelible is nevertheless permanent; and it produces a state of self-abandonment and suppleness. We may explain the symbol by saying that Holy Wisdom dwells habitually in the will, to reign there as Mistress.

Holy Wisdom can reign for no other purpose than to realize the thought of God. She is herself the Thought of God. She extends her conquest, acts and initiates action, only to show forth God's thought for the world, living and concrete, in events and in souls. Through the apostle St. Paul we know what is this eternal purpose of God:

> . . . the dispensation of the mystery which has been hidden from eternity in God, who created all things . . . which in other ages was not known to the sons of men, as now it has been revealed to his holy apostles and prophets in the Spirit; namely, that the Gentiles are joint heirs, and fellow members of the same body, and joint partakers of the promise in Christ Jesus.[18]

God's design is to save all men without distinction by making them all one with Christ Jesus, in the unity of His mystical body.

Already in eternity, God contemplated the whole Christ, the Church, and took His delight in it as in the masterpiece of His mercy. In the exterior works of His creation God moved through all the vicissitudes of the works of His love, toward the realization of His Christ, His Anointed One. *Finis omnium Ecclesia,* the Church is the end of all things, according to Saint Epiphanius. The very vicissitudes, the fall of the angels, the

[17] *Ibid.;* 257.
[18] Eph. 3:5-11.

sin of man, were permitted by God only as an occasion and means for showing forth the whole strength of His arm, the full measure of the love that He would give to the world. Did not Saint Augustine say that God permitted the fall of the angels so as to create man? And the sin of man is a *felix culpa,* a "happy fault," [19] that won for us Christ the Redeemer.

It is through Christ Jesus that God is going to realize His mystery of mercy; through Christ who is generated eternally, for He is the Word of God:

> He is the image of the invisible God, the firstborn of every creature. For in him were created all things in the heavens and on the earth, things visible and things invisible, whether Thrones, or Dominations, or Principalities, or Powers. All things have been created through and unto him, and he is before all creatures, and in him all things hold together.[20]

After the fall of man, the Word became incarnate; and in the new plan of the Redemption God gave to Him, to Christ Jesus, the primacy and plenitude of all things:

> He is the head of his body, the Church; he, who is the beginning, the firstborn from the dead, that in all things he may have the first place. For it has pleased God the Father that in him all his fullness should dwell, and that through him he should reconcile to himself all things, whether on the earth or in the heavens, making peace through the blood of his cross.[21]

The Epistle to the Ephesians testifies also to the eternal plan of God to unite all things in Christ:

> . . . so that he may make known to us the mystery of his will according to his good pleasure. And this his good pleasure he purposed in him to be dispensed in the fulness of the times: to re-establish all things in Christ, both those in the heavens and those on the earth.[22]

In His eternal thought God sees only His Christ; and in Him He sees each one of us, because in Him He has placed us:

[19] Liturgy for Holy Saturday, *Exultet.*
[20] Col. 1:15-7.
[21] *Ibid.;* 18-20.
[22] Eph. 1:9-10.

Even as he chose us in him before the foundation of the world, that we should be holy and without blemish in his sight in love. He predestined us to be adopted through Jesus Christ as his sons, according to the purpose of his will, unto the praise of the glory of his grace, with which he has favored us in this beloved Son.

In him, I say, in whom we also have been called by a special choice, having been predestined in the purpose of him who works all things according to the counsel of his will, to contribute to the praise of his glory—we who before hoped in Christ.[23]

And so, this divine decree that tells us of the eternal love of the Father for His beloved Son, and for us in Christ, causes to surge up from our hearts a hymn of thanksgiving:

Blessed be the God and Father of our Lord Jesus Christ, who has blessed us with every spiritual blessing on high in Christ.[24]

Christ Jesus came on earth to accomplish this divine decree.[25] He disclosed the plan of God only progressively and in veiled words out of regard for the weakness of His listeners, so as not to clash with their egoistic interpretations of the Messianic promises. He speaks of the kingdom of God that He has come to establish, of the laws of its development, of its demands. He calls Himself the way that one must follow, the door of the sheep-fold that must give entrance to all sheep, the good shepherd. He is the light that enlightens, the truth that shines for all, the life that is to be communicated to every soul. He is, finally, the very food of souls: a soul can have life only by eating His Flesh and drinking His Blood:

I am the bread of life. . . . Amen, amen, I say to you, unless you eat the flesh of the Son of Man, and drink his blood, you shall not have life in you. . . . He who eats my flesh, and drinks my blood, abides in me and I in him. As the living Father has sent me, and as I live because of the Father, so he who eats me, he also shall live because of me.[26]

[23] Eph. 1:4-6, 11-2.
[24] Eph. 1:3.
[25] On coming into the world Christ had said: "Behold, I come to do thy will, O God." Heb. 10:7.
[26] John 6:48, 54-7.

Such language seemed hard and incomprehensible to the Jews. And how could it be otherwise, touching as it did so closely upon the hidden mystery to which the previous statements had reference. When the time came to reveal the mystery in full light, all the preaching of Jesus was to find in it its explanation.

This revelation was to be made after the Last Supper to the apostles, now the priests and friends of Christ, at a time when the Eucharistic presence was anointing their soul with the oil that enflames and enlightens. Jesus said to them:

> I am the vine, you are the branches. He who abides in me, and I in him, he bears much fruit; for without me you can do nothing. . . . In this is my Father glorified, that you may bear very much fruit, and become my disciples.[27]

He had already told them about Himself:

> In that day you will know that I am in my Father, and you in me, and I in you. He who has my commandments and keeps them, he it is who loves me. But he who loves me will be loved by my Father, and I will love him and manifest myself to him.[28]

The apostles thrilled at this word that they had been awaiting and that explained, by unifying it, all the previous teaching.

And now Jesus prayed aloud in the presence of His apostles. In His prayer He spoke plainly about Himself, about His mission; He made known the purpose of His earthly life and the intentions of His sacrifice. He had only one purpose and intention for Himself, for His apostles, and for all those who later were to believe in their word:

> . . . that all may be one, even as thou, Father, in me and I in thee; that they also may be one in us, that the world may believe that thou hast sent me. And the glory that thou hast given me, I have given to them, that they may be one, even as we are one: I in them and thou in me; that they may be perfected in unity, and that the world may

27 John 15:5-8.
28 John 14:20-1.
29 John 17:21-3.

know that thou hast sent me, and that thou hast loved them even as thou hast loved me.[29]

Christ died for the unity of His mystical body. The blood that He shed is the blood of the new covenant that God came to enter into with men, the bond that united all that had been separated by sin. God raised Him up; and

> . . . God, who is rich in mercy, by reason of his very great love wherewith he has loved us even when we were dead by reason of our sins, brought us to life together with Christ . . . and raised us up together, and seated us together in heaven in Christ Jesus.[30]

By receiving the body and blood of Christ we enter into Christ and place ourselves under His redemptive and unifying action. It is thus that is formed "one new man," that we are reconciled "in one body to God by the cross," and that "we have access in one Spirit to the Father." [31]

The work goes on throughout all the ages. The plan of God is realized in us and in the world:

> Therefore, you are now no longer strangers and foreigners, but you are citizens with the saints and members of God's household: you are built upon the foundation of the apostles and prophets with Christ Jesus himself as the chief corner stone. In him the whole structure is closely fitted together and grows into a temple holy in the Lord; in him you too are being built together into a dwelling place for God in the Spirit.[32]

This dwelling place, which is the whole Christ, keeps as its essential and vital quality the unity that Christ asked for it:

> One body and one Spirit, even as you were called in one hope of your calling; one Lord, one faith, one Baptism; one God and Father of all, who is above all, and throughout all, and in us all.[33]

Yet, though the body is so perfectly unified, there is variety among the members. This diversity arises from the different measure of grace that Christ has deemed good to grant to each

[30] Eph. 2:4-6.
[31] Eph. 2:15-8.
[32] Eph. 2:19-22.
[33] Eph. 4:4-6.

one of us,[34] and the diversity of functions that He has assigned us:

> And he himself gave some men as apostles, and some as prophets, others again as evangelists, and others as pastors and teachers.[35]
> To one through the Spirit is given the utterance of wisdom; and to another the utterance of knowledge, according to the same Spirit; to another faith, in the same Spirit; to another the gift of healing, in the one Spirit; to another the working of miracles; to another prophecy; to another the distinguishing of spirits; to another various kinds of tongues; to another interpretation of tongues. But all these things are the work of one and the same Spirit, who divides to everyone according as he will.[36]

The plenitude of Christ is poured out upon each one of us. We receive of His grace, by which we share in His divine filiation and in all His privileges. We are sons and heirs of the Father as He is; we are, with Him, priests and kings.

But in us this plenitude shows forth the riches of Christ, reflections of His divine beauty, and the diversity of the functions of His priesthood. Like a prism which, receiving white light, reflects all its tonalities, so the mystical body of Christ tempers to our view through its members the riches that our poor eyes could not in a single glance embrace in the simple and luminous plenitude of Christ Jesus. Divine Wisdom, who made this unity to be, willed also that there be diversity. When He predestined us to be His adopted sons in Christ,[37] God gave us a place in a member of Christ's mystical body, that we might there proclaim a particular perfection in Christ [38] and fulfill a function of His priesthood.

Our participation in Christ is not merely passive; it is active. Christ, on ascending to the Father, sent the Church into the world, as His Father had sent Him, to preach, to baptize, and to save souls. The life that He gives us is love. And this love, because it is goodness communicating itself, is always advancing

[34] Eph. 4:7.
[35] Eph. 4:11.
[36] I Cor. 12:8-11.
[37] Eph. 1-5.
[38] I Pet. 2:9.

to new conquests. Those that it takes captive are, they too, drawn along in its movement and become instruments of its action, channels of the life that it communicates.

Such is the Church of which Christ is the head:

> For from him the whole body (being closely joined and knit together through every joint of the system according to the functioning in due measure of each single part) derives its increase to the building up of itself in love.[39]

Such is the plan of God which is realized progressively but surely, despite all obstacles, on through the ages. It is the great reality, the fact that dominates the history of peoples and of the world. It is the end and the reason for all things. And so when the whole Christ has attained "to perfect manhood, to the mature measure of the fullness of Christ," [40] the figure of this world will pass and the reality will appear: the reality of Christ in whom God has wrought His mighty power "in raising him from the dead, and setting him at his right hand in heaven above every Principality and Power and Virtue and Domination"; in whom He worked His plan by giving Him "as head over all the Church, which indeed is his body," and by ensuring "the fullness of him who is wholly fulfilled in all.[41]

C. The mystery of the Church and the spirituality of Saint Teresa

The mystery of the Church sets before us the design of divine love, its movement. It yields to us the secret of divine government in the world, the meaning of its action within souls and of its activity externally through events. This dogma must not be simply the object of our contemplation. It is essentially practical and must enter into our spiritual life. It tells us that we have a place to occupy, a mission to fulfill in the mystical body of Christ. To occupy that place, to accomplish that mis-

[39] Eph. 4:16.
[40] Eph. 4:13.
[41] Eph. 1:20-3.

sion, these are inseparable from our perfection. Sanctity can be found only in the completion of the plan of God. Any spirituality that would lead us to sanctity must reveal to us that single design of God which is the Church, must guide us to the place reserved in it for us and have us fulfill in it our appointed mission.

This discovery of the Church is the important event that accompanies union of will. The discovery is as yet obscure like the other discoveries of the fifth Mansions. Only later will it shine out in the light, and with full awareness. We have already given the signs that show that it is profound and certain.

God has wrought the ordering of charity in the soul. Its burning love goes beyond Christ Jesus to find Christ communicated and transfused through His members. This love is restless, because it has not yet grasped distinctly its object. It does not know where to abide, but already it suffers much for Christ and His members. And it is fruitful unknowingly.[42] God has effected the ordering of charity in the soul; that is, He has ordered it to its twofold object, God and souls, toward the sole reality in which they are united: the Church.

It might be asked why God waited so long to grant the experience of this mystery and to instill in the soul the spiritual movement corresponding to it. Wisdom proceeds with might and sweetness, with weight and measure. There was need for the soul to be strengthened in its union with God. Saint Teresa has told us that, during the first period, concern for personal perfection was primary; that the beginner had to orientate himself toward God, to organize his asceticism in terms of that quest for God, in order to ensure its efficacy; and that eagerness for the apostolate might be harmful if it diverted one's gaze from God. Later, she pointed out the danger in which the divine outpourings of the first supernatural prayers place the soul by leading it to spend itself without measure profitably for others, at a time when it cannot renew its strength. These illu-

[42] Cf. descriptions given above.

sions arising from activity itself, from pride, from strength received in the prayer of quiet—Saint Teresa has pointed them all out. Now her invitation to enter into the movement of the love of God, as manifest in the Church, is secure and must be followed.

The life of Saint Teresa adds precious confirmation and example to her teaching. The Saint tells us that during the first years of her religious life she was sometimes elevated to the prayer of union.[43] These favors made her very strong to endure the great sufferings of her sickness and enabled her to exercise a fruitful apostolate, especially with her father and several persons of the world. After a long period of waiting, a period that the Saint calls one of lukewarmness, she again experienced the divine captivation of her soul. Among the lofty favors that she then received—visions and revelations which belong, it is true, to the sixth Mansions—was the transverberation,[44] which conferred on her the grace of spiritual maternity. Soon the effect of that grace was apparent in her institution of the Reform and the foundation of the Convent of Saint Joseph of Avila.

It seems certain that the Saint, in founding this convent, had in mind only to create a solitude that would permit her to live in deep intimacy with Christ Jesus.[45] Then, she adds:

> As time went on, my desires to do something for the good of some soul grew greater and greater, and I often felt like one who has a large amount of treasure in her charge and would like everyone to enjoy it but whose hands are tied so that she cannot distribute it. In just this way it seemed to me that my soul was bound; for the favours which the Lord granted it during those years were very great and they all seemed to be ill spent upon me. But I served the Lord with my poor prayers; and I always persuaded the sisters to do the same and to be zealous for the good of souls and the increase of His Church. Thus all who had to do with them were invariably edified, and in this my great desires found satisfaction.[46]

News of the wars of religion that were working havoc in

[43] *Life,* iv; Peers, I, 23.
[44] *Ibid.*, xxix.
[45] *Ibid.*, xxxii; cf. also: *Way of Perfection,* i; Peers, II.
[46] *Foundations,* i; Peers, III, 3.

France,[47] and the visit of the Franciscan Father, home from the West Indies, who told her about "the many millions of souls perishing there for lack of teaching," [48] increased and made more explicit her desires for the apostolate. She decided to found more convents with an apostolic end in view [49] and to extend her Reform to the Friars, since they especially could work for the salvation of souls.

Thus we see how Saint Teresa progressively discovered the Church, which is the whole Christ. We see how she experienced its unity, the deep and living bonds that unite souls to Christ and one another, by bearing in her own heart the wounds that Christ was receiving in France and by suffering, even to tears, from the moral misery of those millions of souls that were being lost in faraway America. Having thus profoundly entered into the Church, she found there the place and the mission that God, in His eternal plan, had assigned to her and to her Reform.

This twofold discovery is not an intellectual one. It comes, profound and living, from an illumination of love that pervades the whole soul, stirs a movement in its inmost depths, and directs thereafter all its interior and exterior activity.

The newly awakened zeal is no longer—as is sometimes said—a simple overflowing of superabundance that still leaves the soul to itself and its concerns for personal perfection, allowing it to use for others only what strength remains over and above this. Rather, it is a vital movement arising deep within, carrying along the whole soul and committing it entire to the Church and her members. The soul now is not as a vase overflowing, but like a reservoir all of whose flood-gates are open to make fruitful the field of the Church. Actual perfection for that soul lies in the complete gift of itself without any reserve to the Church.

[47] *Way of Perfection,* i; Peers, II, 3.
[48] *Foundations,* i; 3.
[49] *Way of Perfection,* i; 3.

But is there not some danger in thus giving oneself without measure? Yes perhaps in these fifth Mansions, and Saint Teresa warns us of it while nonetheless asserting the necessity of the gift; but soon this loss of self will turn to an enrichment. Indeed even now it is necessary for the perfecting of the soul. In order to merit the purification that is essential for this, the soul must first render great services to God; [50] and it is the exercise of zeal that ordinarily will secure it an important part in that very purification. But let us not anticipate.

Right here, however, may we be permitted to call attention to the stumbling-block in the spirituality of anyone who wants to strive only for purity and perfection of soul, who approaches God only to receive from Him and to become a brilliant satellite of the divine Sun. To that end, such a one withdraws, isolates himself, avoids all contacts whether interior or exterior that might be an obstacle to the realization of that beauty, which he wants unspotted and solely divine. Saint Teresa has told us how indispensable is this attitude during the first period of spiritual life. Moreover, there are vocations and states in which one has not the right to give oneself to external works. But, these reservations made, who can not see the subtle spiritual egoism hidden in a conception of perfection that would forever renounce entering into the mystery of the Church? This egoism would check the movement of love, if it did not kill it altogether. The splendid isolation of such a soul would at best resemble those placid lakes that receive waters from the torrent and hold them. It is to be feared lest, in jealously keeping its waters, it oblige the torrent to deflect its course, and soon find, in the emptiness of its soul, only the memory of its former gifts.

Without any doubt, the soul, in these regions, must give itself. Through union of the will, Christ has become its dwelling place. It will progress spiritually only by letting itself be carried away by the movement of the mind and heart of the Christ who "loved the Church, and delivered himself up for

[50] Saint John of the Cross.

her." [51] For the soul as for Christ, the Church has become the living reality in which and for which it must live and work and die. The union of the soul with Christ is orientated toward a higher union, that of Christ with His Church.

Are we faced here with a general law? Can we say that this practical discovery of the Church, after a period of preparation for the divine captivation, is a requisite of all sanctity? Certainly, there are many ways of discovering and of realizing in practice the dogma of the Church. We cannot call Saint Teresa's experience universal. But if we prescind from the external modes and retain only the general lines, do we not find these over again in the spiritual ascent of the giants of sanctity whom the Holy Spirit, in the first centuries of the Church, led to the summits? The Holy Ghost came upon the apostles, enflamed them with ardors of zeal and gave them to the Church so that, in suffering and labors, they might become perfect apostles and saints. Those who are rightly called Fathers of the Church lived at first for the most part in solitude. There the Spirit seized them to send them again into the world as witnesses and instruments of His grace and, in works performed for His glory, had them achieve both their mission and their holiness.

Such is in fact the order of the divine plan: Wisdom takes on a human nature, she immolates it, she gives it as bread of life: the Incarnation, the Redemption, the Church! This is the divine logic of the mysteries, these are the stages in the divine realizations, the Church being the end for all. We must everywhere find again this logic and this order. Consequently, this it is that must mark the stages of sanctity.

And in the spirituality that Saint Teresa presents to us, union of will, which is a laying hold of it by Holy Wisdom, will be followed by the purifying and redeeming labors of the sixth Mansions, which will precede the transforming union of the seventh Mansions and the perfect gift of self to the Church.

[51] Eph. 5:25.

Holiness In Service of the Church

Here dwells the soul that "has been wounded with love for the Spouse," writes Saint Teresa at the threshold of the sixth Mansions. God has taken this soul aside and has manifested Himself to it. In this intimate and profound contact love has been inflamed. Now is a springtime, full with promise; but it is only springtime. The buds swollen with sap need, if they are to open out and bloom, both the burning heat waves of the sun and the generous showers. The soul is not yet sufficiently transparent to reflect the face of its God; nor its gaze pure enough to discover Him. And must it not also become a perfect instrument of love?

Wisdom sets herself to the task. And nowhere else does she display so wonderfully the workings of God's mercy in the soul. She enriches and impoverishes; she reveals herself so as to set the soul on fire, and she hides herself so as to fan the flames of its desires; she crushes it to make it docile and she wounds it to heal. Thus she purifies, transforms, and tranquilizes the soul.

Poor and trusting, supple and strong, the soul comes to the spiritual betrothal. This is a first state. It will later be elevated to spiritual marriage or transforming union, and will then discover in itself the loftiest marvels that God can bring to pass here below in a mere creature.

In these regions where the divine action is transforming and unifying, Saint Teresa finds herself at home. Here she gladly lingers. A hundred pages, more than half of the *Interior Castle,* are given to the description of the sixth Mansions; thirty-five pages, to the seventh Mansions. In all, more than half the treatise. Let us thank the Saint for this. For here is the veritable domain of Wisdom, the realm where she establishes her reign in the soul and completes her great work of sanctification.

These are regions little frequented, it will be said! Yes, we must admit, the saints are rare. As rare as are the souls that surrender themselves unreservedly to the good pleasure and operations of divine love.

Let us not draw back, however, from studying them. The light that shines on the summits is only the more simple and limpid for being sublime. It puts in sharp focus the end to be attained and sends down shafts from its fires upon the slopes where we are journeying. May it enlarge our desires as well and make strong our trust in God!

CHAPTER I

Divine Enrichments

God is granting you the grace of Himself working within you.[1]

On the high plateau of union of will, "for a long time, even years," [2] the soul has enjoyed the restful ease of advance by stages and delectable feeding in high pastures. With the Psalmist it can say:

> The Lord ruleth me . . .
> He hath set me in a place of pasture.
> He hath brought me up on the water of refreshment:
> He hath converted my soul.[3]

The divine Shepherd is thus preparing it for the hard tasks ahead.

Now, on the confines of the plateau, the abrupt and rugged slopes of the dark night of the spirit tower up. At times their austere shadow already falls athwart the road in those signs, the tokens and heralds, of which Saint John of the Cross speaks.[4] The soul has now arrived at the very ascent. Climb it must. Refusal to do this would be to go no farther, perhaps to lose all.

It is fitting that from the beginning of this period of ascent in the sixth Mansions Saint Teresa should speak of the sufferings met with there; it is perhaps still more fitting that Saint John of the Cross, whose whole purpose in treating of the dark

[1] *Living Flame,* iii; Peers, III, 84.
[2] *Dark Night,* Bk. II, i; Peers, I, 374.
[3] Ps. 22:1-3.
[4] *Dark Night, loc. cit.*

night was to aid souls distressed therein, should at once occupy himself with its anguish and obscurity.

But in our case, since we are desirous only of explaining and offering a commentary on the teaching of our Carmelite masters, we think it best to speak first of the divine enrichments of this period. We do this not because of any fear of discouraging souls, but rather in order to put into relief at once the truth which explains this supremely important stage of the soul's ascent, and sets in real and living perspective all the phenomena that one meets here.

The truth in question is: "God is the agent in this state and the soul is the recipient." [5] Although the night veils in darkness the face of the good Shepherd, He is nevertheless present and is more than ever active. He it is who illumines, purifies, enkindles the soul, and unites it with Himself. The night is so dark and painful only because the Shepherd is leading the soul "on the paths of justice, for his own name's sake." [6]

To confirm this truth of God's predominating action, to indicate its characteristic traits and diverse modes, such will be the object of our preliminary study.

A. Holy Wisdom, artificer of sanctity

In the fourth Mansions, God's action in the soul, being intermittent and attaining only to certain powers, was mixed with many human elements and natural activity. Union of will marked a very appreciable progress. The soul, made captive by God, wrested from its usual surroundings, is now orientated by Him who has seized it toward other regions and other tasks. Union of will, a possessing of the soul by God, is a point of departure, for it allows God to act at His good pleasure.

The divine seal which has been set in the soul carries within it the tidings of God's design; but it will reveal its secret only

[5] *Living Flame,* st. iii; Peers, III, 68.
[6] Ps. 22:3.

in the experiences of the higher states. For the moment, all is obscurity and new ardor. Yet even in the darkness one certitude is clear to the soul: it has been in God. An intense nostalgia for Him who held it captive and for the secret regions to which He led it, still enthralls it. The little butterfly is restless, says Teresa, and does not know where to abide.

> But where will the poor little creature go? It cannot return to the place it came from, for, as has been said, however hard we try, it is not in our power to do that until God is pleased once again to grant us this favour.[7]

Such union is exclusively the work of God. This truth, proclaimed by Saint Teresa on the occasion of the mystical grace of the fifth Mansions, was already contained in the classification of the degrees of prayer as given by her in the book of her *Life.* All the forms of prayer higher than that of quiet and sleep of the powers of the fourth Mansions are symbolized by the abundant rain that marks God's full action in the soul. The Saint writes, speaking of the ways in which the garden can be watered:

> . . . by heavy rain, when the Lord waters it with no labour of ours, a way incomparably better than any of those which have been described.[8]

The descriptions given in the *Interior Castle,* finer in precision and shadings, allow us to see still better the degrees and effects of God's hold on the soul; and, it must be noted, God's sovereign action in these regions is present in each case. Saint Teresa rarely repeats this truth, so much does she take it for granted. For her, these regions are the domain of mystical theology or of the secret wisdom of God. They are the divine workshops where our life is hid "in Christ, or in God for that is the same thing." [9] And so the Saint's sole preoccupation here is to expose the counterfeits that sickness, bad faith, or the devil can produce.

[7] V Mansions, ii; Peers, II, 256.
[8] *Life,* xi; Peers, I, 65.
[9] V Mansions, ii; Peers, II, 254.

More explicit is the testimony of Saint John of the Cross. At every step of the ascent, the holy doctor returns to the preponderent and essential part taken by God's action within. Here for instance is a definition of the dark night:

> This dark night is an inflowing of God into the soul, which purges it from its ignorances. . . . Herein God secretly teaches the soul and instructs it in perfection of love, without its doing anything, or understanding of what manner is this infused contemplation. Inasmuch as it is the loving wisdom of God, God produces striking effects in the soul, for, by purging and illumining it, He prepares it for the union of love with God. Therefore the same loving wisdom that purges the blessed spirits and enlightens them is that which here purges the soul and illumines it.[10]

During prolonged silence of the faculties and dryness, "It is God who is working here in the soul." [11]

In the *Living Flame,* that serene and peaceful treatise on the highest states of the spiritual life, the Saint refers back several times to the rugged ascent that preceded them, to reiterate emphatically the same truth:

> First, it must be known that, if a soul is seeking God, its Beloved is seeking it much more.[12]

And again, all this is to prepare the soul for union not only by painful purifications but also by anointings that enrich it:

> And thus the soul must understand that the desire of God in all the favours that He bestows upon it in the unction and fragrance of His ointments is to prepare it for other choicer and more delicate ointments which are more after the temper of God, until it reaches such a delicate and pure state of preparation that it merits union with God and substantial transformation in all its faculties.[13]

In order that the soul may set no obstacle, it is important for it to know that:

> God is the principal agent in this matter, and the guide of its blind self, Who will take it by the hand and lead it where it could not of

[10] *Dark Night,* Bk. II, v; Peers, I, 381.
[11] *Ibid.,* viii; 393.
[12] *Ibid.,* iii; 66.
[13] *Living Flame,* st. iii; Peers, III, 67.

itself go, namely, to the supernatural things which neither its understanding nor its will nor its memory could know as they are.[14]

With still more vigor the Saint recalls this truth to directors bent on applying their own ideas and methods:

Let such as these take heed and remember that the Holy Spirit is the principal agent and mover of souls and never loses His care for them; and that they themselves are not agents, but only instruments.[15]

The preparations ended, God's action goes on increasing and deepening. God makes haste to captivate for Himself the purified soul.

As the sun, when it rises in the morning and shines into your house, will enter if you open the shutter, even so will God, Who keeps Israel [16] and slumbers not, still less sleeps, enter the soul that is empty and will fill it with blessings.[17]

Divine inflowings, wounds from "this flame, which is the Holy Spirit," [18] spiritual espousals, all "the playings of eternal Wisdom," [19] bring the soul to perfect union.

The playings of divine Wisdom continue in the substance of the soul where the Holy Spirit is celebrating the feast of love,[20] and where the Word reposes as it were asleep, arousing Himself at times in marvelous awakenings [21] to disclose to the soul its sublime riches—the delectable burn of the Holy Spirit, the delicate touch of the Word, and the loving hand of the Father.[22] God's action in these lofty spiritual regions is direct, although ordinarily it observes an hierarchical order, as does every providential action. John of the Cross explains:

The very wisdom of God which purges these souls and illumines them purges the angels from their ignorances, giving them knowledge,

[14] *Ibid.*
[15] *Ibid.;* 74.
[16] Ps. 120:4.
[17] *Living Flame,* st. iii; 75.
[18] *Ibid.,* st. i; 114.
[19] *Ibid.;* 21.
[20] *Ibid.*
[21] *Ibid.,* st. iv; 187 f.
[22] *Ibid.,* st. ii; 36.

enlightening them as to that which they knew not, and flowing down from God through the first hierarchies even to the last, and thence to men. All the works, therefore, which are done by the angels, and all their inspirations, are said in the Scriptures, with truth and propriety, to be the work of God and of themselves; for ordinarily these inspirations come through the angels, and they receive them likewise one from another without any delay—as quickly as a ray of sunshine is communicated through many windows arranged in order. For although it is true that the sun's ray itself passes through them all, still each one passes it on and infuses it into the next, in a modified form, according to the nature of the glass, and with rather more or rather less power and brightness, according as it is nearer to the sun or farther from it. . . .

Hence it follows that man, who is the lowest of all those to whom this loving contemplation flows down continually from God, will, when God desires to give it to him, receive it perforce after his own manner in a very limited way and with great pain.[23]

Many extraordinary favors such as visions and even that grace of spiritual fatherhood which ensures the first fruits of the Spirit and provides for their transmission are the work of angels.[24]

The highest favors, however, such as the delectable wound of which the second stanza of the *Living Flame* speaks, are touches

. . . of the Divinity in the soul, without any form or figure whether formal or imaginary.[25]

But whether supernatural communications come to the soul directly by an immediate touch of God or by the instrumental causality of angels, they are the work of Holy Wisdom in the sense that we have indicated, namely, that they exclude human causality; they are the result of God's own initiative in the soul and of His special benevolence toward it.

Besides, the soul which, ordinarily, is not aware of the presence of an intermediary even when there is one (to discover it there is needed the penetration of a Saint John of the Cross or

[23] *Dark Night,* Bk. II, xii; Peers, I, 410-1.
[24] *Living Flame,* st. ii; Peers, III, 40.
[25] *Ibid.;* 39.

a Saint Teresa), is conscious of this particular act of God's benevolence. It feels itself to be the object of a divine seizure which is itself preceded by a divine choice. In the very first page of her *Autobiography,* Saint Therese of the Child Jesus expresses with her delightful simplicity this clear consciousness of the divine choice that explains everything:

> Opening the Gospels, my eyes fell on these words: "*Jesus, going up into a mountain, called unto Him whom He would Himself.*" [26]
> They threw a clear light upon the mystery of my vocation and of my entire life, and above all upon the favours which our Lord has granted to my soul. He does not call those who are worthy, but those whom He will. As St. Paul says: "*God will have mercy on whom He will have mercy.*[27] *So then it is not of him that willeth, nor of him that runneth, but of God that showeth mercy.*[28] [29]

The efficacy of the divine choice is revealed to the soul much more by the marvelous series of graces it has received than by any single favor. Saint Therese writes, addressing herself to God:

> Thy love has gone before me, even from the days of my childhood. It has grown with my growth, and now it is an abyss whose depths I cannot fathom.[30]

The testimony of the little Saint recalls that of the apostle: "By the grace of God I am what I am." [31]

All those saints who have reached to the highest degrees of sanctity are at one in their canticle of gratitude, giving thanks to God for what they have received from Him, their very sanctity.

This consciousness that is then imparted to them and the conviction that it creates, seem to be the most striking testimony to God's sovereign action in the work of sanctification,

[26] Mark 3:13.
[27] Exod. 33:19.
[28] Rom. 9:16.
[29] *Autobiography,* i, 15.
[30] *Ibid.,* xi, 174.
[31] I Cor. 15:10.

especially in these last stages of the spiritual life where loving Wisdom reveals herself by direct interventions.

B. Marks of the divine action

Before studying in detail God's action in the last stage of the spiritual journey, let us pause here to consider what characterizes it, so as to form of it a general idea.

In these regions Wisdom infuses love into the soul, the depths of which indicate its quality. It is a love that purifies the soul while uniting it with God. It is a love that enlightens and progressively reveals an interior divine presence, making of the soul a divine instrument.

1. WISDOM INFUSES LOVE

Union of will was already the fruit of a special inflowing of love; and Saint Teresa notes that the sixth Mansions are the dwelling place of a soul wounded by love.[32] All the favors described later by the Saint have as their principal effect the development of a love that the soul receives passively. Speaking of its delicate and subtle impulsions, she wonders if "God could be described as the fire in a lighted brazier, from which some spark will fly out and touch the soul, in such a way that it will be able to feel the burning heat of the fire." [33] The raptures He bestows seem "to be causing the spark of which we have already spoken to grow within it, so that, like the phoenix, it catches fire and springs into new life." [34] And again the Saint writes: "Indeed, her love is so full of tenderness that any occasion whatever which serves to increase the strength of this fire causes the soul to take flight; and thus in this Mansion raptures occur continually." [35] By turns, trials which are destined

[32] VI Mansions, i; Peers, II.
[33] *Ibid.,* ii; 277.
[34] *Ibid.,* iv; 287.
[35] *Ibid.,* vi; 297.

to set the will "on desiring to have ever-increasing fruition of its Spouse," [36] and visions which reveal His presence, intensify the ardors of love until finally those almost intolerable sufferings begin,[37] which are the prelude to perfect union.

Saint John of the Cross, who previously put emphasis on the effects of the divine light, now speaks practically the same language as Saint Teresa. It is a soul wounded by love that he too presents to us at the beginning of the *Spiritual Canticle* and in the *Living Flame of Love*. The inflowings of divine love, received passively in contemplation, constitute the dark night of the spirit, which he so magnificently terms "the dark night of loving fire." [38] It is the same flame, that is, the Holy Spirit, who, against the day when He will glorify it, now penetrates the substance of the soul in order to purify.[39] These assaults of love in the soul can be compared to a material fire that attacks a log of wood, envelops it, penetrates its substance, and transforms it into fire.[40]

This comparison translates very well the experience of the flames of love that Saint Therese of the Child Jesus had after her act of oblation to Merciful Love. In a few words she expresses it:

> From that day I have been penetrated and surrounded with love. Every moment this Merciful Love renews me and purifies me, leaving in my soul no trace of sin.[41]

God's entire action is an infusion of love. Love it is that conquers the soul, passive under love's assailing.

The word love conveys the whole experience of the soul in its intimate contacts with the sovereign Good communicating Himself. It is this same word which, in all times, has summed up the experience of those who have come nearest to God,

[36] *Ibid.*, iv; 286.
[37] *Ibid.*, xi; 324 ff.
[38] *Dark Night,* Bk. II, xi; Peers, I, 410.
[39] *Living Flame,* st. 1; Peers, III, 25.
[40] *Ibid.* Cf. also *Dark Night,* Bk. II, x; 403 f., where the comparison is more fully developed.
[41] *Autobiography,* viii, 133.

those who have felt the burning dynamism of the Infinite Being stooping down to human misery to communicate to it His all-consuming life and to draw it after Him in the movement of His charity: "God is a consuming fire," [42] "God is love," [43] has been said by Moses, Saint John, Saint Paul.

2. LOVE IS CHARACTERIZED BY THE DEPTHS AT WHICH IT OPERATES

The comparison of the fire assailing the wood suggests, although imperfectly, a progressive penetration of the soul by the fire of love. This must be explained, for depth here signifies quality.

In the mystical union of the fifth Mansions, the divine encounter takes place in "the center of the soul": [44]

> God implants Himself in the interior of that soul in such a way that, when it returns to itself, it cannot possibly doubt that God has been in it and it has been in God.[45]

The deep regions that are discovered in the fifth Mansions are going to open up progressively both to the action of Holy Wisdom and to the gaze of the soul. Hence the Saint, in describing these Mansions, writes:

> Although the experiences of this Mansion and of the next are almost identical, their effects come to have much greater power.[46]

And in the course of the description of the sixth Mansions, she says parenthetically:

> I mean in these two Mansions, for this and the last might be fused in one: there is no closed door to separate the one from the other.[47]

Already in the book of her *Life,* when she had less experi-

[42] Exod. 3:2-6; Deut. 4:24; Heb. 12:29.
[43] I John 4:16.
[44] V Mansions i; Peers, II, 252.
[45] *Ibid.;* 251.
[46] *Ibid.,* ii; 255.
[47] VI Mansions, iv; 287.

ence in the spiritual life it is true, she had grouped the different kinds of prayer of the last three Mansions under the general heading of prayer of union.

Certainly, profound differences justify the division into separate mansions.[48] But the Saint wants to emphasize—and it is important for us at this point—that in the graces characteristic of the fifth Mansions, and more and more habitually so in the following ones, God's action is localized in the inmost depths, namely, in the center of the soul, which is the very dwelling place of God.[49]

Nor does Saint John of the Cross situate elsewhere the workings of love during this period. The contemplative wisdom that the soul is receiving is "the language of God to the soul, addressed by pure spirit to pure spirit; naught that is less than spirit, such as the senses, can perceive it." [50]

In the *Living Flame* the localization is still more precise. The Saint points out that not only the wounds of love that immediately precede union, and the touches of the Word that follow it,[51] but also the subtle and delicate anointings that purify, "penetrate the inmost substance of the depth of the soul." [52]

[48] VII Mansions, i; 329 ff., where are given the differences between simple mystical union and the union of spiritual marriage.
[49] VII Mansions, ii; 334.
[50] *Dark Night,* Bk. II, xvii; Peers, I, 430.
[51] *Living Flame,* st. i;; Peers, III, 42 f.
[52] *Ibid.,* st. iii; 85.

This would be the time to study with the theologians whether this action of God, or infusion of love in the depths of the soul and in its very substance, takes place through the gifts of the Holy Spirit or directly without their mediation.

Such a study would draw us away from the line that our exclusively practical end imposes upon us. We think it permissible, however, to remark that if we consider the gifts of the Holy Spirit not only in their specific diversity (which orientates each one of them to a particular gift of God) but in their essential and common reality, which is the passivity or obediential potency of charity, we do not see why the gifts of the Holy Spirit would not suffice to receive this action of God in the substance of the soul. It would most of all be important then, as we see, that theology apply itself to clarifying the intimate nature of the gifts in order to solve these problems, rather than directing itself to the easier theme of the properties of each separate gift.

These localizations, familiar to all mystics, are not pure symbols created by the imagination. They are the fruit of a very clear experience. Saint Teresa feels herself carried away from the external world by mystical grace and introduced into her own depths; by a flight of the spirit she is drawn into God. And in the grace of spiritual marriage she is brought into the presence of God dwelling in the center of her soul.

Saint John of the Cross seems to have a still sharper sense of the depths of his own soul. After establishing the distinction between the region of the senses or "noisy outskirts," and that of the spirit, a hiding-place secure against all enemies, "a most profound and vast retreat . . . and immense desert, which nowhere has any boundary," [53] he seems constantly preoccupied both for himself and for others, to discover new depths in the soul. His whole spiritual technique lies in a ceaseless outreaching into one's deepest center to find God more and more.

Saint John of the Cross understood that love's depth is equivalent to its quality and strength. He alone can best explain this:

> In the first place, it must be known that the soul, inasmuch as it is spirit, has not height and depth, nor greater or lesser degrees of profundity in its own being, as have bodies that can be measured. For since there are no parts in the soul, there is no difference between its inward and its outward being; it is all the same.[54]

[53] *Dark Night,* Bk. II, xvii; Peers, I, 430-1.

[54] *Living Flame,* st. 1; Peers, III, 22.

This statement as to the simplicity of the soul seems to render the localizations of which we have spoken illusory as well as the mystical experience on which they rest. However, it is nothing of the kind.

Let us first of all note that the simplicity of the soul does not preclude the distinction of the powers from one another and from the essence of the soul. And in the substance itself Saint Teresa discerns a certain difference between soul and spirit, similar to that between the flame and the fire. God's action can then, reasonably, be experienced in a distinct way in each of the faculties or in the substance of the soul.

But it is especially important to note that experience bears more on the dynamism of love than on its field of action. Now this love, infused by God in the substance of the soul, conquers it and progressively penetrates it in the manner of an oil that progressively soaks into and saturates a hard material. It is this conquering advance of love to which experience attains and which it cognizes as a movement. When the soul has received the measure of love for which it is made, or, in other words, when one's love has developed

In ordinary language, however:

> We term the deepest centre of a thing the farthest point to which its being and virtue and the force of its operation and movement can attain, and beyond which they cannot pass.[55]

These preliminaries stated, the Saint continues:

> The centre of the soul is God; and, when the soul has attained to Him according to the whole capacity of its being, and according to the force of its operation, it will have reached the last and the deep centre of the soul, which will be when with all its powers it loves and understands and enjoys God.[56]

This force of interiorization, this weight that draws the soul toward its innermost center is no other thing than love. *Amor, pondus meum,* love is a weight, according to Saint Augustine. We must observe, as Saint John of the Cross explains, that love is an inclination of the soul, a power or a faculty that it has for going to God:

> Love unites the soul with God, and, the more degrees of love the soul has, the more profoundly does it enter into God and the more is it centred in Him; and thus we can say that, as are the degrees of love of God, so are the centres, each one deeper than another, which the soul has in God; these are the many mansions which, He said, were in His Father's house.[57] And thus the soul which has one degree of love is already in its centre in God, since one degree of love suffices for a soul to abide in Him through grace. If it have two degrees of love, it will have entered into another and a more interior centre with God; and, if it attain to three, it will have entered into the third.[58]

Sense and spirit constitute, then, only a first measure or stage in profundity. When the spirit is attained, love, perfecting it-

---

its whole strength by conquering the soul and its faculties according to the perfection that God has fixed for it, this love has attained to the most profound center of the soul and has realized the union of which it is capable. As we see, the substance of the soul is nonetheless simple; but there is a progress made by the conquering action of love, and it is this progress that is experienced as a deepening.

These explanations seem to agree with what Saint John of the Cross then says about the strength of love's penetration.

[55] *Ibid.*

[56] *Ibid.*

[57] John 14:2.

[58] *Living Flame,* st. i; Peers, III, 23.

self, enters more and more deeply into the substance of the soul, to successive depths which are the sign of its quality.

This language is in accord with the Teresian symbolism of the *Interior Castle,* where the development of love and of union with God is indicated by progression through mansions that are more and more interior until the seventh is reached, in which transforming union takes place.

Thus interiorization and depth have to do with the quality and the strength of love. Hence the Saint adds:

> And thus, when the soul says that the flame wounds it in its deepest centre, it means that it wounds it in the farthest point attained by its own substance and virtue and power.[59]

3. LOVE IS PURIFYING AND UNIFYING

We mention this property of love here only as a reminder. It has been mentioned before; and it must yet have longer consideration, for it marks the essential work of love in these regions to such an extent that the sixth Mansions are synonymous with profound purification and progress toward the perfection of union.

4. LOVE IS THE SOURCE OF LIGHT

After stating that the graces of the last three Mansions are all alike in the depths of the center of the soul, Saint Teresa notes as the principal difference between the grace of mystical union of the fifth Mansions and the transforming union of the seventh, the fact that the first is received in complete obscurity:

> The Lord unites it [the soul] with Himself, but He makes it blind and dumb, as He made Saint Paul at his conversion, and so prevents it from having any sense of how or in what way that favour comes which it is enjoying; the great delight of which the soul is then conscious is the realization of its nearness to God. But when He unites it with Him, it understands nothing; the faculties are all lost.
>
> But in this Mansion [transforming union] everything is different. Our good God now desires to remove the scales from the eyes of the

[59] *Ibid.*

soul, so that it may see and understand something of the favour which He is granting it.[60]

Already, light distinguished the preceding favors, those of the sixth Mansions. The Saint, describing them, says:

> The soul has never before been so fully awake to the things of God or had such light or such knowledge of His Majesty.[61]

These lights are "certain mysteries, such as heavenly things and imaginary visions," interior words that the soul can afterwards describe.[62]

They form an integral part of raptures, so that the Saint declares:

> My own belief is that, if the soul to whom God has given these secrets in its raptures never understands any of them, they proceed, not from raptures at all, but from some natural weakness.[63]

These extraordinary favors described by Saint Teresa place in marked relief the special quality of the Mansion in which they take place. They provide, then, precious indications—easily verifiable—for determining the stage in which a soul is.

At the beginning of the spiritual life, love drew its sustenance from a distinct knowledge of the truths of faith, developed according to the usual psychological laws. Then when love sprang directly from the depths of the soul, whether in delightful outpourings or in peaceful dryness, the understanding became powerless. The resulting darkness became deeper at the beginning of the sixth Mansions: here it is fully the dark night of the purification of the spirit. But besides the fact that the nights are at times streaked with lightnings that rend the dark veil, and that the soul is constantly illumined by infused contemplation, receiving light as to itself and the transcendence of God so that

[60] VII Mansions, i; Peers, II, 331.
[61] VI Mansions, iv; 287.
[62] *Ibid.;* 288.
[63] *Ibid.;* 290.

. . . "it learns how base and defective, and, in some measure, how inapt, are all the terms and words which are used in this life to treat of Divine things,"[64]

behold there appears in these sixth Mansions the first rays of dawn. Saint John of the Cross writes:

For, even as the rising of the morning dispels the darkness of the night and reveals the light of the day, even so this spirit that is tranquil and quiet in God is raised from the darkness of natural knowledge to the morning light of the supernatural knowledge of God—not brightly, but, as we say, darkly, like the night at the time of the rising of the dawn; for, even as the night at the time of such rising is neither wholly night nor wholly day, but, as men say, "between two nights," so this Divine tranquillity and solitude . . .[65]

This coming of the dawn is produced by the light that springs from love. John of the Cross explains that supernatural truths are inscribed in our soul in two ways: in the understanding by means of faith and in the will through love. He writes:

She [the soul] says that she bears these truths outlined in her inmost parts—that is to say, in her soul, according to the understanding and the will; for according to the understanding she has these truths infused into her soul by faith. And, because her knowledge of them is not perfect, she says that they are outlined; for, even as an outline is not a perfect painting, so the knowledge of faith is not perfect knowledge. . . .

But besides this outline of faith there is another outline in the soul of the lover, which is of love, and this is according to the will; . . . it is true to say that the Beloved lives in the lover and the lover in the Beloved; and such manner of likeness does love make in the transformation of the two that are in love that it may be said that each is the other and that both are one. The reason for this is that in the union and transformation of love the one gives possession of itself to the other, and each one gives and abandons itself to the other and exchanges itself for the other. Thus each lives in the other, and the one is the other, and both are one through the transformation of love.[66]

The exact terminology of theology clarifies this testimony of Saint John of the Cross. The understanding, enlightened by

[64] *Dark Night,* Bk. II, xvii; Peers, I, 431.
[65] *Spiritual Canticle,* st. xiii-xiv; Peers, II, 83.
[66] *Ibid.,* xi; 65.

faith, can draw from supernatural truths only the knowledge of which it is capable, that is, analogical or conceptual knowledge expressed in dogmatic formulas—an outline that can go on being perfected here below.

But now love begins to operate. It transforms the soul, uniting it to God in a mutual compenetration and resemblance that become every day more perfect. From this compenetration there issues, thanks to the gift of wisdom, an affective experience and fruitive knowledge. Charity, a participation in the life of God, has divinized the soul, causing it to pass into God as a drop of water into the ocean and giving it what is called knowledge by connaturality.[67]

This affective knowledge by connaturality, which proceeds from the outline traced in the will by love, becomes clear enough in the sixth Mansions, to be compared to the rising of the dawn. Ordinarily it will go on developing with progressive inflowings of lôve. Illumined at times by sudden flashes, by "the whisper of the amorous breezes,"—a communication and very high knowledge of God that comes from substantial touches [68]—it is as a rule "general and obscure," [69] subtle and hidden, given to the soul as a "substance of understanding, stripped of accidents and imaginary forms." [70] Yet it is, like the love that engenders it, real and living. And because it proceeds from contact with the depths of God, and stammers the intimate secrets that it has experienced, it corrects the essential imperfection of the simple knowledge of faith, which is bound up with the weakness of our poor human means of knowing. Concludes Saint John of the Cross, speaking of this transformation of love:

> Everything may be called an outline of love by comparison with that perfect image of transformation in glory. But when this outline

[67] For this knowledge by connaturality, cf. the article by J. Maritain in *Etudes Carmélitaines,* Oct. 1938, "L'expérience mystique naturelle et le vide," pp. 116-123.

[68] *Spiritual Canticle,* st. xiii-xiv; Peers, II, 78 ff.

[69] *Living Flame, st.* iii; Peers, III.

[70] *Spiritual Canticle,* ibid.; 79.

of transformation is attained in this life, it is a great and good happiness, because the Beloved is greatly pleased with it.[71]

5. LOVE REALIZES THE DIVINE PRESENCE

Incontestably, the most precious lights cast by the science of love have reference to the divine presence in the soul.

Already in the fourth Mansions, the peace of passive recollection, the floods of quietude which overflow into the will or all the faculties, as in the sleep of the powers, revealed to the soul the presence within it of a fountain that is living and deep.

Yet the fountain itself was a very long way off as is the glacier from him who slakes his thirst in the torrent flowing from it. Perhaps, even, the soul delighted too much in this savor of eternity; and, drowned as it were in that overflowing plenitude that filled its faculties and desires, it believed itself to have attained the summit of mystical experience. Perhaps it was not sufficiently free of those beneficent floods to direct its gaze toward the living fountains whence they came. The savor, more subtle and austere, of contemplative dryness, can produce the same effects of enveloping blindness and limit to its gifts the aspirations of the soul. These delectable riches are nevertheless only the gifts of God. They are very little in comparison with that contact with God Himself which is had in the higher Mansions. The mystical grace of union of the fifth Mansions is a first interview with God which gives Saint Teresa certitude of God's presence in the soul.[72] The favors of the sixth Mansions, the Beloved's calling to the soul, His visits and absences, these enlarge the wound of love made by the first contact. Thus the soul journeys on to the meeting for the divine espousals in which promises are exchanged, and finally to spiritual marriage, which consecrates the mutual possession of the soul and God in an intellectual vision of the Beloved.

In this series of extraordinary favors described by Saint Teresa, the essential grace of this period and its progressive

[71] *Ibid.*, st. xi; 66.
[72] V Mansions, iv; Peers, II, 286 f.

development shine out clear. For all souls whatsoever, "the entire night of the spirit is but the painful journeying toward that experimental knowledge of the divine object." [73]

A painful journeying, for the divine presence manifested to the soul is not sufficiently clear to it, and often enough is veiled with dense clouds. But the soul longs for no other than the Beloved Himself:

> From today do thou send me no other messenger,
> For they cannot tell me what I wish. . . .

> The more the soul knows of God, the more grows her desire to see Him; and when she sees that there is naught that can cure her pain save the sight and the presence of her Beloved, she mistrusts any other remedy.[74]

The yearning for God Himself, beyond all His gifts, His lights and His raptures, forms the dynamism of this period. The progressive realization of His presence within is one of its characteristic traits.

Addressing itself to God, the soul asks that He reveal to it His presence:

> O crystalline fount,
> If on that thy silvered surface
> Thou wouldst of a sudden form the eyes desired
> Which I bear outlined in my inmost parts! [75]

The twofold outline formed by faith and by love that the soul bears within reveals to it first of all God Himself. That formed by love is the less imperfect. Moreover this is the one that surges from the living and immediate contacts characteristic of this period. Toward it the soul turns in order to realize the divine presence for which it has so strong a desire.

It is indeed a matter of realizing, in the modern sense of the word, the divine presence, by enriching it with intimate and

[73] Cf. the article by P. Lucien de Saint Joseph, "*A la recherche d'une structure,*" in *Etudes Carmélitaines,* October 1938, p. 269.
[74] *Spiritual Canticle,* st. vi; Peers, II, 50.
[75] *Ibid.,* st. xi; 63.

deep relations and with direct and living contacts.[76] God does not change. He is uniformly present everywhere. In God there is no question of more and less. What changes is our relations with Him, namely, the love that He diffuses and that which we in turn give Him. These exchanges of love produce knowledge by connaturality, by transforming us and uniting us to God; they create the divine presence within the soul and make us realize it.

Out from the darkness of love there comes the divine presence. And it is in the inmost depths, where love is exchanged and forms a likeness, that the soul takes on the traits of the Beloved. This presence, independent of any vision or extraordinary perception, the first and essential fruit of knowledge by connaturality, is hidden but living, like the loving embrace that produces it. It becomes continual when love has rendered the soul transparent and has sealed the bonds of union.

The realizing of this presence admits of certain stages that we shall have to indicate. For the moment let us gather together a few testimonies as to how living and deep it is in the shadows that envelop it.

Saint John of the Cross speaks to us of the Word reposing asleep "in the center and depth of his soul, which is its pure and inmost substance," and moving at times in sweet and tender awakenings.[77]

Saint Therese of the Child Jesus said to Mother Agnes of Jesus:

> I do not well see what more I shall have in heaven than now. I shall see the good God, it is true; but as for being with Him I already entirely am on earth.[78]

And in order to indicate the obscurity of this living presence that no extraordinary grace reveals, she wrote to her aunt to

[76] It is in this sense of the realization of the divine presence through faith and especially through love that Saint Paul wishes for the Ephesians that God may make them realize the indwelling of Christ in their soul: "That Christ may dwell by faith in your hearts." Eph. 3:17.

[77] *Living Flame,* st. iv; Peers, III, 94.

[78] Process of Beatification, Sum., n. 629.

explain a picture she had painted, "The Dream of the Child Jesus":

> I painted the divine Child to show what He is in regard to me. . . . In plain fact He is almost always asleep. . . . Poor Therese's Jesus does not caress her as once He caressed His saintly Mother.[79]

This realization of the divine presence is not limited to the Godhead; it makes the soul aware of each one of the three divine Persons,[80] in a more or less distinct way according to the soul's grace—of Christ Jesus especially, to whom divine charity likens us as to the Son of God and in whom it incorporates us as members of His Church. Perhaps even it reveals to us the presence of Mary whose role as mother could not remain inactive in this spiritual generation that is taking place within us.[81]

6. LOVE FORMS THE PERFECT APOSTLE

Love establishes itself in the will before enlightening the intellect; it lays hold on the soul, transforms it, and unites it to God, before opening up into knowledge by connaturality. And so it surrenders the soul to God as an instrument of His designs even before, or rather at the same time as, it makes of the soul a contemplative discovering the Divine.

United to God and transformed in Him, the soul can no longer separate itself from Him; it accompanies Him everywhere that His merciful love draws it. With Christ, it turns

[79] Letter to Sister Marie Aloysia Vallée, Visitation Nun at Le Mans, April 3, 1894; *Collected Letters,* p. 222-3.

[80] Certain visions of Saint Teresa of Avila, the symbolism of which is usually so close to the reality, clarify very well this penetrating presence of love that must be realized. The Saint one day saw that the three Divine Persons were reproduced distinctly within her soul (*Relations,* ix), that their image was imprinted in her soul (*Ibid.,* xxxix). Finally one day, speaking of her soul she says: "In the centre of it was a picture of Christ Our Lord as I generally see Him. I seemed to see Him in every part of my soul as clearly as in a mirror, and this mirror—I cannot explain how—was wholly sculptured in the same Lord by a most loving communication which I shall never be able to describe (*Life;* xl; Peers, I, 292).

[81] Cf. P. Marie-Eugène, O.C.D., *La Vie Mariale au Carmel,* "Les Frères de Notre-Dame," pp. 28-35.

back to the world and finds in the Church the fullness of its object: God and neighbor. Active and fruitful, charity cannot but share in the works and immolation of Christ for His Church.

And so in this last spiritual stage, the same inflowings of love which unite the soul to God and cause it to realize His presence form the perfect apostle, who is an instrument of God. This formation may carry with it charismatic graces, such as the assault made by the seraph, "which will pierce the soul, now enkindled like a coal," making it like a vast fire of love, for God bestows upon a person spiritual wealth and strength according to the greater or lesser number of the descendants who are to inherit his doctrine and spirituality.[82] Such a formation always presupposes a divine captivation of the depths of the soul; it involves luminous discoveries of the whole Christ, ardent desire to serve and increase His mystical body, a purification of the operative faculties of the soul and of its exterior works also in the measure required by the particular mission of the soul thus favored.

To speak truly, there is very little in the writings of Saint Teresa and especially in those of Saint John of the Cross regarding the formation of the apostle. Rather are both Saints concerned with insisting on the contemplative virtualities of charity. They did not discover such formation in their own interior experience. Love's power for action is not a conscious psychological experience, as is the realization of God's presence in the soul; external deeds alone reveal it. Thus it is to their life and to the mission accomplished by our spiritual masters that we must turn to supply for the silence of their writings. These will show how it is love that makes perfect apostles, for it alone can form worthy instruments of God, and how its flame alone makes apostolic activity fruitful.

[82] *Living Flame,* st. ii; Peers, III, 130-1.

C. The divine ways of acting

How, or rather under what exterior forms, does God infuse this special love the high virtualities of which manifest themselves in luminous contemplation and a fruitful apostolate? Is there an answer to this question? And is it worth-while?

True, we are now in a domain where Wisdom reigns sovereignly, deploying an almost infinite variety of resources. It is a region without beaten tracks. It is therefore vain to seek them. It might even be dangerous to pretend to find one.

And yet, provided we refrain from any *a priori* systematization and even from any rigorous generalizing, we can profitably study God's ways of acting, to be discerned in the lives of the saints. Their diversity reveals to us the astonishing resources of divine Wisdom and at the same time lets us glimpse an admirable unity in God's action. In exploring them, one learns a few laws of God's action in souls, and especially the suppleness it demands of all those who are willing to submit to it lovingly.

In Carmel, three Saints, who passed through all the stages of the interior life, have opened up their souls to us in their writings, presenting themselves to us for our questioning. Three saints, three different souls, perhaps three ways. But certainly, the same school, and a single holiness.[83]

1. SAINT TERESA OF AVILA

First there is Saint Teresa, who reveals to us the manner of divine action in souls of which she had experience. Hers was a profound, overflowing interior life. Such was her penetration

[83] Systematization is all the more easy and more dangerous in that the experience of these lofty regions is less frequent. For lack of verification from personal experience one cannot distinguish in the teaching of the saints what is personal from what is essential, and one universalizes it confusedly even in its least details. Thus it has been thought that the stages and the extraordinary favors of Saint Teresa should be found in all the saints. A Saint Therese of the Child Jesus will enable us, we hope, to avoid this pitfall or at least will facilitate a few precious and perhaps sufficient distinctions.

and discernment of the human and divine that her descriptions of the sixth and seventh Mansions are pages comparable to none for the divine spirit that breathes through them and the subtlety of human psychology they manifest.[84] The Saint writes:

> Let us now begin to treat of the way in which the Spouse deals with it [the soul], and see how, before it is wholly one with Him, He fills it with fervent desire.[85]

Such is the divine tactic in the sixth Mansions: to cause desire to grow in order to increase love and obtain from the soul a more active and intense preparation for perfect union.

These desires God fans into flame by His callings to the soul, in which He makes Himself felt; or by visits so sudden and so fleeting as hardly to be recognized. The painful and delightful wound made by the first encounter has enlarged. The flame of love leaps forth in greater ardor, and the desires for possessing God become keen and living. God uses means, says Saint Teresa,

> . . . so delicate that the soul itself does not understand them, nor do I think I shall succeed in describing them in such a way as to be understood, except by those who have experienced it; for these are influences so delicate and subtle that they proceed from the very depth of the heart and I know no comparison that I can make which will fit the case. . . .
>
> Often when a person is quite unprepared for such a thing, and is not even thinking of God, he is awakened by His Majesty, as though by a rushing comet or a thunderclap. Although no sound is heard, the soul is very well aware that it has been called by God. . . . It is conscious of having been most delectably wounded, but cannot say how or by whom; but it is certain that this is a precious experience and it would be glad if it were never to be healed of that wound. . . . This is a great grief, though a sweet and delectable one.[86]

[84] In the book of her *Life* (ch. xviii-xxxii and ch. xxxvii-xl), the Saint has already given descriptions of almost all the graces of the sixth Mansions; these are precious because they contain details that one does not find elsewhere. Yet in the *Interior Castle,* which the Saint writes when she has arrived at spiritual marriage, she dominated her subject more perfectly. The description is more sober although always vital; many too warm impressions have fallen away and the vibrations of her soul are more peaceful and more profound; characteristic details are placed in relief, and everything is put in a perspective that the Saint thereafter discovers completely.

[85] VI Mansions, ii; Peers, II, 275.

[86] *Ibid.;* 275-6.

And then, as frequently happens, the Saint very happily makes her point just when she insists on her inability to explain. She writes:

> The Beloved is making it very clear that He is with the soul and seems to be giving it such a clear sign that He is calling it that it cannot doubt the fact, and that call is so penetrating that it cannot fail to hear Him. . . .
>
> I have just been wondering if my God could be described as the fire in a lighted brazier, from which some spark will fly out and touch the soul, in such a way that it will be able to feel the burning heat of the fire; but, as the fire is not hot enough to burn it up, and the experience is very delectable, the soul continues to feel that pain and the mere touch suffices to produce that effect in it. This seems the best comparison that I have been able to find.[87]

The following favor strongly resembles the one just mentioned:

> Quite unexpectedly, when engaged in vocal prayer and not thinking of interior things, it seems, in some wonderful way, to catch fire. It is just as though there suddenly assailed it a fragrance so powerful that it diffused itself through all the senses or something of that kind (I do not say it is a fragrance; I merely make the comparison) in order to convey to it the consciousness that the Spouse is there. . . . The source of this favour is that already referred to.[88]

These favors lift up the whole soul toward the divine presence that it bears within. Besides these, Saint Teresa writes:

> There is another way in which God awakens the soul, and which, although in some respects it seems a greater favour than the others, may also be more perilous. . . . This awakening of the soul is effected by means of locutions, which are of many kinds.[89]

Because of its danger, the Saint wants to "spend a short time in describing it." [90] Since we must return to it and to the favors that follow next, we can now pass on rapidly.

It should be pointed out, however, that these interior words that "oblige the understanding to give all its attention," [91] bear

[87] *Ibid.*; 276-7.
[88] *Ibid.*; 278.
[89] *Ibid.*, iii; 279.
[90] *Ibid.*
[91] *Life*, xxv; Peers, I.

with them "the sense of power and authority . . . both in themselves and in the actions which follow them;" [92] the calm, the strength, the courage, the assurance, the peace and light [93] that they leave, reveal a living presence that is very close, the presence of the Master of all things.

The increase in the depths of love wrought by these visits and by tribulations prepare the soul for that meeting of the espousals at which an exchange of promises is made.

These espousals take place in a rapture, in an encounter in the light, and are sometimes accompanied by transports of the soul, flights of spirit which show the weakness of the body and the irresistible force of the "powerful Giant." [94] The intellectual and imaginary visions that place the soul in the presence of Christ, its guest, and of the saints who form His court, are also a work of light and fix the gaze of the soul entirely on this divine presence; while wounds deeper than all the preceding ones leave in the soul a burning love and desires of such intensity that the bonds of the body would break if God did not cease His action.

Spiritual marriage comes finally to seal the union and change the promises into a communication of persons in the transformation of love. This supreme taking possession of the soul was marked, in the case of Saint Teresa, by a very lofty imaginary vision, the receiving of a nail and a locution from Christ, her Spouse, which explained to her the import of the favor. Henceforth, in mutual possession, God and the soul rejoice in their reciprocal perfect love. The intellectual vision of the soul is constant, though of a clarity which varies and modifies the intensity of its accompanying joy.

And so, according to Saint Teresa's description of her spiritual journey, it appears to us marked at inte 's by extraordinary favors which were powerful means of her sanctification.

[92] VI Mansions, iii; Peers, II, 280.
[93] *Life*, xxv.
[94] VI Mansions, v; 293.

The short cut that she points out in the fifth Mansions continues on through the following stages. Such seems to be the judgment which forces itself upon us after a general survey of the ways followed by the Saint.

But we must be wary of any hasty synthesis and use discretion in accepting conclusions which seem evident. Here the truth is very delicately shaded. Saint Teresa's own experiences far surpassed these favors. She writes:

> You will think, sisters, that so much has been said about this spiritual road that there cannot possibly be any more to say. It would be a great mistake to think that; just as the greatness of God is without limit, even so are His works. . . . Do not be surprised, therefore, at what has been said and at what will be said now, for it is only a fraction of the things that still remain to be related about God.[95]

The Saint has too penetrating a sense of the divine transcendence to place limits to the power of God and to the means He uses in His wisdom. Besides, is she not also dimly aware that all the works that God imposes upon her during this period of ascent from 1560 to 1572—the foundation of the convent at Avila with its accompanying torments, the extension of her Reform to the Friars, the foundation of convents in Castille, and her return as prioress at the Incarnation in 1571—all these were sources of precious and perhaps decisive graces. She does not explicitly say so; it is for us to draw our own conclusions.

Yet she notes the following from her experience, something that is not an extraordinary favor:

> His Majesty also communicates Himself in other ways, which are much more sublime, and are also less dangerous, because, I think, the devil cannot counterfeit them. But, being very secret things, they are difficult to describe, whereas imaginary visions can be explained more readily.[96]

The Saint then describes supernatural perceptions that are purely intellectual; and this brings us to Saint John of the Cross.

[95] VII Mansions, i; 329.
[96] VI Mansions, x; 321.

2. SAINT JOHN OF THE CROSS

In these regions one can speak less than ever of the essential difference between Teresa's experience and that of John of the Cross. Each retains his or her own special grace and genius. Saint Teresa writes from the abundance of her positive experience which, under her supple pen, preserves all its vitality and richness. Saint John of the Cross is the spiritual father and director. He is preoccupied with the difficulties met with by souls. With the precise science of the theologian, he points out the dangers occasioned by divine favors; and, on the other hand, he reveals the treasures concealed in certain states of abnegation and painful experiences of spiritual poverty. Thus the two Saints complement each other, one throwing light on the other's teaching, both together offering a synthesis of spiritual doctrine, which could not without danger be reduced to its separate elements.

But we gather from the life of Saint John of the Cross, as well as from allusions in his writings, that he knows by experience the extraordinary favors described by Saint Teresa. Of certain ones he speaks little, and, apropos of raptures, he gives the reason. In the commentary on the second stanza of the *Spiritual Canticle,* he writes:

> This would be a convenient place for treating of the different kinds of rapture and ecstasy and of other issuings forth and subtle flights of the spirit, which are accustomed to befall spiritual persons. But, since my intent is but to expound these stanzas briefly, as I promised in the prologue, these other things must remain for such as can treat them better than I. And I pass over the subject likewise because the Blessed Teresa of Jesus, our mother, left notes admirably written upon these things of the spirit, the which notes I hope in God will speedily be printed and brought to light.[97]

To the Blessed Teresa, then, he leaves the task of explaining those divine visits which manifest themselves exteriorly. His is another message, which he states for us in his commentary on

[97] *Spiritual Canticle,* st. xii; Peers, II, 69.

the thirteenth and fourteenth stanzas of this same *Spiritual Canticle:*

> It is not to be understood that these visits are always accompanied by these natural distresses and fears, which, as has been said, are the lot of those that are beginning to enter the estate of illumination and perfection, and to experience this kind of communication; for in others these things are accompanied rather by great sweetness.[98]

The Saint then describes a divine communication which takes a different form. It is like a peaceful night:

> In this spiritual sleep which the soul has in the bosom of its Beloved, it possesses and enjoys all the calm and rest and quiet of the peaceful night, and it receives in God, together with this, a profound and dark Divine intelligence.[99]

He is evidently referring to that infused contemplation of which he speaks at length in the *Dark Night of the Soul* and in the *Living Flame:*

> It describes this dark contemplation as 'secret,' since, as we have indicated above, it is mystical theology, which theologians call secret wisdom, and which, as Saint Thomas says, is communicated and infused into the soul through love. This happens secretly and in darkness, so as to be hidden from the work of the understanding and of the other faculties. Wherefore, inasmuch as the faculties aforementioned attain not to it, but the Holy Spirit infuses and orders it in the soul, as says the Bride in the Songs, without either its knowledge or its understanding, it is called secret.[100]

This contemplation "according to the expression of Saint Denis is a ray of darkness for the understanding"; [101] or better still, says our holy doctor, "the language of God to the soul, addressed by pure spirit to pure spirit." [102]

We are here in the same depths of the soul revealed to us by mystical graces. But here all is "deep silence" [103] and darkness for the senses, which know nothing of the divine operations,

98 *Ibid.,* st. xiii-iv; 83.
99 *Ibid.*
100 *Dark Night,* Bk. II, xvii; Peers, I, 428.
101 *Living Flame,* st. iii; Peers, III.
102 *Dark Night, ibid.;* 430.
103 *Living Flame, ibid.;* 70.

as well as for the spiritual director who would try to penetrate them:

This road whereby the soul journeys to God is as secret and as hidden from the sense of the soul as the way of one that walks on the sea, whose paths and footprints are not known.[104]

Thus the soul is carried into a secret abyss of which it is at times clearly aware:

For, besides performing its ordinary function, it sometimes absorbs the soul and engulfs it in its secret abyss, in such a way that the soul clearly sees that it has been carried far away from every creature and has become most remote therefrom; so that it considers itself as having been placed in a most profound and vast retreat, to which no human creature can attain, such an immense desert, which nowhere has any boundary, a desert the more delectable, pleasant and lovely for its secrecy, vastness and solitude, wherein the more the soul is raised up above all temporal creatures, the more deeply does it find itself hidden.[105]

A work of grace, which yields in no way to that of the other divine visits, takes place in this silence:

The interior blessings that this silent contemplation leaves impressed upon the soul without its perception of them are, as I say, inestimable; for they are in fact the most secret and delicate anointings of the Holy Spirit, whereby He secretly fills the soul with riches and gifts and graces.[106]

Greatly does this abyss of wisdom raise up and exalt the soul at this time, making it to penetrate the veins of the science of love.[107]

This contemplation in effect is not the exclusive privilege of souls already purified, as seemed to be implied in the passage [108] from the *Spiritual Canticle* quoted above. It is "a road that guides and leads the soul to the perfection of union with God." [109] It is this which operates when the soul is "in the darknesses and afflictions of purgation." [110] This contemplation

[104] *Dark Night, ibid.;* 432.
[105] *Ibid.;* 430-1.
[106] *Living Flame,* st. iii; 72.
[107] *Dark Night, ibid.;* 431.
[108] *Spiritual Canticle,* st. xiii-xiv; 83.
[109] *Dark Night, ibid.*
[110] *Ibid.;* 428.

"so simple, so general and so spiritual" [111] is "a secret ladder" by which the soul, "disguised," journeys toward God,[112] for

> . . . just as men mount by means of ladders and climb up to possessions and treasures and things that are in strong places, even so also, by means of this secret contemplation, without knowing how, the soul ascends and climbs up to a knowledge and possession of the good things and treasures of Heaven.[113]

The Saint insists, explains, and seems even to repeat himself. He is here in his personal domain. It is his own special message. He affirms this when he says that he proposed to himself "the explanation of this night to many souls who pass through it and yet know nothing about it." [114] It is important for the soul to bear in mind that,

> . . . although it is not conscious of making any progress, it is making much more than when it was walking on foot; for it is because God is bearing it in His arms that it is not conscious of such movement.[115]

These last words make us think of Saint Therese of the Child Jesus. And the whole calls up a beautiful description of a similar state that Saint Teresa of Avila experiences not only during prayer but also during the rest of the day. She writes:

> At other times my soul is troubled by what I should call a kind of foolishness: I seem to be doing neither good nor evil, but to be following the crowd, as they say, without experiencing either suffering or bliss. I care not whether I live or die, nor whether I experience pleasure or pain: I seem to feel nothing. The soul appears to me to be like a little ass, feeding and sustaining its life by means of the food which is given it and which it eats almost unconsciously. For the soul in this state cannot do otherwise than feed on some of God's great favours; it does not mind living this miserable life and bearing its existence with equanimity, but it is quite unconscious of any motions or effects which might help it to understand its condition.[116]

Such a state was a little disconcerting to Saint Teresa, habituated as she was to the divine outpourings. Yet she continues

[111] *Ibid.;* 429.
[112] *Ibid.*
[113] *Ibid.,* xviii; 432.
[114] *Ibid.,* xxii; 446.
[115] *Living Flame,* st. iii; Peers, III, 85.
[116] *Life,* xxx; Peers, I, 202.

with an "it seems to me"—which in her case lessens in no way the value of her testimony:

> This, it now seems to me, is like sailing with a very calm wind: one makes great headway, but without knowing how.[117]

Saint Teresa, then, knows well the calm surface and the fruitfulness of God's action in the hidden depths beneath. Hence one must be careful not to regard the experiences of Saint Teresa as quite apart from those of Saint John of the Cross. Yet it does remain true that Saint John of the Cross is the doctor of this mode of divine action, silent and hidden, which is infused contemplation.

3. SAINT THERESE OF THE CHILD JESUS

Saint John's description of God carrying "the soul in his arms" reminded us just now of Saint Therese of the Child Jesus. The resemblance between the two Saints is not limited to their use of images. It goes so deep that Saint Therese of the Child Jesus can rightly be called the most illustrious of the daughters of Saint John of the Cross. With reference to the point we are treating, we clearly find the same climate of contemplation as we pass from the mystical doctor to the mistress of little souls.

Accounts of her prayer left by the little Saint of Lisieux are well known. During the retreat preceding her clothing with the habit of Carmel she writes:

> In my relations with Jesus, nothing; dryness, sleep.[118]
> Your little lamb can say nothing to Jesus; and more important, Jesus says nothing to her.[119]

And again:

> The lamb is mistaken in thinking that the little lamb is not in darkness; it is plunged in the thick of it. Perhaps, I admit, this darkness is luminous; but nevertheless it is darkness.[120]

[117] *Ibid.*
[118] Letter II to Mother Agnes.
[119] Letter II to Sister Marie of the Sacred Heart.
[120] An unpublished note to Mother Agnes.

A year and a half later, during her profession retreat, she experiences the same powerlessness and the same obscurity. She writes:

> I do not understand the retreat, I can think of nothing; in a word, I am in a very dark subway.[121]

The *Letters* and the *Autobiography* agree in their testimony.[122] The powerlessness seems to increase. Beginning with 1892, she derives no consolation from any of the spiritual writers; she is left in aridity.[123] At no time is she less consoled than during her thanksgivings after Holy Communion.[124]

And yet, one certitude shines out from the darkness: God is instructing her and working in her soul:

> My Beloved is instructing my soul; He speaks to it in the silence, in the darkness.[125]

Even after the offering she makes of herself to merciful Love and the divine outpouring of love that follows it in 1895, God does not change His manner of acting deep in the dryness of her soul:

> Do not think that I am always bathed in consolations; oh! no, my consolation is in not having any on earth. Without showing himself, without making his voice heard, Jesus instructs me in secret. This is not through books, for I do not understand what I read.[126]

The following is a page that the Saint wrote in 1890, in which she indicated the characteristics of her spiritual journey:

> But the little solitary must tell you of the itinerary of her journey. Here it is: Before they started, it seemed that her Spouse asked her in what country she wished to travel, what road she wished to follow . . . the little bride answered she had only one desire, to come to the summit of the *mountain of Love*. . . .
>
> Then Jesus took me by the hand and brought me into a subter-

[121] *Ibid.*
[122] Letter IV to Mother Agnes; Letter to Sister Marie of the Sacred Heart; *Autobiography*, viii, 139 ff.
[123] *Autobiography*, viii, 131.
[124] *Ibid.*, 126.
[125] Unpublished extract from a letter to Céline.
[126] *Autobiography*, xi.

ranean way, where it is neither hot nor cold, where the sun does not shine, and rain and wind do not come; a tunnel where I see nothing but a brightness half-veiled, the glow from the downcast eyes in the Face of my Spouse. . . .

I do not see that we are advancing towards the mountain that is our goal, because our journey is under the earth; yet I have a feeling that we are approaching it, without knowing why.[127]

On reading these lines one can understand how eagerly Saint Therese nourished her spiritual life from the writings of Saint John of the Cross:

I have obtained many spiritual lights through the works of Saint John of the Cross. When I was seventeen and eighteen they were my only food.[128]

At this decisive period of her spiritual ascent, she found reassurance in his writings. She found in them the description of that darkness and peaceful emptiness in which she was then living. She discovered too confirmation that under cover of this darkness and emptiness God was acting silently and profoundly, and that she could confidently rely on this spiritual poverty for the fulfillment of her immense desires for love.

Saint John of the Cross explained Saint Therese of the Child Jesus to herself. He explains her to us also. So true is this, that it seems one can discover all the marvelous depths of the way of spiritual childhood only in the light of the teaching of the mystical doctor.

On the other hand, the Saint of Lisieux enables us to understand Saint John of the Cross by translating him into a language and an experience that we grasp because they are of our time. Translated thus for our benefit, the experience of Saint Therese of the Child Jesus retains all its value: it is a perfect realization of Saint John of the Cross, devoid of extraordinary graces and poor even as regards spiritual delights.

From these austere demands of spiritual poverty during the time of prayer, we are led insensibly as it were by the Saint

[127] Letter to Mother Agnes; *Collected Letters,* 138-9.
[128] *Autobiography,* viii, 131.

toward other modes of divine action, outside the time of prayer properly so-called.

We say "ordinarily," because Teresa of Avila has already warned us, with her experience of God's action in the soul, that souls completely wrapped up in their prayers, who think perfection consists in losing nothing of the devotion they feel, "understand little of the road to the attainment of union." "What the Lord desires is works," she adds, saying that one must never hesitate to leave one's devotions to give help to a sick person.[129] Her apostolic labors for her foundations and the sufferings that she met with contributed largely to meriting for her the abundant inflowings of love that brought her soul to spiritual marriage.

The testimony of John of the Cross on this point is valuable:

> For they to whom God is to grant so notable a favour as to tempt them more interiorly must have rendered Him many services, and have had much patience and constancy for His sake, and be very acceptable in their lives in His sight.[130]

And the Saint cites the example of Job and Tobias who, because they had been faithful, were tried by sufferings that perfected them.

Works and sufferings, then, merit inflowings of love and are even necessary for spiritual ascent in these high regions. Thus it is not only in the extraordinary graces of prayer and in contemplation that God infuses the love that purifies and transforms. Saint Therese of the Child Jesus exemplifies this truth to us still more clearly than do Saint Teresa of Avila and Saint John of the Cross.

It is during the exercise of the Way of the Cross in choir that the Saint of Lisieux receives the wound of merciful Love.[131] But most of the important graces of her life are given her outside of prayer. Such is the grace of Christmas 1886, which works a psychological transformation enabling her "to begin

[129] V Mansions, iii; Peers, II, 262-3.
[130] *Living Flame,* st. ii; Peers, III, 47.
[131] *Novissima Verba,* p. 32.

as it were a giant's race," and which comes to her after an effort to advance in virtue.[132] Such is the burning zeal for souls that "carries her beyond the narrow circle" in which she lives; it took fire in her soul at the sight of a holy picture of our Lord on the Cross that slipped out of her book during Mass, showing only one of His divine hands pierced and bleeding.[133] She herself says that it is for the most part in the midst of daily occupations that lights come to her:

> Our Lord has no need of books or teachers to instruct our souls. He, the Teacher of Teachers, instructs us without any noise of words. I have never heard Him speak, yet I know He is within me. He is there, always guiding and inspiring me; and just when I need them, lights, hitherto unseen, break in. This is not as a rule during my prayers, but in the midst of my daily duties.[134]

And on the other hand, she says that she often fell asleep during prayer. Not sleeping enough at night, she often became drowsy during prayer in choir and during thanksgiving in spite of her efforts. But this does not distress her. She writes:

> That I fall asleep so often during meditation, and thanksgiving after Communion, should distress me. Well, I am not distressed. I reflect that little children are equally dear to their parents whether they are asleep or awake; that, in order to perform operations, doctors put their patients to sleep; and finally that "The Lord knoweth our frame, He remembereth that we are but dust.[135]

There is no doubt, the little Saint thinks that sleep does not hinder God from acting, and even that God profits by it to infuse more deeply His grace.

But laying emphasis on these texts and testimonies do we not prove too much? Could not one draw the conclusion that Saint Therese of the Child Jesus is not at all a contemplative? We do not think so; she evinced an esteem for prayer and a fidelity to it that caused her to overcome all difficulties and to write:

[132] *Autobiography,* vi, 41.
[133] *Ibid.,* 72.
[134] *Ibid.,* viii, 131.
[135] *Autobiography,* viii, 118.

"Give me a lever and a fulcrum on which to lean it," said Archimedes, "and I will lift the world."

What he could not obtain because his request had only a material end, without reference to God, the Saints have obtained in all its fulness. They lean on God Almighty's power itself and their lever is the prayer that inflames with love's fire. With this lever they have raised the world—with this lever the Saints of the Church Militant still raise it, and will raise it to the end of time.[136]

Moreover how could she be sanctified in a contemplative Order such as Carmel, without making full use of its proper means to sanctity, which is mental prayer and contemplation?

It cannot be doubted that Saint Therese of the Child Jesus is a contemplative, and that God poured His love abundantly into her soul in the silence of prayer. Her testimony nevertheless has a more general import. Considered in its ensemble, it shows us God's ways of acting with a soul that He has captivated, and at the same time the attitude of humble, trusting docility that love creates in that soul, to keep it efficaciously under the hold of God.

This brief study of three Carmelite Saints shows us that God used three means to pour into their souls the charity that caused them to mount up to the summit: extraordinary graces, infused contemplation, the activity of love in works. The three ways of acting are to be found in the three Saints but in different degrees. In Saint Teresa extraordinary favors and works of the apostolate stand out in strong relief, while silent infused contemplation seems to take second place. In Saint John of the Cross infused contemplation and divine favors dominate, while apostolic works appear less during the period of spiritual ascent. In Saint Therese of the Child Jesus,[137] there are few extraordinary favors; on the other hand contemplation, the humble accomplishment of the duties of her state, and love for souls were powerful means for drawing down floods of infinite Love.

[136] *Ibid.*, xi, 176.

[137] Even in Saint Therese of the Child Jesus, extraordinary graces, although infrequent, had a decisive influence. Cf. the grace of Christmas 1886, the wound of merciful Love, not to mention her miraculous cure.

If one might draw some general conclusions to embrace all kinds of souls, one might formulate them thus. The divine ways of dealing with souls are as varied as the particular ways of Wisdom and the vocations of souls themselves. Ordinarily it is by a synthesis of the three means we have indicated that perfect love is infused. It seems very rare, though it is possible, that a soul travels exclusively by the way of contemplation, without extraordinary favors and without external works of charity. It seems possible also, although still more rare, that a soul may be elevated to the transforming union of love, even though it is not contemplative and is given uniquely to works of the apostolate.

This psychological analysis and these fine distinctions repeat a more simple and profound truth, namely, that God is Love. It is the infinite force of His love that makes God stoop down to take possession of us and transform us into Himself. This active love, which finds its joy in conquering us and reigning in us, awaits our cooperation in an attitude and in acts expressive of love. This attitude and these acts that God requires are determined more immediately by duties of state, special events, and the interior light of our particular grace. The contemplative will attain to God in the silence of prayer; the apostle will call to Him in the anguish of his difficulties and will merit the divine conquest by his works. Let the proof of love that God asks be given generously, and divine Love comes to dwell in us as in His abode.

> If anyone love me, he will keep my word, and my Father will love him, and we will come to him and make our abode with him.[138]

This love of God urging us on, its invasions into the faithful soul, its profound and painful action to make the soul worthy of such a Guest and fitted for the role it must fulfil, its final abiding in the soul and perfect reign therein—all this forms the thread of the painful and heroic drama that the sixth and seventh Mansions set before us.

[138] John 14:23.

CHAPTER II

Extraordinary Favors Locutions and Visions

If Our Lord had not bestowed on me the favours He has, I should not, I think, have had the courage to perform the works I have. . . .[1]

The divine enrichments of this period are enrichments of love. It is by an abundant infusing of love more and more deep, that God purifies, illumines, transforms the soul and unites it definitively to Himself. A fundamental truth, this, which explains the final ascent to the summit and which, for this reason, cannot be too much emphasized.

In describing this magnificent work of supernatural charity, the most beautiful of God's works that we are permitted to contemplate here below, the great spiritual writers, and Saint Teresa in particular, give a notable place to extraordinary graces. Certainly, these masters know that such graces are not necessary for holiness; yet they point out that extraordinary favors may play an important part in achieving it. For these brilliant phenomena that very happily mark out the stages of the spiritual journey and give light on them have also a singular power for sanctification.

Saint Teresa justifies her long descriptions by writing at the beginning of the sixth Mansions:

There is another way in which God awakens the soul, and which, although in some respects it seems a greater favour than the others,

[1] *Relations,* xxxiv; Peers, I, 351.

may also be more perilous. For this reason I will spend a short time in describing it.[2]

Dangerous indeed supernatural favors can be because they are subject to counterfeit and they sometimes feed pride and illusion; yet not dangerous to the point of justifying the atmosphere of distrust that, because of them, some persons maintain toward the mystical life in general; nor the skeptical if not derisive smile that their very mention provokes.[3]

In order to dispel fears and equivocations, Saint Teresa proposes her usual remedy: bring light to bear on the matter. Let us stay a while to learn from her and Saint John of the Cross what extraordinary favors are, and what are their effects; their frequency and the moment for them; how God produces them; how to discern their divine origin; and finally, what must be the soul's attitude if it would receive them.

A. What is meant by extraordinary favor and what these favors are

1. DEFINITION

The extraordinary favors of which we are here speaking are particular forms of God's direct action on the soul, which produce distinct knowledge either through a sense impression or by an infusion of light in the intellect.

Let us clarify the terms. By direct action of God we mean, as we have previously said, an action of God that does not exclude the action of an instrument, but in the production of which the

[2] VI Mansions, iii; Peers, II, 279.

[3] There are some persons who refuse to study the teaching of the saints on extraordinary favors, and directors who forbid it, on the ground of not wanting to promote illusions. We must of course recognize the fact that this study can, in imaginations that are too active or in unbalanced temperaments, give rise to or develop desires for extraordinary manifestations. On the other hand, ignorance of the teaching of the masters on this subject leaves directors hesitant and fearful in the face of preternatural facts. It is not rare to find that distrust in regard to doctrine goes along with a naive credulity with regard to the marvelous.

soul does not in any way intervene, and which it receives passively.

The word extraordinary qualifies this particular mode of God's direct action, which is action applied directly to the faculties or the senses to produce in them a light or an image.

Hence we consider as belonging to the ordinary mode of the divine action any infusion of charity, whatever be its intensity, as well as the most profound contacts and substantial touches together with the confused light of connaturality they produce, even if that light is strong and clear enough to be compared to a dawn, for it is the normal fruit of charity and of the gifts.

On the other hand, all the supernatural lights that could not be the normal fruit of charity—because they are distinct, or by reason of the mode according to which they are received—and likewise all images in general will be attributed to God's extraordinary action; stooping to our human means of knowing, our senses and our intellect, He infuses light into them directly, by a means adapted to their capacity.

As we see, the term "extraordinary" is not used here to express the abundance and exceptional quality of an inflowing of love, nor the marvelous power of its effects, such as a conversion or an ecstasy,[4] nor even the rarity of a state or of a mystical phenomenon, such as union of will or transforming union. Rather it designates a special mode of the divine action which, by a play of contrasts, is extraordinary only because God, in order to enlighten us, descends even to speaking in a language adapted to our senses and our intellect.

God will speak this human language to the soul often when it is in ecstasy. Ordinarily He will give with it an abundant outpouring of charity. But whatever may be the transcendence

[4] We shall speak later on, after the chapter on the "Dark Night of the Soul," concerning the external and physical effects of God's action, such as those of ecstasy. It seems that actually the suspension of the senses, or ecstasy, is not a direct effect of God's action but is only a reaction because of the weakness of the natural powers under the extraordinary force of the action of God on the soul.

of the divine gifts that accompany it, the extraordinary favor of which we are speaking is God's direct action on the faculties.

Saint John of the Cross classifies this extraordinary knowledge according to the powers that receive it. Thus he distinguishes the communications that come to the soul through the external senses (sight, hearing, smell, taste, touch), such as external visions, locutions, savors, perfumes, and so on; [5] those that are formed supernaturally in the imagination, such as imaginary visions; [6] and finally the clear and distinct knowledge which comes by a supernatural way directly to the understanding by intellectual visions, revelations, interior words, and spiritual feelings.[7] This classification is exhaustive and corresponds with the logical plan of the *Ascent of Mount Carmel.*

On the other hand, the Teresian classification is drawn from experience. The Saint mentions only words and visions. She puts under these two heads, making of course the necessary distinctions, all the modes of God's extraordinary action. Hence between Saint Teresa's classification and Saint John's there is some criss-crossing that might create confusions, if one were to dwell on the terminology without reference to the definition. For instance, what Teresa calls intellectual visions of certain truths are, for John of the Cross, revelations.

We shall adopt the Teresian classification, casting further light on it from the teaching of Saint John of the Cross. We shall thus avoid drawn out discussions, perhaps repetitions, while giving an instruction sufficient for our purpose on the problems raised by the question of extraordinary favors.

2. EXTRAORDINARY FAVORS IN THE LIFE OF SAINT TERESA

a. *Locutions*

The first extraordinary communication with which Saint Teresa was favored took place about 1540. The Saint was then

[5] *Ascent,* Bk. II, xi; Peers, I, 96 ff.
[6] *Ibid.,* xvi; 122 ff.
[7] *Ibid.,* xxiii; 173 ff.

twenty-five. Christ appeared to her with a stern look while she was conversing with a guest in the parlor, to let her know that such friendships were not good for her.[8] This was an isolated manifestation. More than fifteen years were to pass before the period of the great extraordinary favors, the first of which were interior words (1557). She writes:

> There is another way in which God awakens the soul. . . . This awakening of the soul is effected by means of locutions, which are of many kinds. Some of them seem to come from without; others from the innermost depths of the soul; others from its higher part; while others, again, are so completely outside the soul that they can be heard with the ears, and seem to be uttered by a human voice.[9]

The words that Teresa hears, however, are as a rule interior:

> Though perfectly formed, the words are not heard with the bodily ear; yet they are understood much more clearly than if they were so heard, and, however determined one's resistance, it is impossible to fail to hear them.[10]

Saint John of the Cross devotes a very penetrating study to these words. He distinguishes three kinds: successive words, words simply formal, and substantial words.

> 1. I describe as successive certain words and arguments which the spirit is wont to form and fashion when it is inwardly recollected.[11]

If we consider just the definition, successive words are not extraordinary favors since the spirit and not God formulates them. Yet the Saint studies them at some length because

> . . . although it is the spirit itself that works as an instrument, the Holy Spirit oftentimes aids it to produce and form those true reasonings, words and conceptions. And thus it utters them to itself as though to a third person. For, as at that time the understanding is recollected and united with the truth of that whereon it is thinking, and the Divine Spirit is likewise united with it in that truth, as it is always united in all truth, it follows that, when the understanding communicates in this way with the Divine Spirit by means of this truth, it begins to form within itself, successively, those other truths which

[8] *Life*, vii; Peers, I, 40.
[9] VI Mansions, iii; Peers, II, 279.
[10] *Life*, xxv; 156.
[11] *Ascent*, Bk. II, xxviii; Peers, I, 195.

are connected with that whereon it is thinking, the door being opened to it and illumination being given to it continually by the Holy Spirit Who teaches it. For this is one of the ways wherein the Holy Spirit teaches.

And when the understanding is illumined and taught in this way by this master, and comprehends these truths, it begins of its own accord to form the words which relate to the truths that are communicated to it from elsewhere. So that we may say that the voice is the voice of Jacob and the hands are the hands of Esau.[12]

The inflowing of light from the Holy Spirit can give high value to these words, especially when the divine light is abundant. But one easily falls into illusion:

Although it is true that, in this communication and enlightenment of the understanding, no deception is produced in the soul itself, nevertheless, deception may, and does, frequently occur in the formal words and reasonings which the understanding bases upon it.[13]

Understanding began to work under a divine influence; it now continues by its own movement:

There are certain types of understanding so quick and subtle that, when they become recollected during some meditation, they invent conceptions, and begin naturally, and with great facility, to form these conceptions into the most lifelike words and arguments, which they think, without any doubt, come from God. . . . This happens very commonly, and many persons are greatly deceived by it, thinking that they have attained to a high degree of prayer and are receiving communications from God, wherefore they either write this down or cause it to be written. And it turns out to be nothing, and to have the substance of no virtue, and it serves only to encourage them in vanity.[14]

Saint John of the Cross has a wide experience of this sort of thing. And so he never tires of flaying the error. He writes:

I am appalled at what happens in these days—namely, when some soul with the very smallest experience of meditation, if it be conscious of certain locutions of this kind in some state of recollection, at once christens them all as coming from God, and assumes that this is the case, saying: 'God said to me . . .'; 'God answered me . . .'; whereas it is not so at all, but, as we have said, it is for the most part they who are saying these things to themselves.[15]

[12] *Ibid.*, xxix; 196.
[13] *Ibid.*
[14] *Ibid.*; 199.
[15] *Ibid.*; 197.

Moreover the devil can work his way in and follow up by his suggestions the lead of the Holy Spirit.

This evil shows up in every era. We cannot help thinking that many of the divine messages that enjoy great success in our day are composed only of successive words in which divine inspiration was perhaps not lacking at their beginning, but in which it is certainly limited. The doctrine of Saint John of the Cross on this point is therefore still practical. It should be meditated upon.

2. Formal words are authentically supernatural favors.

> The interior words belonging to the second type are formal words, which at certain times come to the spirit by supernatural means, without the intervention of any of the senses, sometimes when the spirit is recollected and at other times when it is not.[16]

Yet they differ in degree:

> These words are sometimes very clearly formed and sometimes less so; for they are frequently like conceptions in which something is said to the spirit, whether in the form of a reply to it or in that of another manner of address. Sometimes there is only one word; sometimes there are two or more; sometimes the words succeed one another like those already described, for they are apt to be continuous, either instructing the soul or discussing something with it; and all this comes to pass without any part being played therein by the spirit, for it is just as though one person were speaking with another. In this way, we read, it came to pass with Daniel,[17] who says that the angel spoke within him.[18]

These words may be simply formal and serve only "to instruct or illumine with respect to one thing." [19] The devil can produce them. And since the effect they have upon the soul is not great, it is not easy to discern them.

3. Substantial words on the other hand are formal words that are clearly marked because they bring to pass in the soul what they signify:

[16] *Ibid.*, xxx; 202.
[17] Daniel 9:22.
[18] *Ascent*, Bk., xxxi; Peers, I, 202.
[19] *Ibid.*

It is as if Our Lord were to say formally to the soul: 'Be thou good'; it would then substantially be good. . . . Or as if it feared greatly and He said to it: 'Fear thou not'; it would at once feel within itself great fortitude and tranquillity. For the saying of God, and His word, as the Wise Man says, is full of power; and thus that which He says to the soul He produces substantially within it. . . . And this is the power of His word in the Gospel, wherewith He healed the sick, raised the dead, etc., by no more than a word. And after this manner He gives certain souls locutions which are substantial; and they are of such moment and price that they are life and virtue and incomparable good to the soul; for one of these words works greater good within the soul than all that the soul itself has done throughout its life.[20]

It belongs only to God to attach such efficacy to formal words. One can have no doubt as to their origin when they are substantial. Saint John of the Cross does however point out an exception, namely, that of a soul that would have given itself up by a voluntary pact to the devil, who could thus impress upon it "effects, not of good, but of evil." [21]

All the words of which Saint Teresa makes explicit mention in her writings seem to be substantial ones. For example she tells us:

When I was in this terrible state of exhaustion . . . these words alone were sufficient: "Be not afraid, daughter, for it is I and I will not forsake thee: fear not." . . . Here I was, calmed by nothing but these words, and given fortitude and courage and conviction and tranquillity and light.[22]

The Lord said to me: "Why dost thou fear? Knowest thou not that I am all-powerful? I will fulfil what I have promised thee." And shortly afterwards this promise was in fact completely fulfilled. But even at that time I began at once to feel so strong that I believe I could have set out on fresh undertakings. . . .

Often He has uttered words of reproof to me in this way, and He does so still when I commit imperfections, which are sufficient to bring about a soul's destruction. And His words always help me to amend my life, for, as I have said, His Majesty supplies both counsel and remedy. At other times the Lord recalls my past sins to me, especially when He wishes to grant me some outstanding favour, so that my soul feels as if it is really at the Judgment; with such com-

[20] *Ibid.*, xxxi; 205-6.
[21] *Ibid.;* 206.
[22] *Life,* xxv; Peers, I, 164.

plete knowledge is the truth presented to it that it knows not where to hide.[23]

When these words announce to her future events, they impress her by the complete certitude they give. The Saint says of any soul that has received such locutions:

Even if many years go by, it never loses its belief that, though God may use other means incomprehensible to men, in the end what He has said will come true; as in fact it does.[24]

The fact that Saint Teresa refers only to substantial words indicates that she recognizes only these as authentically divine.

Saint John of the Cross, guided by his concern to make known the presence of the divine wherever it may be found, usefully extended his field of investigation to words simply formal and even successive, so as to disengage the part flowing from the divine action. Nevertheless he finds that in these two groups, the supernatural and natural influences are so intermingled and the supernatural effects so little defined, there is always a doubt concerning them. Hence it is prudent to reserve, with Saint Teresa, the name of "interior words" to substantial words, which bear within them the authentic sign of their supernatural origin.

b. *Visions.*

The term vision lends itself to confusion. Let us make the meaning exact.

Saint John of the Cross makes the remark, "for the soul to understand is for it to see." [25] In this sense one can say that any act of knowing, whatever be its object or its mode, is a vision of the truth.

Taken in its ordinary and common usage, the word vision has a much more restricted meaning. It is reserved to the perception of a corporeal form by the external sense of sight or by

[23] *Ibid.,* xxvi; 167.
[24] VI Mansions, iii; Peers, II, 281.
[25] *Ascent,* Bk. II, xxiii; Peers, I, 174.

the internal sense of imagination. It is thus that we say Saint Bernadette had an external vision of the Blessed Virgin, and that Saint Teresa had interior visions of the sacred humanity of Jesus Christ.

Saint Teresa does not use the word vision in its widest sense, applying it to any kind of knowledge; neither does she reserve it merely to sense perception of a corporeal form. The first supernatural manifestations with which she is favored after interior words are perceptions of presences, without any sense image. These she calls intellectual visions. Intellectual visions were to be perfected a little later, in her experience, by imaginary visions. Finally there were to be pure intellectual visions having for their object God or His attributes. Before defining them, let us listen to the remarkably vivid descriptions given by the Saint:

1. Intellectual visions of corporeal substances: At the time that Teresa was distressed by a decree of the Inquisition forbidding the reading of a great number of spiritual books written in Castilian, she heard our Lord say to her:

> Be not distressed, for I will give thee a living book." I could not understand why this had been said to me, for I had not then had any visions. But a very few days afterwards, I came to understand it very well.[26]

And she continues:

> I was at prayer on a festival of the glorious Saint Peter when I saw Christ at my side—or, to put it better, I was conscious of Him, for neither with the eyes of the body nor with those of the soul did I see anything. I thought He was quite close to me and I saw that it was He Who, as I thought, was speaking to me. Being completely ignorant that visions of this kind could occur, I was at first very much afraid, and did nothing but weep, though, as soon as He addressed a single word to me to reassure me, I became quiet again, as I had been before, and was quite happy and free from fear. All the time Jesus Christ seemed to be beside me, but, as this was not an imaginary vision, I could not discern in what form: what I felt very clearly was that all the time He was at my right hand, and a witness of everything that I

[26] *Life,* xxvi; Peers, I, 168.

was doing, and that, whenever I became slightly recollected or was not greatly distracted, I could not but be aware of His nearness to me.[27]

This vision is quite different from the experience of the presence of God in the prayer of union or of quiet. For precision, the Saint notes that in these prayers:

> The soul recognizes the presence of God by the effects which, as I say, He produces in the soul, for it is by that means that His Majesty is pleased to make His presence felt: but in a vision the soul distinctly sees that Jesus Christ, the Son of the Virgin, is present.[28]

Thus a true perception is had of a presence acting near. By what name can it be called if not a vision, although the senses do not see the corporeal form of this presence? And most of all, how explain it? Speaking in the third person, Saint Teresa sets forth the difficulties she experienced in trying to do this:

> She went off to her confessor in a state of great perturbation. "If you see nothing," he asked her, "how do you know it is Our Lord?" Then he told her to tell him what His face was like. She replied that she did not know, that she had seen no face, and that she could not tell him more than she had done already: what she did know was that it was He Who was speaking to her and that it was no fancy.[29]

Such assurances were not sufficient, as we can imagine, for a confessor who had only his good common sense to judge of the facts. He multiplied questions:

> My confessor then asked me who told me it was Jesus Christ. "He often tells me so Himself," I replied; "but, before ever He told me so, the fact was impressed upon my understanding, and before that He used to tell me He was there when I could not see Him." [30]

And the vision lasted "for many days—sometimes for more than a year," [31] without the confessor and other experienced advisors being able to decide this embarrassing case. Fortunately, a few years later Saint Peter of Alcantara came to Avila; with the authority of his personal experience and his holiness, he

[27] *Ibid.*, xxvii; 170.
[28] *Ibid.*; 171.
[29] VI Mansions, viii; Peers, II, 310.
[30] *Life*, xxvii; Peers, I, 171-2.
[31] VI Mansions, viii; Peers, II, 310.

was able to reassure the Saint [32] as well as those spiritual men who had been tormenting her by their doubts.[33]

2. Imaginary visions: But Saint Teresa had not yet been reassured about the intellectual visions when she was favored with imaginary visions. She writes:

> Let us now imagine, as I said in the last chapter, that this Lord is here. It is as if in a gold reliquary there were hidden a precious stone of the highest value and the choicest virtues: although we have never seen the stone, we know for certain that it is there and if we carry it about with us we can have the benefit of its virtues. We do not prize it any the less for not having seen it. . . . But we dare not look at it, or open the reliquary in which it is contained, nor are we able to do so; for only the owner of the jewel knows how to open it, and though he has lent it to us so that we may benefit by it, he has kept the key and so it is still his own. He will open it when he wants to show it to us. . . .
>
> And now let us suppose that on some occasion the owner of the reliquary suddenly wants to open it, for the benefit of the person to whom he has lent it. . . . This is what happens here. When Our Lord is pleased to bestow greater consolations upon this soul, He grants it, in whatever way He thinks best, a clear revelation of His sacred Humanity, either as He was when He lived in the world, or as He was after His resurrection; and although He does this so quickly that we might liken the action to a flash of lightning, this most glorious image is so deeply engraven upon the imagination that I do not believe it can possibly disappear until it is seen where it can be enjoyed to all eternity.[34]

The image is a living one and incomparably beautiful:

> The brilliance of this vision is like that of infused light or of a sun covered with some material of the transparency of a diamond, if such a thing could be woven. This raiment looks like the finest cambric.[35]

In the book of her *Life,* the Saint describes at still greater length the brilliance in comparison with which "the brightness of our sun seems quite dim," the "infused radiance which, without wearying the eyes, causes them the greatest delight,"

[32] *Life,* xxx; Peers, I, 194.
[33] *Ibid.,* xxviii; 186.
[34] VI Mansions, ix; Peers, II, 314-5.
[35] *Ibid.;* 315.

the "light which never gives place to night. . . . It is of such a kind, indeed, that no one, however powerful his intellect, could, in the whole course of his life, imagine it as it is." [36]

The soul is overpowered by it:

The soul is very far from expecting to see anything and the thought of such a thing has never even passed through its mind. All of a sudden the whole vision is revealed to it and all its faculties and senses are thrown into the direst fear and confusion, and then sink into that blessed state of peace. It is just as when Saint Paul was thrown to the ground and there came that storm and tumult in the sky; just so, in this interior world, there is a great commotion; and then all at once, as I have said, everything grows calm.[37]

Almost invariably the soul on which God bestows this favour remains in rapture.[38]

And so, out of regard for the natural weakness of the soul, says Saint Teresa, our Lord manifests to it progressively His hands, His divine countenance, and finally:

One year, on Saint Paul's Day, when I was at Mass, I saw a complete representation of this most sacred Humanity, just as in a picture of His resurrected body, in very great beauty and majesty.[39]

Saint Teresa declares that she never contemplated such visions with her bodily eyes but always with the eyes of her soul.[40] She never had external corporeal visions then, but only imaginary ones.

These imaginary visions were usually accompanied by an intellectual vision:

These two kinds of vision almost invariably occur simultaneously, and, as they come in this way, the eyes of the soul see the excellence and the beauty and the glory of the most holy Humanity. And in the other way which has been described it is revealed to us how He is God, and that He is powerful, and can do all things, and commands all things, and rules all things, and fills all things with His love.[41]

[36] *Life,* xxviii; Peers, I, 180.
[37] VI Mansions, ix; Peers, II, 317.
[38] *Ibid.;* 315.
[39] *Life,* xxviii; 179.
[40] *Ibid.;* also, VI Mansions, ix; 315.
[41] *Life,* xxviii; 183.

The imaginary vision clothes the intellectual vision with living and resplendent forms.[42]

All the interior powers of the soul, intellectual and sense, are enraptured by the same presence manifesting itself in a way appropriate to each one. Thus we understand how Saint Teresa can say that imaginary visions, accompanied by intellectual visions,

. . . seem to me in some ways more profitable because they are in closer conformity with our nature.[43]

Elsewhere she explains:

For, though the former type of vision [intellectual] which, as I said, reveals God without presenting any image of Him, is of a higher kind, yet, if the memory of it is to last, despite our weakness, and if the thoughts are to be well occupied, it is a great thing that so Divine a Presence should be presented to the imagination and should remain within it.[44]

3. Visions of spiritual substances: The preceding visions, either imaginary or intellectual, were of bodily substances. Visions of spiritual substances are those which make the soul perceive substances that do not of themselves possess corporeal form, such as truths, angels, or God Himself. These visions can be imaginary or intellectual, according as they are perceived by the senses with the aid of an image or by the intellect with the aid of an infused light.

Visions such as these pose, by their very nature, more delicate problems. But before taking up the problems let us gather the testimony of Saint Teresa who had many experiences, most characteristic, of this kind. Among them we find three categories of visions of spiritual substances: visions of hidden or future events, visions of the divine attributes and of the soul itself, and visions of the Holy Trinity.

[42] In chapter xxxiii of her *Life,* Saint Teresa describes a vision in which she sees Our Lady in both an intellectual and imaginary vision and Saint Joseph in a vision that is only intellectual.

[43] VI Mansions, ix; Peers, II, 314.

[44] *Life,* xxviii; Peers, I, 182.

a. Visions of hidden things: Visions of hidden things, of things at a distance or future events, are rather numerous in Saint Teresa's life; she was favored with them until the end of her life. Ordinarily her visions of this kind were imaginary and intellectual at the same time, the infused light explaining the image and the image drawing the light to a focus in sensible and precise forms.

> Once when I was praying before the Most Holy Sacrament there appeared to me a holy man whose Order had been to some extent in a state of decline. In his hands he was holding a large book; he opened this and told me to read a few words which were in large and very legible print. "In the times to come," they said, "this Order will flourish; it will have many martyrs."
>
> On another occasion when I was at Matins in choir, I saw in front of me the figures of six or seven members of this same Order, with swords in their hands. I take this to mean that they are to defend the Faith. For at another time, when I was in prayer, my spirit was carried away and I thought I was in a great field where many people were fighting and the members of this Order were doing battle with great fervour. They had lovely faces, quite lit up with zeal; many were vanquished and laid low by them; others were killed. This, I thought, was a battle against the heretics.[45]

Purely charismatic, that is, given for the good of others, these visions do not properly speaking enter into the spiritual life of the Saint, nor do they show a progressive development in harmony with her spiritual ascent.

b. Visions of God or the soul: In the book of her *Life,* Saint Teresa notes, among favors received, certain dazzling lights; one, for example, of which she says:

> I was shown so clearly how it was possible for there to be one God alone and Three Persons that it caused me both amazement and much comfort.[46]

Whether this was simply light or a vision, we cannot say.

But on another occasion, there is light on God-Truth which strongly impressed the Saint, and which she considers as "a high

[45] *Life,* xi; 295.
[46] *Life,* xxxix; 289.

favor." She mentions the vision in both the book of her *Life* and the *Interior Castle*.[47] She writes:

> My spirit seemed to be plunged into that Majesty of which I have been conscious on other occasions, and to be filled with it. In this Majesty I was given to understand a truth which is the fulfilment of all truths. . . . Thus I understood what it is for a soul to be walking in truth in the presence of Truth Itself. . . .
>
> This truth which I am referring to and which was taught me is truth in itself, and is without beginning or end. . . . Yet I cannot tell how, for I saw nothing.[48]

This intellectual vision is accompanied by an interior locution and by an image, deeply engraven in her soul.

> From this Divine Truth, which was presented to me without my knowing what it was or how it came, there remained imprinted upon me one truth in particular.[49]

We think we can connect this manifestation of a high truth to "that sort of vision and language" which Saint Teresa describes apropos of intellectual visions [50] and in which:

> The Lord introduces into the inmost part of the soul what He wishes that soul to understand, and presents it, not by means of images or forms of words, but after the manner of this vision aforementioned. Consider carefully this way in which God causes the soul to understand what He wills, and also great truths and mysteries; for often what I understand, when the Lord expounds to me some vision which His Majesty is pleased to present to me, comes in this way. . . .
>
> They occur only from time to time and are quickly over; at other times, as I think, the faculties are not suspended, nor is the soul bereft of its senses, but these remain active, which in contemplation is not always the case—it happens, indeed, very seldom. When it is the case, I believe that we ourselves do nothing and accomplish nothing—the whole thing seems to be the work of the Lord. It is as if food has been introduced into the stomach without our having eaten it or knowing how it got there. We know quite well that it is there. . . . In this experience the soul does nothing. . . . It finds all its food cooked and eaten: it has nothing to do but to enjoy it. . . .
>
> The soul suddenly finds itself learned, and the mystery of the Most Holy Trinity, together with other lofty things, is so clearly explained

[47] *Ibid.*, xl; 290; also, VI Mansions, x.
[48] *Life,* xl; 290-2.
[49] *Ibid.;* 291.
[50] *Ibid.*, xxvii; 172.

to it that there is no theologian with whom it would not have the boldness to contend in defence of the truth of these marvels.[51]

These precise descriptions set in relief both the passivity of the soul and the luminous riches of the treasure that it suddenly discovers within itself; they disclose the workings of a light in the soul directly infused by God, that is called an intellectual vision.

After this intellectual vision of Truth, Saint Teresa tells of another vision—an imaginary one this time—of the soul in which God dwells:

My soul suddenly became recollected and seemed to me to become bright all over like a mirror: no part of it—back, sides, top or bottom—but was completely bright, and in the centre of it was a picture of Christ Our Lord as I generally see Him. I seemed to see Him in every part of my soul as clearly as in a mirror, and this mirror—I cannot explain how—was wholly sculptured in the same Lord by a most loving communication which I shall never be able to describe.[52]

This vision is helpful for recollection, because the light is illustrated by an image that holds the senses. Beyond doubt, the vision is both intellectual and imaginary—the image being superimposed on the intellectual vision—an advantage that Saint Teresa extolled, when speaking of imaginary visions of corporeal substances.

At times the image is much less defined, so that the Saint hesitates to say it is there at all. The intellectual vision then stands out more clearly:

Once, when I was in prayer, I saw, for a very brief time and without any distinctness of form, but with perfect clarity, how all things are seen in God and how within Himself He contains them all. Describe this I cannot, but the vision remained firmly imprinted upon my soul. . . . I cannot say with certainty that I saw nothing, for, as I am able to make this comparison, something must have been visible to me; but the vision comes in so subtle and delicate a way that the understanding cannot grasp it. Or it may be that I cannot understand these visions, which do not seem to be imaginary, though there must be an imaginary element in some of them. . . .

[51] *Ibid.;* 172-3.
[52] *Life,* xl; 292.

> Let us say that the Godhead is like a very clear diamond, much larger than the whole world, or a mirror, like that which symbolized the soul in my account of an earlier vision, . . . furthermore, that all we do is seen in this diamond, which is of such a kind that it contains everything within itself, because there is nothing capable of falling outside such greatness.[53]

Note must be taken that in these visions of spiritual substances we find the same progressive order as in the visions of corporeal substances. The intellectual vision is given first; the imaginary vision is added to the intellectual vision to perfect it and increase the power of its effects. The same progressive development appears in the visions of the Holy Trinity, at least in those that precede spiritual marriage.

c. Visions of the Holy Trinity: Visions of the Holy Trinity mark a singular deepening of the divine life in the soul and bring to it a new element. The first such intellectual vision with which the Saint is favored, causes her a certain surprise.

> On the Tuesday following Ascension Day,[54] I spent some time in prayer, after communicating in a state of distress because I was so distracted as to be incapable of concentration. So I complained of our miserable nature to the Lord. Then my soul began to kindle with fire and I seemed to have the clearest realization of the presence of the Most Holy Trinity in an intellectual vision, through which, in a sort of picture, or figure of the truth, of a kind that even my stupidity could understand, my soul learned how God is Three and One. And thus, it seemed to me, all Three Persons were speaking and were distinctly present within my soul. They told me that from that day onward I should find myself better in three respects, for each of the three Persons was granting me a favour. One would give me charity; One, joy in suffering; and One, a consciousness of that charity, with an enkindled soul. I now realized the meaning of these words spoken by the Lord—that the three Divine Persons will be with the soul that is in grace—for I experienced Their presence within me in the way I have described. . . . These three Persons, Whom I saw, Who are one God alone, seemed to have impressed themselves so deeply upon my soul that I realized, if that deep impression remained, it would be

[53] *Ibid.;* 293-4. Saint Teresa very briefly describes this same vision in the *Interior Castle,* VI Mansions, x.

[54] This incident took place on May 29, 1571, in the Convent of Saint Joseph of Avila.

impossible for me to be other than recollected in such Divine company.[55]

Actually, this intellectual presence continues with her. A month later she says:

I have had with me this presence of the Three Persons, of which I spoke earlier, until today, which is that of the Commemoration of Saint Paul. They have been continually present in my soul; and, as I was accustomed to have only Jesus Christ with me, I had supposed all the time that the presence of the Three Persons was to some extent a hindrance to this, though I know They are all Three One God. Today, while I was thinking about this, the Lord told me I was wrong to think of things of the soul in the same terms as of those of the body: I must realize that the two are very different and that the soul has a capacity for great fruition. This seemed to be shown me by the illustration of a sponge which takes up and absorbs water: just so my soul was filled with the Godhead and in a certain sense it had within itself the fruition and the possession of the Three Persons. I also heard these words: "Labour not to hold Me enclosed within thyself but to enclose thyself within Me." It seemed to me that these Three Persons were present within my soul and that I saw Them there, and that They communicated Themselves to all created things, and never either failed to do this or ceased to be with me.[56]

Saint Teresa writes these "spiritual relations" only a short time after being favored by the visions, the newness of which hampers her pen. When, seven years later, she writes the *Interior Castle,* her pen has recovered its easy flow. Elevated habitually to higher states of the spiritual life, she understands better the nature of these visions and the state they characterize. It is then she tells us that intellectual visions of the Holy Trinity are given to the soul as soon as it enters the seventh Mansions, before it receives the grace of spiritual marriage.

It is brought into this Mansion by means of an intellectual vision, in which, by a representation of the truth in a particular way, the Most Holy Trinity reveals itself, in all three Persons. First of all the spirit becomes enkindled and is illumined, as it were, by a cloud of the greatest brightness. It sees these three Persons, individually, and yet, by a wonderful kind of knowledge which is given to it, the soul realizes that most certainly and truly all these three Persons are one

[55] *Relations,* xvi; Peers, I, 342.
[56] *Ibid.,* xviii; 343.

Substance and one Power and one Knowledge and one God alone; so that what we hold by faith the soul may be said here to grasp by sight, although nothing is seen by the eyes, either of the body or of the soul, for it is no imaginary vision. Here all three Persons communicate Themselves to the soul and speak to the soul and explain to it those words which the Gospel attributes to the Lord—namely, that He and the Father and the Holy Spirit will come to dwell with the soul which loves Him and keeps His commandments. . . .

This Presence is not of course always realized so fully—I mean so clearly—as it is when it first comes. . . . But although the light which accompanies it may not be so clear, the soul is always aware that it is experiencing this companionship.[57]

This information, then, we can gather: Saint Teresa entered the seventh Mansions the Tuesday after the Feast of the Ascension, 1571, when she was favored with the intellectual vision of the Holy Trinity; and from then on the vision was habitual.

Thus the intellectual vision of a particular nature, being produced as it is when the spirit is "enkindled and illumined," will attain its perfection only in spiritual marriage. On reading the *Relations* of Saint Teresa, one has the impression that until then the intellectual vision is in itself sustained and perfected by visions of another kind.

The Saint, in the same year, notes:

Once, when I was in prayer, the Lord showed me, by a strange kind of intellectual vision, the condition of a soul that is in grace. While in its company I saw, in an intellectual vision, the Most Holy Trinity, from Whose companionship there came to the soul a power which had dominion over the whole earth. . . . He also showed me the condition of the soul that is in sin; it is completely devoid of power, like a person securely tied, bound and blindfold, who, desire to do so as he may, can neither see nor hear nor talk, but is in great darkness. I conceived such pity for souls in this state that any trial seems light to me if I can set one of them free.[58]

The following year, September 22, 1572, two months before her spiritual marriage, Teresa is favored by an imaginary vision. She describes this at some length to show the details that the image adds to the intellectual vision:

[57] VII Mansions, i; Peers, II, 331-2.
[58] *Relations,* xxiv; Peers, I, 345.

I was given to understand very clearly, in such a way that, by means of certain methods and comparisons, I saw it in an imaginary vision. And although on other occasions the Most Holy Trinity has been revealed to me through an intellectual vision, the truth has not remained with me for several days—as it has done this time, I mean—so that I can think of it and find comfort in it. Now I realize that this is exactly what I have been taught by learned men, but I have never understood it as I do now. . . .

The revelation which I have received consists of Three distinct Persons, each of Whom can be seen by Himself and each of Whom Himself speaks. Since then I have been thinking that the Son alone took human flesh, through which this truth is made manifest. These Persons have mutual love, communication and knowledge, each in relation to the rest. . . . In all Three Persons there is not more than one will and one power and one dominion, so that none of Them can do anything without Another; so, however many creatures there may be, there is only One Creator.[59]

Finally on November 18, 1572, when she receives the grace of spiritual marriage, Saint Teresa is favored with two visions that have a special character, which she herself emphasizes. First there is an imaginary vision of the sacred humanity of Christ:

When granting this favour the first time, His Majesty is pleased to reveal Himself to the soul through an imaginary vision of His most sacred Humanity, so that it may clearly understand what is taking place and not be ignorant of the fact that it is receiving so sovereign a gift. To other people this experience will come in a different way. . . .

This, you will think, was nothing new, since on other occasions the Lord had revealed Himself to that soul in this way. But it was so different that it left her quite confused and dismayed: for one reason because this vision came with great force; for another, because of the words which He spoke to her; and also because, in the interior of her soul, where He revealed Himself to her, she had never seen any visions but this.[60]

At the same time, there is the union of the soul with God:

This secret union takes place in the deepest centre of the soul, which must be where God Himself dwells, and I do not think there is any need of a door by which to enter it. I say there is no need of a door because all that has so far been described seems to have come through the medium of the senses and faculties and this appearance of the

[59] *Ibid.*, xxxiii; 350.
[60] VII Mansions, ii; Peers, II, 334.

Humanity of the Lord must do so too. But what passes in the union of the Spiritual Marriage is very different. The Lord appears in the centre of the soul, not through an imaginary, but through an intellectual vision (although this is a subtler one than that already mentioned).[61]

That lofty intellectual vision seems to be the discovery of the presence of God in the soul, due to the perfect union which it has contracted with Him; and "although this great favour cannot be fulfilled in us during our lifetime," [62] it marks nevertheless a summit attained and already a definitive possession. Thereafter, Saint Teresa assures us, "the soul remains all the time in that center with its God." [63]

3. QUALITY OF THESE FAVORS

We may wonder whether the divine communications that we have just enumerated, locutions and visions, are all extraordinary favors, that is, favors produced by God's direct action on the faculties or the senses. Let us try to answer this. The classification of these favors as given by Saint John of the Cross will be of help.

a. *Locutions.* If, in the light of the definition given, we examine the interior words that Saint Teresa reports, it appears clear that these words, being substantial ones, are extraordinary favors.

The successive words described by Saint John of the Cross, being pronounced by the soul under the action of the divine light, are not extraordinary favors.

As to words simply formal, they are by definition extraordinary favors, since produced directly by God. Yet, since their effects are scarcely sensible, it is in many cases difficult to distinguish them from successive words. Hence it is prudent to suspend judgment as to their quality.

b. *Visions.* It is less easy to qualify the Teresian visions.

61 *Ibid.*
62 *Ibid.;* 333.
63 *Ibid.;* 335.

Saint John's classification will be especially useful in this domain.

1. Saint John of the Cross distinguishes three kinds of visions: visions properly so-called, revelations, and any knowledge of truths. Visions properly so-called penetrate directly, with the aid of a supernatural light, things that are absent, whether of heaven or of earth; they may be of God, of spiritual or of corporeal realities.

The full vision of God and of spiritual substance is had only in the other life, for one cannot see God without dying. The Saint admits, however, that some such visions are possible in this life,

> . . . occasionally and fleetingly, when, making an exception to the conditions which govern our natural life, God so allows it. At such times He totally withdraws the spirit from this life, and the natural functions of the body are supplied by His favour. . . . But these visions that were so substantial—like that of Saint Paul and Moses, and that of our father Elias, when he covered his face at the gentle whisper of God—although they are fleeting, occur only very rarely—indeed, hardly ever—and to very few.[64]

The visions of corporeal things are those visions of bodily substances about which we spoke before.

All these visions are extraordinary favors.

Revelations consist of the disclosure of hidden secrets and mysteries. They concern God Himself, that is, the mystery of the Trinity and the divine attributes; or again, what God is in His works and in all the other dogmas of faith. Revelation being now closed, having been made once and for all, favors of this kind illumine or make manifest a truth already known and give a better understanding of it. Revelations "come ordinarily through words, figures and similitudes." [65]

Knowledge that consists "in comprehending and seeing within the understanding the truths of God, whether of things that are, that have been or that will be," [66] can have for its object

[64] *Ascent,* Bk. II, xxiv; Peers, I, 177.
[65] *Ibid.,* xxvii; 192.
[66] *Ibid.,* xxvi; 182.

the Creator or creatures. The lofty manifestations of God are pure contemplation. They are the fruit of unitive love. In their perfect form they can come only to the soul

> . . . that attains to union with God, for they are themselves that union; and to receive them is equivalent to a certain contact with the Divinity which the soul experiences, and thus it is God Himself Who is perceived and tasted therein.[67]

Substantial touches, enriching the soul as they do, bring to light these manifestations, which are the most precious of all the gifts, because they proceed from union and are indeed that very union.

These lofty manifestations of the divine are not extraordinary favors, since they are the fruit of connaturality effected by charity. Although most elevated and most desirable, they are in the normal line of the development of grace and are produced by grace.

Manifestations concerning objects inferior to God are quite different; they refer to things in themselves, to facts, to events that take place among men. Saint John of the Cross tells us that this knowledge can proceed from a charism, a particular gift of wisdom or of prophecy, or from an aptitude of the purified spirit which, with the aid of slight external indications, discovers profound realities. In both cases a divine light is needed to actualize the gift or the aptitude.

These manifestations, then, are not as a rule extraordinary favors in the sense that has been pointed out. Saint John of the Cross insists on this, lest one be inclined to trust too much in them.[68]

2. This classification gives us valuable light on the nature of the visions with which Saint Teresa was favored. Let us consider them in succession.

The intellectual and imaginary visions of bodily substances that we have described were visions properly so-called and

[67] *Ibid.;* 184.
[68] *Ibid.;* 186-90.

hence must certainly be considered as extraordinary favors.

Distinctions must be made in the case of the supernatural phenomena that we have grouped under the title of visions of spiritual substances.

Among the visions of spiritual substances described by Saint Teresa are there any that could be called visions of God or of spiritual realities in the sense used by Saint John of the Cross? We do not think so.[69] The highest visions described by Saint Teresa, those of the Holy Trinity, persist for some time, while the visions of God of which Saint John of the Cross speaks last only for an instant. The Teresian visions that we know of can be explained without recourse to so rare and extraordinary a phenomenon as appears to be the favor described by the mystical doctor. If a doubt on this point persisted one would have to clarify it, so it seems, by studying not the Saint's visions of the Holy Trinity but the vision of God-Truth which made so profound an impression on her soul.

The vision of God as Truth, which is accompanied by an interior locution and by an image which is impressed on the soul, the visions of the soul in which Christ dwells, of the soul in the state of grace and in the state of sin, the imaginary vision of the Holy Trinity, all these seem to us to be revelations in the terminology of Saint John of the Cross. He says in fact that the manifestation of divine secrets is made usually with the aid of words, figures, and similitudes. These revelations are extraordinary favors.

The Teresian visions of the future are also extraordinary favors, being revelations proceeding from an extraordinary infusion of distinct divine light.[70]

The intellectual visions of the Holy Trinity with which the soul is favored upon entering the seventh Mansions are not revelations but are manifestations of spiritual knowledge pro-

[69] It is possible that Saint Teresa enjoyed such visions and does not describe them.

[70] *Ascent,* Bk. II, xxvii; 192.

ceeding from the highest degree of charity. Hence they are not extraordinary favors in the strict sense of the definition. In the period that precedes spiritual marriage this intellectual vision lasts for some time, according to Saint Teresa, but seems to grow weaker after a few days.[71] Divine union not being perfect, neither is the intellectual vision; but in Saint Teresa it was sustained by the extraordinary favors that we have qualified as revelations. When the soul has arrived at spiritual marriage, the intellectual vision finds its perfection in the very perfection of the union realized. Thereafter extraordinary favors can cease. The soul is in possession of a light that is superior to them, a light that proceeds from unitive love, revealing constantly the divine Guest who dwells within it and its perfect union with Him.[72]

The experiences of Saint Teresa are in perfect harmony with the teaching of Saint John of the Cross, who places above all the lights received in an extraordinary way the light of dawn, rising from the perfection of unitive love.

B. Effects of extraordinary favors

The perfectly legitimate concern not to encourage desires for extraordinary graces brings one to minimize at times the effects of these favors. We think it preferable to state the truth on this point, even though this might give rise to difficulty in some particular cases. And the truth is that these favors usually have considerable influence in the development of the spiritual life of persons who receive them and in the realization of the mission that is theirs. This was so for Saint Teresa.

1. SANCTIFICATION OF THE SOUL

The first interior word that Saint Teresa hears: "I will have thee converse now, not with men, but with angels," [73] detaches

[71] *Relations,* xxxiii.

[72] One can find farther on in the chapter, "Spiritual Betrothal and Marriage" longer developments on the intellectual vision of the Holy Trinity.

[73] *Life,* xxxiv; Peers, I, 155.

her from conversations in the parlor and from every affection not purely spiritual. She writes:

> Never since then have I been able to maintain firm friendship save with people who I believe love God and try to serve Him. . . . Since that day I have been courageous enough to give up everything for the sake of God, Who in that moment—for I think it happened in no more than a moment—was pleased to make His servant another person. So there was no need for my confessor to give me any further commands.[74]

Visions and revelations are filled with light and grace as much as are interior locutions, if not more than they. They are "the greatest help toward attaining a high degree of perfection in the virtues," [75] and "the soul, completely instructed in such great truths, has no need of another master." [76] They penetrate it with humility [77] and inflame it with love.[78]

> The soul is now a new creature: it is continuously absorbed in God; it seems to me that a new and living love of God is beginning to work within it to a very high degree.[79]

Thus writes the Saint apropos of imaginary visions.

The effects of grace, veritable jewels, were so visible that she could present them to those who doubted, as proofs of the divine action within her soul. She writes:

> And, I said, I could show them these jewels—for all who knew me were well aware how my soul had changed: my confessor himself testified to this, for the difference was very great in every respect, and no fancy, but such as all could clearly see.[80]

The testimony of Saint Teresa is so abundantly confirmed by hagiography that there is scarcely need to insist on it. Like the fishermen of Galilee who, after hearing the call of the Master, contemplating His character, and receiving miraculously His

[74] *Ibid.;* 155-6.
[75] VI Mansions, ix; Peers, II, 320.
[76] *Ibid.;* 317.
[77] *Life,* xxix; Peers, I, 188.
[78] *Ibid.;* 191-f.
[79] *Ibid.,* xxviii; 182.
[80] *Ibid.;* 184.

Spirit, became apostles of nations, many souls have been transformed by a substantial word or a vision and efficaciously orientated toward a mission which was thus revealed to them.

It must be noted, however, that these effects of transformation do not proceed directly from the favor, but rather from a grace that accompanies it.[81]

2. LIGHT

The proper effect of extraordinary favors is light; and this light is of such quality that it can have an extraordinary influence on the spiritual life.

This clear and transcendent light, adapted to man's faculties and flooding them, penetrates even to the most humble of man's knowing powers. It reveals to them supernatural realities in a direct and living way and, imprinting an image or the memory of them in the depths of the soul, enlivens desire for those realities and thereafter facilitates contact with them.

Saint Teresa especially emphasizes how much the intellectual visions which were prolonged brought about the constant companionship of our Lord:

> For though we know quite well that God is present in all that we do, our nature is such that it makes us lose sight of the fact; but when this favour [intellectual vision] is granted it can no longer do so, for the Lord, Who is near at hand, awakens it. And even the favours aforementioned occur much more commonly, as the soul experiences a vivid and almost constant love for Him Whom it sees or knows to be at its side. . . . When the Lord is pleased to withdraw it (this favour), the soul is left in great loneliness.[82]

The imaginary vision is still more useful, according to the Saint,[83] because it is more suited to our ordinary means of knowing through the senses, and it imprints in the memory living images impossible to forget.

[81] A word simply formal is an extraordinary favor, although having little sanctifying effect. Likewise it can be that a revelation gives light only on a particular point, and yet is an extraordinary favor.

[82] VI Mansions, viii; Peers, II, 311-2.

[83] *Life*, xxviii; Peers, I, 182.

Mystical experience finds precious help in the light that comes from extraordinary favors. Such experience is essentially obscure and remains so even when its light merits to be called a brightness of dawn. In the dark period in the night of the spirit, the soul seems to be buried in dark night; it is then, usually, that the greatest number of extraordinary favors come to it, and that it receives from them the most opportune help.

In mystical experience the soul is always certain of possessing a divine treasure. But this treasure is in a reliquary, and the soul can enjoy it at times only by closing its eyes to it. Faith, it is true, makes the hidden mystery explicit in a perfect formula; but this formula itself guards jealously the mystery of the gold of its substance under the veil of its "silvered and luminous surface." An extraordinary favor opens for a moment the reliquary, letting its treasure be seen.[84] It rends the surface of the dogmatic formula which, although luminous, is as a thick covering. It causes the divine life that this formula contains and protects, to shine forth and radiate in a brilliant and living revelation to the faculties, which receive it with surprise and joy.

Peter was sleeping on Thabor, in spite of his ardent faith, while Jesus prayed. Then with James and John, he is given the resplendent vision that makes the interior riches of the Master's prayer perceptible. We can understand why he wants to build a tabernacle on Thabor. Later he was to say that the formulas of faith are more certain than visions: *habemus firmiorem propheticum sermonem;*[85] but this was after appealing to the testimony of his vision of Christ's glory, which had given him a deep and living personal consciousness of that glory.

Extraordinary favors enrich the soul and mark profoundly the whole development of the spiritual life of the saints. Frequently, at the threshold of the narrow way in which he engages His elect, God places an extraordinary favor which, like a

[84] VI Mansions, ix; 314.
[85] II Peter 1:19.

beacon, shows the entrance to it, lights up the way and its steep ascents, and already with its powerful shafts reveals its summit. The visions of Christ Jesus with which Saint Teresa was favored gave to her life, to her doctrine and her mission, that Christocentric character that is part of their wealth. Rightly has it been stressed that the mystery of the Christ is the dominant thought in the preaching and spirituality of Saint Paul; and that this thought is already present in its entirety in the initial vision of Jesus Christ which throws Paul from his horse on the Damascus road, telling him that this is Jesus, the Christ, whom he was persecuting when he persecuted the Christians.[86] Who can say what the repeated visions and words of the Immaculate Virgin left in the soul of Bernadette? Certainly a call to holiness and to the realization of the beauty she had discovered, a call whose efficacious power was made manifest in a rough and poor human setting touched with the delicate charms of divine simplicity. Is not the beauty of the Blessed Virgin and her healing smile imprinted also on the captivating countenance of Saint Therese of the Child Jesus?

3. CHARISMATIC EFFECTS

The immense profit that the soul can derive from them must not hide from us the fact that these extraordinary favors are of themselves charismatic. Hence it is in the good that they procure for one's neighbor and for the Church, rather than in their sanctification of the soul, that we must look for their specific effect and the end to which they are providentially ordered.

These extraordinary favors are given by God to ensure light and strength for the fulfillment of supernatural missions, and to gain the credence of others. This end does not exclude the preceding one, any more than does the good of the Church, the end of all things, exclude the sanctification of the members who work to build it, but on the contrary requires and procures it. The good of the Church and the particular spiritual good of

[86] Cf. Mersch, *The Mystical Body of Christ,* Part I, ch. iv.

souls are harmonized in the divine plan. This appears most clearly in the history of the Hebrew people and in the history of the Church. It alone explains the frequency of perceptible signs of God's action or their absence in the particular ways that lead to sanctity.

Saul is chosen as a vessel of election and apostle of the Gentiles. The vision that converts him assures him of sufficient light and strength to fulfill his mission.

The extraordinary favors that are so powerful an aid to Saint Teresa in arriving at transforming union are an evident preparation for her mission as Reformer and as master of the spiritual life. The vision of the seraph and its assaults visibly confer on her the grace of spiritual maternity. She herself recognizes the light and efficacious support that she found in these favors. In 1572 she writes:

> If Our Lord had not bestowed on me the favours He has, I should not, I think, have had the courage to perform the works I have, nor strength to endure the trials and oppositions and criticisms that I have. And so, since beginning my foundations, I have lost the fears, which had previously troubled me, when I thought I was suffering from delusions, and I have become certain that it was all the work of God. This led me to fling myself into difficult enterprises, though I always acted on advice and under obedience. From this I realize that, when Our Lord was pleased to inspire the beginning of this Order, and of His mercy made me the means of this, His Majesty had to supply all I lacked, which was everything, so that my labours should be effective, and that His greatness should be the more clearly manifested in one so wicked as I.[87]

The very indiscretions, so painful for Saint Teresa, that were to make known her interior life, also won greater credence for her foundations. It is a vision of a just soul that gives her the subject for her masterpiece, the *Interior Castle,* the most important stages of which, she marks with the luminous sign of an extraordinary favor illustrating its special grace.

God, who by means of miracles accredits the cult of the saints, does not hesitate to mark with the sign of an extraor-

[87] *Relations,* xxiv; Peers, I, 351.

dinary favor a doctrine or movement of piety that He wants to make universal in His Church. The revelations made to Saint Margaret Mary spread devotion to the Sacred Heart; the apparitions to Saint Bernadette set crowds moving to Lourdes. The resources of Wisdom are infinite. God could have taken other means to reach the same end. Usually He chooses means that are the most suited and most simple, and by setting His seal of external favors on extraordinary external missions, He brings them into credit.

C. Frequency and moment of extraordinary favors

Extraordinary is almost synonymous with rare. And extraordinary favors are assuredly rare; but with a rarity that has degrees.

Speaking of the Old Testament, Saint John of the Cross remarks:

> At that time faith had no firm foundation, neither was the law of the Gospel established; and thus it was needful that men should enquire of God and that He should speak, whether by words or by visions and revelations or whether by figures and similitudes or by many other ways of expressing His meaning. . . . Such communion with God was employed in the Old Law and was lawful; and not only was it lawful, but God commanded it. And when they used not this opportunity, God reproved them, as is to be seen in Isaias, where God reproves the children of Israel. . . . We see in the Divine Scripture that Moses always enquired of God, as did King David and all the kings of Israel with regard to their wars and necessities, and the priests and prophets of old . . .[88]

Thus in the Old Testament extraordinary favors were part of the normal order of divine Providence, who used them to exercise authority over His chosen people and to make known His good pleasure. Saint John of the Cross adds:

> But now that the faith is founded in Christ, and, in this era of grace, the law of the Gospel has been made manifest, there is no reason to enquire of Him in that manner, nor for Him to speak or to answer as He did then. For, in giving us, as He did, His Son, which is His

[88] *Ascent*, Bk. II, xxii; Peers, I, 162.

Word—and He has no other—He spake to us all together, once and for all, in this single Word, and He has no occasion to speak further.

And this is the sense of that passage with which Saint Paul begins, when he tries to persuade the Hebrews that they should abandon those first manners and ways of converse with God which are in the law of Moses, and should set their eyes on Christ alone, saying: *Multifariam multisque modis olim Deus loquens patribus in Prophetis: novissime autem diebus locutus est nobis in Filio.* And this is as though he had said: That which God spake of old in the prophets to our fathers, in sundry ways and divers manners, He now, at last, in these days, has spoken to us once and for all in the Son.[89] Herein the Apostle declares that God has become, as it were, dumb, and has no more to say, since that which He spake aforetime, in part, to the prophets, He has now spoken altogether in Him, giving us the All, which is His Son.[90]

Revelation was closed at the death of the last apostle, direct witness of Christ Jesus. God has told us all. We have no right to expect new revelations, nor to desire any. Desire and effort now can bear only on opening up the deposit entrusted to the Church and making it progressively more explicit. Nor does this mean that God's sovereign liberty is in any way lessened. He reserves the right to speak, Himself, to men, to make known to them particular truths. And He does so still; but such communication through words or figures has become under the New Law, properly speaking, extraordinary.

Is it possible to determine the frequency of these extraordinary communications? Saint John of the Cross, so intent on mortifying all desire on this point, seems to set down these favors as an almost normal occurrence in the growth of the spiritual life:

God brings man to perfection according to the way of man's own nature, working from what is lowest and most exterior up to what is most interior and highest. First, then, He perfects his bodily senses. . . . And, when these senses are in some degree prepared, He is wont to perfect them still further, by bestowing on them certain supernatural favors and gifts, in order to confirm them the more completely in that which is good, offering them certain supernatural communications, such as visions of saints or holy things, in corporeal shape, the sweetest perfumes, locutions, and exceeding great delights of touch, wherewith

89 Heb. 1:1-2.
90 *Ascent,* Bk. II, xxii; 162-3.

sense is greatly confirmed in virtue and withdrawn from a desire for evil things. And besides this He continues at the same time to perfect the interior bodily senses. . . .

And, when these are prepared by this natural exercise, God is wont to enlighten and spiritualize them still more by means of certain supernatural visions, which are those that we are here calling imaginary; wherein, as we have said, the spirit, at the same time, profits greatly, for both kinds of vision help to take away its grossness and gradually to reform it.

And after this manner God continues to lead the soul step by step till it reaches that which is the most interior of all.[91]

Saint John of the Cross attributed to these extraordinary favors other effects than that of conducing to the progressive detachment of the soul; this we know by parallel passages where he treats of them. But it is interesting to note in this connection that supernatural communications do not appear to him as an unusual and very rare phenomenon among spiritual persons.

During the first twenty years of her religious life, Saint Teresa has only one vision of Christ.[92] She is nearly forty when, about 1555, the period of extraordinary graces opens for her. She is then in the sixth Mansions, and God is preparing her for her mission as a Reformer of her Order. First she hears words, has intellectual visions, and then imaginary ones. The visions disappear progressively at spiritual marriage to give place to the more lofty perceptions that accompany transforming union. The locutions do not cease, however; and the Saint receives through them precious lights on what she is to do.

If we extend our field of observation, we find that there are few canonized saints—few whose light God has placed high to enlighten and guide in His Church—who have not been favored with at least some of these extraordinary favors. Saint Therese of the Child Jesus, so often cited as a perfect model and guide in the ordinary ways of sanctity, was favored with a smile from the Blessed Virgin that cured her, and with a prophetic vision of her father. Moreover, these favors are met

[91] *Ibid.*, xvii; 130-2.
[92] *Life*, vii; Peers, I.

with well beyond the rather restricted circle of canonized saints. Most often they are placed at the beginning of a spiritual life that God wills to be profound; or, later on, in order to make clear a mission and to accredit it.

Yet it cannot be said that such favors are necessary to the development of sanctity, even the highest, nor to the fulfillment of a mission, were it the most brilliant. Neither are they, as such, sufficient proof of holiness. God distributes them as He wills and when He wills, just as He makes His saints by means and ways that He has chosen. Loving Wisdom has no other law than her own good pleasure.

D. How does God produce extraordinary graces?

We are limiting the problem to favors truly extraordinary, to those produced by God's direct action in the faculties. Eliminated, consequently, are not only the mystical experience, but successive words as well, and the intellectual vision of the Holy Trinity.

The question, then, is to know how God acts on the faculties, creating in them a light or an image. In the face of this difficult problem Saint Teresa humbly declares:

> I do not mean that I shall describe how it is that He can introduce this strong light into the inward sense and give the understanding an image so clear that it seems like reality. That is a matter for learned men to explain. The Lord has not been pleased to grant me to understand how it is.[93]

And yet, nothing else that we have is any more clear on this question than is the testimony of Saint Teresa and Saint John of the Cross. And so we shall gather this together. But the difficulty of the problem will oblige us to proceed by a series of statements touching upon it, without laying claim to answering all the questions that might be put on the subject.

[93] *Ibid.*, xxviii; 180-1.

1. DIRECT ACTION

Extraordinary favors are produced by a direct action of God that eliminates all cooperation on the part of the soul other than a passive receptivity.

Imaginary visions and intellectual visions, declare the two Saints, are produced in the faculties without any activity on their part, being communicated to them in a supernatural way. We have already referred to Saint Teresa's testimony on this point wherein she marvels at the "living image"; [94] "so living an image of Himself," adds the Saint, speaking of our Lord, "that He seems to be really present." [95]

Saint John of the Cross includes under the name "imaginary vision"

> . . . all things which can be represented to the imagination supernaturally by means of any image, form, figure and species. For all the apprehensions and species which, through all the five bodily senses, are represented to the soul, and dwell within it, after a natural manner, may likewise occur in the soul after a supernatural manner, and be represented to it without any assistance of the outward senses.[96]

As to the intellectual visions which are produced

> . . . without the intervention of any inward or outward corporeal sense, they present themselves to the understanding, clearly and distinctly, by supernatural means, passively—that is to say, without the performance of any act or operation on the part of the soul itself, at the least actively.[97]

The same is true of interior words. Whether they seem to come from without or from the most intimate depth of the soul, and whether they can be heard in its higher regions or are so exterior that they can be heard like the articulated sound of a voice,[98] they are very distinct—especially interior words, which are perceived much more clearly than one hears through

[94] *Ibid.;* 181.
[95] *Ibid.*
[96] *Ascent,* Bk. II, xvi; Peers, I, 123.
[97] *Ibid.,* xxiii; 173-4.
[98] VI Mansions, iii; Peers, II, 279.

the sense of hearing.[99] Thus we have definitely stated the divine causality and the passivity of the human faculties.[100]

How is this divine causality exercised on the soul? This is the whole problem. It can be solved only by making a distinction between intellectual perceptions and sense perceptions.

2. LIGHTS INFUSED INTO THE INTELLECT

Extarordinary lights, otherwise called intellectual visions of spiritual substances and revelations, are infused by God directly into the intellect.

Speaking of lights that she finds within herself without being able to explain how they came there, Saint Teresa writes:

> The position seems to me to be that the Lord's will is for the soul to have at any rate some idea of what is happening in Heaven, and, just as souls in Heaven understand one another without speaking (which I never knew for certain till the Lord in His goodness willed me to see it and revealed it to me in a rapture), even so it is here. God and the soul understand each other, simply because this is His Majesty's will, and no other means is necessary to express the mutual love of these two friends.[101]

3. SENSE PERCEPTIONS

Can it be said that all extraordinary sense perceptions, such as visions and locutions, are produced by God in the same way, that is, by the creation of an image or a percept in the senses? The fact that beings perceived supernaturally have a body that can be perceived by the senses, changes some aspects of the problem. And so, distinctions must be made.

[99] *Life,* xxv; Peers, I, 156.

[100] From this comparative study of extraordinary favors an explanatory remark suggests itself: Saint John of the Cross is at pains to signalize God's action everywhere that he finds it; Saint Teresa, on the contrary, reserves the name of supernatural to that which seems to be disengaged from all human efficient causality.

Previously, moreover, Saint John of the Cross had noted God's action from the beginning of contemplation, while Saint Teresa reserved the qualification of supernatural for prayers of passive recollection and especially for the prayer of quiet in which the action of God dominates. Thus the field of the supernatural is more vast for Saint John of the Cross; it is more sharply defined with Saint Teresa.

[101] *Life,* xxvii; 173-4.

1. First of all, one can affirm that the persons whose presence the soul perceives in a supernatural vision or by a locution are really present. Our Lord, the Blessed Virgin, the saints are thus near the soul when they manifest themselves in an extraordinary favor. Since God proves by the effects, that He is the author of this vision or interior word and since He creates certainty as to the presence, we cannot suppose that God is creating a false impression and thus placing the soul under an illusion. Hence the reality of this presence seems to us to rest on the very veracity of God.

2. From the reality of the presence one cannot, however, conclude that in extraordinary favors the senses perceive the corporeal reality of the person whose presence is certain.

Saint Teresa actually asserts that all her visions were interior, that is, imaginary. Hence the external senses, the ordinary instruments for the perception of bodies, contributed nothing to them. To admit the real perception of the corporeal presence would serve only to complicate the problem by adding a new one, that of the miraculous perception of an external sensible reality by an interior sense. Thus it seems normal to conclude that the visions Saint Teresa had of corporeal substances were, like the intellectual visions, produced directly by the production of an image in the senses.

3. What are we to think of sensible visions that are exterior and in which, consequently, the external senses might intervene, suited as they are to perceiving sensible realities?

If the persons who appear with a corporeal presence have no body, such as the angels, or do not now have one, such as the saints in heaven, the principle of economy leads us to say that except in a case in which an angel would have an extended mission to fulfill here below. God does not give a borrowed body to those spirits, but rather is pleased to create an image in the senses of the one who is favored with the vision.

If the persons who appear are really possessed of a body, as are our Lord and the Blessed Virgin, is it their real body that, on becoming visible, they manifest? An affirmative answer would not seem doubtful, if Saint Teresa herself did not put forth the opinion that our Lord has never manifested Himself since His Ascension except to the apostle Saint Paul. Saint John of the Cross likewise says that "Christ scarcely ever appears in His actual person." [102] This negative opinion of our two masters inclines us then to think that even the sensible external apparitions, such as those with which Saint Bernadette and Saint Margaret Mary were favored, are ordinarily constituted in the sense order by an image that God impresses in the senses. This invisibility of the real body and the creation of the vision by the impression of an image would explain perfectly why only one or several persons enjoy it while those near them can perceive only the apparition's reflection on the countenance of the person who is supernaturally favored with it.

4. Locutions, interior or exterior words, without any perception of a sensible presence must, it seems, be explained in the same way; the supernatural impression of an auditory perception in the senses suffices to explain all the effects.

We can conclude, then, that extraordinary favors are produced ordinarily, if not always, by a supernatural infusion of light in the intellect or by the impression of an image or of a perception in the senses.

4. GOD MAKES USE OF THE ARCHIVES OF MEMORY

Pursuing our inquiry in these obscure regions with the light that our masters give us, we may ask ourselves what is the personal part of God in the creation and the impression of that light or of that image in the intellect or in the senses.

To solve this problem, let us turn to a general law that Saint John of the Cross enunciates in the *Ascent of Mount Carmel:*

[102] *Dark Night,* Bk. II, xxiii; Peers, I, 450.

With respect to Divine visions and revelations and locutions, God is not wont to reveal them, for He is ever desirous that men should make such use of their own reason as is possible.[103]

God's activity is usually carried on through secondary causes. His creative power and His conserving providence lie willingly hidden in the world, beneath the overflowing activity of the life of creatures. Thus triumphs divine Wisdom, humbly but how magnificently, by remaining concealed under the veil of sensible signs and of beings that He has caused to participate in His power.

What is true of the ordinary providential action of God applies also to His extraordinary action. Here God reduces to a minimum the interventions of His direct and personal action. It is important, especially in the domain of the extraordinary, never to forget this law, and to defend it against the tendency to "miraculism," which quickly sees a personal intervention of God wherever a thing appears marvelous or exceptional. The divine ways oblige us, on the contrary, to admit this practical principle, namely, that each time that a supernatural effect can be explained by the intermediary of a second cause, we are to believe that God used that cause, unless His direct personal action is evident or can be proved.

Visions offer us a good occasion for the application of this principle. God is the author of the visions; but His action need not go so far as to create all the elements that constitute them, since the archives of the memory offer Him an ample reserve of images that He can use for their construction. Actually the resplendent theophanies of the Old Testament are made up of images already known to the prophets who were thus favored.

The architecture of Babylon, familiar to Ezechiel, seems to have supplied the images with which the great vision of the four winged animals is composed. Either in the ancient prophets or in the memories of Saint John, one could probably find all the wealth of images in the visions of the Apocalypse. It

[103] *Ascent,* Bk. II, xxii; Peers, I, 169-70.

would be a very interesting study to seek out the sources that furnished Saint Teresa's visions; by finding the elements from which they are constructed, one would in no way call into question their supernatural origin. God, as author of the vision, acting in a manner analogous to the creative imagination, uses images already possessed to create a new image. But He puts into it a living splendor that is a reflection of His glory and assures it of supernatural effects, which reveal the creative power of His hand. Such is the direct action of God in extraordinary favors.

5. GOD ADAPTS HIMSELF ADMIRABLY

God's direct action, being thus grounded in the human of which it makes use, is marvelously adapted to the psychological life of the soul. This adaptation of God should be underlined as an important characteristic of His interventions.

God, who consents to speak the language of human signs to give us His light, pushes condescendence to the point of adapting Himself to our temperaments and our particular needs in the choice of these signs, so as to reach us more surely. For a faith that has kept its purity and its simplicity, He will speak in a language of external brilliant signs that will make faith vibrate. For a faith that rationalism has rendered prudent and critical, He will have a more intellectual language. Visions and revelations will be more numerous for the Spanish sixteenth century. To reach and touch our modern minds that tend to skepticism, God seems to leave aside the language of extraordinary external signs, to infuse His light directly in souls. Fewer extraordinary favors, but gifts of pure and dry contemplation distributed more widely: thus divine mercy, adapting itself, descends to the spiritual poverty of our time.

The care God takes to adapt Himself to us is manifested with touching delicacy in the extraordinary interventions themselves. Visions and words reveal the transcendence of their origin by the weight they bear and by their effects; but they are so simple, so human, so near to us by their constitutive elements that they do not disturb nor shock us. Through them God comes down near to the soul and makes Himself known as God, but by making Himself into Man. To speak to the Hebrews, He uses the picturesque richness of their symbols in order thus to fix His teachings in their soul. It is in the *patois* of Lourdes that the Blessed Virgin answers Bernadette's question and reveals that she is the Immaculate Conception. The divine and the human, the transcendent and the ordinary are so admirably united in the extraordinary manifestation, that the simple harmony which results becomes a sign of its supernatural origin.

6. GOD USES THE INSTRUMENTAL CAUSALITY OF THE ANGELS

Must this special arrangement of images and marvelous adaptation to the human, a work of God certainly, be attributed to His personal action? The principle enunciated a while ago comes in again here with its rigorous demands, the application of which can be verified by the facts.

To create a vision by imprinting an image in the interior senses, or to give a distinct light by causing a locution to be heard, does not surpass the ordinary power of the angel who as a pure spirit has power over all inferior natures. Hence it is normal that God should use the power of the angel to produce these extraordinary graces. The angel thus becomes an instrumental cause in the hands of God, who is the principal agent.

The Old Testament frequently shows us angels used by God not only as messengers but as instruments, to the point of seeming to be identified with Him. Abraham receives three angels, who inform him of the mission given them to destroy Sodom. While the patriarch accompanies them on the way, behold, the sacred writer tells us,[104] a dramatic dialogue takes place between the Lord Himself and Abraham, prolonging the conversation

[104] Gen. 18:16-33.

that had ensued between the patriarch and the heavenly messengers. It seemed perfectly congruous to the inspired writer, thus suddenly to substitute God Himself for His angels; and the unity of the story in no way suffers, so true is it that the angel is only a divine instrument.

In the description of the manifestations of God to the prophets, the inspired writer mentions almost indifferently the Lord and the angel of the Lord; and, in the same vision, sometimes attributes the words in turn to one and the other. One could not better affirm the instrumental causality of the angel and, consequently, the identification of the messenger and his Master.

A typical and living illustration of this instrumental causality of the angel is presented in the assault of the seraph, known as transverberation.[105] In the *Living Flame,* Saint John of the Cross places this charismatic favor, one of the highest that God grants, close to substantial touches. Yet he carefully distinguishes the two; for, speaking of the substantial touch, he says:

> This is a touch of the Divinity in the soul, without any form or figure whether formal or imaginary,[106]

whereas an angel intervenes in the charismatic favor. Saint Teresa in an interesting description indicates how this is done. She tells us of an angel that the Lord was pleased she should see:

> In his hands I saw a long golden spear and at the end of the iron tip I seemed to see a point of fire. With this he seemed to pierce my heart several times so that it penetrated to my entrails. When he drew it out, I thought he was drawing them out with it and he left me completely afire with a great love for God.[107]

The vision, under sensible forms, shows us how the grace of spiritual fecundity is granted. The love by which God confers

105 *Living Flame,* st. ii; Peers, III, 40-1.
106 *Ibid.;* 39.
107 *Life,* xxix; Peers, I, 192-3; Saint Teresa likewise states that in the sixth Mansions it is not God Himself but an angel who speaks (VI Mansions, iii; Peers, II, 281).

on a soul whom He has chosen to be head of a family "spiritual wealth and strength . . . according as He means his descendants to inherit the first-fruits of the Spirit," [108] can be given only by God. But because a singular favor is to be given, it is an angel of the highest order [109] who is charged with infusing this "point of fire" in the depths of the soul. The angel is a free and living instrument whose action, it seems, God uses for all charismatic graces.

The problem of the instrumental causality of the angel in the production of extraordinary favors calls up another problem: that of the discernment of the divine origin of these extraordinary favors.

E. Discernment of the divine origin of these favors

That which is in the power of the angel by reason of his nature as a pure spirit is also in the power of the devil who, although fallen from God's grace, has retained the gifts of his angelic nature. The devil excels in using the archives of sense and intellectual memory to represent in the memory and the imagination many false forms and ideas, impressing them on the spirit and the senses with such effectiveness and certitude that the soul is persuaded they are true.[110] He can form visions and cause locutions to be heard. He can also give rise to spiritual feelings by his influence on the senses,[111] and use his acuteness of mind to simulate revelations of future events.

[108] *Living Flame,* st. ii; Peers, III, 40.

[109] Saint John of the Cross speaks of the assaults of the seraph; Saint Teresa places among the cherubim the one who appears to her with a golden spear.

Banez thought he should make a correction to Saint Teresa's text by adding a note in which he says: "It seems more like those which are called seraphim." The detail is not important. We may however remark that it is congruous that one of the cherubim, the angels most burning with love, should be the instrument of this grace of fruitful love.

[110] *Ascent,* Bk. III, x; Peers, I, 230.

[111] *Ibid.,* Bk. II, xxxii; 209.

There are many visions and words that come from the devil, says Saint John of the Cross:

> Ordinarily many of these locutions and visions are of the devil; for in his converse with the soul the devil habitually wears the same guise as God assumes in His dealings with it, setting before it things that are very like to those which God communicated to it, insinuating himself, like the wolf in sheep's clothing, among the flock, with a success so nearly complete that he can hardly be recognized.[112]

It is all the more easy for him to imitate God's action and to transform himself into an angel of light, for

> . . . of those favours which come through a good angel God habitually allows the enemy to have knowledge: partly so that he may do that which he can against them according to the measure of justice, and that thus he may not be able to allege with truth that no opportunity is given him for conquering the soul, as he said concerning Job.[113]

In this connection Saint John of the Cross recalls that

> . . . all the genuine signs that Moses wrought were wrought likewise in appearance by the magicians of Pharo.[114]

And he adds:

> Not only does the evil one imitate God in this type of bodily vision, but he also imitates and interferes in spiritual communications which come through the instrumentality of an angel, when he succeeds in seeing them, as we say.[115]

We can at least conclude, then, that the diabolic counterfeits of extraordinary favors are as numerous as are the authentic

[112] *Ibid.*, xxi; 157.
[113] *Dark Night,* II, xxiii; Peers, I, 449.
[114] *Ibid.;* 450.
[115] *Ibid.*
In this connection Saint John of the Cross calls attention to the fact that the power of the good angels is greater than that of the devil. Not only is the action of the good angel marked with the divine seal that assures for it transcendent effects, but the good angel, enjoying supernatural life and acting as an instrument of God near a soul that is open to His action, can give spiritual communications to that soul, while the devil can do no more than counterfeit what is sensible in the divine communications. The devil could, however, act directly in the soul of one who had given himself up to him by a compact (*Ascent,* Bk. II, xxxi; Peers, I, 206).

favors. Psycho-pathological disorders notably increase the number of these counterfeits.[116]

Actually these disorders, which seem to take away the use of certain faculties and thus break the harmonious balance that makes for the value of the person, bring to the maximum on the other hand the virtualities of certain sense powers. All the forces of one's being are held captive by the hypertrophic power which exhausts them by absorbing them. Before total failure sets in, hypertrophy displays itself at times in strange occurrences that might make one think preternatural forces are at work.

The penetrating studies and conclusions of modern psychiatry in this domain would not, we think, have surprised Saint Teresa and Saint John of the Cross; for they simply add fine precisions to what the two Saints had already discovered from their experience of souls and from keen psychological insight. If we compare the diagnosis they make with the technical formulas, unadorned and more succinct, of modern psychiatry, it appears almost too general and too simplified; but the caution that they advise, the remedies they propose, show us that they perfectly understood the cases. Let us hear Saint Teresa on this:

> Sometimes—often, indeed—this may be a fancy, especially in persons who are melancholy—I mean, are affected by real melancholy—or have feeble imaginations.
>
> Of persons of these two kinds no notice should be taken, in my view, even if they say they see or hear or are given to understand things, nor should one upset them by telling them that their experiences come from the devil. One should listen to them as one would to a sick person. . . . If one tells them they are suffering from melancholy, there will be no end to it. They will simply swear they see and hear things, and really believe that they do.[117]

[116] One can find in the *Etudes Carmélitaines,* 2nd series (1931–38), under the direction of P. Bruno, profound studies and an abundant documentation on these questions.

See especially the number for October, 1938, which has studies on P. Surin, signed by P. de Guibert, and P. Olphe-Gaillard; also, on Thérèse Noblet by Pr. Lhermitte, R. Dalbiez, and D'Achille Delmas.

[117] VI Mansions, iii; Peers, II, 279-80.

The attitude of Saint John of the Cross is still more rigorous:

> It is always well, then, that the soul should reject these things, and close its eyes to them, whencesoever they come. For, unless it does so, it will prepare the way for those things that come from the devil, and will give him such influence that, not only will his visions come in place of God's but his visions will begin to increase, and those of God to cease, in such manner that the devil will have all the power and God will have none.[118]

This absolute rejection of visions is the part of prudence and puts in security the harvest of riches in the dark night of faith. Still it is true that the soul needs to know the origin of the extraordinary manifestations of which it is the object, when these impose upon it a mission or definite duties to fulfill. The spiritual director, in these cases at least, must be able to make the necessary distinctions. Saint Teresa has written at such great length on this question simply to give us the signs of God's action in the soul. From her detailed teaching, let us gather the most characteristic traits.

1. NEGATIVE SIGNS

The first sign, negative it is true, but important, of the divine origin of extraordinary favors is that they present nothing that is contrary to reason or to faith. God adapts Himself, even in His extraordinary modes of acting, to the natural order that governs us. Visions and divine revelations do not shock. In them God speaks our language. Everything about them is proportion, sincerity and truth, balance and simplicity.

On the other hand, pathological disturbances and the action of the devil declare themselves by lack of proportion, by strangeness, by ridiculous details, by pride, which shows itself in the care one takes to be seen by others or to surprise them, and by lies that very soon are caught in their own snare. When God manifests Himself, He speaks the language of the good man who is a good Christian; the devil and the mentally sick pose as supermen.

[118] *Ascent,* Bk. II, xi; Peers, I, 100.

2. POSITIVE SIGNS

The positive signs are more convincing if not more clear. One of them alone does not constitute a proof. Each one is an indication; the convergence of all engenders certitude.

a. Although adapting Himself to the human, God could not conceal His transcendence. In extraordinary manifestations, this expresses itself by a certain majesty, a strength, an authority that produce in the soul reverence and humility.

The first and the surest sign that locutions come from God, writes Saint Teresa, is

> . . . the sense of power and authority which they bear with them, both in themselves and in the actions which follow them.[119]

Speaking of visions, she says:

> O my Jesus, if one could but describe the majesty with which Thou dost reveal Thyself! How completely art Thou Lord of the whole world, and of the heavens, and of a thousand other worlds, and of countless worlds and heavens that Thou hast created! And the majesty with which Thou dost reveal Thyself shows the soul that to be Lord of this is nothing for Thee.[120]

One can guess what is the soul's impression in the face of this power that manifests itself and at times overwhelms:

> Sometimes these words are of such majesty that, without our knowing from whom they come, they make us tremble if they are words of reproof and if they are words of love fill us with a love that is all-consuming.[121]

The Saint repeatedly admits that in order to receive these divine favors one must have great courage,[122] and that they always produce humility and confusion:

> Here is shame and genuine repentance for sin; for, though it sees God revealing His love to it, the soul can find no place to hide itself and thus is utterly confounded.[123]

[119] VI Mansions, iii; Peers, II, 280.
[120] *Life,* xxviii; Peers, I, 182.
[121] *Ibid.,* xxv; 159.
[122] VI Mansions, iv; 286 f.
[123] *Life,* xxviii; 285.

b. This humility becomes a certain sign of God's action in the soul. Teresa writes:

> If gifts and favours come to it from the Lord, the soul should consider carefully and see if they make it think any the better of itself; and if, as the words grow more and more precious, it does not suffer increasing confusion, it can be sure that the spirit is not of God.[124]

Even of the intellectual vision, which has nothing sensible, she writes:

> This favour of the Lord brings with it the greatest confusion and humility. If it came from the devil, it would be just the reverse.[125]

The devil can imitate God's action; but in his false creation he cannot counterfeit the "glory" that comes from God, a fact that Saint Teresa often points out:

> Three or four times, I think, he has attempted to present the Lord Himself to me in this way, by making a false likeness of Him. He takes the form of flesh, but he cannot counterfeit the glory which the vision has when it comes from God.[126]

The preternatural forces of the devil are sufficient to create a certain humility or depression. But how different this is from true humility. Saint Teresa says of the soul that has experienced this:

> It then becomes troubled, despondent and restless; loses the devotion and joy which it had before; and is unable to pray.[127]
> This is a false humility. . . . His part in it is evident from the disquiet and unrest with which it begins, from the turmoil which he creates in the soul for so long as his influence lasts, and from the darkness and affliction into which he plunges it, causing it an aridity and an ill-disposition for prayer and for everything that is good. He seems to stifle the soul and to constrain the body, and thus to render both powerless.[128]

The soul possessed of the humility that comes from God experiences the overwhelming power of His transcendence and

[124] VI Mansions, iii; 285.
[125] *Ibid.*, viii; 311.
[126] *Life,* xxviii; Peers, I, 183.
[127] *Ibid.*
[128] *Ibid.*, xxx; 197.

at the same time the sweetness of His love. Saint Teresa says that genuine humility does not cause unrest in the soul:

> It cheers it and produces in it the opposite effects—quietness, sweetness and light. Though it causes us distress, we are comforted to see what a great favour God is granting us by sending us that distress and how well the soul is occupied. Grieved as it is at having offended God, it is also encouraged by His mercy. It is sufficiently enlightened to feel ashamed, but it praises His Majesty, Who for so long has borne with it.[129]

c. Humility is of the truth,[130] for it proceeds from the divine light. And light is another sign of supernatural manifestations.

Words and visions come to the soul without its willing them; and the words especially are distinct and clear even in their expression.[131] They are astonishingly full of meaning:

> In a genuine locution one single word may contain a world of meaning such as the understanding alone could never put rapidly into human language.[132]

And elsewhere the Saint says:

> The Divine words instruct us at once, without any lapse of time, and by their means we can understand things which it would probably take us a month to make up ourselves.[133]

Speaking of one who experiences visions in connection with transports of the spirit, she says:

> In a single instant he is taught so many things all at once that, if he were to labour for years on end in trying to fit them all into his imagination and thought, he could not succeed with a thousandth part of them.[134]

The faculties are at first dazzled by them. The soul cannot keep its gaze fixed on the vision.[135] But the light that is im-

[129] *Ibid.;* 198.
[130] VI Mansions, x; Peers, II, 323.
[131] *Ibid.,* iii; 284.
[132] *Ibid.*
[133] *Life,* xxv; Peers, I, 159.
[134] VI Mansions, v; Peers, II, 295.
[135] *Ibid.,* ix; 315-6.

printed in it and that it will never forget [136] becomes for it like a luminous parchment which, unrolling, progressively reveals its riches; or like a beacon, which at frequent intervals casts its shafts of light over the road the soul is traveling.

Hence it is that Saint Teresa says of interior words that

> . . . frequently, not only can words be heard, but, in a way which I shall never be able to explain, much more can be understood than the words themselves convey and this without any further utterance.[137]

She has in her mind her own experience when she adverts to all the secret things that Moses saw in the burning bush:

> Amid the thorns of that bush he must have learned marvelous things, for it was these things which gave him courage to do what he did for the people of Israel.[138]

d. When these favors are repeated in the soul, as we have said, they singularly enrich and transform it. Their profound effects are one of the most certain signs of God's action within it. "*A fructibus eorum cognoscetis eos.* By their fruits you shall know them," [139] said Jesus, speaking of the prophets. But holiness and fruits of the apostolate stamp a mission with authenticity more than does an isolated extraordinary favor.

Thanks to all these signs, is it going to be easy now to discern the origin of extraordinary manifestations? Who would dare to say so?

Saint Teresa makes a remark which, while diminishing in no way the value of the signs, indicates that their appraisal is not always without difficulty. Good dispositions, she says, are not enough

> . . . as means of distinguishing between a good spirit and an evil one. So it is well for us always to proceed with great caution, for persons who experience visions or revelations and are no farther advanced in prayer than this might easily be deceived.[140]

[136] *Life,* xxv; Peers, I, 159.
[137] VI Mansions, iii; Peers, II, 284.
[138] *Ibid.,* iv; 288.
[139] Matt. 7:16.
[140] *Life,* xxv; Peers, I, 160-1.

And a little farther on she states more precisely that a certain degree of prayer is necessary. She has been speaking of a false vision, and adds:

> It is so very different from a true vision that I think, even if a soul has experienced only the Prayer of Quiet, it will become aware of the difference from the effects which have been described in the chapter on locutions. The thing is very easy to recognize.[141]

One must know by experience, then, at least the supernatural prayer of quiet, a prayer that lets one "taste" God, in order to judge of the quality of God's action. Humility, depression, sweetness, peace and light, the perfume of God—all these traces of His passing—who can discern them with certainty, if not he who is used to experiencing them in his frequent contacts with God? The need to have had this supernatural experience places, in itself, a limit on the number of persons capable of judging experimentally the value of the signs.

It must further be added that this supernatural action is usually accompanied by counterfeits, or at least by diabolic attempts at counterfeit, in the same person or his entourage; and also by natural reactions, at times morbid, in temperaments that are not strong or are simply in course of purification. Consequently, only in certain saints already purified does this supernatural action of God appear, freed from all noxious or inferior elements. Thus the discernment of supernatural favors is an arduous task, full of difficulties—except when it pleases God to sanction them with a miracle. Even more than prudence, there is needed a gift of counsel proper to the task.

F. Attitude of the soul that receives these favors

1. NOT TO BE COMPLACENT IN THEM

The difficulties we have mentioned are one reason justifying the often repeated advice of Saint John of the Cross, namely,

[141] *Ibid.*, xxviii; 183.

to reject any and every extraordinary manifestation, with no obligation on the part of the spiritual directors to discern among them:

> God does not command them to undertake this labour, nor does He desire that sincere and simple souls should be led into this conflict and danger; for they have safe and sound teaching, which is that of the faith, wherein they can go forward.
>
> This, however, cannot be unless they close their eyes to all that is of particular and clear intelligence and sense. For, although Saint Peter was quite certain of that vision of glory which he saw in Christ at the Transfiguration, yet, after having described it in his second canonical Epistle, he desired not that it should be taken for an important and sure testimony, but rather directed his hearers to faith, saying: "*Et habemus firmiorem propheticum sermonem: cui benefacitis attendentes, quasi lucernae lucenti in caliginoso loco, donec dies elucescat.*[142] Which signifies: And we have a surer testimony than this vision of Tabor—namely, the sayings and words of the prophets who bear testimony to Christ, whereunto ye must indeed cling, as to a candle which gives light in a dark place.[143]

In another passage John of the Cross enumerates six disadvantages that follow from desiring to receive these manifestations.[144] The first and most important is that of weakening faith and consequently of withdrawing the soul from the means of union with God.

On the other hand, rejection of favors must not turn to scorn of them, remarks the Saint. Supernatural favors, they too, are a means or even a way to go to God. God's gift must be respected and used:

> For, since they are a means and manner whereby God guides such souls, there is no reason for thinking ill of them or for being alarmed or scandalized by them.[145]

But, insists the holy doctor, the best way to use these apprehensions perfectly is to reject them all, "save occasionally on another person's advice, which should very rarely be given." [146]

[142] II Peter 1:13.
[143] *Ascent,* Bk. II, xvi; Peers, I, 129.
[144] *Ibid.,* xi; 99-100.
[145] *Ibid.,* xxii; 172.
[146] *Ibid.,* xi; 103.

For, by rejection of evil visions, the errors of the devil are avoided, and by the rejection of good visions no hindrance is offered to faith and the spirit harvests the fruit of them.[147]

By becoming attached to the good visions, we develop a spirit of possession. Moreover, we are apt to fall into illusion either because we interpret these communications according to our own view, hence in a false sense, as did the Jews in the case of the prophecies concerning the Messias; or, because God Himself for certain reasons changes their realization, as happened in the case of the destruction of Nineveh, foretold by Jonas.[148]

Certainly these visions

. . . do the soul good by communicating to it intelligence or love or sweetness; but for this effect to be produced by them in the soul it is not necessary that it should desire to receive them. . . . And not only do they produce this joint effect, but principally, although not simultaneously, they produce their effect in the soul passively.[149]

In rejecting them, the soul receives into itself the grace they bring and avoids their dangers. Thus one enters into the designs of God, who makes of these communications a means adapted to our weakness, to lead us on to divine union.[150]

2. NOT TO DESIRE THEM

For the reasons already given these extraordinary communications are not to be desired. Desire blinds: it makes one accept any communications too readily and opens the way to all the snares of the devil. The doctrine of Saint John of the Cross on this point finds precious confirmation in the teaching of Saint Teresa. She gives six reasons why these desires are dangerous.[151]

[147] *Ibid.;* 100.
[148] *Ibid.,* xvi-xviii. In these chapters Saint John of the Cross develops at length this doctrine, which he considers very important. His insistence and the absolute tones that he puts in this advice are explained by the wave of illuminism that was gathering force in his time and which, among spiritual persons, brought extraordinary favors to the fore.
[149] *Ibid.,* xvi; 126-7.
[150] *Ibid.,* xvii; 130 ff.
[151] VI Mansions, ix; Peers, II, 314 ff.

Besides the lack of humility in a person who desires to receive such favors,

> . . . such a person is quite certain to be deceived, or to be in great peril, because the devil has only to see a door left slightly ajar to enter and play a thousand tricks on us. . . .
>
> When a person has a great desire for something, he persuades himself that he is seeing or hearing what he desires [152]

The Saint reminds us too that "to have these favors must be of the greatest help," [153] and yet they are not necessary to perfection:

> There are many saintly people who have never known what it is to receive a favour of this kind, and there are others who receive such favours, although they are not saintly.[154]

3. TO DECLARE THESE FAVORS TO A SPIRITUAL GUIDE

Our two spiritual masters sound a last word of advice on the subject of supernatural communications, which is to lay them open to a spiritual director and leave the matter to his judgment:

> Anything, of whatsoever kind, received by the soul through supernatural means, must clearly and plainly, fully and simply, be at once communicated to the spiritual director. . . . It is very necessary to give an account of all these, although it may seem to the soul that there is no reason for so doing.[155]

Thus the soul is led to spiritual detachment, to humility, and enters into the plan of God, who, by this means, assures to the soul all the benefits of these graces.[156]

Saint Teresa recommends the same simple and sincere openness of soul.[157] She gives precise advice:

> It will be well at first for you to communicate this, in confession, to some very learned man (for it is from such men that we must seek illumination) or to any highly spiritual person if you know one. . . .

[152] *Ibid.*, 319.
[153] *Ibid.*, 320.
[154] *Ibid.*
[155] *Ascent*, Bk. II, xxii; Peers, I, 171.
[156] *Ibid.*
[157] VI Mansions, ix; Peers, II, 317-8.

When you have finished these consultations, calm yourself and do not go on talking about the matter.[158]

To consult too many is to expose oneself to indiscretions:

. . . especially if the confessor has had little experience and treats the matter timorously and enjoins you to go and consult others. In such a case what should by rights be a close secret gets noised abroad and the penitent is persecuted and tormented. . . . Great caution, then, is necessary here and such caution I strongly recommend to prioresses.[159]

Once having made an open statement of these favors, the soul must obey the guide it has chosen:

For this is His Majesty's will, so by carrying it out we are not failing to do what He commands: He has told us that we are to put our confessor in His place, even when it cannot be doubted that the words are His. . . . I consider it very dangerous for a person to do anything but what he has been told to do and to follow his own opinion in this matter; so I admonish you, sisters, in Our Lord's name, never to act thus.[160]

These so wise counsels have for their aim to bring the soul back, as much as is possible, into the ordinary way, by submitting to the authority of the Church any extraordinary interventions of God which, by their nature, seemed as though they might escape it. By these favors, divine mercy testifies to its liberty in the distribution of gifts; but then shows us by the obedience that it imposes, its submission to the eternal and unique plan of Holy Wisdom, which is to restore all things to God by perfectly uniting souls in the whole Christ.

It is in the perspective of this plan of Wisdom that Saint Teresa and Saint John of the Cross have placed extraordinary favors, in order to appraise their value and make clear the conduct of the soul in their regard. Like meteors whose luminous path flashes for a moment in the quiet semi-darkness of a starlit sky, these graces make us aware of the ever active Spirit of

[158] *Ibid.*, viii; 313.

[159] *Ibid.*; 313-4. The Saint is recalling the heavy trials she was caused by the indecisions of P. Balthasar, and the indiscretions of her confessors concerning what she had related to them of her *Life*.

[160] *Ibid.*, iii; 283.

Love abiding in the Church and in souls. Because they are brilliant and extraordinary, such phenomena might come too much to the fore in our preoccupations and desires, or even in our conception of the spiritual life. This would be a usurpation and a danger. They are only means, very useful but extremely delicate, to help the soul in its progress toward union with God. Perfect union with God is the only thing that matters; and so, as between extraordinary favors and the prayer of union, there must be no hesitation: one must orientate the favors to the prayer of union and even sacrifice them if it is necessary; for union with God is the only good that we can desire and ask for absolutely.

> David says concerning Him [Christ]: *Ad Nihilum redactus sum, et nescivi.* This he said that the truly spiritual man may understand the mystery of the gate and of the way of Christ, and so become united with God, and may know that, the more completely he is annihilated for God's sake, according to these two parts, the sensual and the spiritual, the more completely is he united to God and the greater is the work which he accomplishes. And when at last he is reduced to nothing, which will be the greatest extreme of humility, spiritual union will be wrought between the soul and God, which in this life is the greatest and the highest state attainable. This consists not, then, in refreshment and in consolations and spiritual feelings, but in a living death of the Cross, both as to sense and as to spirit—that is, both inwardly and outwardly.[161]

Let us sum up this text of Saint John of the Cross: the most beautiful and most elevated divine riches, outside of the possession of God Himself, are for us the occasion and cause of new impoverishments.

And this brings us to the central core of our study in this last period of spiritual ascent: the purifying nights of the spirit.

[161] *Ascent,* Bk. II, vii; Peers, I, 87.

CHAPTER III

The Dark Night of the Spirit: The Drama

And all Mount Sinai was in a smoke: because the Lord was come down upon it in fire, and the smoke arose from it as out of a furnace. And all the mount was terrible. . . .[1] *The mount burned even unto heaven: and there was darkness, and a cloud and obscurity in it.*[2]

In God's manifestation on Mount Sinai, we have a powerful symbol, almost a description, of the dark night of the spirit. God came down to the Mount to give the Law to His people; and He testified to His authority by letting His power, terrible in its strength, show forth externally. Likewise it is to assert and establish His rule in the soul that God comes to it in the dark night of the spirit. How could He do this without revealing who He is? The enrichments of His love in the dark night are accompanied by witnesses to His power like to flashes of His anger. The divine transcendence is evinced even in the law of love. When God embraces man in the depths of man's soul, the antinomies of the human and the divine declare themselves in terrible force and flame; divine love burns the soul, divine purity blackens it, omnipotence overpowers it, a dazzling light envelops in a cloud of mystery this meeting between God and man. "The mount burned even unto heaven: and there was darkness, and a cloud and obscurity in it. . . . The smoke arose

[1] Exod. 19:18.
[2] Deut. 4:11.

from it as out of a furnace. And the mount was terrible." Such too is the dark night of the spirit. The interior sufferings that it produces, and the failings externally, make of it a drama. Before trying to describe it, let us see what are its causes; at the end we shall indicate the external forms that cloak its terrible splendors.[3]

A. Causes of the dark night of the spirit

Beyond doubt, the dark night of the spirit is caused by the divine invadings of the soul, which we have previously studied.

The definition that Saint John of the Cross gives of it leaves no doubt:

> This dark night is an inflowing of God into the soul, which purges it from its ignorances and imperfections, habitual, natural and spiritual, and which is called by contemplatives infused contemplation, or mystical theology.[4]

This inflowing of God is lofty and direct. It is "the language of God to the soul, addressed by pure spirit to pure spirit."[5] God breaks through into the soul. But we may wonder how it can be that so intimate a visit brings suffering and darkness. It was under such conditions that God spoke "from mouth to mouth"[6] to Moses on Mount Sinai, when He gave him the Law of fear. Are we to conclude, then, that here we find ourselves again faced with a high manifestation of the God of the Old Testament? No indeed. It is "the loving wisdom of God,"

[3] The dark night of the spirit was the subject proposed for the Congress on religious psychology held at the Carmelite monastery at Avon, September 21–25, 1938. The reports that were there presented by theologians, philosophers, neurologists, psychiatrists, have been assembled in the October 1938 number of *Etudes Carmélitaines.* They constitute a penetrating and helpful study on the night of the spirit, its different forms and its counterfeits, the things that accompany it and that follow. We shall use these extensively in this chapter, and we refer the reader to it. Consult also *"Douleurs et stigmatisation," Etudes Carmélitaines.* October 1936, and *"Illuminations et sécheresses,"* October 1937; these give reports from preceding Congresses.

[4] *Dark Night of the Soul,* Bk. II, v; Peers, I, 381.

[5] *Ibid.,* xvii; 430.

[6] *Ibid;* 429.

says Saint John of the Cross, who produces striking effects in the soul, "for, by purging and illumining it, He prepares it for the union of love with God." [7] Loving Wisdom intends only the happiness of the soul. Explaining these painful effects, Saint John of the Cross says:

> . . . the cause of this is that, in contemplation and the Divine inflowing, there is naught that of itself can cause affliction, but that they rather cause great sweetness and delight, as we shall say hereafter.[8]

The real cause of the darkness and of the suffering lies in the soul itself:

> For two reasons this Divine Wisdom is not only night and darkness for the soul, but is likewise affliction and torment. The first is because of the height of Divine Wisdom, which transcends the talent of the soul, and in this way is darkness to it; the second, because of its vileness and impurity, in which respect it is painful and afflictive to it, and is also dark.[9]

Thus the causes of the dark night are clearly indicated. In communicating itself to the soul, Wisdom finds in it two obstacles, its impurities and its unfitness to receive the divine action. These two obstacles provoke combat and violence on the part of Wisdom, and suffering in the soul. The divine torrent lashes against the rock that stops it or restrains its flow. Clash and struggle ensue between the onrushing force of the waters and the resistant obstacle that stands in their way. The limpid torrent roars deep, covering the rock with its foam. Yet more pressure must be put upon the rock. The comparison is crude. Yet it shows the opposition God's action meets with, the violence and suffering that result in the soul. When the rock has given way, that is, when the unfitness and impurities of the soul present no further obstacles, the inflowing torrent will follow its course, rapid but peaceful.

The whole problem of the dark night rests in this play of opposition and contrast. We must add further precisions, how-

[7] *Ibid.*, v; 38.
[8] *Ibid.*, ix; 402.
[9] *Ibid.*, v; 381-2.

ever, for this statement does not explain everything. It does not, for example, say why the opposition is manifest only at this time with this violence. For long years, actually, divine Wisdom has been communicating itself to this soul. The soul has passed through the fourth and fifth Mansions and has experienced the divine riches. The dark night of sense is over and has left its beneficent and peaceful fruits. Why this change now and these new struggles? Saint John of the Cross is to give us the answer.

Certainly, the supernatural communications already received are authentic; they have wrought an important work. They have sufficiently freed the soul from the operations of sense to open it to supernatural contemplation. The calmed senses silently respect God's action within the soul and even taste in their way the divine communications. The passions have been subdued, evil tendencies mortified, especially those capital sins of which Saint John of the Cross gave in detail the evil effects in the spiritual domain.[10]

> The soul is purified and cleansed of the imperfections that were clinging to it because of the desires and affections, which of their own accord deaden and darken the soul.[11]
>
> Its imagination and faculties are no longer bound, as they were before, by meditation and anxiety of spirit, since it now very readily finds in its spirit the most serene and loving contemplation and spiritual sweetness without the labour of meditation.[12]

And yet, the purification of sense is only a prelude. Our mystical doctor says:

> The purgation of sense is only the entrance and beginning of contemplation leading to the purgation of the spirit, which, as we have likewise said, serves rather to accommodate sense to spirit than to unite spirit with God. But there still remain in the spirit the stains of the old man, although the spirit thinks not that this is so, neither can it perceive them.[13]

[10] Cf. *infra.* TO UNION OF THE WILL, ch. iii, "The Dark Nights."
[11] *Dark Night,* Bk. I, xiii; Peers, I, 368.
[12] *Ibid.,* Bk. II, i; 374.
[13] *Ibid.,* ii; 376.

True, the main work remains to be done to accommodate spirit to God, to purify it and thus make union possible. This task will be done by an appropriate action on the part of God. The various communications in the preceding period attained to the faculties. From the deep source which is God present in the soul, living waters sprang up and spread their healing floods over the intellect and will. The aridities of the beginning gave way to a predominance of peace and delight that sweetly held captive the faculties and thus favored a more lofty activity.

The divine communications of this new period are, as we have said, direct and profound in a new way. Since the grace of mystical union and the union of will which is its fruit, God's action has taken place in the substance of the soul. There God speaks a language that is a secret for the senses.[14] He "penetrates into the essence of the soul in that it is pure spirit," [15] so as to establish Himself there as master and from there rule over the whole activity of the faculties. These are henceforth to be under His direction.

This invasion of the divine brings about a veritable psychological revolution. Up to now, intellect and will have acted according to the laws of human action, that is, were guided by following the attraction of their proper object, which was presented to them by the senses or other faculties. From now on they are submissive to God's motion, which comes to them from the depths of the soul.[16] A psychological reversal: previously they moved one another in mutual interdependence and under an influence that came from the outside. Now they are other-

[14] *Ibid.*, xvii; 428.

[15] Cf. Dom Mager, *Fondements psychologiques de la purification passive,* in *Etude Carmélitaines,* October 1938, p. 246.

In this penetrating study, the learned dean of the faculty of theology of Salzburg localizes God's action in each of the various phases of the passive purifications.

[16] "Under this influence, intellect and will no longer act as moved by their proper objects but rather by the most intimate essence of the soul." Cf. Dom Mager, loc. cit.

wise moved; their impulsion to act comes to them from the One who dwells in the essence of the soul.[17]

It is easily conceivable that there should result a certain disarray, and even a painful overthrowing of accustomed ways; for this interior action of God is at times not without violence. Besides, it is always accompanied by a light that dazzles and a force that paralyzes.

The unfitness of the faculties for responding to God's impulse and receiving the inflowings of divine Wisdom comes, as we see, from their normal habits of issuing into act. The resistance they offer to God's directive action which arises from deep within the soul is the first obstacle that the dark night of the spirit will cause to fall, so as to adapt the spirit to God. It will also be first to cause suffering in this night.

The unfitness of the soul is doubled, Saint John of the Cross tells us, by reason of its impurities, the purification of which will constitute the second aim of the dark night and the second cause of suffering.

The consequences of original sin, evil tendencies, attachments, imperfect habits, these still remain in the soul after the purification of sense.[18] This purification cut off their branches, that is, put a stop to their exterior manifestations; but it left trunk and roots in the soul, at the very base of the faculties. These deep-seated tendencies weigh down the soul, draw it to external things, attach it to itself, rendering still more difficult its orientation to God and submission to divine Wisdom.

To these tendencies, which Saint John of the Cross calls habitual imperfections, actual imperfections are added. These differ widely according to souls. Ordinarily they spring from a bad use of the spiritual goods gained in the dark night of sense. The Saint writes:

[17] This psychological reorientation effected by the dark night of the spirit is well explained by R. P. Lucien de Saint Joseph in an article, "*A la recherche d'une structure,*" *Etudes Carmélitaines,* Oct. 1938, pp. 254-81.

[18] *Dark Night,* Bk. II, ii; Peers, I, 376.

Some, whose spiritual good is so superficial and so readily affected by sense, fall into greater difficulties and dangers, which we described at the beginning of this treatise. For, as they find so many and such abundant spiritual communications and apprehensions, both in sense and in spirit, wherein they oftentimes see imaginary and spiritual visions (for all these things, together with other delectable feelings, come to many souls in this state, wherein the devil and their own fancy very commonly practise deceptions on them).[19]

False visions, spiritual pride, presumption, such are the temptations and faults that afflict these souls. The Saint says:

So inveterate do they grow, that it is very doubtful if such souls will return to the pure road of virtue and true spirituality. . . .

None of these proficients, however strenuously he may have labored, is free, at best, from many of those natural affections and imperfect habits . . . they are the more incurable because such souls consider them to be more spiritual than the others . . . wherefore, in order to come to this union, the soul must needs enter into the second night of the spirit.[20]

The dark night of the spirit, painful and purifying, is produced by the encounter in the depths of the soul between the divine action and all the imperfections that are there. John of the Cross explains:

As two contraries cannot coexist in one subject—the soul—it must of necessity have pain and suffering, since it is the subject wherein these two contraries war against each other, working the one against the other.[21]

What is at stake in this encounter between the human and the divine, the purity of God and the soul's impurity, is too important for the devil not to intervene in it with all the power at his disposal. Yet a little while and the soul purified by the dark night will be secure against his attacks and will be to him a terrible thing. Hence the devil makes use of the advantages he still possesses over it because of its imperfections and its attachments to the sensible. Saint John of the Cross notes that

[19] *Ibid.;* 376-7.
[20] *Ibid.;* 377.
[21] *Ibid.*, v; 382.

"the evil one takes his stand, with great cunning, on the road which leads from sense to spirit." [22]

The darkness of these regions, the soul's disarray, disconcerted as it is by the newness of its experiences and the intensity of its suffering, create conditions particularly favorable to the interventions of the prince of darkness and of lies.

By certain exterior signs of calm and of deep silence in the senses, the devil easily guesses that the soul is receiving divine communications. Our mystical doctor says:

> Of those favours which come through a good angel God habitually allows the enemy to have knowledge: partly so that he may do that which he can against them according to the measure of justice, and that thus he may not be able to allege with truth that no opportunity is given him for conquering the soul, as he said concerning Job.[23]

Such are the facts in the problem of the dark night of the spirit, and the causes that produce it. This night is an encounter, or rather a real combat, organized by loving Wisdom. God establishes His perfect reign in the soul only after taking away its unfitness for the divine and conquering all the forces of evil that have any power over it.

The dark night of the spirit is truly a drama. To get some light on its horror and explain its fruitfulness, one must compare it with the drama of Gethsemane, which it prolongs. Gethsemane was witness to the conflict between the purity of God and the sin of the world, waged in the sacred humanity of Christ who bore that twofold weight. In His humanity, He was crushed by it, broken, made into nothingness. A few plaints to the apostles, some groanings heard in the night, the sweat of blood, by these one can guess at the horror of the silent, profound drama that the darkness of mystery enveloped. And yet, the redemption of mankind, the birth and growth of the Church have revealed the stature of the victory won in that combat by the patient Christ. The dark night of the spirit is a participation in that suffering and that victory.

[22] *Living Flame,* st. iii; Peers, III, 83.
[23] *Dark Night,* Bk. II, xxiii; Peers, I, 449.

Yet we must not identify completely the two combats. Some distinctions need be made. Jesus had upon Him the anointing of the Godhead, and the sin of the entire world. However high may be the soul's communications with God, it receives only a created and finite grace; and the sin it bears is its own. Christ's combat had for its stake the salvation of all humanity, and He was victorious. The dark night of the spirit has at stake the lofty perfection of one soul. And yet, not just one soul hangs in the balance. This is no individual combat. He who comes out victorious from the battle becomes necessarily an apostle, a trainer of others. Hence, all proportions kept, it is indeed Gethsemane that is prolonged in the dark night of the spirit that the valiant undergo. The whole Church has an interest in their victory.

B. The drama

> The first purgation or night is bitter and terrible to sense. . . . The second bears no comparison with it, for it is horrible and awful to the spirit.[24]

Thus writes John of the Cross.

The first prepares the second, says the Saint:

> For very great fortitude is needful for so violent and severe a purgation, since, if the weakness of the lower part has not first been corrected and fortitude has not been gained from God through the sweet and delectable communion which the soul has afterwards enjoyed with Him, its nature will not have the strength or the disposition to bear it.[25]

At the beginning of the sixth Mansions, Teresa too cries out:

> Oh, my God, how great are these trials which the soul will suffer, both within and without, before it enters the seventh Mansion! Really, when I think of them, I am sometimes afraid that, if we realized their intensity beforehand, it would be most difficult for us, naturally weak as we are, to muster determination enough to enable us to suffer them or resolution enough for enduring them, however attractively the advantage of so doing might be presented to us.[26]

24 *Ibid.,* Bk. I, viii; 349-50.
25 *Ibid.,* Bk. II, iii; 379.
26 VI Mansions, i; Peers, II, 269.

Saint John of the Cross sums up his experience by saying:

> Of such are they that in truth go down alive into hell, being purged here on earth in the same manner as there.[27]

Thus we are forewarned by the testimony of our two masters, both of whom experienced it. As these sufferings are mysterious to us by their very nature as well as by their intensity, we have no other resource in describing them than to draw largely upon the descriptions left us by those who knew them by experience.

In order to proceed with order, let us, following Saint Teresa's suggestion, divide these sufferings into interior ones and exterior. The first being mainly spiritual, are the most important; the second, more visible, are ordinarily a consequence of the first.

1. INTERIOR SUFFERINGS

The magnificent pages that Saint John of the Cross has devoted to the description of the distress and pain of the soul under God's action make of him the incomparable poet of the dark night.

The order that he adopts in this description is more apparent than real. There is question in fact of only one and the same suffering, of a weight that oppresses, of a darkness that paralyzes, an anguish that suffocates. To mark its intensity and depth, the holy doctor adds one touch after another to the description. He shows forth the suffering in its diverse aspects and places it in different lights. He mentions several particular traits, and then later returns to accentuate them. At times his pen seems to be stopped, powerless. He then appeals to the simple and sublime poetry of Scripture texts, to their inspired power, and lets himself be carried along by them. Thus he introduces us into the abyss of a suffering without name. When we have the impression of sinking with him into despair, he suddenly rises up with serene strength, and upraises us too

[27] *Dark Night,* Bk. II, vi; Peers, I, 387.

into the light and certitude of the approaching triumph of God and His grace.

First we have a *vue d'ensemble:*

In poverty, and without protection or support in all the apprehensions of my soul—that is, in the darkness of my understanding and the constraint of my will, in affliction and anguish with respect to memory, remaining in the dark in pure faith, which is dark night for the said natural faculties, the will alone being touched by grief and afflictions and yearnings for the love of God—I went forth from myself.[28]

Thus declares the soul at the beginning. All the faculties, as we see, are assailed. Yet, although the torment is general, one suffering dominates and seems to be cause of all the others: the dazzle from the divine light within.

When this Divine light of contemplation assails the soul which is not yet wholly enlightened, it causes spiritual darkness in it; for not only does it overcome it, but likewise it overwhelms it and darkens the act of its natural intelligence. For this reason Saint Dionysius and other mystical theologians call this infused contemplation a ray of darkness. . . . Wherefore David likewise said: That near to God and round about Him are darkness and cloud; not that this is so in fact, but that it is so to our weak understanding, which is blinded and darkened by so vast a light, to which it cannot attain. For this cause the same David then explained himself, saying: 'Through the great splendour of His presence passed clouds'—that is, between God and our understanding.[29]

This light, so resplendent that it paralyzes the faculties and reduces to darkness the divine fire whence it proceeds, shows up in astonishing clarity on the other hand the impurities of the soul, placing in strong opposition to them the purity of God. Thus two contraries assert themselves; and contraries cannot co-exist in the same subject. Hence, the struggle and suffering.

When the soul suffers the direct assault of this Divine light, its pain, which results from its impurity, is immense; because, when this pure light assails the soul, it is in order to expel its impurity . . .[30]

[28] *Ibid.*, iv; 380.
[29] *Ibid.*, v; 382.
[30] *Ibid.*, vi; 383.

The soul thus discovers painfully how far it is from God; even, how set in opposition seemingly to Him.

The soul feels itself to be so impure and miserable that it believes God to be against it, and thinks that it has set itself up against God. This causes it sore grief and pain, because it now believes that God has cast it away: this was one of the greatest trials which Job felt when God sent him this experience, and he said: 'Why hast Thou set me contrary to Thee, so that I am grievous and burdensome to myself?' [31]

In its opposition the soul feels the weight of the mighty hand of God, which oppresses and crushes it. This causes it new suffering. As the Saint explains:

When this Divine contemplation assails the soul with a certain force . . . sense and spirit, as if beneath some immense and dark load, are in such great pain and agony that the soul would find advantage and relief in death. This had been experienced by the prophet Job, when he said: 'I desire not that He should have intercourse with me in great strength, lest He oppress me with the weight of His greatness.' [32]

But not only do the human and the divine confront each other exteriorly; a battle unto death is waged within their very substance. This it is that produces the third suffering.

The Divine assails the soul in order to renew it, . . . destroys and consumes its spiritual substance, and absorbs it in deep and profound darkness. As a result of this, the soul feels itself to be perishing and melting away in the presence and sight of its miseries, in a cruel spiritual death, even as if it had been swallowed by a beast and felt itself being devoured in the darkness of its belly, suffering such anguish as was endured by Jonas in the belly of that beast of the sea. . . .

A description of this suffering and pain, although in truth it transcends all description, is given by David, when he says: 'The lamentations of death compassed me about; the pains of hell surrounded me; I cried in my tribulation.' But what the sorrowful soul feels most in this condition is its clear perception, as it thinks, that God has abandoned it, and, in His abhorrence of it, has flung it into darkness. . . . All this is felt by the soul in this condition——yea, and more, for it believes that it is so with it for ever.

It feels, too, that all creatures have forsaken it, and that it is contemned by them, particularly by its friends. Wherefore David presently

[31] *Ibid.*
[32] *Ibid;* 383-4.

continues, saying: 'Thou has put far from me my friends and acquaintances; they have counted me an abomination.'[33]

New depths are thus hollowed out of the soul by God's action within it, causing a painful void. And this is the fourth suffering that the purifying flames produce. Saint John of the Cross writes:

For it feels within itself a profound emptiness and impoverishment of three kinds of good which are ordained for the pleasure of the soul, which are the temporal, the natural and the spiritual; and finds itself set in the midst of the evils contrary to these, namely, miseries of imperfection, aridity and emptiness of the apprehensions of the faculties and abandonment of the spirit in darkness.[34]

In this abandonment and deprivation of all support, the soul experiences the pain of emptiness and of suffocation. The Saint continues:

The soul not only suffers this emptiness and the suspension of these natural supports and perceptions, which is a most afflictive suffering (as if a man were suspended or held in the air so that he could not breathe), but likewise He is purging the soul, annihilating it, emptying it or consuming in it (even as fire consumes the mouldiness and the rust of metal) all the affections and imperfect habits which it has contracted in its whole life. Since these are deeply rooted in the substance of the soul, it is wont to suffer great undoing and inward torment.[35]

With his profound understanding of Sacred Scriptures, the mystical doctor applies to this purifying torment, to this melting of the soul in the divine fire, the vigorous symbol of the bones, taken from Ezechiel:

There may here be fulfilled that passage from Ezechiel which says: 'Heap together the bones and I will burn them in the fire; the flesh shall be consumed and the whole composition shall be burned and the bones shall be destroyed.' Herein is understood the pain which is suffered in the emptiness and poverty of the substance of the soul both in sense and in spirit. And concerning this he then says: 'Set it also empty upon the coals, that its metal may become hot and molten, and its uncleanness may be destroyed within it, and its rust may be

[33] *Ibid.*; 384-5.
[34] *Ibid.*; 386.
[35] *Ibid.*

consumed.' Herein is described the grave suffering which the soul here endures in the purgation of the fire of this contemplation, for the Prophet says here that, in order for the rust of the affections which are within the soul to be purified and destroyed, it is needful that, in a certain manner, the soul itself should be annihilated and destroyed, since these passions and imperfections have become natural to it.[36]

This so expressive comparison shows that there is question not only of a breaking with imperfections, of a superficial purification, but more, of a complete overthrowing interiorly—of a new creating of the soul in the fire. Its wound is not just on the surface; the soul is one great wound, it is molten under the action of the burning fire. Thus it reaches the very limits of human power to suffer. Speaking of how God now humbles the soul, Saint John of the Cross says:

> If He ordained not that, when these feelings arise within the soul, they should speedily be stilled, it would die in a very short space; but there are only occasional periods when it is conscious of their greatest intensity. At times, however, they are so keen that the soul seems to be seeing hell, being purged here on earth in the same manner as there.[37]

The remembrance of past prosperity, that is, of graces with which the soul was favored before entering into the dark night, adds to the weight of the present pain.

> This was also described by Job, who had had experience of it, in these words: "I, who was wont to be wealthy and rich, am suddenly undone and broken to pieces; He hath taken me by my neck; He hath broken me and set me up for His mark to wound me; He hath compassed me round about with His lances; He hath wounded all my loins; He hath not spared; He hath poured out my bowels on the earth; He hath broken me with wound upon wound; He hath assailed me as a strong giant; I have sewed sackcloth upon my skin and have covered my flesh with ashes; my face is become swollen with weeping and mine eyes are blinded.[38]

Job and Jeremias are the great Biblical poets of suffering. After citing the first at length, John of the Cross borrows the pen of the second to give us an idea of the torments of the

[36] *Ibid.;* 386-7.
[37] *Ibid.;* 387.
[38] *Ibid.,* vii; 388.

dark night of the spirit, so numerous and so terrible that he declares himself powerless to describe them.

And, that we may bring the exposition of this line to a close and explain more fully what is worked in the soul by this night, I shall tell what Jeremias felt about it, which, since there is so much of it, he describes and bewails in many words after this manner: "I am the man that sees my poverty in the rod of His indignation; He hath threatened me and brought me into darkness and not into light. So far hath He turned against me and hath converted His hand upon me all the day. My skin and my flesh hath He made old; He hath broken my bones; He hath made a fence around me and compassed me with gall and trial; He hath set me in dark places, as those that are dead for ever. He hath made a fence around me and against me, that I may not go out; He hath made my captivity heavy; Yea, and when I have cried and have entreated, He hath shut out my prayer. He hath enclosed my paths and ways out with square stones; He hath thwarted my steps. He hath set ambushes for me; He hath become to me a lion in a secret place. He hath turned aside my steps and broken me in pieces; He hath made me desolate; He hath bent His bow and set me as a mark for His arrow. He hath shot into my reins the daughters of His quiver. I have become a derision to all the people, and laughter and scorn for them all the day. He hath filled me with bitterness and hath made me drunken with wormwood. He hath broken my teeth by number; He hath fed me with ashes. My soul is cast out from peace; I have forgotten good things. And I said: "Mine end is frustrated and cut short, together with my desire and my hope from the Lord. Remember my poverty and my excess, the wormwood and the gall. I shall be mindful with remembrance and my soul shall be undone within me in pains." [39]

All the lamentations that the soul utters through the mouth of Job and of Jeremias are aimed at God. He it is who causes all its woes. His merciful action is cruel to the soul that it is preparing for perfect union. To purify and adorn it, God wounds it painfully.

There is still another torment: God seems to let loose against the soul the heinous power of Satan. John of the Cross has already warned us that the devil ordinarily knows, by external indications or by God's special permission, the communications God is making to the soul. When these communications take a sensible form, such as feelings, visions, words, his game con-

[39] *Ibid.;* 388-9.

sists in counterfeiting the divine action by producing the same phenomena. Or at other times, he suggests thoughts of presumption and pride, by which he can deceive and seduce the soul.[40] When the regions where purely spiritual communications take place are closed to the devil, he tries to disturb them by indirect action. Saint John of the Cross explains:

> As he sees that he cannot succeed in thwarting them in the depth of the soul, he does what he can to disturb and disquiet the sensual part—that part to which he is able to attain—now by means of afflictions, now by terrors and fears, with intent to disquiet and disturb the higher and spiritual part of the soul by this means, with respect to that blessing which it then receives and enjoys.[41]

When the spiritual communication involves a sensible element, the devil works his way in more easily, troubling the spirit by means of the senses.

> Great are the torment and the affliction which are then caused in the spirit; at times they exceed all that can be expressed. For, when there is a naked contact of spirit with spirit, the horror is intolerable which the evil spirit causes in the good spirit (I mean, in the soul), when its tumult reaches it.[42]

At times the devil succeeds in revealing his presence to the soul in a spiritual way.

> And thus, in order to attack the soul, in the same way as that wherein it is being visited, his fearful spirit presents a similar vision in order to attack and destroy spiritual things by spiritual.[43]

If the soul does not make a quick escape into the obscure regions of faith, the devil seems to prevail

> . . . and encompasses the soul wth a perturbation and horror which is a greater affliction to it than any torment in this life could be. For, as this horrible communication passes direct from spirit to spirit, in something like nakedness and clearly distinguished from all that is corporeal, it is grievous beyond what every sense can feel; and this lasts in the spirit for some time, yet not for long, for otherwise the

[40] *Ibid.*, ii; 377.
[41] *Ibid.*, xxiii; 448.
[42] *Ibid.*; 449.
[43] *Ibid.*; 450.

spirit would be driven forth from the flesh by the vehement communication of the other spirit. Afterwards there remains to it the memory thereof, which is sufficient to cause it great affliction.[44]

The soul, then, finds within itself only causes for suffering. God and Satan seem to have joined forces to torment it. Can it at least hope for a little spiritual consolation from outside? Saint Teresa has reported her trials on this score:

In this spiritual tempest no consolation is possible. If she decides to take up the matter with her confessor, it would look as if the devils have come to his aid so that he may torture her soul the more. A certain confessor, dealing with a person who had been in this state of torment, after it had passed away, thought that the oppression must have been of a dangerous type, since it had involved her in so many trials; so he told her, whenever she was in this state, to report to him; but this made her so much worse that he came to realize that he could no longer do anything with her.[45]

"Wherefore," says Saint John of the Cross, "the soul that God sets in this tempestuous and horrible night is deserving of great compassion." [46]

"Oh, Jesus!" Saint Teresa cries, "how sad it is to see a soul thus forsaken." [47]

[44] *Ibid;* 451.

Concerning the devil's action during this period, Saint Teresa writes: "[this soul] believes what the imagination (now mistress of the understanding) presents to it and the nonsense which the devil attempts to present to it, when Our Lord gives him leave to test her soul, and even to make her think herself cast off by God. For there are many things which assault her soul with an interior oppression so keenly felt and so intolerable that I do not know to what it can be compared, save to the torment of those who suffer in hell." VI Mansions, i; Peers, II, 273.

[45] *Ibid.* In the same chapter Saint Teresa speaks of "the torture which it costs us to have to do with a confessor so scrupulous and inexperienced that he thinks nothing safe: he is afraid of everything, and doubtful about everything, as soon as he sees that he is dealing with anything out of the ordinary. This is particularly so if he sees any imperfection in the soul that is undergoing these experiences . . . he attributes the whole thing to melancholy or to the devil. . . . But, when the poor soul, harassed by the same fear, goes to the confessor as to a judge, and he condemns her, she cannot fail to be upset and tortured by what he says—and only a person who has passed through such a trial will know how great it is." *Ibid.;* 272.

[46] *Ibid.,* vii; 389.

[47] VI Mansions, i; Peers, II, 274.

Avowals of sympathy and encouragement do not succeed, however, in piercing the wall of anguish that surrounds it. Both John of the Cross and Teresa affirm this:

> Although in many ways its director may show it good reason for being comforted because of the blessings which are contained in these afflictions, it cannot believe him. For it is so greatly absorbed and immersed in the realization of those evils wherein it sees its own miseries so clearly, that it thinks that, as its director observes not that which it sees and feels, he is speaking in this manner because he understands it not.[48]

And in her turn Teresa says:

> So do not suppose, sisters, if you ever find yourselves in this condition, that people who are wealthy, or free to do as they like, have any better remedy for such times. No, no; to offer them earthly consolations would be like telling criminals condemned to death about all the joys that there are in the world; not only would this fail to comfort them—it would but increase their torment; comfort must come to them from above, for earthly things are of no value to them any more.[49]

And yet at times the door of the dark prison seems to stand ajar and the soul

> . . . is brought into the recreation of spaciousness and liberty. . . . Occasionally this is so great that the soul believes its trials to be at last over.[50]

But the respite is fleeting:

> When the soul is most secure and least alert, it is dragged down and immersed again in another and a worse degree of affliction which is severer and darker and more grievous than that which is past; and this new affliction will continue for a further period of time, perhaps longer than the first.[51]

These alternations between light and darkness only increase the soul's suffering and make it doubt if the trial will ever end.

Thus everything contributes to making its anguish more acute, even to its great love for God, which makes it see very

[48] *Dark Night,* Bk. II, vii; Peers, I, 390.
[49] VI Mansions, i; Peers, II, 274.
[50] *Dark Night,* Bk. II, vii; Peers, I, 390.
[51] *Ibid.;* 391.

clearly "reasons for deserving to be cast out by Him for Whom it has such great love and desire." [52]

Such are the sufferings that characterize the dark night of the spirit. The echoes from them that we have picked up indicate their depth and intensity. Their diversity is only apparent; it comes from a complexity of reactions to the action of a single cause. This cause is the purifying blade of the divine light which cuts into the wounds of sin at the very root of the faculties to open them up and heal them. The night of the spirit is above all a drama of the inmost depths. And yet this drama, because it is intense and profound, produces repercussions in more external regions; these make more of an impression because more visible.

2. EXTERNAL SUFFERINGS

Sin has accentuated the opposition between body and soul in our human nature; nevertheless, they are so closely united that each takes upon itself the weight of any constraint that burdens the other. And so it is normal that the spiritual suffering of the soul, so intense in the dark night of the spirit, should spread to the body and there have sensible effects. Moreover, since the dark night of the spirit is to bring to completion the purification of the senses, it seems necessary that it assail the sense powers not only by ricochet or rebound, but also directly, if it is indeed to complete its work. From this cleansing, the soul comes forth with that essential purity that disposes it for perfect union with God, and with that suppleness that is to make of it a docile instrument, fit for the tasks God reserves for it in His Church.

For all these reasons, the suffering becomes exterior and sensible. In the external manifestations of the dark night of the spirit, we distinguish three groups of phenomena:

a. Perturbations that are the ordinary consequence of God's action within.

b. Trials brought about by external agents.

[52] *Ibid.*, 393.

c. Phenomena or disorders that take an extraordinary form under the influence either of pathological tendencies or of some agent, supernatural or preternatural.

This study could be extended into very interesting developments, examining to advantage particular cases. In accord with our plan, however, we shall limit ourselves to determining the different categories of phenomena, bringing to bear on them some speculative judgments that may give light as to the practical attitude to be taken in their regard.

a. Ordinary perturbations produced by God's action.

1. *Psychological phenomena*

Ordinarily it is the faculties which perceive with the greatest intensity God's action in the center of the soul. First of all, they are aware of the force of it during this period when it is particularly intense. Beginning with the fifth Mansions, Saint Teresa describes the loss of consciousness and suspension of the faculties produced by the enriching contacts of God with the substance of the soul.[53] And when the soul is carried away in transports or raptures, the faculties are again suspended, being as it were annihilated in their own operations.[54] When they recover consciousness and their liberty, they experience an impression of painful surprise,[55] a certain terror at feeling themselves at the mercy of this mysterious force that suddenly rises up within and masters them as a giant would a straw.[56] Although God's action has put them at peace, they cannot help fearing that they have been victims of an illusion or a trick of the devil.[57] Another rather usual reaction following the return of consciousness is a state of agitation, which may even reach a certain frenzy. The faculties seem in this way to assert their independence after the constraint to which they have been subjected. Or better, like children whom the authority of a

[53] V Mansions, i; Peers, II, 247.
[54] VI Mansions, iv; 291.
[55] V Mansions, i; 251.
[56] VI Mansions, v; 293.
[57] V Mansions, i; 251.

master has kept attentive and diligent for a rather long time, they let go free, disorderly and noisy, the forces eager for life that a superior power has strongly mastered and curbed.

These psychological phenomena are usually transitory, as is the shock from which they are a reaction. There are some that are more constant; these must be attributed to the psychological reorientation caused by the dark night of the spirit.

As God progressively takes over the direction of the soul by imposing upon it from within His lights and impulsions, the normal process of the activity of the faculties is upset; this redirection is furthered by the fact that the senses, which ordinarily supply the faculties their food, are themselves paralyzed. There results in the psychological domain a profound disarray, which is evinced by a powerlessness and painful impressions.

Not only is meditation or the forming of concepts about dogmatic truths impossible, but also that loving attention which was so advantageously substituted for reasoning during the first dark night. Because it now attacks the root of the faculties, the powerlessness is general, extended to all the soul's operations. It even bears on temporal affairs, which the soul no longer seems capable of treating. Lapses in memory make it lose consciousness of time and of what it is doing. To this soul, habituated to enjoying God's action within it in a luminous interior sweetness and a rich balance of the faculties, which were the fruit of that action, this powerlessness and emptiness, and these failures, give the impression, sometimes a certitude, that God has abandoned it, and that it is going to founder in a pathological breakdown. Saint John of the Cross writes:

> It is unable to raise its affection or its mind to God, neither can it pray to Him, thinking, as Jeremias thought concerning himself, that God has set a cloud before it through which its prayer cannot pass. . . . And if it sometimes prays it does so with such lack of strength and of sweetness that it thinks that God neither hears it nor pays heed to it. . . . Hence it can neither pray nor pay attention when it is present at the Divine offices, much less can it attend to other things and affairs which are temporal. Not only so, but it has likewise such distractions and times of such profound forgetfulness of the memory

that frequent periods pass by without its knowing what it has been doing or thinking, or what it is that it is doing or is going to do, neither can it pay attention, although it desire to do so, to anything that occupies it.[58]

The experience of Saint Teresa in these lofty regions does not differ from that of Saint John of the Cross. She speaks of her understanding as being "so dim that it is incapable of seeing the truth," [59] and of its being dominated by the imagination "and the nonsense which the devil attempts to present to it." [60] Prayer is impossible, or at least it seems fruitless. But let us hear what Saint Teresa says :

Now what will a poor creature like that do if such a thing goes on for a very long time? If she prays, she might as well not be doing so at all—I mean for all the comfort it will bring her, for interiorly she is incapable of receiving any comfort, nor, even when her prayer is vocal, can she understand what she is saying; while mental prayer at such a time is certainly impossible—her faculties are not capable of it.

Solitude is still worse for her, though it is also torture for her to be in anyone's company or to be spoken to; and so, despite all her efforts to conceal the fact, she becomes outwardly upset and despondent to a very noticeable extent.

Is it credible that she will be able to say what is the matter with her? The thing is inexpressible, for this distress and oppression are spiritual troubles and cannot be given a name.[61]

This generalized inability, this utter darkness that veils in painful helplessness all the faculties, these are psychological phenomena characteristic of the night of the spirit. In the dark night of sense the depth of the soul still kept life and activity. And later, when the psychological reorientation is completed, there will be trouble and agitation in some faculties—as Saint Teresa mentions having experienced it while writing the Prologue of the *Interior Castle* [62]—but the soul will continue to work in a fruitful fashion.

[58] *Dark Night,* II, viii; Peers, I, 393-4.
[59] VI Mansions, i; Peers, II, 273.
[60] *Ibid.*
[61] *Ibid.;* 294.
[62] "For the last three months I have been suffering from such noises and

This complete powerlessness now, this disorder of the faculties—the consequence, it would seem, of failure in the will—this suffering without discernible cause, in brief, the ensemble of these psychological phenomena in acute form, make one think of pathological cases that psychiatry would make quick work of naming and classifying. And yet these phenomena, which may assume diverse forms according to temperaments and bear the mark of pathological tendencies in the slight degree in which they are found in the well-balanced man, these are the normal consequence of God's action in the soul.

The divine action, powerful and profound, ordinarily produces a shock that jars the soul. The reversal of psychological activity, which is a beneficent effect, cannot, in its first period, but disorient and annihilate painfully the faculties. We must make these statements in order to dispel any ambiguity and set limits to the extraordinary, of which we shall have to speak a little farther on.

2. *Physical phenomena*

The perturbation produced by God's action in the soul spreads out through all its powers like the undulations on the surface of waves; it reaches to the most exterior. Thus are added to the psychological phenomena, which testify to how much the faculties of the soul are affected, physical phenomena, which show the effects of the disturbance in the senses and the

---

weakness in the head that I find it troublesome to write even about necessary business."*Interior Castle,* Prologue; Peers, II, 199.

Farther on she explains: "As I write this, the noises in my head are so loud that I am beginning to wonder what is going on in it. As I said at the outset, they have been making it almost impossible for me to obey those who commanded me to write. My head sounds just as if it were full of brimming rivers, and then as if all the water in those rivers came suddenly rushing downward; and a host of little birds seem to be whistling, not in the ears, but in the upper part of the head, where the higher part of the soul is said to be." IV Mansions, i; 234.

Five months later, she speaks again of the pain in her head which prevents her rereading what she had written. V Mansions, iv; 236.

This interior noise does not hinder her then from writing her masterpiece, the *Interior Castle.*

body. From the beginning of the sixth Mansions, Saint Teresa mentions illness among the trials that the soul meets with in these regions:

> The Lord is also in the habit of sending the most grievous infirmities. This is a much greater trial, especially if the pains are severe.[63]
> I know a person who, for the forty years since God began to grant her the favor of which we have spoken,[64] could say in all truth that she had not passed a single day without suffering and without enduring various pains; I want to speak of her poor health as well as of her great trials.[65]

While Saint Teresa points out the concomitance of mystical graces and illnesses, she does not affirm any relation of causality. The rapprochement that she makes, however, suggests that there is one. Moreover, she says that God's action in the soul in the sixth Mansions affects the senses and the body through visions, ecstasies, elevation of the body.

> Do you suppose it causes but little perturbation to a person in complete possession of his senses when he experiences these transports of the soul? We have even read in some authors that the body is transported as well as the soul, without knowing whither it is going, or who is bearing it away. . . .
> Can any means of resisting this be found? None whatever: on the contrary, resistance only makes matters worse. This I know from a certain person . . . it must realize that it is no longer its own mistress, and so the violence with which it is transported becomes markedly greater. This person, therefore, decided to offer no more resistance than a straw does when it is lifted up by amber (if you have ever observed this). . . . And, speaking of straw, it is a fact that a powerful man cannot bear away a straw more easily than this great and powerful Giant of ours can bear away the spirit.[66]

The comparison with a powerful giant picking up a piece of straw translates well the impression of a transcendent force, such as the Saint experienced in her raptures. In this attack of

[63] VI Mansions, i; 271.

[64] This is the grace of mystical union with which the Saint was favored during her novitiate or the following year. Cf. *Life,* iv; Peers, I.

[65] For these trials of illnessess, Cf. *Life,* v; Peers, I, 26 f. and *Foundations,* passim.

[66] VI Mansions, v; Peers, II, 293.

a supernatural power that makes its action felt even in the body, the physical forces at first exhaust themselves in resisting. Vanquished, they must submit to the domination of that unknown force that destroys their balance and normal activity. Hence there is a veritable breaking physically.

The objection may perhaps be made that this direct action on the body, producing raptures accompanied by levitation, is among the extraordinary graces, and that consequently one cannot draw from it a general law. But in this connection Saint Teresa herself tells us of a purely spiritual action that places one's life in danger. She speaks of a wound made in the inmost depth of the soul by a certain ray of fire:

> I once saw a person in this state who I really believed was dying; and this was not at all surprising, because it does in fact involve great peril of death. Although it lasts only for a short time, it leaves the limbs quite disjointed, and, for as long as it continues, the pulse is as feeble as though the soul were about to render itself up to God. It really is quite as bad as this. For, while the natural heat of the body fails, the soul burns so fiercely within that, if the flame were only a little stronger, God would have fulfilled its desires. It is not that it feels any bodily pain whatsoever, notwithstanding such a dislocation of the limbs that for two or three days afterwards it is in great pain and has not the strength even to write.[67]

Saint John of the Cross gives us the explanation of these dislocations and weaknesses under the influence of spiritual action. He writes at the beginning of the *Dark Night of the Spirit:*

> As, however, this sensual part of the soul is weak and incapable of experiencing the strong things of the spirit, it follows that these proficients, by reason of this spiritual communication which is made to their sensual part, endure therein many frailties and sufferings and weaknesses of the stomach, and in consequence are fatigued in spirit. For, as the Wise Man says: 'The corruptible body presseth down the soul.' Hence comes it that the communications that are granted to these souls cannot be very strong or very intense or very spiritual, as is required for Divine union with God, by reason of the weakness and corruption of the sensual nature which has a part in them. Hence

[67] *Ibid.*, xi; 325.

arise the raptures and trances and dislocations of the bones which always happen when the communications are not purely spiritual—that is, are not given to the spirit alone, as are those of the perfect who are purified by the second night of the spirit, and in whom these raptures and torments of the body no longer exist, since they are enjoying liberty of spirit, and their senses are now neither clouded nor transported.[68]

Some very precious information is summed up in these few lines. First, that spiritual communications received in the spirit redound to the region of sense; [69] also, assurance that the physical failings are produced by the violence of the impact of the spiritual communications against the heaviness, the impurity, the lack of fitness of the senses; the latter place obstacles, thus arresting the force of the communications and their freedom. Hence raptures and ecstasies are weaknesses, the normal consequence of the resistance that comes from lack of suppleness and purity of soul. Actually, as the sense part goes on being purified, it will more and more leave full liberty to the spirit, and these external phenomena will disappear.

Thus is explained the fact that the first spiritual shocks may cause profound physical disturbances. Indeed, the graces of union that Teresa received during the first years of her religious life were not unrelated to that physical breakdown that brought her to the threshold of the grave.[70] And may we not believe that the strange illness from which Saint Therese of the Child Jesus suffered was caused both by God's action in her soul and by the emotional upset she felt at the entrance of her sister Pauline into Carmel.[71]

[68] *Dark Night,* Bk. II, i; Peers, I, 375.

[69] Elsewhere Saint John of the Cross says "each part after its own manner eating of one and the same spiritual food and from one and the same dish." *Ibid.,* iii; 378.

[70] *Life,* v; Peers, I, 31.—Speaking of mystical union in chapter eighteen, Saint Teresa writes on the other hand: "This prayer, for however long it may last, does no harm; at least, it has never done any to me, nor do I ever remember feeling any ill effects after the Lord has granted me this favour, however unwell I may have been; indeed, I am generally much the better for it."

[71] *Autobiography,* iii. In these two cases the intervention of a preternatural cause is not to be excluded.

3. *Physical localizations*

Neurologists who study the reactions that intellectual perceptions have in the body tell us that these are diffuse and extensive. This law must be kept in mind. It allows us to foresee that general conditions of *malaise* will be the normal effect of the purification or dark night of the spirit.[72]

Nevertheless, in certain cases, according to the temperament of the organism affected, this illness will take particular forms or will localize its effects. Just as a shock from the impact of a steel beam vibrates over a whole surface but reveals the hidden air bubble by breaking at that point the thing that was struck, just so the divine impact, the irradiation of which spreads through the whole body, affects more painfully the weak points of that organism and shows up its pathological tendencies.

Such conditions render very difficult a diagnosis of the physical disturbances produced by God's action in the soul. The general *malaise* does not disclose its cause, and the localization that attracts attention may lead astray efforts at diagnosis. The collaboration of a medical doctor and a spiritual director is necessary in such cases. The doctor, even should he be a psychiatrist, could not ordinarily grasp all aspects of the problem and hence would not suffice for the cure. If, deceived by the localization of the malady, he should attribute it to a purely physiological cause and hope to master it solely by an appropriate therapeutic, his interventions might become harmful.[73] The role of

[72] On the subject of the nature of moral suffering and of its physiological transmission to the area of intellectual perceptions by the excitation of the cortical sense centers affected, see the studies made by Pr. Le Grand and Dr. Tinel in *Etudes Carmélitaines*—Oct. 1936, pp. 95 and 115. Dr. Tinel writes: "The higher one goes in the development of the nervous system the more one finds that reactions are naturally more diffuse and more extensive." Art. cit., p. 95.

[73] It would be quite indelicate for the medical science of our day, so much better informed and more penetrating, to recall the treatment that Saint Teresa underwent at Becedas and that almost killed her. Yet it remains true that a treatment, although quite scientific, can be very harmful when it takes no cognizance of the principal supernatural cause that produced the disorder. We are thinking especially of hasty surgery done without a sure and verified diagnosis. Psychoanalysis, too, can have harmful effects for spiritual progress.

the doctor in such a case consists, less than ever, in eradicating pain,[74] the cause of which he cannot actually reach. He must rather sustain and strengthen the organism to bear the physical weight of grace and the disturbances produced by its constant pressure on the soul or by the shock of its extraordinary inflowings. The spiritual director will prudently watch during this time to see that these illnesses and the necessary medication do not turn the soul in upon itself and occupy it too much with its illness and possible relief. More vigorously than ever, he will help it to go out of itself and look to God alone, who wounds only to heal. A long patience, animated by supernatural hope, will be therefore the most efficacious remedy, if not the only one. Since these physical maladies are actually the result of God's intense action within and of the patient's lack of suppleness and purity, the latter's duty is clear: to do nothing that might diminish the supernatural force and efficacy of the divine action and patiently to wait until that action itself produces the purity and suppleness that will neutralize its sensible effects.

b. Trials coming from exterior agents

Everything becomes a cause of suffering for the soul during this period, as it was for Christ Jesus during His passion. Suffering envelops it on all sides. All things seem in league against it. Persecution at the hands of this world is added to the interior sufferings of Gethsemane and to the bloody sweat that manifests exteriorly its violence and depth. Saint Teresa writes

[74] In the study from which we have already quoted (*Etudes Carmélitaines*, Oct. 1936, p. 99) Father Le Grand, in accord with Westfried, notes that pain has a prophylactic function because it draws attention to a defective function of the organism which, without pain, might pass unnoticed. This indication must be used to discover the malady and to cure it. Medication must attain to the root of the evil and not be satisfied with giving momentary relief from the pain, at least when the trouble can truly be eradicated. In the case that we are considering, this remark is of great importance. The abuse of sedatives, by creating a need for immediate relief, diminishes the resistance of the subject and risks neutralizing the spiritual purification which must be wrought in patience, suppleness, purity, and self-renunciation. The problem is delicate. The dosage to be given must be such that it will sustain without weakening, calm the patient and at the same time free him from self.

Oh, my God, how great are these trials which the soul will suffer, both within and without, before it enters the seventh Mansion! . . . I think it will be well if I tell you about some of the things which I know are certain to happen here. . . .

An outcry is made by people with whom such a person is acquainted, and even by those with whom she is not acquainted and who she never in her life supposed would think about her at all. "How holy she's getting!" they exclaim, or "She's only going to those extremes to deceive the world and to make other people look sinful, when really they are better Christians then she is without any of these goings-on!" (Notice, by the way, that she is not really indulging in any "goings-on" at all: she is only trying to live up to her profession.) Then people whom she had thought her friends abandon her and it is they who say the worst things of all and express the deepest regret that (as they put it) she is "going to perdition" and "obviously being deluded," that "this is the devil's work," that "she's going the way of So-and-so and So-and-so, who ruined their own lives and dragged good people down with them," and that "she takes in all her confessors." And they actually go to her confessors and tell them so, illustrating what they say by stories of some who ruined their lives in this way: and they scoff at the poor creature and talk about her like this times without number.

I know of a person to whom these things were happening and who was terribly afraid that there would be nobody willing to hear her confession; but there is so much I could say about that that I will not stop to tell it here.[75]

The Saint here tells her experience and the particular trials that won for her many extraordinary favors.[76] To complete the description, one should recall the troubles that accompanied the foundation of the Convent of Saint Joseph of Avila, the difficulties met with in founding the other convents, and at the beginning of her office as prioress at the Incarnation. One may recall also what Saint John of the Cross suffered in prison at Toledo; the criticisms and persecutions of which the holy Curé of Ars was the target, and with him all the saints whose sanctity radiates exteriorly.

It does not seem that a holy person, in this period in which he is passing through the last stages of the spiritual journey and already manifesting the extraordinary power of sanctity, can avoid such trials, especially the criticisms of well-meaning

[75] VI Mansions, i; Peers, II, 269-70.

[76] *Life,* xxviii; Peers, I, 178 ff.; xxx; 194 ff.

persons such as those who were so trying to Saint Teresa, as she herself says.

Actually, criticism rather readily finds matter to attack in these souls. They are not yet completely purified. God's hold on the will still allows some very natural tendencies to remain in the faculties and to appear. These tendencies show themselves in the soul's relations with God and with neighbor. In the activity of the apostolate, which tends to lessen the soul's control, they find a certain liberty to express themselves, and they stand out in greater relief. Thus there appear ways of thinking, of acting, quick replies, external discourtesies, abrupt words, lack of prudence in the use of supernatural gifts, poorly repressed movements of selfishness and of pride. It is indeed clear that the work of purification is not yet over and that the sweet anointing of grace has not wholly penetrated. Certainly there is no doubt that the divine exists in that soul; but the human displays itself in a contrasting light that puts it in relief. This quite human impurity and rudeness in its relation with God and with men that the soul itself discovers under a clear and humiliating light are evident also to the outside observer, even a benevolent one.

They present a problem: how to reconcile such strength and abundance of divine love with the human imperfections that rather garishly display themselves.[77]

We must not exaggerate the defects of the soul in this period of its spiritual life. Yet neither must we deny them. They will disappear only when the mode of human acting has completely yielded to the divine conquest. And even then, there will still be personal ways of thinking and acting, displeasing to the kindliest entourage. But until love has covered the multitude

[77] We remember that the unfavorable judgement passed by Master Daza and the Council that he had called at Avila to judge of the supernatural origin of the favors which Mother Teresa had received, was motivated by the fact that she did not possess virtues in keeping with the favors accorded to her. Cf. *Life,* xxiii; Peers, I, 150 f.

of sins,[78] the acts that it inspires and directs bear visible traces of the sinful source which is not yet entirely purified. Real defects that seem to mar an authentic action of God explain the scandal of the weak and the double effects that assail the prudent.

The mingling of the perfect and the imperfect does not excuse, nevertheless, and even does not explain all the agitation that goes on about these souls who, as Saint Teresa says, do nothing strange, unless it be that they apply themselves to accomplish well the duties of their state.[79] Seeing the problem as a whole, the most one can say is that such a mixture of bad with good offers an easy occasion for detraction that springs from passion.

The violent opposition and persecutions that these souls undergo find their true cause and source in the hatred that divine charity, by its action and its triumphs, arouses in this world. The world and the prince of this world, the devil, see in it an attack upon their rights. Jesus warned His apostles that it would be so. "If the world hates you, know that it has hated Me. If you were of the world, the world would love that which is its own. But because you are not of the world, and I have drawn you out of the world, that is the reason why the world hates you. Remember the word that I have spoken: the servant is no greater than his master." [80]

God has chosen such a soul, and His hold on it shows that He wants it entirely for His own. The physical disorders, the darkness of the night, the fruits of virtue as well as the extraordinary graces, all bespeak the efficacy of the divine choice. Union of will has already surrendered this soul to its mission

[78] I Peter, 2:8. Our admiring affection for the saints, willing to accept in certain cases a sudden conversion from sin to virtue, tolerates with difficulty the possibility of their spiritual progress otherwise than in the purity of love. To admire them more at our ease, we disembody them from human weakness and from its laws of progress. This lack of perspective falsifies the vision of sanctity and its development and, by depriving us of a living example, makes us unjust towards those around the saint who contributed to his formation through his defects and also his patience.

[79] VI Mansions, i; Peers, II, 270.

[80] John 15:18-20.

in the Church. At this stage of the spiritual life Saint Teresa had already received the grace of spiritual maternity and founded houses of her Order. Saint John of the Cross had carried on his work as a reformer at Duruelo, at Pastraña, and at the Convent of the Incarnation before arriving at spiritual marriage. The light is already on the candlestick and although its radiation is as yet limited, nevertheless it can be seen by "all those who are in the house." [81] A fruitful apostolate reveals already the quality of God's hold on the soul and announces a more powerful action for the day when the instrument has become perfect. Such a choice on God's part and so marked a divine conquest are truly events in the spiritual world of souls. They provoke hate as well as love. The latter rejoices at these divine conquests; the former, irritated, becomes restless and mobilizes all its forces.

Among the powers of evil, Satan stands out as a subtle and powerful strategist. His hateful jealousy cannot remain unmoved in the face of this soul that is about to escape him definitively and very soon to do him considerable harm. Such a soul has become his personal enemy. And so he uses against it all his resources. To the type of action that we have already mentioned, he will certainly join a more exterior activity. In the external domain of the senses, he finds all his best means and a certain superiority. To stop the progress of the soul and paralyze its action, the devil will enlist both persons and things. He will turn everything to his profit, the passions of men as well as their good desires, as also the laws of nature, which he will disturb in order to create agitation and trouble, contradiction and persecutions.

The Book of Job, the Gospels, the lives of saints, the founding of the Convent of Saint Joseph of Avila, the Toledo prison of Saint John of the Cross, the trials of the Curé of Ars, and those strange trials that founders of religious orders sometimes undergo, all these expose to us the secret and powerful trickery

[81] Matt. 5:15.

of the devil. With amazing penetration he discerns among his adversaries the principal supernatural agent, even though its external role be in the background. He strikes it at some sensitive point, constructs subtle and grandiose plans to destroy it, counterfeits with disconcerting art, and becomes violent before yielding to the supernatural force that reduces him to powerlessness.

And yet, a fact worthy of note, these so active interventions of Satan usually take place in the domain of secondary natural causes. Only rarely do they emerge from it. The devil enters the exterior domain of marvelous phenomena only when drawn by his desire to counterfeit a striking external action of God, or when his rage at defeat makes him throw aside all prudence. Why should he uselessly attract attention to himself and give open signs of his presence, when his power of dissimulation is his most effective weapon? For this reason the problem of the discernment of the devil's action becomes only the more difficult.[82]

To solve this problem, we must not forget that the devil has only one end and one tactic: to do harm by deceiving. He is an evil power, holding sway in dark places and by means of lies. It is difficult for us to conceive such black perversity. God, who is truth and light, lays open His action to our rational investigations; He puts upon His works and the mission of His envoys His divine seal. Just as we easily become accustomed to the divine ways, which meet so well our need for clarity, so we have difficulty in adjusting to the methods of the devil, that professional at lying, who always lies. If at times he tells the truth in part, this is only in order the better afterward to deceive. Our ordinary relations with our neighbor, based on good faith and on love of the truth, make us easily naive when faced with the devil and his action. The very request that we have heard made, to submit the devil's interventions to critical and sci-

[82] On the discernment of the diabolic marvels, read the very interesting article of Roland Dalbiez concerning Thérèse Noblet, *Etudes Carmélitaines,* Oct., 1938.

entific investigation in order to authenticate his action, might be taken as an example of such naivete. How is it possible to catch one stronger than ourselves and submit to an examination on sincerity and light an invisible, adept liar who reigns only in dark places? At most, he will let himself be examined, that he may falsify already acquired facts and act on the examiners so as to deceive them more.

The devil obeys only the divine power of the exorcist. The hidden play of that evil spirit is laid bare here only by the supernatural gift of the discernment of spirits. Except in cases in which action takes exterior and extraordinary form, this supernatural gift alone, aided by a more profound light, can interpret indications of it, can discover the plan drawn up by hate, the course of an action that developed in darkness; only this gift can discern the subtle presence of the spirit of evil. His presence once discovered or even suspected, the devil usually tries to disappear. This specialist in trickery would gain a most ruinous victory if, by eluding any inquiry carried on according to the demands of scientific criticism, he could succeed in convincing one of his absence or even his non-existence. The devil does exist, and his noxious action is as certain as is his hateful jealousy.

These exterior tribulations in which the genius of the powers of evil seems to triumph serve, they too, the work of God. God permits them only for that end. They unite the soul more closely to Christ and to the mystery of His complete immolation. After His spiritual agony in the Garden of Gethsemane, Christ Jesus was led before the different praetoriums of Jerusalem where He heard the cries and maledictions of the crowd. "It was necessary that Christ enter thus into His glory." The soul, walking in the bloodstained steps of Christ and participating in His sufferings, draws into all its powers the purifying effects of the redeeming blood. Its identification with the divine Model is expressed in the faculties by a deeper understanding of charity. By a painful experience of its own weakness, of the depths of sin in itself and in others, of the hateful power of sin in the world, of its blind violence in all men, the soul learns humility before God, before itself, before the work to be realized in the Church. It progressively discovers the human-divine conditions in which the kingdom of God is built up here below, the part of God in it and the part of man, the efficacious power of divine charity, the indulgent and silent patience that this charity requires of the human instrument, if it would triumph over the forces of sin.

This exterior suffering is eminently useful even when the devil is its author. It perfects the instrument and serves for the extension of God's kingdom.

Shall we find the same beneficial effects in exterior trials of an extraordinary nature, of which we still have to speak? This is a very complex problem that we must touch upon.

c. Extraordinary external phenomena

Under this title, we group all the exterior phenomena connected with God's action in the soul, or seeming to be so connected, which by their rarity and their extraordinary form seem to bespeak a preternatural or supernatural causality.

We think of Saint Paul falling to the ground on the Damascus road. And Paul "arose from the ground, but when his eyes were opened, he could see nothing." They led him into Damascus, "and for three days he could not see, and he neither ate nor drank," until Ananias laid his hands upon him. "And straightway there fell from his eyes something like scales, and he recovered his sight, and arose, and was baptized. And after taking some food, he regained his strength." [83] Saint Teresa, during ecstasy, was sometimes lifted up from the ground by the divine power. Saint Therese of the Child Jesus suffered from a mysterious illness of which she was cured by a smile from the statue of the Blessed Virgin. Saint Francis of Assisi on the mount of Alverno, after a fast of forty days, received

[83] Acts, 9:7-8; 17-18.

in his hands and feet the stigmata which made of him a crucified Christ living among men. The lives of the saints present to us rather frequently external manifestations of the supernatural that reveal to the faithful their deep union with God.

At times these mystical phenomena, or ones that seem so, are accompanied by troubling circumstances. The holiness of the subject is nothing less than evident. A mystic, a true one or false, is afflicted with illnesses that might explain the external phenomena. Or again, and more frequently, there is a mixture of good and evil, of human and divine, which is disconcerting. Père Surin, for example, writes works that are read with great profit by the faithful and even by Saint Therese of the Child Jesus; on the other hand, his biography presents us with a quantity of facts that he himself explains as diabolic possession, but that almost all his confreres attribute to a psychical unbalance and to insanity.

Setting aside any trickery and bad faith (for we do not intend here to go into historical criticism), and retaining only facts that have been duly proved, we find ourselves faced with a problem: what is the part of God in all this, the part of the devil and of nature? Which phenomena are to be attributed to each one of these causes? The problem is all the more complex since different phenomena appear in the same subject. The stigmatist of Konnersreuth, Teresa Neumann, has ecstasies, visions, speaks various languages, and keeps a perpetual fast. The doctors declare that they found hysteria in Maria-Therese Noblet whose heroic and fruitful missionary life was filled, according to her biographer, with trials from the devil, with visions and revelations, accompanied by stigmata and ecstasies.

Let us add that no two cases are alike. There are only individual cases. One can classify the phenomena; but it is almost impossible to categorize the cases except by a few affinities. Teresa Neumann had visions, but she in no way resembles Teresa of Avila. Père Surin is a spiritual writer; but how could we compare him with John of the Cross?

The complexity of these problems does not, however, seem to be sufficient reason to evade them. The light of the principles that make possible some clarification reaches far beyond the strange cases of the extraordinary which prove so powerful in arousing the curiosity of the multitude. There are numerous borderline cases that spring from the same causes and present the same intersecting of the human and the divine. Hence the difficulties attached to these questions must not prevent us from seeking light to solve them and from a practical line of conduct in their regard.

Among these phenomena we can at once distinguish two kinds: 1) Physical phenomena affecting the body exteriorly; for example, levitation, ecstasy, stigmata. 2) Psychical phenomena, the external manifestations of which indicate that the soul's faculties are undergoing some outside influence; for example, certain intellectual or affective disturbances. The first are more apparent, more easily observable, and seem to call more imperiously for explanation by supernatural causality. The second, more interior, more complex, seem more mysterious. We approach the former with more confidence; of the latter we are more wary. Will these first impressions persist even after a deeper study? [84]

1) *Physical phenomena*

Saint John of the Cross has told us that spiritual communications from God to the soul ordinarily have a rebound in the senses and the body.

[84] One cannot treat these questions without taking into account penetrating studies made by psychiatrists, theologians, philosophers, and published by the *Etudes Carmélitaines* on Madeleine de Pierre Janet (*Etudes Carmélitaines*, Apr. and Oct. 1935: Dom Mager, P. Lavaud, Pr. J. Lhermitte); on stigmatization (*Etudes Carm.*, Oct. 1936; Prof. Lhermitte, Dr. Le Grand, Tinel, Van Gehucten, Wunderle, Vinchon, Dom Mager); on the dark night of sense and of spirit and the cases of P. Surin and Marie-Therese Noblet (*Etudes Carm.*, Oct. 1937, Oct. 1939 and Apr., 1939; Pr. de Greef, J. Lhermitte, Dr. Achille Delmas, Giscard, Pr. Roland Dalbiez, P. de Guibert, Olphe Gaillard, etc.). We have drawn largely upon these articles and the conversations that followed the conferences at the Congress of Psychology held at Avon in 1936–37–38.

As, however, this sensual part of the soul is weak and incapable of experiencing the strong things of the spirit, it follows that these proficients, by reason of this spiritual communication which is made to their sensual part, endure therein many frailties and sufferings and weaknesses of the stomach, and in consequence are fatigued in spirit.[85]

How strong can be the reaction on the senses? What are its limits? What physical phenomena are no longer under the soul's power, requiring for explanation the direct and extraordinary action of God, in the sense previously indicated.[86] Such is the problem before us.

We shall not go into it in full, taking up each category of phenomena. We must limit ourselves. Hence we shall not stop on ecstasies and raptures which, according to Saint John of the Cross, are an effect of the most intense spiritual communication before purification is complete. The Saint writes, speaking of the weakness of the sensual nature:

Hence arise the raptures and trances and dislocations of the bones which always happen when the communications are not purely spiritual—that is, are not given to the spirit alone, as are those of the perfect who are purified by the second night of the spirit.[87]

The problem of God's extraordinary action does not arise, then, in such cases. They can be explained as a radiation of purely spiritual action on temperaments that are weak or imperfectly purified.[88]

[85] *Dark Night,* Bk. II, i; Peers, I, 375.
[86] Cf. *infra,* ch. ii, "Extraordinary Favors."
[87] *Dark Night, ibid.*
[88] In chapter vi of the book of the *Foundations* and in chapter iii of the IV Mansions, Saint Teresa clearly says that swooning under God's action can be the effect of physical weakness. She says: Some persons, "because of prayers, vigils and severe penances, and also for other reasons, have poor health. When they experience any spiritual consolation, therefore, their physical nature is too much for them; and as soon as they feel any interior joy there comes over them a physical weakness and langour. . . . One person was in this state for eight hours; she was not unconscious . . ." (IV Mansions, iii; Peers, II, 245-6). Here we have an example of the reaction that spiritual action can have on the body, an action that is falsely amplified by physical weakness. Saint Teresa considered it necessary to insist on these typical cases; they seem to her extremely important in pointing up the value of external signs in evaluating the spiritual life of souls.

The problem of the extraordinary might present itself in connection with levitation. But this phenomenon is observable with difficulty because transitory.

On the other hand, the stigmata are phenomena that, even though not permanent, at least recur often enough so that learned men, specialists of various kinds, and masters of the spiritual life can observe them under good conditions. These phenomena are so definitely marked and are so extraordinary in themselves that, if it is true that the sense reaction from the spiritual can produce them, they certainly bring us to the limit of what its power can do. Hence we shall retain stigmata as a typical case furnishing us with the most important data of the problem and allowing us, consequently, to envisage the various possible solutions.

a. The case of Teresa Neumann

The stigmata are wounds that appear on the body in the likeness of one or several marks of the Passion. The first of these by date, it seems, and the most well known, are the stigmata with which Saint Francis of Assisi was favored two years before his death, during a forty days' fast on Mount Alverno. The Saint came down from the mountain bearing in his hands, his feet, and his side the bleeding wounds of Jesus crucified.

Since then, similar phenomena have recurred. Doctor Imbert-Goubeyre has drawn up a catalogue of three hundred and twenty-one cases of persons stigmatized, or claiming to be.[89] The majority of these cases, to be sure, do not stand up under a close scrutiny of the documents that testify to them.[90] Yet it would be imprudent to conclude from the absence of the proofs required by modern criticism that all these testimonials are false and the stigmatized merely tricksters. Whatever may be

[89] Cf. Dr. Antoine Imbert-Goubeyre, professor at the Faculty of Medicine at Clermont-Ferrard, *La Stigmatisation, l'extase divine et les miracles de Lourdes. Réponse aux libre-penseurs,* Clermont, 1894.

[90] Cf. the article of P. Debongnie in *Etudes Carmélitaines,* Oct. 1936, pp. 22-59; a critical essay on the history of stigmatizations in the Middle Ages.

true of the past, several cases of stigmatization in our day have been observed in precise and scientific enough a manner to consider them as historically certain facts. Such, for example, are the stigmata of Gemma Galgani and those of Teresa Neumann. The latter will serve as a basis for our study and comments.

Teresa Neumann, the eldest of a family of nine children, was born April 8 or 9, 1898, of a poor peasant family of Konnersreuth, Bavaria. Pious, robust and laborious, she early worked in the fields and entered into the service of a peasant in her village. In 1918, following over-exertion and a chill, she fell sick. Then there is one accident after another: falls, paralysis of different parts of the body, various wounds, blindness; these seem to be the consequence of her general condition. Her doctor makes the following diagnosis: grave hysteria following upon a very serious accident. On April 29, 1923, the day of the beatification of Saint Therese of the Child Jesus, she suddenly recovers her sight. On May 17, 1925, the day of the canonization, she is favored with a luminous apparition from which a mysterious voice announces to her that she will recover the use of her limbs, but the pains will not cease. At the beginning of Lent 1926, Teresa does not feel well. During the night from Thursday to Friday, 4–5 March, she has a vision of our Lord on the Mount of Olives with His apostles. She experiences a violent and sharp pain around her heart. Blood begins to flow from her side; wounds appear in her hands and feet. There is also an effusion of blood from her eyes; this coagulates during the night and on Friday before noon. Since that time her wounds bleed during the night from Thursday to Friday, and on Friday before noon every week, except for the liturgical seasons of Christmas and Easter and holy days of obligation. Since March 1927, there has also been the wound from the crown of thorns.[91] These stigmata bleed during or

[91] Cf. "Konnersreuth comme fait et problème," by Dom Mager, *Etudes Carmélitaines,* Apr., 1933, pp. 39-44.

after visions of the Passion. These visions cause Teresa to follow and to relive the different scenes of the Passion; they take place during the night from Thursday to Friday and until Friday afternoon. Each vision lasts from ten to fifteen minutes and is accompanied by a state of ecstasy, without anyone's being sure whether the ecstasy precedes the vision or is brought about by it. Teresa

> . . . is at the time sitting up in her bed, she has her arms extended, her eyes are open, but looking off as into infinite distances; and she seems to be imitating important gestures.[92]
>
> Her face betrays that her intellect, her will and sensibility are participating intensely in what she is contemplating in vision. All her expressions during the pantomime are closely related to Christ and faith. Enthusiasm, jubilation make the lines of her face resplendent with joy when she recognizes corresponding sentiments in Christ or in other persons in the scene. Then again, there are manifest sentiments of compassion, of fear, of anguish, of disgust or of anger when she sees these in the persons of the vision. These sentiments go beyond natural limits in force and expression, in the sense that opposite states of soul and emotions follow one another with great rapidity without any transition. Scarcely has she evinced joy when, the instant after, tears flow. As quickly as the scenes in the visions change, her expressions as quickly reflect them.[93]

The visions of parts of the Passion succeed one another to the number "of about forty, more or less according to the case," and are accompanied by more or less intense activity of the stigmatic wounds.[94]

The visions are followed by a state of recollection or of absorption in which Teresa Neumann

[92] *Ibid.*, p. 43.

[93] Cf. *Konnersreuth*, ch. vi. pp. 43-46 by Fahsel. Quoted by P. Lavaud in "Les phénomènes extatiques chez Teresa Neumann," *Etudes Carmélitaines*, Apr., 1933, pp. 67-68. Fahsel writes apropos of Teresa Neumann's gaze during an ecstatic vision: "Her eyes follow with a very piercing gaze and with the greatest attention the scene that is taking place, eager to let nothing escape them. If anyone passes his hand in front of her eyes, the direction of her gaze into the distance is not disturbed." *Ibid.*, p. 67.

[94] Cf. The article by P. Lavaud, p. 69. One can find in the same article, pp. 7-75, an account of the visions made by Teresa Neumann herself, showing how sudden they are, how living and precise in what concerns the person of Jesus.

. . . falls back as if abandoned by the strength that was sustaining her. Her eyes close. . . . She hears and can speak.[95] . . . She is ordinarily calm and tranquil, often motionless. But on speaking to her one notices that she is interiorly held and dominated by what she has just seen, when this was a gripping event. Her emotion is expressed in the way she speaks of it, which she willingly does, moreover, and without reserve.[96]

At the time, she enjoys higher lights for the discerning of consecrated objects or persons and the disposition of hearts. Teresa Neumann has another mystical state called the state of ecstatic repose. This is

. . . the repose of a sleep in which her soul is united to God by the highest contemplation and ecstasy, and rests in him. (This sleep) strengthens and restores Teresa physically in a mysterious manner. It intervenes each time that her physical sufferings, either of the Passion on Friday or in its mystical substitutions, have almost attained the limit of what is possible to bear. . . . It manifests itself almost every time that she receives the Holy Eucharist. . . . This state lasts from twelve to twenty minutes, sometimes an hour. . . . During these moments of rest a prompt and marvelous renewal of her exhausted strength takes place in her. . . . The rapid and profound change is evident to everyone. . . . The actual fulfillment of numerous predictions has for several years confirmed the friends of Teresa in their certitude that she enjoys at least at intervals in the state of ecstatic repose, some prophetic gifts, and penetrates the secrets of hearts.[97]

If we add that "since Christmas, 1926, Teresa no longer takes any food, neither solid nor liquid." [98] we shall have given a succinct exposition of the facts of Konnersreuth; these show in what an abundance of extraordinary phenomena the stigmatization of Teresa Neumann is situated, and allow us to glimpse the complexity of problems that it poses.

b. How is stigmatization produced?

1. *Exposition of possible solutions.*—How is stigmatization to be explained? To what causes shall we attribute it? To the action of God or of the devil or to a play of the laws of na-

[95] *Ibid.*, p. 76.
[96] *Ibid.*, p. 65.
[97] *Ibid.*, pp. 81-3.
[98] Cf. The article of Dom Mager already cited, p. 44.

ture? To these different causes simultaneously? And in what measure? Such is the problem.

The simplest solution, once trickery has evidently been eliminated, would be to reserve to God's action the production of so marvelous a phenomenon. But there remains the necessity of determining precisely the nature of God's action in this regard.

Is it God Himself who intervenes with His omnipotence to produce this phenomenon outside the laws of created nature,[99] so that stigmatization would be a miracle in the actual sense of the word, as, for example, is the resurrection of a dead person, the multiplication of the loaves, the instantaneous healing of a bone or a tissue? Certainly not. The wounds of the stigmata can be produced by a man using a suitable instrument or by an angel.

But if He used an angel as the instrumental cause to imprint the stigmata, God would still be their principal author and His action could be called direct, as we have previously said apropos of visions.[100]

Can it be admitted that an indirect divine action, making use of a psycho-physiological process, would suffice to produce this marvelous phenomenon? In this case, God would create in the soul, by a wound of love, very intense sentiments of love and compassion, accompanied ordinarily by an imaginary vision of the scenes of the Passion; and these very deeply living sentiments would be exteriorized as the wounds of Jesus crucified. In brief, the stigmata would be a localized sensible reaction to God's action in the soul.

The devil would likewise have power to produce the stigmata. His action would be exercised directly, or, if one admits the second opinion, by the exteriorization of intense sentiments and of false visions he would have himself produced.

[99] "That is called a miracle which is outside the order of the whole created nature. God alone can perform a miracle, for what an angel or any other creature does through its own power is in the order of a created nature, and for this reason is not a miracle." Such is the definition of miracle according to Saint Thomas (Sum. Theol. I, q. 110, a. 4).

[100] Cf. *supra,* ch. ii; "Extraordinary Favors," pp. 286-94.

Finally, if the stigmata can be produced by a psycho-physiological process, there would be no difficulty, it seems, in admitting that sick persons endowed with a hypersensibility and victims of halucinatory visions might themselves in this way bring on the stigmata, without any preternatural intervention.

Thus we see that two distinct problems present themselves regarding the stigmata. The first is a general problem, which can be thus stated: Can the stigmata be produced by a psycho-physiological process activated by an indirect action of God or of the devil, or by a psycho-pathological cause? Or do they require a direct action of God or of the devil?

The second problem, particular to each case: Which spirit actually did produce the stigmata? Or again, are they not the fruit of a pathological condition, if it be true that this is sufficient to produce them.

The second problem, of major importance, is connected with the general problem of the discernment of spirits, which has been already studied; [101] for the moment, it will not claim our attention. We shall take up the first problem which, although more speculative, has considerable bearing; for it poses in its extreme cases the problem that we are considering, namely, the repercussion of the spiritual on the sensible and the contribution made by temperament to the exterior phenomena of the mystical life.

2. *Discussion*

Direct action of God—That the stigmata require a direct action of God or of the devil, making use of an instrument, is the more current opinion, the one to which the accounts of the stigmatization of Saint Francis of Assisi seem to give credit. During his fast on Mount Alverno about the feast of the Exaltation of the Holy Cross, a crucified seraph appeared to him one day and filled his soul with joy and compassionate love. Writing of this, Saint Bonaventure says:

[101] *Ibid.*

After a heavenly and familiar conversation, the vision disappeared, leaving in the heart of the Saint an ineffable burning and imprinting in his flesh marvelous marks of the Crucified. . . . There appeared in his hands and in his feet the marks of the nails, showing in the inner part of the hands and the upper part of the foot, with the points on the opposite side. His right side, as if transpierced by the lance, was opened by a red wound from which there often flowed blood onto his clothing.[102]

More clearly still, Saint Francis de Sales describes the seraph's direct action in producing the stigmata. He writes of this in the *Treatise on the Love of God:*

But seeing also the lively representation of the marks and wounds of his Saviour crucified, he felt in his soul the merciless sword which transfixed the sacred breast of the virgin-mother on the day of the passion, with as much interior pain as though he had been crucified with his dear Saviour. . . .

This soul then being thus mollified, softened and almost melted away in this lovefull pain, was thereby extremely disposed to receive the impressions and marks of the love and pain of his sovereign lover. . . .

Whence without doubt the soul found herself transformed into a second crucified. Now the soul, as the form and mistress of the body, exercising her authority over it, impressed the pains of the wounds with which she was struck, on the parts corresponding to those wherein her beloved had endured them. Love is admirable in sharpening the imagination to penetrate to the exterior. . . .

But love being within could not well make the holes in the flesh without, and therefore the burning seraph coming to its help, darted rays of so penetrating a light, that it really made in the flesh the exterior wounds of the crucified, which love had imprinted interiorly in the soul.[103]

These accounts seem to affirm the inability of a psychological process to produce external wounds, whatever may be the intensity of the physical suffering by which the body participates in the soul's compassion with the sufferings of Jesus crucified. The stigmata of Saint Francis of Assisi would thus

[102] Cf. Saint Bonaventure, *Life of Saint Francis;* also, the legend in the Breviary for the Feast of the Stigmata of Saint Francis. Celano, in the *Vita prima* does not indicate the direct action of the seraph in producing the stigmata: "His heart was wholly occupied with the apparition when there began to appear in his hands and feet the marks of the nails such as he had just seen them in the Crucified Man above him."

[103] Saint Francis de Sales, *Treatise on the Love of God,* Bk. VI, ch. xv, 277-79. [Translated by the Rev. Henry Mackey, O.S.B., Westminster, Md., 1942.]

be produced by direct action of God, through the instrumental action of the angel.

This opinion is vigorously sustained by eminent neurologists. Professor Jean Lhermitte, member of the Academy of Medicine, writes:

> The process of stigmatization seems to us as something absolutely unintelligible, unthinkable. In truth, there is no physiological process which approaches, near or far, stigmatization. This phenomenon, when it is not trickery, properly belongs to a category of subjects and responds to a mechanism which completely escapes savants. And if I were obliged to follow the terminology employed by M. l'Abbé Journet, I would assert that there is neither psychological stigmatization, nor stigmatization dia-psychological nor extra-physiological.[104]

These categorical statements from an eminent master would settle the question, were it not that other neurologists and experienced psychologists oppose him with better weighed judgments that render plausible another solution to the problem.

Psycho-physiological process—All recognize the fact that among the experiments made up to now in clinics or laboratories, none proves scientifically the psycho-physiological process of stigmata. Hence this process is from the scientific point of view an hypothesis, but a legitimate hypothesis, and one that may be forced upon us.

Professor Paul von Gehuchten writes:

> I do not see any impossibility, in the case of certain very sensitive subjects, in there being produced after a long suggestive preparation, localized vaso-motor manifestations even to the point of the formation of phlyctaena and bleeding. Without doubt, neither anatomy nor physiology can give us the key to the mechanism; but there is needed no more than one case well studied in which suggestion produces bleeding stigmata, for what is considered an hypothesis to become a certitude.[105]

And in his turn Doctor Tinel says:

> One can strictly conceive that a particularly strong representation of the sufferings of Christ on the Cross could, by means of the complete

[104] Prof. J. Lhermitte, "Le problème medical de la stigmatisation," in *Etudes Carmélitaines* Oct. 1936, pp. 72-73.

[105] Professor Paul von Gehuchten, Professor of Neurology at the University of Liège, "Les stigmates de Louise Lateau," in *Etudes Carmélitaines*, Oct. 1936, p. 90.

process of attention, suggestion, psychical exteriorization and mental projection to the periphery bring about cutaneous zones truly and intensely painful in the areas corresponding to the five wounds of the hands, the feet, and the side . . . ; this is the psychological factor.[106]

Doctor George Wunderlé, Professor at the University of Wurzburg, is still more positive. He writes:

For a long time, from a psychological point of view, no one dared to believe in the possibility of bringing on stigmatization. And I admit that it took me a long time, during long years of study of this problem, to be convinced of this possibility. Today I am of the opinion that one cannot just simply reject the fact of natural stigmatization. The case presented by Doctor Lechler, in spite of the gaps in it, is convincing proof of this.[107]

The testimony of Doctor Wunderlé, in his opinion fraught with consequences both for mystical theology and for religious psychology," [108] calls for distinctions. He does not claim to provide a scientific explanation of stigmatization. But basing his judgment on the duly ascertained fact of a wound produced by a psycho-pathological process, he finds himself "capable of understanding that certain stages of the process of stigmatization have not necessarily a supernatural origin." [109] Hence he puts forward as quite plausible the hypothesis of a natural process that would not make necessary God's direct action in the material production of stigmata. The process would develop thus, writes Doctor Wunderlé:

True stigmatization always supposes a profoundly moved state of soul—from a representation of the Crucifixion, for example. All the

[106] Doctor Tinel, "Essai d' interprétation physiologique" *Etudes Carmélitaines,* October 1936, p. 96.

[107] Prof. Georges Wunderlé, "Psychologie de la stigmatisation," in *Etudes Carmélitaines,* October 1936, pp. 157-163. In the same article, p. 158. Professor Wunderlé writes: "For several years they have been talking in Germany of a case of stigmatization in a Protestant woman (in the sanatorium of Doctor Lechler) . . . last year I saw this person in company with Doctor Deutsch, whose works on the subject of Konnersreuth are well known to us. We could take note of the reality of the stigmatization by the marks that she had, and our belief in the effective process of suggestion was confirmed by appropriate experiments."

[108] *Ibid.,* p. 159.

[109] *Ibid.*

descriptions of these events, beginning with the testimony that we have of the stigmatization of Saint Francis of Assisi, confirm this opinion indubitably. Moreover, they agree in saying that spiritual stigmatization is as a foundation for corporal stigmatization.[110]

In fact, the accounts of the stigmatization, as well of Saint Francis of Assisi as of Teresa Neumann, indicate so close a connection between the vision of Jesus crucified and the appearance of the stigmata, that the mind normally establishes a relation of cause and effect. It appears clear that the vision brings to its highest intensity interior compassion or commotion, according to the language of Doctor Wunderlé, and that it produces in the body of the visionary a veritable interior stigmatization; that is, a localization in the visionary's body of the pains of the wounds that it sees. Saint Francis de Sales, speaking of Saint Francis of Assisi, says:

. . . love employed all the forces of the will to enter into and conform itself to the passion of her well-beloved; whence, without doubt, the soul found herself transformed into a second crucified. Now the soul, as the form and mistress of the body, exercising her authority over it, impressed the pains of the wounds with which she was struck, on the parts corresponding to those wherein her beloved had endured them. Love is admirable in sharpening the imagination to penetrate to the exterior.[111]

The psychological process of which Doctor Wunderlé speaks does not stop, however, at that stage. Citing Gorres, he explains the phenomenon by the intervention of "a plastic force which imprints in the body a likeness according to the interior dispositions of compassion of the stigmatized. . . . The transforming spiritual power of the soul, which reacts on the body, comes from its compassion with the sufferings of Christ crucified." [112]

An important detail to be noted in the more precise descriptions of the stigimatization of Teresa Neumann: the vision is accompanied with ecstasy. This ecstasy, far from causing a dimi-

[110] *Ibid*, p. 160.
[111] Text already quoted from the *Treatise on the Love of God,* Bk. VI, Ch. xv, 278. Saint Francis de Sales refuses, however, to interior stigmatization the power of producing external wounds.
[112] Article of Wunderlé, p. 161.

nution in knowledge, as Doctor Wunderlé remarks, indicates on the contrary an extraordinary tension of all the powers toward the object of the vision, a certain domination of the object over all the powers, which are passive under the action of the power emanating from the vision. As a fact, they say of Teresa Neumann, that during ecstasy "her face betrays an intimate participation of intellect, will, and sensibility in what she is contemplating in vision. Almost all her imitative expressions are closely related to Christ and faith." [113] True, it is a long way from these imitations to the impression of the stigmata; but it is not without use to stress these exterior effects which indicate the powerful action of the vision.

A natural process does not exclude divine causality in the production of the stigmata. Evidently, God retains entire liberty to impress them by a direct action. Even when He uses a psycho-physiological process, His action is necessary in order to bring, by a vision He creates or by any other means, the soul's compassion or interior commotion to the high intensity necessary for it to be imprinted corporeally with the exterior signs of the stigmata. Just as in the case of supernatural words some are formal, formulated by God, and others successive, formulated by the soul under the action of an authentic supernatural light, so there might be stigmata produced by a direct action of God, and other stigmata produced by a natural process activated by an indirect divine intervention.

Both these modes, direct and indirect, are at the disposal of the devil to produce stigmata. If we admit the hypothesis of a natural process, we must also admit that a pathological disturbance can, it too, bring about an intensity of interior emotion capable of exteriorizing itself. Consequently, a psychosis can replace the preternatural action that is required in the case of normal temperaments. Doctor Wunderlé recognizes finally "that stigmatization does not take place every time that com-

[113] Article of Konnersreuth, ch. vi, pp. 43-6, by Fahsel, in "Les phénomènes extatiques chez Teresa Neumann."

passion is at its maximum," [114] even when caused by an imaginary vision or by the real sight of something, such as the Virgin Mary experienced on Calvary. Hence the external effectiveness of the plastic force supposes other conditions.

What are these conditions? At times God's special will; but then His intervention is again direct. For the cases in which a natural process has been set going, we know the laws of divine Providence well enough to be able to say that God lets this process run its course under the action of secondary causes, and without direct intervention on His part. Hence it is in the domain of natural conditions that we must above all look for the cause of the development of the process to the point of external stigmata, or of its halt at some stage. The conditions favorable to its development might be a hypersensibility of the subject, or a special disposition of temperament particularly sensitive to plastic force and more apt for external reproduction.

Conclusion—The hypothesis of a natural process of stigmatization does not, as we see, explain everything. It leaves many points obscure in the psychological as well as the physiological domain. Yet it is very attractive and has our favor. It seems to be in the tradition of mystical authors who, according to Doctor Wunderlé,

> . . . see in physical stigmata that bleed, the term of a process that began in the soul elevated to a mystical state.[115]

He cites Gorres and Ruysbroeck. The intervention of the angel that Saint Francis de Sales judges necessary, and such as he explains it, might well not be a direct intervention:

> Therefore the burning seraph coming to its help, darted rays of so penetrating a light, that it really made in the flesh the exterior wounds . . .[116]

Are these, the luminous rays that emanate from the vision,

[114] Cf. article of Doctor Wunderlé, p. 161.
[115] *Ibid.*, p. 160.
[116] Saint Francis de Sales, *Treatise on the Love of God,* Bk. VI, ch. xv, 278.

really different from the plastic force of which Doctor Wunderlé speaks?

An argument of the greatest weight is the very clear testimony of Saint John of the Cross. Here is what he writes apropos of stigmata:

> Let us return, then, to the work done by that seraph, which in truth is to strike and to wound. If the effect of the wound should sometimes be permitted to pass outward to the bodily sense, to an extent corresponding to the interior wound, the effect of the impact and the wound will be felt without, as came to pass when the seraph wounded the soul of Saint Francis with love, and in that way the effect of those wounds became outwardly visible. For God bestows no favours upon the body without bestowing them first and principally upon the soul.[117]

According to Saint John of the Cross, interior stigmatization is the principal favor produced by God's action. The stigmata of the body are only an external manifestation permitted by God in certain cases. A little farther on, in connection with the relations between the sensible and the spiritual in the soul's advance toward God, the Saint makes more precise his thought on the production of stigmata:

> It is quite different when the affection of feeling overflows from spirit into sense, for herein, as Saint Paul says, there may be much spirituality; for, when the intensity of his realization of the sufferings of Christ was so great that it overflowed into the body, he writes to the Galatians, saying: "I bear in my body the marks of my Lord Jesus." [118]

These texts clearly suppose the existence of a psycho-physiological process, manifesting by external wounds an interior stigmatization affected by God's action. This statement is not an abstract observation made by a mystic who has seen only the spiritual aspect of the problem. Saint John of the Cross is an informed psychologist and, it has been said, perfect in clinical studies. The following are clinical observations on stigmata, accompanied by theological and spiritual considerations which show that he has studied, if not experienced, the case:

[117] *Living Flame,* st. ii; Peers, III, 40-1.
[118] *Ibid.;* 42.

And then, the greater is the delight and strength of love which causes the wound within, the greater is the pain of that wound without, and if the one grows, the other grows likewise. This comes to pass because, since these souls have been purged and made strong in God, all that pertains to God and is strong and sweet is a delight to them in their spirits, which are strong and healthy. . . .

But when the wound is within the soul, and is not communicated without, it can be far more intense and sublime; for, as the flesh is the bridle of the spirit, so, when the blessings of the spirit are communicated to it, the flesh draws in the rein and curbs this fleet steed and restrains its great energy.[119]

We do not find in Saint John of the Cross any reference to a direct action of God in the production of external stigmata. He does not even put the question as to whether this direct action is necessary, so clear it seems to him that exterior stigmatization is a result of interior stigmatization. This tranquil assurance in his conviction on the part of a master, so quick to discern God's action under its various forms of all psychological phenomena, compensates largely for all that these savants find obscure and disconcerting in the psycho-physiological process. It is in our opinion the most solid argument for this hypothesis, which still troubles the neurologist, but satisfies the mystic and the psychologist.

In brief, although the natural process of stigmatization presents much that is obscure, it is in harmony with that movement of the spiritual, so often pointed out by Teresa and John of the Cross, which, springing from divine sources in the soul, overflows progressively into the body in

. . . all the substance of sense and all the members of the body and the very marrow and bones . . . even in the remotest joints of the feet and hands.[120]

And it does this with a marvelously active force that is for us still a mystery.

At the risk of appearing subtle, may I add that this natural process seems to me to explain much better than a direct action

[119] *Ibid.;* 41.
[120] *Living Flame,* st. ii; Peers, III, 45.

on the part of God or the devil all the facts it has been possible to observe in the stigmatics of our time, and the atmosphere that reigns around them.

Certainly, we do not want to decide the case of Teresa Neumann; yet it is permissible to call attention to the fact that, however impressive may be her bleeding stigmata and her ecstasies, her perpetual fast and gift of penetration of souls, we cannot forget that all this was preceded by serious accidents coming from hysteria; and that concerning her case, doctors and theologians sometimes carry on heated discussions, without being able to adduce arguments that remove all doubt.

Most of the cases of stigmatization are marked with this same character. Even when a wide spiritual radiation precludes any thought of trickery and seems to guarantee an action of God, nevertheless, antecedents of sickness, or physical loss sometimes, and a general atmosphere of trouble and obscurity that prevails about the persons, seem to indicate a plurality of causes in the production of this phenomenon. And so the Church, while beatifying Gemma Galgani, declared explicitly that it was not pronouncing on the extraordinary graces of her life, of which stigmatization was one of the most striking.

How different this is from Teresa of Avila and Catherine of Siena whose extraordinary graces were under dispute for a while during their lifetime, but whose wonderful human balance, apostolic fruitfulness, and heroic virtues soon made apparent to all, their personal sanctity and the authenticity of the divine grace that held them captive.

In the saints, God's direct and authentic action spreads through the faculties and the senses and seems quickly to free itself from them. On passing through, it neither breaks definitively anything of the human that it finds nor disassociates it; on the contrary, it leaves the human purified, enriched, marvelously uplifted, making of these men and women sublime types of humanity.

In the stigmatics, God's action—when it truly is present—

on overflowing into the senses is deeply and painfully sealed in them. Why this stopping and fixation in the sensible? The special will and direct action of God, some will answer. That is possible, and in some cases it must be the answer. But since ecstasy is a weakness of soul, produced by an inflexibility and lack of purity that impede God's action, could not the stigmata too be a weakness resulting from more serious psychical defects? These would check spiritual action, fixating it painfully in the senses.

Whatever be the case, we must note that while everything is clear, limpid, marvelously human while highly divine in Saint Teresa and Saint Catherine, around the stigmatics known to us we find shadow, a troubling contradiction of signs, uncertainty, lack of limpidity, a mingling of the human with the preternatural, of the marvelous and the unhealthy. Even though the trial may not harm these persons, still they do not come out of it humanly enlarged. The supernatural in it reaches us only through a process of reactions, of passivities, of very natural resonances, too natural in our opinion; we discover it only as immerged in the sensible and probably intermixed with the pathological.[121]

c. General conclusions

It is time to draw a few practical conclusions:

1. Since the most extraordinary sensible phenomena, such as ecstasy and even the stigmata, according to Saint John of the Cross, are only the exteriorization in the senses of an intense spiritual action of God on the soul, and since, according to a plausible hypothesis, these same phenomena can be produced in certain subjects by a psycho-pathological process, prudence and

[121] This judgement or rather these impressions, very definite moreover, concern the cases that it has been possible for us to know through exact information. The stigmatization of Saint Francis of Assisi is on another plane, as Saint John of the Cross makes clear when he speaks of the superabundance of the spiritual which springs from an inner virtue through profoundly purified faculties. Until we have more ample information, the case of Saint Francis seems unique in its elevated order.

the law of economy of causes do not allow us to admit a direct action of God in the production of these phenomena, except when such action is properly proved, if not actually observed. They also place upon us the duty of welcoming with interest, scientific experiments or even reasonable hypotheses that can help us in determining the human part in the process, provided these explanations do not exclude the possibility of a supernatural action, either at the origin of the process or during its development.

2. When this supernatural influence does exist, it reaches us through sensible extraordinary phenomena, through interior activities, resonances and reactions that are purely natural; hence whatever may be its testimony to the spiritual, it is weighted with all these elements, some of which can be questioned.

While he was at the general chapter of his Order at Lisbon, Saint John of the Cross refused, in spite of the urging of P. Mariano, to go to see Maria of the Cross, the much talked of stigmatic who had Spain and Portugal running to her. Maria of the Cross, it is true, was a fake in the grand style. The Saint said that he did not have to see stigmatics in order to strengthen his faith and provide food for his prayer.

We can draw inspiration from the attitude of Saint John of the Cross in regard to sensible phenomena. However extraordinary they may be, they are so complex that, except for cases authenticated by the Church, it is at very least to waste one's precious time and satisfy a vain curiosity, to linger with them in the hope of viewing some manifestation of the supernatural, or even of determining their nature and the kind of testimony that they give.

A few moments of supernatural recollection or of the prayer of quiet, an act of faith and an act of love, these give God to the soul more surely and more directly than do all the extraordinary sensible phenomena.

2. *Physical phenomena and mental disturbances*

a. *Resemblance between the psychological effects of the dark night and the psychical disturbances of mental illnesses.* Psychiatrists point out a certain resemblance between the psychological effects of the dark night and the psychic disturbances met with in mental illnesses. Professor de Greef writes:

> On reading the description of the dark night of sense and of spirit, the psychiatrist is tempted at first to admit the hypothesis that this is a mental state more or less related to the rhythm of cyclothymiacs. And in truth, examined rapidly and not too closely, the phenomena described by Saint John of the Cross lend themselves to being reduced to simple psycho-pathological equivalents. One is especially struck by the sadness and discouragement of the subjects, even by their despair, their more or less expressed ideas of unworthiness, and even their certitude that they are "as if abandoned by God." . . . And the very interpretation that the subject gives of his state suggests melancholy.[122]

The professor's remark does not give us scandal. A subject does not have two different ways of reacting in the same order under a shock; and his sense reaction, although indicating the violence of the shock, does not register the nature of the cause that produced it. Hence it is not surprising that disturbances produced by the power of God's action in the soul in the dark night should be similar to certain psycho-pathological disturbances that have a different cause.

Moreover even if one does not go so far as to say with the psychoanalyst that we all have some pathological tendency, it must be admitted that these tendencies are widely distributed in our poor human nature, and that they now form part of the consequences of original sin, which singularly burden it. These tendencies exist in various degrees—in a benign state most of the time, more or less hidden from ourselves, if not from others, under our daily routines, in the inner subjections or endurances that we impose upon ourselves, or better in the com-

[122] Cf. Professor Etienne de Greef, "Succédanes et concomitances psychopatholigiques de la Nuit obscure" (the case of P. Surin) in *Etudes Carméli-taines*, October 1938, p. 152.

pensations that we seek or that we demand of our entourage. Thus the restless person, the obsessed, the melancholic, the cyclothymiac adapts his life to what his tendencies demand, and more or less peacefully gains admittance for these in his environment. Social life and especially the ordinary daily life are made up of these reciprocal adjustments; so imperious are they and so interwoven with habit that one may be unconscious of them until the divine light of the dark night discloses their fallacious harmony.

The purification of the spirit brings to the surface with a painful awareness these tendencies deeply rooted in the faculties. Saint John of the Cross writes:

> Material fire, acting upon wood, first of all begins to dry it, by driving out its moisture and causing it to shed the water which it contains within itself. Then it begins to make it black, dark and unsightly, and even to give forth a bad odour, and, as it dries it little by little, it brings out and drives away all the dark and unsightly accidents which are contrary to the nature of fire. . . .
>
> In this same way, we have to philosophize with respect to this Divine fire of contemplative love, which, before it unites and transforms the soul in itself, first purges it of all its contrary accidents. It drives out its unsightliness, and makes it black and dark, so that it seems worse than before and more unsightly and abominable than it was wont to be. For this Divine purgation is removing all the evil and vicious humours which the soul has never perceived because they have been so deeply rooted and grounded in it.[123]

The humors in the language of Saint John of the Cross designate the whole psycho-physiological complex of the soul and consequently the pathological tendencies of which we are speaking. The bond these tendencies have with one's personality and habits is broken in the dark night of the spirit. Like the dross which, extracted from the mineral by fire, comes to the surface and covers over the precious metal from which it has been separated, these tendencies display themselves on the surface in all their blackness. Saint John of the Cross has already noted in the dark night of sense a certain influence of melancholy in

[123] *Dark Night,* Bk. II, x; Peers, I, 403.

contemplative dryness [124] and its very clear action in temptations. [125] During the dark night of the spirit these tendencies are brought to sharp maximum. They strongly color the reactions of the soul to God's action within it, and hence offer to the psychiatrist indications that justify his pessimistic diagnosis. It is indeed an obsessed person, a melancholic, a cyclothymiac who is before us with his well-known characteristics.

b. *How to distinguish these different phenomena*—In spite of their resemblances and their interpenetration, the troubles of the dark night can generally be distinguished from the disorders of psychosis. Professor de Greef from whom we borrow the preceding observations adds:

> Yet while considering as probable that a certain number of dark nights (in the sense of those of the spirit) belong more particularly to cyclothymia, it seems that this latter cannot explain everything and that, for a higher per cent than one would think, it is impossible to identify a state of night with a state of melancholy.[126]

The signs of the dark night given by Saint John of the Cross ordinarily allow one to make the necessary discriminations. The Saint has himself taken care to indicate some of the effects proper to melancholy.

And yet, in mixed cases in which, according to Dom Mager, the principal efficient cause is mystical and the instrumental

[124] *Ibid.*, ix; 352: "And, although this may sometimes be increased by melancholy or some other humour (as it frequently is), it fails not for that reason to produce a purgative effect upon the desire."

[125] *Ibid.*, iv; 340: "Those who are affected by this dare not even look at anything or meditate upon anything, because they immediately encounter this temptation. And upon those who are inclined to melancholy this acts with such effect that they become greatly to be pitied since they are suffering so sadly; for this trial reaches such a point in certain persons, when they have this evil humour, that they believe it to be clear that the devil is ever present with them and that they have no power to prevent this."

Saint Teresa consecrated a whole chapter of the book of the *Foundations* (ch. vii) to melancholics and to the forceful and maternal treatment suited to them. She does not seem to say that the manifestations of this melancholy are due in any way to God's action in the soul. Yet what we are saying of the possibilities of a development of the spiritual life concomitant with mental disturbances is applicable to these melancholics of whom the Saint says that "the principal effect of this humor is to obscure reason."

[126] Cf. De Greef, art. cit., p. 152.

cause is more or less pathological,[127] that is, when the subject is affected by pathological tendencies—discernment will be more difficult. Too great haste in judging would have harmful consequences.

The deportment of the soul and its progress—evaluated not according to the violence of crises or their periodic return, but according to views of the whole taken over a wide period—will permit one to determine which predominant influence of the mystical night or of the psychosis will finally triumph.

On the development of the one and of the other, Professor de Greef gives some external signs that are extremely valuable:

> As against a psychosis which, if it does not always destroy the mind, regularly impoverishes it and the personality by its stagnations and aberrations and which, if it produces an intellectual work, is limited to going over indefinitely the same things without any real spiritual creation, an experience like that of Saint John of the Cross appears, from our psychological point of view, as a constant progression, an uninterrupted enrichment, a regular series of daily victories won in most difficult circumstances.[128]

The case of Saint John of the Cross is described as "surnormal" by the eminent professor. Actually, the soul's advance does not as a rule appear so clearly, nor are its victories from the beginning so decisive. Defeats will at times be so numerous that the combat will for a long time be indecisive. The collaboration of the physician and the spiritual director may be necessary; the first, trying to neutralize the physiological and psychological effects of the psychosis, the second, lifting up the soul to God. But it seems to me that as long as genuine signs of the dark night appear, one should not treat the subject as an ordinary sick person; the spiritual director should take the lead in this case. For normally, the pathological tendency will yield under the action of the dark night and disappear. Saint John of the Cross, after pointing out the influence of melancholy in temptations to impurity, adds:

[127] Dom Mager, "Fondements psychologiques de la purification passive," *Etudes Carmélitaines,* October 1938, p. 353.

[128] *Art. cit.,* pp. 159-160.

When these impurities attack such souls through the medium of melancholy, they are not as a rule freed from them until they have been cured of that kind of humour, unless the dark night has entered the soul, and rids them of all impurities, one after another.[129]

Such is the encouraging assurance that the Saint gives us. The pathological tendencies, like the dross in the mineral, come to the surface and stand out in such relief during the dark night, only because they are in eruption. The dark night creates on the surface abcesses of fixation that draw out the malignant humors and eliminate them. It not only ensures the moral purification of the soul but frees it from its pathological tendencies. The soul thus recovers in full liberty of spirit and perfect psychological balance a normal and regular line of ascent toward holiness. This result once obtained, it becomes evident how the pathological tendencies multiplied troubles along the way, added to the sufferings of the soul, prolonged its trial, but that all in all, they were for the soul a means of progress by detaching it from the natural that it found to be so lacking and so vitiated, and by obliging it to plunge itself into the pure supernatural.

When the transformation is effected, the difficulties of the way fade out. The soul is astonished that it could have attached so much importance to them. The spiritual director sees how much he might have retarded the progress of that soul by his hesitations, by his anxiously seeking out the pathological and the spiritual, which would have been for the soul only occasions of useless analyses and loss of time. He understands better how eminently wise is the attitude that Saint John of the Cross advises, of overreaching all sensible phenomena, when God is acting in the soul, and of being continually orientated toward Him by perseverance in anagogical acts. When one has assurance that the soul is advancing towards God, it is high wisdom not to linger over the least psychological troubles that may appear, probing into their origin and nature. This is so, given the

[129] *Dark Night,* Bk. I, iv; Peers, I, 340.

fact that as a general rule they bear some resemblance with certain disorders of psychosis and are rather frequently intermingled with them to some degree, and given especially that the most efficacious means of curing them is in the orientation of the soul to God alone, "the perfect health of the soul." Besides, is it possible to decide just what is the cause of each one of such troubles and the part played by the intervening causes? After the first year of her religious life, which was marked by mystical graces of union, Teresa of Avila falls sick; and the description that she gives us of her illness permits a diagnosis as of nervous trouble. Saint Therese of the Child Jesus suffers at the age of nine from a strange illness of which she is cured by the smile of the Blessed Virgin. God's powerful action, a weakness or defect in temperament, a trick of the devil? Who is able to lift the veil of the mystery so as to ascribe to each one of these determinants its part? Interest in the problem diminishes in face of the marvelous success of high holiness in perfect human balance, making of these souls exceptional types of humanity.

c. *Concomitance of the mystical night and persistent psychoses*—But the success is not always so perfect. Pathological tendencies do not always yield under the action of the dark night.[130] Sometimes they even seem to develop under its influence and become more tyrannical. Witness the case of P. Surin.[131] Can the apparent check put upon grace by psychosis be explained? Is it followed by spiritual check? It belongs to neurologists and psychiatrists to answer the first question. The second presents a difficult problem. To clarify it we might enlarge it somewhat and formulate it thus: How and in what

[130] Saint John of the Cross says explicitly that tendencies of nature in which "the will enlightened by reason has no part either before or after the acts, hinder only a very little the divine union." Again he writes, "It is impossible to make them disappear and to mortify them fully in this life." It is clear that pathological tendencies enter into the category of natural tendencies.

[131] See the articles of Professor de Greef, of P. O. Gaillard, and of P. de Guibert, in *Etudes Carmélitaines,* October, 1938.

measure is a genuine and profound spiritual life reconcilable with mental troubles?

1. *Diverse mental troubles*—Doctor Achille Delmas catalogues mental troubles according to their cause thus:

> Mental illnesses are of two kinds. Those in the first class result from destructive organic lesions of the cerebral substance. These are curable, such as mental confusion, or incurable, such as dementia in general and chronic deliriums; they are incompatible with lucidity, reasoning power, and any high moral sentiment. Those in the second class, on the contrary, without lesions of the nerve centers, limited to variations by excess or by defect of tendencies of temperament and of character, constitute a lack of balance in activity and affectivity. They develop ordinarily in the form of reversible paroxysms and can be, at least in the light of moderate forms of these paroxysms, compatible with lucidity, discernment, and even . . . with great moral elevation.[132]

Let us still further refine this fine distinction. Among the mental illnesses that come from organic disturbances, some are curable and some incurable; certain ones result in complete and persistent insanity; others seem to affect only one faculty or one area; or they are chronic. Most of the mental illnesses of this group do not destroy completely and definitively the mental life of the individual affected.

The second group of illnesses, which consist in lack of balance in activity and affectivity, even if they diminish or destroy at the time of crises the lucidity and liberty of the one sick, do not seem to touch him profoundly outside of these attacks. The alternating states of excitation and depression, called cyclothymic states, are sometimes found in attractive and moving personalities [133] and at times accompany genius.[134]

[132] Cf. Doctor Achille Delmas, "A propos du P. Surin et de M. Th. Noblet," in *Etudes Carmélitaines,* October, 1938, p. 235.

[133] *Ibid.*, p. 237.

[134] Vivid intuitions of genius usually flash during such states. Napoleon, it seems, was a cyclothymiac. Among the saints, God's hold on them certainly creates in the deep regions of the soul a zone of stable peace, but it seems that the region of the faculties, where the faculties act (the outskirts according to Saint John of the Cross) can experience these heights and depths, exaltation under the action of the divine light and depression in the face of one's personal misery and difficulties. Elias was a man like us, says Holy Scripture. A psychological study made of the apostle Saint Paul from this point of view, with the aid of his epistles, would be very interesting.

This means that such mental troubles, at least when they do not attain to great intensity, can allow if not favor the development of a superior intellectual and moral life.

Among these affective troubles hysteria or mythomania is placed in a category apart by psychiatrists. Doctor Delmas says that it is:

> . . . an innate affective unbalance under the pressure of which mythomaniacs have an impulsive and irresistible but conscious urge to misrepresent their behavior and to direct their activity toward the artificial, the lie, and mythical creation under forms more or less picturesque, strange, tumultuous or dramatic. It is essentially an unbalance through excess of vanity. This state is incompatible with sincerity, and is exactly the inverse of it.[135]

We can understand why the doctor thinks himself obliged to make the most express reservations as to the morality of the patient, when he finds himself faced with a marked hysteria that asserts itself in a series of multiple manifestations, accompanied most of the time by a stupefying appearance of sincerity, by extreme cleverness, and an astounding strength of perseverance.[136]

2. *Possibilities of spiritual life in these diverse troubles*—The medical psychiatrist, preoccupied as he is with human equilibrium in a regular and harmonious functioning of the faculties, finds himself disconcerted in the face of such accidents that render all cure impossible. How could this not be so—especially in the face of those tendencies, like hysteria, that falsify all human relations by introducing into them systematic lies? We can understand why he hesitates to admit the possible concomitance of a genuine moral and spiritual life with such disorders. But the psychiatrist, even a very penetrating one, cannot be set up as the sole judge in these matters.

Necessary distinctions—The philosopher and the theologian have their word to say, and perhaps the most important. They

[135] Cf. the Article by Doctor Achille Delmas, p. 238.
[136] *Ibid.*

tell us actually [137] that the field of religious psychology extends over different superposed planes. First there is the empirical plane or the domain of religious phenomena that the man of science and the psychologist experiment with and study, using the scientific method of observation and induction. Beyond this plane of phenomena there is the ontological plane, the domain of the philosopher, in which he tries with the aid of reason to discover the very essence of the things on which religious life is founded. Finally, at the summit, there is the supernatural plane in which the theologian studies, in the light of faith, the essence of our religious acts; he refers these to their ultimate reason, which is God and grace. These three superimposed domains represent three realities, each one having its proper life. The experimental domain attains directly the sensible life; the ontological domain is that of the life of the spirit; the supernatural domain is transcendent; it is that of the divine life in our soul.

These three domains are closely inter-related. The supernatural act of the infused virtues is engrafted in the activity of the human faculties; it must first be human, that it may become supernatural. And this act, both human and supernatural, issues from a preliminary sense experience and will have its rebound in the domain of sense phenomena. Faith comes from hearing, says the apostle. It is only by an act of the intellect that it attains to its divine object. And the act of faith, once posited, will have its effects on the external life of the believer.

This interdependence is not, however, compenetration. There is between these three domains a distinction that is not merely logical, but is real. To these three domains there correspond three realities, three forms of life with their proper operations. And so, whatever be the depths of the subconscious in which it is rooted, the pathological tendency belongs to the domain of sense. Although intervening in the activity of the intellect

[137] Cf. Penido, "Les trois plans de la psychologie religieuse," *Etudes Carmélitaines,* October 1931, p. 127.

and the will, throwing into confusion their exterior manifestations, a psychosis does not alter the health of intellect and will themselves.[138] These remain healthy, even though the organs they use for their operations are sick. Hence these faculties remain apt for producing regularly and soundly their proper acts whenever the pathological tendency is not exercising its disturbing influence. It even seems to me, that throughout the deviation imposed on their activity by the pathological tendency, they can maintain a certain moral rectitude. The patient can be, between crises, an intelligent and virtuous man; and during the crises, at least when they do not take away from him all conscientiousness and inner liberty, he can freely will the good and execute it, such as it appears to him.

For all the more reason must we safeguard the inviolability of the supernatural domain of grace. The organic illness or the psychosis can alter the lights and impulses which descend from that domain, as well as all that rises from the senses to the higher regions. Hence they can throw disorder into the exercise of supernatural virtue by muddling and falsifying the perceptions of the external real world on which this exercise rests. But never can they attain to the transcendent regions where the very life of grace is. That is God's domain and is under His direct action. He Himself directly infuses the divine life. His bounty in that domain is governed by the free movements of His mercy and by the merits the soul has acquired by its supernatural acts of the virtues. The supernatural life of the patient can therefore be enriched by God when He wishes and according to the measure of His choice; it certainly is enriched each time the patient posits a supernatural interior act.

In order to apply these truths to the cases previously mentioned, let us distinguish two categories of mental illnesses. First are those which, proceeding either from deviations in affectivity or from organic changes coming from lesions, have

[138] Cf. P. Gardeil, "Quel rapport y-a-t-il entre la vie des vertus et la santé de l'intelligence," *Etudes Carmélitaines,* October, 1931, p. 127.

effects that are localized or intermittent. In this first group we shall put even hysteria, however unsympathetic and perplexing from the moral point of view be the tendency to lying and to ostentation that characterizes it. In the second category are mental illnesses that result in complete insanity.

Intermittent or localized disturbances.—The localization and intermittence of the troubles leave the patient in the first group with the possibility, at least at times, of exercising his higher faculties normally and of positing moral acts. There can be no doubt of the possibility of a supernatural life, whatever may be the difficulty of discerning in the life of the patient, and especially in his confidences, what is supernatural fruit and what mental pathology; it being possible, moreover, that the supernatural in such cases is ordinarily impregnated with the pathological in its manifestations.

The moral and supernatural life to which psychosis adds such troubling elements can draw from the psychosis itself a singular help. The patient is conscious of his illness, of the disorders to which it leads him, of the discredit if not scorn that it brings upon him, of the suspicion that it casts over his whole interior life. He journeys here below in the most painful humiliation and perhaps in a constraint that paralyzes his external activity and his liberty. If he accepts the trial and all its consequences, is this not heroism and of the highest.[139] Père de Guibert writes:

> This being so, we do not see what would prevent God from communicating to such a soul the highest graces of infused contemplation. No doubt, in the confidences that the soul makes, it will be impossible always to distinguish clearly between what is an infused gift of God and what is mental pathology. . . . But this impossibility does not change the fact of the matter; and we can very well believe that God

[139] Read in the article of Professor de Greef, *Etudes Carmélitaines,* October, 1938, pp.156-7, the case of "Sister Rose-Anne, a missionary religious. . . . Strange comportment. The Blessed Virgin spoke to her. . . . For the rest she is submissive, offers to God the sacrifice of being considered as out of her mind. . . . The case is very clear from the psychiatrists' point of view, but the erudition of the patient, the heroism and the dignity with which she bears this trial, impress very strongly her associates."

particularly favors this soul, by reason of the immense difficulties and hard trials that it meets with in order to realize its ascent in love, in the midst of the obscurities and tempests of its cruel illness.[140]

And the following concerns Père Surin in whom

. . . we can state with certitude that there is an intense love of God in the midst of the worst inconsistencies and oddnesses in his life. . . , the simultaneous presence of the most grave psycho-pathological accidents and states with marked intellectual and moral gifts.[141]

Complete insanity—What are we to think of complete insanity, which paralyzes all reasonable activity of the faculties? No more intellectual life, no moral life, no spiritual life! Is this the death of everything? Who would dare to say no? But under that apparent death caused by a paralysis or lesion of organs, what is left to serve intellectual functions? Is there not under this dread yoke a soul endowed perhaps with a fine intellect, a noble rectitude of will, adorned with the gifts of grace? Is it indeed true that all activity of that twofold life, intellectual and supernatural, is at an end? Let us not be too quick to say so. There are cases of apparent physical death, which are only a paralysis of the organs. Just so, there are fixed attitudes of absolute mutism and total inactivity, which are compatible with lucidity and an elevated interior moral life.[142] And even if it is true that the life of the faculties is immobilized under a shroud of death, the soul may have accepted in advance the trial that was foreseen and desired, not for itself, but as a purifying and redemptive trial. We think of the offering made by Monsieur Martin, the father of Saint Therese of the Child Jesus, which ended in complete paralysis reaching to the mental faculties. Père Piat writes:

140 P. de Guibert, "Les Cas du P. Surin," *Etudes Carmélitaines,* October, 1938, pp. 187-188.

141 *Ibid.,* p. 189.

142 This is the conclusion drawn by Doctor Delmas from observations made on the case of a young girl who continued for years to follow the religious offices, to go to confession and communicate on the major feasts, to observe fasts and abstinences, and that, without coming out of her mutism, inactivity, and fixed attitude. *Etudes Carmélitaines,* October 1938, p. 236.

He himself will keep for a long time enough lucidity to sanctify the bitterness of this annihilation of personality, while his daughters will find in it the principal trial destined to urge them forward on the royal road of the cross.[143]

And we find other examples of such a trial, which seem to have brought souls into humiliating depths of abjection that were for them the summits of a redemptive sacrifice, of which God alone can tell the fruits. We would not wish to merit the reproach of exalting such human failures and crowning them with the supernatural nimbus of glory. Certainly they do not all, in their cause and development, partake of the supernatural. Are the cases that we cite extraordinary then? Who can say? Whatever be the case, we thought we should react against the promptitude some have in passing pessimistic and unjust judgments on all mental deficiencies,[144] against the tendency always to place holiness at the summits of human equilibrium, and not to want to recognize it elsewhere than on this pedestal.[145] How different are the judgments of God. Again Père de Guibert writes:

For God there is no difference among the souls created and redeemed by Him. The soul of the poor hysterical patient, a real human tatter going from clinic to clinic for years, is no less dear to Him than that of the great scientist, humanly magnificent, who studies the case. Why then refuse to believe that in the face of the human poverty of the resources of that soul for moral progress, God will at times have recourse to His great means of sanctification, leaving perhaps untouched the heavy yoke upon this soul, but causing to spring up in its depths

[143] P. Piat, *Histoire d'une famille,* ch. xvi, p. 305.

[144] Saint Therese of the Child Jesus wrote with fine perception of the practice of charity: "Dear Mother . . . I feel that I ought to be as compassionate for the spiritual infirmities of my Sisters as you are for my bodily ills. . . . Imperfect souls are left alone. . . . Their company is avoided. . . . When I say imperfect souls, I am not referring to souls with spiritual imperfections only. . . . I mean those who are also afflicted with want of tact and refinement, as well as ultra-sensitive souls. I know such defects are incurable, but I also know how patient you would be . . . were my illness to last for many years." *Autobiography,* x, pp. 165-6.

[145] We are evidently speaking here of real holiness which is measured by charity and can be found together with pathological defects, and not of canonized holiness which, in order to be proposed for the veneration and imitation of the faithful, must normally be free of all that could tarnish it or diminish it in the judgment of men.

that escape our observation a true and great love infused by Him? There is a holiness that God gives us the consolation of discerning and touching with the finger in this life. But there is also a holiness, the sight of which He reserves to Himself in this world, and which will no doubt singularly astound us when the chrysalis will have become a butterfly.[146]

That which is intrinsically supernatural escapes observation. Its most beautiful triumphs are hidden beneath a very thick wall of painful and mysterious darkness. Thus has love triumphed here below since the drama of Calvary. "To give oneself up to love is to surrender oneself to all sufferings," proclaimed Saint Therese of the Child Jesus. This word gives the final reason for the dark night of the spirit. It explains the darkness that envelopes this drama, from the depths of the soul where it unfolds, even to the external regions of the faculties and the senses, over which it extends its afflictive mystery.

C. Diverse modalities of the dark night

So frightening a description of the drama of the dark night of the spirit might seem to call forth a desire, if not a prayer, to be delivered from sanctity, if it imposes such sufferings, or at least, to make one wonder whether it is possible to find a road to holiness on which such terrible trials are not met with. An exact answer cannot be given to this question. We are here in the domain of loving Wisdom. She directs the drama, a drama of love, merciful but pitiless against sin; for destroy sin she must, in order to bring about her triumph. She directs the drama freely, in accord with her designs. This is a play that does not obey the laws of our reasonable logic; it shows itself quite independent of the fluctuations and stirrings of our sensibility. And yet, the play is not so utterly hidden that we can neither say nor observe anything of its irregular rhythm and exterior modalities.

If we compare actual cases with the descriptions given by John of the Cross, we may say that the reality, as it is lived by

[146] P. de Guibert, article already quoted, *Etudes Carmélitaines,* Oct. 1938, p. 189.

souls, is more painful but at the same time less terrifying than the picture he gives of it. More painful, because the mystical doctor does not describe all the forms of suffering that the soul in fact undergoes; nor could he tell, for each case, all the aggravating incidents—the intensity and depth of the suffering eluding, as it does, even the pen of a Saint John of the Cross. On the other hand, the reality is less terrible, because the description presents in a concentrated picture, and all grouped together, diverse traits which, in the life of souls, are met with successively, or in different subjects, and combined with other circumstances that tone down their external aspect, if not the suffering they cause. Hence, although the description is true, it seems to bring out the dark side. All the traits are exact and in no way forced; but they appear in actual life under other dimensions.

1. INTERRUPTIONS

Saint John of the Cross warns us that during the period of purification, suffering does not always have the same intensity: Speaking of the soul that has not yet reached the summit of the "ladder of contemplation," he writes:

> It never remains in the same state for long together, but is ascending and descending continually. The reason for this is that, as the state of perfection, which consists in the perfect love of God and contempt for self, cannot exist unless it have these two parts, which are the knowledge of God and of oneself, the soul has of necessity to be practised first in the one and then in the other, now being given to taste of the one—that is, exaltation,—and now being made to experience the other—that is, humiliation.[147]

Elsewhere the Saint explains more precisely what causes the diversity of divine action during this period. The soul is more enkindled in love when its inner flame is less burning, hence less purifying and less painful. This surprises us, but the testimony of the mystical doctor is to that point:

> This enkindling of love, however, is not always felt by the soul, but only at times when contemplation assails it less vehemently, for then it

[147] *Dark Night,* Bk. II, xviii; Peers, I, 433-4.

has occasion to see, and even to enjoy, the work which is being wrought in it, and which is then revealed to it. For it seems that the worker takes his hand from the work, and draws the iron out of the furnace, in order that something of the work which is being done may be seen.[148]

O happy respite that brings such relief! happy revelation of work accomplished, the most strengthening of encouragements!

Let us not, however, expect a regular cycle with periodic intervals such as we find them in nature. Wisdom at times seems to be in haste to complete her work in short time. And again, the intervals are long drawn out. God can leave in shadow, at rest as it were, such or such a tendency, putting off till later the refining of the soul on a particular point and the perfect purifying of the virtue. He may let pass many years before His loving wisdom applies again its afflictive fire. He alone knows why.[149]

2. INDIVIDUAL FORMS OF PURIFICATION

The fire that purifies is an intelligent fire. It regulates the violence of its flame according to the effect it wants to produce. Thus the remark that Saint John of the Cross makes apropos of the night of sense may be applied also to the night of the spirit:

All do not experience it after one manner, neither do all encounter the same temptations. For this is meted out by the will of God, in conformity with the greater or the smaller degree of imperfection which each soul has to purge away. In conformity, likewise, with the degree

[148] *Ibid.*, x; 404.

[149] It seems that this purification of the spirit may last not only for years but a whole life long, ending at the moment of death or shortly before in a final flowering, which is transforming union. I think that one must ordinarily explain thus the sufferings that are continued throughout a lifetime; and that some are too hasty in calling certain sufferings redemptive sufferings, under the claim that they are posterior to an external grace indicative of a high degree of union. Assuredly, there must be here below, other than in our Lord and the Blessed Virgin, sufferings that are uniquely redemptive; but let us proclaim them such only if the state of spiritual marriage or transforming union has been clearly manifest. It is more normal, more in conformity with our dual nature of flesh and spirit, that our suffering be both purifying and redemptive. Cf. P. Garrigou-Lagrange, "Nuit réparatrice de Saint Paul de la Croix," *Etudes Carmélitaines*, October 1938, pp. 287-91.

of love of union to which God is pleased to raise it, He will humble it with greater or less intensity or in greater or less time. Those who have the disposition and greater strength to suffer, He purges with greater intensity and more quickly. But those who are very weak are kept for a long time in this night, and these He purges very gently and with slight temptations.[150]

Moreover, since the imperfections are "the material upon which the fire seizes," [151] consequently the sufferings are different according to the sins the flame assails. The result is that the purification of spirit assumes in each soul an individual form, special by reason of the kind of suffering it imposes and the nature of the trials. Hence we must be on our guard against any stereotyped notion of the dark night. The night is always an intervention of divine Wisdom by fire. The divine bellows fan to a blaze the depths of the soul with a force and rhythm as varied as are the designs of God for it and as are the forms of sin of which it must be purified.

3. PURIFICATION MERGED WITH DAILY LIFE

This remark as to the individual nature of the purification of the spirit must be completed by another trait more important still for the outside observer.

The purification of the spirit is not a surgical feat done in a clinic, nor a laboratory experiment; in other words, it is not a supernatural intervention on a subject that has been separated from the world of reality, isolated in a milieu from which everything has been removed that might hinder the success of the operation, and everything that might favor it carefully brought together. Divine Wisdom does not place in a hothouse all the souls it wills to purify. And yet one might be led to think so on reading the Joannine descriptions, so free from all human alloy the divine action appears in them, so pure and lofty; and the soul itself, so uniquely absorbed by its encounter with God deep within and the painful duel that is taking place between

[150] *Dark Night,* Bk. I, xiv; Peers, I, 373.
[151] *Ibid.,* Bk. II, x; 404.

the light that shines upon it and the sin that it bears. The spectacle given us by these descriptions is living and moving with interest. But we have difficulty in placing it in ordinary reality, so uplifted are the forces at play, and so absorbed by the violence of the struggle and its stake.

And yet, it is indeed in the midst of daily life that the battle takes place. Saint John of the Cross owes it to the purity and penetration of his gaze, that he was able to discern the spiritual elements of this drama and abstract them from the rest, so as to present them to us in their essential reality.[152]

More than anyone else, however, is he familiar with that supreme art of Wisdom, all simplicity and suppleness. The divine Artificer excels in using secondary causes, be they persons or events, making of them instruments of His omnipotence in the realization of His sole design, the Church and the sanctification of souls. The action of Wisdom is ordinarily merged with daily life and hidden under the veil of the most ordinary events.

Assuredly, solitude and the desert offer a field of action particularly favorable to the loftiest interior operations of divine Wisdom. God draws, at least for a time, into these special *ateliers* of His grace those souls that He is preparing for high destinies. But external events and the passions of men are instruments of such quality, so quick to act, so easy to manipulate, so perfectly docile to His movements, that He uses them very widely for the purification of His saints. Saint John of the Cross was isolated from everything, in his rough wooden house near the Convent of the Incarnation; and there he was seized by the envoys of the Calced Friars, to undergo in the prison of Toledo the strongest shock of the attack against the Teresian Reform. He came out from the prison of Toledo with

[152] We have already stressed this gift that Saint John of the Cross has of discerning the essentially supernatural wherever it is. Just as he is wary of the supernatural in mode only, that is, of external manifestations that strike the senses, because illusion easily creeps in, just so has he respect for the essentially supernatural. And so he places it in relief lest the least "crumb" of it be neglected and trampled under foot.

the grace of spiritual marriage. The life of Saint Teresa was filled with assaults from external powers, which purified her soul and strengthened her work as a Reformer.

4. MYSTERIOUS AND OFTEN HID FROM VIEW

The agitation of human passions and the still more opaque veil of the ordinariness of daily events under which the divine action is hid envelop with mystery the work of Wisdom—with a mystery that is deepened by the diversity of its exterior forms. And so this action can escape the gaze of the one who is undergoing it and of the most discerning outside observer as well. Perhaps the awareness of it will come easier to the contemplative, habituated to introspection, in whom supernatural phenomena are normally more numerous and more clearly marked.

In the person given to the active life or in the contemplative taken up with exterior works, both of them subject to more numerous vicissitudes, the supernatural will ordinarily stand out less. The discernment of the divine action will also be more difficult, so thick is the cangue that covers it, made up of a multiplicity of external events and interventions of free causes. Nevertheless, divine Wisdom will reveal Himself in sudden and profound lights. In such a person the purification will be made as intense, if not more so, because the fire is fed with more external difficulties and persecutions, with more personal failures, and more anxiety about works that involve grave spiritual interests; and consequently, with more occasions for humiliating oneself, for hoping and loving. The purification might even be more rapid under these conditions, if the soul knew how to use them to flee from its inner torment and go only to God through faith and self-surrender.[153]

[153] The lives of the saints could illustrate marvelously these conditions, which are rather dead because generalized. In these, one would see how divine Wisdom makes admirable use of exterior difficulties (difficulties about money, opposition of friends, etc.), to oblige the saints to perform acts that are purely supernatural and thus to climb the last degrees of perfection. God tortures wonderfully His saints so as to lead them to the supernatural end that He has set for them.

5. ENLIGHTENED BY THE LIGHT AND PRESENCE OF LOVE

In the mystery that envelops God's action, not all is darkness. Rays of light flash through it. First of all, the extraordinary favors of which we have spoken, and which are for the greater number in this period. Then a more general and more constant help that the soul finds in a certain diffused light, in a certain feeling that God is there. Saint John of the Cross writes, speaking of the fire of love:

> For this present kind is an enkindling of spiritual love in the soul, which, in the midst of these dark confines, feels itself to be keenly and sharply wounded in strong Divine love, and to have a certain realization and foretaste of God, although it understands nothing definitely, for, as we say, the understanding is in darkness.[154]

This conjecture is a veritable certitude, which does not as a rule spread its peace over all the faculties; yet its firmness asserts itself in many circumstances, especially each time that the soul might be tempted to despair, or when in its presence someone expresses doubt as to the supernatural nature of the action at work within it. This feeling gives security and immense strength. Constantly it maintains balance in the soul's inmost regions; and it comes to the fore whenever that balance is seriously threatened by temptations to despair.

And so, at the risk of seeming to heap up antinomies, we could not better summarize this description of the dark night of the spirit than by saying that it is not a hell but a purgatory,[155] a realm of suffering, but also one of peace, a realm where love wounds painfully and with violence only to purify, to liberate, to heal the soul and bring it into transforming union.

[154] *Dark Night,* Bk. II, xi; Peers, I, 406.

[155] *Ibid,* x; 404. "We can learn here incidentally in what manner souls are afflicted in purgatory." Cf. also *Living Flame,* st. i; Peers, III, 25 f.

CHAPTER IV

The Conduct of the Soul: Poverty, Hope, Spiritual Childhood

That which is born of the flesh is flesh; and that which is born of the Spirit is spirit. Do not wonder that I said to thee, 'You must be born again.' The wind blows where it will, and thou hearest its sound but dost not know where it comes from or where it goes. So is everyone who is born of the Spirit.[1]

God's action in the soul during the dark night requires the soul's cooperation. We must ask, then, what is the cooperation that will allow the divine fire to burn, full flame, within?

Was not this the problem that urged on Nicodemus when he went during the night to find Jesus who, for the first time, was manifesting Himself to Jerusalem? However paradoxical may appear this comparison, it should be made. It will give us some light. The young Wonderworker of Nazareth had won to Himself this leader among the Jews. Nicodemus had recognized in Jesus the spirit of God. "Rabbi," he says to Him, "we know that thou hast come a teacher from God." [2] These introductory words give the key to an attitude of soul and suggest a question. Nicodemus wanted a doctrine from this teacher come from God, so that he might be a follower. Jesus anticipates the question: "Amen, amen, I say to thee, unless a man

[1] John 3:6-8.
[2] John 3:2.

be born again, he cannot see the kingdom of God." [3] The brave neophyte is disconcerted. This statement comes as a shock to the learning and ways of thinking of that doctor of the Law who moves at ease among the minute details of ritual prescriptions and the subtleties of rabbinical interpretations. And such indeed is the effect that Jesus wants to produce in that soul of good will. And so, He insists:

> Amen, amen, I say to thee, unless a man be born again of water and the Spirit, he cannot enter into the kingdom of God. That which is born of the flesh is flesh; and that which is born of the Spirit is spirit. Do not wonder that I said to thee, 'You must be born again.' The wind blows where it will, and thou hearest its sound but dost not know where it comes from or where it goes. So is everyone who is born of the Spirit.[4]

To enter into the new kingdom, a man must be reborn; only the breath of the Spirit can effect this. This teaching and dialectic are worthy of the mercy of the Master who is giving it, as well as of the elevation of mind and of good will of the disciple listening. But the disciple is not yet ready to receive such teaching. He does not understand and says so:

> "How can these things be?"
> Answering him, Jesus said, "Thou art a teacher in Israel and dost not know these things?" [5]

The reproach seems severe. It is decisive. Nicodemus accepts it; he casts down his poor learning before the transcendence of the Master's. Now light floods his soul. Jesus declares:

> Amen, amen, I say to thee, we speak of what we know, and we bear witness to what we have seen.[6]

Here is a revelation of the mystery of the Incarnation and a foretelling of the approaching realization of the mystery of the Redemption.

[3] John 3:3.
[4] John 3:5-8.
[5] John 3:9-10.
[6] John 3:11.

No one has ascended into heaven except him who has descended from heaven, the Son of Man who is in heaven.

"And as Moses lifted up the serpent in the desert, even so must the Son of Man be lifted up, that those who believe in him may not perish, but may have life everlasting." [7]

The spirit that gives new birth—one must hope for it from Christ Jesus on the cross. Nicodemus keeps in mind this mysterious teaching. He was often to meditate upon it in silence. He was to wait in hope.

When the time comes that Jesus is lifted up on the cross, when the apostles have scattered because of the scandal of the Passion, Nicodemus will come out from his retreat. Taking a hundred pounds of myrrh and aloes, he will go courageously to bury the body of the Crucified.[8] In the darkness of Calvary, he will gather from the transpierced heart of Jesus the fruit of his waiting and of his hope.

This gospel episode, with its play of shadow and of light, holds before us a precious teaching. Nicodemus, humiliated and dazzled, silent and peaceful in his hopeful waiting, found the attitude of soul that prepared it for rebirth under the action of the Spirit. He is a model for every soul that longs to be reborn under the painful assailing of the flame that wonderfully tortures it.

Let us remember this attitude of Nicodemus; it will give light on all that we have to say about the conduct of the soul in the dark night of the spirit.

A. Hope and poverty

Spiritual rebirth is accomplished in its loftiest and most perfect form in the dark night of the spirit under the action of burning fire. It is a veritable combat, the sufferings of which we have already measured—a wondrous torture. Saint John of the Cross writes:

[7] John 3:13-15.
[8] John 19:39.

> But now, being brought near to this flame, the soul clearly sees and feels its miseries, for—oh, wondrous thing!—there arise within it contraries against contraries, some of which, as the philosophers say, become visible in reacting to others; and they make war in the soul, striving to expel each other in order that they may reign within it. . . . In this way the soul has ordinarily to endure the worst possible suffering in its substance and faculties, experiencing great anguish and affliction from the battle which is being waged by the contrary forces within its suffering self. God, Who is all perfection, wars against all the imperfect habits of the soul.[9]

The flame of the spirit is acting and leading the combat that the soul undergoes; a fundamental truth this, that we never tire of repeating, so fully must it command the attitude of the soul during this period.

The flame is divine, is the omnipotent and transcendent Cause. The first duty of the soul is to respect its action and submit to it. The flame is all-consuming, burning, painful. It cloaks the soul in darkness, and wounds deeply. The soul must suffer its assaults patiently. *Pati Deum,* to suffer God, such is the deepest attitude required of the soul.

Pati Deum, to suffer God—not in a Stoic attitude, for this would be pagan, but as a Christian, silently, willingly and lovingly, in the attitude of Christ on the cross. Patience must be bathed in love and must let itself be transformed by Him, in complete surrender to all the divine operations within.

This self-abandonment goes beyond passive resignation and submission to God's action. It involves active cooperation, a veritable asceticism that has been called mystical. A mystical asceticism in this sense that, sovereignly respectful of God's action, the soul acts—but does so energetically—only to open itself wide to the divine action, suppress whatever might hinder that action's development, and thus ensure its complete efficacy. Mystical asceticism, the perfect response of genuine love, is always a delicate art. It must move strongly between that proud activism that believes in its own power and thus checks the expansion and the initiatives of God's love for the soul, and that

[9] *Living Flame,* st. i; Peers, III, 26-8.

selfish and lazy quietism that fixates the soul's love for its God in the immobility of tepidity or of death. Mystical asceticism finds its measure and its expression in the practice of the virtue of hope.

1. HOPE

Hope is an infused theological virtue by which, relying on the omnipotence of God helping us, we hope for God who will be our beatitude and for the means necessary to attain to Him. Faith reveals God to us; hope desires Him and hopes to attain to Him. Like faith, hope is a theological virtue having God for its object and its motive: He it is for whom we hope, and we hope because His omnipotence will be our help.

Saint John of the Cross, following the apostle Saint Paul, points out that:

> All possession is contrary to hope, which, as Saint Paul says, belongs to that which is not possessed.[10]

In the Epistle to the Romans, the apostle is more precise:

> For in hope were we saved. But hope that is seen is not hope. For how can a man hope for what he sees? But if we hope for what we do not see, we wait for it with patience.[11]

The absence of the object that one hopes for gives rise to desire and the movement of hope toward it. Saint Thomas emphasizes that the supernatural virtue of hope is engrafted in a passion of the irascible appetite, which is

> . . . a movement of the appetitive power ensuing from the apprehension of a future good, difficult but possible to obtain; namely, a stretching forth of the appetite to such a good.[12] Hope makes us tend to God as to a good to be obtained finally.[13]

These remarks bring out the dynamic character of the virtue of hope. Faith discovers; charity possesses in an embrace; hope

[10] *Ascent*, Bk. III, vii; Peers, I, 226. Cf. Heb. 11:1.
[11] Rom. 8:24-5.
[12] *Sum. Theol.*, I-II, q. 40, a. 2.
[13] *Ibid.*, II-II, q. 17, a. 6, ad 3.

lies in tending toward the object known by faith and not yet possessed in the full measure of charity's desire. Hope is the virtue of progress in the spiritual life; it is the motor that keeps it moving, the wings that lift it up. A soul that no longer hopes, either because it finds itself filled and satisfied with what it possesses, or because it has given up trying to possess more, has lost its dynamism and advances no more.[14]

The dynamism of hope can be exercised in two different ways. It can produce an effective movement of the soul toward its object, an advance toward the object, arms extended to grasp it. Or again the soul may be paralyzed by a certain force emanating from the object present but hidden; any movement toward it is useless and would even risk causing it to withdraw farther. Then hope cannot but groan and sigh ardently and in silence. In the first case, hope seems more active; in the second, it seems almost passive, with the energies of its restrained dynamism concentrated in its gaze and desires. In the first case hope grasps the object by going toward it; in the second, it obtains its object perhaps more efficaciously by attracting it to itself by the soul's groaning and sighs.

Hence one can understand that in the measure that hope knows better its object and at the same time finds it to be farther away and more difficult of approach, it tends toward it with more strength and with all the energies of its desire. Then is the hour of hope: an hour of painful crisis, but also the hour of its triumph.

The dark night of the spirit brings with it this hour of supernatural hope. God reveals Himself in the inflowings of grace and the extraordinary favors that mark this period, in that wisdom, secret and always acting, which creates a certain obsession for the divine transcendence. The darkness that prevails makes

[14] The Pauline comparison of the runner in the race who puts to use all his strength to arrive at the goal (I Cor. 9:24-27), presents to us in an expressive picture the dynamism of hope, which utilizes all the energies of the soul to attain to God. The apostle even notes that "everyone in a contest abstains from all things." Supernatural hope, too, is sustained by asceticism and by vigorous efforts.

thicker the veil that separates Him, and greater the distance. The soul, crushed by its misery and weakness, experiences an inability to go toward God, the only object that it can thenceforth desire. To go back it cannot, for it is already captivated by His love. It does not succeed in going toward Him and it will not do so, since the divine flame is within it, assailing it. This is the hour of profound hope, ardent and peaceful. God awaits the sighs that mount up from the depths of the soul, opening them to His action. God needs these inner groanings that tell that the work of purification is being accomplished, and that give up to the flame's action all imperfections. Are not these groanings already those of the Spirit of which the apostle has written:

> But in like manner the Spirit also helps our weakness. For we do not know what we should pray for as we ought, but the Spirit himself pleads for us with unutterable groanings. And he who searches the heart knows what the Spirit desires, that he pleads for the saints according to God.[15]

The authentic action of the Holy Spirit does not exclude but calls for the active cooperation of the soul in the exercise of the virtue of hope. It pertains to the soul, and God requires it, to rest in the interior solitude in which God has placed it and to direct its gaze

> . . . upward, but nowhere else; for this is the function which hope habitually performs in the soul, namely, the directing of its eyes upwards to look at God alone, even as David declared that his eyes were directed, when he said: *Oculi mei semper ad Dominum*.[16] He hoped for no good thing elsewhere, save as he himself says in another Psalm: [17] "Even as the eyes of the handmaid are set upon the hands of her mistress, even so are our eyes set upon our Lord God, until He have mercy upon us as we hope in Him." [18]

God heaps up obstacles and trials only to obtain from the soul that constant and purified gaze which, under the impulse

[15] Rom. 8:26-27.
[16] Ps. 24:15.
[17] Ps. 97:2.
[18] *Dark Night*, Bk. II, xxi; Peers, I, 444.

of the Spirit, produces perfect hope, like to that of Abraham who

> . . . hoping against hope believed, so that he became the father of many nations, according to what was said, So shall thy offspring be.[19]

Perfect hope obtains all it desires. So says Saint John of the Cross, comparing this hope to a green tunic with which the soul is clothed. He writes:

> For this reason, because of this green livery (since the soul is ever looking to God and sets its eyes on naught else, neither is pleased with aught save with Him alone), the Beloved has such great pleasure with the soul that it is true to say that the soul obtains from Him as much as it hopes for from Him. Wherefore the Spouse in the Songs tells the Bride that, by looking upon Him with one eye alone, she has wounded His heart.[20] Without this green livery of hope in God alone it would be impossible for the soul to go forth to encompass this loving achievement, for it would have not success, since that which moves and conquers is the importunity of hope.[21]

We would, however, mutilate the teaching of Saint John of the Cross and perhaps favor a false interpretation of his whole spiritual doctrine on hope if we confined ourselves to this explanation alone. For would it not leave the impression that the perfection of hope resides in its intensity and that its triumphs are assured only by its strength and its constancy? But Saint John of the Cross never tires of saying that hope finds its perfection and its efficacy in its purity. In keeping with the holy doctor, we too must repeat and insist on this.

2. SPIRITUAL POVERTY

In spiritual poverty hope finds the purity that makes for its perfection. There is no truth more strongly asserted in the treatises of Saint John of the Cross. He writes:

> That which is hoped for is that which is not possessed, and since, the less we possess of other things, the greater scope and the greater capacity have we for hoping, and consequently the greater hope, there-

[19] Rom. 4:18.
[20] Cant. 4:9.
[21] *Dark Night, ibid.*

fore, the more things we possess, the less scope and capacity is there for hoping, and consequently the less hope have we.[22]

Merely to analyze the definition of the virtue of hope makes us realize that spiritual poverty alone can ensure its perfection. The virtue of hope hopes to attain God, its first and principal object; it hopes for Him because of Himself, that is, because of His helping omnipotence. It will be the more perfect the more it hopes in God solely, to the exclusion of any other motive than God Himself. This purity of object and motive that makes the perfection of hope is obtained by the elimination of all the rest, by that sovereign detachment which is spiritual poverty.

It is indeed to that poverty which no longer hopes for anything but God that is promised, in fact, the kingdom of God. "Blessed are the poor in spirit, for theirs is the kingdom of heaven;" such is the first beatitude proclaimed by the Master in the Sermon on the Mount.[23] The teaching of Saint John of the Cross in the *Ascent of Mount Carmel* and in the book of the *Dark Nights* echoes this beatitude. The Saint wants only to teach the way to realize or to suffer this impoverishment that will set free the movement of hope and ensure its opening out for the attainment of supernatural goods and of God Himself. Hope is a divine seed; God alone can give it increase; to the soul belongs the negative task of preparing the soil and favoring the growth.

Impoverishment must extend to all natural and supernatural riches, to all goods, intellectual and spiritual, outside of God Himself. In the chart of the *Ascent of Mount Carmel,* it is by the path of nothing, repeated four times over, that the soul —leaving at right and at left the spacious highways of the goods of earth and the goods of heaven—makes its way toward the summit. Only the path of nothing, which is total deprivation, perfect detachment and absolute poverty,[24] leads to the All that is God and makes certain the possession of Him.

[22] *Ascent,* Bk. III, xv; Peers, I, 241.
[23] Matt. 5:3.
[24] *Ascent,* Bk. I, xiii; 59-60.

To give in detail the program of detachment traced out by John of the Cross with regard to each category of both natural and supernatural goods affecting the human faculties of intellect, memory, and will, and to indicate the soul's conduct in each case, would oblige us to repeat the whole teaching of the mystical doctor. This can easily be found in his works. It is, however, important to point out the connection the Saint makes between the purification of the memory and the purification of hope.

Memory is a deposit of archives that holds intellectual and spiritual goods already acquired. This deposit, like the library for an intellectual worker, has considerable importance for the contemplative isolated from the external world, and for any spiritual person who consecrates long hours to prayer. In the silence of mental prayer, especially during times of aridity, the faculties normally go to this deposit seeking refuge, occupation, distraction or consolation. These archives are precious. But how much loss of time there can be in perusing them or simply in turning back to them! And especially how many attachments feed on them and grow strong!

To free the soul from so much accumulated wealth that keeps its gaze and will from soaring upward and hinders hope from mounting to God, pure, simple and luminous, Saint John of the Cross would like to burn every entry in the archives. Would not the soul thus take to itself Lady Poverty and make of her once and for all its companion?

For, as has been said, no supernatural forms or kinds of knowledge which can be apprehended by the memory are God, and, in order to reach God, the soul must void itself of all that is not God. The memory must also strip itself of all these forms and kinds of knowledge, that it may unite itself with God in a manner of mystical and perfect hope. For all possession is contrary to hope, which, as Saint Paul says, belongs to that which is not possessed. Wherefore, the more the memory dispossesses itself, the greater is its hope; and the more it has of hope, the more it has of union with God; for, with respect to God, the more the soul hopes, the more it attains. And it hopes most when it is most completely dispossessed; and, when it shall be perfectly dispossessed, it will remain with the perfect possession of God, in Divine union. But there are many who will not deprive themselves of the sweetness and delight which memory finds in those forms and notions, wherefore they attain not to supreme possession and perfect sweetness. For he that renounces not all that he possesses cannot be the disciple of Christ.[25]

Because it is the ark containing the intellectual and spiritual treasures that the soul often enjoys with a great spirit of ownership, the memory is the principal obstacle to the purification of hope. Hence the Saint's insistance on asking us to free it, separate it totally from its possessions. But can we do that? To do away with memories, to check the natural operations of the memory and fix it solely on God through hope is beyond the power of man. Saint John of the Cross is aware of this. He writes:

You will say, perhaps, that the soul will be unable to void and deprive its memory of all forms and fancies to such an extent as to be able to attain to so lofty a state; for there are two things so difficult that their accomplishment surpasses human ability and strength, namely, to throw off with one's natural powers that which is natural, which is hard enough, and to attain and be united to the supernatural, which is much more difficult—indeed, to speak the truth, is impossible with natural ability alone. The truth, I repeat, is that God must place the soul in this supernatural state; but the soul, as far as in it lies, must be continually preparing itself; and this it can do by natural means, especially with the help that God is continually giving it.[26]

This text sets down the part the soul must take. The asceticism God demands of it will be, here again, a mystical asceticism, that is, a cooperation with God's action, which remains the principal agent even in this casting off of natural knowledge and operations.

Once assured of the soul's faithfulness, God will not fail to accomplish His work. John of the Cross indicates the manner of God's action.

As God has no form or image that can be comprehended by the memory, it follows that, when the memory is united with God (as is

[25] *Ibid.*, Bk. III, vi; 226-7.
[26] *Ibid.*, ii; 217.

seen, too, every day by experience), it remains without form and without figure, its imagination being lost and itself being absorbed in a supreme Good, and in a great oblivion, remembering nothing. For that Divine union voids its fancy and sweeps it clean of all forms and kinds of knowledge and raises it to the supernatural.

Now there sometimes comes to pass here a notable thing; for occasionally, when God brings about these touches of union in the memory, the brain (where memory has its seat) is so perceptibly upset that it seems as if it becomes quite inert, and its judgment and sense are lost. This is sometimes more perceptible and sometimes less so, according to the strength of this touch, and then, by reason of this union, the memory is voided and purged, as I say, of all kinds of knowledge. It remains in oblivion—at times in complete oblivion—so that it has to put forth a great effort and to labour greatly in order to remember anything.[27]

This suspension of natural operations that the divine touches bring about suddenly for a short time in souls at the beginning of union,[28] notes the Saint, becomes progressively habitual and definitive in unitive contemplation. Our mystical doctor declares:

The more nearly the memory attains to union with God, the less it heeds distinct kinds of knowledge, until it loses them entirely.[29]

One of the sufferings of the purification of the spirit is this very void, this penury and darkness of the faculties, deprived of their proper operations.[30]

Is it possible to determine what is the soul's cooperation in this divine task? Saint John of the Cross, after explaining it at length in the books of the *Ascent of Mount Carmel,* puts it briefly thus:

This cannot happen unless the memory be annihilated as to all its forms, if it is to be united with God.[31]

I reply that it is not that which is purely God and which aids this simple, pure, universal and confused knowledge that is to be rejected but that which detains (the memory) in images, forms, figures or similitudes of created things. And, speaking of this purgation, in order that God may accomplish it, purity of soul is of the greatest profit,

[27] *Ibid.;* 213-4.
[28] *Ibid.;* 214.
[29] *Ibid.;* 215.
[30] *Dark Night,* Bk. II, vi; Peers, I; *ibid.,* iii.
[31] *Ascent,* Bk. III, ii; Peers, I, 213.

which means that there clings to the soul no creature affection, or temporal affection, or effective advertence; which I believe cannot but cling to the soul because of the imperfection which the faculties have in their own operations. Wherefore it is best to learn to silence the faculties and to cause them to be still, so that God may speak.[32]

To sum up, the asceticism of the soul consists in preparing, by mortification and purity of heart, for the spiritual poverty that God Himself works in it; in bearing humbly and peacefully this poverty when God gives it as a grace; in protecting it and furthering it, according to the grace that is given, by the practice of an interior silence in which are buried the operations of the faculties and especially those of the memory. In this solitude of peace and silence hope is purified and flowers. Is this not the asceticism of which Saint Paul indicates the stages and the fruits when he writes:

We exult in the hope of the glory of the sons of God. And not only this but we exult in tribulations also, knowing that tribulation works out endurance, and endurance tried virtue, and tried virtue hope. And hope does not disappoint, because the charity of God is poured forth in our hearts by the Holy Spirit who has been given to us.[33]

In a different language, Saint John of the Cross expresses the same truths:

As soon as the soul disencumbers these faculties and voids them of all lower things and of all attachment to higher things, leaving them in solitude, with naught else, God at once uses them for the invisible and Divine, and it is God Who guides the soul in this solitude.[34]

In that solitude wherein aforetime she lived, working therein with labour and anguish, because she was not perfect, she has now set her rest and refreshment, since she has now acquired this solitude perfectly in God.[35]

For just as one

. . . clothes a poor man if one sees him naked, just so God clothes with His purity, with His joy and His love the soul that is stripped of its desires and is utterly indifferent to its own will.[36]

[32] *Ibid.;* 220-1.
[33] Rom. 5:3-5.
[34] *Spiritual Canticle,* st. xxxiv; Peers, II, 154-5.
[35] *Ibid.;* 154.
[36] *Sentences* and *Maxims,* n. 360.

Such are the goods that spiritual poverty procures for hope here below, while waiting until the one and the other are buried and disappear in their triumph, humbly and silently, at the threshold of the eternal Vision.

B. Spiritual childhood

We might have developed at greater length the teaching of Saint John of the Cross, and added more detail to the counsels he gives the soul in this period. But we thought it preferable to confine ourselves to a rather sober explanation of the principles. The principles given by John of the Cross are always powerful beacons, projecting their light onto the pathless regions that extend to the infinite. Hope and spiritual poverty are words that evoke profound resonances in souls plunged in the dark night of the spirit. Long reasonings do not reach them in their darksome and burning solitude. Certain words alone break through it, fraught with the light of the divine Word and rich with experience. These leave a luminous trail that marks out the way; they create in the solitude a silent peace already announcing the light of dawn. The words of hope and spiritual poverty pronounced by Saint John of the Cross are surely of that kind.

Still, the beam of light that they cast needs to be construed in a practical way; and this, Saint Therese of the Child Jesus will do.

The Saint of Lisieux is truly a daughter of Saint John of the Cross. There is no doubt. Her doctrine of spiritual childhood rests on the doctrine of the mystical doctor; one can throw light on its depths only by the teaching of John of the Cross on hope and spiritual poverty. Is the way of childhood anything else than a mystical asceticism, the cooperation of the soul with the all-powerful action of God? I do not think so and will try to show why.

But why deny the fact that although the foundations are the

same, the superstructures of the two explanations seem quite different. John of the Cross belongs to the Spain of the sixteenth century. He is a theologian with austere language, a doctor who enunciates principles and in their light classifies his experiences, all the while trying to be as impersonal as possible. Therese of the Child Jesus is more near to us. We have the impression of having known her, so much are our reactions and way of speaking like hers. She is a young teacher who sits down near us to tell us her experiences. She is only a little doctor with notions so simple they seem poor. But she wins us by the singularly high and simplified light with which her words are filled, by her life and her love that radiates outward, by her teaching she touches not only the contemplatives of whom she is one but all little souls by her simple narration, living and picturesque, by the smile, finally, with which she greets us, and which bespeaks the delicacy of the supernatural love that she had for us even before we approached her. That she had at her disposal for enlightening these obscure regions of the night the converging light of two teachings at once so like and so different was a good fortune and a grace by which we must profit.

I. FOUNDATIONS OF THE DOCTRINE OF SPIRITUAL CHILDHOOD

To reveal God as Love to souls is the central and essential point of the mission of Saint Therese of the Child Jesus. This message has as its foundation the most important and deep grace of her life, namely, a very profound experimental knowledge of God inasmuch as He is Love. She writes:

> To me, He has given His Infinite Mercy, and it is in this ineffable mirror that I contemplate His other attributes. Therein all appear to me radiant with Love. His Justice, even more perhaps than the rest, seems to me to be clothed with Love. What joy to think that Our Lord is just, that is to say, that He takes our weakness into account, that He knows perfectly the frailty of our nature! Of what, then, need I be afraid?
>
> Will not the God of Infinite Justice, Who deigns so lovingly to

pardon the sins of the Prodigal Son, be also just to me "who am always with Him?" [37]

Her autobiography makes this manifest; indeed she can see in the course of her life only the history of divine Mercy in her regard. How and when did she receive this so high and simple light? One cannot say; so much does it go along with the development of her spiritual life, its increasing penetration corresponds to the stages of her spiritual ascent. Her first Holy Communion, for which she had longed so ardently for several years as an intimate contact with Jesus and had prepared for so fervently, caused her to experience the unitive overflowings of divine love:

That day our meeting was more than simple recognition, it was perfect union. We were no longer two. Therese had disappeared like a drop of water lost in the immensity of the ocean; Jesus alone remained—He was the Master, the King!" [38]

The sovereign good that is God-Love communicative of Himself, *bonum diffusivum sui,* in giving Himself unites and absorbs in Himself the beloved, since He is infinite and the soul is only a finite creature. He absorbs into Himself without destroying the person but rather by transforming it. The omnipotence of love's transformation is what Therese of Lisieux experienced in a signal grace on Christmas Day, 1886. She writes:

In an instant Our Lord, satisfied with my good will, accomplished the work I had not been able to do during all these years. . . . Love and a spirit of self-forgetfulness took possession of me, and from that time I was perfectly happy.[39]

Divine Love does not want to limit His action to a few privileged souls. He longs to give Himself everywhere—to conquer the entire world. But few souls understand this and respond to His desires. God let the little Saint experience His desires and disappointments in another favor a few months later:

[37] *Autobiography,* xi, 132.
[38] *Ibid.,* iv, 59.
[39] *Ibid.,* v, 72.

> One Sunday, closing my book at the end of Mass, a picture of Our Lord on the Cross half slipped out, showing only one of His Divine Hands, pierced and bleeding. I felt an indescribable thrill, such as I had never felt before. My heart was torn with grief to see that Precious Blood falling to the ground, and no one caring to treasure It as It fell, and I resolved to remain continually in spirit at the foot of the Cross, that I might receive the Divine Dew of Salvation and pour it forth upon souls.[40]

One after another these divine touches revealed experimentally to Saint Therese of the Child Jesus all the attributes, the desires, and even the painful disappointments of the Love that is God; they caused her to go beyond the narrow circle in which she lived, and to forget self. She became an apostle. She gave as the reason of her entry into the Carmel: "I have come to save souls, and especially to pray for Priests."[41] These lights and aspirations go on being purified, gaining in strength and in depth in the solitude of Carmel, in a contemplative dryness that conceals and concentrates the transforming ardors of divine love. In order to bear patiently this working of God in her soul, she seeks the efficacious help of Saint John of the Cross. The descriptions of love that she finds in his writings, that inexpressible something, powerful, ardent, delicate, divine, that stands out in them, making accessible to the senses the poetry of the symbols and the strength of the words, together with the exigencies of love detailed by the mystical doctor with rigorous logic, all this makes luminously explicit for the little Saint her intuitions, and joyously confirms her own certitudes. It is indeed true that divine Love is infinite, that He longs to give Himself and does in fact pour out His love on those who surrender themselves to Him in a faith and hope that are pure because stripped of all else. . . . Thus Saint Therese of Lisieux makes her own the Joannine doctrine of the All by the way of nothing. Or rather this doctrine was already hers; but

[40] *Ibid.* (a grace of July, 1887).

[41] *Ibid.*, vii, 108. Answer given at the time of the canonical examination before her religious profession.

thereafter she rests on it, as on a very firm rock, her whole spiritual life and teaching.[42]

To be sure, the external facing will be a little different, as we have already said. For God does not make two saints alike, even when He unites them by such close and deep bonds of spiritual filiation; this is especially true when they are two masters who are to illumine two different epochs.

The light has made so much progress in her soul that in 1895 Therese of the Child Jesus asks permission to make an act of oblation to merciful Love, to be consumed as a victim in the unfathomable flames that He cannot pour out upon faithless humanity. She wants to become a victim of love to comfort the good God. The act of oblation is made on the feast of the Holy Trinity, June 9, 1895:

> O my God! must Thy Love which is disdained lie hidden in Thy Heart? Methinks, if Thou shouldst find souls offering themselves as victims of holocaust to Thy Love, Thou wouldst consume them rapidly; . . . O Jesus! let me be that happy victim—consume Thy holocaust with the Fire of Divine Love! [43]

Divine Love responds to her offering and comes to take possession of her, wounding her sensibly with His love while she is making the Way of the Cross in choir:

> Dear Mother, you know the love, or rather the oceans of grace which flooded my soul immediately after I made that Act of Oblation on June 9, 1895. From that day I have been penetrated and surrounded with love.[44]

We are here in the presence of a perfect transformation, an identification with divine Love realized. A summit has been reached. The mission of Saint Therese of the Child Jesus and her doctrine are to spring from it, being explicitly unfolded rather quickly.

It is a matter of revealing Love to others, of finding victims

[42] Cf. the development of these thoughts in: "Sainte Thérèse de l'Enfant Jesus, docteur de vie mystique," by P. Marie-Eugene de l'E.J., *Revue de Carmel,* September, 1947, March and September, 1948.

[43] *Autobiography,* viii, 133.

[44] *Ibid.*

who will respond to His need of giving Himself. How is one to dispose oneself to receive Him? How attract Him? What must be the preparation and the cooperation of a soul that wants to become His happy victim? Is this not, in slightly different terms, the same problem that we posed when confronted with the painful divine outpourings of the sixth Mansions? It is a matter of finding a mystical asceticism adapted to God's action in the soul and ensuring its progress.

The response given by the little Saint is no different from that of Saint John of the Cross, although given on a different tone and under a different light. It is the Gospel that ordinarily provides Saint Therese of the Child Jesus with the explicit formula for her interior lights and their exigencies. Jesus in the Gospel requires faith of those who ask a favor. Faith stirs Him when it is ardent [45] and wrests miracles from Him.[46] Through faith, one believes in Christ and expects great things from His omnipotence. Faith, opening out into hope, releases the floodgates of divine love. And so this virtue becomes the deep-seated disposition of Saint Therese's spirituality, the one that was to characterize her way of spiritual childhood.

To her superior's question about her *way* and how she would teach souls about it, she answers without hesitation July 17, 1897:

> Mother, it is the way of spiritual childhood, the path of confidence and total abandonment.[47]

Confidence is theological hope wholly impregnated with love; abandonment is confidence which no longer expresses itself solely through distinct acts but has created an attitude of soul:

> We can never have too much confidence in the Good God, He is so mighty, so merciful. As we hope in Him so shall we receive.[48]

[45] The faith of the Chanaanite woman (Matt. 15:21-28); that of the Centurion (Matt. 8-10).

[46] The faith of the woman with the hemorrhage, in the streets of Capharnaum (Mark 5:25-34).

[47] *Novissima Verba*, p. 56.

[48] *Autobiography*, Epilogue, 213.

In these declarations of the Saint of Lisieux we recognize affirmations of Saint John of the Cross. And the affinities go deeper than these quotations reveal. Let us continue. Saint Therese of the Child Jesus has noted that divine Love takes greater joy when He can give more. Consider the joy of the father of the prodigal child,[49] who makes a banquet in honor of his son; and the statement of Jesus that there is more joy in heaven over one sinner who does penance than for ninety-nine just who persevere; [50] His declaration that Saint Mary Magdalene loved much because He had forgiven her much.[51]

Misery offers to Love a much greater receptive capacity, with fewer strict rights to the divine benefits. Consequently, Love has opportunity to display both the gratuitousness and the power of His outpourings. He is satisfied because He can more perfectly show what He is and has in Himself. This joy of God, however, is somewhat disconcerting to us as it was to the brother of the prodigal son, armed like us with that equitable justice that would like to regularize the outpourings of infinite Love. With Saint Therese of the Child Jesus let us be lifted up to the divine ways of Love and bend to His laws. One must be poor, miserable, and must lay open one's poverty to the enlarging power of divine Love, in order to attract and satisfy Him. Such is His law. The Saint writes to her sister Marie:

> O my dearest Sister, please understand your little sister, understand that to love Jesus, to be His victim of love, the weaker one is, without desires or virtues, the more apt one is for the operations of that consuming and transforming Love. The desire to be a victim is enough of itself, but one must consent to stay always poor and without strength, and that's the difficulty, for where are we to find the man truly poor in spirit.[52]

The vehement tone emphasizes the importance of this declaration. We find ourselves here at the very foundations of the

[49] Luke 15:20-32.
[50] Luke 15:6, 10.
[51] Luke 8:47.
[52] *Collected Letters,* Sept. 17, 1896, p. 289.

spiritual doctrine of Saint Therese of the Child Jesus. Thus she has given to us her secret:

> Dearest Sister, after that how can you say that my desires are the mark of my love? Ah! I realize that what pleases God in my little soul is not that. What pleases Him is to see me love my littleness and poverty, the blind hope I have in His mercy. . . . That is my sole treasure, dearest Godmother; why should not this treasure be yours? [53]

The secret of Therese is no different from that of Saint John of the Cross. The Theresian love of littleness and of poverty united to blind trust in divine mercy, is it not the same as the Joannine hope that is detached from everything and that God immediately fills? For both Saints these two complementary dispositions that purify and perfect one another are not only the foundations of sanctity but also create it by attracting irresistibly the outpourings of divine Love that transform and consume. But while Saint John of the Cross is incomparable and displays his grace as mystical doctor when he establishes and justifies these principles, it belongs more especially to Saint Therese of the Child Jesus to show us their application in the details of daily life.

For Saint Therese of the Child Jesus, trust and poverty are not simply virtues, like so many others, that one must practice at certain times; they are basic virtues, deep-seated dispositions, governing all the movements and attitudes of the soul. They of themselves create and become a complete spirituality; they constitute, as the Saint proclaims, a way to go to the good God.[54]

Because the way of spiritual childhood offers us a felicitous example, in concrete and living form, for the practice of the virtue of hope, its teaching is particularly precious for the period that we are studying. It is truly the mystical asceticism that is adapted to the sixth Mansions.

[53] *Ibid.*

[54] We noted previously that among the theological virtues hope is par excellence the dynamic virtue, the virtue that advances toward God. And so when Saint Therese of the Child Jesus proclaims that her way to go to God will be trust and self-surrender, she gives proof of a deep theological sense.

2. THE WAY OF SPIRITUAL CHILDHOOD

How did the interior lights become explicit in Saint Therese of the Child Jesus under the form of spiritual childhood? It is difficult to say exactly, so diverse are the elements that enter in, many of them unconsciously.[55] She herself has noted how it became more clearly defined in her own mind. She writes in her *Autobiography:*

> I will seek out a means of getting to Heaven by a little way—very short and very straight, a little way that is wholly new. We live in an age of inventions; nowadays the rich need not trouble to climb the stairs, they have lifts instead. . . . I have sought to find in Holy Scripture some suggestion as to what this lift might be which I so much desired, and I read these words uttered by the Eternal Wisdom Itself: "Whosoever is a little one, let him come to Me." [56] Wishing to know further what He would do to the little one, I continued my search and this is what I found: "You shall be carried at the breasts and upon the knees; as one whom the mother caresseth, so will I comfort you."[57]
>
> Never have I been consoled by words more tender and sweet. Thine Arms, then, O Jesus, are the lift which must raise me up even unto Heaven. To get there I need not grow; on the contrary, I must remain little, I must become still less.[58]

Assuredly Therese meditates also on the Gospel scene in which Jesus places a child before His apostles and declares the necessity of being like it, if one would enter into the kingdom of Heaven:

> Amen I say to you, unless you turn and become like little children, you will not enter into the kingdom of heaven.[59]

[55] Cf. Abbé Combes, *Introduction à la spiritualité de Sainte Thérèse de l'Enfant Jésus,* Ch. viii, "La petite voie d'enfance spirituelle." See especially pp. 292-301 for an analysis of several elements that contributed to this discovery, and the note on page 277 giving some chronological indications.

[56] Prov. 9:14.

[57] Isa. 66:12-13.

[58] *Autobiography,* ix, 136. Ch. ix and what follows were written by the Saint in 1897 a few months before her death. As she does not speak of this discovery in the preceding chapters (the first eight), which were finished in January 1896, we are led to believe that her doctrine became thus explicit at the beginning of 1896.

[59] Matt. 18:1-4.

The Scriptural texts grow in light to her mind in an extraordinary way. The light that shines out from them polarizes the elements scattered in her soul—particular lights, convictions, aspirations—and embodies them in a living form, clear and simple: that of the little child who becomes the perfect model to be effectively imitated.

a. *Essential characteristics*

Among the scattered elements thus brought into harmony by the divine light is certainly Therese's natural disposition to be and remain a child. She was always little, both in her family where, the last of nine children, she lived under the affectionate tutelage of her older sisters, and at the Carmel where, preceded by two of her sisters, entering at the age of fifteen and dying at twenty-four, she was never more than the oldest of the novitiate, not reaching that canonical age that confers exercise of the rights of religious profession. She was always the little Therese and was to remain so even in heaven [60] by a grace that made her, with rigorous and absolute logic, like the model presented by Jesus to His most intimate disciples.

It was easy for Therese to copy the exterior attitudes of a child, its affectionate and charming gestures, even to adopt its way of speaking. But these external forms are not the essential elements and might even favor their distortion. The child that Saint Therese takes and presents as a model is not that weak little creature who, by its conquering charms, imposes its own desires and at times caprices. When asked to explain what she meant by the words "to remain as a little child before God," she said:

> It is to recognize our nothingness, to look for everything from God as a little child looks for everything from his father; it is to be disquieted about nothing, and not to be set on gaining our fortune. . . .
> To be little, moreover, is not to attribute to ourselves the virtues we practice, nor to believe ourselves capable of practicing virtue at all.

[60] "You will call me little Therese," she answers, when asked how to pray to her when she will be in heaven. *Autobiography,* "Counsels and Reminiscences."

It is, rather, to recognize the fact that God puts treasures of virtue into the hands of His little children to make use of them in time of need, but they remain always the treasures of the good God.[61]

Such is the child: a being essentially poor and trustful, convinced that its poverty is its most precious treasure. And what a treasure it is! Therese never tires of recounting its riches, drawing upon the Sacred Books and her own discoveries. Of herself she says, "it is my very weakness which makes me dare to offer myself, O Jesus, as victim to Thy Love." [62] As a child she had "taken the good God by the heart" and "it is for that reason," she says, "that she will be so well received." [63] "To him that is little, mercy is granted." [64] "Little children do not damn themselves." [65] "Even among the poor, they give the child all he needs until he grows up; then his father will no longer support him." [66]

And so this poverty must be protected against all the enrichments that might compromise it, against all enemies from without and especially those from within that threaten it. Possessions are not in themselves the enemies, but rather the spirit of ownership by which one attributes them to oneself, the self-sufficiency and pride that take root in them. One must, then, become poor by giving all that one gains or receives. Not even make provisions of one's virtues. It is on this condition that the good God gives in measure what is necessary in order to practice virtue.[67] Poverty must watch with particular care over the confidence that makes it reach up to God and must keep it pure and deprived of all until it has attained its divine object.

Hence we see what a grace it is when God Himself comes to enlarge the spirit of poverty in a soul, and to deepen it by

[61] *Novissima Verba,* August 6, 1897, pp. 87-8.
[62] *Autobiography,* xi, 184.
[63] *Ibid.,* xii.
[64] *Ibid.,* p. 218; Cf. Wisdom 6:7.
[65] *Novissima Verba,* July 10, p. 38.
[66] *Ibid.,* August 6, p. 87.
[67] *Esprit de Sainte Thérèse,* p. 195.

supernatural lights that disclose it better to that soul. Saint Therese of the Child Jesus writes that the "mighty hath done great things to me—and the greatest is that He has shown me my littleness and how incapable I am of anything good." [68]

These lights on her own nothingness do her more good than lights concerning faith.[69] In fact in her soul they unite a delightful experience to profound conviction, causing her to love littleness and poverty. Hence the Saint can say:

> It happens to me often enough also to fail thus, but I am never astonished at it. . . . It is so sweet to feel oneself to be little and weak.[70]
>
> How happy I am to see myself imperfect and to have such need of the mercy of God at the moment of death.[71]
>
> O Sun, my only Love, I am happy to feel myself so small, so frail in Thy sunshine, and I am in peace.[72]

She declares she does not want to grow up; [73] and several days before her death she gives this reassurance:

> It is possible to remain little even when in the most responsible offices, and when living to a great age.
>
> If I died at eighty years of age, if I had been in many monasteries and charged with numerous responsibilities, I should always have remained just as little as I am today.[74]

Hence this spiritual childhood, springing from poverty jealously safeguarded, was within reach of Nicodemus, a considerable man among the Jews. He could make it his without suppressing anything of what was demanded by his rank and the exercise of his functions, without assuming infantile attitudes and language. . . . He had to make it his, for if a man is to be reborn by the breath of the Spirit, he must be poor, trustful, and dependent in all things on God. Or rather, to be reborn is nothing else than progressively to become a child. While in the

[68] *Autobiography,* ix, 138.
[69] *Novissima Verba,* August 13, 1897, p. 98.
[70] *Ibid.,* July 5, pp. 27-8.
[71] *Ibid.,* July 29, p. 67.
[72] *Autobiography,* xi, 187.
[73] *Novissima Verba,* August 4.
[74] *Ibid.,* September 25, p. 132.

natural order generation, realized in the womb of the mother, comes to its perfection in a progressive separation of the child until it can live its perfect and independent life, a spiritual generation comes about inversely by a progressive absorption into unity. Separated from God by sin, we are enlightened by His light, drawn more and more closely into the bonds of His love, until, having become true children, we lose ourselves in Him, living no longer except by His light and His Spirit. "Whoever are led by the Spirit of God, they are the sons of God," [75] that is, those who, by their spiritual poverty and self-renunciation, have relinquished their own operations and entered into the bosom of God, where their life and movements depend in all things on the Spirit who engenders. Such is the meaning and the value of spiritual childhood. Realized perfectly, it is already sanctity. What Saint Therese of the Child Jesus says on this echoes the word of Saint Paul who describes its effects in the bosom of God; she tells us again the dispositions that bring it about in the soul:

> Oh, it is not that! . . . Holiness does not consist in this or that practice; it consists in a disposition of the heart, which makes us always humble and little in the arms of God, well aware of our feebleness, but boldly confident in the Father's goodness.[76]

b. *How to practice it*

A teaching of such importance merits more than merely to be stated. It must be explored in detail to bring out its practical light. Let us pick out at least the principal traits in the life of union with God of Saint Therese of the Child Jesus, and in her way of conceiving and realizing the asceticism that accompanies and sustains such union.

1. *Union with God*—Spiritual poverty kept and cultivated with so much care results in liberating perfectly the filial instinct of sanctifying grace. We are children of God by the

[75] Rom. 8:14.
[76] *Novissima Verba,* August 3, 1897, p. 78.

grace that makes us brothers of Christ Jesus, His Son by nature. The Gospel tells us:

> You have not received a spirit of bondage so as to be again in fear, but you have received a spirit of adoption as sons, by virtue of which we cry, "Abba! Father!" The Spirit himself gives testimony to our spirit that we are sons of God.[77]

When will the filial spirit awaken in us, then, and cry to the Father, if not when it becomes more sharply aware of its own weakness and dependence on the strength of its Father? The child in danger calls instinctively to its mother.

When Therese of the Child Jesus is given charge of the novices, she feels her powerlessness and takes refuge at once in the good God:

> From the moment I entered the sanctuary of souls, I saw at a glance that the task was beyond my strength. Throwing myself without delay into Our Lord's Arms, I imitated those tiny children, who, when they are frightened, hide their faces on their father's shoulder, and I said: "Dear Lord, Thou seest that I am too small to feed these little ones, but if through me Thou wilt give to each what is suitable, then fill my hands, and without leaving the shelter of Thine Arms, or even turning away, I will distribute Thy treasures to the souls who come to me asking for food. . . ."
>
> And indeed my hope has never been deceived; I have always found my hands filled when sustenance was needed for the souls of my Sisters.[78]

This filial recourse to God in a particular need is so perfect in its delicacy and self-surrender that it gives sign of a grace long practiced. The feeling of poverty, although expressed more vigorously on the occasion of extraordinary needs, does not depend on these circumstances. It is constant because rooted in the deepest conviction of the soul, the most keenly experienced spiritually. Hence it creates a constant need of God, a continual call to Him. Such a child is always near its Father; its filial grace, ceaselessly impelled by its poverty, keeps it in close contact with Him. And so Saint Therese of the Child Jesus can say:

[77] Rom. 8:15-6.
[78] *Autobiography*, x, 158-9.

I cannot well see what more I shall have in Heaven than I have now; I shall see God, it is true, but, as to being with Him, I am that already even on earth.[79]

This little Carmelite with a filial sentiment so alive practices excellently the essential precept of her Rule, which obliges her to meditate on the Law of the Lord night and day; nevertheless she has hours specially consecrated to mental prayer. What will she do during these if not satisfy still more her filial instinct? With the aid of the Gospels in which she always discovers "new lights and hidden mysterious meanings," [80] she tries to "penetrate the character of the good God." [81]

It often happens moreover, especially during trials against faith, that she suffers from painful powerlessness, a humiliating dryness; [82] yet she continues to fix her gaze upon the divine Sun with love. In a letter to Sister Marie of the Sacred Heart, a large part of which constitutes chapter xi of the *Autobiography,* she describes thus her contemplative attitude:

Alas! I am but a poor little unfledged bird. I am not an eagle, I have but the eagle's eyes and heart! Yet, notwithstanding my exceeding littleness, I dare to gaze upon the Divine Sun of Love, and I burn to dart upwards unto Him! I would fly, I would imitate the eagles. . . . What is to become of me? Must I die of sorrow because of my helplessness? Oh, no! I will not even grieve. With daring self-abandonment there will I remain until death, my gaze fixed upon that Divine Sun. Nothing shall affright me, nor wind nor rain. And should impenetrable clouds conceal the Orb of Love, and should I seem to believe that beyond this life there is darkness only, that would be the hour of perfect joy, the hour in which to push my confidence to its uttermost bounds. I should not dare to detach my gaze, well knowing that beyond the dark clouds the sweet Sun still shines.[83]

This contemplative gaze fulfils the definition of contemplation, "*simplex intuitus veritatis sub influxu amoris,* a simple gaze on truth under the influence of love;" through the mist that it courageously penetrates, it attains to the divine Sun of

[79] *Ibid.,* Epilogue, p. 195.
[80] *Ibid.,* viii, 131.
[81] *Summarium,* N 1626.
[82] *Autobiography,* viii, 118.
[83] *Ibid.,* xi, 186-7; cf. *Collected Letters,* p. 284.

love and there obtains supernatural riches; let there be no doubt of that. Saint Therese of the Child Jesus herself remarks:

> Our Lord has no need of books or teachers to instruct our souls. He, the Teacher of Teachers, instructs us without any noise of words. I have never heard Him speak, yet I know He is within me. He is there, always guiding and inspiring me; and just when I need them, lights, hitherto unseen, break in. This is not as a rule during my prayers, but in the midst of my daily duties.[84]

At times the divine responses are more sensible, such as the flights of spirit that she knew,[85] the lights with which she said she was flooded in 1866,[86] the wound of love that followed her oblation to merciful Love. She says of this that she was wounded

> . . . by a dart of fire so ardent that death must be near. I have no words to describe it; it was as though an invisible hand had plunged me wholly into fire. And such fire! Yet, at the same time, what sweetness! I was burning up with love, and was convinced that to withstand such an onslaught of love for one minute, nay, for even one second more, was impossible; death must certainly ensue.[87]

Fortunately for us these divine interventions show to what a degree of detachment her spiritual poverty attained. Others would have placed emphasis on these singular graces, at least in an autobiography. She scarcely mentions them. It took a direct question from Mother Agnes of Jesus for her to tell the sensible effects of the wound of love.[88] It was in a chance conversation at the end of her life that she disclosed her flights of spirit and the grace received in 1889 at the grotto of the Magdalene.[89] As we see, the detachment of memory that Saint John of the Cross requires for the purification and perfection of hope is, in her, perfect.

[84] *Autobiography,* viii, p. 131.
[85] *Novissima Verba,* July 7, 1897, p. 32.
[86] *Autobiography,* ix, 185-6.
[87] *Novissima Verba,* July 7, p. 32.
[88] *Ibid.*
[89] *Ibid.,* July 10.

She does not want to have supernatural manifestations, not even to see God or the Blessed Virgin:

I do not long to see God upon earth. Oh, no! And yet I love Him! I love the Blessed Virgin and the saints very much also; yet I do not desire to see them either. I prefer to live by faith.[90]

She knows the true value of things and puts each one in its place:

Believe me, the writing of pious books, the composing of the sublimest poetry, all that does not equal the smallest act of self-denial.[91]

Sanctity lies not in saying beautiful things, or even in thinking them, or feeling them . . .[92]

Speaking of the retreat before her profession, she writes:

Far from receiving consolation, I went through it in a state of utter dryness and as if abandoned by God. Jesus, as was His wont, slept in my little barque. How rarely do souls suffer Him to sleep in peace! This Good Master is so wearied with continually making fresh advances that He eagerly avails Himself of the repose I offer Him, and, no doubt, He will sleep on until my great and everlasting retreat; but, instead of being grieved at this, I am glad.[93]

Can one conceive of a purer detachment from the loftiest spiritual goods, a more thorough realization of the teaching of Saint John of the Cross?

Not only does the spiritual poverty of Saint Therese of the Child Jesus bring her peace; she says that she is happy. And this happiness of having nothing she protects with great care not only in cold and nakedness, but in storm and trial:

Sometimes, of course, the little bird's heart is beaten upon by the storm, it feels as if it believed that nothing exists save the clouds wrapping it round. . . . Then is the moment of *perfect joy* for the *poor feeble little creature.* What happiness for it to *stay there* just the same! to gaze steadily at the invisible light which stays hid from its faith!!! [94]

[90] *Ibid.*, Sept. 11, p. 126.
[91] *Autobiography,* Counsels and Reminiscences, 234.
[92] Letter to Celine, April 26, 1889; *Collected Letters,* p. 101.
[93] *Autobiography,* viii. 118.
[94] Letter to Sister Mary of the Sacred Heart, September 14, 1896; *Collected Letters,* p. 284.

These statements would have delighted the mystical doctor, Saint John of the Cross, justifying as they do magnificently his teaching.[95]

Poverty can be so humbly peaceful and so simply happy only because the gaze of faith that it spiritualizes, the movement of hope that it sets free, have attained their divine object in the dark night in depths that are already filled. There is no doubt, the way of spiritual childhood leads to the highest summits of contemplation and transforming union described by Saint John of the Cross. By it one makes the ascent in peace and joy. The simplicity of the teaching of Saint Therese of the Child Jesus is yet sublimity of doctrine; and the smile with which she adorns all things is perfection of love.

2. *Asceticism of the way of spiritual childhood*

a. *The principles*—To keep one's gaze unswervingly fixed on God in the dark night is already a hard asceticism. And so perhaps the title of this paragraph is ill chosen! Nevertheless, ordinarily the word asceticism has reference to the activity of the virtues outside of mental prayer. And this activity is necessary.

Love is shown by acts. The contemplative, too, comes under this law. But how is the child going to practice virtue? Do not the poverty and weakness of the child create more than one obstacle, a real impossibility for the practice of virtue? In fact, when Saint Therese of the Child Jesus was praised by the doctor for her patience, did she not exclaim:

> How can he say I am patient? That is not true. I am always groaning, sighing, and crying all the time: "My God, oh, my God, my strength is gone . . . have mercy on me—have mercy on me." [96]

[95] A few weeks before her death, on August 31, 1897, the Saint said to her regular confidants: "Ah! it is unbelievable how all my hopes have been realized. When I used to read St. John of the Cross, I would ask God to accomplish in my soul all that I found described therein. I begged Him to sanctify me as much in a few years as if I had lived a long life, so that I might be rapidly consummated in love. . . . And I have been heard . . ." *Novissima Verba,* p. 119.

[96] *Novissima Verba,* September 20, p. 129-30.

And a month before, she had said:

I have never had patience for a single minute! It is not mine! You always make that mistake.[97]

Sister Genevieve of the Holy Face, her sister, notes, however, at the process for beatification, that the characteristic virtue of the Saint was fortitude. Some saw in her a wilful person, headstrong, proud, too tense, and have emphasized in her little way solely a striving for perfection.[98]

What are we to think of these diverse judgments? Let us ask Saint Therese of the Child Jesus who, with the help of one of those gracious comparisons of which she knows the secret, explains to a novice her idea of asceticism:

You make me think of a little child that is learning to stand but does not yet know how to walk. In his desire to reach the top of the stairs to find his mother, he lifts his little foot to climb the first step. It is all in vain, and at each renewed effort he falls. Well, be like that little child. Always keep lifting your foot to climb the ladder of holiness, and do not imagine that you can mount even the first step. All God asks of you is good will. From the top of the ladder He looks lovingly upon you, and soon, touched by your fruitless efforts, He will Himself come down, and, taking you in His Arms, will carry you to His Kingdom never again to leave Him.[99]

Nowhere else, it seems, has Saint Therese of the Child Jesus explained in so clear and complete a way her thought on the asceticism of the virtues.

Note first that Therese presents to us a child "that is learning to stand but does not yet know how to walk." This is the child with whom we are familiar, powerless now, but in whom there is a growing strength that he can use and in which he can already have confidence. He will certainly not succeed in climbing the stairs—the ladder of perfection. That is a work only God can do; from Him alone can we expect it. Saint Therese of the Child Jesus proclaims this truth because she experienced it. Her heroic attitude could be misleading, but she

[97] *Ibid.*, August 18, p. 101.
[98] Van der Mersch, *La Sainte Petite Thérèse*.
[99] *Autobiography*, "Counsels and Reminiscences," p. 225.

insists on stating things exactly. Let us recall the passage quoted above:

> I have never had patience for a single minute! It is not mine! You always make that mistake.[100]

And again:

> You said you wanted to imitate me; but you do not yet know, then, that I am very poor. The good God measures out to me what I need in order to practise virtue.[101]

She loves to repeat:

> Jesus does everything, I nothing.[102]

Apropos of the disposition of self-abandonment in which she is firmly established, she says:

> Those words: "Although he should kill me, I will trust in him,"[103] have fascinated me ever since childhood. But it took me a long time to become established in that degree of abandonment. Now I am there, however. The good God just took me in His Arms and placed me there![104]

Here is a fundamental truth that holds good for the exercise of the active virtues as it does for contemplation: it is God who does everything. Before Him, and on our way to Him, we are helpless little children, not able to climb even the first step. We shall reach the top of the stairs only when God has taken us in His Arms and placed us there.

What can we do that this may happen? The same problem as for contemplation, and the same solution: first, wait in that humble state of poverty that purifies hope; accept the condition of being the weak children that we are, and know how to remain so.

A feeling of poverty and the awareness of our child-like weakness, such are the qualities that we must cultivate and develop; for littleness attracts the good God and draws Him

[100] *Novissima Verba,* August 18, p. 101.
[101] *Esprit,* unpublished reminiscences, p. 195.
[102] Letter to Celine, July 6, 1893; *Collected Letters,* p. 191.
[103] Job 13:15
[104] *Novissima Verba,* July 7, p. 31.

down to the foot of the ladder to carry the child there away in His arms. Thus he renews for each one of us the incarnation of the Word in our sinful nature, carrying us off captives into the depths of the Holy Trinity. God repeats over and over the same actions and His gifts are without repentance, because His mercy is not for a moment in time, but is eternal. But that His mercy may be renewed and carry us along in its movement, we must be, and must be willing to be, poor and little—even when we have worked much. Our little Saint says:

> If I should have accomplished all the works of St. Paul, I should still consider myself an 'unprofitable servant.'[105] I should find that I had empty hands; but it is precisely that which gives me joy, for, having nothing, I shall receive everything from God.[106]

Does this sovereign action of God in the activity of the virtues authorize a completely passive self-abandonment? Certainly not. It is important to note that the general law of contemplation is a law of silence and of peace. The soul must itself become tranquil and purify its atmosphere if the rays of the divine Sun are to act in it with all their strength. In the practice of the virtues a larger share of activity, if not of suffering, too, is left to the soul.

Let us resume: by the practice of the virtues, the child must constantly lift its little foot to climb the stairs. God will be attracted by its littleness and won by its useless efforts. Saint Therese of the Child Jesus replied to someone who called her a saint:

> No, I am not a saint! I have never performed the works of the saints. I am just a little soul whom the good God has overwhelmed with His graces.[107]

But the same day, she had granted that she was a warrior:

> I am not a warrior who fights with earthly weapons, but with the sword of the Spirit which is the word of God.[108] So this sickness has

[105] Luke 17:10.
[106] *Novissima Verba,* June 23, 22-23.
[107] *Ibid.,* August 9, 94.
[108] Eph. 6:17

not beaten me, and it was only last evening that I used my sword with a novice. . . . Have I not said: 'I shall die sword in hand?'[109]

During her novitiate she has to put forth great effort and this she does generously:

. . . because of my great timidity it was very painful to me to ask to perform certain mortifications customary in our convent, but I was very faithful to this practice.[110]

And again:

My first victory was not a great one, but it cost me a good deal. A small jar, left behind a window, was found broken. No one knew who had put it there, but our Mistress was displeased, and, thinking I was to blame in leaving it about, told me I was very untidy and must be more careful in the future. Without answering, I kissed the ground and promised to be more observant.[111]

She assures the novices that "the highest inspirations are of no value without good works;" [112] and she urges them so much to be strong that she was at times thought to be severe with them. She once said:

How many souls plead: 'I have not enough fortitude to accomplish such an act?' But let them put forth some effort! The good God never refused the first grace which imparts courage to act. After that, the heart is strengthened and the soul goes on from victory to victory.[113]

Thus the Theresian soul moves around two poles: a conviction of its nothingness and its weakness in the face of the goal to be reached, and at the same time energetic effort to merit God's intervention. To a novice who asks her how to reconcile these two virtues, she answers:

One must do all in one's power, give without counting, constantly renounce oneself, in a word prove one's love by all the works in one's power. But in truth, since that is very little, it is urgent to put one's confidence in Him who alone sanctifies the works, and to confess oneself to be a useless servant.[114]

[109] *Novissima Verba,* August 9, 93-4.
[110] *Esprit,* p. 20
[111] *Autobiography,* xii, 117
[112] *Ibid.,* x, 155
[113] *Novissima Verba,* August 8, 93.
[114] *Esprit,* pp. 16-7

Such are the general principles of the asceticism of Saint Therese of the Child Jesus. As befits a child, the little Saint states them poorly in simple terms that veil so well their riches that one has some difficulty discovering them. But Therese lived her asceticism with incomparable energy. Her life is the most luminous commentary on her teaching. In order to understand her way of spiritual childhood, therefore, one must examine in detail her slightest actions, observe her spontaneous reactions, listen to her answers to questions. One discovers thus that her attitudes and what she does, embody with precise and rigorous logic the principles she formulated. Her life is the necessary complement of her teaching, the clearest exposition of her mystical asceticism, so rightly called an asceticism of littleness.

b. *Practice of the asceticism of littleness*

1. *Put aside the extraordinary*—On what forms of activity is this generosity of the child, a real warrior courage, going to expend itself? Since this generosity is that of a child convinced of its weakness, it will set aside from the beginning all that is extraordinary. And what will that be? For Therese, extraordinary is everything that is striking or that requires an extra output of strength, not being in the line of ordinary duty. The valor of the saints in general has had a tendency to manifest itself in strong and brilliant expressions of the great love that burned within them. Hagiography, in search of the marvelous so as to edify by striking the imagination and the senses, has gathered all this together and laid so much emphasis on it, we are prone to think that it forms an integral part of sanctity.

Saint Therese of the Child Jesus seems not to have entirely escaped the allurement of this mirage. She writes to the Abbé Bellière:

> When I began to learn the history of France, the story of Joan of Arc's exploits entranced me; I felt in my heart the desire and the courage to imitate her; it seemed to me that Our Lord meant me for great things too.[115]

[115] *Collected Letters*, April 25, p. 327.

How does it happen that the profound, supernatural aspirations that this child had for great things were not carried away toward the extraordinary, which presented itself in so attractive a way? Jesus, her Director, was watching over her, and when the time came He corrected her aspirations:

> Our Lord made me understand that the only true glory is that which lasts forever; and that to attain it there is no necessity to do brilliant deeds, but rather to hide from the eyes of others, and even from oneself, so that "the left hand knows not what the right hand does." [116]

The Saint declares that this light was one of the greatest graces of her life. She turns it toward her mission as a spiritual master—a disciple of Joan of Arc, in fact, could not form a school. But this light was to mark all her spirituality and be one of its characteristic traits. Therese would not do the great deeds of saints but would perform only ordinary actions, those within range of all little souls.

She fell sick from having worn for too long a time a small iron cross, studded with sharp points that became imbedded in her flesh. Afterwards she said:

> Such a trifle would not have caused this, if God had not wished thus to make me understand that the greater austerities of the Saints are not meant for me—nor for the little souls that walk in the path of "spiritual childhood." [117]

Decisive as it is, the light of this grace causes her to enter definitively into the asceticism of littleness. Let us note that her refusal of extraordinary mortifications is not at all an escape. Generosity is not here in question. Actually Therese was to bear physical sufferings, such as those from cold, which were harder than extraordinary macerations. She is no longer drawn toward these latter because God does not require them of her. A feeble child, she thinks she would be sinning by presumption and going aside from the providential plan, in seeking

[116] *Autobiography,* iv, 55
[117] *Ibid.,* xii, 200

sufferings that would thus be of her own planning and which, consequently, she would have to bear alone. As she explained:

> If every soul called to perfection were obliged to perform these austerities in order to enter Heaven, He would have told us, and we should have willingly undertaken them.[118]

Her ardent desire for martyrdom bears testimony to her generosity:

> Above all, I thirst for the Martyr's crown. It was the desire of my earliest days, and the desire has deepened with the years passed in the Carmel's narrow cell. But this too is folly, since I do not sigh for one torment; I need them all to slake my thirst.[119]

The valor of Therese is that of a feeble little child. Her littleness is a treasure that she wants to keep, at all cost, secure against pride. She thinks she has the right to brave heroism only with the assurance that God will sustain her and that divine grace in her will be heroic. Such asceticism of littleness is indeed a mystical asceticism, that is, an asceticism that looks only to cooperation with God's sovereign action within.

II. *Fidelity to duties of state and of charity*

When, then, will Therese be able to have the assurance of that sovereign action of God permitting her to be only a cooperator? The answer is very simple: every time that God manifests to her His will in a definite way. Sufficiently powerful grace is always given with the duty that God imposes. Hence the duties of religious life, observance of the rules, obedience to the orders of superiors, the practice of fraternal charity, all the duties of state and the sufferings that providential events impose or that are the result of God's direct action—all these enter into the will of God; and consequently they open up a vast field for the generosity of Saint Therese of the Child Jesus and her confidence in grace.

The Saint enters into all this with the desire of profiting by the least occasions to prove her love for Jesus. She says:

[118] *Autobiography,* Counsels and Reminiscences, 240.
[119] *Ibid.,* xi, 182

Far from resembling those beautiful souls who have practised all sorts of mortifications from their infancy, I made mine consist in simply checking my inclinations, keeping back an impatient answer, doing little services to those around me without setting store thereby, and a hundred other things of the kind.[120]

And farther on she writes:

The only way I have of proving my love is to strew flowers before Thee—that is to say, I will let no tiny sacrifice pass, no look, no word. I wish to profit by the smallest actions, and to do them for Love. I wish to suffer for Love's sake, and for Love's sake even to rejoice: thus shall I strew flowers. Not one shall I find without scattering its petals before Thee.[121]

Hence she is rigorously faithful to all the precepts of the Rule, to the slightest approved customs, to the minute and sometimes changing prescriptions of her mother prioress or of anyone who has authority over her. These little and painful restraints are precious opportunities for her by which she eagerly profits. She is the most obedient and the most simply mortified of the religious in her convent.

She discloses what she does and what she bears with, when she says to her three sisters:

Attend well to regularity. After you have been to the parlor, do not stop to exchange your reflections, because then you would become like members of a family where one is deprived of nothing!! [122]

Ah! in heaven the good God will pay us back for having worn heavy habits while on earth.[123]

God requires of her certain particular mortifications of the heart, so naturally affectionate in her.

I remember that when I was a postulant I was sometimes so violently tempted to seek my own satisfaction by having a word with you, that I was obliged to hurry past your cell and hold on to the banisters to keep myself from turning back. Numerous permissions I wanted to ask, and a hundred pretexts for yielding to my desires suggested themselves, but now I am truly glad that I did not listen.[124]

120 *Autobiography,* vi, 105.
121 *Ibid.,* xi, 185
122 *Novissima Verba,* August 3, 78.
123 *Ibid.,* April 5.
124 *Autobiography,* x, 158.

But especially she does God's will through the practice of fraternal charity: before dying she writes beautiful pages about this in chapters ix and x, which are her spiritual testament to her sisters, and in which she reveals what she herself practiced with exquisite delicacy. Whether she takes care of bringing to the refectory the paralyzed Sister Saint Pierre, or asks to be placed under a religious who makes maniac demands, whether she smiles from the door of her cell every evening to Sister Marie-Philomène whom she could not otherwise comfort, whether she refuses with so gracious a smile what she is unable to give that the refusal is as pleasing as the gift, or whether she gives away something dear to her, seemingly happy to be rid of it—it is always with the same simplicity and the same delicacy that she responds to the will of the good God and serves Him in the soul of her sisters.

It is more difficult to accept mortification than to choose one's own. And is not the suffering that is imposed the more providential, coming more directly from the good God? Saint Therese of the Child Jesus knows this well. And so, with what love, with what astonishing acceptance she received the divine trials! We read in her *Autobiography:*

> It was always a principle with Therese that "We should go to the end of our strength before we complain." How many times did she assist at Matins suffering from vertigo or violent headaches! "I am able to walk," she would say, "and so I ought to be at my duty. . . ."
>
> It was with difficulty that her delicate stomach accustomed itself to the frugal fare of the Carmel. Certain things made her ill, but she knew so well how to hide this, that no one ever suspected it. Her neighbour at table said that she had tried in vain to discover the dishes she preferred, and the kitchen Sisters, finding her so easy to please, invariably served her with what was left . . .
>
> Lack of heat during winter was the hardest of her physical sufferings in Carmel . . . Sometimes she spent the entire night trembling from cold, without being able to sleep. She would have obtained relief at once, if in her first years there she had told this to the mistress of novices, but she wanted to accept the mortification without complaining. It was only when she was on her death-bed that she made it known in these expressive words: 'What I suffered from physically

the most during my religious life, was the cold; I suffered almost to death from it! [125]

III. *Heroic and joyful asceticism*

Among these crosses must be placed the passive purifications that she underwent, most especially the temptations against faith; these, together with the wound of love, were the divine response to her self-oblation to merciful Love. Under the strain of this trial, "a wall that rises up to the heavens," that she dares not describe for fear of blaspheming, she reacts by writing:

> But, dear Lord, Thy child has understood Thou art the Light Divine; she asks Thy pardon for her unbelieving brethren, and is willing to eat the bread of sorrow as long as Thou mayest wish. For love of Thee she will sit at that table of bitterness where these poor sinners take their food, and she will not stir from it until Thou givest the sign. But may she not say in her own name, and the name of her guilty brethren: "O God, be merciful to us sinners!" Send us away justified. May all those on whom Faith does not shine see the light at last! O my God, if that table which they profane can be purified by one that loves Thee, I am willing to remain there alone to eat the bread of tears, until it shall please Thee to bring me to Thy Kingdom of Light: the only favour I ask is, that I may never give Thee cause for offence. . . .
>
> In spite of this trial, which robs me of all comfort, I still can say: "Thou has given me, O Lord, delight in all Thou dost." For what joy can be greater than to suffer for Thy Love? The more the suffering is and the less it appears before men, the more is it to Thy Honour and Glory. Even if—but I know it to be impossible—Thou shouldst not deign to heed my sufferings, I should still be happy to bear them, in the hope that by my tears I might perhaps prevent or atone for one sin against Faith.[126]

These last words show us another trait of the asceticism of spiritual childhood that we must stress. The child is helpless. It can cover distances and do important and difficult things only if carried by its mother and held up by her. Therese can do nothing, not even love, except with the love of the good

[125] *Autobiography,* xii, 198-9. [Translator's note: The last paragraph of this quotation is not given in the English *Autobiography* I am using; I have made the translation from Father Marie-Eugène's French text.]
[126] *Ibid.*, ix, 140-2.

God.[127] But there is one privilege that is the child's, a gift that is proper to it because it belongs to its weakness: the gift of delicacy and of the smile. The more tender is the stem of the flower, the more supple it is; and the tinier it is, the more captivating are its charms. Scarcely does a smile appear on the lips of a child than its face is alight and irresistibly wins sympathy: *"son doux regard qui brille fait briller tous les yeux,"* says the poet.

In Therese of the Child Jesus, this delicacy and smile of the child were cultivated supernaturally and marvelously refined as divine love developed in her soul. They became, in the expression of her love and on her countenance, the sublime compensation for her littleness and the most evident proof of the plenitude of love in her soul.

She suffers and immolates herself; but she would not want the good God to notice it, if that were possible, so as not to trouble Him:

> If she perspired from the intense heat of summer or if she suffered from the cold in winter, she took exquisite care not to wipe her face nor to rub her hands together unless unnoticeably, as if not to give the good God time to see it.[128]

She tries to smile during mortifications so that the good God, misled by the expression on her face, "will not know that I am suffering." [129] Her special way of putting others on the wrong track was to sing her joy:

> I will sing. . . . I will sing always, even if my roses must be gathered from amidst thorns; and the longer and sharper the thorns, the sweeter shall be my song.[130]

The joy of the good God will be enough for her even in heaven:

> Just to see the good God happy, that will fully suffice for my happiness. . . . It is to please Jesus: I do not want to give to receive.

[127] *Ibid*.
[128] *Esprit*, p. 45.
[129] *Ibid*
[130] *Autobiography*, xi, 186.

If, *per impossible* the good God Himself did not see my good actions, I would not mind. I love Him so much that I would want to be able to give Him pleasure by my love and my little sacrifices, even if He did not know that they come from me: for knowing this and seeing it, He is almost obliged to give me some recompense. I would not want to give Him that trouble.[131]

On hearing these words, one might be inclined to think that we have forgotten the subject we were to treat. They are so different from the painful groanings of the soul in the dark night of the spirit! Can we present to such a soul Saint Therese of the Child Jesus as a model to be imitated? Are not her delicacy and her smile like those snowflowers that bloom only on mountain-tops, or at least that require high altitudes? On going through the *Letters* of Saint Therese of the Child Jesus, we note that at all the stages of her spiritual life, she puts in practice whatever is essential to the asceticism of spiritual childhood. Several weeks after her entrance to Carmel, she writes to Sister Marie of the Sacred Heart:

Pray that your little girl may remain always a little grain of sand, very obscure, hidden from all eyes, that Jesus alone may be able to see it. Let it become smaller and smaller, let it be reduced to a nothing.[132]

At the time when the state of her father's health has become worse in February, 1889, she writes to Céline:

Ah! darling Sister, far from complaining to Jesus of the cross He sends us, I cannot fathom the infinite love which has brought Him to treat us so. Our dearest father must indeed be loved by Jesus, to have to suffer like this! . . . I think many other things of the love of Jesus which are perhaps much stranger. . . . What a happiness it is to be humbled! It is the one way that makes saints! . . . Oh! don't let us waste the trial Jesus sends us; it is a goldmine we must exploit. Shall we let the chance slip? . . . The grain of sand would set herself to the task without joy, without courage, without strength, and all these conditions will make the enterprise easier it wants to work for love.[133]

[131] *Esprit,* p. 39.
[132] Letter to Sister Marie of the Sacred Heart, May, 1888; *Collected Letters,* p. 51
[133] Letter to Céline, February 28, 1889; *Ibid.,* p. 93.

No, the way of spiritual childhood is not a way reserved to the perfect. It is a way of ascent. The perfection with which Saint Therese kept to it, her absolute faithfulness, the heroism of her virtues, the delicacy of her sentiments and the charm of her smile, these are fruits that show us its excellence, but are not conditions for entering upon it. The way of childhood is open to all souls, to those especially that God has taken captive and that He holds in a painful embrace in the dazzling glow of His light.

For these latter as for us all, Saint Therese has known how to discern and lay stress on this truth, namely, that among all the elements in the spiritual life of souls—activity of the faculties, sufferings, even supernatural impressions—the essential element is the love of God in the soul that gives itself up to Him, and His sovereignly efficacious action within it. True, this is a simple Gospel truth. Saint Therese's merit lies in having known how, with the genial simplicity of a child, to make it stand out from all the rest, and in having lived it with the heroic confidence of a child. Simplicity and heroism in her were gifts of the divine mercy; but they were also fruits of an asceticism and a technique solidly based on the teaching of her mystical doctor, Saint John of the Cross.

Such is the truth that the soul in the dark night of the spirit must live in order to draw from it all the grace God means it to have. In humble and peaceful hope, the soul must give itself up to the ardors of the divine breathing that is over it; in a generous asceticism of littleness, it must put all its energies at the service of the divine grace that is carrying it away and wounding it. This is the cooperation that the Holy Spirit awaits from the soul for the work of spiritual rebirth that He is now working.

CHAPTER V

Help and Models in the Dark Night

The good Jesus is too good company for us to forsake Him and His most sacred Mother.[1]

To journey on in the darkness of the night and keep hope strong in the midst of anguish unto death, has the soul the right to seek any help other than that which comes from God's torturing and purifying action? Is there no danger that other help would serve only to dispel the beneficent obscurity of the night? Would it not bring to a stop the purification of the virtue of hope, which can be perfect only when it relies on God alone? This is our problem. We shall try to solve it by developing the following considerations:

God has established between Himself and men mediators whose action is universal and constant at all times of the spiritual life. These mediators are Jesus, sovereign priest, and Mary, mediatrix and mother of grace. Their action is more than ever necessary during the dark night of the spirit. In fact, it shows itself particularly intense here, while taking the special form that the obscurity in which it works imposes.

A. Christ Jesus, priest and victim

1. NECESSARY RECOURSE TO CHRIST IN THE SIXTH MANSIONS

Teresian spirituality is essentially Christocentric. To take from it this character would be, more than to mutilate it, to

[1] VI Mansions, vii; Peers, II, 308.

destroy it. Everywhere in her writings the Saint states the necessity of seeking Christ Jesus and being united with Him.[2] She does not understand how one could pray otherwise than with Him. The prayer of recollection, the Teresian prayer par excellence, is actually nothing else than a collecting of the faculties in the interior of the soul, there to find Christ Jesus and keep Him company.[3]

The search for Christ is not simply a work for beginners; it is necessary at all the stages of the spiritual life, asserts Teresa.

> This method of bringing Christ into our lives is helpful at all stages; it is a most certain means of making progress in the earliest stage, of quickly reaching the second degree of prayer, and, in the final stages, of keeping ourselves safe from the dangers into which the devil may lead us.[4]
>
> Such is the method of prayer by which all must begin, continue and end. This way is an excellent one and very sure, until the Lord raises us to other supernatural things.[5]

We might have left the matter with what has been previously said on the subject, if Saint Teresa herself had not treated the question again with some vigor in the sixth Mansions, after discussing it earlier.[6] It is, in fact, in the dark night of the spirit that the problem becomes sharpest. And so, although today there is no speculative discussion on this point, the Teresian doctrine being admitted by everyone, nevertheless the problem still has practical importance considerable enough for us, following Saint Teresa, to return to it in order to see more clearly the data and the solutions.

a. *The mediation of Christ is universal*

The universal and unique mediation of Christ Jesus in the work of our redemption and our return to God is one of the

[2] Cf. Vol. I, *I Want to See God,* PERSPECTIVES, ch. v, "The Good Jesus," p. 64 ff.

[3] *Ibid.,* THE FIRST STAGES, ch. iv, "The Prayer of Recollection," p. 198 ff.

[4] *Life,* xii; Peers, I, 71. Cf. also *Ibid.,* xii and xxii; *Way of Perfection,* xxvi; *Interior Castle,* VI Mansions, vii.

[5] *Ibid.;* xiii

[6] *Ibid.,* xii and xxii; Way of Perfection, xxvi.

fundamental dogmas of Christianity. This truth was already the essential article of the apostolic catechesis such as we find it in the discourses of the apostles related in the Acts.

Addressing the council of the rulers of the people a few days after Pentecost, Saint Peter, speaking of the cure of a cripple, says to them courageously:

> As to how this man has been made whole, be it known to all of you and to all the people of Israel that in the name of Jesus Christ of Nazareth, whom you crucified, whom God has raised from the dead, even in this name does he stand here before you, sound.
> This is
>
> 'The stone that was rejected by you, the builders,
> which has become the corner stone.'
>
> Neither is there salvation in any other. For there is no other name under heaven given to men by which we must be saved.[7]

The same truth is given by Saint Paul as the keystone of his message:

> Blessed be the God and Father of our Lord Jesus Christ, who has blessed us with every spiritual blessing on high in Christ. Even as he chose us in him before the foundation of the world, that we should be holy and without blemish in his sight in love, He predestined us to be adopted through Jesus Christ as his sons, according to the purpose of his will.[8]

It is on the foundation of Christ and through Christ that God restores all things and builds up the new edifice, a work of His mercy, after the destructions wrought by sin. This edifice is none else but Christ in the full extension of His life and His grace in souls.

> But God, who is rich in mercy, by reason of his very great love wherewith he has loved us even when we were dead by reason of our sins, brought us to life together with Christ. . . .
>
> Therefore, you are now no longer strangers and foreigners, but you are citizens with the saints and members of God's household: you are built upon the foundation of the apostles and prophets with Christ Jesus himself as the chief cornerstone. In him the whole structure is closely fitted together and grows into a temple holy in the Lord; in

[7] Acts 4:10-12; 2:22-36; 3:12-16, etc.
[8] Eph. 1:3-5.

him you, too, are being built together into a dwelling place for God in the Spirit.[9]

The external design of God in Christ is realized by the sacrifice of Jesus and the shedding of His blood. This truth is inseparable from the first one:

> It has pleased God the Father that in him all his fullness should dwell, and that through him he should reconcile to himself all things, whether on the earth or in the heavens, making peace through the blood of his cross.[10]
>
> In him we have redemption through his blood, the remission of sins, according to the riches of his grace.[11]
>
> We have confidence to enter the Holies in virtue of the blood of Christ, a new and living way which he inaugurated for us through the veil (that is, his flesh).[12]

It seems useless to multiply quotations, so penetrated is Saint Paul's teaching with the doctrine of the universal and necessary meditation of Christ through His blood which purifies us, gives us entrance into His spiritual edifice, and unites us to the Father. Every spiritual renewal is owing to the efficacious action of the blood of Christ.

> You yourselves were at one time estranged and enemies in mind through your evil works. But now he has reconciled you in his body of flesh through his death, to present you holy and undefiled and irreproachable before him.[13]

This apostolic teaching serves as a basis for the Church's doctrine on the value of the Sacrifice of the Mass, which prolongs the sacrifice of Calvary, and on the efficacy of participation in this sacrifice through Holy Communion. On the altar Christ renews in an unbloody way His immolation on Calvary. The Christian must assist at Mass and affirm his desire to participate in the fruits of this sacrifice by receiving in Holy Communion Christ Jesus, living and immolated; if not, he is not a Christian possessing within himself the life of Christ.

[9] Eph. 2:4-5; 19-22.
[10] Col. 1:20.
[11] Eph. 1:7-8.
[12] Heb. 10:19-20.
[13] Col. 1:21-2.

Faith in Christ and in the value of His sacrifice is neccessary for salvation. Thus only can one gather the fruits of spiritual renewal, Saint Paul writes to the Colossians:

> For you were buried together with him in Baptism, and in him also rose again through faith in the working of God who raised him from the dead.[14]

This truth is stated still more rigorously in other Epistles, especially in the Epistle to the Romans and the one to the Hebrews.[15] In the Epistle to the Romans the apostle writes:

> But now the Justice of God has been made manifest independently of the Law, being attested by the Law and the Prophets; the justice of God through faith in Jesus Christ upon all who believe. For there is no distinction. . . .
>
> For we reckon that a man is justified by faith independently of the works of the Law.[16]
>
> Having been justified therefore by faith, let us have peace with God through our Lord Jesus Christ.[17]

In the Epistle to the Hebrews, after showing how the great patriarchs and prophets of the Old Testament were justified by faith, Saint Paul concludes:

> Therefore let us also, having such a cloud of witnesses over us, put away every encumbrance and the sin entangling us, and run with patience to the fight set before us; looking towards the author and finisher of faith, Jesus . . .[18]

b. *Mediation more necessary in these Mansions*

Do these so clear statements of doctrine leave one free to think that in a certain period of the spiritual life—assuredly the most difficult, that of the purification of the spirit—the soul has the right and even the duty to have recourse no longer explicity to Christ Jesus, so as to go more rapidly toward union with God? This was a subject of debate between Teresa and certain spiritual men of her time, her contradictors.

[14] Col. 2:12.
[15] Rom. 3-4; Heb. 10-12.
[16] Rom. 3:21-22, 28.
[17] *Ibid.*, 5:1.
[18] Heb. 12:1-2.

The latter rest their contention on the fact that union with God is entirely and uniquely spiritual, and that the soul has already passed the stages where corporeal objects could help it rise to God. They maintain that in these high regions of the spiritual life, the soul would waste its time and would retrogress by adverting to the sacred humanity of Christ. If it would be united with God, no other means would any longer be efficacious except total detachment and abstraction from the corporeal; thus it would surrender itself to the embrace of God Himself.

In support of their theory, these spiritual men quoted the words of Jesus Himself to His apostles before His Passion: "It is expedient for you that I depart. For if I do not go, the Advocate will not come to you; but if I go, I will send him to you." [19] The presence of the humanity of Christ then, according to His own testimony, would be an obstacle to the descent of the plenitude of God.

We know Saint Teresa's reaction. In her humility she is respectful to these spiritual persons who are seemingly learned men. Did she not even for a time yield to their authority? And for this she experienced cutting remorse.[20] Now, while she is writing the *Interior Castle,* her mind is made up. And so she strongly states her thought on the matter, in a doctrine that was little by little to gain the assent of all. She writes:

> This is a thing of which I have written at length elsewhere, and, although I have been contradicted about it and told that I do not understand it, because these are paths along which Our Lord leads us, and that, when we have got over the first stages, we shall do better to occupy ourselves with matters concerning the Godhead and to flee from corporeal things, they will certainly not make me admit that this is a good way. I may be wrong and we may all be meaning the same thing; but it was clear to me that the devil was trying to deceive me in this way; and I have had to learn my lesson. So, although I have often spoken about this, I propose to speak to you about it again, so that you may walk very warily. And observe that I am going so far as to advise you not to believe anyone who tells you otherwise.[21]

[19] John 16:7
[20] *Life,* xxii; Peers, I, 137-8.
[21] VI Mansions, vii; Peers, II, 304.

The Saint explains what she means by recourse to the sacred humanity of Christ. It is well understand that in these regions of the spiritual life one cannot always have Christ present.

When God is pleased to suspend all the faculties, as we have seen that He does in the modes of prayer already described, it is clear that, though we may not desire it to be so, this Presence is taken from us. At such a time as that, let this be done. Blessed is such a loss, since it brings with it the enjoyment of more than we seem to have sacrificed; for the soul can then employ itself wholly in loving One Whom the understanding has been striving hard to know; it loves what it has not comprehended and rejoices in that of which it could not have such great fruition save by losing itself, in order, as I say, the better to gain itself. But that we should exert care and skill to accustom ourselves not to endeavour with all our strength to have always before us—and the Lord grant it be always!—this most sacred Humanity, it is that, I say, which seems to me not to be right.[22]

It is this attitude, or rather this effort at withdrawal, that Saint Teresa condemns; it has most harmful consequences in the spiritual life:

I believe myself that this is the reason why many souls, after succeeding in experiencing the Prayer of Union, do not make further progress and achieve a very great spiritual freedom.[23]

She says things that are still more grave in the *Interior Castle:*

I cannot believe that people can really do this; it must be that they do not understand themselves and thus do harm to themselves and to others. At any rate, I can assure them that they will not enter these last two Mansions; for, if they lose their Guide, the good Jesus, they will be unable to find their way; they will do well if they are able to remain securely in the other Mansions.[24]

Thus the abandonment of Christ Jesus closes access to the summits of the spiritual life. Indeed it scarcely allows one to enjoy without danger the first manifestations of the mystical life proper to the fourth and fifth Mansions. It is a real spiritual obstacle.

The Saint explains it as a lack of humility:

[22] *Life,* xxii; Peers, I, 140.
[23] *Ibid.;* 138.
[24] VI Mansions, vii; Peers, II, 305.

. . . a desire on the soul's part to rise before the Lord raises it. . . . This little mote of deficient humility, though it seems to be of no importance, does a great deal of harm to those who wish to make progress in contemplation. . . .

God is well pleased to see a soul humbly taking His Son as Mediator, and yet loving Him so much that, even if His Majesty is pleased to raise it to the highest contemplation, as I have said it realizes its unworthiness.[25]

Lack of humility deprives the soul of necessary support:

The soul is left, as the phrase has it, in the air; for it has nothing to lean upon, however full it may think itself to be of God.[26]

But perhaps the cause of the error and its baneful consequences must especially be sought in the spiritual gluttony that usually accompanies the first experiences of the mystical life. Again Saint Teresa takes us into her confidence:

When I began to gain some experience of supernatural prayer—I mean of the Prayer of Ouiet—I tried to put aside everything corporeal, though I dared not lift up my soul, for, being always so wicked, I saw that to do this would be presumption. But I thought I was experiencing the presence of God, as proved to be true, and I contrived to remain with Him in a state of recollection. This type of prayer, if God has a part in it, is full of delight, and brings great joy. And in view of the advantage I was deriving from it and the pleasure it was bringing me, no one could have made me return to meditation on the Humanity—on the contrary, this really seemed to me a hindrance.[27]

She admits in the *Interior Castle:*

I would take less pleasure than previously in thinking of Our Lord Jesus Christ and would go about in that state of absorption, expecting to receive spiritual consolation. Then I saw clearly that I was going wrong; for, as it was impossible always to be having consolations, my thoughts would keep passing from one subject to another, until my soul, I think, got like a bird flying round and round in search of a restingplace and losing a great deal of time.[28]

True, few souls have Teresa's fine spiritual sense and her humility. And so it seems to us that, even in our day, many

[25] *Life,* xxii; Peers, I, 140-1.
[26] *Ibid.;* 140
[27] *Ibid.;* 137.
[28] VI Mansions, vii; Peers, II, 309.

persons let themselves be deceived by the delights of the prayer of quiet or, to speak a more modern language, by the delightful obscurity of the dark night. They see in it a summit, whereas it is really only provision for a still longer journey. Their high opinion of it and desire for it keep them from being sufficiently detached to return to a humble seeking of Christ Jesus. Because of this error, as Saint Teresa has already indicated, they remain only with great difficulty in the regions of simple quiet. Access to more elevated regions is closed to them, for entrance to these requires a more complete detachment and explicit recourse to our Lord Jesus Christ.

As to the arguments put forward to justify withdrawal from Christ, Saint Teresa declares that she cannot accept them:

> We are sometimes reminded that the Lord said to His disciples that it was expedient for them that He should go away: I cannot, however, allow that as an argument. He did not say this to His most sacred Mother, because she was firm in the faith and knew that He was God and Man; and, although she loved Him more than they, her love was so perfect that His being on earth was actually a help to her. The Apostles could not at that time have been as firm in the faith as they were later and as we have reason to be now.[29]

Christ's going away, withdrawing His sensible presence from His disciples, was to open their gaze to the divinity that had been veiled from them. It made their faith more perfect and more enlightened by revealing to them His all, namely, His divinity and His humanity, as well as His role of mediator. Christ Jesus disappeared from sensible view only to shine forth in His whole person.

Moreover, this departure was necessary for the fulfillment of His mission and that of the Holy Spirit. The Holy Spirit was to come to strengthen the apostles and form the Church. What we must not see in the departure of Jesus and the descent of the Holy Spirit is an exclusion of the one by substitution of the other. The Holy Spirit is the Spirit of the Son just as He is the Spirit of the Father. Jesus tells us that through Him, He

[29] *Ibid.;* 308-9.

Himself is with us unto the consummation of the world.[30] The Holy Spirit comes not to replace Christ Jesus, but to build up the whole Christ by diffusing His life in all His members by the merits of His sacred blood. The work of the Holy Spirit will be consummated when Christ Jesus will have attained to His fullness as perfect man and to the glorious extension through His members that God willed for Him from all eternity.

In the spiritual growth of the soul as in the development of the Church there is a coming of the Spirit, whose luminous shadow veils the sensible presence of Christ Jesus. The dark night of the spirit is the most painful and obscure moment of that eclipse. The burning flame of the Holy Spirit produces it only to bring faith to perfection, causing it to enter more profoundly into the mystery of Christ and realize perfect union with Him. To use this eclipse as a pretext for withdrawing from Jesus, practically to oppose the action of the Spirit to that of Christ Himself, to withdraw from the one in order to render the other more efficacious—this is to misunderstand the fundamental truths of Christianity, to adopt a definitely anti-Christian attitude, and to render inefficacious the action of the Spirit by separating it from Christ who is its beginning and end.

At most one can grant that implicit recourse to the mediation of Christ is sufficient for the pagan who does not know of the existence and necessity of such mediation. The Christian contemplative could not normally be excused on the plea of ignorance. It is explicitly that he must go to Christ Jesus at all stages of his spiritual life. He has a duty to put forth effort in order to surmount the particular difficulties that this recourse may present in the dark night of the spirit, for never was Christ's action more necessary to him. This is in fact the time when are excellently wrought in his soul both purification and union, two specific effects of the mediation and redemption of Christ. His blood is our propitiation; through it, all that sin had sep-

[30] Matt. 28:20.

arated in heaven and on earth is reunited.[31] These more intense effects can be obtained only by a deeper faith, a more constant recourse to Christ and to the power of His divine blood. This is the hour, or never, to put in practice the counsels of the apostle in the Epistle to the Hebrews:

> Having therefore a great high priest who has passed into the heavens, Jesus the Son of God, let us hold fast our confession. For we have not a high priest who cannot have compassion on our infirmities, but one tried as we are in all things except sin. Let us therefore draw near with confidence to the throne of grace, that we may obtain mercy and find grace to help in time of need.[32]
>
> For if the blood of goats and bulls and the sprinkled ashes of a heifer sanctify the unclean unto the cleansing of the flesh, how much more will the blood of Christ, who through the Holy Spirit offered himself unblemished unto God, cleanse your conscience from dead works to serve the living God? [33]

Saint Teresa, speaking "for those of us who live in this mortal body," completes the thought of Saint Paul with these conclusions:

> We need to cultivate, and think upon, and seek the companionship of those who, though living on earth like ourselves, have accomplished such great deeds for God; the last thing we should do is to withdraw of set purpose from our greatest help and blessing, which is the most sacred Humanity of Our Lord Jesus Christ. . . . For life is long and there are many trials in it and we have need to look at Christ our Pattern, and also at His Apostles and Saints, and to reflect on how they bore these trials, so that we, too, may bear them perfectly. The good Jesus is too good company for us to forsake Him and His most sacred Mother.[34]

c. *Jesus perfect model in the dark night*

During the dark night of the spirit most especially, the soul could find nowhere else than in Christ Jesus the perfect model to imitate, if it would profit by the purifying trial. Between the interior sufferings of Jesus in His Passion and those of the night of the spirit, there is a close resemblance. Saint John of

[31] Eph. 1:10.
[32] Heb. 4:14-6.
[33] Heb. 9:13-4.
[34] VI Mansions, vii; Peers, II, 304-8.

the Cross illustrates this by using extensively to describe these latter the prophetic texts of the Old Testament, which the Church applies to the Passion of Christ.

Christ is the Lamb who takes on Himself the sin of the world. His Passion is caused by the destructive forces of sin let loose, which rise to the attack of His sacred humanity anointed with the oil of the divinity. Everything in that humanity that can be broken and die succumbs under the violence of the shock. The dark night of the spirit too is caused by the clash of two contraries: God's invading love and sin rooted in the depths of the soul. Certainly, there is no common measure between the love with which the soul is invested and the anointing with the divinity, between the sin of the soul and the sin borne by the Lamb of God; but the forces that are engaged being the same, the sufferings will be similar, if not of the same intensity.

Jesus shows us what attitude to maintain in this struggle. The Lamb of God agonizes in Gethsemane; but His groanings and His prayer for deliverance end in complete abandonment to the will of His Father. His patience is sustained by His love for His Father and for souls, by certain hope of His triumph. Near to Jesus weighed down with suffering yet strong in His silence, the soul in the dark night will remain silent and strong in its patience and hope. "Did not the Christ have to suffer these things before entering into His glory?" [35] "No disciple is above his teacher." [36] "He who follows me does not walk in the darkness." [37] "And I, if I be lifted up from the earth, will draw all things to myself." [38] For one in the dark night, these words cast light and give certitude.

"Looking towards the author and finisher of faith, Jesus," [39] the soul is drawn into the unfolding of His mysteries and par-

[35] Luke 24:26.
[36] Matt. 10:24.
[37] John 8:12.
[38] John 12:32.
[39] Heb. 12:2.

ticipates in them. True, in Christ Jesus the mystery of the Incarnation preceded the mystery of the Redemption; suffering in Him is solely redemptive. In us, sinners, suffering that purifies must prepare us for perfect union with God. Although the Lamb of God is entirely pure, He is the victim of the sin of the world; the soul in the dark night bears its own sin and suffers from it. Is its suffering not already redemptive? Who could say not? In any case, it can hold firm in these regions, being under the weight of sin as it is, only if sustained by intimate contact with the divine Victim.

It is through this contact, which a prolonged and penetrating gaze of the soul must maintain, that the soul draws from the sorrowful Face of Christ Jesus the science of divine love. Thus it not only learns the meaning and value of the trial, but grows in sympathy with the Master and in resemblance to Him. "Having this mind in you which was also in Christ Jesus," [40] the apostle tells us. Christian perfection lies in this resemblance and this compassion. Our Christ is nailed to a rough cross solidly set in our earth of sin. To withdraw from this divine model in the decisive period of purification and transformation is to wander off into by-roads, sacrificing to a natural sublimation of our faculties the realization of that Christian perfection of which Jesus is the type.

d. *Examples of the saints*

It is this contact with Christ in His sorrowful mysteries that the saints sought, those in whom we admire the effects of a deep spiritual rebirth.

Did Nicodemus understand the close relation there is between the mysteries of spiritual rebirth, of the Incarnation of the Son of Man, and of elevation on a cross, mysteries to which Jesus had referred in their conversation? Whatever be the case, when Jesus was nailed to the cross Nicodemus rose up, urged on by the light and grace he had received, and courageously

[40] Phil. 2:5.

drew from the sources of life that death had opened up in his heart.

We find the same movement of grace—and how richly defined—in the apostle Saint Paul. Christ, glorious and sorrowing, cast him to the ground on the Damascus road. The burning and luminous wound that Paul kept from this first meeting with his Savior, as it progressively enlarged, revealed to him more and more the mystery of Christ and of Christ crucified, "who has become for us God-given wisdom, and justice, and sanctification, and redemption." [41]

To him, Paul,

> . . . the very least of all saints, there was given this grace, to announce among the Gentiles the good tidings of the unfathomable riches of Christ, and to enlighten all men as to what is the dispensation of the mystery which has been hidden from eternity in God, who created all things.[42]

And so, the apostle sets forth the diverse aspects and the antinomies of that wisdom, lays stress on its incomparable riches for us, reveals the close union of eternal Wisdom with Christ, and consequently the necessity of drawing from the abundant sources of Christ crucified. As for himself, he is determined

> . . . not to know anything among you, except Jesus Christ and him crucified. . . . to the Jews indeed a stumbling-block and to the Gentiles foolishness, but to those who are called, both Jews and Greeks, Christ, the power of God and the wisdom of God.[43]

The union of divine Wisdom and Christ was a matter of experience for Saint John of the Cross, the doctor of detachment. The sweet unction of his language testifies to this, when he speaks of the "mystery of the gate and of the way of Christ" [44] through whom one must pass if he would be united with God, and of the example of Christ "our example and

[41] I Cor. 1:30.
[42] Eph. 3:8-9.
[43] I Cor. 2:2; 1:23-4.
[44] *Ascent,* Bk. II, vii; Peers, II, 87.

light" [45] in the way of complete detachment, which is the way of union.

In the *Spiritual Canticle,* the Saint exalts knowledge of the wisdom of God which one finds in the mystery of Christ:

> The lofty caverns are the lofty and high and deep mysteries in the wisdom of God which are in Christ. . . . There are great depths to be fathomed in Christ. For He is like an abundant mine with many recesses containing treasures, of which, for all that men try to fathom them, the end and bottom is never reached; rather in each recess men continue to find new veins of new riches on all sides, as Saint Paul said of Christ Himself in these words: *In quo sunt omnes thesauri sapientiae et scientiae Dei, absconditi.*[46] Which signifies: In Christ dwell hidden all the treasures and wisdom of God.

And the mystical doctor adds:

> . . . whereinto the soul cannot enter and whereto it cannot attain, unless first, as we have said, it enter and pass into the thicket of exterior and interior suffering.[47]

This knowledge of divine mysteries is the fruit of a purified love and of a certain experience of suffering. Hence the dark night of the spirit, which brings about the one and the other, far from drawing the soul away from Christ leads it wonderfully into the deep caverns of His mysteries. Such is the conclusion drawn from the teachings of John of the Cross.

The saints are numerous whose testimony one could quote to illustrate this doctrine. But let us return to Saint Therese of the Child Jesus; her living teaching is always set forth in such actual and attractive form.

What has been said about the way of spiritual childhood must not make us forget that this little way turns around Christ Jesus. The Saint's search for a lift by which she could be raised to God, since she was "too tiny to climb the steep stairway to perfection," ends in a happy discovery: "Thine Arms, then, O Jesus, are the lift which must raise me up even unto Heaven." [48]

[45] *Ibid.;* 86.
[46] Col. 2:3.
[47] *Spiritual Canticle,* st. xxxvi; Peers, II, 161.
[48] *Autobiography,* ix, 136.

Jesus it is who must carry away the child into the depths of the Holy Trinity. In a letter to Sister Marie of the Sacred Heart, which constitutes chapter xi of the *Autobiography,* Therese writes:

> O divine Word, You are the adored Eagle, I love You, and You *draw* me to You. . . . One day, so I hope, adored Eagle, You will come for Your little bird, and mounting with it to the Fire of Love, You will plunge it for eternity in the burning Abyss of the Love to which it has offered itself as victim.[49]

On entering Carmel, Therese had received as "realm" the Infancy of our Lord, with the name Sister Therese of the Child Jesus. This mystery suited so well her youth and her grace! Yet it was not to suffice for her. Jesus had already disclosed to her the value of the blood that flows from the wounds of the Crucified; and she had resolved, as she says, "to remain continually at the foot of the Cross, that I might receive the Divine Dew of Salvation and pour it forth upon souls." [50]

In Carmel, she enters still more deeply into the riches of the mystery of the Passion of Jesus. To the sufferings of interior dryness and of religious formation that was difficult for her from the beginning, there was added shortly after her clothing (January 10, 1889) the heavy trial that fell upon the family: her father had a paralytic stroke and had to be placed in a hospital in February 1889. She writes:

> Though my suffering seemed to have reached its height, yet my attraction thereto did not grow less, and soon my soul shared in the trials my heart had to bear. My spiritual aridity increased, and I found no comfort either in Heaven or on earth; yet, amid these waters of tribulation that I had so thirsted for, I was the happiest of mortals.[51]

A few months previously, it seems, she had begun to discover the secrets of the Holy Face:

> Until then I had not appreciated the beauties of the Holy Face; it was my dear Mother, Agnes of Jesus, who unveiled them to me.[52]

[49] Letter to Marie of the Sacred Heart, Sept. 14, 1896; *Collected Letters,* pp. 285-6.
[50] *Autobiography,* v, 73.
[51] *Ibid.,* vii, 115.
[52] *Ibid.,* 110.

A providential revelation, surely, and preparation for the trial that was to deepen her understanding of this mystery. On March 15, 1889, one month after Mr. Martin's entrance in the hospital at Caen, Therese for the first time signs a letter to her sister Céline: Sister Therese of the Child Jesus of the Holy Face.[53] Some months later, writing to Céline to comfort her in their trial, she quotes from Isaias and says:

> Céline, it was *so long ago* . . . and already the soul of the prophet Isaias was immersed like ours in the HIDDEN BEAUTIES of Jesus.[54]

She attached to her letter a copy of verses 1-5 of Chapter 53 of the Book of Isaias, in which the prophet describes the sorrowful countenance of the Servant of Jahweh.[55]

From that time on and to the end of her life, the Holy Face was to be before the loving gaze of Therese. She sings of it in a hymn:

> Jesus, your ineffable Face
> Is the star that guides my steps;
> You know well, your sweet countenance
> Is for me heaven here below
> Your beauty that you veil
> Reveals to me your whole mystery.
> Your Face is my only fatherland
> It is my realm of love
> My sweet sun, every day.

[53] Letter to her sister Céline, March 15, 1889; *Collected Letters,* p. 97.

[54] *Ibid.,* July 18, 1890; p. 132.

[55] From the Prophet Isaias (Ch. 53): Who hath believed our report? And to whom is the arm of the Lord revealed? Christ shall grow up as a tender plant before the Lord, and as a root out of a thirsty ground. There is no beauty in Him, nor comeliness: we have seen Him and there was no sightliness that we could be desirous of Him: despised and the most abject of men, a man of sorrows and acquainted with infirmity; His look was as it were hidden and despised. Whereupon we esteemed Him not. Surely He hath borne our infirmities and carried our sorrows. We have thought of Him as it were a leper, and as one struck by God and afflicted. But he was wounded for our iniquities. He was bruised for our sins. The chastisement of our peace was upon Him: and by His bruises we are healed.

To this text were joined verses 1-5 of ch. lxiii of Isaias, verses 14 and 15 of ch. vii of the *Apocalypse,* several verses from the *Canticle of Canticles,* and stanza viii from *The Spiritual Canticle* of Saint John of the Cross. All these texts have to do with the Passion and the attitude of the soul in the presence of the suffering Christ.

It is my rest, my sweetness
And my melodious lyre . . .
Your Face is my only wealth.[56]

She composes an Act of Consecration to the Holy Face.[57] And in the depositions for the process of her beatification, we read:

The Holy Face was the mirror in which Therese saw the soul and the heart of her Beloved. This Holy Face was the meditation book from which she drew her signs of love.

She had an image of it always before her in her office book and in her stall during her prayer. There was a copy attached to the curtains of her bed during her illness; the sight of it helped her to endure her long martyrdom.[58]

She herself says several weeks before her death:

My devotion to the Holy Face, or rather all my spirituality, has been based on these words of Isaias: 'There is no beauty in him, nor comeliness: and we have seen him, and there was no sightliness (in him). . . . Despised and the most abject of men, a man of sorrows, and acquainted with infirmity: and his look was as it were hidden and despised, whereupon we esteemed him not.' [59] I, too, desire to be without glory or beauty, to tread the winepress alone,[60] unknown to any creature.[61]

Contemplation of the Holy Face holds, as we see, a considerable place in the spiritual life of Saint Therese of the Child Jesus, especially at the time of her painful and definite ascent to transforming union.

During this period, interior darkness does not conceal the Holy Face. On the contrary its beauty, arises before her during the night of trial: it is the divine Sun that is to dispel the painful darkness. Saint Therese of the Child Jesus guards and cultivates with a virginal care spiritual poverty, as being the most precious treasure of her hope in God alone. She does not think

[56] *Autobiography,* Poems. [This poem is not found in the English translation.]
[57] *Ibid.*, p. 314.
[58] Summary of the Process for Beatification.
[59] Isa. 53:1-3.
[60] Isa. 63:3.
[61] *Novissima Verba,* August 5, p. 83.

she is tarnishing it by gazing steadfastly at the face of her beloved, to journey into a subterranean way

> . . . where it is neither hot nor cold, where the sun does not shine, and rain and wind do not come; a tunnel where I see nothing but a brightness half-veiled, the glow from the downcast eyes in the Face of my Spouse.[62]

In this half-veiled brightness, ceaselessly she finds patience, consolation, humility, and always more ardent zeal for the salvation of souls. She writes to Céline:

> How can we complain when He Himself was considered "as one struck by God and afflicted"?
> The "charm divine" charms my soul and marvelously consoles it at every instant of the day! Ah! The tears of Jesus, what smiles they are![63]

Truly, under the light that shines from the Holy Face the soul of Therese grows and opens out to the proportions of the universe.

> The Little Flower which had been transplanted to the mountain of Carmel quickly turned to the Director of Directors, and unfolded itself under the shadow of His Cross, having for refreshing dew His Tears, His Precious Blood, and for radiant sun His Adorable Face.[64]

A source of life, a model to be imitated, the Holy Face is the great treasure of Therese, the kingdom that Jesus gave her as a dowry on the day of their divine espousals, so that all its divine traits might be reproduced in her soul. And so she sings:

> Your Face is my sole wealth,
> I ask for nothing more.
> Hiding myself endlessly in it,
> I shall be like you, my Jesus.
> Leave in me the divine imprint
> Of your traits filled with sweetness,
> And soon I shall become holy,
> And shall draw hearts to you.[65]

[62] Letter to Mother Agnes, during Therese's retreat for profession, Sept., 1890; *Collected Letters,* p. 139.
[63] Letter to Celine, July 18, 1890; *Collected Letters,* p. 133.
[64] *Autobiography,* vii, 110.
[65] *Autobiography,* Canticle to the Holy Face.

A touching and enlightening confirmation of a doctrine. Christ in His Passion is the best companion on the way for a soul painfully journeying in the darkness of the night. The soul has, therefore, the duty of staying close to Him, and of drawing at its source the life that surges from His wounds.

There still remains a problem to be solved, the most important perhaps in the opinion of the contradictors of Teresa of Avila:

2. HOW TO REALIZE THIS RECOURSE TO JESUS

a. *Difficulties*

In order to legitimize their voluntary withdrawal from Christ, the contradictors argued the impossibility of dwelling upon the sacred humanity. Saint Teresa sets forth their opinion:

> These writers think that, as this work is entirely spiritual, anything corporeal may disturb or impede it, and that what contemplatives must contrive to do is to think of themselves as circumscribed, but of God as being everywhere, so that they may become absorbed in Him.[66]

It is, in fact, certain that souls elevated to contemplation can no longer meditate and reason in mental prayer as previously. Saint John of the Cross gives this impossibility as a sign that the purgation of sense has begun:

> The third sign . . . is that the soul can no longer meditate or reflect in the imaginative sphere of sense as it was wont, however much it may of itself endeavour to do so. For God now begins to communicate Himself to it, no longer through sense, as He did aforetime, by means of reflections which joined and sundered its knowledge, but by pure spirit, into which consecutive reflections enter not; but He communicates Himself to it by an act of simple contemplation, to which neither the exterior nor the interior senses of the lower part of the soul can attain. From this time forward, therefore, imagination and fancy can find no support in any meditation, and can gain no foothold by means thereof.[67]

Saint Teresa also, speaking of meditation or, "prolonged reasoning with the understanding," recognizes that

[66] *Life,* xxii; Peers, I, 136.
[67] *Dark Night,* Bk. I, ix; Peers, I, 355.

. . . those whom God has raised to supernatural things and to perfect contemplation are right in saying they cannot practise. As I have said, I do not know why this should be the case; but as a rule they are in fact unable to do so.[68]

The Saint concedes also that at moments when contemplation is perfect, that is, for her, when all the faculties are held captive and are drowned in a certain intoxication, they are not able to think but only to love.

But this state could be only fleeting. The Saint would consider suspect the state of any soul that declared it experienced this delight continuously.[69] She insists that one would waste his time by keeping the faculties inactive until it returns.[70]

There remains the habitual inability to use the imagination and discursive reason. Does this powerlessness still allow recourse to the sacred humanity of Christ? On this subject Saint Teresa declares:

A man will not be right, however, to say that he cannot dwell upon these mysteries, for he often has them in his mind, especially when they are being celebrated by the Catholic Church; nor is it possible that a soul which has received so much from God should forget all these precious signs of His love, for they are living sparks which will enkindle the soul more and more in its love for Our Lord.[71]

One might think that Saint Teresa is here referring to the intellectual and imaginary visions of Christ Jesus with which she had been favored, the memory of which would singularly facilitate recourse to our Lord. Certainly, these extraordinary favors had great influence on her mental prayer. It is clear, however, that the recourse to the sacred humanity of which she is speaking is independent of these graces. She goes on to say:

But these mysteries will not be apprehended by the understanding: the soul will understand them in a more perfect way. First, the understanding will picture them to itself, and then they will be impressed upon the memory, so that the mere sight of the Lord on His knees, in the Garden, covered with that terrible sweat, will suffice us, not

[68] VI Mansions, vii; Peers, II, 307.
[69] *Ibid.;* 308.
[70] *Ibid.*
[71] *Ibid.;* 307.

merely for an hour, but for many days. We consider, with a simple regard, Who He is and how ungrateful we have been to One Who has borne such pain for us. Then the will is aroused, not perhaps with deep emotion but with a desire to make some kind of return for this great favour and to suffer something for One Who has suffered so much Himself. And so it is with other subjects, in which both memory and understanding will have a place. This, I think, is why the soul cannot reason properly about the Passion, and it is because of this that it believes itself unable to meditate upon it at all.

But if it does not already meditate in this way, it will be well advised to attempt to do so; for I know that the most sublime kind of prayer will be no obstacle to it and I believe omission to practise it often would be a great mistake.[72]

In this important text, Saint Teresa points out that for the contemplative soul, outside of states in which there is suspension of the faculties, there is always possible an intellectual activity that is beyond discursive reasoning, beyond the activity of the imagination and phantasy—to use the language of Saint John of the Cross. This activity is without doubt a contemplative activity.

This contemplative activity may be theological contemplation, that is, a work of reason enlightened by faith and sustained, at least at times, by the gifts; it fixes its attention on Christ Jesus in order to penetrate into His soul and His suffering. Saint Teresa thinks that such contemplation is possible for souls in this state. Her advice is to practice it rather than let oneself be absorbed by the remembrance of delights, suspending voluntarily the activity of the faculties.

And yet it is not theological contemplation that keeps the soul habitually in the presence of Christ Jesus during this period of the purification of the spirit. During the dark night of the spirit, the powerlessness of the faculties goes deeper than during the dark night of sense. The descriptions given by John of the Cross bear this out. If the soul is still able to fix its gaze or to think, this is only momentarily. There is little probability of its prolonging this gaze and fixing its thought at any length, for it promptly falls into helplessness and darkness. Moreover,

[72] *Ibid.*

the Teresian descriptions that we have just read, as well as the constant and profound devotion of Saint Therese of the Child Jesus to the Holy Face, draw their nourishment from something else, it seems, than theological contemplation.

This something else is an authentic mystical light proceeding from an interior experience and marvelously illuminating the tableau or the mystery of Christ that the mind is considering. This point merits explanation by reason of its importance.

b. *Interior experience and gaze fixed on Christ*

During this period, in spite of the painful darkness, love continues to enrich living faith with the riches of its experience. Faith and experience, both of them essentially obscure, happily share their insights gained from the gaze of the soul on the mystery of Christ.

Interior experience discovers at first that the love we have received is a filial love, that this spirit is not "a spirit of bondage . . . but a spirit of adoption as sons, by virtue of which we cry, 'Abba! Father!' The Spirit himself gives testimony to our spirit that we are sons of God," declares the apostle.[73]

The inner testimony of the Spirit and of grace as to the filial character of the charity that is given us is completed by the experience of connaturality, which exists between Christ Jesus and ourselves. He is the Son by nature, we are sons by adoption through grace; we are "joint heirs with Christ." [74] All that unites the soul to Christ stands out more clearly to its interior gaze as charity grows within it, transforming it and identifying it with Him.[75]

This experience, which in the dark night of the spirit is painful, connected with powerlessness and interior humiliation, has evident affinities with that of Jesus crucified. And so the soul, in gazing on the Passion, finds its proper atmosphere; it is en-

[73] Rom. 8:15-6.
[74] Rom. 8:17.
[75] We shall return to this identification with Christ and the perfect discovery that accompanies it in transforming union.

larged and elucidated. Interior experience and attentive gaze on Jesus mutually enrich by completing each other. Experience makes one enter into the depths of the Passion of Christ; the soul's gaze on Christ suffering reveals to experience its value and an already realized union. In this discovery and awareness what strength there is for the soul, an at-oneness with Christ Jesus whom it finds so near!

The link that is forged by a gaze on Jesus suffering, or simply the remembrance of the Passion, has brought about changes in depth. The external traits of the tableau and conceptual forms of thought disappear. The obscure depths of the soul find repose in the depths of the mystery of Christ suffering, in an outpouring of painful love that finds strength and light in this meeting. The soul that is suffering under love's action joins Christ who is in agony in His love for men until the end of the world.

This meeting and its effects explain what Saint Teresa tells us about the prayer of contemplatives who cannot reason properly about the Passion:

> These mysteries will not be apprehended by the understanding: the soul will understand them in a more perfect way. . . . The mere sight of the Lord on His knees, in the Garden, covered with that terrible sweat, will suffice us, not merely for an hour, but for many days. We consider, with a simple regard, Who He is and how ungrateful we have been. . . . Then the will is aroused, not perhaps with deep emotion but with a desire to make some kind of return for this great favour.[76]

As we see, the faculties are powerless only because overpowered by a more profound and more unifying activity. The gaze on Christ, although no longer sustaining meditation or theological contemplation, becomes in fact much more enriching by drawing strength and clarity from the inner experience that it makes explicit and enlarges. This gaze on Christ not only is useful during the dark night of the spirit; it is necessary if

[76] VI Mansions, vii; Peers, II, 307.

one is to become aware of the riches that afflictive love places in the soul, and truly take possession of them.

c. *Devotion to the Holy Face practiced by Saint Therese of the Child Jesus*

Devotion to the Holy Face as practiced by Saint Therese of the the Child Jesus offers us an example of the marvelous enrichment that interior experience can derive from the soul's gaze on Christ Jesus. Actually, it was this devotion, together with the trial of her father's illness and the interior experience that it illumined, which orientated the Saint toward her oblation to merciful Love and the sublime summits of her spiritual life.

The devotion had come to her from the Carmel of Tours where Sister Marie of Saint Peter had lived, the inspirer and counselor of M. Dupont, the holy man of Tours, zealous propagator of devotion to the Face of Christ. Mother Agnes had revealed to Therese the secrets of this Holy Face,[77] thereby first giving definite form to the interior experience of the Saint, who was then in darkness and powerlessness. It was her father's paralytic stroke that opened this realm to her definitively.

The despised Christ, the last of men, with a hidden look, without splendor or beauty, His eyes lowered, the man of sorrows whom Isaias describes, is this not her father, so cruelly struck after her oblation as a victim? The face of her father, a gentle victim, whose afflicted features a sad trial had just imprinted in her soul, is it not blended with that of the silent and hidden Christ in her mental prayer during this period of powerlessness, but without her losing a sense of each one's presence in the dark night? The two sorrowful faces throw light on each other. That of Christ ennobles with its divine and mysterious majesty that of her beloved father; and the latter makes the Holy Face of Jesus more living. The two are super-

[77] *Autobiography,* vii, 110.

imposed, are unified; they form only one in the soul of Therese, under her loving gaze.

Thus is irresistibly impressed upon her the face of the *Ecce Homo* that the procurator solemnly presented to the world on the lithostrotos. That Holy Face is as a star fascinating her, her "daily sun." Yet it is not like a picture to which one shows devotion at certain times. Imprinted in the depths of her soul both by mystical experience and by trial, it is an interior reality always present, of human aspect with veiled features, eyes lowered, indistinct in its lines yet so living, a face that love perceives in the dark night more than does vision. This living reality forms an integral part of her spiritual life. The journey in the "subterranean way, where it is neither hot nor cold, where the sun does not shine, and rain and wind do not come," is brightened by the half-veiled glow from the downcast eyes of the Face of her Spouse.[78]

Everything in this subterranean way—the silence and the shadow and the mystery of life surging there—everything invites Therese to travel this road, seeing in it a way to go to the deep realities that her living faith reveals, to Love hidden and despised, longing to communicate Himself, to the necessary self-oblation if one's soul is to receive His outpourings. Therese continues thus her journey toward the summits in that dark night faintly illumined by the Face of Jesus, silently, patiently, lovingly. She was to reach it on the day when, having offered herself to merciful Love, she was inundated and wounded by the floods of that overflowing Love and thus identified with the divine Victim.

This journeying of Therese of the Child Jesus in the dark night under the veiled light of the Face of Christ, its marvelous success, illustrates remarkably and testifies to the doctrine of Teresa of Avila, namely, that the living presence of Jesus remains with one in the dark night, hidden from the senses but

[78] Letter to Mother Agnes, during Therese's retreat for profession, Sept., 1890; *Collected Letters, p.* 139.

perceived in deeper regions; and that the soul could travel securely in the darkness and reach the end only in that divine company and in the half-light of the mystery of his suffering.

Nowhere more than in these tormented and obscure regions is there need of the presence and action of Him who is the Way and the Light. Only Jesus can show the way to be followed and give the indispensable light.

Such is the night of the spirit. Brought about by God's action on a soul, the soul must draw strength from its gaze on Christ Jesus. For God "has shone in our hearts, to give enlightenment concerning the knowledge of the glory of God, shining on the face of Christ Jesus." [79] The soul must contemplate this glory to make it its own, for God the Father could embrace as sons only those who bear the living reflection of the lights that shine on the Face of His Christ, His only and true Son.

B. The Virgin Mary, all-mother

In the darkness of Calvary where Nicodemus had come to take possession of the body of Jesus to embalm and bury it, near the Crucified he found Mary, standing and valiant, the mother of Jesus. He who journeys in the dark night of the spirit must likewise find in the darkness, near to Jesus in His Passion, Mary, the virgin mother. This discovery we judge to be necessary; hence we cannot omit speaking of it.

1. JESUS AND MARY IN THE DIVINE PLAN

God has closely united Jesus and Mary for the realization of His designs of mercy. For this common mission, God has made them as like one to the other as the transcendence of the hypostatic union reserved to Christ permits. Hence they cannot be separated.

Actually, it is not possible to construct a rigorous theology of Mary and define its truths except in the light of Christ

[79] II Cor. 4:6.

Jesus. History shows likewise that dogmas concerning the Son and the Mother have been made explicit at the same time throughout the centuries. And so, in order to study the privileges and the role of Mary, one could not do better than attribute to her the threefold primacy of dignity, efficiency and finality that God assured to Christ, and in which Christ certainly had His mother share.[80]

a. *Primacy of dignity*

Christ Jesus was chosen by God to be the foundation of the whole divine work of Redemption. God, who had created all things by His Word, willed after the Fall to restore all things through His incarnate Word. In the Epistle to the Colossians, the apostle develops magnificently this thought:

> He is the image of the invisible God, the firstborn of every creature. For in him were created all things in the heavens and on the earth. . . . All things have been created through and unto him, and he is before all creatures, and in him all things hold together. Again, he is the head of his body, the Church; he, who is the beginning, the firstborn from the dead, that in all things he may have the first place. For it has pleased God the Father that in him all his fullness should dwell, and that through him he should reconcile to himself all things, whether on the earth or in the heavens, making peace through the blood of his cross.[81]

Christ, the stone that was rejected, became the cornerstone of the whole new edifice. Again, writing to the Ephesians, the apostle says:

> In him, I say, in whom we also have been called by a special choice . . .
>
> In him the whole structure is closely fitted together and grows into a temple holy in the Lord; . . .
>
> For from him the whole body (being closely joined and knit together . . .) derives its increase to the building up of itself in love.[82]

[80] One must not expect to find here a complete treatise on Mariology, but only a short exposition of the truths that give light on the relations of the soul in the dark night of the spirit with the Blessed Virgin.

[81] Col. 1:15-20.

[82] Eph. 1:11; 2:21; 4:16

And so God placed His Christ above all creatures, angels and men, as the apostle testifies in the Epistle to the Hebrews: [83]

For to which of the angels has he ever said,
"Thou art my son,
I this day have begotten thee"?
and again,
"I will be to him a father,
and he shall be to me a son"?
And again, when he brings the firstborn into the world, he says,
"And let all the angels of God adore him."

The primacy of dignity rests not only on the divine choice, which makes of Christ an eternal priest, but also on the hypostatic union, which unites in Him, in the Person of the Word, the divine nature and human nature and which, in itself, makes of Him the mediator between heaven and earth.

In this work of mediation, God has given Christ a collaborator. Richard of Saint Laurence puts in the mouth of God, apropos of Christ, the word that He spoke of Adam: It is not good for man to be alone; let us make him a help like unto himself.[84]

Thus with the new Adam we find a new Eve, the Virgin Mary, the mother of the living. It is through her that the Son of God enters into this world, taking from her a human nature which, anointed with the oil of the divinity, becomes Christ Jesus. The mother of God, says the grave Cajetan, Mary: ". . . attains to the confines of divinity by her own operation, in that she conceives God, engenders Him, gives Him birth, and nourishes Him with her milk."

Mary is thus elevated to the plane of the hypostatic union. The good and the graces that she receives from this are in relation to her dignity. Saint Thomas says:

. . . and the Blessed Virgin from the fact that she is the mother of God, have all a certain infinite dignity from the infinite good, which is God. And on this account there cannot be anything better than these; just as there cannot be anything better than God.[85]

[83] Heb. 1:5-6.
[84] Gen. 2:18.
[85] *Sum. Theol.*, I, q. 25, a. 6, ad. 4.

Saint Bernardine of Siena, in other language, emphasizes the same truth:

> For a woman to be worthy to conceive and give birth to God, she had to be, so to speak, elevated to a certain equality with God Himself by a measure of perfection and of grace.

It is this "certain equality with God," to which the divine maternity elevates her, which gains for Mary the extraordinary privileges of her Immaculate Conception, of the plenitude of grace that fills her measure from the beginning; and added to this, the succeeding and marvelous developments by which this plenitude is enlarged to the point of exceeding all measure and all capacity to appreciate it. The human mind cannot reach those confines of the divinity to which Mary attains, to judge and measure her graces.

Truly, as Saint Ephraim affirms: "God alone excepted, she is superior to all." And yet, it would be to limit the dignity of the Virgin Mary to express it only in terms of her divine maternity. She is mother on the plane of the hypostatic union and in the whole plentitude of the term. In the eternal design of God she is to be the collaborator in all the divine fruitfulness. Everywhere that the divine paternity is to act, it will be through the maternity of the Virgin Mother. Thus Mary accompanies Jesus in His redemptive work, and the Holy Spirit in His work of building up the mystical body. She is Mother wherever Jesus is Savior, as well as wherever the Holy Spirit is giver of grace to souls and to the Church.

> God having once decreed that the will of the Virgin should efficaciously cooperate in giving Jesus Christ to men, this first plan never changes; always we shall receive Jesus Christ by the intermediary of her charity.[86]

In saying this, Bossuet speaks for the whole Christian tradition. And this brings us to the primacy of efficiency.

[86] Bossuet, IV, "Sermon on the Annunciation," First Point.

b. *Primacy of efficiency*

The divine choice puts on Christ Jesus a hard task. His office of priestly mediation makes of Him a man who will live in suffering and nakedness, who will bear out infirmities. He will live at Nazareth, will lead an apostolic life, will bury Himself in prayer in the desert and in the night, will meet with the indifference of men and the hatred arising from the world's sin.

He is priest but Savior, and as such, victim in His Passion and on the cross. The sacraments that He institutes, especially the Holy Eucharist, secure for us the benefits of His redemptive suffering, the outpourings of His divine life, and all the privileges of His sacred Person. Priest and victim, light and life, Savior and food, everything comes to us from Him through the merits of His Passion and His priestly action. We are purified, saved, sanctified, introduced into the Holy Trinity, not only in Him, but through Him, through His personal action.

In this domain of the realization of the divine plan we see best the collaboration of Jesus and Mary. In pronouncing the *Fiat* of the Annunciation and giving her consent to the mystery of the Incarnation, Mary already collaborates in the whole work that her Son is to accomplish. She gives us the Savior and already wins for us salvation by her divine maternity.

This maternity establishes an intimate and definitive union between Mother and Son. The Mother gives of her substance; and the unction of the divinity that comes upon it to form the humanity of Christ seems in this contact to flow back upon the Mother, according to some, like a quasi-unction.

As Jesus grows, as His redemptive mission is progressively made manifest and realized, the union between Jesus and Mary by their contemplative gaze, by the strong bonds of mutual love, becomes closer and more active. The *"hoc sentite in vobis quod in Christo Jesu,"* ["have this mind in you which was also in Christ Jesus,"] recommended by the apostle, is in no other realized to an equally high degree. Everything becomes common to them both: oblation, sentiments, thoughts, mission. Mary offers herself, prays, works with Jesus, for the same intentions. They journey on to the same end, enveloped in the same divine plan that united them for the salvation of humanity. When Jesus enters upon His public life, Mary, although remaining in obscurity, accompanies Him by her offering. The work of Jesus is her work; the apostles and disciples of her Son are hers. The hour of trial was to disclose how generous, profound, and absolute was her communion with her Son in His mission. She is present on Calvary. Her attitude tells how her heart had become enlarged to the dimensions of the whole mystical body of Christ. With God the Father, for love of the world she gives her only Son. She hears Jesus sanction, by an efficacious word, the work realized in her by her union with Him and give it officially all its meaning. "Behold thy mother, behold thy son." By this word, Jesus gives Mary to John, John to Mary; Mary is the mother, John is the son and the type of the regenerated humanity that follows Jesus even to Calvary. Mary is truly the Mother of all those who have faith in Christ.

The plan of God is thus unveiled and brought to light. Saint Peter Damien expresses it thus:

> Immediately, from the throne of the divinity, the Lord draws the name of Mary, decreeing that everything should be done through her, in her, with her, and from her; and just as nothing has been made without Him, so nothing is to be remade without her.

Mary becomes the mediatrix of all grace. She is its necessary channel. In the mystical body of which Jesus is the head, she is the neck through which all life passes into the members.

Bossuet, however, does not seem satisfied with this symbolism of the channel of grace. He writes:

> God, having decreed from all eternity, to give us Jesus through Mary, is not content to make use of her simply as an instrument for this glorious ministry; He does not want her to be simply a channel for such a grace, but rather a voluntary instrument contributing to this great work not only by her excellent dispositions, but still more by movement of her will.[87]

[87] Bossuet, IV, "Sermon on the Annunciation," Third Point.

According to Bossuet, the term "channel" suggests too passive a role; but Mary's will has an active part. One can also object to this word on the score that it does not indicate the quality of Mary's action as mediatrix of grace.

Her action is universal in the sense that wherever Jesus is first cause, she herself is second cause. She is mother wherever He is Savior and Head of the mystical body.

This raises the question as to whether the title of mother implies an influence on grace itself—not, certainly, an interior action working some change, but an action that is real while remaining exterior. The maternal function that Mary exercises in the mystery of the Incarnation invites us to pose this problem. Mary receives the Word and gives Him to us in an apparent abasement that does not involve any real modification nor dimunition of the Word. But she enveloped the divinity with the veil of humanity which makes of Jesus the Emmanuel, "God with us." Is not Mary mother of grace in the same way, transmitting to us the divine grace that God alone can produce, but enveloping it, thanks to her maternal function, with a certain veil making it more human, more adapted to our own needs, more within our grasp? It belongs to theology to study this point and to define it, relying on the fact that the gifts of God are without repentance, and that the maternity of Mary, so active in the production of the humanity of Jesus, could not be reduced to the passive role of a "channel," even though a voluntary one in the building up of the mystical body of her Christ.[88] This influence of Mary over grace, that we think it logical to admit, makes grace Marian while leaving it wholly divine. Just as Jesus, of whom Mary makes us brothers, is the Son of God and of Mary, so by this divine and Marian grace, we become truly sons of the Father and sons of Mary.

[88] Some theologians have made a study of the action exercised by the Blessed Virgin in the transmission of grace. Hugon (la Mère de la grace) says that she exercises an instrumental physical causality. Merkelbach (*"Maria Mater gratiae,"* in *Revue ecclésiastique de Liège,* t. X, pp. 23-25) finds a causality that is efficient and dispositive in the intentional order. Bainbel *(Marie, Mère de grace)* admits an efficient moral causality.

c. *Primacy of finality*

Christ's sovereign action establishes us in Him and makes us His subjects. We are His kingdom and His conquest, bought with His blood that we may show forth the perfections of Him who has called us to the marvelous splendors of His light.[89] His work done, God set Him at His right hand in heaven

> . . . above every Principality and Power and Virtue and Domination—in short, above every name that is named, not only in this world, but also in that which is to come. And all things he made subject under his feet, and him he gave as head over all the Church, which indeed is his body, the fullness of him who is wholly fulfilled in all.[90]

At the last judgment, Christ will come with the sceptre of His cross, in the presence of the entire world gathered together, to take possession of His kingdom made up of those who belong to Him. His royalty will show forth in all its splendor in that final triumph. The blessed in heaven will sing His glory with great joy.

> To him who has loved us, and washed us from our sins in his own blood, and made us to be a kingdom, and priests to God his Father—to him being glory and dominion forever and ever. Amen.[91]

In the light of the beatific vision it will then appear how everything is ours, but that we are Christ's and that Christ is God's.[92]

The same light will disclose Mary's role and the place that is due her. Just as the divine anointing that constitutes Jesus mediator assures to Him the adoration reserved to God alone and, by His redemptive action, gives His royalty over all things, so also the dignity of the Mother of God and the proportionate grace accompanying this dignity assures to Mary a cult apart, the cult of hyperdulia; and her universal action in the realization of the designs of God establishes her royalty over all

[89] I Peter 2:9.
[90] Eph. 1:21-2.
[91] Apoc. 1:5-6.
[92] I Cor. 3:23.

things, a royalty that Christians already proclaim. In heaven next to Christ, King by the shedding of His blood, the Virgin Mary is Queen by the exercise of her maternity of grace.

Such are the fundamental truths of the theology of Mary. Although general, they cast light on the particular problem that we are studying. Since Mary's maternity of grace is universal, the soul in the dark night of the spirit must not withdraw from it. Because of its more intense needs and greater difficulties at this time, it has on the contrary the duty to have recourse to this Mother of grace and of fair love, who can so efficaciously and so maternally help it. This is evident. We shall not insist on it, so as to put more stress on the particular role that belongs to the Blessed Virgin in this more troubled period.

2. PROVIDENTIAL ROLE OF THE VIRGIN MARY IN THE DARK NIGHT

a. *Mary, mother of mercy in the dark hours*

The providential role of the Virgin Mary in the dark night is not a theological conclusion; it is a fact of experience.

The religious history of the world shows us that divine Providence does in fact use and cause to shine forth the maternal power of the Blessed Virgin in a very particular way during these hours of darkness and of trouble in which God seems to have disappeared, and in which all recourse to Him has become apparently impossible. There are times when God, offended, like a father legitimately concerned to safeguard the rights of His authority, presents to men only the rigors or the silence of His justice. Then it is that He causes Mary to intervene with the word of salvation that liberates the soul from His just decrees, or at least with consolation enabling the soul to bear their weight. The arm of divine mercy itself is lengthened to its farthest limits by the ministry of Mary.

A medieval author observes in this connection that God reserved to Himself the exercise of justice and entrusted to Mary the exercise of mercy. Saint Therese of the Child Jesus, healed by a smile from the Virgin at a time when all means had failed to check a mysterious illness, enlightened by her experience, sang:

> O thou who cam'st to smile on me at dawn of life's beginning!
> Come once again to smile on me . . . Mother! the night is nigh.[93]

The maternity of the Virgin shines out most brightly in the shadows of evening or the darkness of the night. A glance through history since the beginning of time convinces one of this.

Was there ever sadness greater than that of our first parents after their Fall when they became aware of their nakedness, of that privation of supernatural and preternatural gifts which ensured happiness, peace and harmony to their life and soul, and when they understood that this privation would be the heavy heritage they would transmit to their posterity? The Fall of man became the fall of all humanity. God pronounces the sentence confirming the already perceived fact and stating the consequences for them and their children: struggle, work, suffering, old age, death. There only remains for them, so it seems, to be buried in sadness with the bitter memory of all the happiness lost. But before pronouncing their condemnation, the voice of God resounded terrible in its malediction of the serpent. Our first parents heard and retained those words:

> Because thou hast done this thing, thou art cursed. . . . I will put enmities between thee and the woman, and thy seed and her seed: she shall crush thy head, and thou shalt lie in wait for her heel.[94]

Defeat is not, then, final. The battle is only begun; victory will belong to the woman and her posterity. Thus are announced the Virgin and her revenge on the demon. This promise shines in the far-off distance like a dawning over the actual disaster. And it gives light to the whole life of our first parents. On it rest their faith and their hope.

[93] *Autobiography, Poems,* p. 328.
[94] Gen. 3:14-15. The text of the Vulgate states precisely that it will be the woman who will crush its head, and not her posterity.

The divine promise is made more precise by Isaias at the time of the impious King Achaz who does not even want to ask for a sign of hope, although all sorts of misfortunes threaten the kingdoms of Israel and of Juda. In those sad hours of the history of the people, depositary of the promises, Isaias writes:

> The Lord himself shall give you a sign. Behold a virgin shall conceive and bear a son: and his name shall be called Emmanuel.[95]

The Immaculate Conception is thus announced, and the nature of the fruit that it is to give the world, the Emmanuel, God with us. The most pure rays from the Virgin shine out in the darkest hours to strengthen hope and bespeak the constant solicitude of divine mercy, which remains faithful to the chosen people even in their wanderings.

On reading the Gospel, one easily takes note that Mary is with Jesus during His hidden life, and that she remains hidden at the time of His manifestation to Israel. When hatred makes its appearance, the Virgin too manifests herself. On Calvary, when hatred triumphs and seems to have destroyed everything of the person, the work, and the reputation of Christ Jesus, Mary is standing at the foot of the Cross. By her presence there and her attitude she affirms her strength, her mission, and the triumph of her maternity. Nothing is lost, since the fruitfulness of the Mother is in no way touched but is, on the contrary, proclaimed and exalted. Through it, mercy is to be spread far and spiritual life propagated.

It seems to us that in a tableau of suggestions there is not only food for feeling and piety, but an affirmation of the providential design that makes the maternity of Mary shine out like a star in the night.

The history of the Church shows us that the fine sense of the faithful has always discerned this providential plan. In hours of distress, it leads one toward Mary as to merciful omnipotence and the supreme hope that never deceives. The great victories of the faith against heresies, or of Christianity against

[95] Is. 7:14.

menacing invasions, are for the most part attributed to Mary, help of Christians.

If we enter into the interior domain of souls, we find the same trusting appeal to her intercession, and the same efficacious help of Mary in the most tragic hours. The wearing of the scapular of Mount Carmel and the Marian promise that is attached to it stress this truth so often experienced that it has become a commonplace, namely, that sincere confidence in Mary, asserted by a practice or a prayer, assures to the sinner the grace of final perseverance. While reason seems to rise up against such an assurance, the experience of souls frequently gives moving proof of it.

This experience and the harvest of facts that it reaps allow us to state that if a soul gives up all reception of the sacraments and is left with almost no visible traces of the supernatural edifice of the theological virtues, confidence in Mary can still remain in it and, by being affirmed in certain circumstances, provides a grounded hope that the supernatural bonds with God will be re-established through her.

How can we explain this fact? Perhaps by calling to mind that Mary is a pure creature with whom we can have relations on a natural plane, an ideal creature who attracts us by her beauty, who wins us by her quality as Mother and by her goodness, who answers all prayers; and that she thus extends her spiritual radiation and the influence of her maternity beyond the circle of Christians who are united to her by the supernatural bond of charity.

But beyond all of these motives and making use of all these virtualities conceded to the Virgin, there is the design of God who has made Mary all Mother and entrusted to her the exercise of His mercy.

b. *Intervention of Mary in the dark night of the spirit*

1. *Forms her intervention takes*—This simple exposition suffices to show us how Mary must be solicited through her

heart and her mission to help souls who are undergoing the purification of the dark night of the spirit. These souls are in suffering, the most painful that one can conceive. Her maternal heart cannot be insensible to them, inasmuch as such souls already have a great love for God. The remembrance of her anxious seeking for Jesus on the way home from Jerusalem must oblige her to bend over those who now are bearing the heavy trial of anxious love, in the weariness and depression of all their faculties.

These souls are in the darkness of the night, and the light of the Virgin never shines more sweetly than in darkness. Her providential mission requires her to be the star enlightening the night of the spirit. Mary fulfils her role and efficaciously intervenes in these periods of the spiritual life. She visits John of the Cross in his prison at Toledo, on the vigil of the Assumption, promising that his deliverance is near.[96]

But these exterior and visible interventions do not tell us the usual manner of Mary's interventions during this period. It would be useful to speak of this.

The darkness of the night in which these souls find themselves is salutary; the sufferings and the anguish from which they suffer are inevitable and necessary for the purification and development of love. Hence Mary must not dispel the darkness nor do away with the suffering characteristic of this period.

Moreover, these souls usually seem to themselves to be cut off from the supernatural world, which now seems to them only a void between painful remembrance of the past and anxiety at times for the future. They resemble the sinner separated from God; and they eat the black bread of a seeming deprivation of Him. Yet there is an essential difference even in the psychological field: the sinner, occupied as he is with his business and his pleasures, is little disturbed by the pain of damnation, which, on the other hand, tortures the soul in the dark

[96] Cf. P. Bruno de J. M., *Saint John of the Cross,* p. 183.

night because it loves ardently, and its love meets only with darkness and void. The sinner lives in his sin and suffers from it scarcely at all; the soul in the dark night knows the hard suffering of sin in the light of contrast. Certainly, nothing must be suppressed of this purifying play of contrasts, of the darkness in which it is produced, of its beneficent effects. Peace must not be given by a diminution of light, thus reducing the antinomies, but by a still higher light that will harmonize them by respecting them.

Mary excels in intervening without disturbing the realization of God's design, without diminishing the salutary power of His light, nor the efficacy of His action. She does however intervene; but her manifestations are of a delicacy so subtle, so tender! There may be an apparently chance coincidence, a sudden calm, a light, a meeting, a nothing insignificant in appearance, but in which the soul recognizes with certitude the action, the smile, the perfume, and so the presence of its Mother. A silent shadow in the night, Mary spreads sweetness without suppressing suffering, creates a soft shadow without dissipating the darkness. The sweetness and the shadow are produced by the certitude the soul has of her action and by the obscure awareness of her presence. To know that its Mother is there, watching over it in the night, makes the heart of the child glad, renews its strength, fortifies its hope, gives it light and peace; yet the violence of the crucifying ardors within does not grow less.

A real intimacy is thus established between Mary and the soul, an intimacy that the spiritual life of the saints brings to light when they let us into their confidence. *Novissima Verba,* for example, lets us see in what intimate and familiar relations with the Blessed Virgin, Saint Therese of the Child Jesus lived during the last months of her life, marked nevertheless with hard physical and spiritual sufferings. She asks very little things of the Blessed Virgin:

I asked the Blessed Virgin not to let me be so exhausted and abstracted as I had been these last days. I knew very well that my condition was distressing you.[97]

I asked the Blessed Virgin last evening that I might not cough so that Sister Genevieve might be able to sleep during the night.[98]

But with what delicacy:

I should like to have a beautiful death just to give you pleasure. I have asked this of the Blessed Virgin. To ask something of the Blessed Virgin is not the same as to ask something of the good God. She knows well what to do with my little desires, and it is for her to decide whether to ask for them or not. . . . After all, it is up to her not to force the good God to hear me, but to leave all to His Will.[99]

Describing the life of the Blessed Virgin, Therese speaks of her privileges, of her ordinary life, with a simplicity and a penetration that are signs of an almost continual intimacy with her.[100]

Elsewhere she admits:

No, the Blessed Virgin will never be hidden from me, for I love her too much for that to happen.[101]

2. *How the soul has recourse to Mary in the dark night*

This last statement was made by Therese of the Child Jesus at a time when she was in the greatest darkness and asked prayers for the dying. How explain this contrast? [102] Or more precisely, how can the soul in this night perceive and discern the intervention of the Virgin Mary?

To explain this intimacy, recourse can be had to the sensible and human element that enters into our relations with the Blessed Virgin, and that remains even when the theological

[97] *Novissima Verba,* June 4, p. 14.
[98] *Ibid.,* August 15, p. 99.
[99] *Ibid.,* June 4, pp. 14-15.
[100] *Ibid.,* August 23, p. 107 ff.
[101] *Ibid.,* July 8, p. 35.
[102] While giving these explanations, we do not claim to affirm that Saint Therese of the Child Jesus was at the time in the dark night of the spirit. Her trials then were certainly more reparative and redemptive than they were purifying for her. But whatever may be the nature of the dark night, the same problem arises: how to explain the interventions of the Blessed Virgin that do not dispel the night?

virtues have disappeared. Mary is an ideal creature whose image remains living in our memory, and whom we can continue to love in the midst of the desolation that accompanies the most sad interior disasters.

But in these loving souls other more powerful and deeper forces enter into action. Living faith grows in this night because the love that enlightens it is considerably increased. This love, being filial, bears within it all the potentialities of complete filial love. The loving child not only cries, "Father"; it calls also to the Mother. Perhaps during the night and trial it is the appeal to the Mother that springs first from filial instinct. The dark night that wrests from it this cry for help and sharpens its desire does not prevent it from discovering the object of its desire. The love that illumines faith with its light of connaturality guides it securely in its search in the night and leads it to the restful intimacy of an embrace and a contact which the obscurity, with its darkness and its anguish, contributes to make more ardent and more profound. The child, thanks to the riches of its filial love, has found its Mother and, in the half-light of the mystical experience, no longer leaves her but rests in her arms.

Ineffable grace, powerful help, which is outside all extraordinary manifestations and is more solid, more constant, if not more efficacious than all extraordinary sensible perceptions. And yet these latter are not excluded, for Mary does not fail to use them, as the lives of the Saints prove, when she judges it necessary in order to help the soul undergoing trial and to give it appropriate assistance.

And so, Saint Grignon de Montfort can say in his treatise on *True Devotion to Mary:*

> It is true that we can attain divine union by other roads; but it is by many more crosses and strange deaths, and with many more difficulties, which we shall find it hard to overcome. We must pass through obscure nights, through combats, through strange agonies, over craggy mountains, through cruel thorns and over frightful deserts. But by the path of Mary we pass more gently and more tranquilly.

We do find, it is true, great battles to fight, and great hardships to master; but that good Mother makes herself so present and so near to her faithful servants, to enlighten them in their darknesses and their doubts, to strengthen them in their fears, and to sustain them in their struggles and their difficulties, that in truth this virginal path to find Jesus Christ is a path of roses and honey compared with the other paths.[103]

These lines beautifully tell us the importance of recourse to Mary in the dark night of the spirit and her mission to bring calm and light. In a treatise less well-known and yet more complete on his spiritual doctrine, the *Love of Eternal Wisdom,* Saint Grignon de Montfort does not hesitate to affirm:

It is only through Mary that one can obtain Wisdom.[104]

Such statements must be explained by the context. By taking them in an absolute sense, one would risk excluding from the summits of the spiritual life saints, and even the greatest, such as Saint Paul, in whom one never finds express recourse to Mary, or even a mention of her mission in the redemptive plan and the distribution of grace. Hence we must understand the statement of Grignon de Montfort in the sense of mediation that can be either implicit or explicit. Implicit mediation certainly sufficed in epochs when Mariology was itself poor in explicitation. But now when the writings of the saints and the works of theologians furnish us with luminous precisions on the maternity of Mary, even though these do not yet answer to all the curiosity of our filial love, explicit recourse to Mary seems morally necessary, if one would take possession of Wisdom. Consequently, the statement of Saint Grignon de Montfort takes on its full meaning and its whole imperative force.

3. *Different forms of intimacy with Mary*—But still, account must be taken of different degrees and modes of recourse to Mary and of Mary's influence on souls.

[103] Saint Louis Grignon de Montfort, *True Devotion to the Blessed Virgin Mary,* ch. v, art. 5, p. 117.

[104] Saint Louis Grignon de Montfort, *L'Amour de la Sagesse Eternelle,* ch. xvi, n. 209

Although actually sanctity is one, is wrought by the same Spirit, and makes all share in the same riches of life and of light, yet it displays in each saint different gifts and causes to shine forth a particular virtue of Him who has made us all priests and kings with Him. Thus it is that among souls there are some, like Saint John among the apostles, to whom the Blessed Virgin is especially given. Like the beloved apostle, these souls enjoy in a special way her presence and her action. Life with Mary, through Mary, in Mary becomes sweet to them and a duty. Usually this gift takes at first the form of an active, sensible devotion absorbing their whole spiritual life. Ordinarily this devotion undergoes an eclipse while the soul is advancing in the ways of perfection. Whatever is sensible in the devotion, or distinct and luminous in one's conviction about it, seems to founder in the obscurity of the dark night and under the veil of insensibility that envelops the whole soul. Mary has not disappeared, nor has her love. But the faculties are undergoing the effects of spiritual growth and of the dark night into which they have entered.

Mary will appear again later in an interior light, delicate and delightful, arising from the night. A precious contemplative discovery, made by a gaze of the soul that has been purified and refined in the darkness, that can now discover spiritual realities hidden from the senses and the natural faculties. A new life is taking form, an intimacy is developing based on this dimly perceived presence and these fine perceptions. This life with Mary and in Mary has thereafter its deep foundations in a purified spiritual love; it radiates exteriorly in continual and touching manifestations.

The Carmelite Fathers Bostius [105] and Michael of Saint Au-

[105] Bostius: *De patronatu et patrocinio B. V. Mariae in dicatum sibi Carmelum apud Speculum Carmelitanum, P. Danaielis a Virgine.*

P. Bostius of the Province of Flanders, (died at Gand 1499), wrote a sketch of the contemplative life with Mary and in Mary in the XV century.

Cf. the article by P. Gabriel de S.M.M., *Analecta,* O.C.D., 1931.

gustine [106]—the latter, speaking of his spiritual daughter Marie of Saint Teresa—have explained in detail the developments and riches of this contemplative discovery and this union with Mary through love and contemplative gaze. The treatises of Saint Grignon de Montfort [107] proceed from an experience that must have the same depth, although it is set forth in a different language, because destined for the general run of Christians.

Besides these Marian souls in the full sense of the word, there are others perhaps more numerous whose spiritual life is not centered to the same degree in the Virgin Mary. God has made them another gift, has placed them on another way. They too love the Virgin and have recourse to her divine motherhood. Their devotion is active in the first period. In the second, they also discover Mary in the semi-darkness of the night; her presence becomes known in the light of love. A deep and living intimacy is established. Exterior manifestations are less precise or, rather, less frequent. They are produced only under certain circumstances, although the interior intimacy is constant.

Thus we have the little intimacies in the last months of the life of Saint Therese of the Child Jesus [108] related above, which reveal her profound and marvelous penetration of the life and soul of Mary. Of Saint John of the Cross, Brother Martin of the Assumption, his companion, reports:

> A few years before his death, telling the story of the pool from which the Blessed Virgin drew him out miraculously, Father John of the Cross told him that the numerous favors the Mother of God had accorded him were such that the mere sight of her picture refreshed his soul and filled it with love and light.[109]

[106] P. Michel de Saint Augustin, *Vie, Marie-forme.* Cf. *Etudes Carmélitaines,* 1931–1932. This treatise was published in 1671, two years before the birth of Grignon de Montfort.

[107] *L'Amour de la Sagesse Eternelle,* ch. xvii, written probably in 1703 or 1704. The treatise on *True Devotion* is later and was discovered only in 1842.

[108] As to the Marian life of Saint Therese of the Child Jesus, cf. the penetrating study of P. Louis de Sainte Thérèse, in *Vie Mariale au Carmel* (Editions du Carmel, Petit Castelet). In the same brochure, in *Les Frères de Notre-Dame,* by P. Marie-Eugène, one will find a development of the thoughts expressed here summarily.

[109] Cf. P. Bruno de J.M., *Saint John of the Cross,* ch. xiii, pp. 183-4.

He spoke to them of her with such great tenderness! When traveling, and especially when he was tired or sad, he delighted in recalling thoughts of Mary, or even sang a hymn to the Virgin.[110]

And yet, Saint Therese of the Child Jesus and Saint John of the Cross speak rather little of the Blessed Virgin.[111] Their attention is drawn principally to the mystery of God.

In which souls, those of the first group or those of the second, are the Virgin's love and her action the more powerful and efficacious? How could this be judged? The quality of the love makes its perfection. Would it not be imprudent to base any judgment as to the value of love simply on the multiplicity or the sensible intensity of its manifestations, or on the clarity of the light that sustains it or is its fruit! The purest rays are the least visible, says Saint John of the Cross. And we know that the deepest spiritual realities are not always the most exteriorized.

But what matter if we cannot evaluate it. Let us respect the mystery with which God in His designs envelops souls and His work in them. The essential thing is that each one be convinced that he must go to Mary if he would find Holy Wisdom, and that he must draw upon her to the full measure of his grace and gift.

[110] *Ibid.*

[111] It is true that the references he makes indicate union already realized. Saint John of the Cross speaks of the Blessed Virgin only three or four times in his treatises; but passages in the *Ascent of Mount Carmel,* Bk. III, ch. i, and the *Living Flame,* I, show that when he speaks of the soul arrived at perfect union, he has before his eyes the Virgin Mary in whom are realized all the operations of transforming grace, in an eminent degree.

CHAPTER VI

Effects of the Dark Night of the Spirit

For surely you have heard of him and have been taught in him (as truth is in Jesus) that as regards your former manner of life you are to put off the old man, which is being corrupted through its deceptive lusts. But be renewed in the spirit of your mind, and put on the new man, which has been created according to God in justice and holiness of truth.[1]

Such are the requirements for perfect conversion, as the apostle explains to the Ephesians. A man must be stripped of self and renewed to the very depths of his spirit if he would put on the new man according to the model that is Christ. This is the work of the dark night of the spirit.

This night, as has been abundantly said, is the meeting place of two contraries which cannot coexist in the same subject, and which come to grips on the battlefield of the soul.[2] Love, progressively taking hold of the soul, leads the combat and will gain the victory with the soul's cooperation. The work of love is similar, says John of the Cross, to that of fire assailing wood.

This purgative and loving knowledge or Divine light whereof we here speak acts upon the soul which it is purging and preparing for perfect union with it in the same way as fire acts upon a log of wood in order to transform it into itself; for material fire, acting upon wood, first of all begins to dry it, by driving out its moisture and causing it

[1] Eph. 4:22-4.
[2] *Dark Night,* Bk. II, v; Peers, I, 382.

to shed the water which it contains within itself. Then it begins to make it black, dark and unsightly, and even to give forth a bad odour, and, as it dries it little by little, it brings out and drives away all the dark and unsightly accidents which are contrary to the nature of fire. And, finally, it begins to kindle it externally and give it heat, and at last transforms it into itself and makes it as beautiful as fire. In this respect, the wood has neither passivity nor activity of its own, save for its weight, which is greater, and its substance, which is denser, than that of fire, for it has in itself the properties and activities of fire. Thus it is dry and it dries; it is hot and heats; it is bright and gives brightness; and it is much less heavy than before. All these properties and effects are caused in it by the fire.[3]

These effects show the power of "the fire of love which, as we have said, like the material fire acting upon the wood, begins to take hold upon the soul." [4] The Saint himself writes:

In this way it can be realized in some measure how great and how strong may be this enkindling of love in the spirit, wherein God keeps in recollection all the energies, faculties and desires of the soul, both of spirit and of sense.[5]

Inasmuch as this love is infused, it is passive rather than active, and thus it begets in the soul a strong passion of love.[6]

"Fire of love" kindled by God, "passion of love" produced in the soul, we know what causes are at work in this dark night; and certainly one could never emphasize these too much in explaining all that is to be understood in the great spiritual event that is the night of the spirit. We want to know what are the effects. The comparison with the wood that is first dried out and then inflamed allows us to guess them. But we want precisions. To what in the spiritual life does this transformation of the green wood into a burning brand correspond? Will Saint John of the Cross tell us?

Yes, surely; and probably in the best possible way although somewhat disconcerting. In other matters, this rigorous logician, this penetrating psychologist dissects, analyzes, distin-

[3] *Ibid.* x; 402-3. Cf. also *Ascent,* I, xi; Peers, I, 52; *Living Flame,* Prologue; Peers, III, 14, where he continues the comparison in order to show the action of love in the already perfect soul, st. i, p. 17 ff.

[4] *Ibid,* xi; 406.

[5] *Ibid.;* 407.

[6] *Ibid.;* 406.

guishes so as to set forth everything in clear light. Here, he limits himself to using symbols to mark the finished work, to indicate certain properties of the transformation, to point out a few of its aspects or moments. He seems to leave aside analysis so as not to break the living unity of the work wrought by love.

This work is indeed so much one that to present as distinct its different elements would be to falsify the view of the ensemble. We are no longer at the time when God's action, localized in such or such a faculty, produced in it different effects corresponding to the moment. Now the fire of love is enkindled in the spirit [7] where "all the energies, faculties, and desires of the soul" [8] are recollected. The furnace of this fire is in the depths of the soul. Its radiation is no longer localized. The whole wood is in the fire, and from its inmost depths the flame arises. Thus the whole soul is assailed by the fire and transformed by a single action.

Nevertheless, in one of his definitions of the dark night, Saint John of the Cross speaks of different effects. He says:

> This dark night is an inflowing of God into the soul, purging it from its ignorance and imperfections, habitual, natural and spiritual.[9]

Different aspects of the dark night rather than effects specifically different, these have close bonds of mutual dependence.[10] We shall try not to break, and even to place in relief the bonds created by the living flame, while we consider the following points:

1. The moral purification, which is the best known fruit of the dark night.

[7] *Ibid.*
[8] *Ibid.;* 407.
[9] *Ibid.,* v; Peers, I, 381.
[10] On this question of the structure of the dark night of the spirit, read the remarkable study by R. P. Lucien de Saint Joseph: *"A la recherche d'une structure"* (*Etudes Carmélitaines,* October, 1934, pp. 254-281), which served as a conclusion for the convention on religious psychology held at Avon in September 1938, on the subject of the dark night of the spirit.

2. The psychological reorientation, which makes the faculties apt for the captivating hold of love.

3. The positive effects of love in divine union.

A. Moral purification

1. NECESSITY FOR PURIFICATION

Anyone familiar with the writings of Saint John of the Cross knows well the rigor of his demands, which are those of God, with regard to purity of soul. The *Ascent of Mount Carmel* sets them down with such force that the beginner is frightened:

> It is supreme ignorance for the soul to think that it will be able to pass to this high estate of union with God if first it void not the desire of all things, natural and supernatural, which may hinder it, according as we shall explain hereafter; for there is the greatest possible distance between these things and that which comes to pass in this estate, which is naught else than transformation in God. For this reason Our Lord, when showing us this path, said through Saint Luke: *Qui non renuntiat omnibus quae possidet, non potest meus esse discipulus.* This signifies: He that renounces not all things that he possesses with his will cannot be My disciple.[11]

He draws on many passages in Holy Scripture to prove this statement. God gives the manna, a celestial food, to the Hebrews, only when the flour that they had brought from Egypt has failed them.[12] He stops giving it when they ask for a food other than this noble and simple one, and chastises them.[13] He commands Moses to climb the mountain alone, where He is to speak to him.[14] God, says the Saint, permits not that any other thing should dwell together with him:

> And He permits and wills that there should be only one desire where He is, which is to keep the law of God perfectly, and to bear upon oneself the Cross of Christ. And thus naught else is said in the Divine Scripture to have been commanded by God to be put in the Ark, where the manna was, save the book of the Law, and the rod of Moses,

[11] Luke 14:33, *Ascent,* Bk. I, v; Peers, I, 29.
[12] *Ascent; ibid.*
[13] *Ibid.;* 30.
[14] *Ibid.*

which signifies the Cross. For the soul that aspires to naught else than the keeping of the law of the Lord perfectly and the bearing of the Cross of Christ will be a true Ark, containing within itself the true manna, which is God.[15]

2. ONLY THE DARK NIGHT OF THE SPIRIT EFFECTS PURIFICATION

But is not this reminder of an elementary doctrine useless for souls in the sixth Mansions who have already undergone victoriously the purification of sense? The holy doctor answers:

> The purgation of sense is only the entrance and beginning of contemplation leading to the purgation of the spirit, which . . . serves rather to accommodate sense to spirit than to unite spirit with God. But there still remain in the spirit the stains of the old man, although the spirit thinks not that this is so, neither can it perceive them; if these stains be not removed with the soap and strong lye of the purgation of this night, the spirit will be unable to come to the purity of Divine union.[16]

There is only one veritable and efficacious purification, that of the spirit:

> The difference between the purgation of these and that of this other kind (of sense) is the difference between the root and the branch, or between the removing of a stain which is fresh and one which is old and of long standing.[17]
>
> Wherefore the night which we have called that of sense may and should be called a kind of correction and restraint of the desire rather than purgation.[18]

Even the disorders that the senses manifest are suppressed only by the purification of the spirit. The holy doctor explains:

> The reason is that all the imperfections and disorders of the sensual part have their strength and root in the spirit, where all habits, both good and bad, are brought into subjection, and thus, until these are purged, the rebellions and depravities of sense cannot be purged thoroughly.[19]

15 *Ibid.;* 32.
16 *Dark Night,* II, ii; Peers, I, 376.
17 *Ibid.*
18 *Ibid.,* iii; 378.
19 *Ibid.*

This gives us light on the problem. The work of purification is scarcely begun. The night of sense has secured the calm and strength needed to bear the dark night of the spirit, but it is only a prelude. The night of the spirit alone is a real purification.

3. OBJECT OF THE PURIFICATION

To what does this purification reach? We must first of all distinguish it from the purification effected by the sacrament of Penance. The sacrament, through the infusion of grace, has for its principal effect to take away the stain of sin, that is, to restore the soul to the friendship of God, which it had lost. The purification of the spirit can take place only in a soul already justified. It bears on the very sources of sin, on all sinful tendencies, whether these be in us one of the hereditary forms of original sin, or the consequence of our personal sins.

Saint John of the Cross expresses thus the matter on which the purification of the spirit falls.

> These proficients have two kinds of imperfection: the one kind is habitual; the other actual. The habitual imperfections are the imperfect habits and affections which have remained all the time in the spirit, and are like roots, to which the purgation of sense has been unable to penetrate. . . .
>
> These souls have likewise the *habitudo mentis* and the natural roughness which every man contracts through sin. . . .
>
> To actual imperfections all are not liable in the same way. Some, whose spiritual good is so superficial and so readily affected by sense, fall into greater difficulties and dangers, which we described at the beginning of this treatise. . . .
>
> There is much more that I might say of these imperfections and of how they are the more incurable because such souls consider them to be more spiritual than the others, but I will leave this subject.[20]

This Joannine chart, then, points out to us in proficients upon their entrance into the night of spirit, two kinds of habitual imperfections: evil tendencies already pruned by the purgation of sense, the trunk and roots of which still remain in the spirit, and deep-seated or organic imperfections (heaviness or

[20] *Ibid.*, ii; 376-7.

roughness of spirit) which do not cause one to commit faults properly speaking. Both are attacked by the purification of the spirit; but the second will be directly assailed only by the psychological reorientation.

As to actual imperfections, they appear to be only manifestations of habitual imperfections which, driven back from the domain of sense by the first night, are still active in the domain of spiritual goods.

In short, on the threshold of the dark night of the spirit, the soul bears within it, mortified in certain exterior manifestations but still strong in the depths of the spiritual domain, the spiritual imperfections of which the Saint gave us so living a picture at the beginning of the dark night of sense, and which are a transposition of the seven capital sins. Hence it is these vices, appearing externally in a more or less attenuated form, that must be attacked and destroyed in their deep roots.

Let us try to state more precisely still the object of this purification.

Among the desires or imperfections, Saint John of the Cross distinguishes two kinds: natural desires and voluntary desires:

> The natural desires hinder the soul little, if at all, from attaining to union, when they are not consented to nor pass beyond the first movements (I mean, all those wherein the rational will has had no part, whether at first or afterward); and to take away these—that is, to mortify them wholly in this life—is impossible. And these hinder not the soul in such a way as to prevent its attainment to Divine union, even though they be not, as I say, wholly mortified.[21]

And concerning these faults committed under the impulse of desires that are not completely voluntary it is written, adds the Saint, that "the just man shall fall seven times in the day and shall rise up again." [22] Voluntary desires are much more dangerous.

> But all the other voluntary desires, whether they be of mortal sin, which are the gravest, or of venial sin, which are less grave, or whether

[21] *Ascent,* I, xi; Peers, I, 49.
[22] *Ibid.;* 50.

they be only of imperfections, which are the least grave of all, must be driven away every one, and the soul must be free from them all, howsoever slight they be, if it is to come to this complete union.[23]

The Saint insists, with no fear of repeating himself:

> But of the voluntary desires, which, though they be for very small things, are, as I have said, intentional venial sins, any one that is not conquered suffices to impede union. I mean, if this habit be not mortified; for sometimes certain acts of different desires have not as much power when the habits are mortified.[24]

He gives specific examples:

> These habitual imperfections are, for example, a common custom of much speaking, or some slight attachment which we never quite wish to conquer—such as that to a person, a garment, a book, a cell, a particular kind of food, tittle-tattle, fancies for tasting, knowing or hearing certain things, and suchlike.[25]

A single one of these slight voluntary attachments hinders the divine work in the soul and causes it the harm spoken of at the beginning of the *Ascent of Mount Carmel:*

> These desires are the cause of two serious evils in the soul: the one is that they deprive it of the Spirit of God, and the other is that the soul wherein they dwell is wearied, tormented, darkened, defiled and weakened. . . . Those two evils—namely, the privative and the positive—may be caused by any disordered act of the desire.[26]
>
> For as long as it has this there is no possibility that it will make progress in perfection. . . . It is greatly to be lamented that, when God has granted them strength to break other and stouter cords—namely, affections for sins and vanities—they should fail to attain to such blessing because they have not shaken off some childish thing which God had bidden them conquer for love of Him, and which is nothing more than a thread or a hair.[27]

How explain God's severity in stopping His transforming action in the face of such little nothings? Saint John of the Cross answers:

> The reason is that the state of this Divine union consists in the soul's total transformation, according to the will, in the will of God,

[23] *Ibid.;* 49.
[24] *Ibid.;* 50.
[25] *Ibid.*
[26] *Ibid.,* vi; 33.
[27] *Ibid.,* xi; 50-1.

so that there may be naught in the soul that is contrary to the will of God, but that, in all and through all, its movement may be that of the will of God alone.

It is for this reason that we say of this state that it is the making of two wills into one—namely, into the will of God, which will of God is likewise the will of the soul. For if this soul desired any imperfection that God wills not, there would not be made one will of God, since the soul would have a will for that which God has not. It is clear, then, that for the soul to come to unite itself perfectly with God through love and will, it must first be free from all desire of the will, howsoever slight.[28]

And the Saint clothes this strong truth with a gracious comparison, thus fixing it forever in our mind:

For it comes to the same thing whether a bird be held by a slender cord or by a stout one; since, even if it be slender, the bird will be as well held as though it were stout, for so long as it breaks it not and flies not away. It is true that the slender one is the easier to break; still, easy though it be, the bird will not fly away if it be not broken.[29]

But immediately another problem suggests itself: How is it that a soul that has already fought so generously hesitates in the face of so small an obslacle, "a thread, a hair," that keeps it from advancing? The design of divine providence? Possibly. "God," says Saint John of the Cross, "has granted them strength to break other and stouter cords—namely, affections for sins and vanities." [30] He has left them to themselves to surmount this obstacle, and they seem helpless. Mystery of grace for which God has fixed the measure and the time.

A psychological explanation of this weakness can be given. The obstacle seems on the surface to be little enough; but it probably has powerful substructures. Are not the most dangerous reefs those that scarcely rise above the surface of the water? The will, although presenting so strong and united a front in resistance to sin in general, presents on this point a slight fissure that hardly appears but that runs through to its very depths. Here is indeed the slight crack in the vase through

[28] *Ibid.;* 49.
[29] *Ibid.;* 50-1.
[30] *Ibid.;* 51.

which all the liquid flows out.[31] This so slight yet tenacious "thread" would thus be the external sign of an attachment that still had deep and living roots in the soul although the dark night of sense had clipped it bare of ramifications. Thus the will's weakness would have a reasonable explanation. The will, then, needs to be rectified on this point and strengthened. A thoroughgoing work is necessary, for, says Saint John of the Cross:

> One single affection remaining in the spirit, or one particular thing to which, actually or habitually, it clings, suffices to hinder it from feeling or experiencing or communicating the delicacy and intimate sweetness of the spirit of love.[32]

We have come upon the region where the moral purification must take place. Evidently it is in the depths of the will—there where the evil is that wounds and weakens it. True, the will has already been made docile and conquered by the grace of union of will in the fifth Mansions. A considerable work was then wrought. Since receiving this grace, the will experiences a profound need of adhering wholly to the divine will. But as we see, this adherence is not yet so perfect as not to leave those hardly perceptible yet profound faults, that deep-seated resistance and lack of suppleness, which require an apt purification.

4. HOW IS MORAL PURIFICATION EFFECTED?

Moral purification goes side by side with the psychological redirection, becoming perfect only with and through it. Some of its elements are nevertheless distinct enough from the effects of the psychological reorientation to warrant our setting them forth separately; thus will be manifest all the work accomplished by the dark night of the spirit. The Saint tells us:

> This dark night is an inflowing of God into the soul, which purges it from its ignorances and imperfections, habitual, natural and spiritual, and which is called by contemplatives infused contemplation, or mysti-

[31] *Ibid.*
[32] *Dark Night,* II, ix; Peers, I, 397.

cal theology. . . . Inasmuch as it is the loving wisdom of God, God produces striking effects in the soul, for, by purging and illumining it, He prepares it for the union of love with God.[33]

This passage gives us the essential factors in the work of the dark night of the spirit. Let us sum them up.

The inflowing of God, which constitutes the dark night of the spirit, produces infused contemplation in the soul. This contemplation which is secret Wisdom, springing from love, produces light and love. Saint John of the Cross emphasizes that Wisdom, by illumining the soul, purifies it.

a. *Purifying action of light*

The light given by infused contemplation issues from the connaturality that love creates. Although indistinct and obscure, such contemplation throws light on God and the soul. It makes the soul experience both the riches of the grace coming from God—purity, power, sweetness—and the poverty of the vessel receiving them. The apostle says: We carry this treasure in vessels of clay, to show that the abundance of the power is God's and not ours.[34]

Saint Teresa makes a similar remark:

> We shall never succeed in knowing ourselves unless we seek to know God: let us think of His greatness and then come back to our own baseness; by looking at His purity we shall see our foulness. . . . Anything white looks very much whiter against something black, just as the black looks blacker against the white.[35]

The contrast here is incriminating for the soul. The light shines out from the inner depths where charity is experienced in these sixth Mansions. Hence it reveals in its path all the evil tendencies and their roots, those substructures of the soul ordinarily buried away under a thick veil that conceals them from the most detailed examinations of conscience. The probing inductions of psychoanalysis pierce through the veil only

[33] *Ibid.*, V; 381.
[34] II Cor. 4:7.
[35] I Mansions, ii; Peers, II, 209.

at certain points; and even so, very slowly. Whether the mystical light comes from the sudden and blinding illuminations of extraordinary favors, or from the secret experience of infused contemplation, it shows in full light the depths of the forces of sin in us. Saint Teresa writes:

> It [the soul] also sees clearly how extremely unworthy it is—for in a room bathed in sunlight not a cobweb can remain hidden. It sees its own wretchedness. So far is vainglory from it that it cannot believe it could ever be guilty of such a thing. For now it sees with its own eyes that of itself it can do little or nothing. . . . The soul realizes that it has deserved to go to hell, yet its punishment is to taste glory.[36]
>
> Not only does the soul perceive the cobwebs which disfigure it and its own great faults, but so bright is the sunlight that it sees every little speck of dust, however small; and so, however hard a soul may have laboured to perfect itself, once this Sun really strikes it, it sees that it is wholly unclean. Just so the water in a vessel seems quite clear when the sun is not shining upon it; but the sun shows it to be full of specks.[37]

Like the plow that tears open the bowels of the earth, pulls out the weeds with their roots, and leaves them broken and dried on the ground, this light opens up the depths of the soul and, by laying bare its tendencies, destroys them. Does not the psychoanalyst claim to cause pathological tendencies to disappear by bringing them out from the dark subconscious that shelters them? Thus this light, shining at it does on the vices rooted in the soul and on the dust of their manifestations in the acts of ordinary life, is already purifying.

Again it is this light that produces in the soul the fervent humility that creates a corresponding conviction and attitude. Proceeding from experience and from love, it not only acts upon the intellect but penetrates the whole being, subduing and forming it according to its exigencies. Sweet, strong and efficacious to bring about what it expresses, it bends the soul into an attitude of truth before God and withdraws it from the proud

[36] *Life,* xix; Peers, I, 112.
[37] *Ibid.,* xx; 129-30.

dominion of self.[38] Thus the mystical light owes to its impregnation with love a part of its purifying power; and this lets us foresee a still greater efficacy for love itself.

b. *Purifying action of love*

Saint John of the Cross assigns to love excellence in purifying.

> The soul is purged when it is illumined with this fire of loving wisdom for God never grants mystical wisdom without love, since love itself infuses it.[39]

Of love it is truly written that it "covers a multitude of sins." [40] And Jesus says to the sinner who anointed His feet in the house of Simon the Pharisee: "Thy sins are forgiven." To those who are scandalized by these words, He explains: "Her sins, many as they are, shall be forgiven her, because she has loved much." [41] Nothing can resist the invading and unifying force of love. Its peaceful reign in the soul is established by the submission of all its enemies. Not only does it take away sin, but it attacks and subdues everything that is contrary to its expansion, both capital sins and pathological tendencies.

Love exercises this purifying action in a sovereign way by the complete destruction of evil tendencies only in exceptional cases and at the times ordained by God. Ordinarily love is limited to establishing its perfect domination over the will, and to weakening evil tendencies.

No more than are physical defects, is a natural tendency as such an obstacle to divine union. Only the desires that are voluntary, or rather the deflection of the will under the impulse of desire, hinder this perfect union. The comparision with the thread that does not permit the bird to fly away has shown us that this deflection is due to a wound in the will on some partic-

[38] Cf. Vol. I, *I Want To See God,* CONTEMPLATION AND THE MYSTICAL LIFE, iv, "Humility," p. 389 ff. for what has been said on fervent humility.

[39] *Dark Night,* II, xii; Peers, I, 410.

[40] I Peter, 4:8.

[41] Luke 7:47-50.

ular point, caused by desire. The dark night of the spirit lays bare the subtle but profound wound of the will and heals it by an abundant infusion of love. In this love, the will finds new strength and rectitude, which fortify it against evil endencies and make it secure against their nefarious influence.

Saint John of the Cross, speaking of a reason why the soul journeys securely in darkness, says:

> It is derived from the fortitude by which the soul is at once inspired in these obscure and afflictive dark waters of God. For after all, though the waters be dark, they are none the less waters, and therefore they cannot but refresh and fortify the soul in that which is most needful for it, although in darkness and with affliction. For the soul immediately perceives in itself a genuine determination and an effectual desire to do naught which it understands to be an offence to God, and to omit to do naught that seems to be for His service.[42]

The firmness of this adherence to God and this ardent desire to please Him in all things, which are the essential effects of love, suffice to cut the thread of the attachment that held the will prisoner.

Nevertheless, the liberation of the will does not always make sure the disappearance of the sinful tendency. The moving confidences of the apostle are proof of this. The marvelous transformation that came about on the day of his conversion, and the extraordinary outpourings of grace that followed it, did not extinguish all the fire of evil in him. He wrote to the Romans:

> For I do not do the good that I wish, but the evil that I do not wish, that I perform. Now if I do what I do not wish, it is no longer I who do it, but the sin that dwells in me.[43]

He enlarged upon this when writing to the Corinthians:

> And lest the greatness of the revelations should puff me up, there was given me a thorn for the flesh, a messenger of Satan, to buffet me. Concerning this I thrice besought the Lord that it might leave me. And he has said to me, "My grace is sufficient for thee, for strength is made perfect in weakness." Gladly therefore I will glory in my infirmities, that the strength of Christ may dwell in me. Wherefore I

[42] *Dark Night,* Bk. II, xvi; Peers, I, 427.
[43] Rom. 7:19-20.

am satisfied, for Christ's sake, with infirmities, with insults, with hardships, with persecutions, with distresses. For when I am weak, then I am strong.[44]

Luminous texts these, which show us to what point the purification of the spirit leads, and what are its best fruits. God transforms the soul, destroys certain tendencies, always fortifies and sustains it; but He leaves us with our human nature and our status as sinners. Under the divine light which thereafter dominates, the experience, now become more painful, of the sources of sin remaining in the soul is necessary for safeguarding humility and keeping the living fountain of mercy ever active within.

Let us not then dream of a liberated humanity become angelic on the summits, nor even of that integrity of man as he came from the hands of the Creator, and in whom the preternatural gifts ensured perfect equilibrium.[45] Certainly, such a soul has found a spiritual transparency and capacity that may allow it to receive a degree of divine charity superior to that of some angels, a firmness of adherence to God that will not tolerate a voluntary unfaithfulness even in its first movements. But until death separates it, it remains attached to a body that bears the remains of sin and makes it feel sin's weight. Why should the soul be desolate because of this when the apostle

[44] 2 Cor. 12:7-10.

[45] Saint John of the Cross writes on this subject: ". . . these two portions of the soul, the spiritual and the sensual, which, in order that they may go forth to the Divine union of love, must needs first be reformed, ordered and tranquillized with respect to the sensual and to the spiritual, according to the nature of the state of innocence which was Adam's." (*Dark Night*, Bk. II, xxiv; 454).

The Saint speaks of ordering, of pacifying the desires, not of suppressing them. And even this pacification must be understood in a relative sense as long as the soul lives here below; that is, in the sense that this pacification still leaves a painful view of the tendency, sometimes movements of these desires, and even constant trials which have a redemptive fruit. The Saint has told us that the just man sins seven times a day, and that, because of the ignorance and the natural desires that remain in him (*Ascent*, Bk. I, xi; Peers, I, 50).

The pacification resides then essentially in a rectification and perfect firmness of the will as regards movements that proceed both from the sensitive part and the spiritual part of the soul.

glorified in it? Indeed, just as the wounds of the risen Christ are glorious by reason of the floods of life that flow from them, so the wounds of sin can become so by the cleansing floods of mercy that they draw down.

B. Psychological reorientation

1. WHAT IT IS

The perfect liberation of the will as regards its desires is brought to pass by a certain psychological reorientation. This psychological reorientation, an astonishing fact, almost miraculous in the psychological life of the soul, has effects that extend beyond moral purification. And so it merits an attentive study.

Ordinarily, the faculties of the soul receive their sustenance from the exterior world through the senses, which are, according to the word of John of the Cross, "the windows" of the soul onto the outside world. From the sense perceptions the intellect draws out, by abstraction, ideas on which it then works to feed itself and enlighten the will. In studying the genesis of the act of faith we have seen how faith is nourished by dogmatic truths, the formulas of which have been received through hearing; "faith depends on hearing," says the apostle, and he adds: "How are they to believe him whom they have not heard?" [46] Thus the vital movement goes from the exterior to the interior.

But when God Himself intervenes directly in the spiritual life of the soul by His lights and His impulsions, a movement is set up in the opposite direction. The source is in the inmost center of the soul; the living water springs up direct from the depths of the fountain itself, "from its source, which is God," [47] and spreads out to the exterior. This phenomenon sur-

[46] Rom. 10:14. Cf. Vol. I, *I Want To See God,* CONTEMPLATION AND THE MYSTICAL LIFE, x, "Faith and Supernatural Contemplation," p. 518 ff.

[47] IV Mansions, ii; Peers, II, 237.

prises the faculties; it both calms them and disturbs them. An adjustment takes place in the dark night of sense, which habituates the faculties to receive in peace the food that is coming to them from within. A provisory adjustment only, it no longer suffices under the deep inflowings of grace that create the dark night of the spirit. The secret and burning Wisdom that is enveloping the soul closes the faculties to all that comes to them from the outside through the senses.

> The simpler and the purer is this Divine light in its assault upon the soul, the more does it darken it, void it and annihilate it according to its particular apprehensions and affections, with regard both to things above and to things below.[48]

On the other hand, the faculties themselves no longer find food suited to their activity in what Wisdom gives them.

> As that inward wisdom is so simple, so general and so spiritual that it has not entered into the understanding enwrapped or cloaked in any form or image subject to sense, it follows that sense and imagination (as it has not entered through them nor has taken their form and colour) cannot account for it or imagine it, so as to say anything concerning it.[49]

There results from this the sufferings of the dark night of the spirit, especially that anguish from emptiness and that oppression "as if a man were suspended or held in the air so that he could not breathe." [50] The cord that is holding and afflicting the soul is divine Wisdom hidden from the faculties; the emptiness comes from the powerlessness of the faculties to grasp their object or to act in any domain.

This painful drama has been described. Hence it is useless to insist on it except to emphasize what has reference to the psychological redirection, which Saint John of the Cross sums up in these words:

> The darkness which the soul here describes relates, as we have said, to the desires and faculties, sensual, interior and spiritual, for all these are darkened in this night as to their natural light, so that, being

[48] *Dark Night,* Bk. II, viii; Peers, I, 394.
[49] *Ibid.,* xvii; 429.
[50] *Ibid.,* vi; 386.

purged in this respect, they may be illumined with respect to the supernatural. For the spiritual and the sensual desires are put to sleep and mortified, so that they can experience nothing, either Divine or human; the affections of the soul are oppressed and constrained, so that they can neither move nor find support in anything; the imagination is bound and can make no useful reflection; the memory is gone; the understanding is in darkness, unable to understand anything; and hence the will likewise is arid and constrained and all the faculties are void and useless; and in addition to all this a thick and heavy cloud is upon the soul, keeping it in affliction, and, as it were, far away from God. It is in this kind of 'darkness' that the soul says here it travelled 'securely.' [51]

Where is the soul going, groping thus in the darkness? [52]

As it has never experienced that new feeling which drives it forth and dazzles it and makes it depart recklessly from its former way of life, it thinks itself to be losing ground rather than gaining and progressing, since it sees that it is losing with respect to that which it knew and enjoyed.[53]

This soul is now, as it were, undergoing a cure, in order that it may regain its health—its health being God Himself. . . .

In such a way does this dark night of contemplation absorb and immerse the soul in itself, and so near does it bring the soul to God, that it protects and delivers it from all that is not God.[54]

These statements announce the triumph of God's action in the soul by the elimination of all that formerly came to it through the senses. Apropos of the memory, the Saint explains what happens in the soul in this higher state:

When it has the habit of union, which is a supernatural state, memory and the other faculties fail it completely in their natural functions, and pass beyond their natural limitations, even to God, Who is supernatural. And thus, when the memory is transformed in God, it cannot receive impressions of forms or kinds of knowledge. Wherefore the functions of the memory and of the other faculties in this state are all Divine; for, when at last God possesses the faculties and has become the entire master of them, through their transformation into Himself, it is He Himself Who moves and commands them divinely, according to His Divine Spirit and will; and the result of this is that the operations of the soul are not distinct, but all that it

[51] *Ibid.*, xvi; 421.
[52] *Ibid.*; 424.
[53] *Ibid.*
[54] *Ibid.*; 425.

does is of God, and its operations are Divine, so that, even as Saint Paul says, he that is joined unto God becomes one spirit with Him.[55]

The soul now receives light and movement only from God; of the two contrary currents, coming one from the outside the other from within, which existed at the beginning of the mystical life, there is now only the latter.

Compared to the normal psychological life of man, this new state causes a veritable reorientation of the soul to appear. It is no longer turned toward the senses, its windows open on the external world, there to find its food. It is attentive solely to God, the living fountain springing up in its depths and as it were beyond itself.

Independent of the senses, the soul thus finds itself free from everything in them that vitiated its spiritual operation. Sense tendencies and psychoses cannot directly touch the soul itself nor the spiritual faculties; they can create organic troubles only in the senses where they are seated. As long as the soul uses the senses as receptors and instruments of action, its spiritual activity is burdened with all that encumbers them. The liberation from them that the psychological reorientation procures is a liberation from all the troubles that affect them and from the consequent functional disorders of spiritual activity. It successfully brings to completion the moral purification and, by submitting the soul to God alone, gives the soul "its health—its health being God Himself." [56]

Reorientation assures to the spiritual activity of the soul another benefit still more important: liberation with regard to all the natural operations of the faculties.

The natural faculties can offer the theological virtues only imperfect modes of acting—base and vulgar ways, says John of the Cross.[57] Comparing the passions and desires of the soul to domestics in its house, he says:

[55] *Ascent,* Bk. III, ii; Peers, I, 215.
[56] *Dark Night,* Bk. II, xvi; Peers, I, 425.
[57] *Ibid.,* iii; 378.

They invariably hinder the soul from seeking its good, since they are opposed to its going forth in freedom. These are they of whom Our Saviour speaks in the Gospel,[58] saying that they are the enemies of man.[59]

By turning the soul exclusively toward God, the psychological reorientation withdraws the spiritual activity from the influence of its enemies, the natural faculties. The theological virtues no longer have recourse to them, but receive from God Himself all that they need for their activity. The light and the movement that God assures them, causes them to find their perfect mode of exercise, exclusively theological. Under this action coming henceforth from God alone, the spiritual rebirth is made perfect.

Commenting on the text of Saint John, "*qui non ex sanguinibus, neque ex voluntate carnis, neque ex voluntate viri, sed ex Deo nati sunt.*" [60] Saint John of the Cross explains that herein is included

. . . every way and manner of judging and comprehending with the understanding. He gave power to none of these to become sons of God, but only to those that are born of God—that is, to those who, being born again through grace, and dying first of all to everything that is of the old man, are raised above themselves to the supernatural, and receive from God this rebirth and adoption, which transcends all that can be imagined. For, as Saint John himself says elsewhere: *Nisi quis renatus fuerit ex aqua, et Spiritu Sancto, no potest videre regnum Dei.*[61] This signifies: He that is not born again in the Holy Spirit will not be able to see this kingdom of God, which is that state of perfection.[62]

Complete moral purification, freedom from all enemies, spiritual rebirth, a turning to God alone, all these benefits of the psychological reorientation display their fruits in the new relations of the soul with God, that is, in the new mode of acting of the theological virtues. With Saint John of the Cross let us admire all this more closely.

[58] Matt. 10:36.
[59] *Dark Night,* Bk. II, xiv; Peers, I, 419.
[60] John 1:13.
[61] John 3:5.
[62] *Ascent,* Bk. II, iv; Peers, I, 77.

2. EFFECT ON THE ACTIVITY OF THE THEOLOGICAL VIRTUES

In his symbolic language, Saint John of the Cross compares the three theological virtues to a livery made up of three garments of different colors, which the soul puts on to gain the graces of Christ, its Spouse:

> The soul, then, touched with the love of Christ the Spouse, and longing to attain to His grace and gain His goodwill, goes forth here disguised with that disguise which most vividly represents the affections of its spirit and which will protect it most securely on its journey from its adversaries and enemies, which are the devil, the world and the flesh. Thus the livery which it wears is of three chief colours—white, green and purple—denoting the three theological virtues, faith, hope and charity.[63]

And farther on, the Saint enriches this description. He writes:

> This, then, is the disguise which the soul says that it wears in the night of faith, upon this secret ladder, and these are its three colours. They constitute a most fit preparation for the union of the soul with God, according to its three faculties, which are understanding, memory and will.[64]

In this symbolism of the three colors, Saint John of the Cross sets before us a whole spiritual panorama. In striking parallels, he points out the relations of the theological virtues to the faculties of the soul and to the enemies to be overcome. Thus with large strokes he determines the development of mystical asceticism required by the theological virtues for ascent to the summits of divine union. It gives a synthesis of the essential points of his doctrine with luminous precision:

> Faith engrafted in the understanding protects the soul from the devil.
> Hope engrafted in the memory protects it from the world.
> Charity engrafted in the will protects it from the flesh.

We can be still more precise:

> Faith, understanding, obedience, ruses of the devil;
> hope, memory, poverty, creatures;
> charity, will, virginity, movements of the flesh and of the heart.

[63] *Dark Night,* Bk. II, xxi; 442.
[64] *Ibid.;* 445.

It is very useful to have grasped in a synthetic chart the relations existing among these different realities, if one is to carry on the combats of the spiritual life with a logic that is efficacious, because founded in reason.

Here, the Saint limits himself to recalling a doctrine more fully set forth elsewhere. The words are full of meaning. They show us how, under the apparent imprecision of its symbols and terms, symbolic language can be rich in light and savor. The Saint writes:

> Faith is an inward tunic of a whiteness so pure that it completely dazzles the eyes of the understanding. And thus, when the soul journeys in its vestment of faith, the devil can neither see it nor succeed in harming it. . . .
>
> It is clear that Saint Peter could find no better protection than faith to save him from the devil, when he said: *Cui resistite fortes in fide.*[65] . . . For without it, as the Apostle says, it is impossible to please God,[66] and with it, it is impossible to fail to please Him. For He Himself says through a prophet: *Sponsabo te mihi in fide.*[67] Which is as much as to say: If thou desirest, O soul, to be united and betrothed to Me, thou must come inwardly clad in faith.[68]

Clad in the white garment of faith the soul has passed through the purifying obscurity of the dark night, protected from anything that might tarnish it from either above or below. Now it has arrived at its actual perfection, in which state it depends only on the word of God. Now it can in truth say with David: *"Propter verba labiorum tuorum ego custodivi vias tuas,"* that is, by the words of thy lips I kept hard ways.[69]

The developments on hope are also of a rich sobriety, giving the whole doctrine on this virtue:

> Next, over this white tunic of faith the soul now puts on the second colour, which is a green vestment. By this, as we said, is signified the virtue of hope. . . . This green colour of living hope in God gives the soul such ardour and courage and aspiration to the things of eternal life that, by comparison with what it hopes for therein, all things of

[65] II Peter 5:9.
[66] Heb. 11:6.
[67] Osee 2:20.
[68] *Dark Night,* Bk. II, xxi; Peers, I, 442-3.
[69] Ps. 16:4.

the world seem to it to be, as in truth they are, dry and faded and dead and nothing worth. . . .

And thus, in this green livery and disguise, the soul journeys in complete security from this second enemy, which is the world. For Saint Paul speaks of hope as the helmet of salvation[70]—that is, a piece of armour that protects the whole head, and covers it so that there remains uncovered only a visor through which it may look.[71]

The portrait of the spiritual warrior is picturesque. We have before us a medieval knight equipped with the full defensive armor of Saint Paul—the shield of faith and the helmet of hope—protecting all the senses of the head.

It has a visor, however, which the soul is permitted to use so that its eyes may look upward, but nowhere else; for this is the function which hope habitually performs in the soul, namely, the directing of its eyes upwards to look at God alone, even as David declared that his eyes were directed, when he said:[72] *Oculi mei semper ad Dominum* [My eyes are ever toward the Lord.][73]

Let us not forget that if

. . . faith voids and darkens the understanding as to all its natural intelligence . . . hope voids and withdraws the memory from all creature possessions.[74]

But the most precious garment is incontestably the third,

. . . which is a splendid garment of purple. By this is denoted the third virtue, which is charity. This not only adds grace to the other two colours, but causes the soul to rise to so lofty a point that it is brought near to God.[75]

In elevated language the Saint praises charity, the virtue that assures to all the others strength, beauty, and life.

Without charity no virtue has grace before God. This is the purple which is spoken of in the Songs,[76] upon which God reclines. Clad in this purple livery the soul journeys when (as has been explained above in the first stanza) it goes forth from itself in the dark night, and

[70] I Thess. 5:8.
[71] *Dark Night*, Bk. II, xxi; 443-4.
[72] Ps. 24:15.
[73] *Dark Night, ibid*; 444.
[74] *Ibid.*; 445.
[75] *Ibid.*
[76] *Cant.* 3:10.

from all things created . . . to the perfect union of love of God, its beloved salvation.[77]

This virtue purifies the will and protects the soul against its third enemy, which is the flesh:

For where there is true love of God there enters neither love of self nor that of the things of self.[78]

Freed from all enemies, from the roots of sin that vitiated their activity, and from the natural operations of the faculties that kept them bound to a lower, imperfect way of acting, the theological virtues, now open to God's influence alone, have found with their perfect mode of acting their full efficiency in God, their object and their motive. The moral purification and psychological reorientation, fruits of the dark night of the spirit, have brought the virtues to this perfection. Now with perfected instruments and a perfect activity, the soul must reach the goal. And so Saint John of the Cross can conclude:

To have succeeded in thus clothing itself and persevering until it should obtain the end and aspiration which it had so much desired, which was the union of love, was a great and happy chance, wherefore in this line the soul also says:

Oh, happy chance! [79]

The dark night is indeed an immediate preparation for this perfect loving union with God.

C. Triumph of loving wisdom

Unimpeded by all the obstacles that hindered her advance and her action, loving Wisdom now triumphs in the soul and there realizes her desires. From now on we shall have only to study the successive phases of this triumph, which will go on gathering strength until the beatific vision. Following Saint John of the Cross, let us here point out some general traits of

[77] *Dark Night,* Bk. II, xxi; Peers, I, 445.
[78] *Ibid.*
[79] *Ibid.;* 446.

the reign of Wisdom. This will entail repetitions. But is there not need to repeat many times those things of divine love that yield their riches and depth only to the persevering contemplative gaze?

1. LIGHT AND LOVE

The triumph of loving Wisdom shows itself by diverse and successive manifestations of light and of love, for

> . . . this dark night of contemplation consists of divine light and love, just as fire contains light and heat.[80]

What we said about the manifestations of light and love proper to the dark night of sense and the large part played by temperament in the diversity of these manifestations can still be applied in these higher regions.[81] But it has less bearing. God's action in the soul, having become much more profound, is less indeterminate and leaves less freedom to the faculties to show the nature of their reactions. The faculties do not, as formerly, envelop the divine gift to taste it; they are dominated and inebriated by the effects of the divine touch in the depths of the soul.

Saint John of the Cross attributes the diversity of these manifestations to the passive manner in which the soul receives them. He writes:

> From what we have said it may here be inferred how in these spiritual blessings, which are passively infused by God into the soul, the will may very well love even though the understanding understand not; and similarly the understanding may understand and the will love not.[82]

That is, the difference in the manifestations is in the first place ordained by the divine good pleasure. After saying that at times the dark night of contemplation leaves the understanding in darkness, and at other times enlightens it but leaves the will in aridity, the Saint adds:

[80] *Ibid.*, xii; 412.
[81] *Supra,* UP TO UNION OF THE WILL, ii: "God as Light and God as Love."
[82] *Dark Night;* 412.

> . . . (as it is also true that the heat of the fire can be received without the light being seen, and also the light of it can be seen without the reception of heat); and this is wrought by the Lord, Who infuses as He wills.[83]

This principle applies in full force when the soul is completely subdued, purified, and made supple by loving Wisdom. The Saint's commentaries in the *Spiritual Canticle* and the *Living Flame* repeat this truth and prove it.[84]

But meanwhile, until the purification is ended, the diversity of the manifestations can be explained at least in part by the degree of purification already realized. The soul receives this loving contemplation after its own manner "in a very limited way and with great pain." [85] As the Saint explains:

> In the beginning, when this spiritual purgation commences, all this Divine fire is used in drying up and making ready the wood (which is the soul) rather than in giving it heat.[86]

The soul does not feel the flame of love; it receives nevertheless the precious gift of a very elevated reverent love.

> At the beginning, when this spiritual night commences, this enkindling of love is not felt, because this fire of love has not begun to take a hold, God gives the soul, in place of it, an estimative love of Himself so great that, as we have said, the greatest sufferings and trials of which it is conscious in this night are the anguished thoughts that it has lost God and the fears that He has abandoned it.[87]

[83] *Ibid.;* 412-3.

[84] Cf. *Spiritual Canticle,* st. xvii; Peers, II, 96 ff.; *Living Flame,* st. iii; Peers, III, 145 ff.

In these regions loving Wisdom commands totally as absolute mistress; everything must be attributed directly to her. Yet, we know that Wisdom governs beings with sovereign delicacy, respecting the nature and the temperament that she herself has given them and prepared for the realization of her designs. She disposes all things mightily and sweetly from beginning to end. She seems to break and annihilate only to purify, and in reality because she is constantly building according to her plan which is always the same from beginning to end. Hence the action that proceeds from her will harmonize with the temperament that she herself has prepared for the end that she has set. These thoughts will become clearer when we consider the soul transformed and adapted to God's design.

[85] *Dark Night,* Bk. II, xii; Peers, I, 411.

[86] *Ibid.;* 411-2.

[87] *Ibid.;* 414.

Reverent love is a light proceeding from the gift of understanding and of knowledge. But now there begin to appear the flames of love:

> As time goes on, the fire begins to give heat to the soul, and the soul then very commonly feels this enkindling and heat of love. Further, as the understanding is being more and more purged by means of this darkness, it sometimes comes to pass that this mystical and loving theology, as well as enkindling the will, strikes and illumines the other faculty also—that of the understanding—with a certain Divine light and knowledge, so delectably and delicately that it aids the will to conceive a marvellous fervour, and, without any action of its own, there burns in it this Divine fire of love, in living flames, so that it now appears to the soul a living fire.[88]
>
> This enkindling of love, which accompanies the union of these two faculties, the understanding and the will, which are here united, is for the soul a thing of great richness and delight.[89]

This delight, coming from "a certain touch of the Divinity," is a prelude to the feasts that Wisdom will celebrate in the faculties to affirm her profound triumphs in the substance of the soul.

Saint Teresa has the same experiences in this period of the spiritual life. While in an almost complete powerlessness of the faculties, she knew the marvelous efficacy of that reverent love which is in no way felt. She writes:

> At other times my soul is troubled by what I should call a kind of foolishness: I seem to be doing neither good nor evil, but to be following the crowd, as they say, without experiencing either suffering or bliss. I care not whether I live or die, nor whether I experience pleasure or pain: I seem to feel nothing. The soul appears to me to be like a little ass, feeding and sustaining its life by means of the food which is given it and which it eats almost unconsciously. For the soul in this state cannot do otherwise than feed on some of God's great favours; it does not mind living this miserable life and bears its existence with equanimity, but it is quite unconscious of any motions or effects which might help it to understand its condition.[90]

Saint Teresa is unique for the penetrating finesse of her analyses, the exquisite grace and precision of her comparisons.

[88] *Ibid.;* 412.
[89] *Ibid.*
[90] *Life,* xxx; Peers, I, 202.

Now she too discovers within her soul the burning manifestations of infused love:

> It reminds me of little springs which I have seen gushing up and which keep on incessantly stirring up the sand all around them. This, I think, is a very lifelike illustration or comparison to apply to souls which attain to this state. Love is continually bubbling up in them and thinking of the things it will do: it cannot remain where it is, just as the spring-water seems unable to remain in the earth, but issues forth from it. Just so, as a general rule, is it with the soul: such is the love it has that it can find no rest, nor can it contain itself, and it has already saturated the earth around. It would like others to drink of its love, since it has itself no lack of it, so that they might help it to praise God. Oh, how often do I remember the living water of which the Lord spoke to the woman of Samaria! I am so fond of that Gospel. . . .
>
> This love is also like a great fire, which has always to be fed lest it should go out.[91]

The little donkey that goes on feeding, the spring that keeps bubbling up and stirring up the sand around it, the fire that burns, these show us the external effects of the triumph of loving Wisdom in this period when the triumph is not fully secure. Beyond these manifestations that touch upon the senses, there are others deeper still, more constant also and more characteristic of God's domination finally established in the soul. We shall study them later in detail and mention them now but briefly.

2. TRIUMPH OF LOVE

The Wisdom that triumphs is loving Wisdom. Her essential work consists in communicating love. The apostle Saint Paul emphasizes this when he says: "The charity of God is poured forth in our hearts by the Holy Spirit who has been given to us." [92] Charity is the great supernatural riches; to it alone can one cleave, for all the rest passes away, even faith and hope. Charity alone remains.[93] The apostle extols the excellence of

[91] *Ibid.;* 202-3.
[92] Rom. 5:5.
[93] I Cor. 13:8.

divine charity and its preeminence. Saint John of the Cross writes:

> The purer and the more refined in faith is the soul, the more it has of the infused charity of God; and the more charity it has, the more is it illumined and the more gifts of the Holy Spirit are communicated to it, for charity is the cause and the means whereby they are communicated to it.[94]

Charity is the only perfect gift here below. All the others flow from it and have value through it alone. This fact appears in full light on the summits that we are approaching. There charity reigns and works in the soul. The other gifts are its fruits, or at least are less than it. From it even light proceeds without ever attaining the perfection of the charity that causes it to shine forth. In other words, Wisdom triumphs fully here below only through love. Let us consider a few traits of this triumph of charity.

a. *A love high in quality*

The triumph of Wisdom is perfect only because it infuses into the soul a charity of excellent quality. We have already many times repeated the testimony of our masters, namely, that love is made perfect not by its intensity nor by its external manifestations, but by its quality. Symbolically this quality is expressed by the depth where it resides—the depth bespeaking the soul's detachment from what is human, the exclusiveness of God's action within it, and its high spiritual capacity for receiving God's most elevated gifts.

In the regions to which we have come, the soul is completely purified and detached. It has found an interior desert, a solitude where it belongs henceforth to God alone.

Speaking of favors that are granted to the soul in concealment, Saint John of the Cross says:

> The soul is wont, during some of them, and without knowing how this comes to pass, to see itself so far withdrawn and separated according to the higher and spiritual part, from the sensual and lower por-

[94] *Ascent,* Bk. II, xxix; Peers, I, 198.

tion, that it recognizes in itself two parts so distinct from each other that it believes that the one has naught to do with the other, but that the one is very remote and far withdrawn from the other. And in reality, in a certain way, this is so; for the operation is now wholly spiritual, and the soul receives no communication in its sensual part.[95]

So marked a separation tells us the perfect purity with which God's action is received. The soul experiences such a separation as a fruit of its reorientation toward God. The soul sees that it has been carried far away from every creature:

> It considers itself as having been placed in a most profound and vast retreat, to which no human creature can attain, such as an immense desert, which nowhere has any boundary, a desert the more delectable, pleasant and lovely for its secrecy, vastness and solitude, wherein, the more the soul is raised up above all temporal creatures, the more deeply does it find itself hidden.[96]

This vast solitude is the spiritual depth of the soul where, even beyond the faculties, the soul passively receives the inflowing of God's love. Again Saint John of the Cross relates:

> This passive love does not now directly strike the will, for the will is free, and this enkindling of love is a passion of love rather than the free act of the will; for this heat of love strikes the substance of the soul and thus moves the affections passively. And so this is called passion of love rather than a free act of the will, an act of the will being so called only in so far as it is free.[97]

Thus loving Wisdom flows "down from God through the first hierarchies [of angels] even to the last, and thence to men":[98] the infusions of love become more and more ardent until they are produced by the very touch of God. Wisdom produces a living fire of love that accompanies the union of the understanding and the will. The Saint says of it:

> It is a certain touch of the Divinity and is already the beginning of the perfection of the union of love for which it hopes.[99]

[95] *Dark Night*, Bk. II, xxiii; Peers, I, 453.
[96] *Ibid.*, xvii; 430-1.
[97] *Ibid.*, xii; 414.
[98] *Ibid.*; 410.
[99] *Ibid.*; 412.

When the transformation of love is complete, there will be those delicate touches of the Word which "subtly penetrate the substance of the soul, touching it wholly." [100]

For the moment it suffices to have lifted the veil that conceals from us these mysterious regions and God's working in them, to appreciate the quality of the love that flows into them and the purity in which it is there received.

b. *Unifying effects of love*

The proper and essential effect of charity is to unite and transform. It is more than a bond. It brings about a mutual compenetration of the two beings that it unites, thus producing in them a certain likeness and identity. The supernatural charity which is poured out by God into our souls is a participation in the divine life and makes us children of God. It is the gift of God making us His by adoption.

Once charity has purified and conquered the soul and drawn it away from creatures, it meets no more obstacles. Its unifying and transforming power can be unfolded with the full efficacy that the divine will gives it. Hence it unites "the two wills—namely that of the soul and that of God" so that they are conformed together and "there is naught in the one that is repugnant to the other." [101]

But since its action is localized in the substance of the soul, it effects there what Saint John of the Cross calls a "substantial union." [102] But this union is further a transformation of the soul through charity, and hence we are speaking "not of this substantial union which is continually being wrought, but of the union and transformation of the soul with God." [103] It is a union of likeness that comes from love, hence its name, the union of likeness.

These terms tell us that love in these regions causes us per-

[100] *Living Flame,* st. ii; Peers, III, 43.
[101] *Ascent,* II, v; Peers, I, 76.
[102] *Ibid.*
[103] *Ibid.;* 75.

fectly to realize our supernatural vocation. Its unifying and transforming power brings us to perfect rebirth and gives us full divine filiation, transforming us from glory to glory unto likeness with the Word. It places us in Him in the bosom of the Holy Trinity, causing us to participate in all His operations. This transforming power secures for charity primacy over all the other virtues and renders it supremely desirable. Compared to it and its transforming power, the other gifts of God are only means or fruits. And if these means are to be efficacious, if the fruits are to be delightful or brilliant as are the splendors of union, they must remain in an attitude of dependence as regards charity. The apostle says:

> Strive after the greater gifts. And I point out to you a yet more excellent way . . . aim at charity.[104]

It is of sovereign importance to practise charity, insists Saint John of the Cross, because it is love that works the transformation of the soul in God.[105]

c. *Dynamism of this love*

The transformation having been wrought, that is, the faculties being now purified and perfectly submissive to love's dominion, full liberty is henceforth assured for the dynamism of love. For love is essentially dynamic. *Bonum diffusivum sui.* It is the good communicating itself, always in movement to give itself. It is a participation in the life of God. To come to a stop would be to destroy itself and to die. Its life is in the movement that the constant gift of itself implies.

What is this movement? It is that of the Son of God, of Christ Jesus. With Him in the bosom of the Holy Trinity, love is borne along toward the Father to be continually renewed under the action of His paternity. Thence it descends again to all that it has conquered and captivated, the substance of the soul, its faculties and sense powers, to pour out on them new

[104] I Cor. 12:31 and 14:1.
[105] *Ascent,* Bk. I, iv; Peers, I, 24 ff.

treasures drawn from God. The soul and its faculties henceforth possess only what comes to them through the floods of that love coming down from the Father and weighted with the perfect gifts of God.

This filial love together with that of Jesus descends again over the world and souls. The Love of the Word, which is the Spirit of Love, builds up the Church, the mystical body of Christ. The transformation of love gives over the soul with all its energies to the impulse of this Spirit, and consequently to the realization of the work He has undertaken. In fact, the Spirit of Love takes as collaborators the souls He has conquered.

What will the captivated soul do? What the Spirit of Love requires of it: prayer, immolation, activity. All at the same time, or this or that, following the will of Him who has become its Master, and the impulse of the Spirit. It has no preference, no will, except to be docile to the Beloved and to fulfill the whole task that the Spirit of Love wants done through it.

Will this task be spiritual or material, active or contemplative; will it take the soul to its own depths, there to taste God, or to the extremities of the earth to spend itself? These different movements are for it now only external forms to which it has become indifferent, for it is occupied only with loving. This love is not a resting, but rather a giving of self to the Beloved to take on His sentiments, His thoughts, His desires, to imitate all His attitudes and His deeds, to let oneself be carried away by Him in all His movements, and all His desires. Where could the soul finds Him elsewhere than there where He wants it to be and Himself transports it? To be awaiting an opportunity to taste His love and see Him more closely in a restful intimacy would be actually to lose both His touch and Himself by resuming one's independence. If love would satisfy its desire for ever closer union, it must follow its Beloved wherever He leads it. Only that can be called true loving, and indicates the perfect triumph of love.

d. *Peace and sweetness*

The perfection of this triumph has for its sign peace and sweetness. Formerly the dynamism of love was expressed by a certain violence in the face of an obstacle that still offered resistance, and an impetuosity when the obstacle gave way. Now every obstacle within has fallen. The external ones are overcome by silent patience which is an overflow from love. Love has become an old wine; the lees are settled and the fermentation has ceased; it is sweet, delectable, and strong.[106]

Such in broad lines is the triumph that the dark night of the spirit assures to love. There remains only to mark out more precisely each trait in the different stages that we are going to traverse.

3. THE EXPANSION OF LIGHT

Light is one of the most precious fruits of transforming love. Saint John of the Cross writes:

> This is naught else but His illumination of the understanding with supernatural light, so that it is no more a human understanding but becomes Divine through union with the Divine. In the same way the will is informed with Divine love, so that it is a will that is now no less than Divine, nor does it love otherwise than divinely.[107]

Actually, the light that transforms the understanding and the love that enflames the will both spring from a deeper source, the transformation of love that has been wrought in the substance of the soul. In these regions light proceeds from the connaturality that love creates. Thus light is a fruit of love. Light will regain the ascendency over love only in the beatific vision, when the *lumen gloriae,* the light of glory, will allow us to see God as He is and, consequently, to participate in the operations of God's intimate life in the realm of intellect where they unfold.

[106] *Spiritual Canticle,* st. xvi; Peers, II, 94.
[107] *Dark Night,* Bk. II, xiii; Peers, I, 418.

The light that proceeds from love is most excellent. It bears the mark and the privileges of its divine origin.

a. *The light is hidden*

Its first characteristic is to be hidden, to arise from the darkness and be enveloped by it.

Faith, which leads us to God, reveals Him to us only obscurely. Obscurity is one of its essential traits and cannot be dispelled here below. This obscurity comes from the imperfection of our instrument of knowing; but we assign it to God Himself, and we say with the Psalmist:

> . . . darkness was under his feet.
> And he ascended upon the cherubim, and he flew: he flew upon the wings of the winds.
> And he made darkness his covert, his pavilion round about him: dark waters in the clouds of the air.[108]

Saint John of the Cross, commenting this text, says:

> By his saying that He set darkness beneath His feet, and that He took the darkness for a hiding-place, and that His tabernacle round about Him was in the dark water, is denoted the obscurity of the faith wherein He is concealed.[109]

Even in His highest manifestations, God does not come out from the darkness. Again the Saint writes:

> When Solomon had completed the building of the Temple, God came down in darkness and filled the Temple so that the children of Israel could not see; whereupon Solomon spake and said: [110] 'The Lord hath promised that He will dwell in darkness.' [111]

Likewise God appeared to Moses on the Mount in a dark cloud. Whenever God has made solemn apparitions, He has shown Himself in a dark cloud. We see this again in the book of Job who tells us that God spoke to him from the darkness of the air.[112] This darkness signifies the obscurity of faith in

[108] Psalms 17:10.
[109] *Ascent,* Bk. II, viii; Peers, I, 93.
[110] III Kings 8:12.
[111] *Ascent,* Bk. II, viii; 94.
[112] Job 38:1; 60:1.

which the divinity envelops itself so as to communicate with the soul.[113]

The light that living faith caused to shine out from the darkness was, itself, only darkness for the soul before its purification. Now it has progressively become as the light of dawn, bathed in a semi-darkness that it does not dispel.

Of the loftiest lights that the soul can receive, for example substantial knowledge, Saint John of the Cross says:

> Substance of understanding is given to it, stripped of accidents and imaginary forms, for it is given to the understanding that is called by philosophers 'passive' or 'possible,' because it received it passively, doing naught on its own behalf; . . . although it is free from accidents, it is not for that reason clear, but rather it is dark, for it is contemplation, which, as Saint Dionysius says, is in this life a ray of darkness.[114]

Extraordinary visions themselves, a trail of light in the night, luminous areas that suddenly light up on the fringe of the darkness with which the infinite is clothed, allow some of its hidden marvels to be seen, but they disclose more especially the depths of its mystery. Hence there is in them more of darkness than of light; they would not be divine if this were not so, for Saint John of the Cross says again:

> If we speak of the supernatural (in so far as is possible in this life of our ordinary faculties), the understanding in its bodily prison has no preparation or capacity for receiving the clear knowledge of God; for such knowledge belongs not to this state, and we must either die or remain without receiving it. Wherefore Moses, when he entreated God for this clear knowledge, was told by God that he would be unable to see Him, in these words: [115] 'No man shall see me and remain alive.' Wherefore Saint John says: [116] 'No man hath seen God at any time.' [117]

Like the soldiers of Gideon, the soul carries in its hand a lighted lamp, but hidden in a pitcher. Only when the pitcher is broken will the light appear.[118]

[113] *Ascent, ibid.*
[114] *Spiritual Canticle,* st. xiii; Peers, 79-80.
[115] Exod. 33:20.
[116] John 1:18.
[117] *Ascent,* Bk. II, vii; Peers, I, 90.
[118] *Ibid.,* ix; 94.

b. *It springs from experience*

The ray of darkness, or knowledge of God by negation, is not the fruit of intellectual work; it is "communicated and infused into the soul through love."[119] Since this wisdom comes to the soul not from the outside through the senses but from an inner experience of love; it is a new mode of knowledge.

> It [the soul] is like one who sees something never seen before, whereof he has not even seen the like; although he might understand its nature and have experience of it, he would be unable to give it a name.[120]

The soul is surprised and happy to find within it this inward wisdom so simple, general, spiritual, full of love, so tranquil, solitary, peaceful, sweet, inebriating, arising from the depths of the soul and from all the powers that love has transformed and penetrated.

Inasmuch as it is the fruit of divine connaturality wrought by love in the very substance of the soul, the wisdom of this contemplation is properly speaking "the language of God to the soul, addressed by pure spirit to pure spirit," [121] possessing all the riches of knowledge that result from the divine touch.

Its greatest riches lie in its obscurity. The proper virtue and excellence of this ray of darkness consist in allowing one to find in the delightful experience of the mystery the transcendence of the Being hidden in the depth of darkness. And so the soul desires only to be more engulfed in the dark waters:

> Well protected is the soul in these dark waters, when it is close to God. For, as these waters serve as a tabernacle and dwelling-place for God Himself, they will serve the soul in the same way and for a perfect protection and security.[122]

It longs to be ever more profoundly hidden in the secret of the Face of God and to enter into His tabernacle.[123]

[119] *Dark Night,* Bk. II, xvii; Peers, I, 428.
[120] *Ibid.;* 429.
[121] *Ibid;* 430.
[122] *Ibid.,* xvi; 426.
[123] Cf. Ps. 30:21: "Thou shalt hide them in the secret of thy face from the disturbance of men. Thou shalt protect them in thy tabernacle from the contradiction of tongues."

The simplicity of this knowledge is such that often the soul will be able to say nothing of it except the peace and the joy that it brings. It will be able to describe it abundantly when particular favors and delights supply it with sensible forms which do not escape formulation, at least a symbolic one.[124]

c. *It discovers the divine presence*

Saint John of the Cross points out that the soul discovers within itself a friendly presence in the dark night of the spirit. He writes:

> But in the midst of these dark and loving afflictions the soul feels within itself a certain companionship and strength, which bears it company and greatly strengthens it.[125]

This friendly presence is something new and is characteristic of this period. Previously the soul experienced the upsurge of living water in its faculties, especially in the will; the source of it was profound and far away. A deepening has taken place. God's action now is in the very soul. There are substantial touches; God Himself speaks to the soul the language of pure spirit to pure spirit.

These touches give an experience of the very source of the Being from which they issue. There is no question of a vision, either imaginary or intellectual, but of a purified spirit's perception. This perception, aided by the dogmas of faith, will become more and more clear and substantial in each stage of the ascent until it becomes almost constant; it constitutes a sign of complete transformation. With this perception of the divine Presence it seems we must connect the perception of the devil's presence of which Saint John of the Cross speaks at the end of the *Dark Night of the Soul*.[126] Not that the devil can touch the substance of the soul; these touches are reserved to God alone and "neither angel nor devil can attain to an understand-

[124] *Dark Night*, Bk. II, xvii; 430.
[125] *Ibid.*, xi; 409.
[126] *Ibid.*, xxiii; 450-52.

ing of that which comes to pass." [127] The devil cannot even imitate these spiritual communications which have, as such, neither form nor figure. But,

> . . . in order to attack the soul, in the same way as that wherein it is being visited, his fearful spirit presents a similar vision in order to attack and destroy spiritual things by spiritual.[128]

Thus the devil profits by the greater refinement of the soul's spiritual sense and its experience to make it perceive His presence; and this produces in it "a certain horror and perturbation of spirit which at times is most distressing." [129]

d. *It increases knowledge of God*

We have still to mention as a fruit of the dark night of the spirit the soul's aptitude for receiving in all purity, untarnished by the intervention of the senses, lofty spiritual knowledge concerning particular truths that God is infusing passively into the soul, this being knowledge of God Himself.[130]

This purification brings also an habitual marvelous penetration of the depths of God and even of what is hidden in men. Saint John of the Cross writes:

> It must be known that those whose spirits are purged can learn by natural means with great readiness, and some more readily than others, that which is in the inward spirit or heart, and the inclinations and talents of men, and this by outward indication, albeit very slight ones, as words, movements and other signs. For, even as the devil can do this, since he is spirit, even so likewise can the spiritual man, according to the words of the Apostle, who says: [131] *Spiritualis autem judicat omnia.* 'He that is spiritual judgeth all things.' And again he says: [132] *Spiritus enim omnia scrutatur, etiam profunda Dei.* 'The spirit searcheth all things, yea, the deep things of God.' Wherefore, although spiritual persons cannot by nature know thoughts, or things that are in the minds of others, they may well interpret them through supernatural enlightenment or by signs.[133]

[127] *Ibid.;* 452.
[128] *Ibid.;* 450.
[129] *Ibid.;* 451.
[130] Cf. *infra,* ii, "Extraordinary Favors."
[131] I Cor. 2:15.
[132] *Ibid.;* 2:10.
[133] *Ascent,* Bk. II, xxvi; Peers, I, 188.

As we see, the dark night of the soul detaches and sets wondrously free all the potentialities of the spirit for receiving God's light as also for penetrating under that light all lesser realities. The soul is still a human soul but highly spiritualized.

4. STAGES OF THIS TRIUMPH OF LOVE

a. *A twofold movement: ascending and descending*

In order to appreciate love's triumph in the dark night of the spirit, we must not forget the word of Saint Teresa on which we commented when speaking of spiritual growth.[134] She writes:

> For, as I have already said—and I should not like this to be forgotten—in this life of ours the soul does not grow in the way the body does, though we speak as if it did, and growth does in fact occur. But whereas a child, after attaining to the full stature of a man, does not diminish in size so that his body becomes small again, in spiritual matters the Lord is pleased that such diminution should take place—at least, according to my own observation, for I have no other means of knowing.[135]
>
> No soul on this road is such a giant that it does not often need to become a child at the breast again. (This must never be forgotten: I may repeat it again and again, for it is of great importance.) [136]

Advances in spiritual growth have not the same fixity as do advances in physical growth. The latter present to view a material reality that seems steady. But advances in the spiritual order are less easily discernible, and when discovered, they appear fluctuating. Spiritual growth appears less in exact and stable signs than in a living rhythm which, moreover, has rather clear characteristics.

Saint John of the Cross expresses this fact in the last chapters of the *Dark Night,* by comparing loving Wisdom to a secret ladder.

> When I went forth by the secret ladder, disguised.[137]

[134] Cf. Vol. I, *I Want to See God,* PERSPECTIVES, "Spiritual Growth."
[135] *Life,* xv; Peers, I, 94.
[136] *Ibid.,* xiii; 80.
[137] *Dark Night,* Bk. II, xviii; Peers, I, 432 ff.

A twofold movement of the soul is expressed by this symbolism: an ascent and a descent in dispositions, and a continual ascending movement toward the summits of union. The first seems to take place in the actual dispositions of charity; the second, more deep, corresponds to the very growth of charity. The Saint says:

> We may also call it a ladder because, even as the ladder has those same steps in order that men may mount, it has them also that they may descend; even so is it likewise with this secret contemplation, for those same communications which it causes in the soul raise it up to God, yet humble it with respect to itself.[138]

These ups and downs express not only inner states but also a certain exterior reality. Storms follow prosperity; a period of calm seems given only to prepare for torments, which are themselves followed by an abundance of peace.

In her concrete language, Saint Teresea states:

> There come times when those whose will is so completely subjected to the will of God that they would let themselves be tortured rather than be guilty of one imperfection and die a thousand deaths rather than commit sins, find it necessary, if they are to be free from offending God, when they see themselves assaulted by temptations and persecutions, to make use of the primary weapons—that is, of prayer—and thus to recall to themselves that everything comes to an end, that there is a heaven and a hell, and other truths of the same kind.[139]

Here below the soul does not remain in the same state for long at a time, says Saint John of the Cross; it is ascending and descending continually. He adds:

> The reason for this is that, as the state of perfection, which consists in the perfect love of God and contempt for self, cannot exist unless it have these two parts, which are the knowledge of God and of oneself, the soul has of necessity to be practised first in the one and then in the other.[140]

This up and down movement is especially marked in the dark night of the spirit. It becomes less painful as the soul

[138] *Ibid.;* 433.
[139] *Life,* xv; Peers, I, 94.
[140] *Dark Night, ibid.;* 433-4.

mounts, without however disappearing until the soul finds perfect rest in divine union at the summit of the mystical ladder. Where this summit is, Saint John of the Cross will tell us.

b. *Continuous progression of habitual charity*

The ladder symbolizes also the ascent of the soul toward divine union. Evidently, this movement is the more important. The first refers only to the dispositions of love; the second has to do with the substance of the soul. The Saint writes:

> But, speaking now somewhat more substantially and properly of this ladder of secret contemplation, we shall observe that the principal characteristic of contemplation, on account of which it is here called a ladder, is that it is the science of love. This, as we have said, is an infused and loving knowledge of God, which enlightens the soul and at the same time enkindles it with love, until it is raised up step by step, even unto God its Creator. For it is love alone that unites and joins the soul with God.[141]

Since it is love that brings about union and is, consequently, the criterion of it, the ladder of ascent toward union is a ladder of love. It has ten steps. "We shall therefore distinguish them by their effects, as do Saint Bernard and Saint Thomas," the Saint tells us.[142] And in the following chapter he explains the steps by which the soul mounts, one by one, to God:

> The first step of love causes the soul to languish, and this to its advantage. . . . The second step causes the soul to seek God without ceasing. . . . The third step of the ladder of love is that which causes the soul to work and gives it fervor so that it fails not. . . . The fourth step is that whereby there is caused in the soul an habitual suffering because of the Beloved, yet without weariness. . . . The fifth step makes the soul to desire and long for God impatiently. . . . On the sixth step the soul runs swiftly to God and touches Him again and again. . . . The seventh step of this ladder makes the soul to become vehement in its boldness. . . . The eighth step of love causes the soul to seize Him and hold Him fast without letting Him go. . . . The ninth step of love makes the soul to burn with sweetness. . . . The tenth and last step of this secret ladder of love causes the soul to become wholly assimilated to God, by reason of the clear and immediate vision of God which it then possesses.[143]

141 *Ibid.;* 434.
142 *Ibid.*
143 *Ibid.,* xix and xx; 435-441.

This mystical ladder or ladder of love indicates the different degrees of love or progress in the quality of love by which the soul comes to the fullness of its grace. The essential roles of love in the ascent of the soul is thus clearly marked. The ladder leads from the first inflowings of passive love to the beatific vision. Until this end is reached, there is no halt nor rest for love. It is always in movement—conquering, enlarging, and ascending. Since it is not possible, says Saint John of the Cross,[144] to know them in themselves after a natural manner, the steps or degrees of love are distinguished by their effects.

Certainly the effects are classified in their order of excellence. The penetrating gaze of Saint John of the Cross grasps the relation between the external effects and the inner reality, namely, the love that the effects manifest. Hence it is a logical order of real progress that is thus presented.

And yet we shall not take the steps marked out by this ladder of love as the basis of our study of these last stages. Probably because we know very poorly these regions so familiar to Saint John of the Cross, these steps of love seem to us too detailed and finely shaded to be set forth in a teaching that does not want to sacrifice clarity to precisions that would still remain mysterious.

Moreover, this logical order does not ordinarily appear very clearly in the progress of souls toward the summits. Other traits are more visible—traits that the divine Mercy seems to place in relief because they correspond to His particular will for each soul and the mission with which He entrusts it. Thus in Saint Therese of the Child Jesus, who had come to Carmel to pray for sinners and priests, the last stage of transforming love before the beatific vision was to be certainly a burning love; but the sweetness, pointed out by Saint John of the Cross, was hidden under the redemptive suffering for sin borne by the Saint, giving her a special share in the death of Jesus on the cross. Thus the relative order established by divine Mercy for the

[144] *Ibid.;* 434.

realization of a particular mission replaced the logical order founded on a hierarchy of effects.

Hence we shall not attempt to study one after another each of these steps of the ladder of love. It seems to us preferable to take up the different aspects already mentioned of the triumph of love in this last period: brightening of contemplative light, transformation wrought by love, external effectiveness of this love in the Church. For each one of these aspects, or rather for each of these essential riches of love, we shall try to determine the progress up to its final perfection.

CHAPTER VII

Spiritual Betrothal and Marriage

He who loves me will be loved by my Father, and I will love him and manifest myself to him. . . . If anyone love me, he will keep my word, and my Father will love him, and we will come to him and make our abode with him.[1]

On approaching the summits of the spiritual life, Saint Teresa does not leave off calling on God for help. At the threshold of the sixth Mansions she had written:

> May He be pleased to enable me to explain something of these difficult things, which I know will be impossible unless His Majesty and the Holy Spirit guide my pen.[2]

At the seventh Mansions, her prayer becomes more urgent still:

> If it be His Majesty's will, may it please Him to guide my pen, and give me to understand how I may tell you some of the many things which there are to be said and which God reveals to every soul that He brings into this Mansion. Earnestly have I besought His Majesty.[3]

Saint Teresa at these summits thought herself incapable of putting into words her experience. Would it not seem too rash, any attempt to explain so personal an experience?

And yet the Masters of Carmel cause so simple and clear a light to shine on the summits that even though deprived of this high experience—which alone allows one to understand

[1] John 14:21, 23.
[2] V Mansions, iv; Peers, II, 268.
[3] VII Mansions, i; 329.

the details of their descriptions—one draws great profit from making the ascent in their company. To do so, is to have a cure of pure air and light. With joyful surprise we discover in their lived teaching the perfect realization of the loftiest and most simple statements of the Gospel as to the kingdom of God.

We lay store particularly by this latter aspect. The hope of so great a benefit gives us courage to follow these sublime masters of holiness up to the summits.

The first truths from the Gospel emphasized by Saint Teresa and Saint John of the Cross have reference to the twofold promise made by our Lord to His apostles after the Last Supper; we have quoted them at the head of this chapter:

> He who loves me will be loved by my Father, and I will love him and manifest myself to him.[4]

To him who loves perfectly, Jesus promises a manifestation of Himself. A precious promise, the first fulfillment of which we find in the spiritual betrothal.

> If anyone love me, he will keep my word, and my Father will love him, and we will come to him and make our abode with him.[5]

To perfect fidelity in love, God will answer with perfect love, taking definitive and complete possession of the soul, which will thus become His veritable dwelling place. This promise will have its perfect realization in spiritual marriage.

Spiritual betrothal and spiritual marriage are the terms we have used. This is the symbolism used by Saint Teresa and Saint John of the Cross to indicate and describe the two stages that they distinguish on the summits. The holy mother writes:

> You will often have heard that God betrothes Himself to souls spiritually. Blessed be His mercy, which is pleased so to humble itself! I am only making a rough comparison, but I can find no other which will better explain what I am trying to say than the Sacrament of Matrimony. The two things work differently, for in this matter which

[4] John 14:21.
[5] John 14:23.

we are treating there is nothing that is not spiritual: corporeal union is quite another thing and the spiritual joys and consolations given by the Lord are a thousand leagues removed from those experienced in marriage. It is all a union of love with love, and its operations are entirely pure, and so delicate and gentle that there is no way of describing them; but the Lord can make the soul very deeply conscious of them.[6]

The symbolism may seem daring. Nevertheless it is perfectly justified by the apostle Saint Paul, who affirms that the union of man and woman in marriage is the sign of the union of Christ and His Church and finds in this latter its grace and glory.[7]

Spiritual betrothal and spiritual marriage, these two stages will show us the divine manifestations in their highest developments and the contemplative light in its full brightness in transforming union.

A. Spiritual betrothal

Saint Teresa, in the book of her *Life* and in the sixth Mansions,[8] presents abundant teaching on the spiritual betrothal, as does Saint John of the Cross also, especially in the commentary on stanzas xii to xxvi of the *Spiritual Canticle.*[9] Their teaching here not only is convergent but has striking similitudes, even to identical expressions. In his commentary on stanza xii, where the soul accedes to the spiritual betrothal, Saint John of the Cross writes:

This would be a convenient place for treating of the different kinds of rapture and ecstasy and of other issuings forth and subtle flights of the spirit, which are accustomed to befall spiritual persons. But, since my intent is but to expound these stanzas briefly, as I promised in the prologue, these other things must remain for such as can treat them better than I. And I pass over the subject likewise because the Blessed

[6] V Mansions, iv; 264.

[7] Eph. 5:31, 32—For this reason a man shall leave his father and mother, and shall cleave to his wife; and the two shall become one flesh. This is a great mystery—I mean in reference to Christ and to the Church.

[8] *Life,* xx-xxi; Peers, I, 119-135; VI Mansions, iv-vi; Peers, II, 286-302.

[9] *Spiritual Canticle,* st. xii-xxvii; Peers, II, 66-136.

Teresa of Jesus, our mother, left notes admirably written upon these things of the spirit, the which notes I hope in God will speedily be printed and brought to light.[10]

The reference is explicit to Saint Teresea's descriptions in the book of her *Life* and probably to the book of the *Mansions*. There is a recollection also of the spiritual conversations the two Saints had and the raptures that interrupted them, in the parlor of the Convent of the Incarnation from 1571 to 1574, while Saint Teresa was prioress there and Saint John of the Cross, chaplain and confessor. Then it was that Saint Teresa was elevated to spiritual marriage after a period during which she had numerous raptures. Saint John of the Cross had probably come as yet only to spiritual betrothal, and knew its particular favors. Saint Teresa's experience was at that time more complete. It seems normal, then, that the mystical doctor should have been instructed by her on certain points, and that later in his writings he should refer to himself in this matter as a disciple. However, in his commentary on the stanzas of the *Canticle* and in the *Living Flame,* John of the Cross was to add to the Teresian descriptions very happy precisions that enable us to pick out the essential characteristics of this period.

1. IN WHAT DOES SPIRITUAL BETROTHAL CONSIST?

To this question Saint Teresa answers:

And now you are going to see what His Majesty does to confirm this betrothal, for this, as I understand it, is what happens when He bestows raptures, which carry the soul out of its senses; for if, while still in possession of its senses, the soul saw that it was so near to such great majesty, it might perhaps be unable to remain alive.[11]

In the book of her *Life,* the Saint is more precise:

The Lord gathers up the soul, just (we might say) as the clouds gather up the vapours from the earth, and raises it up till it is right out of itself (I have heard that it is in this way that the clouds or the sun gather up the vapours) and the cloud rises to Heaven and takes the soul with it, and begins to reveal to it things concerning the King-

[10] *Ibid.*, st. xii; 69.
[11] VI Mansions, iv; Peers, II, 286-7.

dom that He has prepared for it. I do not know if the comparison is an exact one, but that is the way it actually happens.

In these raptures the soul seems no longer to animate the body, and thus the natural heat of the body is felt to be very sensibly diminished: it gradually becomes colder, though conscious of the greatest sweetness and delight. No means of resistance is possible, whereas in union, where we are on our own ground, such a means exists: resistance may be painful and violent but it can almost always be effected. But with rapture, as a rule, there is no such possibility. . . . You realize, I repeat, and indeed see, that you are being carried away, you know not whither.[12]

If the soul is in the body or not while all this is happening I cannot say; I would not myself swear that the soul is in the body, nor that the body is bereft of the soul.[13]

In almost identical terms Saint John of the Cross describes this action of God carrying the soul away to its divine betrothal:

As the soul has just now desired these Divine eyes with such great yearning, even as she has just said in the foregoing stanza, the Beloved has revealed to her some rays of His greatness and divinity, as she has desired. These rays were communicated with such loftiness and such power that the soul was made to issue forth from herself in rapture and ecstasy. . . . It seemed to her that her soul was flying out of her body, which is what she desired: for this reason she begged Him to withdraw His eyes—that is, to communicate them no longer to her in the flesh, since in this wise she could neither bear them nor enjoy them as she would desire, but to communicate them to her in the flight which she was about to make from out of the flesh. . . . And that we may the better understand what flight is this, it is to be noted that, as we have said, in that visitation of the Divine Spirit the spirit of the soul is enraptured with great force, to commune with the Spirit, and abandons the body, and ceases to experience feelings and to have its actions in the body, since it has them in God. For this cause said Saint Paul, with respect to that rapture of his, that he knew not if his soul was receiving it in the body, or out of the body.[14]

Concerned with warding off counterfeits, Teresa and John of the Cross both point out that these raptures are "not like other swoons and trances, which are natural, so that their subjects return to themselves with the first touch of pain,"[15]

[12] *Life*, xx; Peers, I, 119-20.

[13] VI Mansions, v; Peers, II, 296. On this occasion the Saint poses the problem of the distinction between soul and spirit. Cf. Vol. I, *I Want to See God*, PERSPECTIVES, "Psychological Knowledge of Self," p. 35 f.

[14] *Spiritual Canticle*, st. xii; Peers, II, 66-9.

[15] *Ibid.*; 69.

weaknesses that can be produced in persons of delicate constitution. For "when a person is enraptured you can be sure that God is taking her entire soul to Himself." [16]

Saint Teresa especially considers it important to mark the differences between the raptures of the betrothal and the mystical grace of union of the fifth Mansions. Thus she carefully points out what distinguishes each stage from the preceding one, and from the progress already achieved.

Certainly, in the mystical union the soul has already had contact with God. A meeting has taken place; nevertheless, speaking of this union, the Saint says:

> It seems to me that this union has not yet reached the point of spiritual betrothal, but is rather like what happens in our earthly life when two people are about to be betrothed. There is a discussion as to whether or no they are suited to each other and are both in love; and then they meet again so that they may learn to appreciate each other better. So it is here. The contract is already drawn up and the soul has been clearly given to understand the happiness of her lot and is determined to do all the will of her Spouse in every way in which she sees that she can give Him pleasure. His Majesty, Who will know quite well if this is the case, is pleased with the soul, so He grants her this mercy, desiring that she shall get to know Him better, and that, as we may say, they shall meet together, and He shall unite her with Himself. We can compare this kind of union to a short meeting of that nature because it is over in the very shortest time.[17]

The first meeting between two persons who desire to be united gives them opportunity to know each other but does not involve any mutual engagement. The betrothal takes place in a meeting of another character that Saint Teresa is to describe.

In the mystical union there is loss of consciousness, complete suspension of the external and internal senses, hence a certain falling of the soul into darkness, a plunge into the center of itself with loss of consciousness. On regaining consciousness, the soul has the certitude of having been in God in its own center. It discovers the riches derived from this contact, but of

[16] VI Mansions, iv; Peers, II, 290.
[17] V Mansions, iv; 264-5.

the contact itself it can say nothing. In the meeting of the betrothal or rapture, the soul, says Saint Teresa,

> . . . is not deprived of its interior senses; for it is not like one who suffers a swoon or a paroxysm so that it can understand nothing either within itself or without.[18]

The soul feels itself uplifted, carried away, according to the Saint, by an irresistible force. Not only is there no loss of consciousness, but, declares Saint Teresa:

> The position, in this case, as I understand it, is that the soul has never before been so fully awake to the things of God or had such light or such knowledge of His Majesty. This may seem impossible; because, if the faculties are so completely absorbed that we might describe them as dead, and the senses are so as well, how can the soul be said to understand this secret? I cannot say, nor perhaps can any creature.[19]

Elsewhere the Saint says:

> It [rapture] is much more beneficial than union: the effects it produces are far more important and it has a great many more operations, for union gives the impression of being just the same at the beginning, in the middle and at the end, and it all happens interiorly. But the ends of these raptures are of a higher degree, and the effects they produce are both interior and exterior.[20]

In the rapture of transport of the betrothal, the soul not only has enriching contact with God, but a veritable penetration into God. Moreover, the darkness of the mystical union is replaced by a dazzling light. The soul gazes into God, eyes open. Thus it is aware of its union and discovers profound secrets of the Divine. Saint Teresa makes use of a comparison to render her teaching more living and pointed.

> You enter a private apartment in the palace of a king or a great lord (I think they call it a *camarin*), where they have an infinite variety of glassware, and earthenware, and all kinds of things, set out in such a way that you can see almost all of them as you enter. I was once taken into a room of this kind in the house of the Duchess of Alba. . . .

[18] VI Mansions, iv; 287.
[19] *Ibid.*
[20] *Life*, xx; Peers, I, 119.

When I went in I was astounded and began to wonder what all this mass of things could be used for, and then I realized that the sight of so many different things might lead one to glorify the Lord. It occurs to me now how useful an experience it was for my present purpose. Although I was there for some time, there was so much to be seen that I could not remember it all, so that I could no more recall what was in those rooms than if I had never seen them. . . .

It is just like that here. The soul becomes one with God. It is brought into this mansion of the empyrean Heaven which we must have in the depths of our souls; for it is clear that, since God dwells in them, He must have one of these Mansions. And although while the soul is in ecstasy the Lord will not always wish it to see these secrets (for it is so much absorbed in its fruition of Him that that great blessing suffices it), He is sometimes pleased that it should emerge from its absorption, and then it will at once see what there is in this room; in which case, after coming to itself, it will remember that revelation of the great things it has seen. It will not, however, be able to describe any of them, nor will its nature be able to apprehend more of the supernatural than God has been pleased to reveal to it.[21]

The powerful force that bears the soul away to these higher regions and the divine outpourings with which the soul there is favored are very different from the quiet produced by the spring of water or the divine spark of the fourth Mansions:

I think that basin of water, of which we spoke in (I believe) the fourth Mansion (but I do not remember exactly where) was being filled at that stage gently and quietly—I mean without any movement. But now this great God, Who controls the sources of the waters and forbids the sea to move beyond its bounds, has loosed the sources whence water has been coming into this basin; and with tremendous force there rises up so powerful a wave that this little ship—our soul—is lifted up on high.[22]

And the light accompanying this force has the same divine character of transcendence. Again the Saint writes:

He feels (a person enraptured) as if he has been in another world, very different from this in which we live, and has been shown a fresh light there, so much unlike any to be found in this life that, if he had been imagining it, and similar things, all his life long, it would have been impossible for him to obtain any idea of them.[23]

[21] VI Mansions, iv; Peers, II, 289.
[22] *Ibid.*, v; 293-4.
[23] *Ibid.*; 295.

He is taught many things all at once. Of this, Saint Teresa says that it is

> . . . an imaginary vision, which is seen with the eyes of the soul very much more clearly than we can ordinarily see things with the eyes of the body; and some of the revelations are communicated to it without words. If, for example, he sees any of the saints, he knows them as well as if he had spent a long time in their company.
>
> Sometimes, in addition to the things which he sees with the eyes of the soul, in intellectual vision, others are revealed to him—in particular, a host of angels, with their Lord.[24]

Extraordinary favors often accompany this higher light proper to the region at which the soul has now arrived. The first time that Saint Teresa was elevated to rapture, she heard our Lord say to her: "I will have thee converse now, not with men, but with angels" [25]—a substantial word, freeing her from all attachments to human communications. At other times, she was favored during transports or raptures with visions, intellectual or imaginary. Such favors are the luminous fringe, better perceived and inscribed in the senses, of a manifestation of God which transcends them.

In fact, it is after spiritual betrothal that Saint Teresa places her exposition of extraordinary graces,[26] for it is in this period that they are ordinarily the most numerous and produce their greatest effects. We do not think them, however, an essential element of the betrothal. Some souls receive them in other circumstances and apart from the profound union that characterizes this meeting.

The spiritual betrothal is marked essentially by the superior quality of the union and the light in which it is concluded. This union and light are of such a nature that, according to Saint Teresa, there is no essential difference between the Mansion in which transport of the soul begins and the Mansion in which perfect union of spiritual marriage takes place. Saint Teresa

[24] *Ibid.*
[25] *Life,* xxiv; Peers, I, 155.
[26] Cf. *Life,* xxv-xxix; VI Mansions, viii-x.

says that only the Creator Himself knows the secret of what happens, she herself cannot say; and she adds:

> . . . nor can I speak of many other things that happen in this state—I mean in these two Mansions, for this and the last might be fused in one: there is no closed door to separate the one from the other. As, however, there are things in the latter Mansion which are not shown to those who have not yet reached it, I have thought it best to separate them.[27]

The remark is to be underscored: The spiritual betrothal bears more resemblance to the spiritual marriage than to the mystical union of the fifth Mansions. It introduces the soul into a higher state and adorns it with precious jewels that prepare it, immediately, for perfect union.

2. THE BETROTHAL JEWELS

Saint John of the Cross describes in fifteen stanzas of the *Spiritual Canticle* "the great gifts and jewels" that the soul receives "through union of love in the Spiritual Betrothal." [28] Saint Teresa gives several chapters of the book of her *Life* and of the *Interior Mansion* to "The jewels which the Spouse is beginning to give to His bride." [29] Let us admire for a moment these treasures.

a. *Discovery of God in divine union*

The most precious of the betrothal jewels is certainly the Word Himself as Spouse, giving Himself and manifesting Himself in more and more frequent visits. Saint John of the Cross writes:

> By this spiritual flight which we have just described is denoted a lofty estate and union of love wherein after much spiritual exercise God is wont to place the soul, which is called spiritual betrothal with the Word, the Son of God. And at the beginning, when this is done for the first time, God communicates to the soul great things concerning Himself, beautifying it with greatness and majesty, decking it with

[27] VI Mansions, iv; Peers, II, 287-8.
[28] *Spiritual Canticle,* st. xxvii; Peers, II, 133.
[29] VI Mansions, v; 297.

gifts and virtues, and clothing it with knowledge and honour of God, just as if it were a bride on the day of her betrothal.[30]

Intimate knowledge of its divine Spouse is truly the soul's most beautiful adornment, its most precious treasure, the source of all its good; it can want no other.

The Bride says that her Beloved is all these things, both in Himself and also for her; for in that which God is wont to communicate in such excesses, the soul feels and knows the truth of that saying which the holy Francis uttered, namely: 'God mine, and all things.' Wherefore, since God is all things to the soul, and the good of them all.[31]

Everything comes to the soul from its union with the Beloved. Saint John of the Cross insists so much on this truth that one might think that the soul had already arrived at spiritual marriage. "Our flowery bed," sings the bride in the fifteenth stanza; Saint John of the Cross comments:

This flowery bed is the bosom and love of the Beloved, wherein the soul, that has become the Bride, is now united; the which bed is flowery for her by reason of the union and bond which has now been made between the two, by means whereof are communicated to her the virtues, graces and gifts of the Beloved.[32]

No, this is not yet spiritual marriage. But we already know that spiritual betrothal is closely related to it, and that between these two Mansions "there is no closed door." [33] Contrary to natural espousals, which are only external meetings, spiritual espousals are visits in which manifestation and union are experienced at the same time. They are a union between God and the soul in light.

The soul becomes one with God.[34]

Manifestation is the effect of union. Saint John of the Cross explains with his customary penetration what these visits are in the depth of the soul, and how the touch of God there produces light.

[30] *Spiritual Canticle,* st. xiii; 72.
[31] *Ibid.;* 74.
[32] *Ibid.,* st. xv; 87.
[33] VI Mansions, iv; Peers, II, 287.
[34] *Ibid.;* 289.

In the commentary on stanzas thirteen and fourteen of the *Canticle,* the Saint points out among the lofty favors that souls in this state receive, some more others less, some after one manner and others after another: [35]

The whisper of the amorous breezes

By the amorous breezes are here understood the virtues and graces of the Beloved, which, by means of the said union of the Spouse, assail the soul, communicate themselves most lovingly and touch it in its substance. And by the whisper of these breezes is meant a most lofty and most delectable knowledge of God, and of His virtues, which overflows into the understanding at the touch which these virtues of God effect in the substance of the soul.[36]

The Saint goes on to explain, so that his teaching may be quite clear.

As two things are perceived in the air—namely, the touch thereof and the sound or whisper—so in this communication of the Spouse two other things are perceived—namely, feeling of delight, and knowledge. . . . The touch of the virtues of the Beloved is felt and enjoyed in the sense of touch of this soul which is in its substance; and the knowledge of these virtues of God is felt in the ear of the soul, which is in the understanding.[37]

Thus has Saint John of the Cross given us the key to the problem of the betrothal. Spiritual betrothal is a touch of God in the substance of the soul. Although this touch is as unifying as spiritual marriage, it is only a touch. By enriching the substance of the soul with manifold goods and especially with love, it produces in the soul a deep satisfaction and fills it with delight.[38] From these goods or amorous breezes produced by the divine touch in the substance of the soul, there comes a whisper which is a very lofty knowledge "derived in the understanding."

This most subtle and delicate knowledge enters with marvellous sweetness and delight into the inmost substance of the soul, which is a far greater delight than any other.[39]

[35] *Spiritual Canticle,* st. xiii; Peers, II, 73.
[36] *Ibid.;* 78.
[37] *Ibid.;* 78-9.
[38] *Ibid.;* 72.
[39] *Ibid.;* 79.

The joy that comes from this lofty knowledge is more elevated than that caused by the substantial touch, for as the Saint explains:

> The sense of hearing is more spiritual (or, to speak more exactly, comes nearer to the spiritual) than the sense of touch.[40]

And so Saint John of the Cross applies himself to analyzing this whisper of delectable knowledge:

> Substance of understanding is given to it [the soul], stripped of accidents and imaginary forms, for it is given to the understanding that is called by philosophers 'passive' or 'possible,' because it receives it passively, doing naught on its own behalf. . . .
> This Divine whisper, which enters by the ear of the soul, is not only substance which I have called that of understanding, but likewise it is the manifestation of truths concerning the Divinity and the revelation of His hidden secrets; for ordinarily, whensoever some communication of God is found in the Divine Scriptures, and is said to enter by the ear, it is found to be a manifestation of these naked truths in the understanding, or a revelation of secrets of God.[41]

Our mystical doctor takes care to distinguish this substantial knowledge from the clear and perfect knowledge had in heaven. Of the knowledge that the "whisper" communicates, he says:

> Although it is free from accidents, it is not for that reason clear, but rather it is dark, for it is contemplation, which, as Saint Dionysius says, is in this life a ray of darkness.[42]

This is lofty knowledge, together with that given by extraordinary favors in this period, constitutes the magnificent and brilliant adornment of light that the soul receives from its Spouse at its betrothal, preparing it for the perfect union of spiritual marriage. Saint John of the Cross seems unable to resign himself to dropping this subject so dear to his contemplative soul. Is it not this "whisper" that brought him in the dark night of his contemplation the greatest joys and most

[40] *Ibid.*
[41] *Ibid.;* 79-80.
[42] *Ibid.;* 80.

precious gifts? And so he dwells on it; and to sum up all his teaching, he comments on a text from the Book of Job which, he says,

> . . . is very much to the point, as confirming a great part of that which I have said of this rapture and betrothal, I will relate it here (although it may delay us a little longer).[43]

Let us too linger with the Saint, even though like him we might fear to delay too long. Here we have one of the most beautiful Scriptural applications made by Saint John of the Cross to his teaching.

> Eliphaz the Themanite, then, in the Book of Job, speaks after this manner: [44] In truth a hidden word was spoken to me, and mine ear received as it were by stealth the veins of its whisper. In the horror of the vision by night, when sleep is wont to occupy men, I was occupied by fear and trembling, and all my bones shook; and, as the spirit passed before my presence, the skin of my flesh shrank; and there came before me One Whose countenance I knew not, an image before mine eyes, and I heard a voice of a gentle breeze. In this passage is contained almost all that we have here said concerning this rapture, from the twelfth stanza, which says: 'Withdraw them, Beloved,' down to this point. For in that which Eliphaz the Themanite says, namely, that a hidden word was spoken to him, is signified that hidden thing which was given to the soul, the greatness whereof it could not suffer, so that it said: 'Withdraw them, Beloved.'
>
> In this saying that his ear received, as it were by stealth, the veins of its whisper, is signified the naked substance which, as we have said, is received by the understanding: for veins here denote inward substance, and the whisper signifies that communication and touch of the virtues from which the said substance of understanding is communicated to the understanding. And the soul here calls it a whisper, because such a communication is very gentle. . . .
>
> And he adds further that all his bones were terrified, or shaken. Which is as though he had said that they were moved and dislocated from out of their places; wherein is described the great dislocation of the bones which, as we have said, is suffered at this time. . . .
>
> The passage continues: 'There was One Whose countenance I knew not, an image before mine eyes.' This One Who he says was present was God, Who communicated Himself after the manner aforementioned. And he says that he knew not His countenance, in order to

[43] *Ibid.;* 81.
[44] Job 4:12-6.

indicate that in this communication and vision, most lofty though it be, the face and the Essence of God are neither known nor seen.[45]

This Scriptural text situates in local color the rapture of the betrothal with its exterior and interior perceptions, its inexpressible sense torment and spiritual delights that the discovery of God stirs in the soul not yet ready to receive Him.

This meeting is not simply a happy meeting with God from which the soul has returned adorned with light as a gift. The betrothal introduces the soul into a new state, which is already unitive. It has received a promise of perfect union. This promise, it too, is one of the betrothal jewels; and in certain hours, the most precious one.

b. *Exchange of promises and mutual fidelity*

Essentially, the spiritual betrothal is a promise of marriage, mutually exchanged.

In the spiritual betrothal, there is no contract. The promises may even be not explicitly spoken. Yet they are certain and very firm. They rest on reality, on a certain union of love that already exists, and that indefectibly assures mutual faithfulness.

Through the meeting for the betrothal, God has revealed the choice He has made of this soul to be His spouse. The choice is final. God manifests it by His gifts, which are to guarantee the soul's fidelity. Promises of union are exchanged; it is God who gives the love that brings it about and is now making ready for it. A divine jewel indeed is this love that God pours out upon the soul He has chosen.

Thereafter God affirms His choice by renewed visits. His hold on the soul becomes progressively more powerful; but already it makes the soul all His. God, says Saint Teresa, is taking the soul to Himself, "as she is His own property and has now become His bride."

[45] *Ibid.;* 81-3. Cf. in *Ephemerides Carmeliticae* (May 1947, pp. 5-53), published by the Faculty of Theology of the Discalced Carmelites, Rome, R. P. Gabriel de Sainte-Madeleine's penetrating and exact study of unitive contemplation produced by these substantial touches.

He will not allow her to be disturbed either by the faculties or by the senses; so He at once commands that all the doors of these Mansions shall be shut, and only the door of the Mansion in which He dwells remains open so that we may enter.[46]

Although the experience of perfect union is fleeting, the soul is thereafter God's own possession. Never will He abandon it, as Saint Teresa testifies:

It seems that Our Lord wants everyone to realize that such a person's soul is now His and that no one must touch it. People are welcome to attack her body, her honour, and her possessions, for any of these attacks will be to His Majesty's honour. But her soul they may not attack, for unless, with most blameworthy presumption, it tears itself away from its Spouse, He will protect it from the whole world, and indeed from all hell.[47]

We may recall that Saint Teresa, after the grace of mystical union in the fifth Mansions, immediately warned the soul to be on its guard against dangerous occasions, withdrawing from them; and she added that, after spiritual betrothal, the soul would be almost invulnerable:

So, Christian souls, whom the Lord has brought to this point on your journey, I beseech you, for His sake, not to be negligent, but to withdraw from occasions of sin—for even in this state the soul is not strong enough to be able to run into them safely, as it is after the betrothal has been made—that is to say, in the Mansions which we shall describe after this one. For this communication has been no more than (as we might say) one single short meeting, and the devil will take great pains about combating it and will try to hinder the betrothal. Afterwards, when he sees that the soul is completely surrendered to the Spouse, he dare not do this, for he is afraid of such a soul as that, and he knows by experience that if he attempts anything of the kind he will come out very much the loser and the soul will achieve a corresponding gain.[48]

The soul derives this firmness, which renders it thereafter invulnerable as it were and terrible to the devil, in the singular gifts with which God has favored it in this betrothal. John of the Cross says that it enjoys three things in particular:

[46] VI Mansions, iv; Peers, II, 290.
[47] *Ibid.;* 292.
[48] V Mansions, iv; 265.

> The first is knowledge of the greatness of God: the more we see of this, the more deeply we are conscious of it. The second is self-knowledge and humility at realizing how a thing like the soul, so base by comparison with One Who is the Creator of such greatness, has dared to offend Him and dares to raise its eyes to Him. The third is a supreme contempt for earthly things, save those which can be employed in the service of so great a God.[49]

In rapture, the soul has experienced God's mighty power; it has felt fear overpowered by deepest love and a strange detachment.[50] Further:

> The soul, while enraptured, is mistress of everything, and in a single hour, or in less, acquires such freedom that it cannot recognize itself. It sees clearly that this state is in no way due to itself, nor does it know who has given it so great a blessing. . . . Nobody will believe this without having had experience of it.[51]
>
> What power is that of a soul brought hither by the Lord, which can look upon everything without being ensnared by it! . . .[52]
>
> Not only does the soul perceive the cobwebs which disfigure it and its own great faults, but so bright is the sunlight that it sees every little speck of dust, however small.[53]

Among God's gifts there is not only light or a new attitude of soul, but also efficacious strength for action:

> When a soul has reached this state, it has not merely desires to serve God: His Majesty also gives it strength to carry these desires into effect. No way in which it thinks it may serve God can be set before it into which it will not fling itself; and yet it is doing nothing, because, as I say, it sees clearly that nothing is of any value save pleasing God.[54]

The soul's fidelity is now unfailing. Its gift of self is perfect.

> The soul has no desire to seek or possess any free-will, even if it so wished, and it is for this that it prays to the Lord, giving Him the keys of its will.[55]

[49] *Ibid.;* 296-7.
[50] *Life,* xx; Peers, I, 121.
[51] *Ibid.;* 128.
[52] *Ibid.*
[53] *Ibid.;* 129.
[54] *Ibid.,* xxi; 132.
[55] *Ibid.,* xx; 127.

God's captivation of the soul and the soul's response with faithfulness and love are described by Saint John of the Cross in several stanzas abounding with divine life and human poetry:

> In the inner cellar,
> Of my Beloved have I drunk,
>
> . . . .
>
> There he gave me his breast;
>
> . . . .
>
> And I gave myself to him indeed,
> Reserving nothing.[56]

The Saint comments:

> In that sweet draught of God, wherein, as we have said, the soul is immersed in God, it surrenders itself, most willingly and with great sweetness, to Him wholly, desiring to be wholly His and never again to have aught in itself that is alien from Him. . . . Inasmuch as He transforms the soul into Himself, He makes it to be wholly His and empties it of all that it possessed and that was alien from God. Wherefore the soul is indeed completely given up to God, reserving naught, not only according to its will, but also according to its works, even as God has given Himself freely to the soul. So these two wills are surrendered, satisfied and given up the one to the other, so that neither shall fail the other, as in the faithfulness and stability of a betrothal.[57]

Spiritual betrothal, then, carries with it mutual pledges and already a union of love. Thus captivated the soul gives itself completely and has no other concern than this love which envelops it and to which it surrenders itself.

And so, in the following stanza it sings:

> My soul has employed itself
> And all my possessions in his service:
>
> . . . .
>
> For now my exercise is in loving alone.[58]

With more insistence the soul repeats what it had previously said, that it no longer keeps the flock that it formerly followed.[59] Reference here is to its appetites and evil tendencies that still

[56] *Spiritual Canticle,* st. xvii-xviii; Peers, II, 96-103.
[57] *Ibid.,* st. xviii; 104.
[58] *Ibid.,* st. xix; 105.
[59] *Ibid.,* st. xvii; 96 and st. xix; 105.

asserted themselves at certain times, and from which its faithfulness and the inflowing of love have freed it.

It is thus that love has brought it into the vast solitude where love alone reigns. From this day on it will no longer be found on the "common land" or the public square where passions are stirred and fed. The Saint says:

> By 'common land' is ordinarily meant a place common to all, where people are wont to come together to have solace and recreation, and where likewise shepherds pasture their flocks.[60]

By public place is not necessarily meant here that part of the world where vices hold forth, but "the common" that the soul frequented before, that is, the milieu in which it lived, were this even a devout and religious one, in which it pursued the flock of its passions.

The soul is now lost to all worldly things and has become wholly God's.

> You will say that I am lost;
> That wandering love-stricken,
> I lost my way and was found.[61]

Does this death of the soul to the world and to its own milieu, this single occupation with loving, involve a flight to the desert? Certainly, the soul desires that complete solitude in which it finds, intense and sustaining, the repose and torment of love. And this repose must needs be assured it at least for periods of time. But if we would understand the movements of this divine love, let us follow the development of the Saint's thought. Both repose and movement, closely united, are expressed in the stanzas with their supple and harmoniously limpid flow—supple yet how strong in their delightful plentitude.

> With flowers and emeralds
> Gathered in the cool mornings
> We will make the garlands flowering in thy love
> And interwoven with one hair from my head.[62]

[60] *Ibid.*, st. xx; 109.
[61] *Ibid.;* 108.
[62] *Ibid.*, st. xxi; 111.

The Saint explains that "the flowers are the virtues of the soul and the emeralds are the gifts which it has of God." [63] Together God and the soul, with God's gifts and the virtues of the soul, weave garlands which are thus the work of their common activity, the fruit of their mutual love which cannot remain inactive. By garlands are understood good works, "all the holy souls begotten by Christ in the Church"; and by the beauteous garlands, "the halos made likewise by Christ and the Church," halos of virgins, halos of holy doctors, halos of the martyrs.[64] These garlands are all the interior and exterior works that Christ and His Church, the Spirit of love and the souls He has conquered produce in the world.

Thus at spiritual betrothal love is already fruitful, comprising as it does domination by God and union with Him. During this period in Saint Teresa's life she establishes her Reform and founds several monasteries.

We shall return to this fruitfulness of the soul under God's domination through the gifts of the Holy Spirit. For the moment we mention it simply to note that in the works the soul produces, God sees only the faithfulness and love to which they testify.

By that hair alone
Which thou regardest fluttering on my neck.[65]

This single hair, tenuous and supple, strong and stirring under the breeze of the Holy Spirit, is love "the bond of perfection," [66] which binds together the flowers of the garlands.[67] The divine Spouse sees it fluttering on the neck, which signifies fortitude, and is captivated by it. Saint John of the Cross comments:

[63] *Ibid.;* 112.
[64] *Ibid.;* 114.
[65] *Ibid.,* xxii; 115.
[66] Col. 3:14.
[67] *Spiritual Canticle,* st. xxi; 115.

Thou wert captivated

Oh, thing that art worthy of all acceptation and joy, that God should be captivated by a hair! [68]

Moreover, this could happen only because the Beloved, the royal eagle flying high over the heights, descends to our lowly love, desiring to be caught.[69]

To fidelity in love made manifest by works there is added the faithfulness shown by the eye's gaze.

And wert wounded by one of mine eyes.[70]

By the eye is here understood faith, which, thereafter purified and simple, remains steadfastly fixed on the Beloved.

And the love wherewith the Spouse is taken captive by the Bride in this singleness and fidelity that He sees in her is so intimate that, if He was taken captive by the hair of her love, by the eye of her faith His captivity is made closer, . . . and she enters into His love the more deeply.[71]

God has been attracted by the perfume of love arising from good works; He is conquered by the soul's silent and ardent gaze. This twofold fidelity of love and of faith assures the soul's victory over God. The soul obtains the perfect fulfillment of the divine promises: God's coming to the soul and His manifestation to it.

If anyone love me, he will keep my word, and my Father will love him and we will come to him and make our abode with him. . . . He who loves me will be loved by my Father and I will love him and manifest myself to him.[72]

Nevertheless, if it is to become the perfect dwelling place of God, the soul, having been purified and adorned, must be dilated and enlarged in proportion to the gift it is to receive. Anguish and great desires are to effect this final preparation. It is the last jewel of the betrothal.

[68] *Ibid.*, st. xxii; 117.
[69] *Ibid.*
[70] *Ibid.*
[71] *Ibid;* 117-8.
[72] John 14:21-3.

c. *Ardent desires and anguish*

After the grace of mystical union of the fifth Mansions the soul was bewildered by the newness of the regions in which it found itself. Saint Teresa insists at length on the restlessness of the poor little butterfly:

> To see, then, the restlessness of this little butterfly—though it has never been quieter or more at rest in its life! . . . It is not surprising, then, that, as this little butterfly feels a stranger to things of the earth, it should be seeking a new resting-place. But where will the poor little creature go? It cannot return to the place it came from, for, as has been said, however hard we try, it is not in our power to do that until God is pleased once again to grant us this favour. . . .[73]
>
> How much rest can this poor little butterfly have amid all these trials and other things that I have described? [74]

The agitation and restlessness are explained also by the complete obscurity in which union took place in that mystical grace. The discovery of the Spouse in the light of the spiritual betrothal dispels the darkness and brings comforting peace to the soul.

Saint John of the Cross explains how this appeasement is brought about:

> Now as this little dove, which is the soul, was flying on the breezes of love above the waters of the flood (namely, those her fatigues and yearnings of love which she has described up to this point) and found no rest for her foot, upon this last flight which we have described, the compassionate father Noe put forth the hand of his mercy and caught her, and brought her into the ark of his charity and love.[75]

In this blessed ark, the dove finally comes to rest:

> And upon this happy day, not only is there an end of the soul's former vehement yearnings and plaints of love, but, being adorned with the good things which I am describing, she enters into an estate of peace and delight and sweetness of love . . . since in this estate all those other things are now ended.[76]

[73] V Mansions, ii; Peers, II, 255-6.
[74] VI Mansions, iv; 286.
[75] *Spiritual Canticle,* st. xiii; Peers, II, 73.
[76] *Ibid.*

What ark is this into which the dove has been drawn by the hand of divine mercy? "It is the bosom of God" Himself. Therein are many mansions and food of all kinds.[77]

> In this Divine union the soul sees and tastes abundance and inestimable riches, finds all the rest and the recreation that it desires, and understands strange kinds of knowledge and secrets of God, which is another of those kinds of food that it likes best. . . . It tastes a marvellous sweetness and spiritual delight, finds true rest and Divine light and has lofty experience of the knowledge of God. . . . And, above all, it experiences, and has fruition of, an inestimable feast of love, which confirms it in love.[78]

This deep peace is only temporary, however. Fortunately so, moreover, for the peace of satiation might well extinguish the soul's desires, arrest its aspirations and its enthusiasm for the ascent. But it is not yet at the summit. God Himself rekindles the flame of great desires, creating in the soul new anguish. This is one of the fruits of the divine visits that recur.

> Having won such great favours, the soul is so anxious to have complete fruition of their Giver that its life becomes sheer, though delectable, torture. It has the keenest longings for death, and so it frequently and tearfully begs God to take it out of this exile. Everything in this life that it sees wearies it; when it finds itself alone it experiences great relief, but immediately this distress returns till it hardly knows itself when it is without it. In short, this little butterfly can find no lasting repose.[79]

A strange torment, but one which, according to Saint Teresa and Saint John of the Cross, marks a happy development of the grace of the betrothal and announces that perfect union is near.

Increased love has greater desires to see and possess God. It tends toward God with all its ardent energy. It no longer wants anything but God and will brook no obstacles that hinder it from enjoying perfectly the Beloved.

[77] These absolute statements of the soul that has arrived at a new spiritual stage correspond to the overflowing fullness of the gifts that it is experiencing and that go beyond all it had dared hope for. These affirmations have only a relative value as long as the soul has not reached the summit—in relation to what it will soon desire and will later receive.

[78] *Ibid.;* 73-4.

[79] VI Mansions, vi; Peers, II, 297.

But whatever may be the purity of the soul, it is bothered by what it calls "foxes"—

> . . . as, for example, all the disturbances, temptations, causes of unrest, desires (if any remain), imaginations and other motions, whether natural or spiritual.[80]

These movements act sometimes like a mist, creating a certain interior agitation which is wont

> . . . to keep from the soul the flower of inward sweetness and quiet and peace, at the time when the soul in her virtues is most contentedly enjoying it, together with her Beloved.[81]

Small spots these may seem; but the purity of the divine light brings them out and shows their blackness painfully.

Moreover, the divine visits, however frequent they may be, are intermittent, leaving long and painful absences. It seems then to the soul that "the dead north wind . . . a cold and dry wind which withers the flowers," blows on it and "kills spiritual sweetness and substance." [82]

And so, in two stanzas the soul begs the angels of God to keep from it the foxes that ruin its vineyard in flower [83] and calls on the Beloved to let the peaceful south breeze blow through its garden, refreshing it with love.[84]

Light mists and passing dryness sharpen the soul's hunger and make it feel the emptiness of its inner depths. This torment becomes habitual.

Saint John of the Cross explains the nature and the cause of the torment. Faculties of the soul, detached and purified, are thereafter empty. Wonderfully has divine Wisdom, both through purification and through visits, hollowed out in them depths like to caverns, that now cry out their emptiness and their hunger, for they are made for plenitude.

[80] *Spiritual Canticle,* st. xxv; Peers, II, 123.
[81] *Ibid.*
[82] *Ibid.,* st. xxvi; 127.
[83] *Ibid.,* st. xxv; 123.
[84] *Ibid.,* st. xxvi; 127.

But, when they are empty and clean, the hunger and thirst and yearning of their spiritual sense become intolerable; for, as the capacities of these caverns are deep, their pain is deep likewise; as is also the food that they lack, which, as I say, is God. And this great feeling of pain commonly occurs towards the close of the illumination and purification of the soul, ere it attain to union, wherein it has satisfaction. For, when the spiritual appetite is empty and purged from every creature and from every creature affection, and its natural temper is lost, and it has become attempered to the Divine, . . . and the Divine communication of union with God has not yet reached it, then the suffering caused by this emptiness and thirst is worse than death, especially when the soul is vouchsafed some foresight or glimpse of the Divine ray and this is not communicated to it.[85]

Oh marvel of divine Wisdom which prepares, hollows out, purifies the vessel, creates in it great longing before filling it with what it has long desired.

At this time God seems to visit the soul only to increase and bring to a higher degree of intensity its habitual torment. Saint Teresa writes:

Very often a desire unexpectedly arises, in a way which I cannot explain. And this desire, which in a single moment penetrates to the very depths of the soul, begins to weary it so much that the soul soars upwards, far above itself and above all created things.[86]

It is a martyrdom, severe but also delectable; for the soul will accept nothing earthly that may be offered it, even though it were the thing which it had been accustomed to enjoy most.[87]

Saint Teresa notes that favors of this kind were granted her after all the others that she mentions in the book of her *Life*.[88] These graces mark the end of the period of the spiritual betrothal.

The description of this suffering and the favors that bring it to its sharpest pain fill the last chapter devoted to the sixth Mansions.[89] The Saint writes, speaking of the soul:

Although she may have been receiving these favours for many years, she is still sighing and weeping, and each of them causes her fresh

[85] *Living Flame,* st. iii; Peers, III, 63.
[86] *Life,* xx; Peers, I, 122.
[87] *Ibid.;* 123.
[88] *Ibid.;* 122-23.
[89] VI Mansions, xi; Peers, II, 323-8.

pain. . . . For the more is revealed to her of how much this great God and Lord deserves to be loved, the more does her love for Him grow. And gradually, during these years, her desire increases, so that she comes to experience great distress, as I will now explain.[90]

But "these yearnings and tears and sighs, together with the strong impulses" are all as nothing by comparison with this other, "a blow" like "an arrow of fire" [91] that sometimes wounds the soul, producing such spiritual distress that

. . . the sufferer cries out aloud. However patient a sufferer she may be, and however accustomed to enduring great pain, she cannot help doing this.[92]

The Saint then tells of an ecstasy she had at Salamanca in 1571, the Tuesday of Eastertide during recreation, while the novice Isabel of Jesus was singing the hymn: "Let mine eyes behold Thee."

Let us now return to what we were discussing when we left this soul in such affliction. It remains in this state only for a short time (three or four hours at most, I should say); for, if the pain lasted long, it would be impossible, save by a miracle, for natural weakness to suffer it. On one occasion it lasted only for a quarter of an hour and yet produced complete prostration. On that occasion, as a matter of fact, the sufferer entirely lost consciousness. The violent attack came on through her hearing some words about "life not ending." She was engaged in conversation at the time—it was the last day of Eastertide, and all that Easter she had been afflicted with such aridity that she hardly knew it was Easter at all. So just imagine anyone thinking that these attacks can be resisted! It is no more possible to resist them than for a person thrown into a fire to make the flames lose their heat and not burn her. She cannot hide her anguish, so all who are present realize the great peril in which she lies, even though they cannot witness what is going on within her.[93]

The day after the ecstasy, Saint Teresa writes this poem:

I live, yet no true life I know,
And, living thus expectantly,
I die because I do not die.

. . . . . .

[90] *Ibid.;* 324.
[91] *Ibid.*
[92] *Ibid.;* 325.
[93] *Ibid.;* 326-7. Cf. also *Relations,* iv.

I'd win thee dying day by day,
Such yearning for my Spouse have I,
Dying because I do not die.[94]

The following year on the octave-day of Saint Martin, Saint Teresa received the grace of spiritual marriage.[95]

Before studying this grace, let us try to determine the time and the duration of the spiritual betrothal.

3. TIME AND DURATION OF THE SPIRITUAL BETROTHAL

1. *Time.* The spiritual betrothal constitutes the central fact of the sixth Mansions, the mark that characterizes them in the soul's progress toward spiritual union. Saint Teresa describes the betrothal in chapters four, five, and six of these Mansions, having previously spoken of purifying sufferings and of the awakenings and words of God in the soul. In the following chapters, after insisting in chapter seven on recourse to the humanity of Christ, she describes extraordinary favors, visions and revelations in chapters eight, nine, and ten. Finally, in chapter eleven, she shows us the ardent anguish of love impatient before spiritual marriage.

This order provides some precious indications as to the time when the betrothal takes place, which will give light on the testimony of Saint John of the Cross.

The mystical doctor gives some signposts which, although precise, leave difficulties in interpretation.

At the beginning of stanza twenty-seven of the *Spiritual Canticle,* the stanza that marks the soul's entrance to the estate of the spiritual marriage, the Saint casts a glance backwards to point out the stages traversed. He writes:

In order that we may expound the arrangement of these stanzas the more clearly, and describe the soul's habitual progress ere it come to this estate of the Spiritual Marriage, . . . it is to be noted that first of all it exercised itself in the trials and bitternesses of mortification, and in meditation, as the soul said at the beginning, from the first

[94] *Poems,* i; Peers, III, 277-9.
[95] *Relations,* xxxv; Peers, I, 351.

stanza down to that which says: 'Scattering a thousand graces.'[96] Afterwards it passed through the pains and straits of love which have been described in the stanzas following, as far as that which says: 'Withdraw them, Beloved.'[97] And in addition to this, the soul then relates how it has received great communications and many visits from its Beloved, wherein it has reached ever-increasing perfection and knowledge in His love, so much so that, passing beyond all things, and even beyond itself, it has surrendered itself to Him through union of love in the Spiritual Betrothal, wherein, as one that is now betrothed, it has received from the Spouse great gifts and jewels, even as it has described in its song, from the stanza wherein this Divine betrothal was made, and which says, 'Withdraw them, Beloved.'[98]

Let us pick out the indications here given. In the three periods that precede spiritual marriage, the first is that of the first preparatory mortifications; in the second, we recognize the passive purifications of the spirit. These open into a period of divine visits that purify and enrich the soul, among which are the spiritual betrothal.

The *Living Flame* supplies other indications:

And this is the lofty state of spiritual betrothal of the soul with the Word, wherein the Spouse grants the soul great favours, and visits it most lovingly and frequently, wherein the soul receives great favours and delights. But these have nothing to do with those of marriage, for they are all preparations for the union of marriage; and, though it is true that they come to the soul when it is completely purged from all creature affection (for spiritual betrothal, as we say, cannot take place until this happens), nevertheless the soul has need of other and positive preparations on the part of God, of His visits and gifts whereby He purifies the soul ever more completely and beautifies and refines it so that it may be fitly prepared for such high union. In some souls more time is necessary than in others, for God works here according to the state of the soul.[99]

These texts show us that Saint John of the Cross distinguishes two phases in the preparation for spiritual marriage—a negative phase of preparation represented by the passive purification and a positive phase of preparation effected by the divine visits. The spiritual betrothal, which inaugurates the sec-

[96] *Spiritual Canticle*, st. v.
[97] *Ibid.*, st. xii.
[98] *Ibid.*, st. xxvii; Peers, II, 132-3.
[99] *Living Flame*, st. iii; Peers, III, 65.

ond phase in its most intense period, would thus be situated between the two phases.

Nevertheless it would be a mistake to separate in airtight compartments the two phases. We already know that the purifications of the spirit are produced by a divine flame, that is, by a very intense divine action in the depths of the soul. Hence the divine visits are not reserved exclusively to the second period. Besides, and this seems to us worth underlining, the visits of the betrothal produce, in the beginning at least, terrors, physical breaking, and raptures. Saint John of the Cross gives these sensible reactions to God's action as a sign of spiritual weakness and of imperfect purification.

> These feelings are experienced in such visitations by those who have not yet arrived at the estate of perfection, but who are travelling along the road in the estate of progressives; for those who have already attained receive all these communications in peace and gentle love, and these raptures cease, since they were communications preparing the soul for the communication which crowns all.[100]

In the *Dark Night of the Spirit,* the Saint states again very plainly:

> Hence comes it that the communications that are granted to these souls cannot be very strong or very intense or very spiritual, as is required for Divine union with God, by reason of the weakness and corruption of the sensual nature which has a part in them. Hence arise the raptures and trances and dislocations of the bones which always happen when the communications are not purely spiritual—that is, are not given to the spirit alone, as are those of the perfect who are purified by the second night of the spirit, and in whom these raptures and torments of the body no longer exist, since they are enjoying liberty of spirit, and their senses are now neither clouded nor transported.[101]

The raptures of the betrothal are thus ascribed to the dark night of the spirit and are a sign that the purification is not complete.

But they bring it to an end, and very happily so, as Saint John of the Cross elsewhere tells us. He writes in the *Ascent of Mount Carmel:*

[100] *Spiritual Canticle,* st. xii; Peers, II, 69.
[101] *Dark Night,* Bk. II, i; Peers, I, 375.

> There are certain kinds of knowledge, and certain of these touches effected by God in the substance of the soul, which enrich it after such wise that not only does one of them suffice to take from the soul once and for all the whole of the imperfections that it had itself been unable to throw off during its whole life, but it leaves the soul full of virtues and blessings from God.[102]

There is no doubt that these are substantial touches proper to the spiritual betrothal.

Thus the divine visits of the betrothal complete the soul's purification, enriching it and preparing it in a positive way for the spiritual marriage. With their extraordinary gifts of love in the depths of the soul, they destroy or render inactive the remaining evil tendencies; the meeting with God in the light, which they procure, perfects the psychological reorientation of the soul; thereafter the soul is wholly turned toward the Beloved.

Hence the spiritual betrothal is placed between the negative phase and the positive phase of preparation for perfect union.

But though these texts provide us with helpful signs, they designedly leave much in the shadows; and so we must guard against mathematically precise statements if we would keep to the truth.

The spiritual betrothal is not a peak or ridge that one goes over, suddenly to arrive on the other side; nor a frontier that one crosses, to find oneself in another country. The divine visits have both negative and positive effects; these bear visible marks of a night that is not ended and are, at the same time, favors preparing the soul for perfect union. They bring to completion the work of purification; and although this is fully effected only in perfect union, nevertheless the visits assure to God's positive action a predominance that goes on increasing until spiritual marriage.

Let us again hear Saint John of the Cross describe, in lan-

[102] *Ascent,* Bk. II, xxvi; Peers, I, 184.

guage that any commentary would mar, the positive action of God during the period of espousals:

> This is prefigured in those maidens who were chosen for King Assuerus;[103] although they had been taken from their own countries and from their fathers' houses, yet, before they were sent to the king's bed, they were kept waiting for a year, albeit within the enclosure of the palace. For one half of the year they were prepared with certain ointments of myrrh and other spices, and for the other half of the year with other and choicer ointments, after which they went to the king's bed.
>
> During the time, then, of this betrothal and expectation of marriage in the unctions of the Holy Spirit, when the ointments that prepare the soul for union with God are very choice, the yearnings of the caverns of the soul are wont to be extreme and delicate. For, as those ointments are a most proximate preparation for union with God, because they are nearest to God and for this cause make the soul more desirous of Him and inspire it with a more delicate affection for Him, the desire is more delicate and also deeper; for the desire for God is a preparation for union with God.[104]

2. *Duration of the period of betrothal.* How much time is given to this positive preparation? In the text that we have just read, Saint John of the Cross speaks of a year's preparation of the maidens in the King's palace. And this corresponds closely with what the symbolism of betrothal suggests. The betrothal is an exchange of promises preceding marriage and, as a rule, announces it as near. And so if we let ourselves be taken and carried away by symbolism—a thing that is particularly easy to do and happens almost unconsciously in these unknown regions—we have the impression that the period of betrothal is to last several months, one or two years at most. But let us examine the problem more closely.

At the beginning of the eleventh chapter of the sixth Mansions, where Saint Teresa describes the great desires that precede spiritual marriage, she gives us a valuable sign:

> For the more is revealed to her of how much this great God and Lord deserves to be loved, the more does her love for Him grow. And gradually, during these years, her desire increases, so that she comes

[103] Esther 2:12-4.
[104] *Living Flame,* st. iii; Peers, III, 65-6.

to experience great distress, as I will now explain. I have spoken of years, because I am writing about the experiences of the particular person about whom I have been speaking here. But it must be clearly understood that no limitations can be set to God's acts, and that He can raise a soul to the highest point here mentioned in a single moment.[105]

While maintaining the rights of divine mercy which, especially in these regions, asserts its independence, Saint Teresa recalls for us the facts of her own experience. Several years passed during which her desires went on increasing under the action of divine visits before she came to know that anguish of love which constitutes the immediate preparation for spiritual marriage. A glance at the book of her *Life* will allow us to give more definite indications.

In chapter twenty-seven of her *Life,* the Saint tells that she had her first rapture during a novena of *Veni Creator's* that one of the Fathers of the Society of Jesus had told her to make for the grace of detachment from certain friendships. During this rapture she heard the words: "I will have thee converse now, not with men, but with angels," and she received an efficacious grace of complete detachment.[106]

When she received this grace, Saint Teresa was still at the Convent of the Incarnation; she was making a visit at the home of her friend Doña Guiomar de Ulloa. The question had not yet arisen, it seems, of the foundation of the reformed Convent of Saint Joseph of Avila. This grace can be situated between 1558 and 1560. Hence the period of the betrothal began at that time and terminated in November 1572, with the favor of spiritual marriage. This period lasted then, for at least twelve years. And we cannot say that it was prolonged by the Saint's infidelities, for this is the period that includes the works of the foundation of Saint Joseph of Avila, the first particularly fervent years of her sojourn in this convent, and finally the first foundations of the Carmelites in Castile, and the exten-

[105] VI Mansions, xi; Peers, II, 324.
[106] *Life,* xxiv; Peers, I, 155.

sion of the Reform to the Friars. Merely to recall these works shows anyone who knows the life of the Saint what extraordinary favors spiritual betrothal brings to a soul, but also the works and fruitfulness which manifest the union already realized.

True, these indications drawn from the life of Saint Teresa are only one example—but it is an example that has particular value in view of the Saint's special mission as spiritual mother, and that harmonizes with the role of positive preparation for spiritual marriage, attributed to this period of betrothal. Hence we cannot neglect it, and we must see in it its general import.

The spiritual betrothal is not, then, a meeting destined to fix the conditions of a union soon to be confirmed. It inaugurates a period of positive preparation that the requirements for spiritual marriage will ordinarily prolong. Moreover, this period is not simply one of waiting; it is already marked by favors and by a supernatural fruitfulness that make it radiant under the light that falls from the summits.

B. Spiritual marriage

Saint John of the Cross writes:

> First, it must be known that, if a soul is seeking God, its Beloved is seeking it much more.[107]

These two loves, seeking each other with such purity and such ardor, meet in the perfect and mutual gift of spiritual marriage. A new state is created of which Saint John of the Cross says, comparing it to the preceding one:

> There is as great a difference between these states as there is between betrothal and marriage. For in betrothal there is only a consent by agreement, and a unity of will between the two parties, and the jewels and the adornment of the bride-to-be, given her graciously by the bridegroom. But in marriage there is likewise communication between the persons, and union. During the betrothal, although from time to

[107] *Living Flame,* st. iii; Peers, III, 66.

time the bridegroom sees the bride and gives her gifts, as we have said, there is no union between them, for that is the end of the betrothal.[108]

Even so is it between God and the soul. The soul has come to the end of its journey, has reached the center of itself which is the seventh Mansion, the dwelling where God Himself abides. In this innermost depth it will henceforth dwell in perfect union with God. This depth is at the same time the summit of the mystical mountain sketched for us by Saint John of the Cross, where is served the perpetual banquet of loving Wisdom. Grace there unfolds all the divine gifts that lay hid in its mystery. Perfect contemplation and sanctity are one.

We have come to a new world of marvels. Saint Teresa and Saint John of the Cross have described it. Dwelling in this new world, they had only to let their pen run on to tell us what was before their eyes. In fifteen days Saint John of the Cross writes the *Living Flame of Love.* These splendors astound us even more than they dazzle us. We have difficulty in adjusting our gaze to them. And yet it is here that Wisdom dwells and manifests herself as she is as light and strength and fruitfulness. We have not the right to draw away on the score that we lack the delightful experience that would allow intimate communion with her teaching.

In order to help those who are less accustomed to meditating upon the texts of Saint Teresa and Saint John of the Cross, we shall try to set up a few guidemarks, a few arrows pointing the way in the luxuriant forest of their descriptions. Thus each one can not only admire them—which would be an insufficient homage—but can discover the profound and practical dogmatic truths on which they are based. We shall have need of these to give light on our own journey toward Christian perfection.

In order to remain faithful to the plan we adopted, we shall study for the moment only God's manifestation in spiritual marriage. The next two chapters will go into the problem more deeply, considering what constitutes essentially this state and

[108] *Ibid.;* 65.

what is God's practical aim in holding souls captive in the bonds of His love.

I. THE GRACE OF SPIRITUAL MARRIAGE

a. *The inaugural imaginary vision*

In one of her spiritual "Relations," Saint Teresa gives the most complete account of this favor:

> When I was at the Incarnation, during the second year I was Prioress there, on the octave-day of Saint Martin, I was making my communion, and the Father, Fray John of the Cross, who was giving me the Most Holy Sacrament, divided the Host between another sister and myself. I thought he was doing this, not for lack of Hosts, but because he wanted to mortify me, for I had told him that I was very pleased when the Hosts were large ones, though I knew I should be receiving the Lord, whole and entire, if I took only the smallest particle. "Have no fear, daughter," His Majesty said to me, "that anyone will be able to part thee from Me." By this He gave me to understand that it was of no moment.
>
> Then He revealed Himself to me, in an imaginery vision, most interiorly, as on other occasions, and He gave me His right hand, saying to me: "Behold this nail. It is a sign that from to-day onward thou shalt be my bride. Until now, thou hadst not merited this; but henceforward thou shalt regard My honour not only as that of thy Creator and King and God but as that of My very bride. My honour is thine, and thine, Mine." This favour produced such an effect upon me that I could not restrain myself but became like a person who is foolish, and begged the Lord either to exalt my lowliness or to show me fewer favours, for I really did not think my nature could endure them. For the whole of that day I remained completely absorbed. Since then I have been conscious of receiving great benefits and of still greater confusion and distress when I see that in exchange for such great favours I am doing nothing.[109]

Writing the *Interior Castle* five years after receiving this favor, Saint Teresa has learned its importance and clearly considers it as the one that secured for her spiritual marriage. She writes:

> When granting this favour for the first time, His Majesty is pleased to reveal Himself to the soul through an imaginary vision of His most sacred Humanity, so that it may clearly understand what is taking

[109] *Relations,* xxxv, November 18, 1572, Avila; Peers, III, 351.

place and not be ignorant of the fact that it is receiving so sovereign a gift. To other people the experience will come in a different way.[110]

She wants to emphasize that this favor has something quite special about it.

This, you will think, was nothing new, since on other occasions the Lord had revealed Himself to that soul in this way. But it was so different that it left her quite confused and dismayed: for one reason, because this vision came with great force; for another, because of the words which He spoke to her; and also because, in the interior of her soul, where He revealed Himself to her, she had never seen any visions but this.[111]

The Saint hastens to warn us that the differences are found not only in the initial vision; they extend to all the manifestations proper to spiritual marriage:

For you must understand that there is the greatest difference between all the other visions we have mentioned and those belonging to this Mansion, and there is the same difference between the Spiritual Betrothal and the Spiritual Marriage as there is between two betrothed persons and two who are united so that they cannot be separated any more.[112]

It seems quite certain that the imaginary vision, with the symbolic nail and the words that give it meaning, is not an essential element of spiritual marriage. In the Teresian ascent we find at each Mansion an extraordinary favor, like a luminous sign marking the entrance and indicating by its special light the stage of progress. This spiritual mother with a universal mission needed to describe and direct, to know how to discern with exactness the entry upon each period and its characteristics. In fact, she notes that this vision was granted her so that she might have full knowledge of the state at which she had arrived. On the other hand, divine Wisdom may dispose all things in other souls in such a way that they do not know the stage at which they have arrived. In one there is complete obscurity, in another explicit light; all is grace for

[110] VII Mansions, ii; Peers, II, 334.
[111] *Ibid.*
[112] *Ibid.*

the realization of God's design over each soul. And so, to desire a ceremonial at the entrance of the seventh Mansions seems to us dangerous and childish. To look for such signs in the lives of the saints and to interpret here or there such or such a word or divine manifestation as proof of a union perfectly realized, can be the source of regrettable errors.

The authentic signs of spiritual marriage lie elsewhere. Divine union consists of something else than symbols, or rather, the symbol has value only through the reality that it signifies and exteriorly illustrates.

b. *Union of betrothal and union of spiritual marriage*

In one passage after another Saint Teresa points out admirably the distinction between the betrothal and spiritual marriage. Let us follow her thought:

> When Our Lord is pleased to have pity upon this soul, which suffers and has suffered so much out of desire for Him, and which He has now taken spiritually to be His bride, He brings her into this Mansion of His, which is the seventh, before consummating the Spiritual Marriage. For He must needs have an abiding-place in the soul, just as He has one in Heaven, where His Majesty alone dwells: so let us call this a second Heaven.[113]

To enter into the Mansion where God dwells means for Saint Teresa to be united with Him. All the Mansions symbolize, in fact, a degree of union.

But the soul has already known perfect union with God in the spiritual betrothal. Saint Teresa explains what differentiates these two ways of entering into God's Mansion: by the betrothal, and by spiritual marriage.

> Now, when His Majesty is pleased to grant the soul the aforementioned favour of this Divine Marriage, He first of all brings it into His own Mansion. And His Majesty is pleased that it should not be as on other occasions, when He has granted it raptures, in which I certainly think it is united with Him, as it is in the above-mentioned Prayer of Union, although the soul does not feel called to enter into

[113] *Ibid.*, i; 330.

its own centre, as here in this Mansion, but is affected only in its higher part.[114]

We recall that in the rapture of the betrothal, there was a certain separation of soul and spirit, the spirit rising up above the soul—like the flame mounting up from the furnace—and being carried away in God.

In spiritual marriage, union is complete. No longer the spirit alone but the whole soul is drawn into its center where God is. And so in this union there is no transport felt nor separation between the parts of the soul. All is peace and inner unity.

This may lead you to think that such a person will not remain in possession of her senses but will be so completely absorbed that she will be able to fix her mind upon nothing. But no: in all that belongs to the service of God she is more alert than before.[115]

The Saint adds another and still more important difference: the union of spiritual marriage is not only complete but is definitive.

The Spiritual Betrothal is different: here the two persons are frequently separated, as is the case with union, for, although by union is meant the joining of two things into one, each of the two, as is a matter of common observation, can be separated and remain a thing by itself. This favour of the Lord passes quickly and afterwards the soul is deprived of that companionship—I mean so far as it can understand. In this other favour of the Lord it is not so: the soul remains all the time in that centre with its God.[116]

A union that is complete and definitive, such are the essential characteristics of spiritual marriage that Saint Teresa and Saint John of the Cross stress, and that the symbolism of the betrothal and of marriage illustrates. Saint John of the Cross writes:

There is as great a difference between these states as there is between betrothal and marriage. . . . But in marriage there is likewise communication between the persons, and union. During the betrothal,

[114] *Ibid.;* 331.
[115] *Ibid.;* 332.
[116] *Ibid.,* ii; 335.

although from time to time the bridegroom sees the bride and gives her gifts, as we have said, there is no union between them, for that is the end of betrothal.[117]

This union seems to join two beings to one another, for it is a union by transformation:

. . . wherein on either side there is made surrender, by total possession, of the one to the other in consummate union of love, as far as may be in this life. . . . For, even as in the consummation of marriage according to the flesh the two become one flesh, as says the Divine Scripture, even so, when this Spiritual Marriage between God and the soul is consummated, there are two natures in one spirit and love of God.[118]

These strong statements of Saint John of the Cross place before us truths that we shall have to go into more deeply in order to make explicit a few of the substantial riches that they enclose. We have already had to mention them in explaining the light and peace that accompany spiritual marriage.

c. *Intellectual vision of the Holy Trinity*

The imaginary vision of the sacred humanity of Christ was fleeting. For Saint Teresa it was the beacon showing her the entry to the port to which the wind of the Spirit was carrying her. Spiritual marriage brings a deeper and more enduring manifestation of God, the fruit of the union that it procures.

Let us turn again to the confidence of the Saint, who will instruct us in precise language. Continuing to compare the grace of spiritual marriage with the graces of union previously received, she says:

When He unites it with Him, it understands nothing; the faculties are all lost. . . . Whatever it does, the Lord unites it with Himself, but He makes it blind and dumb, as He made Saint Paul at his conversion, and so prevents it from having any sense of how or in what way that favour comes which it is enjoying; the great delight of which the soul is then conscious is the realization of its nearness to God.

But in this Mansion everything is different. Our good God now desires to remove the scales from the eyes of the soul, so that it may

[117] *Living Flame,* st. iii; Peers, III, 65.
[118] *Spiritual Canticle,* st. xxvii; Peers, II, 133.

see and understand something of the favour which He is granting it, although He is doing this in a strange manner. It is brought into this Mansion by means of an intellectual vision, in which, by a representation of the truth in a particular way, the Most Holy Trinity reveals Itself, in all three Persons. First of all the spirit becomes enkindled and is illumined, as it were, by a cloud of the greatest brightness. It sees these three Persons, individually, and yet, by a wonderful kind of knowledge which is given to it, the soul realizes that most certainly and truly all these three Persons are one Substance and one Power and one Knowledge and one God alone; so that what we hold by faith the soul may be said here to grasp by sight, although nothing is seen by the eyes, either of the body or of the soul, for it is no imaginary vision. Here all three Persons communicate Themselves to the soul and speak to the soul and explain to it those words which the Gospel attributes to the Lord—namely, that He and the Father and the Holy Spirit will come to dwell with the soul which loves Him and keeps His commandments.[119]

With words inadequate to the task Saint Teresa tried to describe the vision of God's Mansion and the light that illumines it. To discover all its precise richness, we must have recourse, it seems to me, to mystical theology.

We have already seen that the word vision, for Saint Teresa, does not necessarily mean a sense perception.

We must remark that this intellectual vision is not of the same order as the imaginary vision of the humanity of Christ, which marked the entry to spiritual marriage. The imaginary vision is an extraordinary favor, in the sense previously indicated,[120] being directly produced by God in the faculties and giving a distinct light. The intellectual vision or knowledge of the Holy Trinity is of another order. It proceeds from perfect union and is a fruit of the connaturality that this union establishes between God and the soul.

A union quite fleeting and less profound took place in the most complete darkness, in the mystical grace of union of the fifth Mansions. It left only the certitude that there had been contact with God. In the rapture of the betrothal, the union that was realized in a simple meeting produced an intoxication

[119] VII Mansions, i; Peers, II, 331-2.
[120] Cf. *infra,* ch. ii, "Extraordinary Favors."

and a dazzling. The soul experienced divine union and in this contact discovered great divine secrets. But like Saint Paul on the Damascus road, blind and dumb, it was not able to explain how, nor to tell what it had discovered. The rapture of the betrothal carried it away for a moment into a state higher than that in which it ordinarily lived. The meeting was a sudden and fleeting plunge into the depths of perfect union. And so it was violent and sweet, blinding with its light.

In spiritual marriage, perfect union is no longer just a happy incident along the way; it is thereafter a thing confirmed, a fact that imposes itself with all its consequences. The fleeting substantial touch is replaced by the substantial penetration of habitual union. The soul is immersed in God like a sponge in the ocean; it rests in the transforming love that has taken it captive and that continues its working.

The perfection and stability of this union give to the knowledge of connaturality, which is proper to it, perfection and continuity. The experential light from it, perfect according to its mode, is only a light of dawn, but of a dawning that will give way only to the full light of the beatific vision in unending day.

The soul already knows that light, having found it in the whisper of the breezes[121] or again in certain visions of the Holy Trinity with which it has been favored.[122] But mingled with it were extraordinary favors which, while completing it, gave evidence that it had not reached its perfection. But above all, it was fleeting and died away with the substantial touch from which it came.

The compenetration realized by perfect union now produces a purer light and a higher one which will never be completely extinguished. We understand why Saint Teresa calls this mode of knowing new by reason of its actual perfection.

This light of dawn is sufficient to illumine God's dwelling

[121] Cf. *infra,* "The Spiritual Betrothal."
[122] *Spiritual Canticle,* st. xiv; Peers, II.

place in the soul. It is of this light, which radiates from the seventh Mansions, that Saint Teresa is speaking when she writes:

> It is very important, sisters, that we should not think of the soul as of something dark. It must seem dark to most of us, as we cannot see it, for we forget that there is not only a light which we can see, but also an interior light, and so we think that within our soul there is some kind of darkness.[123]

Assuredly, this light is not the lamp that is the Lamb, which is the whole light of the celestial city,[124] although it too proceeds from God. Nevertheless, issuing as it does from the perfect connaturality of the soul with its God, it suffices to reveal to the soul the Mansion in which it is, the supernatural realities with which it is in loving contact, the divine Persons who, by a common working in the soul, are divinizing it. Speaking of how the most Holy Trinity reveals Itself, in all three Persons, to the soul, Saint Teresa writes: "First of all the spirit becomes enkindled and is illumined as is were, by a cloud of the greatest brightness." [125] How could one better speak of the transcendence, the clarity, and the mystery of that light arising from love, in which the soul is granted an intellectual vision of the Holy Trinity?

The clarity of this vision can, and actually does, vary. But the experience of the presence of the three divine Persons remains, and the soul has only to turn its gaze within to find again that living and luminous Presence. Saint Teresa writes:

> This Presence is not of course always realized so fully—I mean so clearly—as it is when it first comes, or on certain other occasions when God grants the soul this consolation. . . . But although the light which

[123] VII Mansions, i; Peers, II, 330.

[124] Cf. Apocalypse 21:23: "And the city has no need of the sun or the moon to shine upon it. For the glory of God lights it up, and the Lamb is the lamp thereof."

[125] VII Mansions, i; Peers, II, 331. In the book on *Conceptions of the Love of God* the Saint says again very happily, speaking of the shadow of the Godhead: ". . . well termed "shadow," for we cannot see it clearly on earth but only beneath this cloud dwells that resplendent Sun, Who sends out to the soul a message of love, communicating His Majesty's nearness to it—a nearness which is ineffable." Peers, II, 389.

accompanies it may not be so clear, the soul is always aware that it is experiencing this companionship. We might compare the soul to a person who is with others in a very bright room; and then suppose that the shutters are closed so that the people are all in darkness.[126]

The light has not always the same intensity. At times it is strong and at times weak; but this is not within the power of the soul to determine, Saint Teresa assures us.[127] But beneath these variable intensities the experience of light remains, making the soul aware that it has attained to God's dwelling place, or rather, that the three divine Persons are present in its inmost center, that they have taken possession of it and have made of it their dwelling place. This light of love whence proceeds the intellectual vision of the Holy Trinity brings to realization, as Saint Teresa notes, the promise of Jesus in the Gospel:

> If anyone love me, he will keep my word, and my Father will love him, and we will come to him and make our abode with him.[128]

That this knowledge or vision can discover the distinction and unity of the divine Persons, the operations common to the Three, and the constituent attribute of each one, gives evidence of the high quality of light issuing from the transforming union.

Nevertheless, a problem that we must not avoid arises. It can be expressed thus: loving knowledge, whatever be the degree of union from which it proceeds and its penetration into the nature and most intimate secrets of the soul, is still an intuitive knowledge through sympathy and contact, a knowledge that is profound but is in itself rebellious to fixed formulas. Love expresses its science by deeds and attitudes; love's words are frought with meaning but are simple when obliged to break the silence in which it finds its most perfect expression. Whence does love derive its exact formulas given by Saint Teresa when she describes the intellectual vision?

If we would explain this depth of knowledge together with

[126] *Ibid.*, iii; 332.
[127] *Ibid.*
[128] John 14:23.

precision in its formula and the clarity of the vision that flows from it, we must recall what faith is.

Faith presents to us divine truth in formulas of dogma; it gives us the gold of the divine substance in a conceptual covering with silvered surfaces. At first the soul drew sustenance from these dogmatic formulas, which presented it divine truth in analogical human terms. When living faith brought the soul into the gold of the substance, it was at first dazzled, especially in the deep and obscure contact of the fifth Mansions. The clear light of the formula, such as the soul had grasped it, and the light proceeding from the substance seemed to be in opposition. This was a part of the drama of the dark night of the spirit. The sixth Mansions brought some conciliatory lights: the divine secrets perceived in the meeting of the betrothal transcend formulas, but show forth their truth. The light that comes from the experience of love in spiritual marriage reveals their perfect harmony. No longer is there apparent contradiction, no longer clashings, nor dark breach between the light coming from the experience of the substance and that from the silvered surface. The formula is no longer an obstacle; it has become a help. The experience of love triumphs; the soul's loving gaze into divine truth penetrates so deep, is so enlightening and so perfect, that it serves to confirm the precision of the formula. Better still, the knowledge proceeding from connaturality of love needs the dogmatic formula in order to make itself explicit; and in fact it consents to express itself explicitly only in this formula, for there is no other that better translates what it found through substantial contact, and what it continually experiences through loving union. God and the Church have spoken well, the soul would readily say. And in so saying, it shows that its experience of love is genuine, for it coincides with the truth in the precise formulation that the infallible magisterium of the Church proposes.[129]

[129] Consequently, it seems we can suppose that an authentic mystical experience of perfect union in the case of a man who did not know the mystery of the Holy Trinity would cause him truly to experience the unity and distinc-

The brightness of the intellectual vision of the Trinity is caused by the meeting of the two lights, that of the formula and that of experience, in a harmonious fusion in which they both triumph by being united and mutually serving each other. The affirmations of Saint Teresa that we have already read thus assume their full meaning, almost a new sense:

> It sees these three Persons, individually, and yet, by a wonderful kind of knowledge which is given to it, the soul realizes that most certainly and truly all these three Persons are one Substance and one Power and one Knowledge and one God alone; so that what we hold by faith the soul may be said here to grasp by sight, although nothing is seen by the eyes, either of the body or of the soul, for it is no imaginary vision.[130]

The soul understands and sees in some dim way, yet the greatest of mysteries retains its obscurity. Triumph of living faith, the fruit of union. How strong and pure is the light of that dawning, which thus causes to shine in their very depths the limpid springs that flow from the word of God!

Saint Teresa seems to give as a characteristic sign of spiritual marriage the intellectual vision of the Holy Trinity, such as she describes it. Must we take her testimony literally? Actually, Saint John of the Cross does not express it in this same form. Saint Therese of the Child Jesus does not explicitly speak of it.

We think we can find in what has just been said an explanation of these apparent divergencies, an explanation that adds a fortunate precision.

The knowledge essential to spiritual marriage is the knowledge by connaturality, which proceeds from the transforming union. Saint Therese herself has told us that its brightness had its high points and low, but that it always remained in the depths of the soul. It is this deep knowledge of the Holy Trinity through experience, of the unity and distinction of Persons—a

---

tion of persons; but he would not know how to express it or would do so imperfectly.

[130] VII Mansions, i; Peers, II, 331-2.

veritable dawning of eternal life—that we shall find in all the saints who have reached this high degree.

But since the explicitness belongs not properly to the knowledge itself but to the dogmatic formula, we can understand how it happens that here or there it is made, in such or such a soul, under an external form which, while remaining in conformity with the truth, varies in different cases. Thus when Saint Therese of the Child Jesus lets her pen run on so as to express her inner experience after the wound of love which elevated her to transforming union, she makes explicit references to the Holy Trinity and to each one of the divine Persons in their relations with her soul, which show a perception of the distinction and unity of the divine Persons. Nevertheless, she was to express her constant experience of transforming union, not by an intellectual vision of the Holy Trinity, but by this avowal concerning the "oceans of grace" that had flooded her soul since her Act of Oblation (June 9, 1895) to merciful Love:

> From that day I have been penetrated and surrounded with love. Every moment this merciful Love renews me and purifies me, leaving in my soul no trace of sins.[131]

What conclusion can we draw from this avowal if not that the Saint was more aware of her experience of merciful Love, by reason of her particular mission, and consequently found it easier to express explicitly; and that this experience veiled in a certain measure the experience of the Holy Trinity which was, however, real, as the outpourings of chapter ix of the *Autobiography* prove.

We shall have similar remarks to make concerning the experience of the summits of Saint John of the Cross and his description of it.

Let us conclude by saying that with spiritual marriage comes an experience of God and of the Holy Trinity, of the nature and distinction of the divine Persons; but that this very lofty

[131] *Autobiography,* viii, 133.

and clear knowledge can be made explicit under different forms, which are not always an intellectual vision of the Holy Trinity, in the Teresian sense of the word.

d. *The peace of spiritual marriage*

Peace is also one of the characteristic and essential fruits of spiritual marriage. Saint Teresa writes:

> The soul, as I have said, neither moves from that centre nor loses its peace, for He who gave His peace to the Apostles when they were all together [132] can give peace to the soul.
>
> It has occurred to me that this salutation of the Lord must mean much more than the mere words suggest, as must also His telling the glorious Magdalen to go in peace; [133] for the words of the Lord are like acts wrought in us, and so they must have produced some effect in those who were already prepared to put away from them everything corporeal and to leave the soul in a state of pure spirituality, so that it might be joined with Uncreated Spirit in this celestial union.[134]

And Saint John of the Cross writes that "the grandeur and stability of the soul in this estate are complete." [135]

Peace comes from the possession of God in that light of dawn that satisfies the faculties. We are made for God who is our end. It is normal that the soul that has attained to Him with certitude should find peace, which is the tranquillity of order realized. As Saint Teresa says:

> This little butterfly has now died, full of joy at having found rest, and within her lives Christ. . . . In short, the desires of these souls are no longer for consolations or favours, for they have with them the Lord Himself and it is His Majesty Who now lives in them.[136]

The soul's possession of God is peaceful because it is stable and secure thereafter against the attacks and dangers that up to now troubled it. It is protected by

> . . . the rampart of peace and virtues and perfections which the soul now has, and by which it is now protected, which is the wall and defense of the garden of its Beloved.[137]

[132] John 20:19.
[133] Luke 7:50.
[134] VII Mansions, ii; Peers, II, 336.
[135] *Spiritual Canticle,* st. xxx; Peers, II, 142.
[136] VII Mansions, iii; 338-40.
[137] *Spiritual Canticle,* st. xxx; 144.

In the last stanza of the *Spiritual Canticle,*[138] Saint John of the Cross sings of the peacefulness of this security and the interior harmony that it creates:

For none saw it,
Neither did Aminadab appear,
And there was a rest from the siege
And the cavalry came down at the sight of the waters.

Thus the soul lets us know that it is far withdrawn from creatures in that deep center where it dwells with God; that Aminadab, the devil, can no longer reach it; that the passions that formerly assailed it can no longer trouble its interior peace; and that the senses now purified and adapted to the spiritual come down like cavalry at the sight of the divine waters.

Saint Teresa describes this peace that comes from detachment, from solitude and inner harmony, by saying to what it extends. No more dryness and disturbance, no more weakness under God's action:

> The difference between this Mansion and the rest has already been explained. There are hardly any of the periods of aridity or interior disturbance in it which at one time or another have occurred in all the rest, but the soul is almost always in tranquillity. It is not afraid that this sublime favour may be counterfeited by the devil. . . . And I am quite dazed myself when I observe that, on reaching this state, the soul has no more raptures (accompanied, that is to say, by the suspension of the senses), save very occasionally, and even then it has not the same transports and flights of the spirit.[139]

In other words, raptures are no longer accompanied by physical weakness and suffering. In this estate the soul is detached from everything, wholly satisfied with the loving union it is enjoying. Could this then be a beatitude without shadows, a silence and a peace without turmoil or trouble?

In the twenty-ninth stanza of the *Spiritual Canticle* Saint John of the Cross addresses the "birds of swift wing," or the digressions of the imagination, the "lions, harts, leaping does," which represent the ardors or weaknesses of the concupiscible

[138] *Ibid.,* st. xxxix; 173.
[139] VII Mansions, iii; Peers, II, 341-2.

power, the "mountains, valleys, banks," as he designates the inordinate acts of the three faculties of the soul (understanding, will, and memory), the "waters, breezes, heats, and terrors that keep watch by night," which are the four passions of the soul—namely, grief, hope, joy, and fear.[140] He asks them, as he asks also the movements of sensuality, to be still, to cease from their operations and not "to trouble or harass the higher and spiritual part of the soul, lest it should be kept, by any motion, howsoever small, from the blessing and sweetness which it enjoys." [141]

Thus we see that these powers are not destroyed, that they still carry on an activity that is not entirely under subjection. No one could deny this. Saint John of the Cross testifies, speaking of the Bride:

> She sees that in her lower part—namely, sensuality—there may be impediments, as in fact there are, which disturb so great a blessing.[142]

Ordinarily, however, they do not succeed. Their motions are, moreover, outside the profound regions where the soul now dwells in loving union. The enemy is powerless to penetrate into this inmost Mansion and cannot draw the soul away from union; at most, he can hinder the enjoyment of that union.

These psychological precisions seem to us useful. Some, commenting on certain symbols used by John of the Cross, make of spiritual marriage a refuge of absolute and unalterable peace, reaching from the depths of one's being to its outermost limits, a paradisiac abode that has nothing left of the human or earthly. The truth is quite otherwise; and it must be stated, so as to dispel illusions and reaffirm that grace does not destroy nature.

God asks of the saint works and sufferings. He may even permit one to be troubled by sensible affliction and pain.[143] It

[140] *Spiritual Canticle,* st. xxix-xxx; Peers, II, 138-47.
[141] *Ibid.,* st. xxxi; 145.
[142] *Ibid.*
[143] *Ibid.,* st. xxx; 141.

may be that the saint has within himself the cause of this, at least for a certain time.

Let us again turn to Saint Teresa for light on the peace proper to spiritual marriage, to get a clearer idea of it.

When Our Lord brings the soul into this Mansion of His, which is the centre of the soul itself (for they say that the empyrean heaven, where Our Lord is, does not move like the other heavens), it seems, on entering, to be subject to none of the usual movements of the faculties and the imagination, which injure it and take away its peace.[144]

This statement finds happy confirmation in the description the Saint gave of her condition at the time she was writing the "Fourth Mansions" of the *Interior Castle*. She had for several years been experiencing the favor of spiritual marriage, and yet she said:

As I write this, the noises in my head are so loud that I am beginning to wonder what is going on in it. As I said at the outset, they have been making it almost impossible for me to obey those who commanded me to write. My head sounds just as if it were full of brimming rivers, and then as if all the water in those rivers came suddenly rushing downward; and a host of little birds seem to be whistling, not in the ears, but in the upper part of the head, where the higher part of the soul is said to be.[145]

Yet while experiencing all that, the Saint remained united with God and could continue writing. To conclude, let us hear her tell in her figurative but precise way in what this peace consists and what are its limits:

This "centre" of our soul, or "spirit," is something so difficult to describe, and indeed to believe, that I think, sisters, as I am so bad at explaining myself, I will not subject you to the temptation of disbelieving what I say, for it is difficult to understand how the soul can have trials and afflictions and yet be in peace. I want to be put before you one or two comparisons: God grant they may be of some value, but, if they are not, I know that what I have said is the truth.

A king is living in His palace: many wars are waged in his kingdom and many other distressing things happen there, but he remains where he is despite them all. So it is here: although in the other Mansions there are many disturbances and poisonous creatures, and the noise

[144] VII Mansions, ii; Peers, II, 337.
[145] IV Mansions, i; 234.

of all this can be heard, nobody enters this Mansion and forces the soul to leave it; and, although the things which the soul hears cause it some distress, they are not of a kind to disturb it or to take away its peace, for the passions are already vanquished, and thus are afraid to enter there because to do so would only exhaust them further. Our whole body may be in pain, yet if our head is sound the fact that the body is in pain will not cause it to ache as well. These comparisons make me smile and I do not like them at all, but I know no others. Think what you will; what I have said is the truth.[146]

2. GROWTH OF THE GRACE OF SPIRITUAL MARRIAGE

Saint John of the Cross tells us that spiritual marriage is "the highest estate which in this life is attainable." [147] When the soul has come to it, "it is just that it should take its repose and rest after it has labored." [148] But is spiritual marriage a goal, a summit beyond which one cannot go, where the soul takes its stand immobile in the repose of its peace and the brilliance of its light?

At the outset, Saint Teresa says speaking of spiritual marriage:

> This great favor cannot be fulfilled perfectly in us during our lifetime.[149]

Saint John of the Cross too interrupts at times his description of the ineffable riches that overflow from the plentitude of his soul, to tell us that all this is not eternal life but is only shadow and imperfection when compared with the longed-for vision face to face.

In spiritual marriage, then, the soul continues its progress toward God. Its love possesses its object as yet only in shadow. The living faith that illumines it becomes each day more desirous of light. Its hope, purified by love, grows more ardent although peaceful. Love itself remains the self-communicative good, the impulse of which nothing thereafter could check. It is more dynamic than ever. Living faith supplies it with certitudes that give light in the shadows. Hope puts at love's service

[146] VII Mansions, ii; 338.
[147] *Spiritual Canticle,* st. xxvii; Peers, II, 134.
[148] *Ibid,;* 135.
[149] VII Mansions, ii; Peers, II, 333.

fleet wings to pass with sure and rapid flight through the distances that lie between it and its infinite object. Love becomes one living flame in making a more and more complete gift of itself.

In the Prologue of the *Living Flame of Love,* Saint John of the Cross describes both the stability and the ceaseless movement of transforming love.

> Although in the stanzas which we expounded above (in the *Spiritual Canticle*) we spoke of the most perfect degree of perfection to which a man may attain in this life, which is transformation in God, nevertheless these stanzas treat of a love which is even more completed and perfected within this same state of transformation. For, although it is true that both these stanzas and those speak of a state of transformation beyond which, as such, a soul cannot pass, yet none the less, with time and practice, as I say, the soul may become more completely perfected and grounded in love. Even so, when a log of wood has been set upon the fire, it is transformed into fire and united with it; yet, as the fire grows hotter and the wood remains upon it for a longer time, it glows much more and becomes more completely enkindled, until it gives out sparks of fire and flame.
>
> And it is of this degree of enkindled love that the soul must be understood as speaking when it is at last transformed and perfected interiorly in the fire of love.[150]

From the beginning of the commentary on the first stanza, the Saint sets forth his thought.

> The soul feels itself to be at last wholly enkindled in Divine union, its palate to be wholly bathed in glory and love, and from the very inmost part of its substance to be flowing veritable rivers of glory, abounding in delights, for it perceives that from its belly are flowing the rivers of living water which the Son of God said would flow from such souls.[151]

The bursts of flame do not send out their sparks at random; the rivers of living water do not flow by a chance way. The force of divine love is not blind. It is at the service of Wisdom, obeys her laws and is directly guided by her. This love is holy Wisdom. It mounts up to God and works for the realization of His designs here below.

[150] *Living Flame,* Prologue; Peers, III, 14.
[151] *Ibid.,* st. i; 17.

Here we are only stating these truths, which we shall soon take up again. For now we have only to consider the developments of the grace of spiritual marriage in the discovery of God and supernatural realities.

Under the growing light of dawn, the soul becomes a daring explorer into the depths of divine life. In the *Spiritual Canticle,* Saint John of the Cross points out love's penetrating curiosity and some of its fruits.

> And let us go to see ourselves in thy beauty,
> To the mountain or the hill where flows the pure water;
> Let us enter farther into the thicket.[152]

Thus speaks the Bride to her Beloved. But it is especially in the *Living Flame* that Saint John of the Cross has let overflow, like the lava that runs burning and peaceful down the slopes of the mountain, the riches that rose up from the flaming depths of his soul. In spite of the unwillingness he felt and his difficulty in speaking "of that which passes in the depths of the spirit," [153] he consented upon urgent request to expound the four stanzas that he was to use as a basis for describing some effects of the light produced by the bursts of flame in the shadow of the divine mystery.

These stanzas show less the progress of the soul in the higher regions than the diverse aspects that one discovers of the summits. These aspects are dogmatic truths having reference to the divine life within us and practical truths concerning the spiritual life—both illumined by the glowing light from the flame of transforming union. And so the *Living Flame,* the most elevated treatise of Saint John of the Cross, is at the same time the most simple and practical, the one in which his doctrine and his soul are nearest to us.

Love's light discovers the flame whence it proceeds, the ardent and sweet flame, living and delicate, the flame that is the Holy Spirit, ceaselessly singing love's triumph in the sub-

[152] *Spiritual Canticle,* st. xxxv; Peers, II, 156.
[153] *Living Flame,* Prologue; Peers, III, 13.

stance of the soul. It sets on fire the whole dwelling where God abides with the soul; in this fire they are united. This takes place in the inmost depths in the center of the soul, which the flame dilates and ever deepens, for depth is synonmous with love's quality. Although formerly the flame of love had obstacles to overcome and triumphed only after painful combats, now it sweetly consumes. It uses and spiritualizes everything that is opposed to its triumph, all the barriers or veils that prevent the perfect grasp of its divine object in the light. To break the last fine web that will release the soul from the body does not depend on it. Certainly, it does not lack the power, but it must wait upon the divine hour and order. A sign from God, and all the force of love will have soon carried away the soul, triumphant, to the bosom of God for the "sweet meeting" in the beatific vision. Such is the commentary on the first stanza.

In the second stanza, the soul contemplates the divine Persons. They are within it, distinct in unity of nature. They cause the burning of love, but their distinction is perceived by the effect of each. The "burn" is attributed to the Holy Spirit; the "burn" itself proceeds from the delicate touch of the Word. The Saint writes:

> Oh, then, thou delicate touch, Thou Word, Son of God, Who, through the delicateness of Thy Divine Being, dost subtly penetrate the substance of my soul, and, touching it wholly and delicately, dost absorb it wholly in Thyself.[154]

The touch is the hand of "the merciful and omnipotent Father" [155] gently laid upon the soul.

In this furnace which is the soul, there is still place for sweet and burning wounds that come at times from the very Godhead and assail its substance without any intermediary. These are the ones that have made the furnace as it is, with its intensity and the quality of its fire. There are other wounds also that are sublime, and that the Saint mentions because of their ex-

[154] *Ibid.*, st. ii; 134.
[155] *Ibid.*, st. ii; 133.

traordinary charismatic effects. Of these there is the wound of fecundity made by the seraph's dart, which those receive who are to transmit spiritual wealth and strength to a greater or lesser number of descendants. Also, the wound of the stigmata, a sensible exteriorization of an interior wound, it too caused by the seraph, uniting its recipient in a special way to the Passion of Christ. All these wounds savor of eternal life, by reason both of the joy they give and the suffering they cause.

The three divine Persons are distinct, but their work of sanctification is one. In his commentary on the third stanza Saint John of the Cross explores this single operation. Grace is a participation in the life of God. The riches that it shows forth are as diverse as are the divine attributes from which they flow. These attributes, diverse in the unity of God, shine like lamps of fire casting their splendors or shadows upon the soul. These —the divine reflections, the savors, the diverse properties of grace in the souls—bear within them, each one, all the substantial riches of grace, just as the divine attributes from which they flow are, each one of them, the very essence of God. In other words, God's action in the soul is one in its substance; it is diverse in its virtualities and its effects, as are the divine attributes in the single essence of God.

The Saint profits by this consideration of God's transforming action in the soul to point out the enemies that set for it snares and obstacles. These enemies are—who would have believed it! in the first place spiritual directors; then come the devil and the soul itself.

In the center of all these marvels, there is an experience more lofty and more intimate, more constant and nearer to what we know, the experience and the manifestation of the Word as Spouse. This is how the promise of Jesus is realized profoundly and magnificently in the center of the soul:

> He who loves me will be loved by my Father, and I will love him and manifest myself to him.[156]

[156] John 14:21.

This manifestation of the Word as Spouse fills the fourth stanza.

In the center and depth of the soul, in its pure and inmost substance, the Word and Spouse dwells secretly and in silence; He is there as in His own house, on His own bed of repose.[157] He rules it as master, and holds the soul intimately and closely united to Himself. Thus He makes the soul His, and the soul can call Him its Spouse. Does not the love given it by the single operation of the Holy Trinity identify it with the Word, Son of God? It is daughter by grace as the Word is Son by nature. By its union with the Word, it enters into the cycle of the Triune life and participates in the divine operations. It breathes the Holy Spirit by grace as the Word does by nature.[158]

Deep within, the soul has an experience of the Word-Spouse, the source of all its good. He rests in the shadows, asleep, it seems. Yet His breathing evinces His presence and His action. What great desires the soul has to know Him! When it begs to enter farther into its depths,[159] it is in truth a more profound penetration and more intimate knowledge of Christ and His mysteries that it longs for.

The Word-Spouse is the soul's, and the soul is His. This mutual possession and compenetration bring the soul effectively into the deep caverns that are the mysteries of Christ, into that inexhaustible mine with its countless veins enclosing riches ever new.[160] The mysteries that the soul has known by faith, has studied in theology, or penetrated with the simple gaze of its prayer, become more clear in its depths. The light that illumines them, the gaze that grasps them, are no longer from the outside. The experience of love has entered farther into "the thicket of wisdom," where the multitude of God's marvelous works are seen under the light of an inner fire.

This perception ordinarily takes place as a subtle awareness

[157] *Living Flame,* st. iv; Peers, III, 188.
[158] *Ibid.;* 187-194.
[159] *Spiritual Canticle,* st. xxxv; Peers, II, 158 ff.
[160] *Ibid.,* st. xxxvi; 160 ff.

of the presence of the Word in the shadows. The divine Spouse seems to sleep in the bosom of the soul.[161] But now the Word, the Spouse, awakens. He appears to move on the bed where He lies. Saint John of the Cross writes:

> This awakening is a movement of the Word in the substance of the soul, of such greatness and dominion and glory, and of such intimate sweetness, that it seems to the soul that all the balms and perfumed spices and flowers in the world are mingled and shaken and revolved together to give their sweetness; and that all the kingdoms and dominions of the world and all the powers and virtues of Heaven are moved.[162]

By this simple movement, the Word, the Spouse of the soul, reveals His intimate secrets, causes His treasures to shine forth, communicates His excellences. In Him all things are life; in Him they live and are and move. Hence, when this great Lord moves, He seems to carry with Him all creation, of which He is the center. Such is the Spouse who dwells in the inmost substance of the soul, holding it in the sweet and close embrace of His love.

For the sake of precision, the mystical doctor adds that in these awakenings, it is the soul that awakens a moment to the great reality it is perceiving; the movement is in the soul and not in the Word, who is immovable. Yet the soul participates a little in the divine immutability, for it "faints not away and fears not in this awakening which is so powerful and glorious." [163]

In the *Spiritual Canticle,* the Saint tries to make more explicit something of the breathing that accompanies the awakening, the breathing of the Holy Spirit that the transformed soul breathes in God and the breathing of the Holy Spirit into it:

> She [the soul] calls it the breathing of the air, because it is a most delicate touch and feeling of love which habitually in this estate is caused in the soul by the communication of the Holy Spirit. Breathing with that His Divine breath, He raises the soul most sublimely, and

[161] *Living Flame,* st. iv; Peers, III, 194.
[162] *Ibid.;* 188.
[163] *Ibid.;* 191-2.

informs her, that she may breathe in God the same breath of love that the Father breathes in the Son and the Son in the Father.[164]

But in the *Living Flame,* the awakening has become so powerful, the breathing so delicate and sublime, that the Saint can only put down his pen and withdraw in silent praise

> . . . in the deep things of God, to Whom be honour and glory. Amen.[165]

Not all the veils are drawn back from the face of God, says Saint John of the Cross, but the soul has been able to see Him somewhat darkly.[166]

We are here at the confines of the eternal vision. We had to come thus far to follow the luminous discoveries of spiritual marriage.

[164] *Spiritual Canticle,* st. xxxviii; Peers, II, 168.
[165] *Living Flame,* st. iv; Peers, III, 195.
[166] *Ibid.;* 190.

CHAPTER VIII

Transforming Union

I am the vine, you are the branches.[1]
As if the ends of two wax candles were joined so that the light they give is one.[2]

Does it not seem to be a descent, to speak of transforming union after the high mystical experiences of spiritual marriage? Is there even any use in making a special study of transforming union, when Saint Teresa and Saint John of the Cross, in their descriptions, seem to assimilate it to spiritual marriage. We shall answer these questions before defining the transforming union and its properties.

A. Spiritual marriage and transforming union

Spiritual marriage and transforming union do not designate two different spiritual states, but rather two aspects of the same interior reality, namely, the summit of the spiritual life.

Spiritual marriage calls to mind that spiritual state with all its cortege of manifestations, extraordinary favors, and contemplative lights, indicating that a soul has arrived thus far. Transforming union designates the reality that constitutes this state, namely, the degree of charity that brings about this perfect union with God through the transformation and likeness of love. Spiritual marriage places in relief what might be called the phenomenal aspect of the union, on condition that the phenomenal be not made to mean the superficial, and that the most

[1] John 15:5.
[2] VII Mansions, ii; Peers, II, 335.

profound and authentic manifestations of this interior state be understood. Transforming union is this spiritual state itself in its ontological constitution, that is, charity in its transforming and unifying plenitude.

To ascertain whether it is useful to distinguish clearly between spiritual marriage and transforming union, between the manifestations and the reality of which they are signs, one need only cast a glance at spiritual literature, and especially biographies. Confusions between the mystical phenomenon and the reality are frequent, in favor of the phenomenon, which is sought out and emphasized as if it were the principal element. This is because the mystical phenomenon that marks the summits generally exercises a strong attraction on the mass of the faithful, eager for signs and for the extraordinary, the miraculous.

Even among spiritual persons, it is not rare to find more lively desire for mystical experience than for supernatural charity, which is its source—an unavowed desire, often unconscious, but nevertheless disclosing the scale of spiritual values according to which the person is forming his judgments and building his spiritual life.

Some even make of spiritual marriage a state superior to transforming union.

The judgments passed on Saint Therese of the Child Jesus and her spirituality have brought to light the incorrectness of these notions and allow us to guess the harmful influence they could exercise on the spiritual life of souls. Actually, some hesitated to recognize in Saint Therese of the Child Jesus the highest states of the spiritual life, because in her they were not accompanied and proven by the mystical phenomena that they thought to be inseparable from these states. And yet, with that luminous simplicity that comes from detachment and purity of soul, the little Saint of Lisieux took care to warn us that when perfection is in question, appearing perfect is of small importance compared with being so. And apropos of her death of love she said, a few weeks before it, July 10, 1897:

> It does not matter whether it appears provided it be so. Our Lord died of love on the Cross, and see what His agony was.[3]

Confusion between being and appearing, more importance given to the appearing that is brilliant and showy than to the being that is hidden and obscure, these give rise to practical errors as to the nature of perfection and the goal to be attained, and may occasion errors in direction from the very beginning of the spiritual life. Souls are thus retarded in the way of perfection or even brought to a definite standstill. The road of the imperfect soul, in the chart of Saint John of the Cross, that ends at an impasse, is indeed the road on which the soul seeks as an end the goods of heaven, of glory, joy, consolatioin, security, light, in short, all the goods that accompany union but are not union, and even hinder one from attaining it, if desired for themselves.

Let us try to situate transforming union in reference to the manifestations of spiritual marriage that go with it, pointing out the relations between them and their respective value.

1. MANIFESTATIONS, THE FRUIT OF LOVE

These manifestations, the fruit of transforming union, take different forms and expressions.

Among these manifestations, we distinguish first of all the extraordinary favors of contemplative lights properly so-called. The first favors procure the advancement of the soul, but usually have a clearly charismatic character, that is, they are given for the good of the Church.[4] They prepare the soul for the

[3] *Esprit de Sainte Thérèse de l'E. J.*, p. 126.

[4] The charismatic character of the extraordinary favors that Saint Teresa received appears plainly. This reformer needed very particular divine assurances; this mistress of the spiritual life had to be able to situate in a precise way the stages of the spiritual life and the characteristics of each one of them. Extraordinary favors provided her with the luminous guideposts that she needed.

accomplishment of a special mission and provide the means for its execution. God gives them what He wills and as He wills by direct action. Hence they are not the specific fruit of the union of the soul with God. And so, whatever be the power and the light accompanying them, these extraordinary favors could never, of themselves alone, be considered as sufficient proof of sanctity.[5] They may, however, add confirmation to more certain proofs, making them more explicit.[6]

In treating of the relations of transforming union with spiritual marriage, we do not intend to speak of those favors that are not specifically manifestations of transforming union, but only of the contemplative lights proceeding from the connaturality of love. These latter—the riches of which, Saint John of the Cross has set forth in his commentary on the *Spiritual Canticle* and the *Living Flame,* and whose quality Saint Teresa has shown in her description of the intellectual vision of the Holy Trinity—are presented by both these masters as fruits of union.

Let us here recall that "the whisper of the amorous breezes" —that lofty knowledge, that "substance of understanding" given to the soul, that "manifestation of new truths"—is produced by a substantial touch. Certainly, the sense of hearing experiences greater delight in it than does the sense of touch, being more spiritual, but there is no doubt that all such lofty knowledge has as its orgin the unifying contact of God with the substance of the soul.[7] Saint John of the Cross writes speaking of the soul:

> She desires to see the face of God, which is essential communication of His Divinity, without any kind of intermediary in the soul, through certain contact thereof with the Divinity. This a thing far removed

[5] *Ascent,* Bk. II, xvii; Peers, I, 191 ff.

[6] Thus it would be imprudent to believe that a soul has arrived at transforming union because our Lord called it His spouse. Such an interior word, even authentic, can be interpreted in different ways. Nevertheless, it could give assurance that this soul has arrived at transforming union, if it presents objective signs.

[7] *Spiritual Canticle,* st. xiii and xiv; Peers, II, 72.

from all sense and accidents, inasmuch as it is the touch of pure substances—that is, of the soul and the Divinity.[8]

These divine manifestations of knowledge are so closely dependent on the union that produces them, that Saint John of the Cross assimilates them to the union itself.

> These lofty manifestations of knowledge can come only to the soul that attains to union with God, for they are themselves that union; and to receive them is equivalent to a certain contact with the Divinity which the soul experiences.[9]

In the *Living Flame,* the Saint sets forth the lofty experiences of God with which the soul is favored as sparklings from the flame of love, flashes and effects from the light of the blazing fire that the soul has become under the action of increasing love. These descriptions are a canticle to the living flame of love. And so:

> The soul magnifies its Spouse and gives Him thanks for the great favours which it receives from the union that it has with Him, by means whereof it says here that it receives abundant and great knowledge of Himself, all full of love.[10]

This great knowledge filled with love, accompanying spiritual marriage, proceeds in fact from the experience of connaturality. But there can be no experience of connaturality except in the union and transformation wrought by love. The manifestations of knowledge are so lofty only because the union and transformation are perfect. Such is the truth underlying the testimony of Saint John of the Cross and giving us certitude that the riches of light issue from transforming union.

Although proceeding from the same experience of love, these manifestations differ in form and expression in different saints. Saint John of the Cross affirms this when describing the effects of the substantial touch of the betrothal. He writes:

> It is not to be understood that to all such as arrive at this estate He communicates all that is expounded in these two stanzas, nor that He

[8] *Ibid.,* st. xxxii; 149.
[9] *Ascent,* Bk. II, xxvi; Peers, I, 183-4.
[10] *Living Flame,* st. iii; Peers, III, 145.

does so according to one single way and degree of knowledge and feeling. For to some souls He gives more and to others less; to some after one manner and to others after another; though souls belonging to either category can be in this estate of the Spiritual Betrothal.[11]

We have already noted how in spiritual marriage the experience of God and of the three divine Persons, although identical in its essential element, assumes different forms and expressions in different saints. The gifts of God are diverse even on the summits. The infinite treasure whence comes the contact of perfect union is constantly yielding to souls new riches, and adapting these to temperament and to grace. Moreover, temperament and grace intervene in their turn in the expression of what the soul has received in its experience of that perfect union.

Saint John of the Cross, using in the service of his powerful intellect and fine spiritual sense his gifts as artist and theologian, expresses, in a language that is precise although brilliant with symbols, the abundant light that he found in his soul for all the generations entrusted by the Holy Spirit to his grace as spiritual father. Saint Therese of the Child Jesus seems on the contrary to have wanted not to know these contemplative riches, to leave them buried in forgetfulness. It is a chance conversation at the end of her life that lets us know she had had transports of the spirit.[12] Through the insistence of her sister, Sister Marie of the Sacred Heart, we have been allowed to glimpse the depths of her experience. But of all that, she says:

> In fact they are the spiritual riches that make us *unjust*—when we rest in them complacently and think they are *something great.*[13]

Thus to our century, proud and covetous of all goods, even the spiritual, the little Saint was to preach humility and spiritual poverty.

[11] *Spiritual Canticle,* st. xiii; Peers, II, 73.
[12] *Novissima Verba,* 42-3.
[13] To Sister Marie of the Sacred Heart, Sept. 17, 1896; *Letters,* p. 288. Saint Therese said this especially in reference to her desires for martyrdom that her sister had stressed; but she meant it for all the riches that she had disclosed in her letter constituting chapter xi of the *Autobiography.*

The holy Curé of Ars buried his mystical experience in the darkness of his confessional. It revealed itself only in his tears in the presence of sin and his wholly divine mercy toward sinners; or again, in the light of his eyes and the sweet unction of his language. Thus could one guess how strong was the flame burning deep within his soul.

These examples show how varied are the flames from the blaze of love that rises up, singing and triumphant, from the consuming fires of transforming union. Are not the marvelous reflections from that blaze too volatile to fixate our desires? Certainly, the fire of love that produces them is alone desirable. When our soul is ablaze with love, then will God cause to rise from it the flame that is in keeping with His designs.

2. CONTEMPLATIVE LIGHT

Contemplative lights are sovereignly useful. They are a means ordered to the development of love.

To belittle the riches of light that proceed from the fire of transforming union would be wrong. They are divine riches, among the purest and most useful that God dispenses here below. They disclose to the contemplative gaze, as much as can be on earth, the secrets of God's very being. They derive their excellence from the fact that they issue from the soul's contact with supernatural realities. They are not the fruit of a passing play of the spirit nor a lightning flash of the intellect. The love that produces them continues to hold in embrace the divine realities they illumine. Light and life, thought and being, join in this unifying contact that love establishes between two spirits and two substances, that of God and that of the soul.

Could there be here below any realism more objective or knowledge more immediate that this perception, through contact and union, of being in its plenitude? And so we understand why modern philosophy, having cast aside the constructive dialectics of reason to seek a simple vision of reality and direct perception of values, professes high esteem for mystical knowledge that is the fruit of union, seeking in it support for itself in that depth of realism that is the whole life of the spirit.[14]

This contribution to modern philosophy, although precious, is only one of the benefits afforded by lofty knowledge through connaturality of love. Saint John of the Cross too professes high esteem for it, but for other reasons:

> These touches are so delectable to the soul . . . that if it received only one of them it would consider itself well rewarded for all the trials that it had suffered in this life, even had they been innumerable.[15]

The lights on God that these divine touches give, and the vision of the world that they procure, lift the soul up above the contingencies of this world and natural ways of knowing. This "knowledge of the morning, as theologians say, which is knowledge in the divine Word . . . and the knowledge of the evening, which is the wisdom of God in His creatures and works and wondrous ordinances . . ." [16] make of the soul a royal soul whose eagle gaze penetrates to the depths of God and of men.

Such lights are one of the most precious treasures of the Church, one of its most efficacious means of evangelization and teaching. From works written under their influence there flows out a delightful and luminous plenitude of love that enlightens and draws. They are the rivers of living water which, according to the promise of Jesus, flow from him who believes.[17] They reveal God living and acting here below; they illumine and rejoice all those who are in the house. Merely to go through the treatises of Saint Teresa of Avila and Saint John of the Cross, and the *Autobiography* of Saint Therese of the Child Jesus, is enough to make one aware of the supernatural power and the wealth of light and of recollection that emanate from

[14] Cf. The doctrine of Saint John of the Cross and contemporary thought, by A. Forest, Professor on the faculty at Montpellier, in *Saint Jean de la Croix et la pensée contemporaine* (Editions du Carmel) where these thoughts are very happily developed.

[15] *Ascent,* Bk. II, xxvi; Peers, I, 184.

[16] *Spiritual Canticle,* st. xxxv; Peers, II, 157.

[17] John, 7:38.

writings "composed under the influence of a love which comes from abounding mystical understanding." [18]

All the lights that issue from love are loving knowledge and must return to love. Saint John of the Cross writes:

> The soul is dissolved in that transformation wherein, inflamed and changed in love, it was annihilated and undone as to all that which was not love, and left so that it knew naught else save love.[19]

This is the effect of the grace of spiritual betrothal. On revealing the divine Spouse, the light that proceeds from His touch calms the soul and at the same time creates in it new desires, even to the point of anguish. This has already been said. In the mutual possession of spiritual marriage knowledge becomes more clear; and it keeps alive desire to enter more deeply into the depths of Wisdom, at the price of new sufferings. Saint John of the Cross gives us the reason:

> The end for which the soul desired to enter those caverns aforementioned was that she might reach (at least in so far as this estate of life permits) the consummation of that which she had ever desired, which is the complete and perfect love communicated in this communication, for love is the end of all.[20]

Love is the end of all; this we must repeat with Saint John of the Cross. The beatific vision is alone more desirable, but that is not of earth. All light here below must, then, turn to love and intensify love's fire.

It would be vain to be attached to these lofty manifestations of knowledge, and to want to use them for themselves. That would be to try to grasp with the hand the flame leaping up from the fire or the light coming from it, so as to carry it away and make it one's own. The saints have felt the thrill, the refreshment that love's light brings, the desires that it keeps alive and creates; but they never thought that one could use it otherwise than to love more. Separated from the fire from which it emanates, turned aside from the end towards which

[18] *Spiritual Canticle,* Prologue; 24.
[19] *Ibid.,* st. xvii; 101.
[20] *Ibid.,* st. xxxvii; 164.

of itself it tends, the noetic value of love is withdrawn from its rightful setting. It seems profaned and loses its living force.

To her sister, Sister Genevieve of the Holy Face, who asked a word of farewell, Saint Therese of the Child Jesus whispered, the eve of her death:

> I have said all . . . all is accomplished! . . . It is love alone that counts.[21]

Love alone has absolute value here below. The last remark that we shall make on this point bears this out again.

3. THE BEATIFIC VISION

The beatific vision is in the measure of transforming love and issues from it.

Contemplative lights lead the soul up to the transparent veil that conceals the dazzling majesty of God in Himself. One might think that when death, or rather the force of love, has torn asunder the veil, the lofty knowledge experienced in transforming union would, through the rent veil, be made perfect in the presence of its divine object. Not so. The light of connaturality proceeding from a union that is already perfect here below could not receive, from the divine embrace in heaven, a new perfection that would change it essentially. For it is light coming from the experience of divine contact, and this will not change after death. Vivified by love that puts in all things a leaven of immortality, it does not disappear but rather, remains on a secondary plane.

The direct vision of God pertains to a new power that is given the soul, the *lumen gloriae,* the light of glory; issuing from love, its strength is in the measure of the love that engenders it.

The contemplative lights that so happily perfect and sustain the supernatural life here below, the beginning of eternal life, do not, then, of themselves, bring that life to its perfection in heaven. After perfecting faith in its exercise so as to ensure its

[21] *Novissima Verba,* 135.

progress in obscurity, they are in heaven on a plane notably lower than the beatific vision, complementing it in an accidental way.

Hence love and the union that it effects between God and the soul transcend all spiritual goods of this world, however elevated they may be.

> I do not repent of having delivered myself up to Love,[22]

said Saint Therese of the Child Jesus during her death agony, shortly before dying. And she had good reason, for

> At eventide they will examine thee in love,[23]

—and love alone will receive as its reward the vision and possession of God. Did not the apostle write to the Corinthians:

> If I have prophecy and know all mysteries and all knowledge, and if I have all faith so as to remove mountains, yet do not have charity, I am nothing.[24]

As we stand among the dazzling marvels at the summit, it is important to recall this great truth affirmed by the apostle, if we would place all things according to their true value; thus we can see clearly the only goal worthy of all our desire.

B. Transforming union

In the *Ascent of Mount Carmel,* Saint John of the Cross stresses how important it is to know in what the transforming union consists:

> That we may proceed with less confusion, I think it will be necessary to describe, in the following chapter, the nature of this that we call union of the soul with God; for, when this is understood, that which we shall say hereafter will become much clearer. And so I think the treatment of this union comes well at this point, as in its proper place.[25]

[22] *Ibid.,* 138.
[23] Saint John of the Cross, *Spiritual Sentences and Maxims,* n. 57; Peers, III, 225.
[24] I Cor. 13:2.
[25] *Ascent,* Bk. II, iv; Peers, I, 73-4.

This definition is to give us, in fact, the true notion of sanctity.

And the Saint fulfils his promise in a more precise exposition of the union of the soul with God. He writes:

In order, then, to understand what is meant by this union whereof we are treating, it must be known that God dwells and is present substantially in every soul, even in that of the greatest sinner in the world. And this kind of union is ever wrought between God and all the creatures, for in it He is preserving their being: if union of this kind were to fail them, they would at once become annihilated and would cease to be.[26]

Such a union is in the purely natural order, the effect of the divine presence of immensity. The transforming union of which we are speaking is a supernatural union. It comes to be through grace, a participation in the divine life. It can be produced only in those souls, consequently, who are in the state of grace. It consists in perfect union of wills and comes to pass,

. . . when the two wills—namely that of the soul and that of God—are conformed together in one, and there is naught in the one that is repugnant to the other. And thus, when the soul rids itself totally of that which is repugnant to the Divine will and conforms not with it, it is transformed in God through love. . . .

Wherefore God communicates Himself most to that soul that has progressed farthest in love; namely, that has its will in closest conformity with the will of God. And the soul that has attained complete conformity and likeness of will is totally united and transformed in God supernaturally.[27]

Perfect conformity with the will of God; such, then, is the essential effect and practical criterion of perfect union. Perfect union cannot exist without perfect purity; Saint John of the Cross stresses this in his treatise on mystical asceticism, the *Ascent:*

As there can be no perfect transformation if there be not perfect purity, and as the enlightenment, illumination and union of the soul with God will be according to the proportion of its purity, in greater

[26] *Ibid.*, v; 75.
[27] *Ibid.*; 76.

or in less degree; yet the soul will not be perfect, as I say, if it be not wholly and perfectly bright and clean.[28]

Purity in the soul is its capacity to receive God and be united with Him. It is to union with God what clear vision is to a picture seen. Just as one whose vision is more excellent and refined sees in it more beauties and perfection, so the soul can penetrate into God and receive Him into itself in the measure of its purity.[29]

But, adds the Saint, this aptitude for union differs according to souls, being determined, it seems, by a design of God:

> Although it is true that a soul, according to its greater or lesser capacity, may have attained to union, yet not all do so in an equal degree, for this depends upon what the Lord is pleased to grant to each one. It is in this way that souls see God in Heaven; some more, some less; but all see Him, and all are content, for their capacity is satisfied.
>
> Wherefore, although in this life here below we find certain souls enjoying equal peace and tranquillity in the state of perfection, and each one of them satisfied, yet some of them may be many degrees higher than others. All, however, will be equally satisfied, because the capacity of each one is satisfied.[30]

The important thing for each soul, then, is to perfect the capacity that God has given it, by arriving at the purity that this perfection requires:

> But the soul that attains not to such a measure of purity as is in conformity with its capacity never attains true peace and satisfaction, since it has not attained to the possession of that detachment and emptiness in its faculties which is required for simple union.[31]

Thus each soul is called to a certain degree of union. When this degree is realized, can it be assimilated to the transforming union? Could one consequently say of an infant that died after baptism that it had arrived at transforming union? That is a problem difficult to solve.

The problem is more difficult in that the criterion of peace,

[28] *Ibid.;* 78.
[29] *Ibid.,* v; 79.
[30] *Ibid.*
[31] *Ibid.*

which marks the realization of the capacity given by God, is verifiable with difficulty; and even when verified, it still can lead into error. At each stage, the soul receives a certain peace as a sign of its victory. Thus peace succeeds peace, giving way each time very happily to new lights presenting new divine demands. The tranquil possession of a spiritual good, even of a rather high mystical experience, might proceed equally from a constant faithfulness that has reached its whole capacity, and from a fidelity which, without a real lapse, has lost some of its fervor and its dynamism and has thus ceased to attract divine lights which might have disclosed to the soul new exigencies and prepared it for further ascent. Here we are confronted with the mystery of souls, more troubling than the mystery of God; and it would be vain to try to penetrate it completely here below.

However that may be, it seems clear to us that we cannot assimilate this relative divine union, appeasing the desires of many spiritual persons and corresponding perhaps to God's demands on them, to the transforming union described by Saint Teresa and Saint John of the Cross. The transforming union they present to us has its positive criteria that isolate it from the divine union realized by the majority of spiritual persons and place it on a summit, while presenting it as a legitimate object of our supernatural hope.

These criteria, although mysterious in themselves, are precise and certain. We shall group them under three headings: transforming plenitude of grace, sovereignly dominating presence of the Holy Spirit, identification with Christ Jesus.

1. TRANSFORMING PLENITUDE OF GRACE

The term transforming union evokes in the first place spiritual regeneration and complete transformation of the soul through love. The soul "is made divine and becomes God by participation, in so far as may be in this life." [32] Its union with

[32] *Spiritual Canticle,* st. xxvii; Peers, II, 133.

God is such that they have become "two natures in one spirit and love of God." [33] The full meaning of these words yields its secrets only in the light of the definitions of sanctifying grace and its properties.

Sanctifying grace, first given at baptism, is a real participation in the divine life. It enters into the soul, establishes its reign in the very substance as an entitative quality, and takes possession of the faculties by means of the infused virtues. It is not on the surface like a varnish, nor on the outside like something engrafted. It is truly infused and, simple, it penetrates to the inmost depths like an oil poured out or a leaven, the penetrating and invading action of which one could not stop. The soul and its faculties are thus both enveloped and penetrated by this divine life. In fact, the spiritual life is nothing else than the conquering progression of the divine life by progressive interiorization. Grace is truly the leaven that a woman put in three measures of flour.

Saint John of the Cross emphasizes the fact that this conquest takes place especially in the direction of increased penetration to the soul's center:

> Love unites the soul with God, and, the more degrees of love the soul has, the more profoundly does it enter into God and the more is it centred in Him; and thus we can say that, as are the degrees of love of God, so are the centres, each one deeper than another, which the soul has in God. . . . And thus the soul which has one degree of love is already in its centre in God, since one degree of love suffices for a soul to abide in Him through grace. If it have two degrees of love, it will have entered into another and a more interior centre with God; and, if it attain to three, it will have entered into the third. If it attain to the last degree, the love of God will succeed in wounding the soul even in its deepest centre—that is, in transforming and enlightening it as regards all the being and power and virtue of the soul, such as it is capable of receiving, until it be brought into such a state that it appears to be God. In this state the soul is like the crystal that is clear and pure; the more degrees of light it receives, the greater concentration of light there is in it, and this enlightenment continues to such a degree that at last it attains a point at which the light is centred in it with such copiousness that it comes to appear to be wholly light, and cannot be dis-

[33] *Ibid.*

tinguished from the light, for it is enlightened to the greatest possible extent and thus appears to be light itself.[34]

Using the same comparision in the *Ascent of Mount Carmel,* the Saint completes the description:

Although in reality the window has a nature distinct from that of the ray itself, however much it may resemble it, yet we may say that that window is a ray of the sun or is light by participation.[35]

These comparisons show how grace, participation in the divine life, by penetrating into the depths of the soul, realizes there progressively its work of conquest and transformation, dominating the natural powers without destroying them, and imposing on them its properties. The soul thus becomes God by participation.

Grace transforms the soul only to unite it more closely to God. Union and transformation go along together. Such in fact is the essential property of love; and grace is charity, as God is love.

Love establishes close communication between those who love. Through it one gives to the other; it effects between them a compenetration. Through love the two beings who love live one in the other. Matter and flesh impose limits and reserves to this reciprocal communication and compenetration. Supernatural love finds none in simple and spiritual beings, as are God and the perfectly purified soul. The soul is in God, and God is in it.

The comparison dear to Saint John of the Cross, of wood thrown into the fire and become in its turn fire in the bosom of the furnace, expresses this aspect of transforming union:

Even so, when a log of wood has been set upon the fire, it is transformed into fire and united with it.[36]

The grace or love that flows into the soul and transforms it is only a created participation of the divine nature. It belongs

[34] *Living Flame,* st. i; Peers, III, 23.
[35] *Ascent,* Bk. II, v; Peers, I, 77.
[36] *Living Flame,* Prologue; 14.

in its own right to the soul and remains distinct from God. Nevertheless, it is given only for the purpose of uniting the soul with the principle from which it proceeds. It casts the soul into the infinite fire that is God Himself and keeps it there by constant union, as in its life-giving element. Again the Saint writes:

> That which God communicates to the soul in this most intimate union is completely ineffable, so that naught can be said thereof, even as naught can be said concerning God Himself which may describe Him; for it is God Himself Who communicates this to the soul, and transforms her into Himself with marvelous glory, so that they are both in one, as we should say the window is one with the sun's ray, or coal with the fire, or the light of the stars with that of the sun.[37]

Transforming union consists in this mutual complete compenetration and the perfect love that brings it to pass. In the spiritual betrothal, says Saint Teresa, the soul "is affected only in its higher part," whereas now the soul is drawn completely into its center where God dwells.[38]

This Mansion of God becomes that of the soul, where henceforward it will dwell. For transforming union is stable and definitive. Its stability is secured by a confirmation in grace, which is part of the transforming union,[39] and by the mutual gift that God and the soul have made.

This essential character, the stability of the union, is illustrated especially by the symbolism of marriage, indissoluble union in the mutual gift of the persons married.

> For in betrothal there is only a consent by agreement, and a unity of will between the two parties. . . . But in marriage there is likewise communication between the persons, and union.[40]

Saint Teresa in turn writes:

> The Spiritual Betrothal is different: here the two persons are frequently separated, as is the case with union, for, although by union is meant the joining of two things into one, each of the two, as is a mat-

[37] *Spiritual Canticle,* st. xvii; Peers, II, 97.
[38] VII Mansions, i; Peers, II, 331.
[39] *Spiritual Canticle,* st. xxvii; 133.
[40] *Living Flame,* st. iii; Peers, III, 65.

ter of common observation, can be separated and remain a thing by itself. This favour of the Lord passes quickly. . . . In this other favour of the Lord it is not so: the soul remains all the time in that centre with its God.[41]

This union draws its stability from the transformation which is its basis. No longer brought about by a passing touch, it is confirmed by an abiding contact with God. Saint John of the Cross writes:

It is a total transformation in the Beloved (and thus I think that this estate is never without confirmation in grace, because the faithfulness of both is confirmed, that of the soul being confirmed in God), wherein on either side there is made surrender, by total possession, of the one to the other in consummate union of love, as far as may be in this life.[42]

The Saint continues by explaining how this transformation comes about by a certain absorption of the soul in God, yet leaving the two natures distinct.

When this Spiritual Marriage between God and the soul is consummated, there are two natures in one spirit and love of God. It is as when the light of the star or of the candle is joined and united with the sun, so that that which shines is not the star or the candle but the sun, which has absorbed the other lights in itself. And of this estate the Spouse treats in the present line, saying: 'The Bride has entered.' [43]

To make clear what this transforming union is and to express the various aspects of it that we have just analyzed—transformation, union of two natures through communication, stability in a certain absorption in God—Saint Teresa eagerly multiplies comparisons and symbols:

We might say that union is as if the ends of two wax candles were joined so that the light they give is one: the wicks and the wax and the light are all one; yet afterwards the one candle can be perfectly well separated from the other and the candles become two again, or the wick may be withdrawn from the wax. But here it is like rain falling from the heavens into a river or a spring; there is nothing but water there and it is impossible to divide or separate the water belonging to the river from that which fell from the heavens. Or it is as if a tiny streamlet enters the sea, from which it will find no way of separating

[41] VII Mansions, ii; Peers, II, 335.
[42] *Spiritual Canticle,* st. xxvii; Peers, II, 133.
[43] *Ibid.*

itself, or as if in a room there were two large windows through which the light streamed in: it enters in different places but it all becomes one.

Perhaps when St. Paul says: "He who is joined to God becomes one spirit with Him," he is referring to this sovereign Marriage, which presupposes the entrance of His Majesty into the soul by union.[44]

Each one of these comparisons casts some light on an aspect of transforming union. They must be brought together, if we would throw sufficient light on this profound spiritual reality. For a reality indeed is here in question, not merely a symbolic vision or a mystical experience. To have a firm conviction of it, we must draw it out from that mist in which we are wont respectfully to place all that is beyond the common measure and capacities of the average Christian, and, by enveloping all higher manifestations in mystery, seemingly to take away from them real and concrete existence. The transforming union is a fact that shows us, in the saints, the living realization of all the virtualities of the divine life in souls. It is only that; but it is all that.

Although stable and permanent, transforming union appears nevertheless in different states and is susceptible of progress.

In the *Ascent of Mount Carmel,* Saint John of the Cross had stated his plan:

Here I treat only of this permanent and total union according to the substance of the soul and its faculties with respect to the obscure habit of union: for with respect to the act, we shall explain later, with the Divine favour.[45]

Later he was to say explicitly that this abiding and habitual union is that of the transforming union or spiritual marriage. He writes:

Although the soul is for ever in this high estate of marriage after God has placed it therein, yet it is not for ever in actual union according to the said faculties, although it is so according to the substance of the soul. But in this substantial union of the soul the faculties are also very frequently in union, and drink in this cellar.[46]

[44] VII Mansions, ii; Peers, II, 335.
[45] *Ascent,* Bk. II, v; Peers, I, 75.
[46] *Spiritual Canticle,* xvii; Peers, II, 99.

By habitual union a transformation takes place in the substance of the soul and in the deep roots of the faculties. It passes into act as the here and now influence of that union and of God Himself on the activity of the faculties, an influence that is ordinarily accompanied by a keener awareness of the reality of that union and its effects.

Saint Teresa, speaking of the intellectual vision of the Holy Trinity, explained how constant it is in the darkness as a living and profound fact, and how at times it declares itself in act, in light and joy.[47] Saint John of the Cross, in his commentary on the fourth stanza of the *Living Flame,* wonderfully describes the habitual presence of the Word asleep, as it were, in the bosom of the soul, and moving at times in marvelous awakenings.[48] These descriptions tell us what habitual transforming union is, and its actualization in the powers that enjoy it.

The stability of love, then, is not uniformity, nor even immobility. The Holy Spirit is a living breath that "brings to pass the glorious vibrations of His flame" [49] and increases also the ardors of the fire that consumes the soul. In transforming union, the fire has penetrated the log of wood that is the soul, says Saint John of the Cross.

> Even so, when a log of wood has been set upon the fire, it is transformed into fire and united with it; yet, as the fire grows hotter and the wood remains upon it for a longer time, it glows much more and becomes more completely enkindled, until it gives out sparks of fire and flame. . . . Such the soul feels itself to be.[50]

Thus the progress of the soul does not come to a standstill in transforming union. The fire of love increases in intensity. Farther on the Saint explains this progress:

> For that which we are describing as coming to pass in it, through the operation of the Holy Spirit which He brings about in it, is much greater than that which comes to pass in the communication and transformation of love. For the one is like a burning coal; but the other, as

[47] VII Mansions, i; Peers, II, 332.
[48] *Living Flame,* iv; Peers, III, 93-102.
[49] *Ibid.,* i; 24.
[50] *Ibid.,* Prologue; 14.

we have said, is like a coal heated with such fervency that it not only burns, but gives forth living flame. And thus these two kinds of union —that is, of union alone, and of love and union with enkindling of love—are in a certain way comparable respectively to the fire of God which, says Isaias, is in Sion, and to the furnace of God which is in Jerusalem.[51] The one signifies the Church Militant, wherein the fire of charity is enkindled to no extreme degree; and the other signifies the vision of peace, which is the Church triumphant, where this fire is as in a furnace enkindled in perfection of love.

Although, as we said, this soul has not attained to such perfection as this, yet, in comparison with the other and common union, it is like a furnace enkindled.[52]

Thus transforming union becomes an ordinary union in relation to those new effects of transforming love that announce eternal life.

These effects do not indicate a change in the nature of union. Transforming union does not change; but the love that brings it to pass can reach greater degrees of perfection and intensity. When the soul arrives at transforming union, all its natural tendencies and properties are absorbed by love. It is wholly filled with love according to its measure. But the measure or capacity of the soul can ceaselessly be enlarged; love can go on progressing in new perfection and intensity. In the furnace of the purified transformed soul, love continues to kindle divine fires more and more subtle, until it carries away the soul as its spouse and its conquest into eternal life.

2. PRESENCE OF THE HOLY SPIRIT

On the day of Annunciation, the Archangel Gabriel hails in the Virgin Mary her fullness of grace and the presence of the Lord within her: "Hail, full of grace, the Lord is with thee." Participation in the divine life and the presence of God, these are the two constitutive elements of sanctifying grace received at Baptism; and these are developed in their plenitude in the transforming union.

Charity, which transforms and deifies the soul, also ensures

[51] Isaias 31:9.
[52] *Living Flame,* st. i; Peers, III, 113-4.

union with God, the principle from which it proceeds. The log of wood is enkindled in the furnace; there it remains. Thus the transformed soul possesses a divine presence distinct from the participation in the divine life that has become habitual. As the apostle says:

> The charity of God is poured forth in our hearts by the Holy Spirit who has been given to us.[53]

All this has already been said. But because in transforming union the divine presence, by its activity and the domination it exercises over the soul, becomes as it were the central fact around which the whole life of the soul gravitates, we have the duty to consider it specially.

a. *Active presence of the Holy Spirit*

Need we recall that the divine presence is constituted by a relation of God with His creatures. God is everywhere by His infinitude, which knows neither limits nor degrees. His infinity therefore has no limitation, no more or less, no here or there. Yet we say that God is here or there, in one way or another, because He is acting there according to different modes. This presence or activity of God does not change God, who is immutable; it affects only the creature. Hence it is a relation of God with His creature.

All God's activity belongs to the divine nature. Hence it is common to the three Persons. Nevertheless, in the language of Scripture and of theology, such or such form of divine activity is attributed by appropriation to one divine Person in particular, by reason of the relation between this activity and the divine relation that is personified in it. Thus the divine work of sanctification of the Church and of souls is attributed to the Holy Spirit, because it is par excellence a work of love, and the Holy Spirit is the spiration of love proceeding from the Father and the Son.

Thus our Lord promises His apostles to send them the Holy

[53] Rom. 5:5.

Spirit to establish His kingdom. On the day of Pentecost, the Spirit descends upon the apostles, visibly takes possession of them, and through them begins His action in the world of souls for the building up of the Church. His manifestations in the primitive Church are frequent and visible. The Holy Spirit is a Person living in the midst of His own. The apostles, by an imposition of hands, give Him to others; and Simon wants to buy this marvelous power.[54] The deacons are filled with His presence. We know that by the Holy Spirit the deacon Philip is led away, after his conversation with the eunuch of Candace.[55] Saint Peter accuses Ananias and Saphira of having lied to the Holy Spirit, and they immediately die at his feet.[56] To support the decisions of the Council of Jerusalem, the apostles declare: "For the Holy Spirit and we have decided. . . ." [57]

Saint Paul's teaching is filled with allusions and testimony concerning the active presence of the Holy Spirit. His doctrine on the charity given by the Spirit and on the Holy Spirit Himself, who abides with us, is fundamental. On this truth, he was to rest his theology and his moral teaching. To the Corinthians, living in the midst of pagan corruption, he happily recalls what respect they owe to themselves and to their own bodies:

> Do you not know that you are the temple of God and that the Spirit of God dwells in you? [58]
>
> Or do you not know that your members are the temple of the Holy Spirit, who is in you, whom you have from God, and that you are not your own? [59]
>
> Do not bear the yoke with unbelievers. . . . What agreement has the temple of God with idols? For you are the temple of the living God.[60]

These exhortations show us how familiar and living this doctrine was among the first Christian communities, since it could serve as an argument and foundation for the precepts of

[54] Acts 8:19.
[55] Acts 8:39.
[56] Acts 5:3.
[57] Acts 15:28.
[58] I Cor. 3:16.
[59] I Cor. 6:19.
[60] II Cor. 6:16.

ordinary moral life. In the mind of the apostle and the first converts, the presence and action of the Holy Spirit in the soul is the specific mark of the Christian; it is the veritable barrier placed by God between Christianity and paganism.

In our time, faith has cooled; it no longer turns with the same warm clarity to that divine Presence, who nevertheless is still acting and living in souls. The Holy Spirit continues to pour out His charity; He gives Himself to every Christian at baptism.

In the brightness of the dawn that comes with the experience of transforming union, the saint recovers these profound realities of the supernatural life—especially the living presence of the Holy Spirit. John of the Cross and Teresa have penetrated to these ever flowing sources of Christian doctrine and life, and have related it to us in descriptions full of savor. The first pages of the *Living Flame* are remarkable in this respect; they offer us precious help in preparing, ourselves, for this divine presence.

b. *Objective presence of the Holy Spirit and the life of love.* The presence of the Holy Spirit in us is not only an active one. It is objective, as we have said; [61] that is, it can be grasped by us through the means of grace. For grace is a participation in the divine life, an aptitude for sharing in the divine operations of knowledge and love. God gives Himself to us; and we know Him and love Him as He knows and loves Himself.

The progressive stages of this discovery through the development of charity, we know. In the first three Mansions, the soul can dispose only of ordinary grace and the efforts of its own faculties. In the fourth Mansions, the divine presence reveals itself deep within by the delightful inflowings of love and light that captivate the faculties, especially the will. The real contact in the fifth Mansions, although obscure and fleeting, holds the will bound, but leaves the soul restless in its loving ardors. In the sixth Mansions, the divine presence lets itself be

[61] Cf. *I Want to See God,* pp. 21-2.

glimpsed for an instant in enrapturing light, so clear is it and dazzling. There is an exchange of promise of abiding union. In order to win the constant presence of its Spouse, the soul, under the influence of His love for it, decides to leave all, to forget all, to be occupied only with loving. God has become the All of the soul—the divine presence, its sole aspiration and its life. The discoveries made at each new visit intensify its desires; so burning are its ardors, they bring it near to death.

This whole work, the discoveries and increase in desire, is of the Holy Spirit. They are the playings and ruses of His love; they prepare for the coming of the Spouse, adorning His dwelling place with virtue and desire.

The divine Spouse Himself has sent before Him the Holy Spirit. Is this not the teaching of the Gospel? Let us hear Saint John of the Cross:

> To this end He first sends His Spirit, Who is His forerunner, as He did to the Apostles, to prepare for Him a dwelling for the soul His Bride, raising her up in delight, setting her garden in order, causing its flowers to open, revealing its gifts, and adorning her with the tapestry of His graces and riches.[62]

The Holy Spirit, forerunner of the Spouse, what a delightful discovery! Thanks to His discreet care and to the "loyal love of those that are betrothed" [63] that the soul gives to its Spouse, He brings it into the dwelling of perfect union.

And the forerunner is there with the soul. His good services are never terminated. They were in fact never more assiduous than now in this estate of transforming union. Is it not in Him that this so lofty union is realized? Is He not the fire that consumes without pain? The flame of love, whose playings and conquests Saint John of the Cross describes in the *Living Flame,* is in truth the Holy Spirit:

> This flame of love is the Spirit of its Spouse—that is, the Holy Spirit. And this flame the soul feels within it, not only as a fire that has consumed and transformed it in sweet love, but also as a fire which

[62] *Spiritual Canticle,* st. xxvi; Peers, II, 129.
[63] *Ibid.,* st. xxvii; 134.

burns within it and sends out flame, as I have said, and that flame bathes the soul in glory and refreshes it with the temper of Divine life. And this is the operation of the Holy Spirit in the soul that is transformed in love.[64]

It is the Holy Spirit who communicates to the soul His flames, producing in it the wounds and burnings of love. He causes it to realize perfectly the divine operations for which it has the capacity in the plenitude of its grace.

Breathing with that His Divine breath, He raises the soul most sublimely, and informs her, that she may breathe in God the same breath of love that the Father breathes in the Son and the Son in the Father, which is the same Holy Spirit that They breathe into her in the said transformation.[65]

It is the Spirit of love, the divine flame, that will draw aside the last veil for the divine meeting in the beatific vision. And until love claims the soul in death, He assures it a perfect life of love.

Here is how Saint John of the Cross describes magnificently, by a comparison of the air and the flame, this life of love of the soul and the Holy Spirit:

The soul that is in union shines forth in splendour. . . . And so we shall say that it is like the air which is within the flame and is enkindled and transformed into fire, for flame is naught else but enkindled air; and the movements made by this flame are not simply those of air nor simply those of fire, but of air and fire together, and the fire causes the air that is enkindled within it to burn.

And in this way we shall understand that the soul with its faculties is illumined within the splendours of God. And the movements of this flame, which are the flickerings and the flamings forth that we have described above, are not wrought only by the soul that is transformed in the flame of the Holy Spirit, neither are they wrought by Him alone; but by Him and by the soul together, the Spirit moving the soul, even as fire moves air that is enkindled. And thus these movements of God and the soul together are not only splendours, but also glorifications which God works in the soul. For these movements or flickerings are the fires and the joyful festivals which we said, in the second line of the first stanza, the Holy Spirit brings to pass within the soul.[66]

[64] *Living Flame,* st. i; Peers, III, 18.
[65] *Spiritual Canticle,* st. xxxviii; Peers, II, 168.
[66] *Living Flame,* st. iii; 58-9.

In these festivals of joy and light, how could the soul not glorify Him who is the forerunner of all these goods, the sweet Guest dwelling within it and in whom it lives. This Father of the poor, this attentive and peaceful Provider, this divine Friend collaborates with the soul and sweetly absorbs it in order to captivate it. Light of its heart and refreshment of all its being, the Flame shines in the darkness and teaches in sweet annointings—as a wound that heals and calms while burning, a subtle flame that envelops and penetrates, a consuming fire that is everywhere and yet eludes any grasp, for, if it is Love, it is also Spirit. The Spirit of Love giving itself, the friendly Flame that consumes, how dear it is to the soul! And the soul's joy is in feeling Love's flame within it; and to feel itself so profoundly, so intimately united with God, that henceforth nothing will be able to separate them. The apostle cried out:

> Who shall separate us from the love of Christ? Shall tribulation, or distress, or persecution, or hunger, or nakedness, or danger, or the sword? . . . But in all these things we overcome because of him who has loved us. For I am sure that neither death, nor life, nor angels, nor principalities, nor things present, nor things to come, nor powers, nor height, nor depth, nor any other creature will be able to separate us from the love of God, which is in Christ Jesus our Lord.[67]

The Spirit of Love has given everything to the soul in this union; and Himself, with all His treasures. He belongs to the soul as the soul belongs to Him. Saint John of the Cross, speaking of the breath of love, that the Father breathes in the Son and the Son in the Father, says that it is "the same Holy Spirit that They breathe into her [the soul] in the said transformation. For it would not be a true transformation if the soul were not united and transformed in the Holy Spirit." [68] Thereafter they, God and the soul, love each other by ceaselessly renewing the communication of their persons; better still, by mutually

[67] Rom. 8:35-39.
[68] *Spiritual Canticle,* st. xxxviii; Peers, II, 168.

giving back all that each has received from the other. Saint John of the Cross writes on this subject:

> Even as God is giving Himself to the soul with free and gracious will, even so likewise the soul, having a will that is the freer and the more generous in proportion as it has a greater degree of union with God, is giving God in God to God Himself, and thus the gift of the soul to God is true and entire. For in this state the soul truly sees that God belongs to it, and that it possesses Him with hereditary possession, as an adopted child of God, by rightful ownership, through the grace that God gave to it of Himself, and it sees that, since He belongs to it, it may give and communicate Him to whomsoever it desires; and thus it gives Him to its Beloved, Who is the very God that gave Himself to it. And herein the soul pays all that it owes; for, of its own will, it gives as much as it has received with inestimable delight and joy.[69]

Thus is realized that equality of love between God and the soul of which Saint John of the Cross has already spoken in the *Spiritual Canticle.*

> I do not mean that she will love God as much as He loves Himself, for this cannot be, but as much as she is loved by Him.[70]

For the soul to love God as much as it is loved by Him, it is necessary but sufficient that it love Him as perfectly and with the same generosity. In fact, the soul now loves God with the love that the Holy Spirit has put at its disposal; it gives Him purely and completely all that it has received from Him, including the gift of God Himself. The transformation of love and perfect union with the Holy Spirit make possible this exchange and equality of love.

c. *Dominating presence of the Holy Spirit and His perfect reign in the soul*

Equality of love, fruit of the mutual gift in transforming union, leaves to the divine transcendence all its rights. The soul could not perfectly possess the Spirit of Love unless it were also perfected by filial fear.[71]

[69] *Living Flame,* st. iii; Peers, III, 90-1.
[70] *Spiritual Canticle,* st. xxxvii; Peers, II, 166.
[71] *Ibid.,* st. xvii; 97.

In this transforming union, the soul is the trickle of water, the drop of water, that falls into the ocean. The drop of water becomes ocean while remaining itself. Yet it takes on the properties of the ocean; and, immersed in the waves, it follows the movements of the moving mass. So it is with the soul.

Transforming union is a victory of God, crowning the long assailings of His love. From now on God rules in the peace of established order. The transformation that has been realized in the soul, and God's hold on it, ensure the stability of His conquest.

In the center of the soul where God dwells, peace is perfect. Habitual union is confirmed there and makes all its effects to be felt. In what measure is this sovereign rule of God through love extended to the faculties, the operative antennae of which reach very far on the outside into regions of noise and disturbance?

Saint John of the Cross answers:

> All the movements and operations and inclinations which the soul had aforetime, and which belonged to the principle and strength of its natural life, are now in this union changed into Divine movements, dead to their own operation and inclination and alive in God. For the soul, like the true daughter of God that it now is, is moved wholly by the Spirit of God, even as Saint Paul teaches, saying: 'They that are moved by the Spirit of God are sons of God Himself.' [72]

In the *Ascent of Mount Carmel,* the Saint had given the same teaching:

> Wherefore the functions of the memory and of the other faculties in this state are all Divine; for, when at last God possesses the faculties and has become the entire master of them, through their transformation into Himself, it is He Himself Who moves and commands them divinely, according to His Divine Spirit and will; and the result of this is that the operations of the soul are not distinct, but all that it does is of God, and its operations are Divine, so that, even as Saint Paul says,[73] that is joined unto God becomes one spirit with Him.
>
> Hence it comes to pass that the operations of the soul in union are of the Divine Spirit and are Divine.[74]

[72] *Living Flame,* st. ii; Peers, III, 143.
[73] I Cor. 6:17.
[74] *Ascent,* Bk. III, i; Peers, I, 215.

Thus Saint John of the Cross presents to us the soul transformed not only in its substances by grace, but also in its powers by the infused virtues. These virtues themselves have been brought under perfect rule by the constant action of the light and impulse of the Holy Spirit.

It is not, then, a wish impossible of fulfillment that Saint Therese of the Child Jesus expressed when, after a conversation on magnetism, she said the next day:

> Your conversation yesterday did me so much good! How I long to be hypnotised by Our Lord! It was my waking thought, and verily it was sweet to surrender Him my will. I want Him to take possession of my faculties in such wise that my acts may no more be mine, or human, but Divine—inspired and guided by the Spirit of Love.[75]

This hold of the Holy Spirit on the faculties and their activity will have considerable consequences in the domain of external fruitfulness and the apostolate, as we shall see in the next chapter. Thus the Spirit is to extend His reign.

But without contradicting these statements of Saint John of the Cross, enunciating a principle and a fundamental truth, should we not show precisely how they apply in actual practice? The Teresian comparison with the king in his palace, whom troubles and numerous wars no longer disturb nor draw out from his dwelling, urges us to do this.[76] We have not forgotten that, according to her own admission, while writing the *Interior Castle* Saint Teresa heard a deafening noise in the upper part of her head, and that during the trials she had to undergo after spiritual marriage she was at times painfully oppressed.

Certainly, the hypostatic union ensured Christ Jesus a perfect control and mastery of every activity of his faculties and powers. The plenitude of grace of the divine maternity was to procure the Virgin Mary the same privilege. But in the redeemed soul, even one that has arrived at transforming union,

[75] *Autobiography,* "Counsels and Reminiscences," 250.
[76] VII Mansions, ii; Peers, II, 338.

does one find the same mastery of the Spirit of Love over all the acts and movements of its powers? Is not such domination reserved for the state of glory in which the soul and all its powers will be caught up and held fixed by the beatific vision?

Here we must recall the distinction already made between habitual union and union in act. The powers, like the branches of a trunk, participate constantly through their roots in habitual union and are thus under the real and profound hold of the Holy Spirit. But when this union is not in act, the faculties and powers remain what they are by nature, changing, fickle, swayed by external influences. The trunk is fixed in God, but the extremity of its antennae, little end branches and leaves, are still stirred and shaken by the winds. There is no voluntary movement, even the first, that escapes the domination and control of the Holy Spirit, sovereign master in the soul. Yet certain reflexes still exist, external influences make themselves felt, which, without disturbing the depths nor harming union with God, show their influence by ripples on the surface of calmed waters.

This triumph of love and dominion of the Holy Spirit in a soul is attested to less by a regulation of all its external acts and attitudes than by a unity wrought in its depths, by the accomplishment of the work God wants of it, by an ardent and peaceful breathing of the Spirit in its whole being, by a love which grows ever greater and is stronger against everything opposed to its desires for more intense union and more complete triumph. Let us point out one last trait, the sovereign liberty of the soul that is thus held by the Holy Spirit. Saint Teresa tells us, and she speaks from intimate experience, that in this union God and the soul command in turn.

> He begins to make such a friend of the soul that not only does He restore its will to it but He gives it His own also. For, now that He is making a friend of it, He is glad to allow it to rule with Him, as we say, turn and turn about.[77]

[77] *Way of Perfection,* xxxii; Peers, II, 139.

Assuredly, the Holy Spirit is the master, and the soul's love is pervaded with filial fear. Yet it is a union of love the Holy Spirit has brought to pass with the soul; His conquest is founded on love. But love has its rights and its demands. The Spirit of Love is caught in His own game. He has made a child of God, and now He must recognize its rights as a Son. "For whoever are led by the Spirit of God, they are the sons of God." [78] It is this work, the most lofty, that we must now consider.

3. IDENTIFICATION WITH CHRIST JESUS

Transforming union ends in identification with Christ Jesus, its most perfect expression and work. "I am the vine, you are the branches." [79] It is only that, but it is that fully and perfectly.

Why not confess our surprise? We had left Christ Jesus in the Mansions of the first phase. The features of His countenance had seemed to lose their luminous and attractive contours under the inflowing of the light of Wisdom. His sacred humanity had disappeared in the dazzle of the substantial contacts with the divinity. Extraordinary favors alone, visions or interior words, recalled His presence. The soul's inability to grasp Him was such that grave warnings from Saint Teresa were needed, lest it abandon Him. During that dark night, the soul wanted only purification and spiritualization and longed only for the flame of love that was burning in the darkness. Everything seemed to it an obstacle to the manifestation and perception of that divine presence. And now this inner flame reveals to it Christ Jesus and causes it to be made into Him. The soul was thinking only of the divinization of itself; and the end that appears to it is an incarnation of the divine life within it. It had forgotten, or did not know with sufficiently deep conviction, that Christ Jesus is not only the light and the way, but that He is veritably the goal of perfection, God's

[78] Rom. 8:14.
[79] John 15:5.

masterpiece in the world; and that we must not only make use of His light, but must be transformed into Him.

Christ Jesus, God's masterpiece, is the work of the Holy Spirit. We know the Archangel Gabriel's answer to the Virgin Mary, when she asks how the great mystery that he is announcing shall take place: "The Holy Spirit shall come upon thee and the power of the Most High shall overshadow thee." [80] The Word takes flesh in the womb of Mary under the fructifying shadow of the Father and by the operation of the Holy Spirit. Every incarnation of the divine life here below is to take place under the same conditions and according to the same laws. "Every good gift and every perfect gift is from above, coming down from the Father of Lights," [81] and it is the Spirit who is to be their distributor and agent here on earth.

The Holy Spirit descends upon the apostles the day of Pentecost; He takes possession of the soul as of a temple at baptism, to effect in it the incarnation of the divine life. We know the work that is His, the eternal design of God that unifies the action of the Holy Spirit in the Church and in souls.

> God the Father . . . has blessed us with every spiritual blessing on high in Christ. Even as he chose us in him before the foundation of the world. . . . He predestined us to be adopted through Jesus Christ as his sons, according to the purpose of his will, unto the praise of the glory of his grace, with which he has favored us in his beloved Son.[82]

The action of the Holy Spirit is entirely orientated toward that effective realization of the divine adoption and that extension of Christ Jesus into our souls by the communication of His grace. The Spirit, in each soul and in the Church, builds up the fullness of Christ, the whole Christ, which is the Church.

The grace that He pours out into souls is in fact a filial grace, which likens us closely to the Word by making us sons by adoption, as He Himself is Son by nature. The apostle says:

[80] Luke 1:35.
[81] James 1:17.
[82] Eph. 1:4-6.

You have received a spirit of adoption as sons, by virtue of which we cry, "Abba! Father!" The Spirit himself gives testimony to our spirit that we are sons of God. But if we are sons, we are heirs also: heirs indeed of God and joint heirs with Christ.[83]

This grace which thus proclaims its name makes us like the Word, when we make it ours by that contemplation in which again the Holy Spirit intervenes. Again the apostle says:

But we all, with faces unveiled, reflecting as in a mirror the glory of the Lord, are being transformed into his very image from glory to glory, as through the Spirit of the Lord.[84]

But the source par excellence of the divine life here below is the Holy Eucharist. Principal channel of grace, whence flow all the others, it is especially through the Eucharist that the Holy Spirit sanctifies souls and builds up the Church. This sacrament, a necessary condition for supernatural life, gives Christ and His life—not only the grace of the Word, but the very flesh and blood of His sacred humanity.

"I am the bread of life," Jesus insistently repeats. And He says precisely:

Amen, amen, I say to you, unless you eat the flesh of the Son of Man, and drink his blood, you shall not have life in you. He who eats my flesh and drinks my blood has life everlasting. . . . He who eats my flesh, and drinks my blood, abides in me and I in him.[85]

The Holy Eucharist, by giving Christ, gives the life of God. It gives life to souls by uniting them to Christ Jesus. It is par excellence the sanctifying sacrament, because it is the sacrament of the soul's union with Christ Jesus. By thus diffusing His life in all the members, it is at the same time the sacrament which forms the unity of the Church.

Holiness and the plan of God are summed up in a few words in the priestly prayer of Jesus:

That they may be one, even as we are one: I in them and thou in me; that they may be perfected in unity.[86]

[83] Rom. 8:15-7.
[84] II Cor. 3:18.
[85] John 6:48-54.
[86] John 17:23.

I am the vine, you are the branches. He who abides in me, and I in him, he bears much fruit; for without me you can do nothing. If anyone does not abide in me, he shall be cast outside as the branch and wither; and they shall gather them up and cast them into the fire, and they shall burn.[87]

These statements are firm and exact. The divine life in us is the life of Christ; it proceeds from Him and unites us to Him to constitute with Him a new reality, the entire vine, the whole Christ made up of Christ and His members. This essential truth must be realized and manifested in the transforming union.

Certainly, we cannot ask of divine grace to reveal all its potentialities during the period of growth. The seed that dies, the delicate shoot that comes up, do not tell exactly what they bear within them. Every germination and all growth take place in darkness or at least in mystery. Only the full flowering shows forth the properties of the life and the quality of the fruit. So too, after the periods of obscurity that have hidden from us some of its properties, grace, in the transforming union, is to reveal its essential riches, showing us that it is working a transformation by a likeness of love to Christ Jesus.

The exterior revelation of Christ in souls will take different forms. The grace of Christ is actually multiform and shines out in diverse reflections; but transformation in Him must be real and deep. It must be attested to by the likeness that love creates in the will, thoughts, sentiments, and external activity.

In the soul and life of the contemplatives we are studying, this loving likeness with Christ has been realized, and we need not, for the moment, point it out. But we must note that it was in the light of transforming union that they discovered this fulfillment of their grace.

The Epistles of Saint Paul abound in testimony to this discovery and this awareness of Christ within him:

For I know that this will turn out for my salvation, . . . in accord with my eager longing and hope that in nothing I shall be put to

[87] John 15:56.

shame, but that with complete assurance now as at all times Christ will be glorified in my body, whether through life or through death. For to me to live is Christ and to die is gain.[88]

He wants to know nothing else than Christ:

For I determined not to know anything among you, except Jesus Christ and Him crucified.[89]

He is concerned not with speculative science, but with that practical wisdom that is life and practical fulfillment. And so he preferred it to all the rest:

But the things that were gain to me, these, for the sake of Christ, I have counted loss. Nay more, I count everything loss because of the excelling knowledge of Jesus Christ, my Lord. For his sake I have suffered the loss of all things, and I count them as dung that I may gain Christ and be found in him.[90]

And so, what can he desire for his faithful, especially for his dear Ephesians, if not this realization of Christ in them, and knowledge of all things through charity.

. . . and to have Christ dwelling through faith in your hearts: so that, being rooted and grounded in love, you may be able to comprehend with all the saints what is the breadth and length and height and depth, and to know Christ's love which surpasses knowledge, in order that you may be filled unto all the fullness of God.[91]

This profound penetration into the charity of Christ and this transformation in Him, together with the lights of living faith that accompany it—what a happy definition of transforming union, the fullness of God in the soul!

In Saint Teresa this is what we do in fact discover. After describing the wondrous union with God that spiritual marriage brings to pass, the Saint immediately adds, recalling the word of Saint Paul:

"For to me, to live is Christ; and to die is gain." This I think, the soul may say here, for it is here that the little butterfly to which we

[88] Philip 1:20-1.
[89] I Cor. 2:2.
[90] Philip 3:7-9.
[91] Eph. 3:17-9.

have referred dies, and with the greatest joy, because Christ is now its life.[92]

As happens to her rather frequently, the Saint has not followed the logic of her thought, but has been drawn along by a reality she perceives, interrupting thus her chain of thought. A little farther on, she insists with enthusiasm on the discovery she has just made. Speaking of Christ's praying for His apostles, she says:

> His Majesty went on to say: "Not for them alone do I pray, but also for all who believe in Me"; and again: "I am in them."
>
> Oh God help me! How true are these words and how well the soul understands them, for in this state it can actually see their truth for itself.[93]

It is in very truth with Christ Jesus that the spiritual marriage has been concluded. An extraordinary favor, an imaginary vision of the sacred humanity has come to the soul, as ordinarily happens at the different Teresian stages, to make explicit the meaning of the interior grace that is given it.[94] Transforming union is thus a union and communion of persons, realized with Jesus Christ.

Saint John of the Cross, that great explorer of the divine, could not fail to discover Christ in the riches of his grace. Over and over he mentions the divine filiation in grace that comes to us through the Spirit of God. Especially on the summits of transforming union, he insists on the discovery of Christ Jesus and His mysteries. We should reread the whole commentary on the twenty-sixth stanza. It begins:

> And then we shall go forth
> To the lofty caverns of the rock . . .
>
> One of the causes which move the soul most to desire to enter into this thicket of the wisdom of God and to have a knowledge of suffering very deeply in His judgments, as we have said, is that it may be able to pass on thence to a union of its understanding and to a knowl-

[92] VII Mansions, ii; Peers, II, 335-6.
[93] *Ibid.;* 337.
[94] *Ibid.;* 334.

edge of the high mysteries of the Incarnation of the Word, as of the soul's highest and most delectable wisdom.[95]

This knowledge is an experimental knowledge proceeding from connaturality with Christ through grace as well as through suffering. The soul plunges into this knowledge, sweetest fruit of transforming union. Thus the Saint, speaking of the Bride and her Spouse, says:

> They will proceed farther still to a knowledge of the sublime mysteries of God and man, which are sublimest in wisdom, and are hidden in God; and that there they will enter, and the soul will be engulfed and absorbed in them.[96]

The treasures of these mysteries are inexhaustible:

> So much so that, despite all the mysteries and wonders which have been discovered by holy doctors and understood by holy souls in this estate of life, there has remained much more to be said, and even to be understood.[97]

There are indeed "great depths to be fathomed in Christ. For He is like an abundant mine with many recesses containing treasures." And the Saint adds that knowledge of these "is the loftiest wisdom attainable in this life." [98] Knowledge of the mysteries, attained in the riches of grace given by Christ, is enriched still more by the awareness of the presence of the Word in the bosom of the soul. This perception of the Word as Spouse, His marvelous awakenings under the breathing of the Spirit of Love, such are the last confidences that we have gathered from Saint John of the Cross, confidences that died away in the silence of his powerlessness to say more.

We are truly on the summit. We have gathered the last and highest fruit of the transforming union, the most beautiful and also the most simple: union with Christ Jesus and a likeness to Him through love, for the realization of the whole Christ.

[95] *Spiritual Canticle,* st. xxxvi; Peers, II, 160.
[96] *Ibid.*
[97] *Ibid.;* 161.
[98] *Ibid.*

Christian perfection and contemplative perfection lie in this union and this realization of Jesus Christ our Lord.

To conclude, let us affirm that transforming union is a transformation through loving resemblance with Christ Jesus, the God-Man. The saint is the branch brought to fullness of life by the sap of the vine that is Christ.

Against the naturalistic tendencies in the spirituality of those who, in order better to embrace Christ Jesus as a brother and make of Him the companion of their labor, envisage Him in their own measure, making of Him a perfect type of humanity, a superman whose countenance is enlightened by a reflection from on high but in whom the divinity is not only hidden but absent, let us assert that Jesus is God, and that transformation in Him is a divinization demanding the violence of the Joannine detachment and self-denial.

Against Angelism, which seeks perfecton in a disincarnate purity, and against Neoplatonism, which places perfection in the very high intellectuality of mystical perception, against both, which speak of divinization only as a surpassing of everything human and a sublimation of the intellectual powers, we must declare that perfection consists in the likeness of love with Jesus, God and Man, and that this resemblance is wrought in us by an incarnation of the divine life, which transforms but does not destroy human nature.

Divinization of human nature, that we may be the children of God; incarnation of the divine life that we may be Christians—such is the twofold realism we must find in transforming union if it be genuine and authentically Christian.

CHAPTER IX

The Saint in the Whole Christ

I have chosen you, and have appointed you that you should go and bear fruit, and that your fruit should remain.[1]

This declaration of Jesus in His parting words to the apostles after the Last Supper, followed what He had said about the close bonds that were to unite Him with them henceforward:

I am the vine, you are the branches. He who abides in me, and I in him, he bears much fruit; for without me you can do nothing.[2]

The branch lives by the sap that rises in the vine. Its function is to transform the sap into fruits. That is its *raison d'être.* If, then, the branch does not bear fruit, it normally should be cut off and cast into the fire. Such is the order of things.

Jesus stresses this point to indicate that fruitfulness is the reason for His choice of apostles and His action in their regard. They are to go into the world and bear fruit for the glory of the Father. The world into which He sends them is wicked and dangerous; it will persecute them. And so He prays for them, adding:

I do not pray that you take them out of the world, but that thou keep them from evil.[3]

After His resurrection, Jesus again declares:

As the Father has sent me, I also send you.[4]

[1] John 15:16.
[2] John 15:5.
[3] John 17:15.
[4] John 20:21.

Consequently there can be no doubt. The work of sanctification wrought by Jesus in His apostles, the mysterious bonds of grace that He created between them and Himself, as well as the astounding powers that He gave them, all this is in view of their mission in the world. The fullness of grace and the fullness of powers conferred are to assure Jesus of apostles who will continue His mission. They have been chosen by Jesus; they will be transformed by His Spirit to become other Christs here below, and bear fruits in the world.

Saint Teresa grasped this truth perfectly:

It will be a good thing, sisters, if I tell you why it is that the Lord grants so many favours in this world. Although you will have learned this from the effects they produce, if you have observed them, I will speak about it further here, so that none of you shall think that He does it simply to give these souls pleasure. That would be to make a great error. For His Majesty can do nothing greater for us than grant us a life which is an imitation of that lived by His Beloved Son. I feel certain, therefore, that these favours are given us to strengthen our weakness, as I have sometimes said here, so that we may be able to imitate Him in His great sufferings.[5]

The Saint insists and states her thought more precisely:

For if the soul [that has arrived at transforming union] is much with Him, as it is right it should be, it will very seldom think of itself; its whole thought will be concentrated upon finding ways to please Him and upon showing Him how it loves Him. This, my daughters, is the aim of prayer: this is the purpose of the Spiritual Marriage, of which are born works and good works alone.[6]

She wants to be well understood. She is not speaking of beginners but of those who have arrived at transforming union:

You may think that I am speaking about beginners, and that later on one may rest: but, as I have already told you, the only repose that these souls enjoy is of an interior kind; of outward repose they get less and less, and they have no wish to get more. . . . It did not then understand what great gain can be derived from trials . . . nor did it realize how the companionship which it now enjoys would give it much greater strength than it ever had before. For if, as David says, with the holy we shall be holy, it cannot be doubted that, if we are

[5] VII Mansions, iv; Peers, II, 345.
[6] *Ibid.;* 346.

made one with the Strong, we shall gain strength through the most sovereign union of spirit with Spirit.[7]

These texts sum up Saint Teresa's teaching in the last chapter of the seventh Mansions. They are a commentary on the last words of our Lord, already quoted. "I have appointed you that you should go and bear fruit." The end of the work of sanctification wrought by God, including contemplation and transforming union, is here clearly stated. It seems to us simple and normal. Why delay over it!

Yet, on comparing these Teresian texts with the last pages of the *Spiritual Canticle* and the *Living Flame,* we have the surprise of finding in the soul of Saint John of the Cross other aspirations, another movement. On the same summit, the two Saints seem not to live in the same atmosphere. Teresa's only desire is to live the life of Christ here below, to give herself like Him to works that will procure the glory of His Father and the salvation of souls. John of the Cross longs for the depths of God, their peace and their light, and for the vision face to face of eternal life. There is scarcely need to cite texts to find again that movement of the Joannine soul that carried us away with its peaceful and ardent force, in the preceding chapters:

> Let us rejoice, Beloved,
> And let us go to see ourselves in thy beauty,
> To the mountain or the hill where flows the pure water;
> Let us enter farther into the thicket.[8]

The *Canticle* closes in the joy of peace finally found:

. . . all these faculties descend and come down from their natural operations, from which they cease, to interior recollection; whereto may the Lord Jesus, the sweetest Spouse, be pleased to bring all such as invoke His Most Holy Name, to Whom belong honour and glory together with the Father and the Holy Spirit forever and forever. Amen.[9]

[7] *Ibid.;* 347.
[8] *Spiritual Canticle,* st. xxxv; Peers, II, 156.
[9] *Ibid.,* xxxix; 176.

This hymn to the divine peace of transforming union at the end of the *Spiritual Canticle* is taken up again with more sublime accents in the *Living Flame,* until it dies away in the silence of the ineffable:

> Oh, how happy is this soul that is ever conscious of God reposing and resting within its breast! Oh, how well it is that it should withdraw from all things, flee from business and live in boundless tranquillity, lest anything, however small, should disturb or move the bosom of the Beloved within it.[10]

These two contemplatives arrived at transforming union, both by the same way. Many times in the course of the journey, especially in the turmoil of the sixth Mansions, they had compared their experiences and recognized their unity of thought. Now on the summit, their aspirations seem divergent.

Each one of them, moreover, has a school. Among their disciples, there are some for whom transforming union is a haven of peace in which the soul, having finally found God, can do nothing better than love Him in solitude, enjoying His intimacy, counting the love that it gives Him preferable to all else, especially to external works. Others consider the tranquil possession of God in transforming union as a means to serve God more freely and more effectively. The latter adopt the definition given by Saint Teresa of the truly spiritual person:

> Do you know when people really become spiritual? It is when they become the slaves of God and are branded with His sign, which is the sign of the Cross, in token that they have given Him their freedom. Then He can sell them as slaves to the whole world, as He Himself was sold.[11]

How solve the problem posed by the divergence of these two tendencies on the heights of transforming union? To be satisfied with saying that the one who wants to be buried in God is a contemplative soul, and that the other, who longs to work for the Church, is active, would be to do injury to Saint Teresa and offer as a solution a mere label. The problem lies

[10] *Living Flame,* st. iv; Peers, III, 100.
[11] VII Mansions, iv; Peers, II, 346.

deeper; it has to do with the finality of transforming union here on earth and of the love that brings it to pass. Let us try to solve it.

A. The twofold movement of love

1. FILIAL MOVEMENT TOWARD GOD

The charity that is poured into our hearts by the Holy Spirit makes us children of God and relates us to the Word in the bosom of the Holy Trinity. It finds, in this filial character, its essential movement. The spirit that is given us cries: Abba, Father! It makes us co-heirs with Christ. Through it, the soul sighs after its share in the heritage that is God Himself. We come from God, and we return to Him. This is the law of the whole of creation; but it is especially marked in man, the head of creation.

Saint Paul, the herald of the great mystery, plumbed the depth of this yearning of all creatures, of which the loftiest form and most perfect expression is the divine filiation of the Christian. He puts into words the painful force of it and its amplitude:

> The eager longing of creation awaits the revelation of the sons of God. . . . For we know that all creation groans and travails in pain until now. And not only it, but we ourselves also who have the first-fruits of the Spirit—we ourselves groan within ourselves, waiting for the adoption as sons, the redemption of our body. For in hope were we saved.[12]

While waiting until hope is fulfilled in the bosom of the Father, the Holy Spirit sustains and guides the longing of the soul in the dark night of here below.

> But in like manner the Spirit also helps our weakness. For we do not know what we should pray for as we ought, but the Spirit himself pleads for us with unutterable groanings. And he who searches the hearts knows what the Spirit desires, that he pleads for the saints according to God.[13]

[12] Rom. 8:19-25.
[13] Rom. 8:26-7.

Both supernatural charity and the Holy Spirit who is given to us with it, unite to lift us up in our yearning toward God our Father.

This primary exigency of filial love is what Jesus first expresses in His priestly prayer:

> Father, the hour has come! Glorify thy Son, that thy Son may glorify thee. . . . I have glorified thee on earth; I have accomplished the work that thou hast given me to do. And now do thou, Father, glorify me with thyself, with the glory that I had with thee before the world existed.[14]

To return to its divine source, such is the desire of filial love. To enter into it more profoundly and be lost in its depths, this is the wages of the loving soul. Its recompense is a greater love, a closer union with its God. Saint John of the Cross writes:

> The which wages and recompense are naught else, nor can the soul desire aught else, than greater love. . . . The soul that loves awaits not the end of its labour, but the end of its work. For its work is to love, and of this work, which is to love, the soul awaits the end and termination, which is the perfection and fulfilment of loving God.[15]

For the loving soul who possesses God here on earth in the darkness of faith, the perfect fulfillment is to possess Him in the beatific vision, for "this is everlasting life, that they may know thee, the only true God, and him whom thou hast sent, Jesus Christ." [16]

2. MOVEMENT TOWARD SOULS

Although essential to it, this yearning to possess God in perfect vision is not the only movement issuing from the depths of our supernatural charity.

While the other-worldly philosophies of Plotinus and Plato declare themselves fully satisfied when they have grasped in some way the idea or the spirit divinized by their love; and while the natural mystics think to reach the goal of their aspira-

[14] John 17:1-5.
[15] *Spiritual Canticle,* st. ix; Peers, II, 60.
[16] John 17:3.

tions when they can plunge into the bosom of the great pantheistic all and there lose themselves, Christian charity longs for something else in God than the possession of God Himself. When it has come to perfect union with God, our supernatural charity finds in Him Persons, and is united with each one of them. A love that tends only to union with being can rest in its possession. Love united to living persons is bound to their thought, their life, their movement. Grappled to these persons, it cannot leave their side. All that is theirs belongs to it also. Its urge is to follow them, to share their desires, their preoccupations, to work with them. Its rest is in being united with their movement, their activity. Such is the happy destiny of our supernatural charity; it causes us to enter into the rhythm of the Triune Life, uniting us to each one of the three divine Persons.

Divine charity is poured out upon us by the Holy Spirit; with it and through it, He Himself comes to take possession of our soul. In the measure that charity works in us a transformation of love, it surrenders us to the Spirit of Love. When the transformation is complete, all our movements, all our aspirations are regulated and ordered by Love. Having become the sovereign master and lord of the soul by His hold on it—from the depths where He dwells to the most exterior of the faculties, which posit divine acts under His impulse—the Holy Spirit binds us to all the movements, the aspirations of substantial Love, which is Himself, in the bosom of God. And He associates us with His works.

We know that it is the Spirit of Love who carries out the eternal design of God. He placed the foundations for it by bringing to pass the mystery of the Incarnation in the womb of Mary. Since then, He continues His work by pouring into our souls a filial charity that identifies us with the Incarnate Word, Christ Jesus. This grace makes us one with Christ, that we may form with Him the whole Christ.

Such is the destiny of our grace: it makes us into Christ, subjecting us perfectly to the lights and movements of the same

Spirit of Love who guided Christ Himself. Thus are we bound to Christ; in Him and His mystical body, the Church, we are to follow all the impulses of the Spirit of Love.

We know the movements that Love imposed upon the Incarnate Word.

For God so loved the world that he gave his only-begotten Son.[17] The Word came down among us. He took on our flesh. He humbled Himself to the depths of our sinful humanity, taking the form of a slave [18] and making Himself into sin for our sakes.[19] Thus Jesus Christ came here below not to judge but to save by bringing His light and the fire of His love. He dwelt among us. "Having loved his own who were in the world," writes the evangelist Saint John, "he loved them to the end." [20] And this end is His sacred Passion, and Calvary, and the Eucharist—mysteries orientated toward the building up of the Church, the whole Christ. The Word incarnate wills to carry us away, as members of His mystical body, into the unity of the Holy Trinity, there to share in His divine operations.

Such is the life and movement of the Word under the impulse of love. We recall the parable of the eagle coming down for her young, helpless to fly with their tiny wings.

> As the eagle enticing her young to fly,
> And hovering over them,
> He spreads his wings: and hath taken him
> And carried him on his shoulders.[21]

Saint John of the Cross took up and developed this gracious and strong image used by Moses in a hymn of thanksgiving.

> This love could not soar so high as to attain to the capture of this Divine Bird of the heights. But since He humbled Himself to look upon us and to incite us to fly upward ever higher, and thus gave worth to our love, He Himself was taken captive . . . — that is, He Himself was glad and pleased and for that reason was captivated.

[17] John 3:16.
[18] Phil. 2:7.
[19] II Cor. 5:21.
[20] John 13:1.
[21] Deut. 32:11.

> . . . And thus it is a credible thing that a bird of lowly flight may capture a royal eagle flying high, if the eagle descends to its lowliness, desiring to be caught.[22]

This means that the royal Eagle still descends; that His love is always hovering over us and lets itself be taken captive so as more easily to carry us away up to the heights,[23] prisoners in the bonds of His love. And so Saint Therese of the Child Jesus asks Him to do this for her. All her hope lies in this habitual movement of the Incarnate Word. She writes to her sister:

> My folly consists in begging the Eagles, my brothers, to obtain for me the favour of flying upward to the Sun of Love with the divine Eagle's own wings. . . .
>
> One day, so I hope, adored Eagle, You will come for Your little bird, and mounting with it to the Fire of Love, You will plunge it for eternity in the burning Abyss of the Love to which it has offered itself as victim.[24]

This parable of the divine Eagle descending to sieze its prey and carry it away, ascending on high, represents the action that love renews ceaselessly through those it has conquered and identified with Christ Jesus. At the same time that love introduces them into the depths of the life that is in God, it causes them to descend to the depths of the sin of humanity here below. With them and through them, love continues to make incarnate the divine life in souls, to groan and to carry on the combat unto the complete triumph willed by the Father.

Transforming union, by introducing the soul into God, does not isolate it from the world. Such union associates the soul with the intense life of the Church. The more the saints are held captive by love, the nearer they are to us; for in divinizing them, charity causes them to enter into the depths of sin, the great suffering of humanity. If it were otherwise, it would not be true that they are identified with Christ. Their charity would not be Christian, for Jesus has expressly said:

[22] *Spiritual Canticle,* st. xxii; Peers, II, 117.
[23] Eph. 4:8-10.
[24] To Sister Marie of the Sacred Heart, September 14, 1896; *Letters,* p. 286.

By this will all men know that you are my disciples, if you have love for one another.[25]

The measure of this love for neighbor is Christ's own, the love that He Himself gave:

This is my commandment, that you love one another as I have loved you.[26]

We know what this measure is; a simple reference suffices:

Greater love than this no one has, that one lay down his life for his friends.[27]

In the evening of this life, we shall be judged on love, so that the degree of our love may be taken as the degree of our glory and our capacity for the beatific vision. But Jesus, describing the circumstances of this judgment, states exactly the proof of love that will be asked for:

Come, blessed of my Father, take possession of the kingdom prepared for you from the foundation of the world; for I was hungry and you gave me to eat; I was thirsty and you gave me drink.[28]

The choice of such a criterion surprises us, as it astonishes those to whom it is applied:

Then the just will answer him saying, "Lord, when did we see thee hungry, and feed thee"; . . . and answering the king will say to them, "Amen I say to you, as long as you did it for one of these, the least of my brethren, you did it for me." [29]

The objection brought forth an insistence and a happy precision that leave no more doubt. The love on which we shall be judged is the love that we have given to God in our brothers.

Of the two movements of supernatural charity in us, the first is essential to it, the second is imposed by the Spirit of Love and by Christ Jesus, with whom it unifies the soul. The two are sanctioned by precept:

[25] John 13:35.
[26] John 15:12.
[27] John 15:13.
[28] Matt. 25:34-5.
[29] Matt. 25:37, 40.

Jesus said:

> "Thou shalt love the Lord thy God
> with thy whole heart
> and with thy whole soul,
> and with thy whole mind."

This is the greatest and the first commandment. And the second is like it,

> "Thou shalt love thy neighbor as thyself."

On these two commandments depend the whole Law and the Prophets.[30]

Of these two similar commandments that sum up the whole law, the first is the greater; but it is the accomplishment of the second that guarantees the value and quality of charity by evincing its efficacy.

3. THESE TWO MOVEMENTS ARE UNITED IN LOVE FOR CHRIST

Thus we have a twofold commandment corresponding to the twofold movement of divine love. Are these two movements contrary to one another? Our mind is so prone to set things in opposition in order better to distinguish them, especially when there is real opposition between the symbols that express the realities. Such is the case here. Filial love for God seems to mount upward and lift us up; love for neighbor seems to descend and draw us downward. The first divinizes; the second renders carnal. But let us not allow our mind to play upon the symbols. Let us go to the living concrete reality of love and its activity.

The saint that has arrived at transforming union is no longer on the edge where the mind considers and disputes. He is plunged in the work of love; and in his experience he meets with a light that blinds the understanding, but reduces all antinomies.

These antinomies or apparent oppositions are one of the laws

[30] Matt. 22:37-40.

of divine love, and love bears them within it as one of its riches; they mark its works as with a personal seal. This love both takes on flesh and divinizes, it spreads both joy and tribulation, it produces a light that is darkness. Christ Jesus, who assures its reign here below, is the Word made flesh who, without ceasing to enjoy the beatific vision, knew the most painful suffering that man has borne here on earth, and finally triumphed by dying on the cross.

How could the saint, transformed by love and identified with Christ, not bear within him these riches characteristic of divine love? Indeed, the love that divinizes him leave him a man like us; he bears within him both Thabor and Gethsemane; he is the happiest of men because he enjoys the presence of the Word in his bosom, and the most unhappy because he bears the sin of the world. Confirmed in God by transforming union, he is nevertheless the man and the saint of a particular epoch, of a people, of a very definite age of the mystical body of Christ in its growth. The divine and the eternal in him do not hinder but rather oblige him to be incarnate in what is the most humanly temporal of his time.

The signs and the words accompanying and explaining the favor of spiritual marriage granted to Saint Teresa bring out and clarify these remarkable antinomies. The Saint writes, speaking of our Lord:

> Then He revealed Himself to me, in an imaginary vision, most interiorly, as on other occasions, and He gave me His right hand, saying to me: "Behold this nail. It is a sign that from to-day onward thou shalt be My Bride. Until now, thou hadst not merited this; but henceforward thou shalt regard My honour not only as that of thy Creator and King and God but as that of My very bride. My honour is thine, and thine, Mine." [31]

The union is thereafter perfectly confirmed. Teresa belongs to Christ and Christ to Teresa. Jesus appears to her to give her assurance of this. But let us look at the fact, let us consider the meaning of the words. On carrying her away with Him into the

[31] *Spiritual Relations,* xxxv; Peers, I, 352.

bosom of God, the incarnate Word vows her to the service of His honor here below, like a true bride. The wedding ring is replaced by a nail that attaches her to the cross. Contradictions these? Who would dare to say so? Teresa is not surprised. She knows the privileges and the duties of love. The Christ who unites her perfectly to Himself is Christ Jesus, triumphant in Heaven and militant and suffering on earth. It is rather this latter Christ that she is to live and prolong while she is on earth. Spiritual marriage brings to pass perfect union with Christ Jesus in the plenitude of His mystical body.

The divergencies that we pointed out between Saint John of the Cross and Saint Teresa are resolved in this light. Having arrived at transforming union they both bear within them the fullness of Christ with His antinomial riches and the twofold movement of His love for God and for souls. In order to explain how some particular riches or how one of the movements of love is more clearly explicit in one Saint or the other, it is enough to recall that God's gifts are displayed in the saints with diverse tonalities corresponding to the particular grace, the mission, and the temperament of each one.

Saint John of the Cross, reformer, confessor, writer, superior of a monastery, his days given to apostolic works, is taken up with the cares of his charges, with anxieties concerning the government and future of the undertaken Reform. How, in the midst of these works and preoccupations, so heavy at times, could this contemplative with penetrating gaze and refined spiritual sense not entertain the ardent desire to rest in the depths of the luminous darkness of the Beloved who, seeming to sleep in his bosom, whispers to him so many and such sweet secrets?

Moreover, it is his special mission to unveil the secret works of the Spirit of Love in all those who surrender themselves to Him and allow Him to operate in the silence of the dark night. It is his task to awaken those who sleep, to aid all who are held back by their ignorance, to speak vigorously to the agitated and the impassioned of his time, to the activists of all times, the spiritually superficial who live at the periphery of their souls, the illuminists in quest of extraordinary favors, the quietists drowned in delight. He must make them hear the voice of Holy Wisdom who, from the profound regions where she distributes her treasures, cries out to them:

> O souls created for these grandeurs and called thereto! What do ye do? Wherein do ye occupy yourselves? Your desires are meannesses, and your possessions miseries. O wretched blindness of the eyes of your souls, which are blind to so great a light and deaf to so clear a voice, seeing not that for so long as ye seek grandeurs and glories ye remain miserable and deprived of so many blessings, and have become ignorant and unworthy! [32]

Saint John of the Cross is concerned with extolling the divine riches of Wisdom, because it was his mission to reveal them to the world and sharpen desire for them. He proclaims how few are those who know them and numerous, on the other hand, those who tarry along the way, because it was his mission to guide souls to the divine Source by the painful road of the dark night. He himself groans in sight of these treasures because, at grips with the sin of the world, he does not yet possess them in the measure of his boundless hope.

Did not the saintly Curé of Ars, he too, long for the solitude of La Trappe, to which he twice stole away? We can understand the anguish and flight of this man, bound as he was by love, spending long hours in his confessional where sin poured in and whence there issued in abundance divine mercy. Of the two aspirations of love, toward God and toward souls, the one that is not satisfied makes itself felt in painful groanings of the spirit.

Thus we understand why Saint Teresa of Avila, hearing of the increasing ruins in France because of the wars of religion, lamented in her cloister her powerlessness as a woman to give aid.

[32] *Spiritual Canticle,* st. xxxviii; Peers, II, 170.

This troubled me very much, and, as though I could do anything, or be of any help in the matter, I wept before the Lord and entreated Him to remedy this great evil. I felt that I would have laid down a thousand lives to save a single one of all the souls that were being lost there. And, seeing that I was a woman, and a sinner, and incapable of doing all I should like in the Lord's service. . . .

Oh, my Redeemer, my heart cannot conceive this without being sorely distressed.[33]

Several years in the reformed Convent of Saint Joseph, which she had founded, sufficed for Saint Teresa to develop in a marvelous way her love for God, to discover its riches and its demands.

As time went on, my desires to do something for the good of some soul grew greater and greater, and I often felt like one who has a large amount of treasure in her charge and would like everyone to enjoy it but whose hands are tied so that she cannot distribute it. In just this way it seemed to me that my soul was bound; for the favours which the Lord granted it during those years were very great and they all seemed to be ill spent upon me.[34]

This is a surprise for Saint Teresa more than for us. Such love needs to communicate itself. It has a mission of conquest. The cloister that love had built itself to secure its own development and intimacy with God now only intensifies love's desires.

But there is no room for doubt; desires to do more good for souls are not passing velleities, a mere natural need for change. They bear authentic testimony to a divine mission. The external deeds and inner reactions of Saint Teresa prove this superabundantly.

And then the accounts given by the Franciscan Maldonado cast oil on the burning fire:

He had only a little while previously returned from the Indies. He began to tell me about the many millions of souls perishing there for lack of teaching, and, before going away, he gave us a sermon and a talk inciting us to penitence. I was so distressed at the way all these souls were being lost that I could not contain myself. I went to one of the hermitages, weeping sorely, and called upon Our Lord, beseeching Him to find me a means of gaining some soul for His service when

[33] *Way of Perfection,* i; Peers, II, 3-4.
[34] *Foundations,* i; Peers, III, 3.

so many were being carried away by the devil. . . . How I envied those who could spend their lives ministering to others for the love of Our Lord, even though they might suffer a thousand deaths! Whenever I read in the lives of saints of how they converted souls, I seem to feel much more devout, tender and envious of them than when I read of all the martyrdoms that they suffered. This is an inclination given me by Our Lord; and I think He prizes one soul which by His mercy, and through our diligence and prayer, we may have gained for Him, more than all the other services we can render Him.[35]

Obeying the imperious impulse of her love, this contemplative, who was dreaming only of being alone with God alone, undertakes the foundation of many convents. To her daughters she presents as a vocation the fruit of her successive discoveries. She procures solitude for them so that, in profound inner contacts with God, their love may be enkindled and put at the service of the Church. The external works that she cannot herself do, this genial woman will bring to pass by extending her Reform to the Friars animated with her spirit and her desires. Thus this contemplative pursues her way, sacrificing her tranquility and her soul for a work that can be only for the Church. And it is when she has sacrificed all, even the work of her Reform by accepting to return as prioress at the Convent of the Incarnation, that Jesus comes to her for the perfect union of spiritual marriage. Thus it appears clearly that the two movements of love diverge only apparently and only on the external plane, that in reality they mutually sustain one another; their diversity is profound harmony and riches.

Saint Therese of the Child Jesus offers us an example of the harmonious synthesis of the two movements of love toward God and toward souls. By touch after touch, delicate, yet ever more profound, God produces this masterpiece, this great apostle of modern times. The grace of conversion of Christman 1886 is followed by the gratuitous grace that kindles in her great zeal for souls: a picture of our Lord on the cross, half-slipped out of her missal, showing His hand pierced and bleeding. The sight of this enkindles that thirst for souls that goes on increasing

[35] *Ibid.*; 3-4.

after the conversion of Pranzini,[36] a notorious criminal. But she refuses, during her journey to Rome, to read the *Annals* of missionary religious, because for the moment she wants to sacrifice everything to the increase of love. Yet she enters the Carmel "to save souls and pray for priests." [37] Her great desires grow as love grows, desires to suffer for Christ and souls, boundless desires for the apostolate that become a veritable martyrdom.[38] Love allows her to realize all her aspirations—the love that places her at the center of the Church, there to pour out life as does the heart in the whole body. She longs to have this gift to the Church take on all forms and all means to be efficacious and complete. A few weeks before her death the little Saint says as she looks at a picture of Joan of Arc in prison:

> The saints encourage me also in my prison. They say to me: "As long as you are in chains, you cannot fulfil your mission; but later on, after your death, then shall come the time of your conquest:" [39]

Love imprisoned Therese of the Child Jesus and forged chains that held her bound. The next life was to give her love full liberty to display all its power and exercise all its virtualities. Therese returns to aid all apostles, especially the victors. She will always come to give Love and make Love loved.

Speaking of eternal beatitude, the Saint said:

> Oh, it is love! To love and to be loved and to return to earth to make Love to be loved! [40]

What attracts her to heaven is the certitude of being able to fulfil this mission unto the end of time.

This movement of love descending to conquer by loving and then carrying its prey to the heights is the synthesis of the twofold movement of love; it is the action of the perfect apostolate because in accord with the movement and action of Jesus Himself.

[36] *Autobiography,* v, 73.
[37] *Ibid.,* vii, 89.
[38] *Ibid.,* xi, 182.
[39] *Novissima Verba,* August 10, 1897, p. 94.
[40] *Ibid.,* July 18, p. 59.

But is it only on the summits that harmony is achieved in the spiritual life, between these two aspirations or movements of love? Must one await perfect identification with Christ Jesus before working efficaciously for the building up of His mystical body? In other words, is the apostolate the exclusive privilege of love, and of love in its overflowing fullness? Difficult problems, certainly, but of so great practical importance that we think we should examine them under the light that comes from these summits of transforming union.

B. Apostolate of love and missions of the apostolate

Faced with the complexity of this problem, we can proceed only by a series of affirmations. This is the only means in our power to try to bring a little light to the multiplicity of thoughts that arise in this connection.

1. THERE ARE DIVINE MISSIONS OF THE APOSTOLATE DISTINCT FROM THE APOSTOLATE OF LOVE

It is incontestable that the transforming union, by submitting the saint to the Holy Spirit and identifying him with Christ Jesus, makes of him a perfect apostle; yet it is also true that spiritual fecundity is not the exclusive privilege of love that has reached this degree; true also that efficacious power of action in the Church is not reserved to supernatural charity. The apostolate is in fact a duty not only for the saint, but for every Christian, whatever be his degree of charity. The Holy Spirit uses souls at all stages of their spiritual life for His work in the Church; and the missions with which He entrusts them are not according to the measure of their love.

With respect to the principle that animates it, then, the apostolate can be considered under two forms: that which proceeds directly from supernatural charity and that which is exercised in virtue of a special mission from God.

We could find a foundation for this distinction in the two

aspects of the priestly mediation exercised by Jesus Christ. Jesus is in truth a mediator by the union in the Person of the Word of the two terms to be united, divinity and humanity. This mediation, in the physical order, was realized in Christ following a choice or mission conferred by God. The apostle writes:

> And no man takes the honor to himself; he takes it who is called by God, as Aaron was. So also Christ did not glorify himself with the high priesthood, but he who spoke to him.
>
> "Thou art my son,
> I this day have begotten thee."

As he says also in another place,

> "Thou art a priest forever,
> according to the order of Melchisedech."
>
> For Jesus, in the days of his earthly life, with a loud cry and tears, offered up prayers and supplications. . . . And when perfected, he became to all who obey him the cause of eternal salvation, called by God a high priest according to the order of Melchisedech.[41]

In Jesus Christ the mission of mediation and its realization through the hypostatic union and fullness of grace coincide perfectly, and thus are one and the same thing. This perfect union is an ideal presented to the Christian, in whom a mission and the fullness of charity to fulfil it perfectly, are two distinct realities.[42]

The Holy Spirit, the agent charged with carrying out the divine plans, entrusts important missions for the realization of those plans and for the common good to persons whose previous life does not seem to justify such a choice, and whose life is not transformed by the imposition of such a mission. The distinction between the mission received and the person's charity shows up clearly to the detriment of the latter. We need only read the books of the Old Testament to be convinced of this.

[41] Heb. 5:4-10.

[42] The priestly character does not do away with the distinction between mission and grace. This character is a mark of Christ, says Saint Thomas; it conforms one to Christ and makes one participate in the priesthood, of which Christ possesses the fullness by His nature, by giving to the ordained priest a certain spiritual power as regards the Sacraments and what concerns divine worship. (*Sum. Theol.* III, q. 63, a. 3-5.)

Judges, Kings, Prophets even, ancestors of Christ, these are not always worthy of the high mission entrusted to them. Yet their faults and even their idolatry do not place in question the legitimacy and efficacy of the mission they are called on to fulfil.

The apostle Saint Paul was pleased to stress how, in the Church, the Holy Spirit distributes gifts or charisms for the common good. He writes:

> Now there are varieties of gifts, but the same Spirit; and there are varieties of ministries, but the same Lord; and there are varieties of workings, but the same God, who works all things in all. Now the manifestation of the Spirit is given to everyone for profit. To one through the Spirit is given the utterance of wisdom; and to another the utterance of knowledge, according to the same Spirit; to another faith, in the same Spirit; to another the gift of healing, in the one Spirit; to another the working of miracles; to another prophecy; to another the distinguishing of spirits; to another various kinds of tongues; to another interpretation of tongues.[43]

Along with these charismatic gifts of the Holy Spirit for the building up of the Church, Saint Paul places certain pastoral functions.

> And God indeed has placed some in the Church, first apostles, secondly prophets, thirdly teachers; after that miracles, then gifts of healing, services of help, power of administration, and the speaking of various tongues.[44]

Powers given to the hierarchy, august functions of the priesthood, charisms, these are all distinct from charity; the subsequent statements of the apostle attest to this. Speaking of these charisms of the apostolate, he continues:

> Yet strive after the greater gifts. And I point out to you a yet more excellent way.[45]

This way, excellent among all, is charity, praise of which fills the following chapter.

Although bestowed and exercised in external form less striking now than formerly, these functions and charismatic graces are still to be found in the Church. The Church herself

[43] I Cor. 12:4-11.
[44] I Cor. 12:28.
[45] I Cor. 12:31.

provides for the choice of her ministers. Particular vocations for the apostolate are grouped together and organized in institutes and religious orders. The direct action of the Holy Spirit is revealed in our day only rarely in extraordinary charisms. Although less apparent and marked by less brilliant signs, His action is only the more profound and more certain in the choice of vocations and the conferring of powers. But the organization with which human prudence now surrounds it maintains a distinction of right between function and charity, and even a cleavage in actual fact that is, alas, at times only too noticeable.

Yet in our endeavor to distinguish properly, let us be careful not to separate. The functions of the apostolate, which can be called charismatic graces in the generic sense of the word, are accompanied by grace; and they ought ordinarily to contribute to the sanctification of the soul that receives them. Hence a second affirmation.

2. GRACE ACCOMPANIES THE MISSIONS OF THE APOSTOLATE

Grace can immediately elevate a soul to the height of its mission, that is, establish an equality between the soul's charity and the functions entrusted to it. The soul becomes at once a perfect instrument. Charity and function coincide perfectly as in Christ Jesus Himself, in whom mediatorship is engrafted in the hypostatic union, which is already a mediation in the physical order. It was so for the Virgin Mary whose fullness of grace was enlarged by the action of the Holy Spirit on the day of the Annunciation to the measure of her dignity and her functions as Mother of God.

That this privilege was given to the Virgin Mother of God, we have certitude. But even if a saint here or there has been so favored, this privilege is exceptional. Ordinarily, grace and mission are not only distinct, but are conferred at the beginning in unequal proportions.

Grace does exist, however. Let us try to analyze it.

a. *Grace of preparation*

The Holy Spirit does nothing by chance. He prepares His instruments. Abraham goes out of his country by successive stages at God's order, to take possession of the country that is to be the inheritance of the numerous posterity of which he is to be the father. Moses is saved from the water and brought up at Pharaoh's court, where he receives the best education of his time. He is led to the desert, where for forty years he is to live the solitary life of a shepherd, before God appears to him in the burning bush and confers on him his mission as liberator and leader of the Hebrew people. How admirable also are the ways by which the Holy Spirit leads John the Baptist and Saint Paul, to prepare them for their exceptional mission.

Guided by the Holy Spirit, the Church imposes on her ministers a period of obligatory preparation before bestowing upon them the powers of the priesthood. Preceded by a divine choice, this preparation is a part of the unfolding of providential events and of the inner working of the Holy Spirit, which it is meant to assist and bring to fruition.

b. *God bestows powers*

In conferring a charism or a mission of the apostolate, God gives powers that have a sure efficacy. The judges chosen by God deliver Israel each time from its enemies. The king anointed by God's order is clothed with a power enabling him to rule over his people and overcome his enemies. God wants his envoys to be convinced of the efficacy of the mission with which they are entrusted. Gideon can ask for contradictory signs.[46] God does not weary of granting them. God answers Moses' objections and reveals to him the power of working wonders, which He is giving him.[47] The victory that Gideon wins with a few soldiers without arms, and the marvelous accounts of the Exodus, all show that the signs given by God

[46] Judges 6.
[47] Exodus 3.

authenticated a divine mission and the supernatural power to fulfil it.

It is in this mission and this power that the charism bestowed by the Holy Spirit for the common good essentially resides; one could not deny their efficacy and fruitfulness. The judge of the Old Testament, Gideon or Jephthe, no matter what his own dispositions, acted in the name of God and freed His people.

In the New Law, the priest receives on the day of his ordination all powers over the body of Christ, to diffuse the divine life. He consecrates, validly absolves, distributes grace to souls, even if he has lost it himself. With the charism of his vocation, the teaching religious can cause light to penetrate minds with certain efficacy, without his own spiritual life's entering directly into play. An apostolic activity can bear fruit, whatever be the degree of charity that animates it.

Fruitfulness is not necessarily bound up with the supernatural charity of the instrument. It is God who gives the increase.[48] He can attach it permanently to gifts, such as the charismatic graces, as well as to any human activity of his choice.

c. *Grace for the accomplishment of the mission*

God owes it to the instrument to sustain its weakness and help it fulfil worthily the mission or the functions with which he has entrusted it. And so, with these powers and mission, God always gives appropriate grace to exercise them worthily according to the divine good pleasure.

It is touching to note in Holy Scripture, with what affectionate solicitude God watches over the instruments He has chosen. "I will be with thee," [49] He says to Moses, who was uneasy about the difficulties of his mission. And He was also with Abraham, with Jacob, with Joseph, with Samuel the judge. He lay hold upon Saul immediately after his anointing.[50] When Samuel had anointed David, "The spirit of the Lord

[48] I Cor. 3:6, "God gives the increase."
[49] Exod. 3:12.
[50] I Kings 10:9.

came upon David from that day forward." [51] This assistance appears in outward works, to the point that every one takes note of the fact; it is many times stressed in the Sacred Writings.

The assistance, or the presence of God with His servant is manifest in the blessings with which God crowns him, the protection He assures to him, and the servant's fidelity through grace. It is not written of all God's servants, that He is with them. God is no longer with Saul, when Saul becomes unfaithful; His spirit rests on David instead, although Saul continues to rule.[52]

This almost visible hold of God on the patriarch, the king, or the prophet of the Old Testament makes one think of the character imprinted by the sacrament of Holy Orders in the soul of the priest. The first effect of the priestly character is the conferring of powers, but it also carries with it the grace to exercise them worthily. The holy anointing puts the priest at the service of God and His people; it penetrates him profoundly, surrounds him as it were with a luminous nimbus that makes him shine before the eyes of all, and assures him of all efficacious means to become another living Christ.

In the experience of the anointing that is poured out into his whole being, the new priest might be led to think he has already arrived at that identification with Christ for which he so ardently longs. Such an illusion is easy, as easy as for the religious who may think, in the fervor of his religious profession, that he has made the complete gift of self of which he dreams. However sensible and powerful this grace may be, it is only a blossom in bud, a first grace destined to ensure faithfulness in the exercise of duty and in making perfect the gift of self. It is only later, perhaps after long years of fidelity, that the priest will bring to his ministry a supernatural charity that will truly make him the worthy instrument of it; then will he realize in its fruitful plenitude the priesthood of Christ.

[51] I Kings 16:13.
[52] I Kings 18:12.

3. FULFILLMENT OF THE MISSION AND PERFECTION OF CHARITY

To insist at length on distinctions is to end by creating oppositions. Thus the mission of the apostlate and supernatural charity might well now appear to us as hostile powers that must be kept apart lest they harm one another. Yet actually, each one finds its perfection in their union; and therein resides the secret of sanctity. Let us try to determine their inner connections.

The care that God gives to the providential preparation of His instruments indicates the value He attaches to this human collaboration with Him. The action of the instrument is written into the divine designs as an indispensable means to their realization. And so the Holy Spirit stipulates fidelity of the instrument to the mission received as the condition of His friendship. Faithfulness is the great proof of love that God requires. "If you love me, keep my commandments," says our Lord.[53] Are there any commandments more important than those that flow from the divine choice, fixing our task and our mission here below? The proof of love, like the precept, is not limited to some one particular point; it applies to a whole life and affects the very realization of the divine plan.

Divine choices are fraught with all the richness of the grace and the mission on which they bear. And so Saul, the object of an extraordinary divine choice, is rejected for having spared Agag, king of Amalec, whom he ought to have killed with his people,[54] and God sharply rebukes Samuel for carrying on mourning over the rejection of this first king whom he himself had anointed in the name of the Lord.[55] David and his people are severely chastised because of David's adultery, for he had "given occasion to the enemies of the Lord to blaspheme."[56] Moses and Aaron are not to enter into the promised land because, says the Lord:

[53] John 14:15.
[54] I Kings 15:20-30.
[55] I Kings 16:1.
[56] II Kings 12:14.

You offended me in the desert of Sin in the contradiction of the multitude: neither would you sanctify me before them at the waters.[57]

These severities of God must be judged in the light of the gift made by God, the importance of the mission, and the divine exigencies accompanying it.

In the primitive Church, the Holy Spirit lays wide open His action as the veritable founder of the Church. Ananias and his wife, Saphira, sold their goods and brought a part of the fruit of the sale to the apostles, saying that they have given them everything. To Ananias, Peter says:

Thou hast not lied to men, but to God. And Ananias, hearing these words, fell down and expired. And great fear came upon all who heard it.[58]

A few minutes later, Saphira arrives and receives the same terrible chastisement, which is in proportion to the action of the Holy Spirit who has been offended. Like the action, the punishment is powerful and external, so that worthy reparation may be assured.

Saint Teresa has a vision of hell, "one of the most signal favours which the Lord has bestowed upon me," she says.[59] In it she sees the place prepared for her there, if she were unfaithful to divine graces.

These terrifying examples show us the value God attaches to the mission He confers, and the response of generous rectitude and fidelity He demands of those to whom He has revealed the power of His grace.

But also, what blessings there are, and what flowering of divine charity for the soul that is faithful. Besides the success of the mission, which is extended marvelously, the soul is made holy by this faithfulness of love.

God never tires of rewarding the good servant who has fulfilled his task. To have buried the talent received entails the

[57] Numb. 27:14.
[58] Acts 5:4-5.
[59] *Life*, xxxii; Peers, I, 217.

pain of hell; to have made several talents bear fruit for the Master merits the governance of a kingdom.[60]

Abraham shows heroic faith in the word of God and is rewarded:

> Abraham believed God and it was credited to him as justice. . . . Abraham hoping against hope believed, so that he became the father of many nations.[61]

This paternity extends not only to the Hebrew people; Saint Paul claims it jealously for all believers and hence for all Christians.[62] Thus Abraham's justice merited for Abraham to become a friend of God, a friend whose intercession was to be forever powerful for all his sons according to the flesh and by faith.

Moses, in spite of a passing neglect, responds to God's mission with a faithfulnes that makes of him an incomparable leader of the people, the lawgiver of Israel, a prophet so remarkable that it is written:

> There arose no more a prophet in Israel like unto Moses, whom the Lord knew face to face.[63]

Having become the confident and the familiar friend of God, Moses dares to ask to see His face. And the Spirit renders to him this testimony:

> . . . my servant Moses . . . is most faithful in all my house. For I speak to him mouth to mouth, and plainly: and not by riddles and figures doth he see the Lord.[64]

The throne of David, too, is strengthened among all his posterity by reason of his fidelity; his psalms tell us the depth and sweet intimacy of his relations with God. The vessel of election, Saint Paul, becomes by his works the veritable apostle of the Gentiles. His contemplative epistles, called "of the cap-

[60] Matt. 15:14-30.
[61] Rom. 4:4, 18.
[62] Gal. 4:22-31; Rom. 4:17.
[63] Deut. 34:10.
[64] Numb. 12:7-8.

tivity," show us how, by faithfulness to his mission, he penetrated to the depths of the great mystery that he preached; and how ardent became his charity in the perfect union realized with Christ Jesus. Saint Teresa, as we have said, is elevated to spiritual marriage when she has given herself for ten years to her task as foundress, and sacrificed all to the Church.

A divine mission of the apostolate is an afflictive weight of grace that may precipitate a soul into abysses of perdition; but by humble and loving loyalty the soul is drawn toward the unsoundable depths of intimacy and familiarity with God. The charism, through this faithfulness, leads to transforming union.

Perfect accomplishment of one's mission is, then, the great proof of love that God requires of those upon whom He has conferred it. In one of His last appearances, Jesus asks of Peter: "Simon, son of John, dost thou love me more than these do?" And upon receiving an affirmative answer, He says: "Feed my lambs." Three times He asks the same question. Peter was grieved. Jesus concludes again the same way: "Feed my sheep." [65]

Probably reparation for Peter's triple denial; but especially, an exact indication that the greatest proof of love that is asked of Peter is to fulfil his mission as shepherd of all souls.

The truth that is brought out by these words and these great examples looks beyond the particular instance of an extraordinary divine mission. It applies to every soul. Each Christian incorporated in the whole Christ by baptism has his mission, his vocation in the Church. This social role is his *raison d'être,* since in the divine plan the Church is the end of all things. The realization of his vocation, the accomplishment of his duties of state, the acceptance of providential offices, faithfulness to all duties incumbent upon him as a member of the Church, these constitute the proof of love that God asks of every Christian.

To have received only one talent while others receive two or

[65] John 21:15-7.

five exposes one more to the temptation of burying it: this is what the gospel parable of the talents seems to suggest. Yet, the obligation is the same for all. He too who has received less will be severely punished, if he is unfaithful. The single talent received obligates him to the work of the Master, to the fidelity that kills selfishness and sustains love. Saint John of the Cross assures us that these are the services rendered to God which will obtain for the soul the light and the trials which purify the simple regard of faith that irresistibly attracts God. It is the humble daily faithfulness to grace that spins the slender thread of love, binding us to God in perfect union.

The evidence of these truths appears when we have the advantage of meeting along the way one of those humble workmen of God who have spent their life in the accomplishment of the ordinary duties of the religious or priestly life, or of family life still more complex. These unconsciously, but with attractive supernatural charm, show forth in the limpid simplicity of their gaze of faith, in the overflowing peace of their charity, the fruits of their loving fidelity and the dawning light of a union that is realized. Thus they testify in their way that in order to love one must serve, and that in serving one arrives at the perfection of love.

In this domain, illusions are numerous and widespread. It is so easy to think that in order to serve one must do extraordinary things or sacrifice everything to particular works, which, although good, are on the margin of one's personal duty of state. This duty is the most important and inalienable part of the social service we owe to God and to the Church. It is easy too for authentic generosity to deviate under the influences that come from one's temperament or under the light of those half-truths, which are as dangerous as the half-learned men that Saint Teresa feared.

And so to these affirmations, let us add a few practical corollaries to define more precisely certain aspects.

4. COROLLARIES

a. *God demands faithfulness*

In the accomplishment of the mission with which He entrusts us, God asks loving fidelity.

This fidelity consists in collaboration with the action of the Holy Spirit who is building up the Church. The Holy Spirit is the Spirit of Love, who builds with love. Collaboration must be of the same nature as the principal action. The good instrument must be pliant to the workman's ways of acting. Thus the instrument of the Holy Spirit will be perfect only when it will be itself moved and animated solely by love.

God can make fruitful any human activity and use it for His ends. He orientates too toward the realization of His designs the action of physical causes, and even that of the devil. But from loveless collaboration, the human instrument draws nothing for itself except chastisement for its refusal to give God the love He expected of it. The scene of the last judgement described by our Lord casts harsh light on this problem:

> Many will say to me in that day, 'Lord, Lord, did we not prophesy in thy name, and cast out devils in thy name, and work many miracles in they name?' And then I will declare to them, 'I never knew you. Depart from me, you workers of iniquity!' [66]

Marvels done in His name do not ensure God's friendship and eternal reward. This reward is for him alone who loves, in doing the will of God. Before pronouncing the above condemnation, Jesus said as much:

> Not everyone who says to me, 'Lord, Lord,' shall enter the kingdom of heaven; but he who does the will of my Father in heaven shall enter the kingdom of heaven.[67]

Saint Paul's well known praise of charity is placed in the First Epistle to the Corinthians, following the doctrine on charisms, which it completes by comparing charisms with charity.

[66] Matt. 7:22-3.
[67] Matt. 7:21.

If I should speak with the tongues of men and of angels, but do not have charity, I have become as sounding brass or a tinkling cymbal. And if I have prophecy and know all mysteries and all knowledge, . . . I am nothing. And if I distribute all my goods to feed the poor, and if I deliver my body to be burned, yet do not have charity, it profits me nothing.[68]

The doctrine is very clear: the most brilliant charisms, whatever may be their practical efficacy for the good of the neighbor and the building up of the Church, have no value whatever for one who possesses them without charity. Charity alone remains and has value for eternity, because it is a participation in the life of God.

Saint Teresa comments thus on this teaching:

The Lord does not look so much at the magnitude of anything we do as at the love with which we do it.[69]

As for Saint Therese of the Child Jesus, she is inexhaustible when she takes up this theme, one of the basic principles of her way of spiritual childhood:

If weak and imperfect souls like mine felt what I feel, none would despair of reaching the summit of the Mountain of Love, since Jesus does not ask for great deeds, but only for gratitude and self-surrender. He says: "I will not take the he-goats from out of thy flocks, for all the beasts of the forests are mine. . . . Offer to God the sacrifice of praise and thanksgiving." [70]

This is all Our Lord claims from us. He has need of our love—He has no need of our works.[71]

Activism which in the apostolate places works above union with God, the source of charity, by sacrificing in practice divine union to works, has in these texts so evident a condemnation that there is no use insisting on it. Works without love, or works that hinder the soul from drawing strength from the living waters of divine life, can be only a cause of perdition for him who is their instrument, even should he be favored with most powerful charisms.

[68] I Cor. 13:1-3.
[69] VII Mansions, iv; Peers, II, 350.
[70] Ps. 49:9, 14.
[71] *Autobiography,* xi, 178.

b. *Works have value and are necessary*

On the other hand works do have value and are necessary. Ceaseless battle against activism can become a perilous game. To exalt only love to the detriment of works can lead one to depreciate activity and falsify values. The danger is actual. Certain idealist tendencies do not escape it.

This idealism thinks of love as a perfume, a slender thread, a reflection, a lofty and very pure sentiment that needs to be withdrawn from all that could tarnish or alter it. All its beauty and fruitfulness would shine forth only in the repose of inactivity. The life of love must be sheltered from any contact that might soil it and any activity that might dissipate. And the death that comes of love is for these idealists, the scarcely perceptible disincarnate breath arising from a diaphanous countenance; it is the last brilliant gaze from flames that have ceased consuming.

Certainly, we do not mean to diminish the value of a love that has so well used and refined its corporeal covering that its plays of light shine through the body's transparence. But to make of such disincarnation and such visible effects an absolute requirement of love and a condition of its perfection is to confuse, it seems to us, one of its forms and expressions with the supernatural reality. Especially does it falsify the true notion and exigencies of supernatural charity.

Love caused the Word to become incarnate in the midst of us. Jesus manifested Himself with His human nature, conquering by all the strength and life that it showed forth, by its human gifts and divine radiance. In the synagogue of Nazareth where He had been brought up, He stands before His own people, reading the words that Isaias had written of Him:

> "The Spirit of the Lord is upon me;
> because he has anointed me;
> To bring good news to the poor he has sent me,
> to proclaim to the captives release,
> and sight to the blind;

> To set at liberty the oppressed,
> to proclaim the acceptable year of the Lord,
> and the day of recompense." [72]

A very clear statement: He has been anointed with the oil of the divinity that He might go to His people, to the poverty and misery of the sinner. And Jesus does go to them. He eats with sinners. His life is all of love. He dies of love on the cross in circumstances that disconcert our terrestrial idealizations and all our human conceptions. On the gibet His human flesh is exposed, its nakedness veiled only by wounds and by blood. In this sinful clay that He had taken on Himself, His incarnate love does not shrink from appearing overwhelmed, even to the stifling of the last agony. Before dying Jesus murmurs verses from the Psalm that the prophet had composed for Him and for this hour: "O God, my God, look upon me: Why hast thou forsaken me?" [73] Sublime agony, yes; but what an incarnation of love in our flesh of misery and sin! Love is finally set free in a cry that at the same time tells its triumph, the reality and depth of its incarnation.

When faced with this life and death of Jesus from very love, how poor in genuine love appear the vaporous idealizations of those who, thinking to live love in its fullness and be completely consumed by love, refuse any contact with our world of sin, with the works and sufferings that are its consequence. Illusions springing from laziness or from generosity, or symptoms of a coming psychosis? Who could say?

At least let us say against these tendencies that love is an unction which flows down to every misery here below, including sin, in order to cure it; it is as a slender thread, but a strong thread, binding the sheath of good works; a fragrance arising from fields made fruitful by its work and its suffering. Works and the greatest charisms are nothing without love's anointing, without this thread and this perfume. The grandeur of works

[72] Luke 4:18-9; Isa. 61:1-2.
[73] Ps. 21.

matters little; alone the quality of love has value in itself. But love could not live, grow, and come to its fullness here on earth without accomplishing perfectly the whole task with which God has entrusted it in His eternal designs.

C. The apostolate and the growth of love

Apostolate and love dwell in perfect harmony only on the summit of the transforming union. As a child Saint Teresa goes away in the hope of seeing God. She finds Him fully only after discovering the Church and giving herself completely to the mission that is hers in it. And this mission she fulfils perfectly only when she has arrived at transforming union. On the slopes there are antinomies. Thus our attempts to determine the rights and value of the apostolate and of love remain on a theoretic level; they cannot supply the practical light needed at each stage.

Hence, a problem must still be solved: that of the apostolate in terms of the growth of love. The apostolate is peremptory. Yet, only love has value for eternity. How fulfil one's duty to the apostolate while developing the life of love?

Solutions to this problem are numerous. Each school of spirituality offers one in conformity with its spirit and its grace. Actually, Saint Teresa does not give us hers. This contemplative, who built a cloister for herself and her daughters, was too humble to dare to construct a doctrine of the apostolate. On the other hand, she had too great a love for souls, too burning a solicitude for the perfection of those with whom she was in contact, not to give them on occasion in her writings appropriate advice for their external apostolate. These counsels follow the progress of the contemplative ascent. They are so exact at each stage, and so luminous is the line they trace out, that by gathering and codifying them one could, we think, prepare an excellent treatise for the formation of apostles who, remaining contemplatives under the action of the Holy Spirit, would for that very reason be only the better apostles.

And so we think that the following pages will be not the least important in this commentary on Teresian thought.

1. THE APOSTOLATE IN THE FIRST THREE MANSIONS

In the first three Mansions or the first phase, characterized by the general help of God, God's action in the soul remains secondary, leaving the initiative to the soul in the direction of its spiritual life. We must note that this reserve on God's part comes not from His particular willing but from lack of charity in the soul.

Charity in such a soul is still weak; all its efforts at growth meet with numerous obstacles. Evil tendencies are not yet dominated; through them, the devil has easy access to the faculties and senses. The soul is able to keep from sin and succced in drawing habitually from the sources of divine grace in the sacraments and prayer only thanks to a strong organization of its life, which ensures the mortification of its passions and its habitual union with God. This organization takes effort and a long patience. And even when it has been effected in the third Mansions, and the soul has triumphed over enemies within and without, Saint Teresa thinks that its charity is still too feeble to be shared with others. In her opinion, during this period the soul's own spiritual life and its search for God must absorb all its energies and be its single and constant preoccupation. She does not even want to speak of the apostolate, so convinced is she that it would be perilous for the soul and bear little fruit for the neighbor.

Need we recall that Saint Teresa is not legislating here for Christians in general but is addressing her daughters, contemplatives. Contemplation has its special requirements of silence and solitude. The noises of the world and the bustle of business disturb, if not stifle it, in the beginning. Besides, these contemplatives are not called to an external apostolate. Their apostolate can and must proceed from the radiating power of their supernatural charity. But it is evident that, at the beginning, their love is as yet in its first human stammerings. It advances only as sustained by reason, like the child that must still be held up by its mother to take its first steps. Later it will come to its perfection and full liberty as a child of God. Like any new life, it must for the moment provide simply for its own growth; it will be fruitful when it has attained a certain maturity.

Rather notably different is the situation of the soul engaged by vocation in the apostolate. It has received the priestly character or the charism relative to its particular vocation. This it must use for the good of the Church. The priest must administer the sacraments and prepare Christians for them; men and women in the religious life must give themselves to the works of their Institute; the Christian has an apostolic duty to exercise in his family and social group. These duties are independent of the degree of charity of the one on whom they are incumbent. Better still, the apostolate constitutes an obligatory exercise of charity toward the neighbor and thus happily ensures the growth of charity. The apostle loves his brothers while working for them; and, by the same token, he would fail in the love he owes them, should he shun the essential task of his vocation.

And yet, can the apostle neglect Saint Teresa's remarks and the practical conclusions she draws from them for her contemplatives? These remarks emphasize a spiritual state that is the same for the apostle and the contemplative. In one as in the other the flesh is weak, the passions not yet dominated; and supernatural charity, with its imperfect channels for acting, feels more closely the pressure of external influences.

The charism of the apostolate and the priesthood have their proper efficacy and guarantee the grace of fidelity. But it is not exact to say that they preserve one from the dangers of the world. In the apostle—and at times with more rage than in the contemplative—flesh and spirit confront each other. The sin of the world, with which the apostle must be in contact and over which he carries off many victories, sets before him its seductions along with its ugliness; and while offering material for his zeal, insidiously provides support and food for his desires. The latter, not yet purified, do not know how to refuse it completely; they draw from it sustenance. There is no doubt, the solicitations of the world are much more dangerous for the apostle than for the contemplative, sheltered as he is by his solitude.

At the beginning, the apostle's charity is weak. The sensible ardors that animate him must not delude him. There is certainly a breach between his mission and the charity at his command. This must be filled. The charism calls for union with Christ corresponding to its power. The priesthood requires for its perfection identification with Christ, priest and victim. True, the very exercise of the charism ensures precious sustenance for charity; its value must not be belittled. But it is surely not enough. Charity flows from the bosom of God. The apostle must go to the sources of this divine life, the sacraments. But less than others, can he rest contented even with this. A friend of God, he must stay habitually near to the inner Guest, who pours out this charity in our souls. A chosen instrument of the Holy Spirit—forerunner of the divine works and builder of the Church—he can fulfil worthily his mission only by cultivating intimacy with Him. Thus will the instrument be made pliant to the lights and movements of the Spirit. More than any other, the apostle has need of that habitual commerce with God that is prayer, and must comply with its essential conditions.

What would become, then, of the apostle who, relying too much on the young ardors of his grace and the conquering dynamism of his zeal, would throw himself into the combat without any other gauge than the victory to be won over the evil he discovers, without other protection than confidence in his love for God and for souls? In this combat, entered upon with presumption and imprudently carried on, the energies of the soul cannot but be used up and progressively weakened. The too natural ardors will ordinarily burn out; evil tendencies will develop; and supernatural charity, little or irregularly fed, will become anemic. Please God the apostle may not himself go down, victim of the sin against which he fought, buried under exterior triumphs that seemed complete because brilliant.

To avoid these dangers and ensure the growth of his supernatural charity, the apostle has the imperious duty in this period to preserve his soul from the sin he meets with and to be fed spiritually in superabundance. Prudence requires him to replace the solitude that safeguards the contemplative by an organization of life that is all the stronger since he is weaker and meets with greater dangers. In enemy country, an army is on greater guard than is a batallion enclosed in a fortress. Vigilance and asceticism are necessary to keep watch over the senses, the windows of the soul, and prevent dissipation of the faculties. Without a rule, it is impossible for the apostle to bring his soul frequently back to the living sources of grace and remain there.

Will these precautions and this rule be sufficient? We might have an answer from those who have charge of sending workers into the fields of the apostolate, and who can then follow the vicissitudes of their interior combats. But a lesson of incomparably superior value and import is afforded us by Jesus Himself, who formed His own apostles.

For three years, Jesus keeps near Him those whom He has chosen to be His apostles, having them witness His teachings and His movements, often instructing them apart. He sends them on mission at times, reluctantly, as it were, setting a rendezvous for their return. Before His Passion, He bestows upon them His priesthood and establishes them as His successors. The outpourings of divine grace in their souls, the master's intimate confidences of the last hour, the presumptuous ardors of Peter, these do not keep the apostles from weakening when confronted with the mystery of the Cross. The experience seems to bring everything to an end. Jesus had foreseen and announced their abandonment of Him. Yet He scarcely refers to it after His Resurrection, bringing them the peace of pardon. He confirms the mission already assigned; but before the apostles enter upon it they are to await in prayer at Jerusalem the coming of the Holy Spirit. It is only on the day of Pentecost, when the Holy Spirit has descended upon them and transformed them, that they become true apostles, capable of fulfilling their mission. And not until three years after his conversion was the apostle Saint Paul to be invested officially with his mission of preaching to the Gentiles; and in the course of these three years there is a sojourn in Arabia. And it is from solitude that have come forth too the majority of the great bishops, builders of the Christian civilization in the great nations of the West.

Such are the laws exemplified by the practical teaching of Jesus and by the tradition of the apostolic ages. One becomes a perfect apostle by being held and possessed by the Holy Spirit. This captivation is distinct from the bestowal of the mission, and even from the priestly ordination. The Spirit comes only when one has prepared oneself to receive Him. These laws for the formation of apostles are for all times. The urgency and extent of the needs of our own time, the intelligent power of the forces of hatred that threaten us and their genius for organizing, ought to make us more thoughtful about these laws for spiritual formation. Fortunately, threats against us turn our minds to new techniques in the apostolate. But if these techniques should cause us to forget and neglect the primary technique of spiritual formation taught us by Christ Jesus, then, like Peter's sword, they would be in our hands but vain defense for proud and boastful presumption.

Saint Teresa's thought on the apostolate and her directives are modeled, it seems to me, on this spiritual technique of Jesus for the formation of apostles, and show precisely its practical bearing for each stage of the spiritual life. This is what gives incomparable value to her teaching—value to its substance and practice, which the following explanation hopes not to diminish by its succinctness.

2. THE APOSTOLATE UNDER THE FIRST DIVINE RAPTURES

In the fourth Mansions, loving Wisdom intervenes directly in the spiritual life of the soul with special help. Saint Teresa and Saint John of the Cross point out the effects of these divine interventions, especially in prayer, which they transform into contemplation. These interventions of God have undoubtedly a parallel development, however, all through the gifts of the Holy Spirit, intellectual and practical; and they make at the same time the contemplative and the apostle.

Saint Teresa, moreover, likes to emphasize how, in the prayer of quiet—the form of contemplation characteristic of this period—the will alone is held captive by the inflowings of love. Love is experienced as a sweet savor, a living water springing up, a flame burning deep within the soul and giving riches of light and strength to the will that becomes its captive. This experience lasts only as long as the prayer, but the riches remain. Can the soul now distribute them? Does it truly move under the impulse of God? Is it now truly fit for the apostolate?

A soul might incline to think so, so notably do the supernatural savor and light overflow from its faculties, and already show forth in its action. It has luminous and deep thoughts, words spiritually full and sweet, views whose penetration certainly goes beyond that of an ordinary intelligence. They provide a feast for those who listen, success for those who follow their counsel. The Spirit of God is there; His action often shines out clearly. And so the apostolate of this soul is fruitful. Why not encourage such a soul to give itself zealously, since God already is leading it. Let us hear the advice of Saint Teresa:

> There is one earnest warning which I must give those who find themselves in this state: namely, that they exert the very greatest care to

keep themselves from occasions of offending God. For as yet the soul is not even weaned but is like a child beginning to suck the breast. If it be taken from its mother, what can it be expected to do but die? That, I am very much afraid, will be the lot of anyone to whom God has granted this favour if he gives up prayer; unless he does so for some very exceptional reason.[74]

In the book of her *Life,* the Saint points out the snare that the devil lays for these souls:

When a soul finds itself very near to God. . . . It seems to have a clear vision of the reward and believes that it cannot now possibly leave something which even in this life is so sweet and delectable for anything as base and soiled as earthly pleasure. Because it has this confidence, the devil is able to deprive it of the misgivings which it ought to have about itself; and, as I say, it runs into many dangers, and in its zeal begins to give away its fruit without stint, thinking that it has now nothing to fear. This condition is not a concomitant of pride, for the soul clearly understands that of itself it can do nothing; it is the result of its extreme confidence in God, which knows no discretion. The soul does not realize that it is like a bird still unfledged. It is able to come out of the nest, and God is taking it out, but it is not yet ready to fly, for its virtues are not yet strong and it has no experience which will warn it of dangers, nor is it aware of the harm done by self-confidence.[75]

The warning is clear and justified. Although at times experiencing the divine hold, and already filled with genuine supernatural riches that make fruitful its action, such a soul must still use prudence and reserve in sharing with others. The interventions of God are intermittent only; the soul is not yet strong enough always to resist when in occasions of sin. It exhausts itself by giving of its treasures; and it would yield to a subtle temptation of presumption by distributing without measure riches that it itself needs—especially since the source that must renew them is only intermittent and does not spring up at the soul's bidding.

How much more useful even for the apostle are these grave warnings of Saint Teresa. If the dangers that she points out are occasional for the contemplative, they are almost constant

[74] IV Mansions, iii; Peers, II, 245.
[75] *Life,* xix; Peers, I, 118.

and pressing for one engaged in the works of the apostolate. To give what he possesses of the spiritual is for him a duty. How shall he regulate the gift? How refuse the solicitations of those he has the duty to sustain, and who come in numbers because attracted by the supernatural fragrance of the riches he communicates? Will he know how to find the measure, and will he have the courage? Divine Wisdom will give him strength, light, and counsel. Through Saint Teresa, He will insistently repeat:

> They are not yet weaned and for some time yet need to be fed with the milk of which I first spoke. Let them remain near those Divine breasts; and, when they have sufficient strength, the Lord will take care to lead them on farther. If they advanced now, they would not do others as much good as they think, but would only harm themselves.[76]

To give without measure would be to spend oneself before the time, to sin by presumption, and perhaps deprive oneself of the grace and strength to mount higher. It would be to cut the wheat in the blade and thus lose the harvest, for having failed to wait for the ripening.

3. THE APOSTOLATE WHEN THE SOUL HAS COME TO UNION OF WILL

Does the union of will realized in the fifth Mansions ensure the perfect maturation necessary for gathering all the fruits? At least, it gives promise that the time is near.

Union of will is already an habitual hold of God upon the soul, although limited to this faculty. Fruit of a divine contact deep within that causes an abundant inflowing of love, it leaves the will in the hands of God. Alone, the will is made captive; but the will has command in the whole soul. Through it, the divine captivation exercises its influence on the other faculties not yet fully purified nor docile.

Such an habitual inflowing of God must bear great fruits. Saint Teresa points this out:

[76] *Conceptions of the Love of God,* vii; Peers, II, 399. Cf. also *Life,* xiii; Peers, I, 74 ff.

> I believe it is God's will that so great a favour should not be given in vain, and that if the soul that receives it does not profit by it others will do so. For, as the soul possesses these aforementioned desires and virtues, it will always profit other souls so long as it leads a good life, and from its own heat new heat will be transmitted to them. Even after losing this, it may still desire others to profit, and take pleasure in describing the favours given by God to those who love and serve Him.[77]

These souls are already conquered. They work for God, even if they have dropped to a state of less fervor, as the Saint says of herself:

> I knew a person [herself] to whom this happened, and who . . . was glad that others should profit by the favours God had shown her; she would describe the way of prayer to those who did not understand it, and she brought them very, very great profit.[78]

God uses His hold on such a soul, then, for the apostolate. Saint Teresa states this first by an allusion:

> But how many are called by the Lord to apostleship, as Judas was, and enjoy communion with Him, or are called to be made kings, as Saul was, and afterwards, through their own fault, are lost![79]

This way of speaking is rather frequent with Saint Teresa. An allusion, a comparison, a single stroke or a longer description bring out a dominant thought that lies close to it. The reference to Judas and to Saul shows that for Saint Teresa union of will is a hold, an anointing, a seal [80] that marks a soul for a mission. In this allusion there appears also the painful preoccupation that distresses the Saint, the faithlessness that still is possible, ending in an irremediable fall. The main thought and the preoccupation, moreover, are to cast light on one another.

Captivation by God is a grace of divine choice, dedicating the soul to great things. Its power asserts itself and stirs up the devil's jealous hatred. What defeats are in store for him if the

[77] V Mansions, iii; Peers, II, 259.
[78] *Ibid.*
[79] *Ibid.*
[80] *Ibid.*, ii; 257.

soul escapes him, and what profit if he makes it fall, or at least brings it to a halt. Saint Teresa writes:

> As I have often said, if he wins a single soul in this way he will win a whole multitude. The devil has much experience in this matter. If we consider what a large number of people God can draw to Himself through the agency of a single soul, the thought of the thousands converted by the martyrs gives us great cause for praising God. Think of a maiden like Saint Ursula. And of the souls whom the devil must have lost through Saint Dominic and Saint Francis and other founders of Orders, and is losing now through Father Ignatius, who founded the Company of Jesus.[81]

And so the devil is going to let loose a hard combat against this soul, who very soon will be totally beyond his reach. Now for the last time perhaps, he will be able to array against it all his power and the close and subtle network of his ruses. He can still attack it. How?

Saint Teresa considers this a difficult problem, and important enough to delay over.[82]

God's domination of the soul in the union of will is nevertheless only the beginning of the great things that will later come to pass. The newness of the experience, the rarity of domination extending to all the faculties, and the darkness in which it takes place, make the soul more restless and ardent than calmed and satisfied, and leave the impression of a detachment from everything rather than a positive experience of actual union. The Saint writes:

> Despite all I have said, this Mansion seems to me a little obscure.[83]

This very obscurity distinguishes it from the following Mansions, where the rays of dawn begin to give their light. Hence the devil takes advantage of the darkness to lay his hidden snares.

Teresa warns us:

[81] *Ibid.*, iv; 265-6.
[82] *Ibid.*; 266 ff.
[83] *Ibid.*, iii; 259.

The devil comes with his artful wiles, and, under colour of doing good, sets about undermining it in trivial ways, and involving it in practices which, so he gives it to understand, are not wrong; little by little he darkens its understanding, and weakens its will, and causes its self-love to increase, until in one way and another he begins to withdraw it from the love of God and to persuade it to indulge its own wishes.[84]

And again:

I tell you, daughters, I have known people of a very high degree of spirituality who have reached this state, and whom, notwithstanding, the devil, with great subtlety and craft, has won back to himself.[85]

Prudence, then, is necessary. The contemplative soul or the apostle—probably both at once—cannot sleep in false security. It must be watchful, if it would not lose all, as did Saul and Judas. Saint Teresa's admonitions become more importunate than ever. The stake is of first importance; these are the last battles in which the soul risks losing all.

So, Christian souls, whom the Lord has brought to this point on your journey, I beseech you, for His sake, not to be negligent, but to withdraw from occasions of sin—for even in this state the soul is not strong enough to be able to run into them safely, as it is after the betrothal has been made—that is to say, in the Mansion which we shall describe after this one.[86]

4. THE PERFECT APOSTOLATE OF THE SIXTH AND THE SEVENTH MANSIONS

These high regions have been described at length. Here we shall lay emphasis only on what concerns the apostolate.

Let us first recall that for Saint Teresa there is no door separating the sixth and the seventh Mansions. It is only a question of love's attaining the perfection that makes it completely transforming in the seventh Mansions, and gives to union all its stability. Yet even in the spiritual betrothal of the sixth Mansions, God touches the deep substance of the soul and there dwells in habitual union. And so, although the manifesta-

[84] *Ibid.*, iv; 266.
[85] *Ibid.*; 265.
[86] *Ibid.*

tions and effects of love are of a higher quality in spiritual marriage, they are not specifically different in the sixth and the seventh Mansions. The perfection of contemplation and the perfection of the apostolate are realized, although in different degrees, in both. Hence we are justified in putting these two Mansions together, to consider the characteristic traits of the perfect apostolate at the summits of the spiritual life.

a. *The perfect apostolate is the fruit of perfect love*

Love in these lofty regions, because it is perfect, is transforming and unifying. The soul has become the living branch of the vine, the log of wood cast into the fire and like it, completely enflamed. Divine union is confirmed in those depths that are the very substance of the soul. This union produces a certain equality between God and the soul, but by an assimilation of the soul by God. God's transcendence has acted with all its power. The drop of water has been cast into the ocean, and it remains distinct; but the ocean, on receiving it into its bosom, has communicated to it its own properties and qualities. The soul has become God by participation.

This transformation reaches into the substance of the soul. But, say the Schoolmen, operation follows being. The transformation wrought in the soul's being has normal repercussions in its faculties. God's hold on the soul, brought about through love, shows forth in what the person does. Saint John of the Cross writes:

> All that it does is of God, and its operations are Divine, so that, even as Saint Paul says, he that is joined unto God becomes one spirit with Him. Hence it comes to pass that the operations of the soul in union are of the Divine Spirit and are Divine.[87]

God's captivation of the whole soul finds the soul perfectly docile. The transforming union brings to pass at the same time loving rapture and loving submission.

[87] *Ascent,* Bk. III, ii; Peers, I, 215.

Saint Teresa insists on submission as one of the characteristics of the perfection attained on the summits. She writes:

> The highest perfection consists not in interior favours or in great raptures or in visions or in the spirit of prophecy, but in the bringing of our wills so closely into conformity with the will of God that, as soon as we realize He wills anything, we desire it ourselves with all our might, and take the bitter with the sweet, knowing that to be His Majesty's will.[88]

This disposition is not simply submission to God's will; it is the soul's placing itself entirely and in all things at the disposal of the divine good pleasure. Saint Teresa writes:

> Do you know when people really become spiritual? It is when they become the slaves of God and are branded with His sign, which is the sign of the Cross, in token that they have given Him their freedom. Then He can sell them as slaves to the whole world, as He Himself was sold.[89]

Saint Therese of the Child Jesus finds in hypnotism, which surrenders the patient to the will of another, a comparison illustrating what she wants to be under God's impulse. In the transforming union, in fact, love pours out into the whole being of the soul and its faculties a sweet anointing, thus keeping them open to its lights and docile to its delicate impulses.

In the divine plan, the union of love between two human beings is orientated to fruitfulness. The transforming union of the soul with its God is not outside this law. The Holy Spirit's hold on the soul and the soul's surrender create a working as one for the realization of the great design that is the Church. The fruit of the over-shadowing of the Holy Spirit and the *Fiat* of the Virgin was Christ Jesus and the whole Christ that is daily being formed.

By His perfect laying hold of the soul in transforming union, the Holy Spirit associates it with His fecundity and that of the Virgin Mary. In union with these higher divine agents, souls who abandon themselves to divine love build up the Church.

[88] *Foundations,* v; Peers, III, 23.
[89] VII Mansions, iv; Peers, II, 346.

Saint Teresa very well grasped this finality of perfect union which frees the soul from self and subjects it to the designs of God.

> Oh, my sisters, how little one should think about resting, and how little one should care about honours, and how far one ought to be from wishing to be esteemed in the very least if the Lord makes His special abode in the soul. For if the soul is much with Him, as it is right it should be, it will very seldom think of itself; its whole thought will be concentrated upon finding ways to please Him and upon showing Him how it loves Him. This, my daughters, is the aim of prayer: this is the purpose of the Spiritual Marriage, of which are born good works and good works alone.[90]

By His enrapturing and the charity He pours out, the Holy Spirit has identified the soul with Christ Jesus. It must follow the way traced out by Christ, the Word Incarnate, who moved through the mystery of the Redemption toward the realization of the mystery of the Church. These three mysteries—Incarnation, Redemption, the Church—are bound one to the other. How change this divine ordering, sanctioned and fulfilled by the life of Jesus. All the communications of grace are orientated to it. This truth appears clearly to Teresa:

> It will be a good thing, sisters, if I tell you why it is that the Lord grants so many favours in this world. Although you will have learned this from the effects they produce, if you have observed them, I will speak about it further here, so that none of you shall think that He does it simply to give these souls pleasure. That would be to make a great error. For His Majesty can do nothing greater for us than grant us a life which is an imitation of that lived by His Beloved Son. I feel certain, therefore, that these favours are given us to strengthen our weakness, as I have sometimes said here, so that we may be able to imitate Him in His great sufferings.[91]

The activity of the soul perfectly amenable under the impulse of the Holy Spirit, builder of the Church, constitutes the apostolate at the summits of the spiritual life. It is the fruit of the transforming union. Perfect love is its activating element; love gives it its perfection and characteristic notes.

[90] *Ibid.*
[91] *Ibid.;* 345.

b. *This perfect apostolate is exercised in special missions in the church*

In the building up of the Church, only Christ Jesus and His divine Mother are on the plane of universal causality. To all the members indiscriminately, who participate in the plenitude of the Spirit and the priesthood of Christ, the law applies that was enunciated by the apostle concerning the diversity of functions and of graces. This law stands out clearly on the summit of transforming union. The perfection of love in each saint causes to shine out resplendently, in identification with Christ, the depths of the unity of His mystical body. At the same time it reveals, in the special grace and mission given to each one of them, the division among the members of the riches of the incomparable plenitude of Christ Jesus.

Just as in His first intuitive gaze upon entering this world, Christ discovered the anointing of the divinity that penetrated Him, together with the redemptive mission that was His and was the end of the Incarnation,[92] so the soul in these raptures of the sixth Mansions that yield to it divine secrets, or better still, in the growing light of dawn, discovers some of the riches of its grace and consequently its place in the whole Christ. A precious discovery, made in different ways and under a light more or less clear.

Saint Teresa recalls in this connection the dazzling vision with which the apostle Saint Paul is favored on the Damascus road. The vision that throws him to the ground, converts him, and reveals to him his mission, is, the Saint assures us, a grace of the sixth Mansions. She refers to it as an exception to general rule:

> . . . the case of anyone to whom Our Lord addresses a special call, as when He at once raised Saint Paul to the summit of contemplation and appeared to him and spoke to him in such a way as to raise him immediately to great heights.[93]

[92] Heb. 5:5-9.
[93] *Conceptions of the Love of God,* v; Peers, II, 388.

This vision, in the judgment of Saint Teresa, is an exceptional favor. Instantaneously Saint Paul receives the degree of charity that places him at once in lofty regions of the spiritual life. From then on he is the vessel of election, elevated by grace to the height of his mission. But ordinarily God does not proceed this way:

> He gives these sublime consolations, and grants these great favours, to persons who have laboured greatly in His service and desired His love and tried to live so that all their actions may be pleasing to His Majesty. Such souls have fatigued themselves by long years of meditation and by long seeking of their Spouse.[94]

Works prepare the soul but do not, properly speaking, merit this favor, which brings with it an inflowing of light and charity for fulfilling a mission, the secret of which it now discloses. Might we think that the descent of the Holy Spirit upon the apostles the day of Pentecost was a grace of this kind? Or was it a grace of transforming union? It is difficult to judge. The first hypothesis seems the more plausible, for it places Paul and all the apostles on the same level at the beginning of their apostolate.[95]

Whatever the case, it is in the sixth Mansions that Saint Teresa discovers her mission as foundress. The raptures of her spiritual betrothal, strengthening her to give up everything for the sake of God,[96] give rise to new exigencies in her soul. The assaults of the seraph, or the transverberation, that make of her a spiritual mother, take place also—at least, the first time—in this period.[97]

[94] *Ibid.*

[95] It must be noted in this connection that favors can be of the same kind and be put consequently in the same category, and yet carry with them an inflowing of charity differing in quality and intensity. Thus, it would be puerile to assimilate to the vision on the Damascus road every rapture that involves the discovery of a mission.

[96] *Life,* xxiv; Peers, I, 156. Cf. *supra* "Spiritual Betrothal," where we placed this grace about 1558–1560.

[97] Saint Teresa describes the transverberation when speaking of raptures in the book of her *Life,* (ch. xxix; 192) which she wrote about 1565, hence before attaining to spiritual marriage.

From the description Saint John of the Cross gives of this favor in the *Living Flame,* one can, it seems to me, draw precious indications as to the nature of the grace that marks a soul for a particular mission:

> It will come to pass that, when the soul is enkindled in the love of God, . . . it will be conscious of an assault upon it made by a seraph with an arrow or a dart completely enkindled in fire of love, which will pierce the soul, now enkindles like a coal, or, to speak more truly, like a flame, and will cauterize it in a sublime manner. . . .
>
> The soul feels, as it were, a grain of mustard seed, most minute, highly enkindled and wondrous keen, which sends out from itself to its circumference a keen and enkindled fire of love; which fire, arising from the substance and virtue of that keen point, wherein lies the substance and the virtue of the herb, is felt by the soul to be subtly diffused through all its spiritual and substantial veins, according to its potentiality and strength. . . .
>
> And that whereof the soul now has fruition cannot be further described, save by saying that the soul is now conscious of the aptness of the comparison made in the Gospel between the Kingdom of Heaven and the grain of mustard seed; which grain, because of its great heat, although small, grows into a great tree. For the soul sees that it has become like a vast fire of love which arises from that enkindled point in the heart of the spirit.
>
> Few souls attain to a state as high as this, but some have done so, especially those whose virtue and spirituality was to be transmitted to the succession of their children. For God bestows spiritual wealth and strength upon the head of a house, together with the first-fruits of the Spirit, according to the greater or lesser number of the descendants who are to inherit his doctrine and spirituality.[98]

This is clearly an extraordinary favor which Saint John of the Cross describes in these pages. Several times we have laid stress on the fact that the symbolism of these extraordinary favors and the form of the experience that accompanies them ordinarily reveal and admirably illustrate the supernatural grace that they bring, and that characterizes the period in which the favor appears. And so it does not seem rash to seek in this description the character of the grace of fecundity which, in this period, marks out a soul for a particular mission; and to conclude that this grace, given through the instrumentality of a

[98] *Living Flame,* st. ii; Peers, III, 130-1.

seraph to a soul already enkindled with love, consists in a special inflowing of love bearing supernatural riches together with the power to communicate them to others.

The granting of a particular grace of fecundity is not bound up with this extraordinary manner of conferring it as described by Saint John of the Cross, nor with any other. It may even not be accompanied by any clear awareness of it. Thus on following the spiritual ascent of Saint Therese of the Child Jesus, we find that the Saint discovers progressively, and at a time difficult to determine before her oblation to merciful Love, the way of spiritual childhood and her mission to teach it to souls.

These graces of fecundity and of the apostolate must be distinguished, it seems to me, from charismatic missions previously entrusted to the soul. The latter confer certain powers and a grace of fidelity; in their case, the divine hold on the soul is, in itself, exterior to sanctifying grace, so that the soul might even exercise its powers without possessing grace.

The missions conferred in the sixth Mansions spring from sanctifying grace itself. They arise from a discovery of the special virtualities of the charity that is given. Under the light of the sixth Mansions, the soul sees in the riches and quality of its grace its place in the divine plan and the particular cooperation the Holy Spirit expects of it.

But the soul's mission does not date from that time. It may have been made known to the soul before, as to Saint John of the Cross, to whom it was foretold that he would reform the Order that he entered. Or it may actually have been conferred by an extraordinary charism or by a special vocation to the apostolate. But in the sixth Mansions, the soul receives grace adequate to fulfil it perfectly; and finds in this grace the light that confirms the mission and makes it explicit.

We have distinguished in Christ Jesus mediation in the physical order, realized by the hypostatic union, and mediation in the moral order, which is the priestly mission He received from the Father; the latter finding in the first its efficacy. We observe in the soul an inverse order. The mission and powers are given in advance; the fullness of grace to exercise it perfectly is received only on the summits of the spiritual life.

Thereafter the apostle will be a perfect apostle, enjoying the full effectiveness of his powers and the special gifts of charity corresponding to them. The priest now exercises the functions of his priesthood not only with the priestly character of his ordination and the grace that is proper to it, but with an identification with Christ that is even now realized. Thus he is truly another Christ before God and in the eyes of the faithful.

The light of this discovery becomes more and more clear, and the riches of its grace develop as love continues its work of transformation. The apostle Saint Paul makes explicit in his teaching and progressively realizes the mission revealed to him on the road to Damascus. Saint Teresa, after founding her first convent of the Reform, discovers the Church; she extends her Reform to meet the measure of her mission and the needs of the Church.

Such deepenings and precisions of one's mission issue from the interior impacts of grace and from events that bring it into sharper focus, confirming one's intuitions concerning it. The soul finds itself at the converging point of marvelous providential preparations. Their meeting in events that appear to the senses gives light on the harmony of the divine plan. Indeed it is true that loving Wisdom directs all things, from far and near, to the end she has assigned them, by ways that are ways of might and sweetness.

Better to appreciate the simplicity and depth of the light coming from inner experience and confirmed by providential events, one would do well to reread the Epistles of Saint Paul: "For those who love God all things work together unto good," he writes to the Romans.[99] In his epistles to the Galatians, to the Ephesians, to the Colossians, he never tires of repeating this great mystery of God that divine Mercy had made known

[99] Rom. 8:28.

to him through experience, that he might become its herald. The supernatural charm of the *Autobiography,* so winning in its simplicity, comes from the particulars Saint Therese of the Child Jesus gives on that love of God of which she says, "Thy love has gone before me, even from the days of my childhood. It has grown with my growth, and now it is an abyss whose depths I cannot fathom." [100]

"At last I have found my vocation. My vocation is love!" cries out Saint Therese of the Child Jesus.[101] This discovery is a source of joy, of a peaceful and inexhaustible enthusiasm, because it springs from the depths of the truth of God's designs. All her reserves of humanity fall away as she daringly proclaims these designs of God. At the end of her life, Saint Therese of the Child Jesus affirms her mission with a clarity and assurance that might disconcert us in a soul so humbly little and poor. Before her, Saint Paul too had affirmed with unmistakable force his role as apostle and the extent of his special mission.

These affirmations draw their strength from inner certitudes readily accepted by the soul. Certitude of its mission, certitude of the love that is invading it, both go together, for they engender each other. The apostle cries out:

> Who shall separate us from the love of Christ? Shall tribulation, or distress, or persecution, or hunger, or nakedness, or danger, or the sword? Even as it is written,
>
> "For thy sake we are put to death all the day long.
> We are regarded as sheep for the slaughter."
>
> But in all these things we overcome because of him who has loved us.[102]

Saint Teresa finds in the intellectual vision of the Holy Trinity the same security and help. She writes:

> While the soul is enjoying the delight which has been described, it seems to be wholly engulfed and protected by a shadow, and, as it were, a cloud of the Godhead, whence come to it certain influences

[100] *Autobiography,* xi, 175.
[101] *Ibid.,* 182.
[102] Rom. 8 35-7.

and a dew so delectable as to free it immediately, and with good reason, from the weariness caused it by the things of the world.[103]

Saint Therese of the Child Jesus feels herself constantly penetrated and purified by divine Mercy; thus even in the dark "subterranean" hole of temptations against faith, she maintains her peace and the certitude of her mission.

c. *In this apostolate action and contemplation are united*

The particular missions that the Holy Spirit imposes on souls are as diverse as are the functions of the priesthood of Christ and the needs of the Church. Mission for silent prayer or hidden self-immolation, mission for teaching, or for an active life in the exercise of the spiritual or corporal works of mercy, all are divine missions through which the Spirit builds up the Church in every epoch of its growth.

The docile soul lets itself be led by the good pleasure of the Holy Spirit; and if it had to make known its desires, this would be, says Saint Teresa, to undertake works and undergo trials for the reign of God:

> To a soul that is surrounded by crosses—that is, by trials and persecutions—it is a great help not to be habitually enjoying the delight of contemplation. . . . I particularly notice in certain persons (there are not many of them, on account of our sins) that the farther they advance in this prayer and the more favours they receive from Our Lord, the more attentive they are to the needs of their neighbors, especially to those of the soul; as I said at the beginning, they would give their lives again and again to save one person from mortal sin.[104]

Moreover, on these summits, Martha and Mary resemble each other and unite to fulfil the same office. "Believe me," writes Saint Teresa,

> Martha and Mary must work together when they offer the Lord lodging, and must have Him ever with them, and they must not entertain Him badly and give Him nothing to eat. . . . His food consists in our bringing Him souls, in every possible way, so that they may be saved and may praise Him for ever.[105]

[103] *Conceptions of the Love of God,* v; Peers, II, 388-9.
[104] *Ibid.,* vii; 398-9.
[105] VII Mansions, iv; Peers, II, 348.

Action and contemplation are united and merged. In order to remain with God, the soul must obey the impulse of the Holy Spirit, who leads it here or there to accomplish His work. And everywhere the Spirit leads it in this manner, it finds God; for it bears God within and enjoys Him in the sweet light of its inner experience. It is never more active nor more powerful than when God keeps it in solitude and contemplation; it is never more united to God nor more contemplative than when engaged in works to do God's will, under the impulse of the Holy Spirit. Let us hear Saint Teresa on this:

> It is here, my daughters, that love is to be found—not hidden away in corners but in the midst of occasions of sin; and believe me, although we may more often fail and commit small lapses, our gain will be incomparably the greater. Remember I am assuming all the time that we are acting in this way out of obedience or charity: if one of these motives is not involved, I do not hesitate to say that solitude is best.[106]

And she adds:

> It would be a bad business if we could practise prayer only by getting alone in corners.[107]

The Saint has some fear lest these statements seem contrary to what she has said on the necessity of recollection and solitude for contemplatives, and scandalize certain souls:

> Who will ever instil this truth into people to whom Our Lord is only beginning to grant favours? Perhaps they think that these others make little progress in their lives and that the important thing is that they should stay in their own little corner and enjoy themselves. I think it is by the Lord's providence that such people do not realize how high these other souls have risen; for, if they did, the fervour which beginners always have would make them want to go rushing after them, and that would not be good for them, for they are not yet weaned and for some time yet need to be fed with the milk of which I first spoke. Let them remain near those Divine breasts; and, when they have sufficient strength, the Lord will take care to lead them on farther. If they advanced now, they would not do others as much good as they think, but would only harm themselves.[108]

[106] *Foundations,* v; Peers, III, 25.
[107] *Ibid.*
[108] *Conceptions of the Love of God,* vii; Peers, II, 399.

In this advice we see the prudence of the holy mother as well as the suppleness of her teaching. Each stage has its grace and its demands. In transforming union, love has acquired a freedom by which it must profit, if it would obey the impulses of the Spirit of Love. Love and do what you will, said Saint Augustine. Love, on the summits, may claim this liberty, for its pleasures are God's good pleasure; nothing could any longer harm it, for it has conquered all.

d. *Fruitful apostolate and delicate collaboration*

There is scarcely need to speak of the fecundity of this apostolate, so evident does it appear. Thanks to the docility of the soul, the Holy Spirit can lead it as He wills and where He wills. Whether it prays or works, the soul does what it does under the light and impulse of the Spirit. Its acts are become divine, according to Saint John of the Cross; and thus they bear in them the efficacy that the divine power assures. Moreover, this captivation by God has for its purpose to use the soul for the realization of the great work that is the Church. The soul's activity under the motion of the Spirit joins with God's design and takes on the sovereign strength that God puts into the realization of His eternal decrees.

God's hold on the soul through the transforming union, and the Spirit's special captivation of it for the realization of its particular mission, create in this transformed soul, now become an apostle, a plenitude of God that cannot but appear in its movements and words, and show itself in their effects. Thus after reading the letter in which Saint Therese of the Child Jesus told her her aspirations, Sister Marie of the Sacred Heart, her sister, could answer in all truth:

> May I tell you? I will: you are possessed by the good God: literally *possessed,* exactly as the wicked are by the devil.[109]

The saints are in truth actually possessed by God. "Behold, I am with you all days, even unto the consummation of the

[109] *Letters of Saint Therese of Lisieux,* Sept. 16, 1896, p. 288.

world," our Lord assures us.[110] His mysterious presence is revealed by fruitfulness. "By their fruits you will know them." [111] This is the sign He gives for recognizing His authentic ambassadors. And the fruit is a fruit that is to evince its quality by its perennity. "I have chosen you and have appointed you that you should go and bear fruit, and that your fruit should remain." [112]

This fruit that remains, the great works, the institutions, the strong organizations wrought by holiness in every epoch, defy the centuries. This fruit is the Church itself, which the Holy Spirit is constantly building up with the activity of the saints He has transformed and conquered, through the love with which He has invaded them. We must note this fact: the power of a thaumaturgist who works a few prodigies is of small account compared with the fruitfulness attached to the daily activity of saints. Through this activity the Spirit, mysteriously but surely, affirms His power and brings to fulfillment His eternal plan.

This omnipotence, this divine presence, does not crush the apostle it uses. Such an apostle is not a common instrument, still less a slave, nor even a simple workman.

> No longer do I call you servants, because the servant does not know what his master does. But I have called you friends, because all things that I have heard from my Father I have make known to you.[113]

So speaks Jesus to His apostles after the Last Supper. The apostle is the friend of the Master. Affectionate trust goes deeper than confidences concerning God's plan. It is a veritable friendship, with all its depths of affection and mutual respect. The soul is entirely docile in the hands of God, and God Himself yields to the good pleasure of the soul. Let us hear Saint Teresa's personal confidences on this point:

[110] Matt. 28:20.
[111] Matt. 7:16.
[112] John 15:16.
[113] John 15:15.

> He begins to make such a friend of the soul that not only does He restore its will to it but He gives it His own also. For, now that He is making a friend of it, He is glad to allow it to rule with Him, as we say, turn and turn about.[114]

Saint Therese of the Child Jesus is so strongly aware of her power over the will of God that, through delicacy, so as not to annoy Him, she does not directly present her requests but offers them through the Blessed Virgin, leaving her to decide if they are according to God's will before presenting them.

Delightful assaults, marvelous playings of a love that has no more ardent desire than to fuse its will with that of the beloved. This is true of the love God bears for us, and it must be true of ours for Him.

And so the Spirit of Jesus, who came not to be served but to serve us,[115] after conquering His apostles by love, gladly disappears behind their personality and their action. Love humbles itself, even when it is omnipotent love, to exalt those it loves.

The apostle, like Christ Jesus, is glorified by the Spirit of Love who possesses him. His personality is exalted and enlarged by the presence and domination of the Holy Spirit. His senses are purified, his intelligence is refined, his will is strengthened, a whole human balance is established, a certain gift of integrity is recovered under the mysterious inflowing of the divine Presence. Fishermen of Galilee become apostles who go up and down the world and transform the Roman Empire. The natural gifts of Saul, the young and brilliant Pharisee, are elevated to the height of the genius of Paul, the universal apostle. One may well question if it is in the power of man to attain to the superman, that haunting goal of his pride; but it is certain that in each epoch the Holy Spirit makes giants of the saints on whom He lays hold. We have only to look to see them: Saint Benedict, Saint Francis of Assisi, Saint Dominic, Saint Teresa, Saint John of the Cross, Saint Vincent

[114] *Way of Perfection,* xxxii; Peers, II, 139.
[115] Matt. 20:28.

de Paul, and so many others, perfect types in a century and a civilization—the highest qualities of which they embody, and the most beautiful ideal.

It is especially in their common work that the Holy Spirit glorifies the instruments He has chosen. The Holy Spirit makes Himself lowly with saints in order to glorify them. Inspirer of the work by His light, efficacious agent by His omnipotence, yet He hides Himself under the human traits of the apostle. Anyone wanting to analyze the character of the works could, in fact, find the *raison d'être* of each one of them in the personality of the saint. The manifold works and institutions in which the Spirit has put His leaven of immortality and in which the Church takes just pride, show forth admirably the gifts, the desires, the diverse genius of their founder. The Holy Spirit appears in this world under a thousand human faces that reflect the power and grace of His hidden presence. The Spirit never repeats Himself in the exterior forms He chooses. Is this not the reason why Saint John of the Cross asks us never to take a saint for our model? This would be to expose oneself to failure in suppleness, in fidelity to the movement of the Spirit, who manifests His power and perfection as Spirit in the variety of His works and the perfection of His incarnation in each one of His instruments.

The delicate charms of this loving collaboration of God and the soul, these playings of the love that unites them, in turn brilliant and hidden, all these splendors of lowliness and of power are only beauties of here below, a reflection that reaches us from the beauty of the work the Holy Spirit is building. This work is the Spouse who comes up from the desert, flowing with delights, leaning upon her Beloved; [116] this is the masterpiece of Divine Mercy, the whole Christ in whom God has brought together and orientated all things. For the beauty of the Church of God, Jesus gave His blood; and the Spirit con-

[116] Cant. 8:5.

tinues to immolate His victims after filling them with the marvelous gifts of His grace.[117] We are all dedicated to the consummation of this work. Our gaze must rest on it lovingly and there remain fixed.

The saint is such only because he has entered by transforming union into the whole Christ. Identified with Christ Jesus, he continues Christ's priestly prayer for union. With the Spirit of Love, he groans within himself, "waiting for the adoption as sons"; [118] and under Love's captivation, works to consummate in unity all those whom God has "predestined to become conformed to the image of his Son." [119]

Saint Therese of the Child Jesus, that victim of the Spirit of Love, who espoused His movements with so marvelous a suppleness and expressed His desires with so much delicacy, said a few weeks before her death:

> No, I shall not be able to take any rest until the end of the world, as long as there are souls to be saved. But when the angel shall declare, "Time shall be no longer," then shall I take my rest, because the number of the elect will be complete, and all souls shall have entered into their joy and their rest. My heart thrills at that thought.[120]

Like Christ Jesus, the saint will enjoy the whole flowering of the riches of his grace and will be perfectly glorified only when Christ shall have reached His stature of the perfect Man. In the whole Christ, which is the Church, he too finds his end, his perfection, and his glory.

While awaiting the day when Jesus will appear on the clouds in all His splendor, the saint is formed here below in that light of dawn which reveals to him his place in the Church and gives him assurance of his triumph.

"I am a daughter of the Church," Saint Teresa repeated on her death bed in the overflowing joy of ecstasy. And complet-

[117] "Wisdom hath built herself a house: she hath hewn her out seven pillars. She hath slain her victims." Prov. 9:1-2.
[118] Rom. 8:23.
[119] Rom. 8:29.
[120] *Novissima Verba,* July 17, p. 56.

ing the thought of the Reformer of Carmel, Saint Therese of the Child Jesus wrote:

> "I am a child of Holy Church. . . . My own glory shall be the radiance that streams from the queenly brow of my Mother." [121]

[121] *Autobiography,* xi, p. 185.